The Biology of the Guinea Pig

CONTRIBUTORS

James E. Breazile
Esther M. Brown
Raymond D. Ediger
Michael F. W. Festing
H. L. Foster
James R. Ganaway
Lawrence V. Harper
Richard M. Hoar
Charles E. Hunt
James G. McCormick
Patrick J. Manning
Juan M. Navia
Alfred L. Nuttall
L. R. Robinette
N. C. Ronald
Dudley B. Sisk
Ronald F. Sprouse
G. L. Van Hoosier, Jr.
John M. Vetterling
Joseph E. Wagner
Richard B. Wescott

The Biology of the Guinea Pig

EDITED BY

Joseph E. Wagner

Department of Veterinary Pathology
Veterinary Medical Diagnostic Laboratory
College of Veterinary Medicine
University of Missouri-Columbia
Columbia, Missouri

Patrick J. Manning

Department of Laboratory Medicine and Pathology
and Research Animal Resources
Unit of Comparative Medicine
University of Minnesota Health Sciences
Minneapolis, Minnesota

ACADEMIC PRESS New York San Francisco London

A Subsidiary of Harcourt Brace Jovanovich, Publishers

ACADEMIC PRESS, INC.
111 Fifth Avenue, New York, New York 10003

United Kingdom Edition published by
ACADEMIC PRESS, INC. (LONDON) LTD.
24/28 Oval Road, London NW1

Library of Congress Cataloging in Publication Data
Main entry under title:

The Biology of the guinea pig.

"All chapters . . . were delivered in part at one of three symposia co-sponsored by ACLAM."
Includes bibliographies and index.
1. Guinea-pigs. 2. Guinea-pigs--Diseases.
3. Guinea-pigs as laboratory animals. I. Wagner, Joseph E. II. Manning, Patrick J. III. American College of Laboratory Animal Medicine.
[DNLM: 1. Guinea pigs. 2. Animals, Laboratory. QY50 B615]
QL737.R634B56 599'.3234 75-13096
ISBN 0-12-730050-3

PRINTED IN THE UNITED STATES OF AMERICA

Contents

CHAPTER 17 NUTRITION, NUTRITIONAL DISEASES, AND NUTRITION RESEARCH APPLICATIONS

Juan M. Navia and Charles E. Hunt

CHAPTER 18 TOXICOLOGY AND TERATOLOGY

Richard M. Hoar

CHAPTER 19 AUDITORY RESEARCH

James G. McCormick and Alfred L. Nuttall

List of Contributors

Numbers in parentheses indicate the pages on which the authors' contributions begin.

James E. Breazile (53), Department of Anatomy-Physiology, College of Veterinary Medicine, University of Missouri-Columbia, Columbia, Missouri

Esther M. Brown (53), Department of Anatomy-Physiology, College of Veterinary Medicine, University of Missouri-Columbia, Columbia, Missouri

Raymond D. Ediger (5), Litton Bionetics, Inc., Frederick Cancer Research Center, Frederick, Maryland

Michael F. W. Festing (99), Medical Research Council Laboratory Animals Centre, Carshalton, Surrey, England

H. L. Foster (21), The Charles River Breeding Laboratories, Inc., Wilmington, Massachusetts

James R. Ganaway (121), Comparative Pathology Section, Veterinary Resources Branch, National Institutes of Health, Bethesda, Maryland

Lawrence V. Harper (31), Department of Applied Behavioral Sciences, University of California, Davis, California

Richard M. Hoar (13, 269), Department of Toxicology, Hoffmann-La Roche, Inc., Nutley, New Jersey

Charles E. Hunt (235), Department of Comparative Medicine and Institute of Dental Research, School of Dentistry and Medicine, University of Alabama, Birmingham, Alabama

James G. McCormick (281), Department of Surgery, Section of Otolaryngology, Bowman Gray School of Medicine, Wake Forest University, Winston-Salem, North Carolina

Patrick J. Manning (211), Department of Laboratory Medicine and Pathology and Research Animal Resources, Unit of Comparative Medicine, University of Minnesota Health Sciences, Minneapolis, Minnesota

Juan M. Navia (235), Institute of Dental Research and Department of Comparative Medicine, School of Dentistry and Medicine, University of Alabama, Birmingham, Alabama

Alfred L. Nuttall (281), Kresge Hearing Research Institute, Department of Otolaryngology, University of Michigan School of Medicine, Ann Arbor, Michigan

L. R. Robinette* (137), Department of Veterinary Pathology and Office of Laboratory Animal Resources, Washington State University, Pullman, Washington

N. C. Ronald (201), Department of Veterinary Parasitology, Texas A & M University, College of Veterinary Medicine, College Station, Texas

Dudley B. Sisk† (63), Department of Anatomy-Physiology, College of Veterinary Medicine, University of Missouri-Columbia, Columbia, Missouri

Ronald F. Sprouse (153), Department of Veterinary Microbiology, College of Veterinary Medicine and Departments of Microbiology and Medicine-Dermatology, School of Medicine, University of Missouri-Columbia, Columbia, Missouri

G. L. Van Hoosier, Jr., (137), Department of Veterinary Pathology and Office of Laboratory Animal Resources, Washington State University, Pullman, Washington

*Present address: Alpine Animal Hospital, Route 3, Moscow, Idaho

†Present address: Central Kentucky Animal Disease Diagnostic Laboratory, Lexington, Kentucky

John M. Vetterling (163), Animal Parasitology Institute, Beltsville Agricultural Research Center, Agricultural Research Service, United States Department of Agriculture, Beltsville, Maryland

Joseph E. Wagner (1, 21, 201, 227), Department of Veterinary Pathology, Veterinary Medical Diagnostic Laboratory, College of Veterinary Medicine, University of Missouri-Columbia, Columbia, Missouri

Richard B. Wescott (197), Department of Veterinary Pathology, College of Veterinary Medicine, Washington State University, Pullman, Washington

Preface

The American College of Laboratory Animal Medicine (ACLAM) was founded in 1957 to encourage education, training, and research in laboratory animal medicine. Its primary goals include professional certification of veterinarians in laboratory animal medicine (diplomates) and continuing education. This monograph represents a part of a program developed to further the educational goals of ACLAM.

"The Biology of the Guinea Pig" is patterned after the first ACLAM book, "The Biology of the Laboratory Rabbit," edited by S. H. Weisbroth, R. E. Flatt, and A. L. Kraus, published by Academic Press in 1974. Development of this book was formulated on the belief that there was a need for a comprehensive review of literature pertaining to the use of the guinea pig as a substrate in research. All of the contributions were delivered in part at one of three symposia cosponsored by ACLAM. The chapters on husbandry, history, physiology, behavior, genetics, reproduction, biomethodology, and specific pathogen-free and germfree techniques were presented as an ACLAM cosponsored seminar at the 23rd Annual Session of the American Association for Laboratory Animal Science in St. Louis, Missouri, in October of 1972. Chapters on research uses of guinea pigs were presented at the annual meeting of the Federation of American Societies of Experimental Biology in Atlantic City, New Jersey, in April of 1973. Chapters on diseases of guinea pigs were presented at the July, 1973 meeting of the American Veterinary Medical Association in New Orleans, Louisiana.

The goal of ACLAM and the editors has been to produce a monograph on the guinea pig useful to the widest possible audience, i.e., the general scientific community including investigators using or considering the use of guinea pigs in research, veterinarians, students of veterinary medicine, and others professionally concerned with the care and management of guinea pigs (supervisory personnel, animal technicians, and technologists concerned with day to day applied care of research guinea pigs) as well as commercial producers of guinea pigs and cavy fanciers. The contributors were assembled based on their recognition as experts in their specific disciplines. With their detailed presentations we have hopefully assembled an authoritative reference work that will be of interest to almost anyone utilizing guinea pigs.

The strengths of this book lie in its comprehensive coverage of material related to applied care and management of guinea pigs and their diseases. The chapters on guinea pig behavior, genetics, specific pathogen-free technique, biomethodology, and colony husbandry represent exhaustive and authoritative treatises. The reader will also find that noninduced diseases of guinea pigs have been emphasized in an organized review form. They constitute potentially one of the most limiting factors to the utility of the guinea pig in biomedical research, which makes their early detection and elimination or recognition per se of paramount importance. Other noninduced diseases of guinea pigs are of substantial value as models for the study of similar diseases in man.

The compilation of chapters on research uses of the guinea pig proved to be a difficult task. Thousands of research papers are published annually in which the guinea pig has been the experimental subject. We initiated a series of computer-assisted literature searches of current and recent journals keying only on the words "guinea pig." Several of the topics and authors were selected as a result of these searches, based on the number of citations in which guinea pigs were used in certain research areas. We perceived use of the guinea pig in nutrition research, otologic research, toxicology, and teratology as the areas of research in which the guinea pig is most widely used, and selected these topics for review in this book. Obviously research in dozens of other disciplines could have been selected as well.

While this represents the first attempt at assembling a massive amount of authoritative information on the guinea pig per se, we look forward to new editions. Certainly, as research use of the guinea pig changes, topics not included will deserve emphasis in future editions. We therefore solicit and welcome suggestions and comments on errors, significant omissions, and content.

We particularily would like to express appreciation to the 1972 ACLAM Board of Directors for committing the resources and support of ACLAM to this endeavor and for selecting us as editors. We acknowledge our indebtedness to our administrative superiors for allowing us freedom to assemble this monograph: Dr. W. H. Eyestone, Chairman, Department of Veterinary Pathology; Dr. L. G. Morehouse, Director, Veterinary Medical Diagnostic Laboratory; Dr. C. C. Middleton, Director, Sinclair Comparative Medicine Research Farm; and Dean K. D. Weide, all of the College of Veterinary Medicine, University of Missouri-Columbia, Columbia, Missouri. We acknowledge the editorial assistance of Joel Morganstern and Ellen Maring and the typographical assistance of Sylvia Bradfield. Last but not least we are indebted in a special way to all the contributing authors who so generously gave of their time and talent in writing their respective chapters. Furthermore they, like the editors, have signed royalities from this work to the coffers of ACLAM for further professional and educational missions in Laboratory Animal Medicine.

To economize, we have kept illustrations to a minimum in the belief that readers with continued interest in a topic will consult the original works liberally referenced in this monograph.

Joseph E. Wagner
Patrick J. Manning

Chapter 1

Introduction and Taxonomy

Joseph E. Wagner

I. INTRODUCTION

The importance of the guinea pig to medical research is symbolized by its synonymity with "experimental subject" in the English language. One of the earliest records in English concerning the biology of the guinea pig is that of Goldsmith (1791). Lavoisier in 1780 (Lane-Petter, 1963) is commonly credited with being one of the first to use the guinea pig in research, having used it to measure heat production.

Weir (1974) reviewed the origin of the domestic guinea pig and its interrelationships with other species of cavies. The wild guinea pig (*Cavia aperea*) is widely distributed in Argentina, Uruguay, and Brazil (Weir, 1970). Another wild ancestor, *C. cutleri,* is still found in Peru (Paterson, 1972). Cumberland (1886) stated "I do not believe that the Cavy ever existed in Brazil as a domestic animal, in the sense of being used for food, as stated by some naturalists, or that it was known there at all before the arrival of the Portuguese."

Wild guinea pigs inhabit open grassland, where they nest and make paths in taller vegetation. They feed in more open areas at dawn and dusk (Weir, 1970). They live in a small societies of from several to several dozen individuals. Waterhouse (1848) related the guinea pig's one useful property was that of banishing rats from its vicinity. The guinea pig is considered a culinary delight by the natives of the Bolivian and Peruvian high country, where the animal is killed, scalded, and scraped to remove the fur and then either roasted or fried whole and served with a hot sauce known as *picante.*

II. HISTORY AND ETYMOLOGY

The most extensive inquiry into the history of the guinea pig outside of South America is that of Cumberland (1886), and the second edition of that work by Gardner (1913). Cumberland (1886) concluded that the original importers of the cavy into Europe were probably responsible for the nomen "guinea pig." According to Cumberland (1886):

> Previous to the arrival of Europeans on the West Coast of South America, the only domestic animals which could be used as food were the llama, alpaca, Coy or Guinea Pig, and a bird called Tuya, about the size of a large duck. Under these circumstances, Cavies must have been of great importance as a food supply, and are in fact so mentioned by the early writers, who, however, generally speak of them as rabbits (Conejo), the name by which they are still called by those Peruvians and Bolivians who speak Spanish.
>
> Velasco, in his "Historia de Quito," says that the Indians had great numbers of Cavies in their houses. We may fairly conclude

that they would bestow the same elaborate care in "breeding and selecting these small rodents as we know they bestowed upon the llamas and alpacas." We are told that these latter animals were kept in separate flocks of different colours; and if, by any chance, a young one was born of a wrong colour, it was immediately moved into a different flock.

If this system were applied to the Cavies, many distinct varieties would be evolved. This careful breeding of the Cavy, and a very remote period for its first domestication, are circumstances both needed to account for the extremely artificial colour and marking of the animals; and we may also reason inversely, from the permanence and obstinate irregularity of the markings, as well as from the colours, so distinct from any wild form, that the domestication took place at a very remote epoch.

We are at first puzzled to know how this little animal, which is neither a pig nor a native of Guinea, came by its absurd misnomer. This is, however, soon explained, if we consider the circumstances under which Europeans must have made its acquaintance. The Spaniards, on their first going into the Peruvian markets, would see exposed for sale, in large numbers, a little animal looking remarkably like a sucking pig, and would give it that name, to which they would add the distinctive term, "Indian," because the early navigators spoke of South America as a part of the Indies: thus, we have Porco da India, Porcella da India, Cochon d'Inde, and Topsell's term, "the Indian Little Pig Coney." The name of "Guinea Pig" is of a later date, and was, probably a further confusion of our own, caused by the circumstance that we had more traffic with the coast of Guinea than with that of South America, and also were accustomed to consider Guinea as a part of the Indies. The pig-like appearance of which I have spoken results from the mode of preparing Cavies for cooking–namely, by scalding and scraping them in the same manner as we should treat a pig.

The Guinea Pig was first described scientifically by Aldrovandus, and his contemporary, Gesner. Aldrovandus was born A.D. 1522, and died in 1607. Gesner was born in 1516, and died in 1605. The great victory of Pizarro over the Peruvians, when he seized the person of the Inca, and decided the fate of the country, was gained on 16th November, 1532, shortly after the Spaniards arrived in Peru. It is clear, therefore, that the figures of the Guinea Pig, and the descriptions of them, which still accurately represent and describe the animal, must have been done soon after its arrival in Europe. It is usual to fix this event, vaguely, as occurring about fifty years after the discovery of Peru, or about A.D. 1580.

In Topsell's "Historie of Foure-footed Beastes, from Gesner and Others," 1607, which contains what I believe to be the first English reference to the Guinea Pig, it is called "the Indian Little Pig Coney." The description, which I conclude is Gesner's, is as follows: "Five claws upon a foot behind, and six before: teeth like a mouse, and no tail, and the colours variable. I have seen them all white and all yellow, and also different from both these." Topsell's "Gesner" makes a curious mistake as to the number of claws–mine certainly have only three on a foot behind, and four before. It is clear that the pure white breed existed at this early period, and was, probably, a result of Peruvian cultivation under the Incas.

Pennant, feeling, no doubt, the inappropriateness of the term "Guinea Pig," called this animal the "Restless Cavy." This name is, however, inaccurate, for Cavies, when there is no exciting cause, such as fear or hunger, are very quiet animals, and will lie side by side for hours, until one or other of these disturbing causes rouses them to activity. The date of the first edition of Pennant's "Hist. Quad." is 1781. It is evident that Pennant has followed Buffon, who, in this instance at least, is not a safe guide. He says: "Colour white, varied with orange and black in irregular blotches; no tail; inhabits Brazil; a restless, grumbling little animal, perpetually running from corner to corner; breeds when two months old, has from four to twelve young at a time; would be innumerable, but numbers of the young are eaten by cats, others killed by the males; are very tender, multitudes of them dying of cold." A great part of Pennant's description of the habits of the Guinea Pig is incorrect. There are many curious misstatements in Buffon, and these have been repeated, upon his authority, by Pennant and subsequent naturalists, evidently without any practical acquaintance with the subject.

In Peru, the Cavy seems to have been reared running loose in the kitchens of the Indian houses; and this appears to be still done in the more rural parts of the country, where the Guinea Pig still holds its own in the struggle with European cattle and poultry.

It is apparent that *Cavia cutleri* had been domesticated for some time by Andean Indians when Pizarro conquered Peru around 1530 (Sire, 1968). Up until that time little is known about the domestication of the guinea pig in Peru; however, the Incas, induced by an absence of large meat providing animals, used the guinea pig for food and sacrifices to their gods. After the Spanish conquest the domestic guinea pig became established for food and fancy in many places of the Spanish Colonial Empire. It was apparently in the sixteenth century that Dutch sailors introduced the small, easily transported guinea pig into Europe. From there the guinea pig spread rapidly to other parts of Europe and the British Isles but failed to gain widespread acceptance as a food source in the latter countries. As a result of this travel, it acquired many common names. They were bred for show and fancy and as pets in Europe for up to 300 years before they were introduced into research. Their introduction into medical research was a matter of convenience. They probably first reached the United States in the early part of the seventeenth century from Europe as pets and fancy animals. Their movement from continent to continent was sporadic and incidental to other travel. Therefore there are no accurate and reliable records of their movement.

The common name of the guinea pig, *cavy*, probably derives from its generic name, Cavia. However, the native Indian name *coüy*, is easily formed into *cavy* or *cavia* which may have influenced its initial generic name. It is interesting to note that people with a "fancy" interest in *Cavia porcellus* have adopted the more "scientific" terminology *cavy*, while the research community continues to utilize *guinea pig*, a term of obscure origin.

The origin of the name *guinea pig* is indeed obscure. Most European nationalities perceived the animal as a small pig that arrived from across the sea and adopted fitting names: *Meerschweinchen* (little sea pig); *cochon de mer* (sea pig); *lapin de*

Barbarie (Barbary rabbit). Paterson (1972) noted that the name *guinea* may have come from "Guiana" or more simply that in another era may have meant "foreign." Could it be that the guinea pig was so named because it arrived in Europe via ships from Guiana, a country in northeastern South America? There is no reference to the domestic *cavy* ever having been found there. Could it have arrived in the English speaking world by slave ships via the coast of Guinea in West Africa? Could it have been named for the coin, guinea, for which it could be purchased in England in the sixteenth and seventeenth centuries?

Sire (1968) suggested that porcellus may have resulted from comparing the animal's nails to small wooden shoes (*petits sabots*). However, porcellus is the Latin name for "little pig." Also, the guinea pig, when prepared for the table, resembles a whole roasted suckling pig.

Obviously the origin and name of the guinea pig as well as the history of its introduction into Europe has been the subject of much curiosity. The names by which the common domestic guinea pig, *Cavia porcellus* Linn., is known throughout the world include:

English	Indian Little Pig Coney (Topsell's "Gresner," 1607), restless cavy (Pennant), Domestic cavy (Cumberland), cavy, guinea pig
French	Cobaye, cochon d'Inde, cochon d'Inde d'Angora (Peruvian)
Spanish	Conejillo de Indias
Italian	Procella de India, porchita da India
Portuguese	Porquinho da India
German	Meeerschwein
Dutch	Indianach varken
Spanish Peruvian	Conejo, cuis, curso
Peruvian Indian or Quichua	Coüi, couy
Russian	Morskaya svinka

Just as the matter of nomenclature is unsettled so is the matter of from which wild species of *Cavia* was *Cavia porcellus* descended. Based primarily on morphological features, Waterhouse (1848) held that *Cavia cobaya* or *porcellus, C. aperea*, and *C. cuteri* might all be placed in the same species. Darwin (quoted by Detlefsen, 1914) held that *C. aperea* was not an ancestor of the domestic guinea pig because a distinct genus of lice infested each form. Detlefsen (1914) suggested that *C. aperea* was more closely related to the domestic guinea pig than *C. rufescens* because the latter gave sterile male offspring in a cross with the tame guinea pig. Male offspring from *C. aperea* were fertile. Thomas (1917) discussed 12 species and subspecies of the genus *Cavia.* Ellermen (1940) reviewed the family *Caviidae.* He referenced and listed 17 "named forms" or species in the genus *Cavia.*

Landry (1957) and Patterson and Pascual (1972) have reviewed the paleontology of the South American hystricomorph rodents. While caviomorphs are descendents of African Phiomorpha of the Oligocene epoch, Caviidae first appeared in South America in the Late Miocene (26 to 7 million years ago) or a later period. More recently Lavocat (1974) reviewed many of the osteological features and other characters of the histricomorphous rodents and discussed the use of the word "hystricomorph." At the same symposium Wood (1974) also discussed the evolution of the Old and New World histricomorphs, the sciurognathous hystricomorphs and hystricognaths. He also discussed the distribution among rodents of features supposed to characterize the "hystricomorpha."

Much of the cultivation of the guinea pig as a fancy may be attributed to the excellent publication of Cumberland (1886) who predicted cultivation of the cavy as a fancy because a wire-haired breed, inappropriately named the Abyssinian, had appeared in England. Also a long silky-haired cavy had appeared in Paris, which was later named *Peruvian* by T. L. Sclater, Esq., of the Zoological Society of London. Daubigny (quoted by Cumberland, 1886) stated that "the Cobaye has been remarkably modified by cultivation," and "cultivation has greatly increased its size." House (1906) expounds at length on the very active fancy cavy industry in England before 1906.

Many laboratory guinea pigs derive from a strain established by Dunkin and Hartley in 1926 (1930). During a life time of genetic studies Sewell Wright (1960) founded a number of inbred strains of guinea pigs. The genetics of the guinea pig are covered in Chapter 8 of this treatise.

Many North American sources of guinea pigs for research, testing, and teaching are listed in a handbook "Animals for Research" compiled and edited by the Institute for Laboratory Animal Resources (Joseph Henry Building, 2100 Pennsylvania Avenue, N.W., Washington D.C.), National Research Council, National Academy of Sciences. Today most of the guinea pigs raised in the United States are for laboratory use; however, guinea pigs raised for fancy and companion uses are also popular. While the path of the guinea pig from barren floor of the earthen hut of the Andean native to the research laboratory cannot be traced with accuracy, we fully appreciate that this path has involved its use as a staple food, a fancy show species, and a pet or companion animal.

III. TAXONOMY

Taxonomic Outline (after Simpson, 1945)

Kingdom—Animal
 Phylum—Chordata: Animals with notochord and gills
  Subphylum—Craniata (Vertebrata): Chordates with organized head region
   Class—Mammalia: Warm-blooded craniates with hair coat. Young nourished from mammary glands

Subclass–Theira: Viviparous mammals
Infraclass–Eutheria: Placental mammals (as compared with marsupials–Metatheria and egg layers–Protheria)
Order–Rodentia
Suborder–Hystricomorpha: This group includes chinchillas, porcupines, and others, distinguished by a zygomatic arch in which the jugal bone forms the center block. These are "porcupine"-like animals compared with squirrel-like (Sciuromorpha) or rat-like (Myomorpha) animals
Superfamily–Cavioidae
Family–Caviidae: More or less tailless South American rodents that have one pair of mammae, four digits on the forefoot and three on the hindfoot. Six genera are generally listed in this family
Subfamily–Caviinae:
Genus–*Cavia,* Pallas (1766) Misc. Zool. p. 30
Type Species–*Cavia cobaya,* Pallas = *Mus porcellus* Linnaeus

ACKNOWLEDGMENTS

This work supported in part by NIH Research Grant RR-00471 from the Division of Research Resources.

REFERENCES

Cumberland, C. (1886). "The Guinea Pig or Domestic Cavy, for Food, Fur, and Fancy." L. Upcott Gill, London.

Detlefsen, J.A. (1914). Genetic studies on a cavy species cross. *Carnegie Inst. Wash. Publ.* **205.**

Dunkin, G.W., Hartley, P., Lewis-Faning, E., and Russell, W.T. (1930). Comparative biometric study of albino and coloured guinea-pigs from the point of view of their stability for experimental use. *J. Hyg.* **30,** 311–319.

Ellerman, J.R. (1940). The families and genera of living rodents. *Brit. Mus. Natur. Hist.* **1,** 237–248.

Gardner, G. (1913). "Cavies or Guinea Pigs." L. Upcott Gill, London.

Goldsmith, O. (1791). "An History of the Earth and Animated Nature," Vol. IV, pp. 53–59. London.

House, C.A. (1906). "Cavies: Their Varieties, Breeding and Management," 3rd ed. Fur and Feather, Idle, Bradord.

Landry, S.O. (1957). The interrelationships of the New and Old World hystricomorph rodents. *Univ. Calif., Berkeley, Publ. Zool.* **56,** 1–118.

Lane-Petter, W., ed. (1963). "Animals for Research: Principals of Breeding and Management." Academic Press, New York.

Lavocat, R. (1974). What is an histricomorph? *In* Symposia of the Zoological Society of London, Number 34, "The Biology of Hystricomorph Rodents" (I.W. Rowlands and B.J. Weir, eds.), pp. 7–20. Academic Press, London.

Paterson, J.W. (1972). The Guinea-pig or cavy. *In* "The UFAW Handbook on the Care and Management of Laboratory Animals" (UFAW, ed.), 4th edition, pp. 223–241. Williams & Wilkins, Baltimore, Maryland.

Patterson, B., and Pascual, R. (1972). The fossil mammal fauna of South America. *In* "Evolution, Mammals, and Southern Continents" (A. Keast, F.C. Erk, and B. Glass, eds.), pp. 247–309. State Univ. of New York Press, Albany.

Simpson, G.G. (1945). The principles of classification and a classification of mammals. *Bull. Amer. Mus. Natur. Hist.* **85,** 93–99.

Sire, M. (1968). "Les'Élévages des Petits Animaux," Vol. II. Editions Paul Lechevelier, Paris.

Thomas, O. (1917). Notes on the species of the genus *Cavia. Ann. Mag. Natur. Hist.* [8] **19,** 152–160.

Waterhouse, G.R. (1848). "Natural History of the Mammalia." Vol. II, pp. 147–207. Baillière, London.

Weir, B.J. (1970). The management and breeding of some more hystricomorph rodents. *Lab. Anim.* **4,** 83–97.

Weir, B.J. (1974). Notes on the origin of the domestic guinea-pig. *In* Symposia of the Zoological Society of London, Number 34. "The Biology of Hystricomorph Rodents" (I.W. Rowlands and B.J. Weir, eds.), pp. 437–446. Academic Press, London.

Wood, A.E. (1974). The evolution of the old world and new world hystricomorphs. *In* Symposia of the Zoological Society of London, Number 34. "The Biology of Hystricomorph Rodents" (I.W. Rowlands and B.J. Weir, eds.), pp. 21–54. Academic Press, London.

Wright, S. (1960). Life genetics of vital characteristics of the guinea pig. *J. Cell. Comp. Physiol.* **56,** 123.

Chapter 2

Care and Management

Raymond D. Ediger

I. HOUSING

The general design criteria used in buildings to hold rats, mice, and hamsters are applicable for the guinea pig. Design and construction of facilities must not only conform to local building codes, but should also comply with the recommendations of the Institute of Laboratory Animal Resources (1972), published in the "Guide for the Care and Use of Laboratory Animals."

In planning individual animal rooms, one must consider the nature of the activity to be performed, such as maintenance of animals for quarantine, long-term holding, breeding, or research requiring special facilities. The functional and spatial requirements for each of these activities will vary; therefore, the room dimensions, spatial relation of rooms to each other, and the designation of space within the room for servicing both animals and equipment will likewise vary.

Control of infectious disease is best accomplished by use of several small rooms, as contrasted with one large room, because the former design minimizes transfer of disease and is a useful form of isolation. It is advisable that each small room be confined to one activity and at no time should healthy animals be housed in the same room as animals undergoing experimental procedures with infectious agents or with animals of another species. Ideally, animals on experiment should be in a different building with its own sterilizing equipment, feed, bedding, and animal attendants. If guinea pigs are procured from an outside source, they should be quarantined in a room remote from all other guinea pigs.

The arrangement of caging within each room depends on the activity and the unit of animal accommodation chosen (see caging requirements, Table I). Maximum use of space is an important factor in design, and caging equipment within the

Table I
Space Recommendations for the Guinea Pig[a]

Weight (gm)	Floor area per animal (cm^2)	Height (cm)
Up to 250	277 (43 inches)	17.8 (7 inches)
250–350	374 (58 inches)	17.8 (7 inches)
Over 350	652 (101 inches)	17.8 (7 inches)

[a]Institute of Laboratory Animal Resources (1972) space recommendations for the guinea pig published in the "Guide for the Care and Use of Laboratory Animals."

room should be arranged to allow easy access to all animals for both observation and handling. Portable racks with tiered caging are popular and increase the capacity of the room; however, there is a loss of efficiency in servicing tiered caging which exceeds the reach of a person of average height. In addition to floor space allotted for holding animals, sufficient space must be reserved for servicing the room, handling animals, tattooing, weighing, experimental manipulations, and for maintenance and storage of records.

A. Temperature, Ventilation, and Humidity Control

Special attention should be given to ventilation systems to control temperature, humidity, air velocity, and air pressure within the animal room. Guinea pigs are extremely susceptible to respiratory disease, and a well-designed, efficiently operating system provides the environmental stability requisite for respiratory disease control.

There should be 10–15 changes of air per hour and no air should be recirculated unless it has been filtered to remove airborne contaminants. Care must be taken to control velocity and direction of air flow to produce a draftless and even distribution of air to all areas of a room. An ideal state of mass air displacement is, in some instances, difficult to achieve in a room filled with animals and cages, and in these circumstances cages can be designed or arranged to minimize drafts.

The compact body of the guinea pig conserves heat well but dissipates it poorly. Thus the guinea pig is more likely to tolerate cold than heat. The average heat production from 350- to 410-gm guinea pigs is 5.0 to 5.7 BTU per animal per hour (Dick and Hanel, 1970; Hill, 1971). Maximum or peak heat production from an animal of similar size is approximately 47 BTU per animal per hour (Brewer, 1964). Therefore, factors such as the number of animals per room and especially the type of caging affect optimal temperature requirements. Guinea pigs kept singly in wire cages with wire bottoms obviously require a higher room temperature than those maintained several to a cage with solid sides and bottom and 2 inches of bedding. My experience has been with a system about midway between the two cage examples just given. Our animals are on bedding, but the sides of their cages are woven wire or perforated panels which provide added ventilation.

Reported optimal temperatures for maintenance and breeding of guinea pigs vary; however, most references indicate an ideal temperature range is 65°–75°F. If allowed to exceed 90°F, heat prostration and death may occur, particularly in sows in advanced pregnancy. Young (1927) reported sterile matings when testicles of male guinea pigs were exposed to high temperatures. In my experience rooms maintained at 72°±2°F were very satisfactory for all age groups. Relative humidity should be maintained at about 50%. One of the strongest reasons for adopting this level is that the survival of airborne microorganisms is lowest at this point (Weihe, 1971).

To maintain an ideal room environment each room or group of rooms serving a common purpose should have individual controls for room temperature and humidity. The sensing element should be located at the level of the animal cages. There should be an alarm system to indicate whenever temperature or humidity deviate from an acceptable range, and the environmental control system should have a "standby" capability to supply auxiliary power if necessary.

B. Caging and Space Requirements

Paterson (1967) described different types of indoor guinea pig caging as (1) floor pens, (2) tiered compartments, fixed or portable, and (3) cages either mobile on trolleys or portable on racking. Portable racks with plastic or metal cages have a distinct advantage over floor pens and other types of permanent caging either single or tiered because permanent caging is generally difficult to disinfect satisfactorily and wasteful of both labor and space. When considering cages of metal or plastic on portable racks, there are many different cage designs from which to choose and the choice must be based primarily on the intended use of the guinea pigs. If they are to be held in a laboratory environment, one determines the number of animals and the size of the animals to be held per cage. The cage size should comply with the Institute of Laboratory Animal Resource's (1972) space recommendations for guinea pigs published in the "Guide for the Care and Use of Laboratory Animals," and with Public Law 89-544 as amended by Public Law 91-579, The Animal Welfare Act of 1970. Attached accessory equipment, such as watering devices and feeders, must take into consideration anatomy as well as the eating and drinking habits of the guinea pig. After 6 months of age females of heavier strains commonly weigh over 800 gm and males over 1000 gm. Provide space accordingly.

Caging for a production colony is more complex and depends on the the breeding system. There may be several animals per cage and provisions must be made for accommodating young. The Tumblebrook cage, a solid floor cage, modeled after those used at Brant Laboratory, New York, has been used for over 20 years with reasonable success at the Fort Detrick production colony (Fig. 1). Each cage is 30 × 30 × 10 inches, made of stainless steel, and has both a solid bottom and front panel. The other three panels are solid 4 inches from the bottom and have ¼ inch mesh, woven wire, or ½ inch perforated holes in the top 6 inches. In both designs, the openings are equivalent to 40% of the panel. Except for the top drawer no cover is necessary. For the top cage a 4-inch removable guard around the perimeter of the cage (Fig. 2) prevents escape by jumping. Each rack is portable on four 5-inch locking casters and holds five cages, which rest on side runners 1.25 inches wide.

Bedding is provided in the solid bottom cages. Numerous materials have been used as bedding, such as peat moss, dried corn cobs, cedar shavings, and a flax by-product. The product most satisfactory in my experience is seasoned ponderosa pine shavings. It consists of large, thin curls of pine, generally obtained from planing mills. In our colony we cover the bottom of the cage with about 2 inches of pine bedding. It is constantly aerated as pigs move through it, and the feces tend to work through the shavings to the floor of the cage. It does not pack as readily as small-particle bedding, such as sawdust. Plank and Irwin (1966) reported that sawdust caused infertility in guinea pigs. They concluded that sawdust particles adhere to the genital mucosa and interfere with copulation. Care must be exercised in procurement of all bedding. It must be free of dust, sharp particles, and excreta of other animals. Although several bedding products are highly satisfactory without sterilization, the only way to be sure that bedding is free of infectious agents is to sterilize the product prior to use and then to prevent poststerilization contamination.

Fig. 1. The Tumblebrook cage.

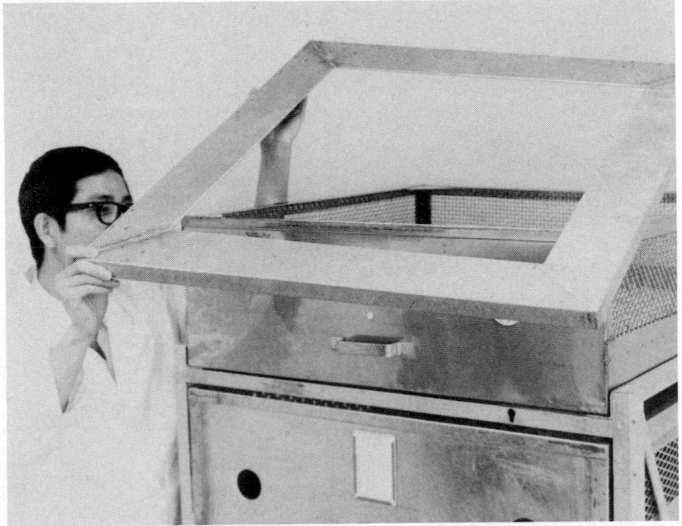

Fig. 2. Four-inch removable guard for prevention of escape by jumping.

Fig. 3. Wire-bottom cages.

There is a great difference of opinion about whether guinea pig cages should have solid or wire floors. Cages with wire floors have been used by a number of competent breeders and researchers. Some claim excellent breeding and rearing results; others have been less successful. The advantage of cages with wire floors is that bedding is not needed, and there are substantial savings in labor in the washing process. The pigs should stay cleaner and drier because water passes through the wire floor to the pan below, and there is no contact with wet or soggy bedding. These cages need not be changed as frequently as those with bedding. The most important feature of wire flooring is the size of the wire mesh. It must be large enough to let the droppings fall through, but not of a size to catch and break legs. Various sizes of wire mesh flooring have been used. Paterson (1962) and Porter (1962) used wire floors with mesh size 76.2 × 12.7 mm. Lane-Petter and Porter (1963) indicated that a mesh of about 18 × 18 mm is satisfactory but that a mesh size of about 75 × 12 is best. They stated that in the case of oblong mesh, longitudinal wires (those at 12 mm intervals) should be on top. In all cases the wires should be straight, not crinkled, and welded at their intersections. Wire floors must be designed to offer no lodgment for droppings at corners, along edges, or at intersections of reinforcing wires.

Several articles, particularly in the British literature, describe the successful use of wire floor cages in guinea pig breeding colonies. Therefore a room of wire-bottom cages (Fig. 3) was designed and installed in the Fort Detrick breeding colony to test the desirability of wire floor cages versus solid floor cages. Two hundred females were maintained in this room for 3 years of testing. From almost every aspect, the use of wire-bottom cages in this breeding colony was unsatisfactory. The production rate was 22% below that of the colony on solid-bottom cages and the young weighed 25% less at weaning. Bacterial pneumonia was the principle cause of a higher mortality rate among both adults and offspring. Other guinea pigs had to be eliminated because of emaciation and debility. The wire mesh floor was essentially devoid of sharp projections yet many animals had to be culled because of pododermatitis. Hairlessness increased significantly in this colony, and guinea pigs turned a dirty rust color on their ventral surfaces. Many young were caught in the wire mesh, suffered fractured legs, and had to be destroyed. The dimensions of the stainless steel wire mesh used was 12.7 × 38.1 mm.

In conclusion, it appears that wire floor cages may have advantages for short-term holding and rearing of guinea pigs provided the wire mesh is of the dimensions necessary to minimize the catching and breaking of legs. Solid floor cages with bedding, on the other hand, appear to have a decided advantage for studies where animals are maintained for an extended period of time and in breeding colonies where each cage usually contains animals of various sizes, from newborn to adults.

Points which must be emphasized when considering caging requirements include: the cage should be designed after consideration of the use to which the animal will be put, such as aging, holding, breeding, quarantine, and the length of holding time required. At all times the comfort of the animal should be considered. The cage should have adequate ventilation without drafts. Either plastic or metal is preferable in cage construction, and joints should be seamless for ease of cleaning and sanitizing. Sufficient space must be provided.

For convenience in identification and record keeping, a card holder, either permanently attached or removable, should be on each cage. Mobile racks, with shelves and removable cages, are popular. These racks are versatile, save labor, and lend themselves to maximal use of space. They should be constructed with a minimum of crevices or joints where dirt might accumulate.

C. Sanitation Procedures

Attention to details of thorough cleaning is an integral part of the success of maintaining guinea pigs. Obnoxious odors, accumulation of mineral scale from the high concentration of mineral salts in guinea pig urine, and spread of infectious diseases between animals and cages are minimized with proper sanitation of cages and racks.

Cages in which bedding is used should be cleaned and sanitized often enough to prevent an accumulation of excreta or debris. In our experience these cages should be sanitized at least once each week, and all new bedding should be added each time the cage is sanitized. Although wire floor cages do not have to be cleaned as frequently, they should be sanitized at least once every 2 weeks. The pan under the cage however must be cleaned frequently to prevent the accumulation of excreta. If large numbers of animals are maintained in each cage, daily cleaning of the pans may be necessary to maintain a high level of sanitation. Soiled bedding should be disposed of promptly either by incineration or in a way that will not contaminate other animal areas or areas of human inhabitation.

Mechanical equipment for cleaning and sanitizing cages and accessory equipment is usually located in a central area which has been specifically designed for this purpose. A cage-washing machine is highly recommended and where the size of the facility warrants the investment, a large washing machine for racks is useful. For thorough cleaning and destruction of most pathogenic organisms, the wash cycle of the machine should use water heated to not less than 180°F. When using cages made of stainless steel, weekly rotation of acid and alkaline detergents has proved to be effective in removal of urinary salt accumulations. Care must be exercised when using acid detergents to wash cages of plastic or metal, other than stainless steel, as they may corrode the cage material. Following the wash cycle, a rinse cycle is necessary to remove residue left on the cage during washing. Periodically, several randomly chosen sanitized cages should be swabbed, and the swab cultured in an effort to isolate and identify microorganisms that may have been left by the sanitation routine. The latter procedure is a valuable quality control method for determining the efficacy of the washing and sanitization cycle.

Routine sterilization of cages and bedding is not considered necessary if care is taken to assure that the washing equipment is sanitizing properly and that clean bedding is used. Where pathogenic organisms are under investigation, autoclaving animal cages and accessory equipment from the holding area is essential to prevent spread of infectious agents to man or other animals.

When washing equipment is not available, the task of cleaning cages is greatly increased. Cleaning can be done by vigorous scrubbing with appropriate detergents followed by thorough rinsing; however, in the case of the large harem-size cage, this operation would not only be cumbersome but time consuming. Cages washed in this manner should not be hand dried, but allowed to air dry in a clean area. Rinsing the cages in hot water will hasten drying.

In conclusion, all activities to acquire, breed, and house guinea pigs free of pathogenic organisms are in vain if a sanitary program is not instituted and adhered to. The "Guide for the Care and Use of Laboratory Animals" (Institute of Laboratory Animal Resources, 1972) has sections dealing specifically with personal hygiene, cleanliness, and sanitation of equipment and facilities. The well-indoctrinated animal care technician who adheres rigorously to the tenets of sanitation is an equal partner in the effort to maintain a colony of high quality guinea pigs.

II. BREEDING

The age at which sexual maturity is attained varies with sex differentiation, environment, and genetic background. Puberty in the female guinea pig may occur as early as 4–5 weeks of age. Wright (1922) found that many young females were mated by their sires before weaning at 33 days of age. Males are slower to reach maturity and although they demonstrate sexual activity at an early age, fertile matings are unusual before 8–10 weeks of age.

Guinea pigs are best mated when they are approximately 2.5 to 3 months old or when they weigh 450–600 gm, depending on the strain in question. If the female is bred before 6 months of age, there is less likelihood of the animal becoming excessively fat or having firm fusion of the symphysis pubis. For normal parturition in the guinea pig, the symphysis pubis must separate approximately the width of the index finger to permit passage of the fetus. Fusion of the symphysis pubis may lead to failure of the fetus to pass, and dystocia results.

The reproductive potential of the guinea pig is high. Generally, a litter of 3–4 young and a reproductive index of 1.0 weanling per female per month is considered standard in outbred colonies whereas in the commercial inbred guinea pig colony the standard reproductive index is 0.7 weanling per female per month. The decline in reproductive potential of inbred guinea pigs has been attributed to a decline in vigor and fertility as displayed by a reduced frequency of littering and smaller litter size.

Unless interrupted by pregnancy, pseudopregnancy, or other disturbances of the reproductive tract, the guinea pig displays signs of estrus every 13–20 days. The average interval between ovulations in unmated animals is about 16 days. The estrous cycle in the guinea pig was described by Baosich and Wyburn (1939) as having four stages: diestrus, proestrus, estrus, and metestrus. The duration of estrus is approximately 50 hours. The female will accept the male for up to 15 hours of this period, generally between 5:00 PM and 5:00 AM (Lane-Petter and Porter, 1963). Ovulation is spontaneous and occurs approximately 10 hours after the beginning of estrus and also within 2–3 hours postpartum.

Mating in the guinea pig is normally detected by either presence of sperm in the vagina or by the presence of a vaginal plug. The plug consists of a central core formed by a mixture of secretions from the male's vesicular and coagulating glands and is enclosed by a mass of flat epithelial cells apparently derived from the vaginal wall (Stockard and Papanicolaou, 1919). The plug usually fills the vagina from cervix to vulva. A few hours after its formation the plug falls out of the vagina and can often be observed as a waxy mass on the cage floor. The efficiency of utilizing plugs to predict pregnancy is usually high. Live sperm, on the other hand, can be found routinely in vaginal smears for only a few hours after copulation.

When not in estrus the vagina of the sexually immature as well as the multiparous female is closed by a cellular membrane which Stockard and Papanicolaou (1919) called the vaginal closure membrane. The epithelial membrane unites the labia of the vulva so that the vaginal opening is completely closed. This membrane is formed shortly after estrus in females that have not copulated and following expulsion of the vaginal plug in those that have copulated. It persists in pregnant animals throughout pregnancy and ruptures when the vulva swells shortly before parturition.

In colonies where intensive or continuous breeding is practiced, the male and female remain together as a static group. With this practice, maximum advantage is taken of the postpartum estrus. Our experience is similar to Rowlands (1949) in that 80% of mated guinea pigs conceived in postpartum estrus; consequently, gestation and lactation proceed simultaneously. This method reduces the time interval between litters and allows for maximum production per female.

The gestation period of the guinea pig is 59–72 days; the average is 63 days. The length of the pregnancy decreases as the litter size increases (McKeown and Macmahon, 1956). In many instances, it has been shown that the female guinea pig doubles her weight during pregnancy.

In 277 genetically heterogeneous females observed daily by Goy *et al.* (1957), 23 or 8.3% of the pregnancies were terminated by abortion. McKeown and Macmahon (1956) concluded that abortions were independent of litter size, but the stillbirth rate was directly proportional to litter size. High stillbirth rates are frequently observed in primaparous animals. Embryonic resorption, uterine hemorrhage, pregnancy toxemia, dystocias, and exhaustion from prolonged labor are common causes of death in a breeding colony.

Individual birth weights depend on nutrition, genetics, and litter size. The average individual body weight in a litter of 3 to 4 is 85 to 95 gm. Young weighing less than 50 gm at birth usually die. Young should be weaned when about 21 days old when they weigh 165 to 240 gm. Development is rapid and young should gain 2.5 to 3.5 gm per day during the first 2 months; at the end of which they should weigh 370 to 475 gm. After 2 months, growth slows and they reach maturity at 5 months; however, weight gain continues until 12 to 15 months of age, when it levels off at 700 to 850 gm for females and 950 to 1200 gm for males.

The art of breeding high quality guinea pigs has been discussed in many texts. Success has been claimed for several breeding systems; however, the system selected by a breeder will be based on the type of equipment, housing, and caretaker personnel available and the purposes for which the animals are required.

Breeding systems may be divided into two groups, each with several variations; these are (1) monogamous pairs and (2) polygamous groups.

1. Monogamous Pairs

With this system a paired male and female of breeding age are mated in a single cage. Monogamous pair breeding is used widely in inbreeding, which requires brother × sister matings, for the issue of littermates, or for selection of stock most suitable for intensive breeding in polygamous groups. Record keeping is simple; however, this system requires maintaining a large number of boars, is less efficient, and requires more space and labor. If the pair is maintained together continually, there is the advantage of the postpartum mating, and it is generally believed that there is a greater number of young weaned per female.

2. Polygamous Groups

This system consists of mating a select number of sows to one boar. Opinions vary regarding the optimum number of sows for a polygamous group; however, the most important factor appears not to be the number of sows which a boar can successfully service, but rather the space available per sow. It is recommended that each sow be provided with 180 square inches of floor space. Due to the aggressive nature of males, when using this system, best results are obtained when there is not more than one boar per pen.

Polygamous groups may be handled several ways: (a) They may be maintained as a static colony and held intact throughout their useful breeding life. This maximizes the advantage of postpartum breeding and communal rearing of young. (b) Sows in advanced pregnancy may be isolated individually for farrowing. After the young are weaned, the sow is again returned to the mating pen and the cycle continues. (c) In the communal farrowing and rearing method, advanced pregnant sows are removed from mating pens and allowed to litter in groups, young are reared communally, and after weaning, the sows are returned to the mating pens.

Monogamous pairs produce the greatest number of offspring per female, but considering the saving in space and the number of animals required, the ratio of 1 male to 4 or 5 females is usually a more efficient housing method. The efficient breeding life of guinea pigs varies and is dependent on many factors including the number of animals per cage as well as genetic and environmental variables. Under ideal management, most guinea pigs reproduce efficiently until 27–30 months of age.

III. WATERING

Most facilities supply water by means of a water bottle and sipper tube. Theoretically, a 32-oz bottle filled daily should supply sufficient water to a breeding cage of 5 adults. However, guinea pigs have a tendency to play with the sipper tube and rapidly empty the bottles. Most of the water ends up in the bedding or on the floor. Collins (1972) reported wastage of water can be reduced by fitting drinking bottles with ball-bearing equipped drinking tubes instead of standard valveless tubes. Presently, the Fort Detrick colony uses automatic water devices mounted about ¾ inch outside the cage thus allowing excess water to drop to the floor and exit through a centrally located floor drain. This system was installed in 1965 and has functioned very satisfactorily. Most important, water is available 24 hours a day. Automatic watering is not recommended for use in guinea pigs housed in solid-bottom cages, unless it is of the design to prevent drippage and leakage into the cage.

The "Nutritive Requirement of Laboratory Animals," second edition (1972), published by the National Academy of Sciences, indicates that adult guinea pigs receiving a green food supplement (usually kale or lettuce) require 50 to 100 ml of water per day. Without a supply of green food, 250 to 1000 ml per day are required because of spillage. As the amount of "greens" in the diet increases, the amount of water required decreases. The reverse is true as well; however, Bruce (1950) indicated that guinea pigs whose water was supplied wholly by green food were less thrifty than those having access to water. She indicated that the amount of water they consumed in green food was below their optimum needs. Mortality rates increase significantly when animals are deprived water. Pregnant and lactating females are affected first followed by young, rapidly growing animals.

IV. NUTRITION

Among the commonly used laboratory species, only guinea pigs and primates require a dietary source of vitamin C (ascorbic acid). Collins and Elvehjem (1958) reported the ascorbic acid requirement for growth of immature guinea pigs is 0.5 mg per 100 gm body weight per day. Nungester and Ames (1948) indicated that a 300-gm guinea pig requires a daily intake of approximately 6 mg of vitamin C to provide adequate protection against infection. Under intensive breeding conditions, the requirement of the adult female that is pregnant or lactating during most of her breeding life is at least 20 mg per day (Bruce and Parker, 1947).

Commercial pelleted diets are manufactured to meet the requirements of the guinea pig for ascorbic acid. Additionally, they are usually fortified to compensate for ascorbic acid losses in storage. In general, most commercial guinea pig feeds are satisfactory in regard to vitamin C content. Laboratory animal feeds must not be maintained too long in storage and must be fresh when used. This is not a pious platitude when referring to guinea pig feed. Ideally, guinea pig feeds should be stored in rooms where the temperature is 50°F or less, and should not be stored in the animal room. The date of manufacture is commonly given or coded on each feed bag, and a strong effort should be made to store feed for no longer than 4 to 6 weeks from the date of manufacture. This is especially important where no green vegetable supplement is offered. Feeders should be designed to prevent guinea pigs from climbing into them. For this purpose the standard "J" type feeder works very well.

Feeding guinea pigs green vegetables in addition to the pelleted diet has been a subject of continuing controversy. A "green" supplement on a regular basis may provide insurance against vitamin C deficiency; however, its benefits go beyond this one advantage. These benefits are most apparent in a production colony under an intensive breeding system where there is heavy stress on the pregnant or lactating female. We have concluded that such supplements enhance the ability of breeding animals to maintain body weight. Based on the results of feeding experiments in which four different commercially prepared diets were compared using large numbers of animals held for breeding periods of 18–24 months, we have observed that the feeding of green supplement resulted in an average increase of 10 to 44% in weaned offspring over the same pelleted feeds without green supplement. Dean and Duell (1963) compared several pelletted diets with and without supplementation. They reinforce our belief that in comparison of diets for breeding guinea pigs, tests for nutrient adequacy must involve long-term studies of breeding animals, preferably for several subsequent generations.

Guinea pigs on short-term experiments can be maintained on fresh pelleted feed and water without provision of green supplement, but care must be taken to provide an adequate water supply.

Maintenance and therapeutic levels of ascorbic acid can be given through the water supply. Ascorbic acid given in this manner is effective at 0.2 gm/liter when added to distilled or resin column deionized water (Paterson, 1962). Ascorbic acid undergoes rapid oxidation, which is enhanced by heat and catalyzed by copper; therefore, if vitamin C is to be given at an effective level in the water supply, a non-copper water system and frequent preparation of the drinking solution are required. Paterson (1962) indicated that approximately 50% of the vitamin activity was present after 24 hours when glass or plastic bottles were employed.

Although a number of vegetable supplements such as carrots, cabbage, sprouted grain, chicory, and mangolds have been used, kale is routinely fed in our colony because it has one of the highest vitamin C levels of all commonly available vegetables. One hundred grams of kale contains 115 mg of ascorbic acid (Heinz and Co., 1959). Also, kale is totally edible, eagerly accepted by guinea pigs, and is available all year in our area. The supplier is required to maintain on his premises automatic equipment for washing the kale in a chlorinated solution in order to provide a product free of chemical residue and minimal surface bacteria. After washing the kale it is immediately iced in disposable plastic bags and delivered daily. Kale has not been implicated at any time as a source of contamination in our colony. Colony contamination by way of the feed, however, is of considerable concern. *Salmonella* species or chemical residues used to control crop insects could be introduced into a colony via the feed. Fluorosis (Hard and Atkinson, 1967), estrogens (Wright and Seibold, 1958), *Pasteurella pseudotuberculosis* (Paterson *et al.*, 1962), *Histoplasma capsulatum* (Correa and Pacheco, 1967), and *Aspergillus flavus* (Paterson *et al.*, 1962) have also been introduced by contaminated feed. These reports illustrate that feed contamination can and does occur in dry pelleted feeds as well as vegetable supplements. Although many of the more intricate quality control tests are beyond the capability of most colonies, maximal effort must be made to ensure that the feed is of highest quality.

Guinea pigs have unusually high requirement for certain amino acids and this is usually met by providing a diet of 20% protein (cf. Chapter 17), usually of plant origin (Reid, 1958). In England, animal protein in fish meal or meat meal is often used quite successfully in guinea pig feeds.

Guinea pigs appear to have definite taste preferences and alterations in the composition of a feed or the introduction of a new feed may result in a sharp decline in feed consumption to the point of starvation or where clinical symptoms of vitamin deficiency rapidly appear. In one instance in our experience the animals refused to eat pelleted feed from our usual supplier. Within 10 days the death rate increased in younger animals with some showing signs of lameness and paralysis. These pigs were found to be suffering from a form of muscular dystrophy. Since we were able to reverse the process with injection of α-tocopherol, we attributed the condition to hypovitaminosis E due to drastically reduced food intake. We later determined that the feed in question contained about five times the amount of NaCl called for in the formula and was thus unpalatable.

V. QUALITY CONTROL

In surveillance of colony health, access to a diagnostic laboratory capable of bacteriological and parasitological tests is an important part of colony management. It allows one to readily confirm or disprove the presence or absence of disease which may adversely affect colony health. Grossly, guinea pigs should be observed daily for signs of disease or any abnormality. Gross observation is not sufficient to detect all diseases, so it is advisable in production colonies to remove representative guinea pigs periodically for necropsy. This can be done by examining approximately 10% of retired breeders. Dead and sick animals should be similarly evaluated. To confirm the cause of disease in select cases, it may be necessary for affected tissues to be examined histologically by a pathologist familiar with laboratory animal diseases.

Guinea pig sera have been tested against many of the latent viruses affecting rats, mice, and hamsters. There is little work which substantiates actual infection by these viruses, and it is quite obvious that much work will be necessary to define the viral flora of the guinea pig and the role which each virus plays.

Cesarian derivation of the guinea pig is a relatively easy surgical procedure. The primary need for this operation, however, is not for production of germfree animals, but rather for obtaining animals aseptically derived and reared in an environment free of pathogenic contamination of parents, thus breaking disease cycles. Although transplacental transfer of disease and mycoplasma infection of the uterus (Juhr and Obi, 1970) are possible sources for contamination of cesarian-derived young, successful derivations and gnotobiotic rearing of guinea pigs have established nucleus colonies free of disease. From these nuclei, new foundation colonies free of communicable diseases can be populated.

To assure that the disease-free status is maintained and that the introduction of pathogenic organisms has not occurred, there must be continuous monitoring of holding and production colonies, as described previously. The entry of new animals with undefined flora into such a colony is considered a great risk. If animals are introduced from an outside source, diagnostic monitoring and a quarantine period of at least 2 weeks are recommended.

REFERENCES

Bacsich, P., and Wyburn, G. M. (1939). Observations on the estrus cycle of the guinea pig. *Proc. Roy. Soc. Edinburgh* **60,** 33–39.

Brewer, N. R. (1964). Estimating heat produced by laboratory animals. *Heat., Piping Air Cond.* **36,** 139–141.

Bruce, H. M. (1950). The water requirement of laboratory animals. *J. Anim. Tech. Ass.* **1,** 2–8.

Bruce, H. M., and Parker, A. S. (1947). Feeding and breeding of laboratory animals. III. Observations on the feeding of guinea pigs. *J. Hyg.* **45,** 70–78.

Collins, G. R. (1972). The relative efficiencies of ball bearing equipped drinking tubes. *Lab. Anim. Sci.* **22,** 507–508.

Collins, M., and Elvehjem, C. A. (1958). Ascorbic acid requirement of the guinea pig using growth and tissue ascorbic acid concentrations as criteria. *J. Nutr.* **64,** 503–511.

Correa, W. M., and Pacheco, A. C. (1967). Naturally occurring histoplasmosis in guinea pigs. *Can. J. Comp. Med. Vet. Sci.* **31,** 203–205.

Dean, D. J., and Duell, C. (1963). Diets without green food for guinea pigs. *Lab. Anim. Care* **13,** 191–196.

Dick, M., and Hanel, E. (1970). *In* "Design Criteria," Vol. II, p. 228. Dept. of the Army, Fort Detrick, Frederick, Maryland.

Goy, R. W., Hoar, R. M., and Young, W. C. (1957). Length of gestation in the guinea pig with data on the frequency and time of abortion and still birth. *Anat. Rec.* **128,** 747–757.

Hard, G. C., and Atkinson, F. F. V. (1967). The aetiology of "slobbers" (chronic fluorosis) in the guinea pig. *J. Pathol. Bacteriol.* **94,** 103–111.

Heinz, H. J. and Co. (1959). *In* "Nutritional Data," 3rd ed., p. 124. H. J. Heinz and Co., Pittsburgh, Pennsylvania.

Hill, B. F. (1971). Some physiological parameters of small animals. *Charles River Dig.* **10,** No. 4.

Institute of Laboratory Animal Resources (1972). "Guide for the Care and Use of Laboratory Animals," 4th ed. National Research Council, Washington D.C.

Juhr, N. C., and Obi, S. (1970). Uterine infection in guinea pigs. *Z. Versuchstierk.* **12,** 383–387.

Lane-Petter, W., and Porter, G. (1963). *In* "Animals for Research" (W. Lane-Petter, ed.), pp. 287–321. Academic Press, New York.

McKeown, T., and Macmahon, B. (1956). The influence of litter size and litter order on length of gestation and early postnatal growth in guinea pigs. *Endocrinology* **13,** 195–200.

Nungester, W. J., and Ames, A. M. (1948). The relationship between ascorbic acid and phagocytic activity. *J. Infec. Dis.* **83,** 50–54.

Paterson, J. S. (1962). Guinea-pig disease. *In* "The Problems of Laboratory Animal Disease" (R.J.C. Harris, ed.), Part II, pp. 169–184. Academic Press, New York.

Paterson, J. S. (1967). *In* "The UFAW Handbook on the Care and Management of Laboratory Animals" (UFAW, ed.), 3rd ed. pp. 241–287. Williams & Wilkins, Baltimore, Maryland.

Paterson, J. S., Crook, J. C., Shand, A., Lewis, G., and Allcroft, R. (1962). Groundnut toxicity as the cause of exudative hepatitis of guinea pigs. *Vet. Rec.* **74,** 639–640.

Plank, J. S., and Irwin, R. (1966). Infertility of guinea pigs on sawdust bedding. *Lab. Anim. Care* **16,** 9–11.

Porter, G. (1962). Keeping guinea-pigs on wire-mesh floors. *In* "Notes for Breeders of Common Laboratory Animals" (G. Porter and W. Lane-Petter eds.), 1st ed., pp. 23–25. Academic Press, New York.

Reid, M. E. (1958). "The Guinea Pig in Research." Human Factors Research Bur., Inc., Publ. No. 557, Washington, D.C.

Rowlands, I. W. (1949). Postpartum breeding in the guinea pig. *J. Hyg.* **47,** 281–287.

Stockard, C. R., and Papanicolaou, G. N. (1919). The vaginal closure membrane, copulation, and the vaginal plug in the guinea pig, with further consideration of estrus rhythm. *Biol. Bull.* **37,** 222–245.

Weihe, W. H. (1971). The significance of the physical environment for the health and state of adaption of laboratory animals. *In* "Defining the Laboratory Animal." *Proc. Symp. ICLA, NCS, 4th, 1969* pp. 353–378.

Wright, J. E., and Seibold, J. R. (1958). Estrogen contamination of pelleted feed for laboratory animals–effect on guinea pig reproduction. *J. Amer. Vet. Med. Ass.* **132,** 258–261.

Wright, S. (1922). The effects of inbreeding and cross breeding on guinea pigs. *U.S. Dep. Agr., Bull.* **1090.**

Young, W. C. (1927). The influence of high temperature on the guinea pig testis. *J. Exp. Zool.* **49,** 459–499.

Chapter 3

Biomethodology

Richard M. Hoar

I. INTRODUCTION

Extensive use of the guinea pig in a variety of experimental procedures ranging from inhalation studies to induced endocrine deficiencies has given rise to modifications of common biomethodology as well as the introduction of specialized techniques. These are presented below according to the system or organ involved except for common surgical techniques and procedures involving the uterus and placenta which are included under Surgery (Section III).

II. ANESTHESIOLOGY

Anesthetic techniques in guinea pigs were reviewed by Hoar (1965, 1969), who discussed handling, restraint, resuscitation, postanesthetic care, and euthanasia as well as intravascular and inhalant anesthetic agents, adjuvants, and respiratory stimulants. As reported in these reviews, methoxyflurane was an excellent anesthetic. Ether was relatively unsafe in guinea pigs (Hoar, 1969) and halothane produced hepatic lesions (Hughes and Lang, 1972). However, Künzel (1970) successfully employed a combination of halothane and nitrous oxide with a breathing mask to induce surgical anesthesia. Of various injectable anesthetics, pentobarbital has a somewhat unpredictable effect (Hoar, 1969). Ketamine hydrochloride (44 mg/kg) given im together with atropine to control salivation will abolish pain perception for 15 to 25 minutes with rapid recovery (Weisbroth and Fudens, 1972). Rubright and Thayer (1970) reported that a mixture of droperidol and fentanyl citrate (Innovar-Vet*) was a "safe and profound surgical anesthetic drug for the guinea pig" at levels of 0.66 to 0.88 ml/kg im. Lewis and Jennings (1972) reported that 0.08 mg/kg Innovar-Vet given im was sufficient for cardiac punctures. However, Leash *et al.* (1973) reported that although Innovar-Vet was an excellent anesthetic, it produced swelling and lameness followed by self-mutilation of the injected leg. They attributed these sequelae to the effects of the acidic solution and recommended that Innovar-Vet not be used in guinea pigs.

Hopcroft (1966) suggested epidural anesthesia in guinea pigs. Initially an intraaxillary injection of chlorpromazine (5 to 10 mg) was given followed by 0.2 to 0.25 ml of warm 0.5 to 1% xylocaine given as a lumbosacral epidural injection to produce anesthesia and relaxation for up to 45 minutes. Continuous epidural anesthesia, with a 1% lidocaine solution with epinephrine (1:100,000), provided good anesthesia of the lower abdomen (Tan and Snow, 1968). Patent intervertebral foramina and fat in the epidural space may interfere with the spread of the anesthetic solution and so limit its effectiveness.

Special anesthetic techniques are required to investigate the living guinea pig fetus. Schwartze *et al.* (1971) combined a local anesthetic, procaine, with tracheostomy followed by succinylcholine (1 mg/kg, iv) for immediate immobilization, lumbar intervertebral injection of absolute alcohol (0.1 to 0.2 ml) for spinal anesthesia, and continuous infusion of NaCl (0.9%) plus succinylcholine (0.03 mg/kg/minute) to maintain paralysis.

The effectiveness of local anesthetics such as procaine, cocaine, and lidocaine may be increased by intraperitoneal administration of an imidazole base, although this compound does not appear to exhibit any anesthetic properties by itself (Parellada *et al.*, 1971). Continued investigation of possible local anesthetic agents has led to the observation that tertiary haloalkylamines enter the cell and form a cyclic quaternary ammonium derivative which could have local anesthetic action (Ross and Akerman, 1971). Similarly, phenothiazine derivatives have been investigated as local anesthetics and compared with lidocaine, procaine, and cocaine with encouraging results (Sharma *et al.*, 1971).

III. SURGERY

A. Adrenalectomy

A technique for bilateral adrenalectomy of guinea pigs in two stages was presented by Hoar (1966). The presentation includes a review of the literature, photographs of the operation, a list of equipment, and comments on anesthetic techniques and postoperative care. Hopcroft (1966) used a transverse abdominal incision to remove both adrenals in a single stage operation. This approach allowed better exposure of both adrenals and, with the intestines limited within a plastic bag containing normal saline, it also allowed more space in which to maneuver within the abdominal cavity.

B. Thyroidectomy

Surgical thyroidectomy in guinea pigs is a relatively simple procedure but care must be used to avoid injury to the recurrent laryngeal nerves. Williams *et al.* (1941), Young *et al.* (1952), and Peterson *et al.* (1952) were among the first to describe a thyroidectomy technique while Fabre and Marescaux (1966, 1969) and Fabre *et al.* (1970) noted and measured the rapid recovery of thyroid activity due to the development of unseen thyroid "rests." Kromka and Hoar (1975) drew from all these sources and added some procedural refinements in their presentation of an improved thyroidectomy technique.

C. Lobectomy

Berstein and Agee (1964) described a method for lobectomy in guinea pigs which required a skillful blending of assisted respiration during the surgical procedure and careful postoperative care. The reported mortality rate (55%) could be significantly reduced by modifying the respiratory apparatus to include an inhalant anesthetic rather than using sodium pentobarbital (Nembutal†) anesthesia.

D. Uterus and Placenta

Uterine surgery has also been described. Rowlands (1961) removed the uterus through a small midline incision with the aid of electrocautery. Bland (1970) developed a two-stage operation for autotransplantation of the uterus to the abdominal wall. The latter technique requires extensive use of electrocautery. Uterine surgery has been combined with the development of techniques for studying placental transport *in situ* including perfusion and recovery of test substances from both the maternal and fetal sides of the placenta (Money and Dancis, 1960).

E. Ovariectomy

Ovariectomy is accomplished through bilateral dorsal incisions ½ inch long, commencing ½ inch posterior to the last rib and proceeding parallel to the erector spinae muscles

*Innovar-Vet, Pitman-Moore, Inc., Washington Crossing, New Jersey.

†Nembutal, Abbott Laboratories, North Chicago, Illinois.

on the dorsum of each flank. A loose fat pad surrounding the ovary and oviduct, located just posterior to the inferior pole of the kidney, may be reached with blunt-tipped forceps and pulled through the incision. Electrocautery or sutures may be used to prevent bleeding as the ovary and *the entire oviduct* are excised. Potential endocrine tissue, "ovarian rests," located along the length of the oviduct, can restore a normal estrous cycle (without ovulation) in a substantial number of ovariectomized guinea pigs.

IV. INTUBATIONS AND INJECTIONS

Liquids or solids, particularly materials which create problems of contamination such as radioisotopes or microorganisms, may be administered in a gelatin capsule with a small version of a large animal balling gun (Nelson and Hoar, 1969). Solutions or suspensions may be introduced into the bronchopulmonary circulation by occluding the esophagus with a special probe and allowing normal respiratory movements to aspirate liquids placed in the animal's oral pharynx (Vlad *et al.*, 1970). Quantities of fluids, up to 5 ml, may be deposited in the axilla or the nape of the neck with the aid of a syringe and needle. However, the most common procedure for the introduction of materials in various forms is by injection, either subcutaneous, intramuscular, intraperitoneal, intrathoracic, intracardiac, or intravenous. Intravenous injections have been administered to guinea pigs by way of the dorsal metatarsal vein (Nobunaga *et al.*, 1966), lateral marginal vein of the leg (Grice, 1964), lateral metatarsal vein (Dolence and Jones, 1975), dorsolateral veins of the penis (Karlson, 1959; Grice, 1964), superficial veins of the ventral abdominal wall (Johnson, 1950), or the marginal ear veins (Markam and Kent, 1951; Karlson and Feldman, 1953; Grice, 1964). A restraining apparatus was designed by McKeon (1963) which facilitated ear vein injections. An indwelling cannula was used successfully in guinea pigs for both repeated injections and blood sampling by Shrader and Everson (1968).

V. BLOOD, BLOOD FLOW, AND BLOOD PRESSURE

Obtaining blood samples from guinea pigs is almost as difficult as intravenous injections. Methods commonly employed include cutting the nail bed (Vallejo-Freire, 1951; Lehnert, 1967; Enta *et al.*, 1968), puncture of the dorsal metatarsal vein (Nobunaga *et al.*, 1966) or marginal ear vein (Markam and Kent, 1951; Karlson and Feldman, 1953; Grice, 1964), puncture of the orbital sinus (Sorg and Buckner, 1964), vacuum-assisted bleeding of either the lateral marginal vein of the hind limb (Sandiford, 1965; Rosenhaft *et al.*, 1971), or the lateral metatarsal vein (Dolence and Jones, 1975), cardiac puncture, or via the indwelling cannula technique of Shrader and Everson (1968). Stone *et al.* (1961) reported that carbon dioxide anesthesia increased the yields of blood and serum particularly when exsanguinating the animal. A method for obtaining 3 to 6 ml of blood from the fetal aorta was described by Simpson *et al.* (1967) and Burnette *et al.* (1968).

Blood flow through the spleen has been determined with xenon-133. The method is based on measurement of the rate of disappearance of xenon-133 from the spleen (Sandberg, 1972). Similarly, uterine blood flow was measured near term by Künzel and Moll (1972) and a technique for recording the blood pressure of fetal guinea pigs was described briefly by Davitaya and Nadirashvili (1971).

VI. ELECTROENCEPHALOGRAPHY AND ELECTROCARDIOGRAPHY

The guinea pig is preferred by many investigators for study of antenatal cardiac or cortical activities under various maternal conditions. The technique of Flexner *et al.* (1950) for determining fetal EEG involved delivery by cesarian section into a bath of warm Ringer's solution while maintaining an intact umbilical circulation. Following craniotomy, electrodes were placed on the cerebral cortex. Bergström *et al.* (1961) and Bergström (1962) modified this procedure by pushing hook electrodes directly through the fetal skull where they would rest on or perhaps 1 to 2 mm into the fetal cortex. Rosen and McLaughlin (1966a,b) and Singer *et al.* (1973) further modified this technique. In order to prevent loss of amniotic fluid and avoid the trauma of hysterotomy, they compressed the fetal vertex against the uterine wall and then pushed the needle electrodes through the myometrium, scalp, and skull to reach the cerebral cortex. A third electrode was sutured to the myometrium over the fetal thorax to record the fetal ECG. Schwartze *et al.* (1971) delivered the fetus via hysterotomy into warm Tyrodes' solution, incised the skin above the sagittal suture and inserted electrodes through the skull onto the brain surface. The electrodes were of two varieties depending upon whether only prenatal or peri- and postnatal EEG's were to be recorded. Electrocardiograms were recorded through six barbed, hook electrodes implanted subcutaneously. A method for measuring nerve conduction velocity of fibers supplying muscles on the plantar surface of the hind foot was described by Fullerton (1966).

Richtarik *et al.* (1965) described a device for measuring ECG's in an unanesthetized guinea pig resting quietly in a normal standing position. Their technique seems preferable to the sling method of Pratt (1938), as modified by Corwin *et al.* (1963), or the supine position utilized by Bartmann and Reinert (1952) and modified by Lukoschek and Thiesen (1954) and Eichbaum and Britto-Pereira (1964). Greenfield and Shepherd (1953) measured fetal heart rate, particularly in response to occlusion of the umbilical cord, with a plethysmograph in a constant temperature saline bath.

VII. RESPIRATION

Normal average values for tidal volume (1.68 ml), respiratory rate (84/minute), minute volume (139 ml), resistance (0.73 cm H_2O/ml/second), and compliance (0.20 ml/cm H_2O) were reported by Amdur and Mead (1958) following their development of techniques for the measurement of intrapleural pressure and ventilatory activity. Intrapleural pressures were measured by a fluid-filled tube inserted into the chest cavity and connected to pressure recorders, while ventilatory measurements were determined by a body plethysomograph. Murphy and Ulrich (1964) altered these techniques to produce a multianimal test system and Swann *et al.* (1965) modified them further to increase the ease of operation. In particular, they added a face mask pneumotachograph to record respiratory activity and a camera to record oscilloscopic vectors of flow and pressure. Alarie *et al.* (1970) modified this system further by adding on-line data extraction with an IBM 1800 digital computer system.

To test the anaphylactic or toxic effect of various compounds upon the lungs, inhalation chambers have been developed including: a modified desiccator with an atomizer (Loew *et al.*, 1945); a 4 liter bottle with a screw cap and an attached nebulizer (Siegmund *et al.*, 1947); a Lucite* exposure chamber complete with humidity and air flow controls (Amdur *et al.*, 1952); complex exposure chambers with extensive controls and sampling devices (Siegel, 1961; Rector *et al.*, 1966; Rose *et al.*, 1970).

Special chambers have been developed for hyperbaric exposures (Rose *et al.*, 1970), to measure respiratory minute volumes with a modified spirometer (Hoebel *et al.*, 1971), and to test the effects of cigarette smoke (Hughes *et al.*, 1970; Lewis and Nicholls, 1972). Two valve methods and one modified oscilloscopic respirograph method were presented by Guyton (1947) for the measurement of respiratory volume.

Fetuses damaged by asphyxia *in utero* show physical signs of distress at the time of the insult (Greenfield and Shepherd, 1953) as well as behavioral deficits when tested as young adults. Becker and Donnell (1952) described a "problem box" and a testing procedure for determining learning deficits after *in utero* asphyxia.

VIII. SKIN

The guinea pig has been used extensively in immunology and studies of inflammatory reactions. The physiological characteristics of its skin are similar to that of man which has led to other areas of investigation such as that of wounds and burns.

*Lucite, DuPont DeNemours and Co., Wilmington, Delaware.

Expressing these injuries as a percentage of the total surface area requires a nomograph to estimate body surface areas of guinea pigs (Ilahi *et al.*, 1971). Studies of wound healing lacked standardization until Must *et al.* (1965) designed a machine to produce and suture a uniform wound on the backs of anesthetized guinea pigs thus eliminating variables of depth, length, angle, and skin apposition. White *et al.* (1971) summarized the basic techniques and provided a standardized method for determining the tensile strength of wounded and unwounded skin.

To examine inflammatory responses more precisely Lambelin *et al.* (1971) utilized cutaneous thermometry to evaluate erythema induced by ultraviolet light and Davies *et al.* (1971) measured edema in the foot with a linear displacement transducer connected with a computer to allow large-scale screening and rapid calculations of antinflammatory activity. Shukla (1969) developed a method for determining the total and differential melanocyte count and intermediate cells of Billingham and Medawar in the skin of black guinea pigs.

Hair color may be used to identify individual animals. As drawing the sometimes complex patterns of multicolored guinea pigs is time consuming at best, the electronic flash photographic method of Roberts (1961) is both fast and accurate. Through the use of mirrors the photographer can obtain the color patterns of both flanks as well as the back of the animal in a single picture.

IX. GASTRIC SECRETIONS AND PERITONEAL FLUIDS

Methods for measuring gastric secretion are essential to studies of peptic ulcers. Techniques include chronic gastric fistulas (Ragins and Wincze, 1969), peroral intubation (Watt, 1955; Watt and Wilson, 1957, 1958), gastrostomy and pyloric ligation with or without partial devascularization of the stomach (Johnson and Fjeld, 1971a,b), and an improved peroral intubation method which through prior training of the animal and the presence of a rubber mouth adapter allowed collection of gastric secretions without anesthesia (Capoferro and Torgersen, 1971).

Measurement of gas exchange between various body compartments through continuous measurement of PCO_2 in the peritoneal fluid was reported by Harichaux *et al.* (1971). Their technique involved extracorporal circulation of fluid through a measuring cell with an electrometer and recording potentiometer attached. The guinea pig is anesthetized and ventilated through a pump attached to a tracheal cannula.

The *in vivo* potential differences between various fluid compartments in pregnant guinea pigs, i.e., the maternal peritoneal cavity versus the amniotic fluid, fetal stomach, and fetal peritoneal cavity, may be determined with a salt bridge technique developed by Mellor (1969).

X. EAR

Methods for measuring cochlear microphonics in guinea pigs with implanted intracochlear electrodes were reported by Tasaki *et al.* (1952). Benson and Eldredge (1955) demonstrated with a small acoustic probe that variations in sound pressure could be induced by normal and abnormal tympanic membranes, and Pestalloza and Davis (1956) measured electric responses induced in the guinea pig ear by high audiofrequencies. Tonndorf (1958) modified some of Tasaki's techniques and Laszlo *et al.* (1970) modified the techniques of previous investigators to insure a constant input stimulus to the ear to establish an accurate mathematical model. A sound-proof chamber, an acoustic generator, and the pinna reflex of Preyers were combined by Finkiewicz-Murawiejska (1971) to determine the threshold values of sound intensity for individual frequencies of pure tones.

A rheographic method to determine the degree of filling of blood vessels and the velocity of blood movement was adapted by Romanov (1971) to assess circulation in the labyrinth; a technique for which he suggests the term rheocochleography.

XI. MILK

A miniature milking machine for guinea pigs was designed by Gilmstedt *et al.* (1937) and modified by Nelson *et al.* (1951); the latter report was accompanied by a detailed description of milking technique and composition of the milk itself. Gupta *et al.* (1970) constructed a very simple device for collecting milk from guinea pigs; however, its very simplicity reduced the milk yield and standardization of technique so necessary for long-term daily milkings.

XII. SPERM

Electrical ejaculation was considered by Dalziel and Phillips (1948) who included a historical review with their description of an improved technique. Further modifications of the electroejaculation technique were described by Freund (1958) in a preliminary report which included a liquifaction method utilizing chymotrypsin. These techniques were detailed further in a report of the characteristics of guinea pig semen collected in this manner (Freund, 1969). Employing sperm collected by electroejaculation, Shulman *et al.* (1971) developed a spermagglutination technique for producing antibodies to spermatozoa.

XIII. MISCELLANEOUS

For those interested in counting bone marrow cells from guinea pig femurs, a comparison of techniques for differential counting was presented by Epstein and Tompkins (1943) together with tables characterizing bone marrow cells and giving differential counts.

A method for measuring delayed hypersensitivity in guinea pigs using the cornea was described by Raffel *et al.* (1949). As these measurements were subjective, Herbert *et al.* (1970) modified the procedure to include a spectrophotometer which eliminated observer variations.

Kirkpatrick and Silver (1970) presented the details of a simple method for lymphography in small laboratory animals such as guinea pigs. The procedure employed only standard materials and although it cannot be used to visualize lymphatics in the extremities, it was useful for examination of the lymphatics in the pelvis, abdomen, and thorax.

REFERENCES

Alarie, Y., Ulrich, C. E., and Haddock, R. H. (1970). Respiratory system flow resistance with digital computer techniques measured in cynomolgus monkeys and guinea pigs. *Arch. Environ. Health* **21**, 483–491.

Amdur, M. O., and Mead, J. (1958). Mechanics of respiration in unanesthetized guinea pigs. *Amer. J. Physiol.* **192**, 364–368.

Amdur, M. O., Schulz, R. L., and Drinker, P. (1952). Toxicity of sulfuric acid mist to guinea pigs. *Arch. Ind. Hyg. Occup. Med.* **5**, 318–329.

Bartmann, K., and Reinert, H. (1952). Das Extramitäten–und Brustwandelektrokardiogramm des nichtnarkotisierten Meerschweinchens. *Naunyn-Schmiedebergs Arch. Exp. Pathol. Pharmakol.* **216**, 258–267.

Becker, R. F., and Donnell, W. (1952). Learning behavior in guinea pigs subjected to asphyxia at birth. *J. Comp. Physiol. Psychol.* **45**, 153–162.

Benson, R. W., and Eldredge, D. H. (1955). Variations in sound pressure produced in guinea-pig ears due to normal and abnormal eardrums. *J. Acoust. Soc. Amer.* **27**, 373–375.

Bergström, R. M. (1962). A surgical technique for the study of brain, muscle and ECG potentials in the foetus. *Ann. Chir. Gynaecol. Fenn.* **51**, 504–510.

Bergström, R. M., Hellström, P.-E., and Stenberg, D. (1961). An intrauterine technique for recording the foetal EEG in animals. *Ann. Chir. Gynaecol. Fenn.* **50**, 430–433.

Bernstein, I. L., and Agee, J. (1964). Successful lobectomy in the guinea pig. *Lab. Anim. Care* **14**, 519–523.

Bland, K. P. (1970). Uterine autotransplantation to the abdominal wall in the guinea-pig. *J. Endocrinol.* **48**, 615–620.

Burnette, J. C., Simpson, D. M., Chandler, D. C., Jr., and Bawden, J. W. (1968). Fetal blood calcium response to maternal parathyroid and vitamin D administration in guinea pigs. *J. Dent. Res.* **47**, 444–446.

Capoferro, R., and Torgersen, O. (1971). A gastric secretion test in the intact guinea-pig. *Scand. J. Gastroenterol.* **6**, 429–433.

Corwin, A. H., Dukes-Dobos, F. N., and Hamberger, M. (1963). Bioassay of blood allergens. II. Food-induced reactions of the heart rate of guinea pigs. *Ann. Allergy* **21**, 547–562.

Dalziel, C. F., and Phillips, C. L. (1948). Electric ejaculation. Determination of optimum electric shock to produce ejaculation in chinchillas and guinea pigs. *Amer. J. Vet. Res.* 9, 225–232.

Davies, G. E., Evans, D. P., and Horsefall, G. B. (1971). An automatic device for the measurement of oedema in the feet of rats and guinea pigs. *Med. Biol. Eng.* **9**, 567–570.

Davitaya, M. D., and Nadirashvili, S. A. (1971). Method of recording blood pressure in the umbilical arteries of guinea pig fetuses with the placental circulation intact. *Bull. Exp. Biol. Med. (USSR)* **71**, 119–120.

Dolence, D., and Jones, H. E. (1975). Pericutaneous phlebotomy and intravenous injection in the guinea pig. *Lab. Anim. Sci.* **25**, 106–107.

Eichbaum, E. W., and Britto-Pereira, C. (1964). Effect of cranial trauma on the electrocardiogram experiments in guinea pigs. *Cardiologia* **44**, 46–56.

Enta, T., Lockey, S. D., Jr., and Reed, C. E. (1968). A rapid safe technique for repeated blood collection from small laboratory animals. The farmer's wife method. *Proc. Soc. Exp. Biol. Med.* **127**, 136–137.

Epstein, R. D., and Tompkins, E. H. (1943). A comparison of techniques for the differential counting of bone marrow cells (guinea pig). *Amer. J. Med. Sci.* **206**, 249–260.

Fabre, M., and Marescaux, J. (1966). Mise en évidence d'une hyperexcrétion hormonale par des régénérats thyroïdiens après thyroïdectomie chirurgicale chez le cobaye. *C. R. Soc. Biol.* **160**, 1955–1958.

Fabre, M., and Marescaux, J. (1969). Valeur fonctionnelle des régénérats thyroïdiens développés chez le cobaye après thyroïdectomie chirurgicale. Recherches morphologiques, radiobiologiques et biochimiques. *Arch. Biol.* **80**, 413–442.

Fabre, M., Marescaux, J., and Vivien-Roels, B. (1970). Compensatory hormonogenic hyperactivity of thyroid homo- and autografts, as well as of regenerates *in situ*, in the thyroidectomized guinea pig–comparative chemical and radiobiological study. *Comp. Biochem. Physiol.* **35**, 945–951.

Finkiewicz-Murawiejska, L. (1971). Methods of audiometric investigations in laboratory animals. (In Polish.) *Otolaryngol. Pol.* **25**, 11–15.

Flexner, L. B., Tyler, D. B., and Gallant, L. J. (1950). Biochemical and physiological differentiation during morphogenesis. X. Onset of electrical activity in developing cerebral cortex of fetal guinea pig. *J. Neurophysiol.* **13**, 427–430.

Freund, M. (1958). Collection and liquification of guinea pig semen. *Proc. Soc. Exp. Biol. Med.* **98**, 538–540.

Freund, M. (1969). Interrelationships among the characteristics of guinea-pig semen collected by electro-ejaculation. *J. Reprod. Fert.* **19**, 393–403.

Fullerton, P. M. (1966). Chronic peripheral neuropathy produced by lead poisoning in guinea-pigs. *J. Neuropathol. Exp. Neurol.* **25**, 214–236.

Glimstedt, G., Moberg, H. A., and Widmark, E. M. P. (1937). Der Stoffwechsel bakterienfreier Tiere. III. Die Gewinnung von Meerschweinchenmilch. *Skand. Arch. Physiol.* **76**, 148–157.

Greenfield, A. D. M., and Shepherd, J. T. (1953). Cardiovascular responses to asphyxia in the foetal guinea-pig. *J. Physiol. (London)* **120**, 538–549.

Grice, H. C. (1964). Methods for obtaining blood and for intravenous injections in laboratory animals. *Lab. Anim. Care* **14**, 483–493.

Gupta, B. N., Conner, G. H., and Langham, R. F. (1970). A device for collecting milk from guinea-pigs. *Amer. J. Vet. Res.* **31**, 557–559.

Guyton, A. C. (1947). Measurement of the respiratory volumes of laboratory animals. *Amer. J. Physiol.* **150**, 70–77.

Harichaux, P., Freville, M., Lienard, J., Denoeux, J. P., and Bonn, G. (1971). Continuous measurement of variations of P_{CO_2} in peritoneal fluid. *Can. J. Physiol. Pharmacol.* **49**, 621–623.

Herbert, W. J., Horne, C. H., and White, R. G. (1970). A new method for the quantitation of cell-mediated hypersensitivity in the eye of the guinea-pig. *Immunology* **18**, 545–549.

Hoar, R. M. (1965). Anesthetic technics of the rat and guinea pig. *In* "Experimental Animal Anesthesiology" (D. C. Sawyer, ed.), Chapter 17, pp. 325–343. USAF School of Aerospace Medicine, Brooks Air Force Base, Texas.

Hoar, R. M. (1966). A technique for bilateral adrenalectomy in guinea pigs. *Lab. Anim. Care* **16**, 410–416.

Hoar, R. M. (1969). Anaesthesia in the guinea-pig. *Fed. Proc., Fed. Amer. Soc. Exp. Biol.* **28**, 1517–1521.

Hoebel, M., Maroske, D., and Eichler, O. (1971). Eine einfache Methode zur Bestimmung des Atemminuten-volumens von Ratten und Meerschweinchen. *Arch. Int. Pharmacodyn. Ther.* **194**, 371–374.

Hopcroft, S. C. (1966). A technique for the simultaneous bilateral removal of the adrenal glands in guinea pigs, using a new type of safe anaesthetic. *Exp. Med. Surg.* **24**, 12–19.

Hughes, H. C., Jr., and Lang, C. M. (1972). Hepatic necrosis produced by repeated administration of halothane to guinea pigs. *Anesthesiology* **36**, 466–471.

Hughes, R. E., Jones, P. R., and Nicholas, P. (1970). Some effects of experimentally-produced cigarette smoke on the growth, vitamin C metabolism and organ weights of guinea-pigs. *J. Pharm. Pharmacol.* **22**, 823–827.

Ilahi, M. A., Barnes, B. A., and Burke, J. F. (1971). A nomogram for surface area of guinea pig. *J. Surg. Res.* **11**, 308–310.

Johnson, D. D. (1950). Alloxan administration in the guinea pig: A study of the histological changes in the islets of Langerhans, the blood sugar fluctuations, and changes in the glucose tolerance. *Endocrinology* **46**, 135–156.

Johnson, J. A., and Fjeld, N. B. (1971a). A method for measuring gastric secretion in the guinea pig. *Acta Chir. Scand.* **137**, 676–678.

Johnson, J. A., and Fjeld, N. B. (1971b). Reduction of acidity in the guinea pig by partial devascularization of the stomach. *Acta Chir. Scand.* **137**, 679–681.

Karlson, A. G. (1959). Intravenous injections in guinea pigs via veins of the penis. *Lab. Invest.* **8**, 987–989.

Karlson, A. G., and Feldman, W. H. (1953). Method for repeated intravenous injections into guinea pigs. *Lab. Invest.* **2**, 451–453.

Kirkpatrick, D., and Silver, D. (1970). A simplified technique of lymphography for the small laboratory animal. *J. Surg. Res.* **10**, 147–150.

Kromka, M. C., and Hoar, R. M. (1975). An improved technique for thyroidectomy in guinea pigs. *Lab. Anim. Sci.* **25**, 82–84.

Künzel, W. (1970). Der Einfluss von Narkotica auf die Sauerstoffaufnahme des trächtigen Uterus. *Arch. Gynaekol.* **209**, 262–275.

Künzel, W., and Moll, W. (1972). Uterine O_2 consumption and blood flow of the pregnant uterus. Experiments in pregnant guinea pigs. *Z. Geburtsh. Perinatologie* **176**, 108–117.

Lambelin, G., Vassart-Thys, D., and Roba, J. (1971). Cutaneous thermometry for topical therapy evaluation of U.V. erythema in the guinea-pig. *Arzneim. Forsch.* **21**, 44–47.

Laszlo, C. A., Gannon, R. P., and Milsum, J. H. (1970). Measurement of the cochlear potentials of the guinea pig at constant sound-pressure level at the eardrum. I. Cochlear-microphonic amplitude and phase. *J. Acoust. Soc. Amer.* **47**, 1055–1062.

Leash, A. M., Beyer, R. D., and Wilber, R. G. (1973). Self-mutilation following Innovar-Vet® injection in the guinea pig. *Lab. Anim. Sci.* **23**, 720–721.

Lehnert, J. P. (1967). Laboratory suggestion. New method for bleeding guinea pigs. *Tech. Bull. Regist. Med. Technol.* **37**, 52–53.

Lewis, A. J., and Nicholls, P. J. (1972). Effect of inhaled cigarette smoke on content, release and breakdown of histamine in guinea-pig lung. *Life Sci.* **11**, 1167–1171.

Lewis, G. E., Jr., and Jennings, P. B., Jr. (1972). Effective sedation of laboratory animals using Innovar-Vet®. *Lab. Anim. Sci.* **22**, 430–432.

Loew, E. R., Kaiser, M. E., and Moore, V. (1945). Synthetic benzhydryl alkamine ethers effective in preventing fatal experimental asthma in guinea pigs exposed to atomized histamine. *J. Pharmacol. Exp. Ther.* **83**, 120–129.

Lukoschek, P., and Thiesen, J. (1954). Das normale Meerschweinchen-Ekg. *Z. Kreislaufforsch.* **43**, 172–180.

McKeon, W. B., Jr. (1963). A critical evaluation of the antagonism of drugs to intravenous histamine in the guinea pig. *Arch. Int. Pharmacodyn. Ther.* **141**, 565–576.

Markham, N. P., and Kent, J. (1951). A technique for the repeated intravenous injections of guinea-pigs. *Brit. J. Exp. Pathol.* **32**, 366–367.

Mellor, D. J. (1969). Potential differences between mother and foetus at different gestational ages in the rat, rabbit and guinea-pig. *J. Physiol. (London)* **204**, 395–405.

Money, W. L., and Dancis, J. (1960). Technique for the *in situ* study of placental transport in the pregnant guinea pig. *Amer. J. Obstet. Gynecol.* **80**, 209–214.

Murphy, S. D., and Ulrich, C. E. (1964). Multi-animal test system for measuring effects of irritant gases and vapors on respiratory function of guinea pigs. *Amer. Ind. Hyg. Ass., J.* **25**, 28–36.

Must, J. S., Brody, G. G., Prevenslik, T., Beckwith, T. G., Glaser, A. A., and Marangoni, R. D. (1965). Apparatus designed to produce uniform experimental wounds. *Med. Electron. Biol. Eng.* **3**, 407–409.

Nelson, N. S., and Hoar, R. M. (1969). A small animal balling gun for oral administration of experimental compounds. *Lab. Anim. Care* **19**, 871–872.

Nelson, W. L., Kaye, A., Moore, M., Williams, H. H., and Harrington, B. L. (1951). Milking techniques and the composition of guinea pig milk. *J. Nutr.* **44**, 585–594.

Nobunaga, T., Nakamura, K., and Imamichi, T. (1966). A method for intravenous injection and collection of blood from rats and mice without restraint and anesthesia. *Lab. Anim. Care* **16**, 40–49.

Parellada, P. P., Gasulla, G. G., and Muset, P. P. (1971). Local anesthetics imidazole and calcium. *Pharmacol. Res. Commun.* **3**, 215–220.

Pestalloza, G., and Davis, H. (1956). Electric respones of the guinea-pig ear to high audio frequencies. *Amer. J. Physiol.* **185**, 595–600.

Peterson, R. R., Webster, R. C., Rayner, B., and Young, W. C. (1952). The thyroid and reproductive performance in the adult female guinea pig. *Endocrinology* **51**, 504–518.

Pratt, C. L. G. (1938). The electrocardiogram of the guinea pig. *J. Physiol. (London)* **92**, 268–272.

Raffel, S., Arnaud, L. E., Dukes, C. D., and Huang, J. S. (1949). The role of the "wax" of the tubercle bacillus in establishing delayed hypersensitivity. II. Hypersensitivity to a protein antigen, egg albumin. *J. Exp. Med.* **90**, 53–59.

Ragins, H., and Wincze, F. (1969). Acid secretion in guinea-pigs with chronic gastric fistulas. *J. Surg. Res.* **9**, 217–221.

Rector, D. E., Steadman, B. J., Jones, R. A., and Siegel, J. (1966). Effects on experimental animals of long-term inhalation exposure to mineral spirits. *Toxicol. Appl. Pharmacol.* **9**, 257–268.

Richtarik, A., Woolsey, T. A. .and Valdivia, E. (1965). Method for recording ECG's in unanesthetized guinea pigs. *J. Appl. Physiol.* **20**, 1091–1093.

Roberts, W. H. (1961). Identification of multicoloured laboratory animals using electronic flash photography. *J. Anim. Tech. Ass.* **12**, 11–14.

Romanov, V. A. (1971). Investigation of the cochlear circulation of the inner ear in animals by a rheographic method. *Bull. Exp. Biol. Med. (USSR)* **71**, 343–345.

Rose, C. S., Jones, R. A., Jenkins, L. J., Jr., and Siegel, J. (1970). The acute hyperbaric toxicity of carbon monoxide. *Toxicol. Appl. Pharmacol.* **17**, 752–760.

Rosen, M. G., and McLaughlin, A. (1966a). Maternal and fetal electroencephalography in the guinea pig. *Amer. J. Obstet. Gynecol.* **95**, 997–1000.

Rosen, M. G., and McLaughlin, A. (1966b). Fetal and maternal electroencephalography in the guinea pig. *Exp. Neurol.* **16**, 181–190.

Rosenhaft, M. E., Bing, D. H., and Knudson, K. C. (1971). A vacuum-assisted method for repetitive blood sampling in guinea pigs. *Lab. Anim. Sci.* **21**, 598–599.

Ross, S. B., and Akerman, S. B. A. (1971). Formation of a piperidinium derivative from *N*-(5′-chloropentyl)-*N*-methylaminoaceto-2,6-xylidide in relation to the sustained local anaesthetic action on the sciatic nerve of the guinea-pig *in vivo*. *Nature (London), New Biol.* **230**, 274–275.

Rowlands, I. W. (1961). Effect of hysterectomy at different stages in the life cycle of the corpus luteum in the guinea pig. *J. Reprod. Fert.* **2**, 341–350.

Rubright, W. C., and Thayer, C. B. (1970). The use of Innovar-Vet® as a surgical anesthetic for the guinea pig. *Lab. Anim. Care* **20**, 989–991.

Sandberg, G. (1972). Splenic blood flow in the guinea-pig measured with xenon 133, and calculation of the venous output of lymphocytes from the spleen. *Acta Physiol. Scand.* **84**, 208–216.

Sandiford, M. (1965). Some methods of collecting blood from small animals. *J. Anim. Tech. Ass.* **16**, 9–14.

Schwartze, H., Schwartze, P., and Schönfelder, J. (1971). Living fetuses of guinea pigs in acute experiments. Methods of anesthesia and operation in the adult pregnant animal; pre- and postnatal vectorcardiographic and electroencephalographic recordings in the developing animals. *Biol. Neonate* **17**, 238–248.

Sharma, V. N., Mital, R. L., Banerjee, S. P., and Sharma, H. L. (1971). Phenothiazines as local anesthetics. *J. Med. Chem.* **14**, 68–70.

Shrader, R. E., and Everson, G. J. (1968). Intravenous injection and blood sampling using cannulated guinea pigs. *Lab. Anim. Care* **18**, 214–219.

Shukla, R. C. (1969). Une méthode pour déterminer le compte total et différentiel des mélanocytes et des cellules intermédiaires de Billingham et Medawar dans la peau du cobaye noir. *Arch. Anat., Histol. Embryol.* **52**, 27–32.

Shulman, S., Hekman, A., and Pann, C. (1971). Antibodies to spermatozoa. II. Spermagglutination techniques for guinea-pig and human cells. *J. Reprod. Fert.* **27**, 31–41.

Siegel, J. (1961). Operational toxicology in the Navy. *Mil. Med.* **126**, 340–346.

Siegmund, O. H., Granger, H. R., and Lands, A. M. (1947). The bronchodilator action of compounds structurally related to epinephrine. *J. Pharmacol. Exp. Ther.* **90**, 254–259.

Simpson, D. M., Burnette, J. C., and Bawden, J. W. (1967). Maternal-fetal blood tetracycline levels in guinea pigs. *J. Oral Ther. Pharmacol.* **3**, 403–408.

Singer, P. R., Scibetta, J. J., and Rosen, M. G. (1973). Simulated marihuana smoking in the maternal and fetal guinea pig. *Amer. J. Obstet. Gynecol.* **117**, 331–340.

Sorg, D. A., and Buckner, B. A. (1964). Simple method of obtaining venous blood from small lab animals. *Proc. Soc. Exp. Biol. Med.* **115**, 1131–1132.

Stone, W. S., Amiraian, K., Duell, C., and Schadler, C. (1961). Carbon dioxide anesthetization of guinea pigs to increase yields of blood and serum. *Proc. Anim. Care Panel* **11**, 299–303.

Swann, H. E., Jr., Brunol, D., and Balchum, O. J. (1965). Pulmonary resistance measurements of guinea pigs. *Arch. Environ. Health* **10**, 24–32.

Tan, E-J., and Snow, H. D. (1968). Continuous epidural anesthesia in the guinea pig. *Amer. J. Vet. Res.* **29**, 487–490.

Tasaki, I., Davis, H., and Legouix, J-P. (1952). The space-time pattern of the cochlar microphonics (guinea pig) as recorded by differential electrodes. *J. Acoust. Soc. Amer.* **24**, 502–519.

Tonndorf, J. (1958). Localization of aural harmonics along the basilar membrane of guinea pigs. *J. Acoust. Soc. Amer.* **30**, 938–943.

Vallejo-Freire, A. (1951). A simple technique for repeated collection of blood samples from guinea pigs. *Science* **114**, 524–525.

Vlad, A., Winter, D., Sauvard, S., Stanescu, C., and Pal, B. (1970). A new method for tracheal instillation without oesophageal obstruction in laboratory animals. *Arzneim. Forsch.* **20**, 861.

Watt, J. (1955). Gastric acidity in the guinea-pig. *Quart. J. Exp. Physiol. Cog. Med. Sci.* **40**, 364–369.

Watt, J., and Wilson, C. W. M. (1957). A method of obtaining the gastric secretion from the unanaesthetized guinea-pig. *J. Physiol. (London)* **135**, 22P–23P.

Watt, J., and Wilson, C. W. M. (1958). Gastric secretion in the normal guinea-pig. *J. Physiol. (London)* **142**, 233–241.

Weisbroth, S. H., and Fudens, J. H. (1972). Use of ketamine hydrochloride as an anesthetic in laboratory rabbits, rats, mice, and guinea pigs. *Lab. Anim. Sci.* **22**, 904–906.

White, W. L., Brody, G. S., Glaser, A. A., Marangoni, R. D., Beckwith, T. G., Must, J. S., and Lehman, J. A. (1971). Tensiometric studies of unwounded and wounded skin: Results using a standardized testing method. *Ann Surg.* **173**, 19–25.

Williams, C., Phelps, D., and Burch, J. C. (1941). Observations on the effect of hypothyroidism on ovarian function in the guinea pig. *Endocrinology* **29**, 373–385.

Young, W. C., Rayner, B., Peterson, R. R., and Brown, M. N. (1952). The thyroid and reproductive performance in the adult male guinea pig. *Endocrinology* **51**, 12–20.

Chapter 4

Germfree and Specific Pathogen-Free

J. E. Wagner and H. L. Foster

I. INTRODUCTION

Technological advances in the last 15 to 20 years have made it possible to utilize germfree animals of many species in many parts of the world. It is the purpose of this chapter to review basic features relevant to deriving and utilizing germfree and specific pathogen free (SPF) guinea pigs in medical research. It is not the purpose of this chapter to review the great diversity of apparatus available for gnotobiology but merely to discuss those facets of germfree methodology commonly utilized and relevant to derivation and germfree studies on guinea pigs. Additionally, it is beyond the scope of this presentation to review comprehensively procedures for monitoring germfree systems. Pleasants (1974) recently reviewed the technical requirements for gnotobiotic research and listed a variety of information sources in the gnotobiotic field.

Once an institution or investigator has decided germfree or SPF guinea pigs are essential to planned investigation, they must decide whether to derive animals in their facility or to purchase them commercially if available. Generally, it is thought to be impractical to maintain breeding colonies of germfree guinea pigs because the animals are of comparatively large size (compared to mice and rats), have a long gestation with small litters, and are difficult to breed because of their generally enlarged cecum. Therefore, unless experimental design dictates otherwise, it is more economical to obtain germfree guinea pigs for research by hysterotomy or hysterectomy of conventional healthy dams. It is usually more economical for investigators to purchase germfree and SPF animals from commercial sources than to establish facilities and assemble expertise necessary for germfree derivations. Newly derived germfree guinea pigs are markedly precocious, requiring little or no nursing or hand feeding. They are rather easily reared to maturity (Institute of Laboratory Animal Resources, 1970).

Nuttall and Thierfelder (1895, 1896, 1897) were the first to derive germfree guinea pigs by cesarean section. They reared them free of microbial agents for up to 10 days. The fact that the guinea pig was the first of the common laboratory animals to be reared successfully germfree attests to the relative simplicity of germfree derivation for the species, i.e., the tedious chore of hand rearing with sterile milk is unnecessary. Later, Cohendy and Wollman (1914) reared guinea pigs germfree for a period of 29 days. Glimstedt (1932, 1936) maintained germfree guinea pigs for up to 2 months and Miyakawa (1955) reared them germfree for 150 days. In 1946 Reyniers reported germfree guinea pigs living as long as 8 months; however, most died around 2 to 3 months. They had brittle bones, showed slow weight gain, and were considered malnourished.

The SPF or disease-free animal lies somewhere between the germfree and conventional animal. The most common approach to obtaining the disease-free animal is through the germfree route, probably because it is more economical to rid the animal of all flora than to attempt selective decontamination. This is especially true with the guinea pig because of his relative precocious state at birth than with other relatively altricial laboratory animal species.

II. METHODOLOGY

Phillips *et al.* (1959) studied a variety of procedures for deriving germfree guinea pigs at maximal gestational age. At approximately 2 weeks prior to parturition the symphysis pubis has separated approximately 6 mm. They reported that germfree guinea pigs derived from dams with a palpatable pubic diastatis spread of 16 mm or more, about the distance accommodated by the thumb, could usually be reared without complications of immaturity. Gilmstedt (1936) reported a technique for radiological observation of diastatic spread of the symphysis pubis of pregnant guinea pigs. However, Phillips *et al.* (1959) mentioned that expression of milk from the teats and radiological observation of the young are not as reliable predictors of pregnancy as pubic spread. Additional evidence of pending parturition can be obtained by plotting body weight gains.

A. Surgical Derivation

The fetal guinea pig at 65 days of gestation is a relatively precocious animal and will not survive in the uterus for more than 2 or 3 minutes after hysterectomy or death of the female. Therefore surgery must be performed very rapidly or the pregnant female must be kept alive during hysterotomy or hysterectomy. This contrasts to derivation of rats and mice with prolonged intrauterine survivability following cervical dislocation. The female guinea pig can be lightly anesthetized with about 15 mg of Nembutal intramuscularly and/or use of a local anesthetic along the anticipated incision line, usually midventral.

Prior to surgery, hair covering the abdominal cavity of the animal is clipped. The animal is tied down on an operating table and abdomen is washed thoroughly with a disinfectant soap and rinsed with sterile water. The abdomen may be shaved or a depilatory agent applied. The area is again washed with soap and rinsed with sterile water. The belly region is covered with a sterile towel with a precut opening, flooded with disinfectant, and the abdominal cavity opened with a sterile scalpel or cautery pistol. The entire gravid uterus is removed (hysterectomy) and subsequently passed into a sterile chamber via a germicidal dunk tank. As an alternative technique the intact uterus may be incised from within a sterile chamber with the surgeon's arms and hands in rubber sleeves and gloves attached to the chamber wall and the young removed individually (hysterotomy or cesarian section).

The hysterectomy technique is, in many ways, the simplest and requires less sophisticated equipment and operating units. In this technique the entire clamped uterus is removed from the abdominal cavity and aseptically passed into the sterile isolator via a liquid germicide (1:10 Clorox* or benzalkonium chloride, 1:100) in a trap or tube in the wall of the isolator (Foster, 1959; Landy *et al.,* 1960). The young are then removed from the uterus and freed from their fetal membranes within the sterile environment of the isolator. This whole process must be accomplished within a few minutes.

If one desires to use a hysterotomy technique, surgery may be performed from within the sterile surgical isolator. An electocautery blade is preferred by some for making skin incisions because of its sterilizing effect. In this procedure the prepped abdomen of the pregnant guinea pig is brought against the wall of the isolator and an incision is made through the wall of the isolator and the abdominal wall of the guinea pig (Reyniers, 1956). Fetuses are then removed from the uterus directly into the sterile environment. Once inside the sterile chamber, be it plastic or steel, the umbilical cord is clamped after removal from the uterus and the membranes are removed from the animal, particularly from the head and nostrils. The animal is then sponged dry and gently cleansed with warm sterile saline. Generally, rhythmic pressing of the thorax forces artificial respiration. A sterile semiliquid food and water are offered within 24 hours. Swabs are taken immediately to reconfirm total sterility. The hysterotomy technique has the advantage that the dam can recover and be rebred if donor stock is highly valuable or limited.

*Clorox Co., Oakland, California.

B. Microbiological Monitoring

Methods for microbiological monitoring of guinea pigs are similar to procedures recommended for rats and mice (Institute of Laboratory Animal Resources, 1970). Typically, weekly samples of feces and other suitable materials are inoculated into thioglycolate broth, blood agar, and Sabouraud's agar and incubated aerobically at room temperature, 37°, and 55°C. Bacteriological testing procedures for germfree animals have been described by Wagner (1959).

It is not usually feasible to search for antibodies against specific viruses because of the dearth of information concerning viral diseases of guinea pigs. Personnel working with germfree guinea pigs should be cognizant of the possibility for the salivary gland virus to vertically pass into germfree animals (Cole and Kuttner, 1926).

C. Equipment

Barriers that maintain absolute sterility are essential for germfree or gnotobiotic operations. Flexible laminated vinyl film isolators are widely used and are sterilized with either peracetic acid or ETO (ethylene oxide) (Trexler and Reynolds, 1957). Sterilizing cylinders of stainless steel or aluminum are used for servicing heat-sensitive flexible isolators. These cylinders are usually perforated and covered with fiber-glass filter material to permit withdrawal of air and subsequent steam penetration. The mouth or loading opening at the end is sealed with Mylar film. Sterilization in cyclic high vacuum autoclaves is preferred for most materials (Trexler, 1963; Foster *et al.*, 1964). Heat-stable porous items are generally sterilized by steam under pressure, e.g., diet, water, and bedding. Air for ventilation is commonly sterilized by filtration through four layers of fiber glass medium FM004. Incineration may also be used to sterilize the air supply (Miyakawa, 1959a; Gustafsson, 1959). Peracetic acid, 2% containing 0.1% alkyl-aryl sulfonate detergent as a wetting agent is commonly used on flexible film units and other nonporous or heat-sensitive materials (Trexler and Reynolds, 1957). Diet sterilization by irradiation is commonly utilized in England and can successfully be utilized when the radiation source is economically competitive. Ethylene oxide is sometimes used to sterilize heat- and moisture-sensitive items; however, it is flammable and may be toxic (Perkins, 1969). It is also used for diets (Charles and Walker, 1967; H. L. Foster, personal communication, 1974). A mixture of 88% ETO and 12% Freon produces minimal nutrient damage (H. L. Foster, personal communication, 1974) (reported by authors in Germany and the United Kingdom). However, thiamine and riboflavin may have to be supplemented (Luckey, 1963). The most common causes of "breaks" in the germfree barrier are (1) failure to sterilize diet; (2) puncture of gloves or isolator; (3) contaminated materials being passed into the isolator; (4) contaminated inocula; (5) faulty air filters or traps; and (6) poor technique when transferring materials in or out of the isolator.

A great variety of pens and cages has been used for housing germfree guinea pigs within the isolator. Those housed in steel isolators can be allowed to run free on the floor. Whether a bedding material or mesh bottom cages without bedding are used is largely a matter of individual preference. Young germfree guinea pigs have a tendency to "nurse at the anal end of cagemates." Additionally, when animals are allowed to run together hair pulling and chewing ensues. Therefore, it may be advantageous to individually house guinea pigs in the germfree environment, although others have reported success while keeping guinea pigs together in harem groups (Pleasants *et al.*, 1967).

III. GERMFREE VS. CONVENTIONAL

In general, germfree guinea pigs compare favorably to conventional counterparts in physical size and appearance. While abnormal cecal distention occurs in other germfree species, i.e., rats and mice, it appears to be a greater problem in germfree guinea pigs. The cecum often exceeds 30% of total body weight (Newton, 1965). Abrams and Bishop (1961) reported the cecum of germfree guinea pigs constituted 25% of body weight, while in conventional animals it was about 10%. While germfree guinea pigs were slightly heavier than conventional counterparts, they were of equal weight when weights were corrected for increased cecal size. The cecum constitutes the anatomical abnormality of greatest magnitude in germfree guinea pigs. Cecal distention appears to be due to a lack of resistance to stretching in the cecal wall (Phillips *et al.*, 1959). It occasionally affects the overall health of animals. Germfree guinea pigs must be handled delicately because the unusually large cecum predisposes to rupture, herniation, torsion, vulvulus, and uterine prolapse. Anal and rectal prolapse occurs in higher incidence than in conventional controls, averaging around 5%. Cecal distention does not appear to affect passage of ingesta through the digestive tract, although sawdust used for bedding may impact the cecum (Phillips *et al.*, 1959). Fecal pellet formation in the large intestine appears normal in spite of cecal distention.

Phillips *et al.* (1959) remarked the Kurloff bodies were not observed in normal germfree guinea pigs that had passed the ages in which these bodies appeared in conventional guinea pigs of the same strain. However, they were observed in germfree guinea pigs with induced protozoan infections. Whether or not this is due to an incompletely developed lymphatic system has not been determined.

It is generally accepted that lymph nodes and lymphatics of the gastrointestinal tract are markedly hypoplastic in germfree animals as compared to conventional animals (Miyakawa, 1959b; Abrams and Bishop, 1961). In addition to underdeveloped lymphatics, Chakhaven (1973) concludes that decreased antigenic stimulation causes hypercorticism, hypoglycoproteinemina, increased deposition of ascorbic acid in adrenals, and secondary depression of lymphatic tissues. The changes in morphology in germfree life are less striking in the spleen than other lymphatic organs.

Total white blood cell counts are lower in germfree guinea pigs than conventional counterparts, e.g., 1900 in germfree vs. 5 to 12,000/mm^3 in conventional animals. Additionally, the percent of neutrophils is higher in germfree guinea pigs: an average of 55% compared to 10 to 20% in conventional animals. Conversely, the lymphocyte percentage of germfree animals is substantially reduced from that of conventional counterparts: 42% vs. approximately 80%, respectively (Phillips *et al.*, 1959).

Pneumonic disease syndromes have been described in germfree guinea pigs; however, they have not been directly associated with an etiological agent (Phillips and Wolfe, 1961; Miyakawa, 1959a).

Geever and Levenson (1964) found that germfree guinea pigs had little or no iron pigment in the tunica propria of the intestinal tract; whereas it was heavily concentrated in the cecum and less concentrated in scattered foci throughout the small intestine of conventionalized guinea pigs. They suggested that the finding reflected an effect of microorganisms on iron metabolism.

The effects of intestinal microflora on levels of serum γ-globulin appear at around 8 to 10 weeks of age (Wostmann, 1961). Until that time germfree and conventional guinea pigs have similar levels of γ-globulin. Newton (1965) has shown that γ-globulin values in germfree guinea pigs range from 20 to 50% of normal. Frederick and Chorpenning (1973) found IgG levels to be lower in germfree guinea pigs, probably due to exposure to fewer antigens; however, they concluded that high levels of natural circulating antibodies indicate that germfree guinea pigs do not differ in immunological competence. Newton *et al.* (1960a) and Tanami (1959) found that germfree guinea pigs had hemolytic complement activity equal to that of conventional animals.

Pregnancies occur frequently in germfree guinea pigs but infrequently go to term. Dams frequently abort and prolapse the uterus after delivery. Many young are born dead or die shortly after birth. It has been speculated that the presence of the enlarged cecal mass in the abdominal cavity could have a profound deleterious effect and may be the cause of premature deaths and difficulties in maintaining pregnancy (Newton, 1965).

Other abnormalities observed occasionally in germfree guinea pigs include: greatly enlarged gallbladder, reduced muscle tone, thin gut wall, and reduced lymphoid tissue (Newton, 1965). To what extent these are due to nutritional inadequacies of absence of bacterial flora has not been completely quantified. It is generally perceived that the gastrointestinal microflora relates to the animal's nutrition and physiology in complicated ways yet to be elucidated.

Conventional guinea pigs develop signs of scurvy much more quickly than do germfree counterparts suggesting that bacteria compete with the host for vitamin C (Levenson *et al.*, 1962; Thompson and Trexler, 1971).

In some instances it may be difficult to have good "control" animals in germfree studies. Particularly, one must recognize the early postnatal differences between conventional and germfree subjects. If conventional controls are used and allowed to deliver normally, they will have suckled for a few days. If one removes them from the dam and does not allow them to suckle, they may be susceptible to postpartum infections and early death. Germfree guinea pigs taken by cesarian section do not receive colostrum from the mother, but this is not of great practical importance in the absence of microorganisms.

Warren and Newton (1959) noted that germfree guinea pigs had approximately one-quarter as much ammonia derived nitrogen in the portal system as did conventional animals. They concluded that bacteria of the gastrointestinal tract contributed markedly to portal blood ammonia concentration through deamination of ingested protein.

IV. NUTRITION

Unlike rabbits, rats, and mice, neonatal germfree guinea pigs, because of their prolonged gestation period, are sufficiently developed to eat semisolid or solid diets. They need not be fed artificial milk formulas nor foster suckled. Cesarian-derived guinea pigs consume very little food during the first 24 hours of life. Although they start eating during this period, they have a substantial weight loss, largely due to dehydration.

A. Diets

For germfree or SPF animals under 3 days of age, a semisolid diet, L-445 (Table I), fortified with vitamin supplement VC-2 (Philips *et al.*, 1959) has been recommended (Institute of Laboratory Animal Resources, 1970). This diet is diluted with water to a creamy consistency.

In addition to the L-445 diet each animal should receive

Table I
Composition of L-445 Diet

Component L-445 S diet	Amount (gm)
Ground Purina Laboratory Chow	100
Rolled oats	100
Dextrose	10
Sodium chloride	5
Whole active dry yeast	15
Water	1000

approximately 1 ml of vitamin supplement VC-2 daily (Table II) (Philips *et al.*, 1959).

After the third day, less water is added to the L-445 diet (Institute of Laboratory Animal Resources, 1970). When the animals are 3 to 4 days old, the L-477 diet (Table III) (Pleasants *et al.*, 1967) is also fed (Institute of Laboratory Animal Resources, 1970). The animals continue to receive approximately 1 ml of VC-2 supplement daily. The amount of semisolid L-445 diet is gradually reduced and discontinued completely at about 21 days of age. Germfree guinea pigs are then maintained on L-477 plus 1 ml of VC-2 supplement daily and water *ad libitum*. The L-477 diet can be pelleted to facilitate feeding.

The L-477 diet supplemented with ascorbic acid and thiamine either mixed in moist diet or in drinking water may be used as the only diet for rearing germfree guinea pigs from birth (Pleasants *et al.*, 1967). Guinea pigs surgically derived and maintained on diet L-477 autoclaved with 25% added moisture, without a milk substitute, maintained a normal cecal size for nearly 6 months, although distention did occur in later life. On the other hand, guinea pigs born naturally germfree and suckled had enlarged ceca by 5 months of age (Pleasants *et al.*, 1967).

Vitamin A and certain B vitamins are particularly heat labile. Additionally, specific amino acids are reduced upon heat sterilization: lysine, methionine, arginine, and tryptophan. These products must be supplemented in excess to provide adequate levels after heat sterilization (Institute of Laboratory Animal Resources, 1970).

Currently it appears that most germfree guinea pigs are being reared on the diet of Pleasants *et al.* (1967) or Philips *et al.*

Table II
Vitamin Supplement VC-2

Component VC-2	Amount (gm)
Ascorbic acid	1
Thiamine HCl	0.05
Distilled water	100

Table III
Composition of L-477 Diet for Germfree Guinea Pigs
(Major ingredients / kilogram)

Component diet L-477	Amount (gm)
Ground whole wheat	320
Ground yellow corn (maize)	145
Rolled oats	220
Lactalbumin	100
Technical casein	78
Alfalfa meal (dehydrated; 17% protein)	20
Desiccated liver	20
Corn oil	30
Salt mix 24	**Amount (gm)**
$CaCO_3$	11
$CaHPO_4 \cdot 2H_2O$	4
$KC_2H_3O_2$	9
$Mg(C_2H_3O_2)_2 \cdot 4H_2O$	9.5
Iso-inositol	0.5
Supplement VC-2	1 ml/day
$MgSO_4$	4
Iodized NaCl	5.3
$Fe(C_6H_5O_7)_2$	0.6
$MnCO_3$	42 mg
CuO	25
ZnO	25
$CaCl_2 \cdot 6H_2O$	4
NaF	0.22
MoO_3	0.15
KBr	0.10
Na_2SeO_3	0.10
Oil-soluble vitamins	**Amount**
Vitamin A concentrate, (200,000 IU/gm)	8,000 IU
Vitamin D_2 (Dawsterol) (200,000 IU/gm)	1,000 IU
Mixed tocopherols (253 IU vit.E/gm)	380 IU
DL-Tocopherol acetate	100 mg
Vitamin K_3, menadione	100 mg
Corn oil carrier	20 gm
B-Vitamin mix	**Amount (mg)**
Thiamine HCl	30
Riboflavin	15
Nicotinamide	25
Niacin	25
Calcium pantothenate	150
Pyridoxine HCl	10
Pyridoxamine 2HCl	2
Biotin	0.5
Folic acid	5
p-Aminobenzoic acid	25
B_{12} (0.1% trituration in mannitol)	125
Choline Cl	1,000
Cornstarch	1,087.5

(1959) or modifications thereof. Basically, the diet of Phillips *et al.* (1959) consists of ground Purina Laboratory Chow* (a rodent diet), oatmeal, dextrose, salt, and dried whole yeast. The mixture is brought to boiling in water, the quantity of which is reduced as animals age up to 2 to 3 weeks. This diet is supplemented with thiamine and ascorbic acid. Others use a commercial guinea pig diet or diet pellet instead of rodent chow (Warren and Newton, 1959). Fortified semipurified diets containing casein, oatmeal, cornstarch, vitamins, and minerals sterilized by irradiation have been used (Horton and Hickey, 1961).

B. Irradiated Diets

Chakhava *et al.* (1968) found that most guinea pigs on a regular diet consisting of beets, carrots, oats, bran, potassium chloride, cod liver oil, and ascorbic acid was irradiated with 3×10^6 rad of γ-rays of ^{60}Co most animals suffered paralysis of the hind legs and subsequently died. The paralyzed animals recovered quickly if fed unsterilized diet for 2 or 3 days. Guinea pigs fed an autoclaved diet survived. These findings are contradictory to those of Goldblith (1966), who found irradiated diets acceptable. Irradiated diets are commonly utilized for germfree research in England (Pleasants, 1974).

V. RESEARCH USES

Cohendy and Wollman (1922) utilized germfree guinea pigs in the study of cholera. *Vibrio cholerae* caused death in monognotophoric guinea pigs while classic animals survived. Since that time a host of studies have been performed on monognotophoric guinea pigs (Luckey, 1968) including inoculations with *Escherichia coli.* In some cases they produced no lesions (Newton, 1963). As a result of these inoculations a serum bactericidal factor was identified in germfree guinea pigs (Sprinz *et al.*, 1961; Formal *et al.*, 1961).

Shigella flexneri caused ulcerative lesions in the colon of germfree guinea pigs (Dammin, 1959) and was fatal (Uyei and Midorikawa, 1961; Sprinz *et al.*, 1961; Newton, 1963). Germfree guinea pigs die within 48 hours when fed *Shigella flexneri* orally while conventional animals are not susceptible (Sprinz *et al.*, 1961). When germfree guinea pigs were inoculated with *E. coli* they were protected against *Shigella.*

Abernathy and Landy (1967) demonstrated that *Salmonella typhosa* endotoxin was lethal to both germfree and conventional guinea pigs; however, only one-third the amount of endotoxin was required to produce hypothermia and leukopenia in conventional animals as compared to germfree guinea pigs. Germfree animals offer a unique opportunity to study endotoxins in the absence of bacteria.

Agrobacterium and *Staphylococcus mesenterious* had no effect on germfree guinea pigs (Cohendy and Wollman, 1922). A rougher strain of *Staphylococcus* spp. was recovered by Maggini (1942) after germfree guinea pigs were inoculated. Minimal reaction was obtained when *Lactobacillus acidophilus* and *Lactobacillus bifidus* were inoculated (Tanami 1959). *Bacillus subtilis* is lethal to germfree guinea pigs (Wagner, 1959). Miyakawa and Kishimoto (1962) found that *Mycobacterium tuberculosis* causes fewer lesions in germfree than conventional guinea pigs.

Horton *et al.* (1970) reported that germfree guinea pigs died of acute enterotoxemia after oral inoculation with *Clostridium perfringens* types B, C, D, and E. Type A was innocuous. Conventional guinea pigs were unaffected by the five agents.

Madden *et al.* (1970) found that germfree guinea pigs died of a form of enterotoxemia following removal to a conventional environment. *Clostridium perfringens* type E was then recovered from intestinal contents, blood, and other organs. The culture was pathogenic for germfree guinea pigs upon experimental feeding.

Newton (1965) found that germfree guinea pigs often die in less than 18 hours after being removed from the germfree to a conventional environment.

Seeliger and Werner (1962) found that alteration of intestinal flora causes death of penicillin-treated conventional guinea pigs. Formal *et al.* (1963) observed that germfree guinea pigs were more resistant to the effects of penicillin than their conventional counterparts, suggesting that "penicillin toxicity" of guinea pigs may be due to an enterocolitis rather than direct toxic actions (Hamre *et al.*, 1943; Koch *et al.*, 1953).

Tabachnick and LaBadie (1970) observed that there was a lower level of nitrogen compounds in the epidermis of germfree guinea pigs when compared to conventional animals. This was attributed to an impairment of protein digestion in the gut due to lack of microbial flora.

It has been suggested that germfree animals may be useful as a "culture medium" for infective agents which otherwise cannot be grown in the laboratory (Abrams and Bishop, 1961).

Podoprigora (1970) observed that there was a significant lag in the development of aseptic inflammation in germfree animals compared to conventional guinea pigs. A benefit of having germfree animals is that rather elaborate operative procedures can be accomplished without secondary infections and wound abscesses.

Newton *et al.* (1959) found that mouse helminths *Nematospiroides dubius* and *Hymenolepis nana* developed to maturity in germfree guinea pigs; whereas they did not in conventional subjects. It appears that a lack of flora allowed the abnormal

*Ralston Purina Co., St. Louis, Missouri.

host to become susceptible to these parasites. Newton *et al.* (1960b) found that *Trichomonas vaginalis* produced large lesions in germfree guinea pigs, whereas no lesions were produced in conventional animals. Phillips (1964, 1968), Phillips and Gorstein (1966), Phillips and Wolfe (1959), and Phillips *et al.* (1955, 1958, 1972) have studied the effects of amebiasis in germfree guinea pigs both with and without bacterial contamination. They concluded that bacteria of certain genera along with ameba were involved in the pathogenesis of human enteric amebiasis.

In some cases germfree guinea pigs have a more pronounced reaction than conventional counterparts, e.g., more severe ocular inflammation in response to acacia extract (Aronson and McMaster, 1972).

Germfree and conventional guinea pigs respond similarily in many studies, e.g., intraperitoneal injection of sterile agar (Brody and Bishop, 1963), contact sensitivity to chemicals (Friedlaender *et al.*, 1972), and response to injected treponems (Fitzgerald *et al.*, 1958).

In other cases germfree animals have a less pronounced response than conventional counterparts, e.g., absence of "blastogenic control" in lymphocytes of immunized germfree guinea pigs (Gris *et al.*, 1972); less response to suture material in the cornea probably due to elimination of microbial contamination (McMaster *et al.*, 1970); defective delayed hypersensitivity responses (Lev and Battisto 1970). Germfree guinea pigs were reported not to develop rigor mortis (Reyniers, 1946). Sera of germfree guinea pigs is less bactericidal than that of conventional animals (Tanami, 1959). Phagocytic activity of leukocytes of germfree guinea pigs is less than that of conventional animals (Tanami, 1959).

VI. DISCUSSION AND SUMMARY

The term "specific pathogen free" or SPF has been used widely to describe an animal which lies somewhere between the truly germfree gnotobiote and the conventional animal. The term, when properly used, means that the animals were originally derived into a germfree system and confirmed to be microbiologically sterile. At a subsequent time the animals were associated with a defined microflora also within an isolator system and allowed to stablize. Subsequently, they were transferred into a barrier facility designed to preclude entrance of pathogens. They are maintained with a regime whereby personnel enter via a rigid procedure of decontamination through entry locks and all supplies coming in contact with the animals are sterilized with steam or ethylene oxide, depending upon the product. Feed is pasteurized.

SPF has been loosely used to describe a conventional colony that has been rid of a single pathogen, e.g., *Salmonella,* through culturing and elimination of carrier animals. Specific pathogen free by definition could mean free of specified pathogens. It is unfortunate that the loose definition of the term has been perpetuated to the point that when single pathogens have been removed or proved nonexistent in conventional colonies, the colony in some cases is referred to as "specific pathogen free."

Rather than going through the laborious task of attempting elimination of individual pathogens and parasites through test, eradication, and chemotherapy, one can eliminate, in one fell swoop through cesarean section, all known pathogenic agents of guinea pigs with the exception of the few transferred vertically or transplacentally. Perhaps the most valuable contribution rendered the research community by gnotobiotic technology is the availability of germfree animals for seed stock to produce disease-free colonies. Based on this concept a large-scale commercial colony was established in September of 1971 (H. L. Foster, personal communication, 1974). Key factors in developing this colony are discussed in the following paragraphs.

Between 50 and 60 cesareans were performed on Duncan–Hartley guinea pigs obtained from the Medical Research Council at Mill Hill, England. Thumb palpation to measure separation of the symphysis pubis was utilized to determine the time for cesarean delivery with excellent success. The abdomen of a pregnant sow was shaved in preparation for surgery. She was killed by cervical separation. Standard techniques were used to perform a hysterectomy and the gravid uterus was introduced via a chlorine dunk tank and sleeve into a sterile chamber where the fetuses were freed of their membranes, washed, massaged, and then transferred into a rearing unit. Neonates were fed sterilized diet commencing 24 hours after birth. After approximately 7 to 10 days when microbiological sterility was reconfirmed, young guinea pigs were given a modified Schaedler flora (Schaedler *et al.*, 1965) and transferred via gnotobiotic techniques into barrier rooms utilizing a germfree shipper attached to a port in the room wall.

The barrier room of approximately 25,000 cubic feet is operated in principle as though it were an oversized isolator, with the exception of people working inside. Personnel enter via a series of electrically interlocked chambers commonly referred to as personnel entry locks. The first lock is entered directly from outdoors and has an automatically activated knock-down aerosol for flying insects. The second room is for clothes removal, the third is a pass-through shower, and the fourth is to dress in sterilized garments that remain in the barrier. Clothing consists of washable coveralls, disposable cap, face mask, and gloves. Clothing is washed within the barrier.

All food is pasteurized in a vacuum-steam autoclave. Other materials passed into the barrier are sterilized by steam or ethylene oxide and subsequently brought into the room via a port transfer wherein they are decontaminated with peracetic acid. Articles too large to fit into the port are passaged through the shower locks wherein they are decontaminated with peracetic acid. The air is filtered by Cambridge 95* aerosol filters, which remove 95% of 0.35-μm particles. Temperature is controlled at 72°F ± 2° and relative humidity maintained between 50 and 60%.

The guinea pigs are kept in large plastic tubs measuring 3 feet 4 inches × 2 feet 5 inches × 9 inches. Automatic watering devices, "L25 Mini-Lixit,"† are used. There are 880 plastic tubs in a room of approximately 2500 square feet. Each breeding cage contains up to 5 sows and one boar. Autoclaved pine shavings are used for bedding and changed twice a week or more frequently if needed.

The animals are feed Charles River Guinea Pig Diet manufactured by Agway, Inc., Syracuse, New York. This diet is fortified with 400 mg of ascorbic acid per 100 gm of diet. The colony receives no roughage supplement or hay. Additional ascorbic acid is introduced daily into the drinking water by a proportioning pump at a rate of 30 mg per 100 ml of water. While these measures to ensure adequate ascorbic acid seem extreme, they were adopted because of an episode of scorbutis characterized by high mortality caused by vitamin C deficiency resulting from a combination of (1) minimal amounts of ascorbic acid in the diet initially; (2) insufficient compensation for destruction during pelleting, pasteurization, and storage coupled with (3) lengthy storage during the summer months. It is recommended that weekly ascorbic acid assays be performed on both raw and pasteurized diet as well as on drinking water when water supplementation is used. The COBS (cesarean originated barrier sustained) guinea pigs in this colony may very well require larger amounts of vitamin C under the stress of reproduction. However, researchers are routinely using these animals and feeding them standard unpasteurized and unsupplemented guinea pig rations.

Production in June of 1974 in a colony with about 4600 breeding sows indicates that a 3.2 litter average at weaning is commonplace. The minimum rule of thumb of one offspring per sow per month, or 12 per annum, is readily being obtained. It is hope that as the colony matures and breeding stock is selected for larger litters up to 15 per annum may be attainable as reported by laboratories in the United Kingdom. Routine microbiological monitoring has demonstrated the colony to be free of *Bordetella bronchiseptica, Streptococcus* Type C, and *Salmonella,* as well as both external and internal parasites. Antibodies to common rodent viruses have not been detected to date. A formalized *Bordetella* vaccine has been prepared by the technique described by Ganaway *et al.* (1965) and will be held in storage for use in the event of an unfortunate *Bordetella* contamination. Without the presence of conventional guinea pigs on the premises, it is believed that such a break in the barrier is relatively unlikely.

It appears that the colony started in December of 1971 through cesarean technique has been successful in that common guinea pig pathogens have been bypassed and all indications are that good reproduction will follow. It is hoped that with selection over a period of time productivity and viability will exceed those reported in conventional guinea pig colonies.

*Cambridge Filter Corporation, Syracuse, New York, Model Number 3A95.

†Systems Engineering, Napa, California.

REFERENCES

Abernathy, R. S., and Landy, J. J. (1967). Increased resistance to endotoxin in germ free guinea pigs. *Proc. Soc. Exp. Biol. Med.* **124,** 1279–83.

Abrams, G. D., and Bishop, J. E. (1961). Germfree technique in experimental pathology: A survey of morphologic changes in, and the research of, the germfree guinea pig. *Univ. Mich. Med. Bull.* **27,** 136–147.

Aronson, S. B., and McMaster, P. R. B. (1972). Mechanisms of the host response in the eye. VI. Immune and toxic stimulation of inflammation in the germfree guinea pig. *Arch. Ophthalmol.* **88,** [N.S.] 533–539.

Brody, G. L., and Bishop, J. E. (1963). Agar peritonitis in the germfree guinea pig. *Arch. Pathol.* **76,** 126–132.

Chakhava, O. V. (1973). Ascorbic acid and glucocorticoid levels in relation to underdeveloped lympatic tissue in guinea pigs. *In* "Germfree Research: Biological Effect of Gnotobiotic Environments" (J. B. Heneghan, ed.), pp. 507–511. Academic Press, New York.

Chakhava, O. V., Zenkevich, M. V., and Zazenkina, T. I. (1968). Some results with diets designed for rearing germfree guinea pigs. *In* "Advances in Germfree Research and Methodology" (M. Miyakawa and T. D. Luckey, eds.) pp. 102–106. CRC Press, Cleveland, Ohio.

Charles, R. J., and Walker, A. I. T. (1967). The use of ethylene oxide for the sterilization of laboratory animal foodstuffs and bedding. *J. Anim. Tech. Ass.* **15,** 44–47.

Cohendy, M., and Wollman, E. (1914). Expériences sur la vie sans microbes. Elévage aseptique de cobayes. *C. R. Acad. Sci.,* **158;** 283–1284.

Cohendy, M., and Wollman, E. (1922). Quelques resultats acquis par la méthode des élévages aseptiques. I. Scorbut experimental. II. Infection cholérique du cobaye aseptique. *C. R. Acad. Sci.* **174,** 1082–1084.

Cole, R., and Kuttner, A. G. (1926). A filterable virus present in the submaxillary glands of guinea pigs. *J. Exp. Med.* **44,** 855–873.

Dammin, G. J. (1959). Part V. Present status and future development of germfree life studies–panel discussion. *Ann. N.Y. Acd. Sci.* **78,** 381.

Fitzgerald, R. J., Hampp, E. G., and Newton, W. L. (1958). Infectivity of oral spirochetes in cortisone-treated and germfree guinea pigs. *J. Dent. Res.* **37,** 11.

Formal, S. B., Dammin, G., Sprinz, H., Kundel, D., Schneider, H., Horowitz, R. E., and Forbes, M. (1961). Infections. V. Studies in germfree guinea pigs. *J. Bacteriol.* **82,** 284–287.

Formal, S. B., Abrams, G. D., Schneider, H., and Sandy, R. (1963). Penicillin in germfree guinea pigs. *Nature (London)* **198,** 172.

Foster, H. L. (1959). A procedure for obtaining nucleus stock for a pathogen-free animal colony. *Proc. Anim. Care Panel* **9**, 135.

Foster, H. L., (1974). Personal communication. The Charles River Breeding Laboratories, Inc., Wilmington, Massachusetts 01887.

Foster, H. L., Black, C. L., and Pfau, E. S. (1964). A pasteurization process for pelleted diets. *Lab. Anim. Care* **14,** 373–381.

Frederick, G. T., and Chorpenning, F. W. (1973). Comparisons of natural and immune antibodies to teichoic acids in germfree and conventional guinea pigs. *In* "Germfree Research: Biological Effect of Gnotobiotic Environments" (J. B. Heneghan, ed.), pp. 493–499. Academic Press, New York.

Friedlaender, M. H., Baer, H., and McMaster, P. R. B. (1972). Contact sensitivity and immunologic tolerance in germfree guinea pigs. *Proc. Soc. Exp. Biol. Med.* **141,** 522–526.

Ganaway, J. R., Allen, A. M., and McPherson, L. W. (1965). Prevention of acute *Bordetella bronchiseptica* penumonia in a guinea pig colony. *Lab. Anim. Care* **15,** 156–162.

Geever, E. F., and Levenson, S. M. (1964). Iron pigmentation of the gut of germfree and coventionalized guinea pigs. *Experientia* **20,** 391–92.

Gilmstedt, G. (1932). Das Leben ohne Bakterien. Sterile Aufziehung von Meerschweinchen. *Verh. Anat. Ges.* **41**:79–89.

Gilmstedt, G. (1936). Bakterienfreie Meerschweinchen. *Acta Pathol. Microbiol. Scand. Suppl.* **30**:1–295.

Goldblith, S. A. (1966). Radiation, sterilization of food. *Nature (London)* **210,** 433.

Gris, Y., Lev. M., and Battisto, J. R. (1972). Absence of "blastogenic control" in immunized germ-free guinea pig lymphoid cells. *Fed. Amer. Soc. Exp. Biol. Proc.*, **31,** A796.

Gustafsson, B. E. (1959). Lightweight stainless steel systems for rearing germ-free animals. *Ann. N. Y. Acad. Sci.* **78,** 17.

Hamre, D. M., Rake, G., McKee, C. M., and MacPhillammy, H. B. (1943). The toxicity of penicillin as prepared for clinical use. *Amer. J. Med. Sci.* **206,** 642.

Horton, R. E., and Hickey, J. L. S. (1961). Irradiated diets for rearing germfree guinea pigs. *Proc. Anim. Care Panel* **11,** 93–106.

Horton, R. E., Madden, D. O., and McCullough, N. B. (1970). Pathogenicity of *Clostridium perfringens* for germ free guinea pigs after oral ingestion. *Appl. Microbiol.* **19,** 314–316.

Institute of Laboratory Animal Resources (1970). "Gnotobiotes; Standards and Guidelines for the Breeding, Care, and Management of Laboratory Animals." Nat. Acad. Sci., Washington, D.C.

Koch, E., Bohn, H., Heiss, F., and Schneider, R. (1953). Cerebral origin of clinical standard syndromes; penicillinase activity of brain and other protective mechanisms. *Naunyn-Schmiedebergs Arch. Exp. Pathol. Pharmakol.* **220,** 157–183.

Landy, J. J., Yerasimides, T. G., Growdon, J. H., and Bausor, S. C. (1960). Germfree guinea pig delivery by hysterectomy. *Surg. Forum* **11,** 425–426.

Lev, M., and Battisto, J. R. (1970). Impaired delayed hypersensitivity in germ free guinea pigs. *Immunology* **19,** 47–54.

Levenson, S. M., Tennant, B., Geever, E., Laundy, R., and Daft, F. (1962). Influence of microorganisms on scurvey. *Arch Intern. Med.* **110,** 693–702.

Luckey, T. D. (1963). "Germfree Life and Gnotobiology." Academic Press, New York.

Luckey, T. D. (1968). Gnotobiology and aerospace systems. *In* "Advances in Germfree Research and Gnotobiology" (M. Miyakawa and T. D. Luckey, eds.), pp. 317–353. CRC Press, Cleveland, Ohio.

McMaster, P. R. B., Aronson, S. B., and Moore, T. E. (1970). Suture toxicity in the germfree guinea pig. *Arch. Ophthalmol.* **84,** [N.S.] 776–782.

Madden, D. L., Horton, R. E., and McCullough, N. B. (1970). Spontaneous infection in ex-germfree guinea pigs due to *Clostridium perfringens. Lab. Anim. Care* **20,** 454–455.

Maggini, A. (1942). M.S. Thesis, University of Notre Dame, Notre Dame, Indiana.

Miyakawa, M. (1955). Germfree rearing of experimental animals. (In Japanese.) *Jap. J. Med. Progr.* **42,** 553–566.

Miyakawa, M. (1959a). The Miyakawa remote-control germ-free rearing unit. *Ann. N.Y. Acad. Sci.* **78,** 37.

Miyakawa, M. (1959b). The lymphatic system of germfree guinea pigs. *Ann. N.Y. Acad. Sci.* **78,** 221–236.

Miyakawa, M., and Kishimoto, H. (1962). Infection of bacteria-free animals with tubercle bacilli. *Kekkaku* **37,** 332–337.

Newton, W. L. (1963). The response of the germfree animal to infection. *Proc. Int. Congr. Zool, 16th, 1963* 1963 abstract.

Newton, W. L. (1965). Methods in germfree animal research. *In* "Methods of Animal Experimentation" (W. I. Gay, ed.), Vol. 1, pp. 215–271. Academic Press, New York.

Newton, W. L., Weinstein, P. P., and Jones, M. F. (1959). A comparison of the development of some rat and mouse helminths in germfree and conventional guinea pigs. *Ann. N.Y. Acad. Sci.* **78,** 290–306.

Newton, W. L., Pennington, R. M., and Lieberman, J. E. (1960a). Comparative hemolytic complement activities of germfree and conventional guinea pig serum. *Proc. Soc. Exp. Biol. Med.* **104,** 486.

Newton, W. L., Reardon, L. V., and Deleva, A. M. (1960b). A comparative study of the subcutaneous innoculation of germfree and conventional guinea pigs with two strains of *Trichomonas vaginalis. Amer. J. Trop. Med. Hyg.* **9,** 56–61.

Nuttall, G. H. F., and Thierfelder, H. (1895). Thierisches Leben ohne Bakterien im Verdauungskanal. *Hoppe-Seyler's Z. Physiol. Chem.* **21,** 109–121.

Nuttall, G. H. F., and Thierfelder, H. (1896). Thierisches Leben ohne Bakterien im Verdauungekanal. II. *Hoppe-Seyler's Z. Physiol. Chem.* **22,** 62–73.

Nuttall, G. H. F., and Thierfelder, H. (1897). Thierisches Leben ohne Bakterien im Verdauungskanal. III. *Hoppe-Seyler's Z. Physiol. Chem.* **23,** 231–235.

Perkins, J. J. (1969). "Principles and Methods of Sterilization in Health Sciences," 2nd ed. Thomas, Springfield, Illinois.

Phillips, B. P. (1964). Studies on the ameba-bacteria relationship of amebiasis. III. Induced amebic lesions in the germfree guinea pig. *Amer. J. Trop. Med. Hyg.* **13,** 391–395.

Phillips, B. P. (1968). Induced amebic enteritis in the germfree, monoinoculated and conventional guinea pig. *In* "Advances in Germfree Research and Gnotobiology" (M. Miyakawa and T. D. Luckey, eds.), pp. 279–286. CRC Press, Cleveland, Ohio.

Phillips, B. P., and Gorstein, F. (1966). Effects of different species of bacteria on the pathology of enteric amebiasis in monocontaminated guinea pigs. *Amer. J. Trop. Med. Hyg.* **15,** 863–868.

Phillips, B. P., and Wolfe, P. A. (1959). The use of germfree guinea pigs in studies on the microbial interrelationshps in amebiasis. *Ann. N.Y. Acad. Sci.* **78,** 308–314.

Phillips, B. P., and Wolfe, P. A. (1961). Pneumonic disease in germfree animals. *J. Infec. Dis.* **108,** 12.

Phillips, B. P., Wolfe, C., Rees, H. A., Gordon, H. A., Wright, W. H., and Reyniers, J. A. (1955). Studies on the ameba-bacterial relationship in amebiasis. Comparative results of the intracecal inoculation of germfree monocontaminated, and conventional guinea pigs with *Entamoeba histolytica. Amer. J. Trop. Med. Hyg.* **4,** 675–592.

Phillips, B. P., Wolfe, P. A., and Bartgis, I. L. (1958). Studies on the amebic-bacteria relationship in amebiasis. II. Some concepts on the etiology of the disease. *Amer. J. Trop. Med. Hyg.* **7,** 392–399.

Phillips, B. P., Wolfe, P. A., and Gordon, H. A. (1959). Studies on rearing the guinea pig germfree. *Ann. N.Y. Acad. Sci.* **78,** 183–207.

Phillips, B. P., Diamond, C. S., Bartgis, I. L., and Stuppler, S. A. (1972). Results of intracecal inoculation of germfree and conventional guinea pigs and germfree rats with atenically cultivated *Entamoeba histolytica. J. Protozool.* **19,** 498–499.

Pleasants, J. R., Reddy, B. S., Zimmerman, D. R., Bruckner-Kardoss, E., and Wostmann, B. S. (1967). Growth, reproduction and morphology of naturally born normally suckled germfree guinea pigs. *Z. Versuchstierk.* **95,** 195–204.

Pleasants, J. R. (1974). Gnotobiotics. In "Handbook of Laboratory Animal Science" (E. C. Melby, Jr. and N. H. Altman, eds.), Vol-1, pp. 117–174. CRC Press, Cleveland, Ohio.

Podoprigora, G. I. (1970. Characteristics of aseptic inflammation in germfree guinea pigs. *Byull. Eksp. Biol. Med.* **70,** 35–8.

Reyniers, J. A. (1946). Germfree life applied to nutrition studies. *Lobund Rep.* **1,** 867–120.

Reyniers, J. A. (1956). Germfree life methodology (gnotobiotics) and experimental nutrition. *Proc. Int. Congr. Biochem., 3rd, 1955* pp. 458–466.

Schaedler, R. W., Dubos, R., and Costello, R. (1965). Association of gremfree mice with bacteria isolated from normal mice. *J. Exp. Med.* **122,** 77.

Seeliger, H. P. R., and Werner, H. (1962). Die toxische Wirkung des Methicillins (2,6-Dimethoxy-benzamidopenicillin-Natrium) auf Meerschweinchen im Vergleich zu Seinz Atoxichen Wirkung be Ratten. *Pathol. Microbiol.* **25,** 153–169.

Sprinz, H., Kundel, D. W., Dammin, G. J., Horowitz, R. E., Schneider, H., and Formal, S. R. (1961). The response of the germ-free guinea pig to oral bacterial challenge with *Escherichia coli* and *Shigella flexneri. Amer. J. Pathol.* **39,** 681–695.

Tabachnick, J., and LaBadie, J. H. (1970). Studies on the Biochemistry of Epidermis. IV. The free amino acids, ammonia, urea, and pyrrolidone carboxylic acid content of conventional and germ-free albino guinea pig epidermis. *J. Invest. Dermatol.* **54,** 24–31.

Tanami, J. (1959). Studies of germfree animals: First Report. *J. Chiba Med. Soc.* **35,** 1–21.

Thompson, G. R., and Trexler, P. C. (1971). Gastrointestinal structure and function in germfree or gnotobiotic animals. *Gut* **12,** 230–235.

Trexler, P. C. (1963). An isolator system for control of contamination. *Lab. Anim. Care* **13,** 572–581.

Trexler, P. C., and Reynolds, L. I. (1957). Flexible film apparatus for the rearing and use of germ-free animals. *Appl. Microbiol.* **5,** 406–412.

Uyei, Y., and Midorikawa, H. (1961). Experimental shigellosis in germfree guinea pigs. *Acta Pathol. Jap.* **2,** 162.

Wagner, M. (1959). Determination of germfree status. *Ann. N.Y. Acad. Sci.* **78,** 89–100.

Warren, K. S., and Newton, W. L. (1959). Portal and peripheral blood ammonia concentrations in germfree and conventional guinea pigs. *Amer. J. Physiol.* **197,** 717–720.

Wostmann, B. S. (1961). Recent studies on the serum proteins of germfree animals. *Ann. N.Y. Acad. Sci.* **94,** 272–83.

Chapter 5

Behavior

Lawrence V. Harper

I. INTRODUCTION

Although cavies were present in Europe as pets from the mid-1500's, the first records of their use in biological experiments date from the middle of the eighteenth century (Mason, 1939). Scientific studies of behavior appeared near the end of the nineteenth century and were concerned with prenatal reflex development (Preyer, 1885), "associative phenomena" (Allen, 1904), and the biology of reproduction (Loeb and Lathrop, 1914; Stockard and Papanicolaou, 1919). The first systematic descriptions and analyses of guinea pigs' behavioral patterns appeared in English in the 1920's. Notable among these were work on prenatal development of behavior (Avery, 1928; Carmichael, 1934) and descriptive studies of reproductive behavior (Avery, 1925; Louttit, 1927, 1929a). Further detailed accounts of the motor patterns of guinea pigs appeared only recently (Coulon, 1971; Grant and Mackintosh, 1963; von Kunkel and Kunkel, 1964; Rood, 1972).

Only two published studies are available in English concerning behavior of domestic cavies under "natural" conditions (King, 1956; Rood, 1972). Relatively little is known about guinea pigs' social organization or enemies in the wild. However, a full understanding of the species' behavior must ultimately be based upon an analysis of its adaptations in natural habitats. Thus, a brief attempt will be made to describe the behavior of guinea pigs in the field.

Cavia porcellus (King, 1956), *C. aperea* (Rood, 1972), and *C.*

cutleri (Castle and Wright, 1916) do not dig burrows; digging in *C. porcellus* is more related to the existence of conflict between impulses than to a tendency to construct a nest or shelter (Grant and Mackintosh, 1963; Rood, 1972). In the wild, guinea pigs use burrows excavated by other animals, crevices in natural or man-made rock formations, or shelter provided by stalks and branches of shrubs (Castle and Wright, 1916; King, 1956; Rood, 1972).

Although available data are not consistent, some form of polygynous social organization exists under natural conditions. (Beauchamp *et al.,* 1971; King, 1956; von Kunkel and Kunkel, 1964; Rood, 1972). Adult males tend to form a linear dominance hierarchy; the alpha male is generally intolerant of sexual activity on the part of lower ranking males (King, 1956; von Kunkel and Kunkel, 1964; Rood, 1972). With ample space, dominant males from different groups may establish a system of mutual avoidance in the areas in which their home ranges overlap (King, 1956; Rood, 1972). When large groups are confined to a relatively restricted area, small "family" subgroups may remain together; the females are usually subordinate to the alpha male, or "their" male, but may also have a loosely defined dominance hierarchy of their own (von Kunkel and Kunkel, 1964).

Guinea pigs actively seek contact with one another but mutual grooming is not extensive, except for brief maternal solicitude for the highly precocious young (Grant and Mackintosh, 1963; King, 1956; von Kunkel and Kunkel, 1964; Rood, 1972). There is little obvious social greeting activity within established groups; strangers introduced into an existing group are investigated by nose to nose contact and anogenital nuzzling (King, 1956; von Kunkel and Kunkel, 1964). The alpha male may attack strange males (Rood, 1972). Young animals frequently follow adults about; when there is a change in setting, animals of all ages tend to venture forth from cover in a single file, moving hesitantly.

In the wild, as in captivity, guinea pigs feed on green grass and vegetables; they are especially fond of alfalfa. According to King (1956) and Rood (1972), they tend to eat in groups with little or no competition; they do not cache or store food.

King's (1956) and Rood's (1972) observations of groups in large outdoor pens suggested that daily periods of activity were governed by temperature and sunlight intensity. Animals were most active in the morning and evening, avoiding the midday sun. On overcast days, they were more active throughout the day and remained under cover most of the night. In King's (1956) colony there was no apparent breeding season and litters were born throughout the year; however, Rood and Weir (1970) and Rood (1972) reported a spring peak in births among *C. aperea* and suggested that the onset of reproduction may be delayed in guinea pigs born in autumn and spring. The young remained under shelter for the first few days after birth and were active outside with adults by the fourth day (King, 1956). There is little evidence of parental defense of the young. The most common responses to danger seem to be immobility, or sudden, explosive, scattering with each animal seeking a different route to shelter (Grant and Mackintosh, 1963; King, 1956).

II. PERCEPTION AND INDIVIDUAL BEHAVIOR PATTERNS

A. Perception

1. Vision

According to Allen (1904), despite the fact that their eyes are open at birth, newborn guinea pigs' object discrimination and depth vision seem to be poorly developed. However, adults rely partly upon vision in learning problems. Using a modified Skinner box, Miles *et al.* (1956) found that brightness discriminations for food reward were made with ease, but hue could not be discriminated. Using a "visual-cliff" apparatus, Schiffman (1970) found that 25-day-old Hartley guinea pigs showed more trembling when placed on the glass over the "deep" side than when placed over the "shallow" side. Further, more locomotor activity was observed on the shallow side. When 30-day-old pups were placed on a board between the shallow and deep sides, 14 of 17 descended to the shallow side and only 3 to the deep side. However, in comparison to species which are more dependent upon visual cues, guinea pigs did not show as much apparent discomfort when placed over the deep side. Schiffman (1970) concluded that haptic information was sufficient to overcome visually indicated absence of support.

2. Audition

Investigations of the auditory capacities of guinea pigs have been conducted since the late nineteenth century (Horton, 1933). A variety of responses have been used as measures of acuity, including the pinna reflex (Preyer, 1885), changes in respiration rate (Horton, 1933; Sherrick and Bilger, 1959), and cochlear potentials (Davis *et al.,* 1935). Miller and Murray (1966) used the guinea pigs' tendency to "freeze" in response to novel sounds as a measure of auditory acuity. Water-deprived subjects were allowed to habituate to a test chamber containing lettuce leaves. When the animals were eating they were presented with sounds from 125 to 32,000 hertz (Hz). Using the least intense level that produced an immobility response as threshold, Miller and Murray discovered that guinea pigs were responsive to all frequencies tested and showed maximum sensitivity between 500 and 8000 Hz. From their own work and review of earlier studies, they concluded that the upper limit of guinea pigs' auditory sensitivity was probably 40,000 to 50,000 Hz.

3. Gustation

Little systematic evidence is available on gustatory sensitivity of this species. Bauer (1971) reported that guinea pigs preferred glucose solutions (anhydrous dextrose) of 0.10 *M* and 0.20 *M* to water, but rejected 0.50 *M* solutions. Maximally preferred glucose strength appeared to be near 0.20 *M*, suggesting that guinea pigs avoid sweet foods. With respect to responses to bitter tasting compounds, Warren and Pfaffman (1959) found that sucrose octa-acetate (SOA) was rejected by guinea pigs when added to water at concentrations of $2 \times 10^{-3} M$, about one-tenth the strength of a quinine solution required to achieve the same effect. Rearing pups in isolation with SOA-treated water or socially, with mothers whose nipples were periodically painted with SOA solution, caused little preference to be shown for plain water over concentrations that were clearly rejected by control subjects. However, retesting 3 to 4 months later indicated that the tendency to accept SOA was not stable. Stark (1963) reported similar results and showed with repeated tests that even control animals' intake of $10^{-3} M$ SOA solutions increased.

4. Other Senses

Little systematic evidence is available concerning other sensory capacities of guinea pigs, although olfaction probably plays an important role in social behavior (see Section III, B).

B. Activity Patterns

While King's (1956) and Rood's (1972) observations indicated a crepuscular activity rhythm, laboratory studies of sleep–activity cycles under conditions of relatively uniform temperature, humidity, and illumination revealed almost continual activity, mostly feeding and self-grooming. Nicholls (1922) found that with only 15 minutes of light per day (at feeding time) there were no prolonged periods of inactivity; the longest periods of quiet rarely exceeded 10 minutes; in the 23-hour periods during which animals were undisturbed, there was an average of 20 hours activity. The same results were obtained when animals 1 to 8 months of age were kept under constant illumination. Males were slightly more active than females. Hunger, short of debilitation, had little effect on this rhythm but under extreme food or water deprivation, physical activity varied with the method of measurement (Campbell *et al.*, 1966). In excessive heat (75°–85°F) animals spent more time inactive, stretched out on the cage bottoms. At 79°F animals were active for 19 hours per day, but when the temperature was increased to 85°F daily activity fell to just over 12 hours (Nicholls, 1922).

Similar patterns of activity have been reported in electrophysiological studies of sleep. Adult animals bearing permanently implanted electrodes which allowed them freedom of movement in sound-shielded, naturally illuminated cages spent 72% of their time awake and 52% of awake time in a state of alertness. Only 4% of the animals' daily cycle was spent in paradoxical sleep (PS). There appeared to be no circadian periodicity of sleep bouts (Pellet and Beraud, 1967). These figures agree with Nicholl's (1922) data since sleep periods can be very brief or broken by sudden startles.

Malven and Sawyer (1966) investigated the effects of the estrous cycle on sleep in ovariectomized adult females. Like Pellet and Beraud (1967), they found that there was only about 4% PS, as recorded by implanted cortical electrodes. Sleep periods were brief; no episode lasted longer than 6 minutes, and 88% of the episodes of PS were of 20 seconds to 3 minutes duration. These periods of PS were always followed by periods of arousal. Behaviorally, PS episodes in subjects well-habituated to the test situation were distinguishable by relaxation of the neck musculature and drooping or closed eyelids. When estrus was induced by two daily estrogen injections followed by an injection of progesterone on the third day, the percentage of sleep was decreased just prior to and during the period of behavioral sexual receptivity. On the following day the amounts of arousal and sleep were at pretreatment levels. There seemed to be no minimum period of quiet sleep necessary prior to the onset of PS.

C. Flight and Exploration

1. Responses to Danger

According to King (1956), guinea pig responses to danger depended upon the sensory modality involved; for example, to unfamiliar, sudden sounds, they tended to freeze rather than flee. Miller and Murray (1966) described laboratory animals' immobility response to sound as characterized by an arched posture with the forefeet extended, the head up, and the eyes opened wide giving the impression of exopthalmus. High frequency sounds were particularly likely to elicit this response. In response to sudden, very loud sounds, immobility was maintained for as long as 20 minutes. They suggested that such immobility minimized stimuli for predators.

Similar inhibition of activity occurs when guinea pigs are placed in unfamiliar surroundings; it is not uncommon to find that an exposure period of 1 to 2 days is necessary in order for animals to habituate to a new cage or piece of testing equipment (Nicholls, 1922; Malven and Sawyer, 1966). In a study of oxygen intake, Gerall and Berg (1964) found that about 20 hours' exposure over a period of 4 days was required before stable baseline measures could be obtained. On the first day in the apparatus, the animals' oxygen intake was the highest recorded, on the second and third days, intake was significantly below levels recorded when the animals had habituated to the apparatus.

Olfactory stimulation appears to play an important role in the guinea pig's response to a setting. Carter (1972) reared litters in environments in which air was scented with either acetophenone or ethyl benzoate or was unscented. Between 25 and 65 days of age the animals were tested in a two-choice apparatus baited with lettuce; the delay between the beginning of the test and the onset of eating was recorded under different odor conditions. The subjects of both sexes generally spent more time in the presence of familiar odors, and male eating responses tended to be inhibited in the presence of unfamiliar odors.

Sansone and Bovet (1970) reported little evidence of freezing in response to electric shock in tests of avoidance learning; however, earlier detailed descriptions suggested that, once guinea pigs reacted to the shock, they tended to remain immobile for some time (Louttit, 1929b; James, 1934). In the absence of systematic data on the subject, it would seem advisable for those contemplating the experimental use of shock as a "reinforcer" with guinea pig subjects to conduct fairly extensive pilot work using various intensities, durations, etc., before undertaking studies of learning or other behavior (see also Section IV, B).

Although its function is not entirely clear, the tonic immobility response is presumably related to self-protection, perhaps as a last resort in response to capture. According to Bayard (1957) immobility could be evoked by holding animals on their backs against a flat surface and pressing down gently. The durations of the bouts of immobility varied from less than 1 minute to over 10 minutes. Bayard found that with repeated testing most young animals became refractory; however, once immobility had been induced, its duration was not directly related to prior test experience.

In response to sudden or unexpected movement guinea pigs usually flee (King, 1956). When a group of animals is thus startled, the net impression is of an explosion, guinea pigs "scattering" in every direction, including toward the source of the disturbance. Such behavior may be adaptive; a predator may be so alarmed or confused by the apparent attack and the random pattern of dispersal that capture may be aborted. In intraspecific fights, scattering may serve to protect the intended victim of an attack by diverting the aggressor's attention (Grant and Mackintosh, 1963).

2. Exploratory Behavior

When introduced into a novel setting or reacting to a new object or change in a familiar setting, guinea pigs move in a series of starts and stops in which the steps are taken slowly and cautiously. Their bodies are usually held low to the ground and fully extended (Rood, 1972). This "extend" position may also be adopted when investigating a novel object and, in the early phases of investigation, such sniffing or nosing is frequently interrrupted by pulling the head back suddenly.

In King's (1956) study it took 9 animals a period of 8 weeks to utilize a 15 × 15 m enclosure; they moved out gradually from their huts and the paths between them. Platt *et al.* (1971) found that, in a Y-maze with a black and a white goal box, guinea pigs, 180 days old, showed no apparent preference for novelty. Rather, despite having had a preliminary opportunity to explore the maze (without goal boxes), 9 of 10 subjects showed strong position preferences across trials. Tobach and Gold (1966) found that guinea pigs tended to remain immobile in the center of a circular enclosure rather than exploring or moving rapidly to the shelter of the wall. Defecation, often considered to be an index of "emotionality" in laboratory animals, occurred in the open field in only one of 15 subjects; however, upon return to their home cages, the animals defecated sooner than when they received comparable handling in the course of routine colony maintenance. After 2 more days, the animals were given an opportunity to leave the home cage and enter a new cage; only 4 of 15 subjects did so despite the fact that 1 day earlier 12 of 13 of the same animals left a transfer bucket to enter an unfamiliar enclosure. Similarly, a comparison of the open field responses of guinea pigs, hamsters, and rats led Lin and Mogenson (1968) to the conclusion that, relative to other laboratory rodents, guinea pigs were unlikely to explore and were most likely to freeze in a novel setting.

This lack of activity does not represent unresponsiveness to the environment. Fara and Catlett (1971) studied guinea pig cardiac responses to changes in stimulation, such as opening the cage door, reaching toward the animal, placing a small object in the cage, or introducing a wood rat (*Neotoma fuscipes*) into the cage. They found that, although the animals displayed a minimum of overt motor reaction, their heart rates showed statistically reliable fluctuations in response to the stimuli (see also Section II, C, 1).

Porter *et al.* (1973a) found that guinea pigs, 1 to 4 weeks old, locomoted more in an open field when their mother and siblings were in an adjacent cage separated only by a wire partition than pups placed in the same enclosure while the adjacent cage was empty. Like Harper (1968) and Nagy and Misanin (1970), Coulon (1971) found that hand-reared animals locomoted more and began to move with shorter latencies in an open field situation than did mother-reared animals. While the hand-reared subjects rapidly ran to the wall, vocalizing, the socially reared animals proceeded cautiously a step at a time (see also Section IV, A). Consistent with the suggestion that younger animals tended to adapt more rapidly to unfamiliar surroundings, Coulon (1971) also noted that pups explored more than did older animals.

It is possible that olfaction may play a part in evoking exploration in guinea pigs. Donovan and Kopriva (1965) reported that electrical stimulation of the olfactory bulbs of adult female guinea pigs tended to elicit increased exploration, although Carter (1972) found that olfactory novelty inhibited the activity of guinea pigs, especially males (see Section II, C, 1).

D. Feeding and Eliminative Behavior

1. Feeding Behavior

Under naturalistic conditions guinea pigs generally feed during the daylight hours, especially around dawn and dusk (King, 1956; Rood, 1972); however, laboratory-reared animals feed throughout the day and night (Nicholls, 1922; Pellet and Beraud, 1967). King's (1956) suggestion that social facilitation of feeding is common among guinea pigs was supported by the finding that isolation reared pups gained weight more slowly than colony reared animals (Harper, 1968). In the field, guinea pigs commonly feed on grass (King, 1956; Rood, 1972); feeding is accomplished by grasping a stalk in the mouth near the ground and tearing it off with a backward and upward thrust of the head (Rood, 1972). The morsel is then drawn into the mouth; chewing and swallowing occur in a coordinated pattern (Smith, 1938).

Much of the feral guinea pig's water requirement may be met by succulent greens. In the laboratory, the guinea pig's water intake generally varies inversely with the amount of fresh greens in the diet (Dutch and Brown, 1968). When supplied water through a drinking tube, guinea pigs do not lick; rather, they put their mouths around the tube and pull their heads back thus drawing out the water (Alvord *et al.,* 1971). With 13-mm diameter tubes fitted with ball bearing antidrip devices, animals gnaw upon the end of the tube to express water (L. V. Harper, personal observation). Although they do not naturally lick from a tube, guinea pigs can be trained to do so by gradually withdrawing the end of the spout into the side of the cage (Alvord *et al.,* 1971). In drinking from a water dish, the forepaws rest on the edge and the head is tilted back after each sip (Rood, 1972).

Experiments suggest that guinea pigs require a fairly regular water intake. Dutch and Brown (1968) reported that young adult females became moribund about 10 days on a schedule permitting access to water for only 1 hour per day unless they were allowed to adjust gradually and were given supplements of fresh grass. Lollier *et al.* (1968) reported that young adult males could survive relatively mild water deprivation but became physiologically distressed on more severe schedules.

Campbell *et al.* (1966) found that under conditions of total food or water deprivation juvenile and young adult guinea pigs survived until about 30% of their original weight had been lost; the slopes of the weight loss curves were very similar for both food and water deprivation. Kutscher (1969) reported that adult male guinea pigs subjected to total water deprivation reduced their dry food intake to about 80% of baseline levels. By the end of deprivation at 5 days, body weight declined 28%. Withholding food for 7 days produced adipsia. Allowing animals access to food for only 2 hours per day produced some decrement in water intake; they ingested only around 30% of their normal daily food intake. Even after 3 weeks on this feeding schedule they were unable to adjust their feeding habits. The decline in drinking under food deprivation may be a function of the degree of deprivation; animals kept on a 50% baseline food deprivation schedule showed a transient increase in water intake, while 0, 25, and 75% rations yielded decreased water intake. The foregoing results generally are consistent with the data on daily activity. Guinea pigs appear to have difficulty in adapting to limited feeding times as one might expect from their tendencies to feed throughout the day.

Smith (1938) reported that decorticate subjects were unable to coordinate normal chewing and swallowing movements. Since mortality in this experiment was high, it would be of interest to see results obtained under modern operative conditions. More recently, Phillips and Valenstein (1969) have shown that bilateral hypothalamic stimulation elicited eating and occasionally drinking behavior. Unlike the rat, the percentage of sites eliciting eating exceeded the percentage of sites eliciting drinking; feeding in guinea pigs could be elicited by stimulation of a greater number of hypothalamic sites than in rats.

While gnawing behavior does not appear to be directly related to feeding (Phillips and Valenstein, 1969), it does involve biting and chewing. Like other rodents, guinea pigs spend considerable amounts of time gnawing on drinking tubes, wood chips, the edge of feeding dishes, etc. Not only will hypothalamic stimulation elicit gnawing (Phillips and Valenstein, 1969), but Srimal and Dhawan (1970) have reported that apomorphine, amphetamine, and methylphenidate all induced vigorous gnawing in guinea pigs. The mechanisms of drug induced gnawing have not been determined.

2. Elimination

Although urine may play some role in social communication (see Section IV), both King (1956) and Rood (1972) observed that feces were dropped indiscriminately about the pen and nestboxes. Tobach and Gold's (1966) data suggested that elimination may be inhibited in strange settings. While Rood (1972) mentioned a slight elevation of the perineal region during urination, the writer feels that this posture is more characteristic of defecation and has described a distinctive pattern of backing up accompanied by a quivering of the rump prior to micturition (Harper, 1972).

Despite their precocity, newborn guinea pigs usually are incapable of voluntary micturition for several days postpartum. Maternal licking stimulates both defecation and urination during this period (Beach, 1966; King, 1956). Even gentle tactual stimulation of the lumbar region often suffices to elicit defecation in hand-reared young (L. V. Harper, personal observation).

Adults and weaning-age young commonly exhibit coprophagy (King, 1956). Most often, the animal "doubles over" forward from a sitting posture, lowering its snout to the anal region to take the fecal pellet as it is passed (von Kunkel and Kunkel, 1964; Rood, 1972). Females whose mobility is severely restricted in the later stages of pregnancy may simply turn around to locate the pellet with or without first attempting to double over (L. V. Harper, personal observation). Pups may occasionally ingest parental feces (von Kunkel and Kunkel, 1964).

III. SOCIAL BEHAVIOR

A. Contactual Patterns

Guinea pigs not only tolerate close physical proximity when at rest but seem to seek contact with one another when they are moving about. The following taxonomy of forms of contact is drawn largely from Grant and Mackintosh (1963) and Rood (1972).

1. General

The most common investigatory movement is extending the snout toward another animal. The regions most frequently approached in this manner are the other animal's snout, ears, or perineum. When nose to nose contact occurs it may be protracted with both parties active in maintaining the interaction. In sexual or parental encounters, perineal investigations may include anogenital licking and nibbling.

During periods of inactivity in moderate or cooler temperatures, guinea pigs characteristically rest in contact with one another, usually huddled in parallel facing in the same or in opposite directions. Another common form of contact while at rest is resting the chin upon the body of another animal. A similar and perhaps related posture is one in which the forequarters and the venter are in contact with the partner, the forepaws usually resting upon the partner's body. An abbreviated form of this response may serve to displace another animal from a desired site (S. Reisbick, personal communication, 1973). The young may actually sit or lie on top of the mother. Lactating females characteristically adopt a sitting posture for nursing while the young crawl under their mother, aligned parallel to her body, to reach the mammae. While under, the pups occasionally "root," raising the head up and back.

When guinea pigs in a group move about while feeding, etc., they often make fleeting contacts, sometimes appearing to go out of their way to "sideswipe" each other. Similarly, when an animal attempts to join a group at rest or at a feeding dish, it often will squeeze in between two others rather than alongside. During periods of excited activity, such as the male's mating attempts, one may crawl under another's abdomen or climb over its back. In attempts to gain access to food, water, or resting sites or to discourage contact, animals may employ what appears to be a variant of the crawling under or rooting patterns to move another out of the way (L. V. Harper, personal observation).

2. Grooming

Little mutual grooming occurs with the exception of early maternal care of the young or occasional nibbling or nosing in the region of the ears or eyes (King, 1956). Self-grooming can be observed in pups on the day of birth. Grooming generally occurs in periods of calm, after a feed, or after resting (Coulon, 1971). The adult pattern usually starts with licking the forepaws and wiping the face. At full intensity the animal sits on its haunches and uses both forepaws simultaneously drawn over the head from behind the ears to the snout. The fur is then groomed with teeth and tongue from breast rearward. Often the snout is rapidly moved back and forth through the fur laterally in a wiping movement accompanied by a lateral combing action of the forepaw on the same side while the animal is sitting (Grant and Mackintosh, 1963; Rood, 1972). Scratching by the hind feet during a bout of grooming is often followed by drawing the nails through the teeth (L. V. Harper, personal observation). Shaking the body also occurs (Rood, 1972) and may be accompanied by a brief rearing of the forequarters (L. V. Harper, personal observation).

Possibly related to, or derived from grooming and perhaps also involving an element of aggression (Grant and Mackintosh, 1963) is one animal grasping the hair of another in its teeth and pulling it out; the mouthful is often ingested. Hair pulling is a common pattern in pups; it is directed toward the mother and usually occurs during or shortly after the end of lactation (Coulon, 1971; Harper, 1968). Occasionally hair pulling will persist into adulthood and it is the writer's impression that it may be contagious. Hair pulling was observed when animals attempted to displace one another at water spouts and feeding dishes. Especially under conditions of crowding or stress, hair pulling and ear nibbling may become so exaggerated that they become a mild form of cannibalism resulting in markedly cropped pinnae and sparse pelage.

B. Communication

Postural signals will be discussed in conjunction with other functional categories. This section will be limited to olfactory and auditory communication.

1. Olfactory Signals

According to Rood (1972), scent marking with the adanal glands is common among cavies. The animal squats and drags the perineal region along the ground (see also von Kunkel and Kunkel, 1964). This response occurs particularly often in mating encounters, after micturition, and when animals are adjusting to strange surroundings, perhaps to denote familiar territory (Ewer, 1968). The supracaudal gland of the male is also used in marking; the male makes side to side movements of the rump against objects (von Kunkel and Kunkel, 1964; Rood, 1972). Although the effects of supracaudal secretions are unknown, they may serve to delimit the male's homesite. (see von Kunkel and Kunkel, 1964). A hand-reared male occasionally responded in this way to the writer's hand, suggesting that supracaudal marking may also be used to identify members of the male's group (Ewer, 1968).

Urine seems to have communicative value for guinea pigs. In attempts to repulse a persistent male's investigation of her perineal region, an unreceptive female may flatten her back, raise the perineum as in the lordosis response, and emit a jet of urine toward the male (Grant and Mackintosh, 1963; Rood, 1972). The male may sniff or lick this emission, and the female may make her escape while the male is so occupied (Louttit, 1927). When a male is attempting to mate with an unreceptive female, he may move by her with a skipping motion, throw his hindquarters toward her (sometimes making contact), and eject a stream of urine at her (Louttit, 1927; Rood, 1972). The function of this response is unclear; the male's scent may affect pair synchronization or serve to identify the female as member of the male's group (Ewer, 1968).

2. Auditory Signals

A variety of calls (see Table I) have been recognized in domestic guinea pigs for some time (Allen, 1904 Avery, 1925). Nearly 20 years ago, Anderson (1954) reported that some audible sounds of guinea pigs had appreciable ultrasonic components above 20 kHz. However, until very recently most attempts to analyze the calls of the guinea pig have been based upon the discriminative ability of the human ear.

Berryman (1970 and personal communication, 1972) has conducted a series of sound-spectrographic analyses of guinea pig calls distinguishing 11 distinct sound patterns. "Chutts" are brief (0.05 second) wide band (0 to 3 kHz) vocalizations occurring singly or in pairs, separated by 0.02- to 0.05-second intervals and are emitted during general activity and exploration.

The "chutter" consists of chains of 2 to 4 components, 0.15 to 0.3 seconds per component, with intervals of 0.1 to 0.15 seconds. It occurs in long bouts with an audibly rising and falling frequency range from 0.5 to 3.5 kHz. The chutter is often followed by the "whine," in which the frequency range is slightly greater (0.5 to 4 kHz), with higher dominant frequencies, lacking regularly occurring components so that the observer has the impression of a quavering call. They are emitted in situations of flight, discomfort, or evasion.

Table I
Analysis of Common Guinea Pig Vocalizations[a]

Call type	Call/component number	Frequency (kHz)	Component duration (sec)	Intercall component interval (sec)	Associated activity
Chutt	1–2 calls	0–3	0.05	0.02–0.05	General activity; exploration
Chutter	2–4 calls	0.5–3.5	0.15–0.3	0.1–0.15	Flight, evasion, defense
Whine	Variable number of calls	0.5–4	0.15–0.3	0.1–0.15	Defense, evasion
Tweet	Variable number of calls	0.5–4	0.1	0.1–0.2	Maternal licking of pups' anogenital region
Whistle	2 components	0–3 and 3–20	0.15–0.65	0.1	Separation; caretaker feeding
Low Whistle	1 component 10–20 calls	0–3	0.05–0.125	0.05–0.1	Separation; caretaker feeding
Purr	Up to 50 components	0–3.5	0.1–0.3	0.025	Seeking contact
Drr	3–14 components	0–3.5	0.1–0.3	0.025	Freezing in response to sudden change in environment
Scream	Variable number of calls	0.25–32	0.15–0.25	0.1	Loser cornered in a fight
Squeal	Single calls	1–16	0.1–0.2	–	Response to injury

[a]From Berryman (1970).

The "tweet" is a 0.1-second call occurring in multiples with 0.1 to 0.2 seconds between sounds, and a rising frequency range of 0.5 to 4 kHz. This is emitted by the young when the mother grooms their anogenital regions (Berryman, 1970; Coulon, 1971).

The "whistle" is a two-part call, from 0 to 3 kHz rising steeply to 8 to 20 kHz in the latter part; whistles occur singly or in long bouts, lasting 0.15 to 0.65 seconds with intercall intervals of at least 0.1 second. "Low whistles" may precede the "whistle" or they may occur alone. Low whistles rise in pitch to only 3 kHz and last 0.05 to 0.125 seconds. They occur in bouts of 10 to 20 with interbout intervals of 0.05 to 0.1 seconds; they are most frequently encountered upon separation from others or in association with a caretaker's providing food (Berryman, 1970; Coulon, 1971; Rood, 1972).

The "purr" is a burst of noise from 0 to 3.5 kHz, 0.1 to 0.03 seconds long, with intervals between bursts of 0.025 seconds, and with as many as 50 bursts per bout. This is the purring call described in conjunction with mating behavior (Avery, 1925; Louttit, 1927) and filial behavior (Harper, 1972). Berryman (1970) characterized it as occurring when contact is allowed or sought.

The "drr" is a short purr composed of only 3 to 14 bursts of noise, usually 6 to 7. Drr's usually are given in response to sudden environmental change (Berryman, 1970), especially sudden auditory stimuli, and seem to function as warning signals (King, 1956).

The "scream" is comparable to a whistle without the low component but with a wider frequency range of 0.25 to 12 to 32 kHz, lasting 0.15 to 0.25 second, and occurs in bouts with 0.1-second intervals between sounds. It is typically emitted by the cornered participant in a fight (Berryman, 1970).

The "squeal" is emitted singly with a frequency range of 1 to 16 kHz, lasting 0.1 to 0.2 second; it lacks the ascending pitch of the scream. Squeals are emitted in response to injury (Berryman, 1970; Rood, 1972).

Since the publication of the foregoing, J. Berryman (personal communication, 1972) has added the "chirp" to her list. This call is provisionally believed to be a low intensity distress call (Berryman) or perhaps a warning (Rood, 1972).

Rood (1972) also described a "grunt" emitted by dominant animals when interacting with subordinates. He felt that the call signified an intention to attack. "Tooth chattering" is a common response of many laboratory rodents including the guinea pig in situations of threat or overt conflict (Grant and Mackintosh, 1963; von Kunkel and Kunkel, 1964; King, 1956; Rood, 1972).

C. Aggression and Dominance Relations

Conflict among guinea pigs occurs in a variety of situations. Commonly, laboratory-housed animals quarrel over space; for access to food, drink, or objects to gnaw upon; to discourage contact, especially during weaning and in mating encounters and, among males, for access to females (Beauchamp *et al.*, 1971; von Kunkel and Kunkel, 1964). The motor patterns involved in such altercations may, for convenience, be divided into offensive and defensive elements (Rood, 1972).

1. Offensive Responses

A threatening guinea pig orients toward its adversary with its head raised, mouth partially open, forelegs semi-extended, and hindquarters in a crouch; this posture is frequently accompanied by tooth chattering and piloerection about the shoulders (von Kunkel and Kunkel, 1964; Rood, 1972). Some males may turn partially broadside and evert the rectal mucosa (Rood, 1972). In some cases, a hip swaying, purring display may occur in the context of threat or an assertion of dominance; piloerection and exposure of the rectal mucosa accompany the display.

The commonest attack pattern involves raising the head slightly, then thrusting it downward and foward toward the opponent. The mouth may be opened making an audible sound and several thrusts may be repeated. Contact is rarely made (Grant and Mackintosh, 1963; Rood, 1972). At higher intensities of attack, this head thrust is accompanied by a jump or short run toward the opponent. If the latter flees, this may result in a chase; in serious conflicts fairly deep bites may be delivered to the nearest part of the retreating animal (Grant and Mackintosh, 1963; von Kunkel and Kunkel, 1964; Rood, 1972).

When two adult males vie for dominance, conflicts may be particularly severe and repeated, especially when they are caged together with females, and may result in the death of a combatant (Avery, 1925). The challenger purrs and sways his hips from side to side or approaches while chattering his teeth. The males circle, threatening, and, if neither backs down, they leap upward and toward each other as if to strike at their adversaries' heads (Avery, 1925; King, 1956; von Kunkel and Kunkel, 1964). These clashes can result in tearing of the nose and lips (King, 1956) and, when one flees, deep wounds over much of the body during the ensuing chase (Grant and Mackintosh, 1963). Even young littermate males may engage in several such contests before they reach full sexual maturity. Females display such leaping attacks, but much less frequently and at lower intensities (L. V. Harper, personal observation). According to King (1956), when two animals are fairly evenly matched and have access to a relatively large area, a standoff may be reached wherein both limit themselves to aggressive displays.

2. Defensive Responses

Submissive cutoff postures are infrequently used by guinea pigs to inhibit an adversary's aggression (Grant and Mackintosh, 1963). Nevertheless, several postures and patterns are common in defensive contexts.

The lordosis-like urination pattern of the nonreceptive female in response to a male's investigation has been considered a defensive act; Rood (1972) also suggests that a lordosis-like posture may function as a defensive or submissive signal. The female turning about to face a courting male and her tendency to kick backward with one or both hind feet when the male begins licking also have been classified as defensive acts by Rood (1972). Kicking back or a variant, a forward downward thrust of the hind foot, and pushing away with lateral movements of the forepaws may be used to discourage the nursing attempts of pups (Rood, 1972). Pointing the nose up is considered to be a defensive (submissive) signal to a more dominant guinea pig; or, in courting males, a conciliatory response to the female's rebuff (Rood, 1972). Grant and Mackintosh (1963) also describe a posture in which the animal on defense is oriented perpendicular to the aggressor with its head oriented slightly away.

Although the above postures frequently can be observed, the predominant defensive maneuver among guinea pigs is flight. According to Coulon (1971), isolation-reared males did not respond to threat postures of socially reared males and, consequently, suffered severe attacks. However, Harper (1970c) observed a hand-reared male respond to the tooth chattering of a socially reared male with flight and tooth chattering.

D. Mating Behavior

The mating pattern is the most extensively researched facet of guinea pig behavior. Most work before 1964 has been reviewed in depth by Young (1969); unless otherwise indicated, the following discussion draws from that review.

1. Male Behavior

a. The Mating Pattern. In guinea pigs, the male coital pattern usually consists of anogenital investigation by sniffing or licking; pursuit by following or circling; running the chin up on the female's hindquarters; mounting with a forepaw clasp, which may include palpation of the female's flanks; pelvic thrusts; intromission; indicated by longer, deeper, thrusts, and ejaculation, indicated by prolonged, convulsive thrust. Whether or not ejaculation occurs, intromissions are followed by genital grooming. After the postejaculatory groom, or even before it, the male may drag his perineum along the substrate (Avery, 1925; Coulon, 1972; Grant and Mackintosh, 1963; Harper, 1968; Louttit, 1927; Rood, 1972; Young, 1969).

Upon introduction of a female, the male usually purrs and rhythmically sways his hindquarters from side to side; he locomotes around the female in this fashion (Avery, 1925; Louttit, 1927) sometimes brushing against her as he goes by. This courtship display usually precedes the display of the basic mating pattern and is more pronounced when the female is not fully receptive (Avery, 1925). When the female is unreceptive, the male may bite the hair on the female's neck and shoulders (Avery, 1925). Improperly oriented mounts at the head or across the body may also occur in mating attempts by highly aroused males (Avery, 1925; Gerall, 1965; Harper, 1968).

In laboratory tests, ejaculation occurs most frequently during the first intromission and, among males caged singly, during the first minute of a 10-minute mating test. After ejaculation, the male loses interest on the female for nearly an hour (the postejaculatory interval). This period of refractoriness may be abbreviated by introduction of another receptive female as early as 30 minutes after ejaculation, but not by removing and replacing the same female. In contrast to laboratory conditions, in outdoor colonies with many animals where the alpha male may have to guard his female from subordinates, Rood (1972) reported that the alpha male mounts about 6 times with intromission before ejaculation is achieved. Subsequently, after a mating chase, highly aroused subordinate males may ejaculate on the first intromission.

b. Detecting Receptive Females. Evidence concerning the male's ability to detect an estrous female is inconsistent. The fact that the introduction of another female shortens the postejaculatory interval suggests that males do distinguish among females. Beauchamp *et al.* (1971) and Rood (1972) observed that males appear to be able to detect and to be attracted to pregnant females near term (and thus, an impending postpartum estrus). Von Kunkel and Kunkel (1964) and Avery (1925) described dominant males guarding receptive females against overtures of other males. However, other observers report that a male locating a female in heat depends upon periodic testing of all the members of the group; his response being determined by the reaction to his investigatory attempts (von Kunkel and Kunkel, 1964; Loeb and Lathrop, 1914 Louttit, 1927). Despite the apparently prominent role of anogenital investigation, Avery (1925) reported that males with transected olfactory bulbs sired litters when permanently caged with fertile females. Beyond this, little else is known.

c. Early Experience. Only 5 minutes of daily exposure to a female peer (Louttit, 1929a), contact with females restricted by a chickenwire screen, or first exposure to receptive females at or before the age of 60 days (Gerall, 1963) seem to suffice for the development of normal mating behavior in male guinea pigs that were isolated by the tenth day of age. However, delaying exposure to congeners until day 77 or later has been found to lead to apparent deficits in male mating behavior (Gerall, 1963; Young, 1969). In such studies, only about one-third of the isolated males achieved normal mounts when social isolation was instituted on the tenth day (Young, 1969), or second day (Gerall, 1965), or immediately after birth (Coulon, 1971; Harper, 1968). In the most intensive study of this phenomenon to date, Coulon (1971) reported that the first mating attempts of males isolated from birth appeared to be much less rigidly patterned than those of socially reared animals. After a period of cohabitation, more typical patterning was observed and successful matings were achieved by most isolated animals. However, Harper (1968) reported that two of five males which were isolated from birth achieved normal mounts in their initial tests and that the pattern of successful mounts was species typical; Coulon's (1971) analysis was based upon a composite of all mating attempts displayed by his isolated subjects.

Although no decline in sexual arousal is apparent, there is a marked tendency for male isolates to display play in mating tests (see Section III, F). This behavior per se is not antithetical to mating (Gerall, 1965; Harper, 1968). While Coulon (1971) and Young (1969) felt that the data indicated that social experience was a necessary condition for the development of species typical social behavior, Harper (1968, 1970c) argued that isolation may affect the expression rather than the organization of coital behavior (see also Section III, F).

d. Effects of Dominance Relations. Dominant male guinea pigs are intolerant of the mating attempts of adolescent or subordinate males (King, 1956; Rood, 1972). When several males are reared together in the same cage, one tends to dominate the others (Avery, 1925). Riss and Goy (1957) found males that were more aggressive toward other males in the presence of females were also more inclined to fight after the females were removed.

There is some evidence that early competition may affect subsequent sexual performance. Harper (1968) found that males, reared in litters of 3, mated more readily in an unfamiliar setting if their littermates were both female than if they had had one male sibling. Martan (1968) reported that when group-reared males were placed in individual cages, the more dominant animals showed higher rates of spontaneous ejaculations and a greater weight of emitted ejaculate than did the more submissive males. During a subsequent period of isolation, emission rates declined for both dominant and submissive animals. The dominants' rate of spontaneous ejaculation returned to high levels after postisolation cohabitation with unreceptive females; in contrast, the submissive animals' spontaneous ejaculation rate was not markedly affected by cohabitation. However, Riss and Goy (1957) reported that even where 4 males competed for a single receptive female, sexual activity was higher than when the males were housed individually. Further, although relatively inactive in an all male group, submissive males' average sexual performance with unfamiliar females was the same as that of the dominant males when tested in a cage in which they had lived alone for several days (see also Harper, 1968).

The necessity for learning in the development of mating behavior in male guinea pigs is debatable, but the display of mating behavior can be modified by experience. The frequency of physical contact between a male and female was reduced by administering electric shock in one of two easily distinguishable compartments of a shuttle box (Louttit, 1929b). Shock-induced avoidance of contact endured for over 200 days. However, the inhibition was limited to the punishment compartment; in the nonpunished side the male remained sexually aggressive. In view of the uncertainty concerning the role of learning in the development of copulatory patterns, it would be of some interest to see if one could manipulate the mating sequence by the use of operant techniques.

e. Genetic and Physiological Determinants. Male guinea pigs from the Kansas strain 2 and a heterogeneous stock, "strain T," showed significant differences in the ages of first mounting, intromission, and ejaculation. The average age of first mounting was 4.4 weeks for "strain T," and 10.4 for strain 2; strain T achieved intromission at 7.3 weeks, and strain 2 at 11.3 weeks; strain T first ejaculated at 7.9 weeks, and strain 2 at 11.7 weeks of age. These differences seemed not to be hormonal since they persisted even when neonatally castrated pups from both strains were given equal, above maintenance level, injections of testosterone. The more rapidly maturing and sexually vigorous animals from strain T had to be isolated by the tenth day of age in order to achieve effects comparable to isolation initiated on day 20 in inbred animals (Young, 1969). Strain differences have also been demonstrated in the frequency with which components of the mating pattern are displayed. Strain 2 males displayed more anogenital investigation, mounting, and intromissions per test than did males from Kansas strain 13. From an intensive study of the patterns of inheritance of elements of the male coital pattern in strains 2 and 13, Jackway (1959) concluded that there were two genetically independent clusters of behavior: circling, sniffing–licking, and mounting; and intromission and ejaculation.

While relative rates of maturation of the elements of the coital pattern seem to be independent of levels of circulating androgen, high levels of exogenous testosterone propionate (TP; 500 μg/100 gm body weight) accelerate the appearance of certain coitus-related responses. Organization of the copulatory act apparently does not depend upon postnatal androgen since animals castrated on day 2 mated normally when given androgen replacement in adulthood. Sensitization to androgens of structures mediating masculine sexual behavior seems to depend upon androgenic stimulation beginning sometime between the twenty-fourth and thirtieth days of gestation (Beach, 1971; Goy *et al.*, 1967; Young, 1969).

Although development of the male coital pattern does not depend upon the postnatal presence of androgens, its display does. Castration at birth depresses the rate of development and display of coitus-related responses while exogenous androgen restores such behavior to control levels (Harper, 1970b;

Young, 1969). Similarly, castration of adult males leads to a marked decline in sexual activity; depending on their initial vigor, they cease to ejaculate within 1 to 9 weeks. The decline in intromission is more gradual and some animals continue to show mounting almost indefinitely. Exogenous TP restores the male mating respones to precastration levels without changing relative standing among similarly treated animals. Varying TP replacement therapy in castrates from 12.5 to 500 μg/100 gm body weight indicated that the normal display of sexual vigor can be maintained with dose levels around 25 μg/100 gm body weight per day (Young, 1969).

The thyroid does not seem to play an important role in the sexual behavior of the male. Although the number of fertile matings decreased after male guinea pigs were thyroidectomized, the percent of live born young issuing from those matings that were fertile did not deviate significantly from control levels (Young, 1969).

Several studies have identified neural structures involved in male sexual behavior. Brookhart and Dey (1941) found that males subjected to bilateral lesions in the ventral hypothalamus between the optic chiasma and the pituitary stalk failed to sire litters despite evidence of active spermatogenesis. Similarly, Phoenix (1961) reported that hypothalamic lesions resulted in an immediate and almost complete cessation of copulatory behavior which could not be reversed by androgen therapy.

2. Female Behavior

a. Receptivity. During periods of sexual activity, normal female guinea pigs may display all the postures and patterns typical of the male (except intromission and ejaculation) and show, in addition, lordosis, flattening of the back, raised pudendum, a wide stance with the hind feet spread, and perineal dilation. Depending upon the strain, receptivity in females is often indicated by the hip swaying, purring display, or mounting activity. Other females, however, may give little indication of receptivity except for assuming the lordosis posture when contacted on the rump by another animal. A few fertile, cycling females may exhibit hip swaying and purring throughout the estrous cycle (Loeb and Lathrop, 1914).

The typical mating sequence involves the female's submitting to investigation by the male, briefly moving away, assuming the lordosis posture as the male mounts, and cleaning the genitalia in a doubled-over posture after the male's dismount (Avery, 1925; Louttit, 1927; Rood, 1972). Occasionally, the female may assume a lordosis posture before actual contact is made (Avery, 1925). In some cases the pursuit phase may occur while the male attempts to mount (Rood, 1972) or takes the form of a rapid mutual circling (Avery, 1925; Louttit, 1927).

b. Early Experience. Isolation from social contact between the ages of 10 and 50 days reduced the frequency of mounting behavior, length of receptivity, and lordosis bout duration (in response to human stroking) in spayed females that were brought into heat by exogenous hormones (Young, 1969). However, Harper (1968) found that, in natural estrus, females isolated from birth until the age of 80 days maintained the lordosis posture at least as long as did socially reared females when mounted by a male guinea pig. However, the duration of the isolates' postcopulatory anogenital grooming was significantly shorter than that of socially reared control animals.

c. Estrous Cycle. The average duration of behavioral estrus is about 8 hours and is usually shorter than the period during which the vaginal closure membrane is open. The best indication of behavioral receptivity is the lordosis posture in response to a male or to gentle stroking of the rump in a caudocephalad direction. The duration between periods of receptivity is usually between 16 and 18 days with females showing stable individual differences in cycle length. In older animals, Young (1969) occasionally observed a "split estrus," an interruption in the period of receptivity lasting several hours after which lordosis responses could again be elicited.

As indicated by vaginal smears, the estrous cycling of females caged in groups is more synchronous than in animals which are caged singly (Donovan and Kopriva, 1965). Under cyclical light–dark conditions or constant illumination, estrus tends to occur nocturnally, with no evidence of seasonal variation (Nicol, 1933; Rood and Weir, 1970; Young, 1969). In constant darkness, estrus occurs at any time of the day. Since parturition occurs at any time of the day, the postpartum estrus is not predominantly nocturnal as is the estrus of regularly cycling females, and it is shorter, lasting 3½ hours on the average, than the receptive periods of the same animals before pregnancy, which averaged 8½ hours (Young, 1969).

The duration of heat appears to be affected by mating. Stockard and Papanicolaou (1919) reported that estrus was shorter in females which were allowed to mate than in those that did not copulate with a male. These findings were replicated by Goldfoot and Goy (1970) who found, among females in spontaneous estrus, those copulating to ejaculation with a male or vaginally stimulated with a glass rod ceased responding to human stimulation with lordoses 3 to 4 hours sooner than did females receiving no vaginal stimulation. Glass-rod stimulated animals, however, responded significantly longer (2 hours) after stimulation than did mated females (1 hour). In ovariectomized females, the amount of exogenous estrogen used to induce estrus did not influence the effect of mating, and hypophysectomized females also had a shortened estrus in response to mating similar to that shown by intact females.

d. Genetic and Physiological Determinants. An extensive literature now exists on the hormonal determinants of sexual receptivity in guinea pigs.

While Loeb and Lathrop (1914) reported that thyroidectomy had no apparent effect upon the occurrence of heat, later work indicated that thyroidectomized female guinea pigs displayed less copulatory behavior than did intact controls; females receiving exogenous thyroxine displayed more sexual behavior than did intact animals (Young, 1969).

Although a few ovariectomized female guinea pigs may show signs of sexual receptivity after the injection of exogenous estrogens (estrone, estradiol), in most cases, in order to induce full behavioral estrus in adult females, estrogen administration (4 to 7 μg estradiol) must be followed between 24 and 60 hours after the last dose of estrogen by the administration of progesterone (0.2 to 0.4 mg). Estrogen-induced heat differs from estrogen–progesterone-induced receptivity in that the onset of the former is less well defined, the duration is longer, and an injection of progesterone will induce a second period of heat, whereas further progesterone after progesterone induced receptivity is ineffective. Latency to heat, duration of lordosis, and frequency of mounting in ovariectomized females does not vary as a function of estradiol injections in excess of 6.64 μg, but the duration of estrus does increase with larger doses of estradiol. Although the frequency of mounting behavior of spayed females is not related to the quantity of exogenous hormone injected to induce heat, the frequency of mounting in intact females has been related to the number of rupturing follicles. Females were sacrificed after the onset of behavioral estrus; those that displayed vigorous mounting during estrus averaged more ruptured follicles per ovary than females that did not mount when in heat (Young, 1969). The amount of estrogen required to prime mating behavior is less than the amount needed to lead to vaginal estrus. The role of progesterone seems to be quite specific; several related compounds were found to be without effect in inducing estrus in spayed, estrogen-primed females (Young, 1969).

Hormonal control of sexual receptivity in female guinea pigs was characterized by Young (1969) as follows:

> The rise in estrogen level which occurs toward the end of the cycle conditions the animal for estrus. The appearance of estrus itself, however, depends on the subsequent action of progesterone which is produced in the still unruptured follicle after it has been acted on by the LH from the hypophysis (Young, 1969, p. 61).

Recent work by Zucker (1966) has shown that there is a 90- to 130-hour postestrous refractory period during which further administration of progesterone alone, or combinations of estrogen and progesterone, are ineffective in inducing heat in ovariectomized females. Progesterone administered simultaneously with estrogen seemed to block temporarily the priming effect of estrogen and a second injection of progesterone 36 hours later had much less effect than one delayed for 60 hours. Inhibition of estrogen-induced heat during the luteal phase of the estrous cycle could be removed by ovariectomy at least 18 hours before progesterone injection, and estrogen priming could occur even during the period of maximal endogenous progesterone output. Thus, Zucker (1968) postulated a "biphasic" effect of progesterone on receptivity in the intact female, both facilitating the expression of estrogen-primed activity and, subsequently, blocking sexual behavior during the luteal phase.

Postnatal integrity of the gonads is not necessary for the ontogeny of female mating behavior; females spayed shortly after birth display normal mating responses after estrogen–progesterone treatment in adulthood. However, prenatal treatment of the dam with androgen in the first trimester of gestation reduces later sensitivity of female offspring to ovarian hormones while increasing their responsiveness to androgenic stimulation. Postnatal androgen injections have only temporary depressive effects; females recover responsiveness to ovarian hormones. Responsiveness to ovarian hormones does not seem to require prenatal hormonal priming; it develops if no androgenic stimulation occurs during the first trimester of gestation (Beach, 1966, 1971; Goy *et al.,* 1967; Young, 1969).

Strain differences in female mating behavior have been observed. In ovariectomized females of inbred Kansas strains 2 and 13 and a heterogeneous stock, "strain T." Females from strain 2 showed estrous reactions more frequently than strain T or 13 females in response to estrogen alone (Goy and Young, 1957). When injected with estrogen and, 36 hours later, progesterone, strain 2 females came into heat more rapidly and remained receptive longer than females from strains 13 and T. Whereas strains T and 13 displayed maximal lordosis in the first 2 hours of heat, strain 2 displayed a maximum in the third hour. Strain differences were also found in the display of male typical behavior.

Cross-breeding experiments using animals from strains 2 and 13 suggested that three genetically independent clusters of behavior could be identified in ovariectomized females receiving exogenous estrogen and progesterone: the first was the latency to come into estrus after injection and the duration of heat, the second was the duration of lordosis in response to stroking by the experimenter, and the third was the number of mounts shown by the females (Goy and Jackway, 1959).

Goldfoot and Goy (1970) observed afferent influences on behavioral receptivity (see Section III, D, 2, c). Although no effect on the estrous cycle per se was noted, Donovan and Kopriva (1965) observed that females subjected to bilateral olfactory bulbectomy mated less readily than did sham-operated females. Electrical stimulation of the olfactory bulbs in intact females did not modify the length or regularity of the estrous cycle.

Brookhart *et al.* (1940) found that midventral anterior hypothalamic lesions blocked the display of estrus without apparent effect on the vaginal cycle. These effects were considered to be independent of anterior pituitary function since fairly extensive hypophyseal lesions appeared to have considerably less effect upon mating behavior (Dey *et al.*, 1942). Goy and Phoenix (1963) replicated the above findings and also observed that 2 ovariectomized females whose lesions were more anterior and more medial than lesions blocking estrous responses displayed lordosis even without exogenous estrogen–progesterone. They suggested that hypothalamic loci exist that are involved in both facilitation and inhibition of female sexual behavior. Goy and Phoenix' (1963) data also supported the independence of lordosis and mounting behavior suggested by genetic analysis. Of 9 females that ceased to lordose after hypothalamic lesions, 3 continued to display mounting, albeit at a reduced level, and 4 females in which mounting was reduced showed little or no change in the intensity or duration of lordoses.

E. Parental Behavior

1. Gestation and Parturition

The duration of gestation varies according to strain; it also varies inversely with parity and the size of the litter (Rood and Weir, 1970; Young, 1969). Primiparous guinea pigs litter earlier than multipara even when litter size is held constant. Although gestation varies between 65 and 70 days, most investigators agree that the average duration of gestation is about 68 days.

The later stages of pregnancy in the guinea pig do not appear to be accompanied by increased attentiveness to young. A few females may display solicitude toward very small pups just before labor begins (L. V. Harper, personal observation). In most cases, the onset of apparent abdominal contractions is relatively abrupt and the first pup is usually born within 5 minutes. During labor the female assumes a quadrupedal squatting posture much like that adopted when defecating. When the pup is expelled through the birth canal, her girth permitting, the mother will double over to grasp or lick the fetus in the same manner used to ingest fecal pellets. Pups are usually born head first; the mother licks and nibbles until fetal membranes are consumed and the pup is cleaned. Since the interval between births is usually less than 3 to 4 minutes, pups may not be fully attended to until the last one is born. The placentae usually are expelled after the pups are born; most of the placentae are devoured (Avery, 1925; Boling *et al.*, 1939; Rood, 1972). Although the mother is typically the most attentive to neonate pups, all animals in the pen appear to be attracted by the fetal membranes and birth fluids (Avery, 1928; Rood, 1972). Indeed, males and pregnant and nulliparous females may also devour the placentae. B. D. Sachs (personal communication, 1972) observed that 5 of 7 adult males and 5 of 6 adult females ate rat placentae when offered, and displayed no apparent discrimination between rat and guinea pig placentae.

2. Maternal Solicitude

According to von Kunkel and Kunkel (1964) and Rood (1972), once a female comes into the postpartum estrus she shows little further interest in her offspring until after she has mated.

Observers generally agree that maternal care in this species is minimal (King 1956; von Kunkel and Kunkel, 1964; Rood, 1972). From the writer's experience, the mother seldom initiates nursing; rather, she passively allows nursing. Grooming of the litter is not marked except for maternal licking of the pups' anogenital region in the first 2 to 3 weeks (Beach, 1966; Harper, 1972). However, as measured by the latency to negotiate an obstruction to reach her litter, mothers displayed maximal interest in young in the first few days after littering; the latency to cross the hurdle increased progressively as a function of days postpartum. Although the sample tested was small, experiments using foster young indicated that this effect was not a function of the age of the test young or time since last nursing (Seward and Seward, 1940).

Generally speaking, when housed in groups containing several breeding females, lactating sows show little discrimination between their own and offspring of other animals (von Kunkel and Kunkel, 1964). Litter size often exceeds the number of mammae; when several litters differ in age or size, larger, stronger pups may prevent weaker animals from nursing (L. V. Harper, personal observation). According to von Kunkel and Kunkel (1964), some sows housed with one other female may distinguish their offspring from pups that are older than theirs by 1 week or more. Porter *et al.* (1973b) observed that 11 of 12, 36- to 48-hour postparturient females tested singly in a two-choice situation spent more time next to a screened-off compartment housing their litters than to a similar compartment containing an unfamiliar litter of the same size and age as their own. Olfactory cues may have been involved; a second experiment with animals whose litters had been painted with ethyl benzoate or acetophenone from birth revealed that 11 of the 12 mothers spent more time near the familiar odor. There was no evidence of an intrinsic preference for either odor.

Current evidence suggests that maternal behavior in guinea pigs is relatively unscathed as a result of hand rearing. Incidental observations by the writer of 2 hand reared females, including behavior at parturition, provided no evidence of behavioral abnormality. Stern and Hoffman (1970) compared the maternal behavior of 10 mother reared primipara to that of 5 primiparous females isolated at birth and hand reared until the age of 3 months. The amount of time the isolates spent nursing their young and the frequency of anogenital grooming did not distinguish the two groups.

3. Lactation

The duration of lactation seems to vary according to the colony. Von Kunkel and Kunkel (1964) reported the nursing period as ranging between 14 and 22 days. King (1956) observed some females nursing through day 28 and Nagasawa *et al.* (1960) stated that lactation continued from 27 to 35 days in multiparous animals. Some of these reported differences may relate to parity, since the latter authors noted that lactation in primipara usually lasted only 21 to 28 days.

For primipara, at least, the smaller the litter, the greater the weight gain of offspring during the nursing period (Stern, 1971). Nagasawa *et al.* (1960) used litter weight gains to measure milk yield in primiparous, biparous, and triparous sows. The peak yield occurred between days 3 and 7 postpartum in multipara, but in primipara lactation was not maximal until between days 5 and 11. Studies of pituitaries from lactating females have shown a rapid postpartum increase and a subsequent steady decline in prolactin output from days 2 to 10 followed by a more gradual reduction to levels typical of cycling, nonparous females by day 30 (Holst and Turner, 1939). Although more data are needed, it has been suggested that irregularities in the postpartum estrous cycle may indicate the existence of a nursing-induced diestrus in guinea pigs (Nicol, 1933).

4. Physiological Substrates

Relative to the data on coital behavior in the guinea pig, little is known about the neural and endocrine determinants of parental solicitude. According to Donovan and Kopriva (1965) anosmic females delivered offspring normally, although no mention was made of further caretaking. Stern and Siepierski (1971) found that application of 20% potassium chloride through indwelling cannulas to the occipital–parietal brain regions of lactating female guinea pigs had no apparent effect on the amount of time the sows spent nursing their offspring. They also reported that postpartum ovariectomy appeared to be without effect on subsequent caretaking. Hopefully, recent work by Tindal *et al.* (1968) on the neural pathways involved in milk letdown in guinea pigs will stimulate further work in this area.

F. Filial Behavior and Play

1. Nursing

Precocity of the neonatal guinea pig is so marked that litters may be weaned by the third or fourth day postpartum without high mortality (Gerall, 1965; Read, 1912); however, pups normally nurse for at least 3 weeks (see Section III, E, 2). Beach (1966) and Coulon (1971) report a strong sucking impulse which, in grouped, hand-reared pups, is manifested by mutual ear and anogenital sucking of considerable intensity and duration. Although litter size usually exceeds the number of mammae, there is little conflict over opportunities to nurse beyond scrambles to reach the nipple when a female does permit nursing (Coulon, 1971).

In nursing attempts, the young of either sex occasionally display a back flattening and perineal dilation similar to the adult female lordosis response (Beach, 1966; Harper, 1972). This seems to facilitate mothers licking the pups' anogenital region to stimulate urination (Beach, 1966; Rood, 1972). Filial lordosis in 1-week-old pups occurs more frequently as the time since they were last stimulated to urinate increases (Harper, 1972). Also associated with both filial and adult copulatory behavior is the purr call, the ontogeny of which follows the same growth curve as filial lordosis, although filial purring seems to be less involved with the release of maternal anogenital licking (Harper, 1972). Berryman (1970) suggested that the purr is a contact call. This seems to be the best explanation to date of the function served by this response in pups.

2. Attachment Behavior

Avery (1925) and Allen (1904) reported that early nursing attempts by pups were not restricted to the mother; very young pups may even attempt to crawl under nonlactating females or males. Porter *et al.* (1973b) reported that up to the age of 27 days pups did not spend more time in the end of a two-choice discrimination box that contained their mother behind a wire screen than in the other end, next to a compartment containing a nonlactating female. The latter authors, however, noted that proximal cues, precluded by their apparatus, may be involved in mother recognition. Porter *et al.* (1973a) found that individual pups were more likely to move about an open field when their mothers and siblings were confined in an adjacent holding pen separated by a wire screen than when the holding pen was vacant. Nevertheless, the pups also spent more time next to the holding pen when mother and siblings were in it than when they were not. Seward (1940) found that although pups would more rapidly negotiate a barrier to reach their mothers when hungry, they crossed a hurdle to the mother's compartment even when warm and satiated and did so despite the fact that they did not suck once they reached her. Under any conditions, the mother was found to be a much stronger incentive than an empty goal box.

Gray (1958) and Hess (1959) suggested that the "following response" in infant guinea pigs waned rapidly if not elicited in the first day or two postpartum. Since then, a number of reports have claimed to have demonstrated imprinting in young guinea pigs to visual stimuli (Gaston *et al.*, 1969; Shipley, 1963; Sluckin and Fullerton, 1969), to auditory stimuli (Rickman, 1970), and to olfactory stimuli (Carter and Marr, 1970). The latter authors reported that litters reared from 24 hours postpartum to day 22 with artificial odors (ethyl benzoate or acetophenone) spent more time in the portion of a multiple choice test chamber containing a similarly scented animal than did normally reared controls or animals reared with the other odor. While brief exposures usually did not overcome the animals' tendencies to be attracted to "normal" guinea pig odors, exposure to an odor during the first week influenced later choices more than equally extended periods of exposure initiated at later ages, which suggests the existence of a sensitive period.

Two studies indicated that pups with either prior or postexposure experience with other guinea pigs appeared to be less responsive to moving objects (Gaston *et al.*, 1969; Shipley, 1963). However, Sluckin (1968) and Sluckin and Fullerton (1969) reported that despite delaying isolation until days 4 to 6, training with a cube or tennis ball induced the display of a preference for the familiar object. Like Shipley (1963), the latter authors found no clear evidence for a critical period for visually elicited approach.

In most studies, the responses investigated were not typical filial behavior e.g., huddling, sitting on top of the surrogate, crawling under, and rooting. Several reported only the time spent actively following or near the preferred object. In cases in which pups had a choice, it is not clear whether proximity measures reflected neophobia or the attractiveness of the familiar object.

Harper (1970a) isolated neonatal pups and exposed them to a furry or a smooth textured, intermittently moving model of a guinea pig in the nursing posture. For some pups the models emitted tape recorded (colony) guinea pig calls through a loudspeaker. During the first 3 days of life, the pups exposed to guinea pig calls displayed higher rates of nosing, huddling, and crawling under than pups exposed to a silent model. Those exposed to a furry surface texture displayed greater contact bout duration than pups exposed to a smooth model, especially when under. In preference tests conducted 5 days after exposure, pups exposed to the furry, vocalizing model learned to run a T-maze to reach the model in preference to an empty goal box. Mother-exposed pups did not show preferential maze running until the mother was the incentive, then they ran to the mother, not the model. The model-exposed pups still ran preferentially to the model. Delaying exposure to a model for 4 to 6 days or returning model-exposed pups and no-model controls to the colony on day 9 yielded no evidence of waning social responsiveness.

In an earlier study, Harper (1968) found strong tendencies to approach a peer in animals that were isolated from birth to the age of 80 days. Nagy and Misanin (1970), although finding a reduced tendency on the part of early isolated guinea pigs to remain near a caged conspecific in a tilt box, also concluded that there was little evidence for the existence of a critical period for social attachment in this species.

In addition to influencing filial attachment, imprinting is thought to influence later sexual behavior (Hess, 1959). Beauchamp and Hess (1971) reared pups from day 1 with domestic chicks; these subjects showed a tendency to spend more time huddling or under a chick than a rabbit or a guinea pig in tests conducted during the first through the third weeks. Guinea pig-reared subjects made a substantial number of chick contacts in the early tests, although they spent more time with a guinea pig. When chick reared male animals began to display copulatory behavior, they increasingly responded preferentially to a test guinea pig, although their early precopulatory responses were also directed toward a chick and a rabbit, but not a rat. In the later tests, guinea pigs were chosen preferentially, regardless of prior cohabitation. Harper (1970c) and von Kunkel and Kunkel (1964) also reported that early social experience with another species served to render males sexually responsive to that species. Although von Kunkel and Kunkel (1964) concluded that the atypical responsiveness was irreversible, neither Harper (1970c) nor Beauchamp and Hess (1971) found this to be the case.

Current evidence indicates "exposure learning" (Sluckin and Fullerton, 1969) may account for the development of approach tendencies in young guinea pigs and that the early development of filial or social attachments is not restricted to a critical period. The data suggest that neonate guinea pigs are initially responsive to a variety of stimuli and, although biased toward conspecific-like qualities (Beauchamp and Hess, 1971), when socially reared, become increasingly unresponsive to stimuli that are both unfamiliar and "un-guinea pig" (Harper, 1970a). The data are not conclusive since in none of the studies reviewed have the young been both isolated at birth and denied olfactory stimulation from their own bodies or auditory stimulation from other animals. Until such time as stimulation in these modalities have been adequately controlled, the question of the existence of a critical period for the receipt of social stimulation remains unanswered. It may yet be shown that for the development of some aspects of conspecific recognition, e.g., olfaction, there is a critical period, while for others, e.g., visual stimuli, none may exist.

3. Peer-Directed Behavior

Neonate (Allen, 1904; Coulon, 1971) and prematurely delivered (Avery, 1928) guinea pigs tend to seek contact with their littermates and adults. Pups isolated from birth and hand reared for 3 to 6 days contacted one another within 1 minute and maintained mutual contact (huddling) whether or not they had previously displayed filial or social responses to a moving surrogate (L. V. Harper, unpublished observation).

A variety of locomotor patterns appear during the litter

period and, for the want of a better term, may provisonally be subsumed under the heading of "play." Among these responses are "frisky hops" (Rood, 1972), including hopping vertically into the air (Avery, 1928), hopping with a change in direction (Beauchamp and Hess, 1971), hopping with a shake of the head to one side (Harper, 1973), and a "prancing" gait (Beauchamp and Hess, 1971). Beauchamp and Hess (1971), Coulon (1971), and Harper (1968) all agree that these responses are first observable within 3 days of birth and are most prominent around the third postnatal week. An analysis of the behavioral context in which socially reared animals displayed hopping with a shake of the head indicated that running was most frequently associated with this response and that it usually was bounded by bouts of social contact. Hopping with a shake of the head most often occurred when other animals were emitting the same behavior (Harper, 1973). Thus, it has many of the characteristics of social play.

Since courtship and hopping with a shake of the head become associated as male pups mature, Coulon (1971) suggested that play could be a derived activity for the exercise of coitus-related motor patterns and that isolation caused dissociation of precopulatory and play behavior, the latter providing self-generated stimulation for male isolates. In contrast, Harper's (1973) analysis of the ontogenetic relations between play responses and early precopulatory behavior led to the conclusion that isolation did not cause such a dissociation, but rather led to an apparent intensification of the infantile relationships between play and coitus-related responses in males.

IV. DEVELOPMENT OF BEHAVIOR

A. Ontogeny of Species Typical Behavior

Two classic studies have described the prenatal behavioral development of guinea pigs (Avery, 1928; Carmichael, 1934). By the sixty-third day of gestation most of the fetuses observed by Avery (1928) could walk and avoid obstacles visually during locomotion. Spontaneous suckling and flight from sudden loud noises were observed by the sixty-fifth day. Filial lordosis was observed 1 day earlier (Beach, 1966) and rooting was observed by at least day 67. Strong gregarious tendencies of guinea pigs were apparent by the sixty-fourth day (Avery, 1928). Although not usually emitted regularly until several days postpartum, Avery (1928) reported observing hopping within 1 hour after birth, and Coulon (1971) noted leaping within 12 hours postpartum.

Guinea pigs can eat (or at least nibble upon) solid food within the first day after birth (Coulon, 1971; Read, 1912). Reisbick (1973) found that 1- to 9-day-old pups could discriminate between food and non-food items more rapidly after the fifth day. Eight-day-old pups exposed once for 10 minutes to lettuce alone, or a choice among lettuce, thin plastic sheets, and a paper towel developed a preference for lettuce if 8 hours or more were allowed to elapse between exposure and testing. Coulon (1971) reported that pups learned to drink from a tube within 48 hours of birth.

Although the development of adult feeding thus occurs within the first week or so, there is some evidence that the capacity for voluntary micturition does not fully mature until around the second week (Beach, 1966; Harper, 1972). The full adult grooming pattern gradually appears during the first week (Coulon, 1971).

As Avery (1928) and Carmichael (1934) have shown, the tendencies to flee at sudden sounds or movement are apparent in prematurely delivered young, and Avery (1928) reported that among 3-day premature pups as little as 10 hours experience with littermates and a lactating female sufficed for development of withdrawal responses to humans. The ontogeny of active exploration has been less extensively studied. According to Porter *et al.* (1973a), the maximum amount of open field ambulation displayed by individual pups was obtained during the second and third weeks; the amount of time spent exploring increased between birth and the second week and declined to week-1 levels by the end of the fourth week. According to Coulon (1971), postures associated with sniffing or exploration can be observed shortly after birth. Coulon (1971) also reported that isolation rearing seemed to facilitate movement in an open field, at least among pups which had transferred many responses to the human handler. These data and the reviewer's own observations suggest that the observer may have functioned to inhibit hand-reared isolates' flight or freezing in the same way as the mother and littermates facilitated mother-reared pups' exploration in the Porter *et al.* (1973a) study.

Many vocalizations peculiar to the species are present in the repertoire of the neonatal animal. Avery (1928) reported that calls, presumably the whistle, were emitted by 3-day premature pups that were separated from one another. Chirping calls (probably putts and chutts) may be present from birth. Similarly, the tweet can be heard on the first day of life (Berryman, 1970; Coulon, 1971). Harper (1972) heard purrs from hand reared pups as early as the first day.

While lordosis, purring, anogenital nosing, and pursuit (following) occur within the first few days after birth, there is a sequential development of organized, coitus-related behaviors. Young males begin to perform the precoital hip swaying, purring response as early as the second postnatal week (Harper, 1968, 1972; Louttit, 1929a). Mounting behavior usually occurs later, between the third and seventh weeks (Harper, 1968; Louttit, 1929a; Young, 1969). Pelvic thrusts then begin to accompany mounting, and the full coital pattern, including intromission and ejaculation, develops after mounting and thrusting behavior (Young, 1969).

Although present in the neonate female's behavioral repertoire, the lordosis response and purring are not organized in the copulatory system until some weeks after birth. According to Boling *et al.* (1939), despite the presence of filial lordosis, young females did not respond with lordosis to estrogen–progesterone treatments in an adult typical fashion until after the third postpartum week. Similarly, Harper (1972) observed that although they emitted filial purrs, the hip swaying, purring response in young androgen-injected females could not be elicited until the age at which males begin this response spontaneously. Whereas coitus-related responses and estrous-like behavior can be elicited from females by exogenous hormones between the third and fourth postnatal weeks, spontaneous or natural estrus and mounting usually does not occur until after the seventh week (Avery, 1925; Young, 1969).

The ontogeny of intraspecific fighting patterns has not been systematically studied. The writer's unpublished observations suggest that head thrust, threat, and defensive postures occur within 4 weeks of birth. Higher intensity attacks and chasing appear later, especially among young males when conflicts arise as a result of precopulatory displays between 5 and 7 weeks of age (King, 1956).

Although only lactating females show consistent interest in young, the writer observed pups under 3 weeks of age licking neonates and nibbling on the fetal membranes. Most maternal care, e.g., licking the anogenital region and the upright sitting (nursing) posture, are present in the behavioral repertoires of very young animals. As in the development of copulatory behavior, the ways in which these elements become (re)-combined into the appropriate adult reproductive patterns remain to be elucidated (Beach, 1966).

B. Learning

Contrary to Coulon's (1971) suggestion that trial-and-error learning may account for species-specific motor patterns in adult guinea pigs, there is evidence that, for several elements of adult copulatory behavior (Harper, 1968, 1972, 1973) and parental behavior (Stern and Hoffman, 1970), conventional learning paradigms may not provide an adequate model. Nonetheless, experience appears to facilitate development or at least expression of copulatory behavior in isolated animals whose postisolation test performances appear to be inadequate (Coulon, 1971; Harper, 1968; Young, 1969; see Section III, D).

Guinea pigs have been used to evaluate traditional conceptions of learning phenomena since the turn of the century. Allen (1904) concluded that cavies could not solve problems requiring "ingenuity" such as puzzle boxes but they could be trained to master tasks that involved "activity" such as simple mazes. Allen felt that kinesthetic stimulation and then vision were the most important bases for learning in this species. Studies by Sedlacek *et al.* (1964) indicate that simple conditioning of alerting responses to acoustic stimuli may be obtained in pups that were delivered 3 to 6 days before term. Insofar as the development of avoidance responses to other animals represents learning, Avery's (1928) finding that 3-day premature young avoided human handlers after 12 hours contact with a lactating female guinea pig provides another example of early learning ability in guinea pigs. Many of the studies purporting to have demonstrated some form of imprinting have at least made clear that exposure learning occurs in this species (see Section III, F, 2).

Guinea pigs have solved visual discrimination problems which required them to learn to respond appropriately to the smaller of two targets (7.5 and 20 cm^2) or to choose the more brightly illuminated target, regardless of its size, in order to obtain a piece of carrot (Hadley, 1927). Interocular transfer of brightness and pattern cues for avoiding shock was demonstrated by Lynch and Sheridan (1970) in both pigmented and albino animals. Burnstein and Wolff (1967) reported that the pitch of male animal calls could be altered by reinforcement. (It would be interesting to know which of the calls of the species were involved, unfortunately, only the frequencies were reported.) Although only with difficulty, James (1934) used electrical shock to obtain conditioned foreleg withdrawal to the sound of a metronome. The difficulty appeared to stem from the animals' tendencies to freeze, moving only at the shock. One may suspect that the metronome click may have contributed to the freezing behavior (see Section II, B, 2). Khallli and Cheney (1970) used a lever pressing response to compare the relative efficacies of cutaneous (foot pad) or subcutaneously administered electric shock; they concluded that the former was both more economical and more effective. Sherrick and Bilger (1959) used shock to condition slow, regular breathing as a response to low frequency tones in order to investigate the auditory discrimination capacities of their subjects.

In addition to the more traditional uses of food and water (see Section II, C) and electric shock as incentives for learning, intracranial electrical (self-)stimualtion (ICS) has proved to be an effective reinforcer for operant learning. Wolff *et al.* (1966) used visual size discrimination as a cue for bar pressing responses to deliver stimulation to the posterior hypothalamus. They found that guinea pigs could be shaped to respond to several schedules of fixed ratio and variable interval reinforcement. Using supramammillary electrode placements, Burnstein *et al.* (1967) investigated a variety of schedules of reinforcement and concluded that, with ICS, "response output can be considerable; schedule control is dramatic, and transitions in performance from one reinforcement schedule to another are easily obtained" (Burnstein *et al.*, 1967, p. 385). Using bar pressing for ICS, Merril *et al.* (1969) demonstrated that withdrawal of ICS, like the withdrawal of other classes of reward, led to an increase in the rate or amplitude of the conditioned response.

Unlike rats, guinea pigs given a series of trials in a shock-avoidance learning situation (a shuttle box) show relatively little evidence that learning occurs during any particular block of trials, while considerable learning may be observed across daily blocks. Webster *et al.* (1965) found that interblock improvement depended to some degree upon the number of trials administered within each block and that learning improved by increasing the intertrial interval within a block. Even in the absence of shock during retest, animals trained with longer intertrial intervals showed improvement. Sansone and Bovet (1970) replicated the above finding of enhanced learning with extended intertrial intervals. They also found that a 15-second interval between the onset of the conditioned stimulus (light) and the unconditioned stimulus (shock) was more effective in producing an association than was a 5-second interval. Sansone and Bovet (1970) reported an actual decrement in performance in the early phases of training, and speculated that the relatively greater improvement across than within blocks might be related to temporal parameters of memory consolidation peculiar to guinea pigs. In another study of the phenomenon, the same authors found that *dl*-amphetamine reduced the performance decrement observed in untreated controls, although the interblock gains again exceeded the intrablock improvement (Sansone and Bovet, 1969).

The explanation for this consolidation phenomenon is unclear. It could be related to a peculiarity of the guinea pigs' capacity to store information, or, perhaps, the apparent lack of intertrial learning may be better explained in terms of the species typical response to danger. With respect to the latter interpretation, however, it should be noted that Sansone and Bovet (1970) reported that their animals were not freezing during the trials; unfortunately, they did not include a detailed description of what the animals did do.

In two-way avoidance training it was found that a reduction in guinea pigs' ability to perceive visual cues may lead to an apparent enhancement of learning. Dyer (1971) found peripheral blinding, training the animals in darkness, or placing lesions in the posterior cortical (visual) areas improved the animals' ability to avoid grid shock by moving from one of two compartments to the other at the onset of a buzzer. An analysis of the blind animals' performance and insertion of an obstruction between compartments indicated that they walked in an eliptical path, following the walls of the box, until the buzzer terminated.

The temporal relations among cue, response, and reinforcement have been shown to be important considerations when working with cavies. Reisbick's (1973) data indicated that the intertrial delay was important in the development of discrimative feeding responses. Webster and Walsh (1968) trained guinea pigs to avoid shocks by pressing and holding down a bar after the onset of either a light or a tone. They found that when the control of the discriminative stimulus (light or tone) was contingent upon the animals' responses, either holding the bar or rapid release could be obtained readily in the same subjects; however, when cue stimulus conditions varied automatically, rapid bar release was more difficult to obtain.

In general, when investigating any aspect of guinea pig behavior, one must always ensure that the animals are thoroughly familiar with being handled and the setting. When subjects are reacting to the novelty of the test situation or the presence of an experimenter, it may be difficult and often impossible to evaluate the effects of other conditions. More attention to the details of the subjects' motor and vocal responses to reinforcement and all other experimental variables would markedly clarify the nature of avoidance and other types of learning. In the evaluation of the effects of drugs on behavior, it is absolutely essential to carefully record and compare not only the nature and frequency of each response but the patterns of responses emitted in any particular situation. As Coulon (1971) has shown for isolated subjects, behavioral patterning may be a more significant and sensitive measure than the mere tallying or cataloging gross activity or "correct" solutions to problems.

On the other hand, when combined with an appreciation for the species-specific adaptations of *C. porcellus*, detailed analysis of the animals' behavior in various settings and under different experimental conditions promises to reveal much concerning the behavior of guinea pigs. New developments, such as a detailed atlas of the guinea pig brain (Tindal *et al.*, 1968), techniques for investigating the course of postnatal neurogenesis (Altman and Das, 1967), microrecording of single cell activity (Desole and Pallestrini, 1969), and recording the neuroelectrical activity of free-moving animals (Stainsbury, 1970), all offer exciting prospects for the future.

REFERENCES

Allen, J. (1904). Associative processes of the guinea pig. A study of the psychical development of an animal with a nervous system well medullated at birth. *J. Comp. Neurol. Psychol.* **14,** 294–359.

Altman, J., and Das, G. D. (1967). Postnatal neurogenesis in the guinea pig. *Nature (London)* **214,** 1098–1101.

Alvord, J., Cheney, C., and Daley, M. (1971). Development and control of licking in the guinea pig. *Behav. Res. Methods Instrum.* **3,** 14–15.

Anderson, J. W. (1954). The production of ultrasonic sounds by laboratory rats and other mammals. *Science* **119,** 808–809.

Avery, G. T. (1925). Notes on reproduction in guinea pigs. *J. Comp. Psychol.* **5,** 373–396.

Avery, G. T. (1928). Responses of foetal guinea pigs prematurely delivered. *Genet. Psychol. Monogr.* **3,** 247–331.

Bauer, F. S. (1971). Glucose preference in the guinea pig. *Physiol. & Behav.* **6,**75–76.

Bayard, J. (1957). The duration of tonic immobility in guinea pigs. *J. Comp. Physiol. Psychol.* **57,** 130–133.

Beach, F. A. (1966). Ontogeny of "coitus-related" reflexes in the female guinea pig. *Proc. Nat. Acad. Sci. U.S.* **56,** 526–533.

Beach, F. A. (1971). Hormonal factors controlling the differentiation, development, and display of copulatory behavior of the ramstergig and related species. *In* "Biopsychology of Development" (E. Tobach, L. R. Aronson, and E. Shaw, eds.), pp. 249–296. Academic Press, New York.

Beauchamp, G., and Hess, E. (1971). The effects of cross-species rearing on the social and sexual preferences of guinea pigs. *Z. Tierpsychol.* **28,** 69–76.

Beauchamp, G., Jacobs, W. W., and Hess, E. H. (1971). Male sexual behavior in a colony of domestic guinea pigs. *Amer. Zool.* **11,** 618.

Berryman, J. (1970). Guinea-pig vocalizations. *Guinea Pig Newslett.* No. 2.

Boling, J. L., Blandau, R. J., Wilson, J. G., and Young, W. C. (1939). Postparturitional heat responses of newborn and adult guinea pigs. Data on parturition. *Proc. Soc. Exp. Biol. Med.* **42,** 128–132.

Brookhart, J. M., and Dey, F. L. (1941). Reduction of sexual behavior in male guinea pigs by hypothalamic lesions. *Amer. J. Physiol.* **133,** 551–554.

Brookhart, J. M., Dey, F. L., and Ranson, S. W. (1940). Failure of ovarian hormones to cause mating reactions in spayed guinea pigs with hypothalamic lesions. *Proc. Soc. Exp. Biol. Med.* **44,** 61–64.

Burnstein, D. D., and Wolff, P. C. (1967). Vocal conditioning in the guinea pig. *Psychon. Sci.* **8,** 39–40.

Burnstein, D. D., Wolff, P. C., and Daley, M. (1967). Concurrent schedules of reinforcement in the guinea pig. *Psychol. Rec.* **17,** 379–385.

Campbell, B. A., Smith, N. F., Misanin, J. R., and Jaynes, J. (1966). Species differences in activity during hunger and thirst. *J. Comp. Physiol. Psychol.* **61,** 123–127.

Carmichael, L. (1934). An experimental study in the prenatal guinea-pig of the origin and development of reflexes and patterns of behavior in relation to the stimulation of specific receptor areas during the period of active fetal life. *Genet. Psychol. Monogr.* **16,** 337–491.

Carter, C. S. (1972). Effects of olfactory experience on the behaviour of the guinea pig (*Cavia porcellus*). *Anim. Behav.* **20,** 54–60.

Carter, C. S., and Marr, J. N. (1970). Olfactory imprinting and age variables in the guinea pig. *Cavia porcellus. Anim. Behav.* **18,** 238–244.

Castle, W. E., and Wright, S. (1916). "Studies of Inheritance in Guinea Pigs and Rats." Carnegie Institute, Washington, D. C.

Coulon, J. (1971). L'influence de l'isolement social sur le comportement du cobaye. *Behaviour* **38,** 93–120.

Davis, H., Derbyshire, A. J., Kemp, E. H., Lurie, M. H., and Upton, M. (1935). Functional and histological changes in the cochlea of the guinea pig resulting from prolonged stimulation. *J. Gen. Psychol.* **13,** 251–278.

Desole, C., and Pallestrini, R. (1969). Responses of vestibular units to stimulation of individual semicircular canals. *Exp. Neurol.* **24,** 310–324.

Dey, F. L., Leininger, C. R., and Ranson, S. W. (1942). The effect of hypophyseal lesions on mating behavior in female guinea pigs. *Endocrinology* **30,** 323–326.

Donovan, B. T., and Kopriva, P. C. (1965). Effect of removal or stimulation of olfactory bulbs on the estrous cycle of the guinea pig. *Endocrinology* **77,** 213–217.

Dutch, J. and Brown, L. B. (1968). Adaptation to a water-deprivation schedule in guinea pigs. *Psychol. Rep.* **23,** 737–738.

Dyer, R. (1971). Influences of the visual system upon two-way avoidance learning on the guinea pig. *J. Comp. Physiol. Psychol.* **76,** 434–440.

Ewer, R. F. (1968). "Ethology of Mammals." Plenum, New York.

Fara, J. W., and Catlett, R. H. (1971). Cardiac response and social behavior in the guinea pig *Cavia porcellus. Anim. Behav.* **19,** 514–523.

Gaston, M. G., Stout, R., and Tom, R. (1969). Imprinting in guinea pigs. *Psychon. Sci.* **16,** 53–54.

Gerall, A. A. (1963). An exploratory study of the effect of social isolation variables on the sexual behavior of male guinea pigs. *Anim. Behav.* **11,** 274–282.

Gerall, A. A., and Berg, W. S. (1964). Effect of novel situation and modification in sexual drive on rate of oxygen consumption in guinea pigs. *Psychol. Rep.* **15,** 311–317.

Gerall, H. D. (1965). Effect of social isolation and physical confinement on motor and sexual behavior of guinea pigs. *J. Pers. Soc. Psychol.* **2,** 460–464.

Goldfoot, D. A., and Goy, R. W. (1970). Abbreviation of behavioral estrus in guinea pigs by coital and vagino-cervical stimulation. *J. Comp. Physiol. Psychol.* **72,** 426–434.

Goy, R. W., and Jackway, J. S. (1959). The inheritance of patterns of sexual behaviour in female guinea pigs. *Anim. Behav.* **7,** 142–149.

Goy, R. W., and Phoenix, C. H. (1963). Hypothalamic regulation of female sexual behaviour: Establishment of behavioural oestrus in spayed guinea-pigs following hypothalamic lesions. *J. Reprod. Fert.* **5,** 23–40.

Goy, R. W., and Young, W. C. (1957). Somatic basis of sexual behavior patterns in guinea pigs: Factors involved in the determination of the character of the soma in the female. *Psychosom. Med.* **19,** 144–151.

Goy, R. W., Phoenix, C. H., and Meidinger, R. (1967). Postnatal development of sensitivity to estrogen and androgen in male, female and pseudohermaphroditic guinea pigs. *Anat. Rec.* **157,** 87–96.

Grant, E. C., and Mackintosh, J. H. (1963). A comparison of the social postures of some common laboratory rodents. *Behaviour* **21,** 246–259.

Gray, P. H. (1958). Theory and evidence of imprinting in human infants. *J. Psychol.* **46,** 155–166.

Hadley, C. V. D. (1927). Transfer experiments with guinea-pigs. *Brit. J. Med. Psychol.* **18,** 189–224.

Harper, L. V. (1968). The effects of isolation from birth on the social behaviour of guinea pigs in adulthood. *Anim. Behav.* **16,** 58–64.

Harper, L. V. (1970a). Role of contact and sound in eliciting filial responses and development of social attachments in domestic guinea pigs. *J. Comp. Physiol. Psychol.* **73,** 427–435.

Harper, L. V. (1970b). Effects of pre- and post-natal androgen on the development of coitus-related responses in young guinea pigs. *Amer. Zool.* **10,** 477.

Harper, L. V. (1970c). Ontogenetic and phylogenetic functions of the parent-offspring relationship in mammals. *Advan. Study Behav.* **3,** 75–117.

Harper, L. V. (1972). The transition from filial to reproductive function of coitus-related responses in young guinea pigs. *Develop. Psychobiol.* **5,** 21–34.

Harper, L. V. (1973). Ontogeny of "aberrant" responses in the mating pattern of male guinea pigs. *Develop. Psychobiol.* **6**, 311–317.

Hess, E. H. (1959). Imprinting. *Science* **130**, 133–141.

Holst, S., and Turner, C. W. (1939). Lactogen content of pituitary of pregnant and lactating rabbits and guinea pigs. *Proc. Soc. Exp. Biol. Med.* **42**, 479–482.

Horton, G. P. (1933). A quantitative study of hearing in the guinea pig (*Cavia cobaya*). *J. Comp. Psychol.* **15**, 59–73.

Jackway, J. S. (1959). Inheritance of patterns of mating behaviour in the male guinea pig. *Anim. Behav.* **7**, 150–162.

James, W. T. (1934). A conditioned response of two escape reflex systems of the guinea pig and the significance of the study for comparative work. *Pedag. Semin.* **44**, 449–453.

Khalili, J., and Cheney, C. (1970). Grid vs. subcutaneously delivered shock in escape schedules with guinea pigs. *Behav. Res. Methods Instrum.* **2**, 25–27.

King, J. A. (1956). Social relations of the domestic guinea pigs living under semi-natural conditions. *Ecology* **37**, 221–228.

Kutscher, C. L. (1969). Species differences in the interaction of feeding and drinking. *Ann. N.Y. Acad. Sci.* **157**, 539–552.

Lin, J. J., and Mogenson, G. J. (1968). Avoidance learning in the guinea pig, hamster, and rat. *Psychol. Rep.* **22**, 431–439.

Loeb, L., and Lathrop, A. E. (1914). Correlation between the cyclic changes in the uterus and the ovaries in the guinea pig. *Biol. Bull.* **27**, 32–44.

Lollier, G., Levitsky, D., and Weinberg, C. (1968). Body weight loss as a measure of motivation in thirsty guinea pigs. *Psychon. Sci.* **19**, 27–28.

Louttit, C. M. (1927). Reproductive behavior of the guinea pig. I. The normal mating pattern. *J. Comp. Psychol.* **7**, 247–263.

Louttit, C. M. (1929a). Reproductive behavior of the guinea pig. II. Ontogenesis of the reproductive behavior pattern. *J. Comp. Psychol.* **9**, 293–304.

Louttit, C. M. (1929b). Reproductive behavior of the guinea pig. III. Modification of the behavior pattern. *J. Comp. Psychol.* **9**, 305–316.

Lynch, K. A. B., and Sheridan, C. L. (1970). Interocular transfer of a brightness and of a pattern discrimination in albino and pigmented guinea pigs. *Psychon. Sci.* **20**, 277–279.

Malven, P. V., and Sawyer, C. H. (1966). Sleeping patterns in female guinea pigs: Effects of sex hormones. *Exp. Neurol.* **15**, 229–239.

Martan, J. (1968). Factors affecting spontaneous ejaculation of male guinea pigs. *J. Reprod. Fert.* **17**, 161–163.

Mason, J. H. (1939). The date of the first use of guinea-pigs and mice in biological research. *S. Afr. Vet. Med. J.* **10**, 22–25.

Merril, K. H., Bromley, B. L., and Porter, P. B. (1969). "Frustration" from witholding reinforcing intracranial stimulation. *Physiol. & Behav.* **4**, 345–349.

Miles, R. C., Ratoosh, P., and Meyer, D. R. (1956). Absence of color vision in guinea pig. *J. Neurophysiol.* **19**, 254–258.

Miller, D. and Murray, F. S. (1966). Guinea pig's immobility response to sound: Threshold and habituation. *J. Comp. Physiol. Psychol.* **61**, 227–233.

Nagasawa, H., Takayoshi, T., Shoda, Y., and Naito, M. (1960). Lactation curve of guinea pig. *Jap. J. Zootech. Sci.* **31**, 195–199.

Nagy, Z. M., and Misanin, J. R. (1970). Social preference in the guinea pig as a function of social rearing conditions and age of separation from the mother. *Psychon. Sci.* **19**, 309–311.

Nicholls, E. E. (1922). A study of the spontaneous activity of the guinea pig. *J. Comp. Psychol.* **2**, 303–330.

Nicol, T. (1933). Studies on the reproductive system of the guinea-pig: Variations in the oestrous cycle in the virgin animal, after parturition, and during pregnancy. *Proc. Roy. Soc. Edinburgh* **53**, 220–238.

Pellet, J., and Béraud, G. (1967). Organisation nycthémérale de la veille et du sommeil chez le cobaye (*Cavia porcellus*). *Physiol. & Behav.* **2**, 131–137.

Phillips, A. and Valenstein, E. S. (1969). Elicitation of stimulus-bound behaviour in guinea pigs. *Psychon. Sci.* **17**, 131–132.

Phoenix, C. H. (1961). Hypothalamic regulation of sexual behavior in male guinea pigs. *J. Comp. Physiol. Psychol.* **54**, 72–77.

Platt, J. J., Reiser, D. L., and Merker, J. (1971). Response to stimulus change and related temporal parameters in rabbits and guinea pigs. *J. Genet. Psychol.* **118**, 173–178.

Porter, R. H., Berryman, J. C., and Fullerton, C. (1973a). Exploration and attachment behaviour in infant guinea pigs. *Behaviour* **45**, 312–322.

Porter, R. H., Fullerton, C., and Berryman, J. C. (1973b). Guinea-pig maternal-young attachment behaviour. *Z. Tierpsychol.* **32**, 489–495.

Preyer, W. (1885). "Specielle Physiologie des Embryo," pp. 586–595. Grieben, Leipzig.

Read, M. J. (1912). Observations on the suckling period in the guinea pig. *Univ. Calif. Berkeley, Publ. Zool.* **9**, 341–351.

Reisbick, S. H. (1973). Development of food preferences in newborn guinea pigs. *J. Comp. Physiol. Psychol.* **85**, 427–442.

Rickman, W. G., Jr. (1970). Early experience and imprinting to music in the guinea pig. *Diss. Abstr.* **31**, 423–424.

Riss, W., and Goy, R. W. (1957). Modification of sex drive and 0_2 consumption by isolating and grouping male guinea pigs. *J. Comp. Physiol. Psychol.* **50**, 151–154.

Rood, J. P. (1972). Ecological and behavioral comparisons of three genera of Argentine cavies. *Anim. Behav. Monogr.* **5**, 1–83.

Rood, J. P., and Weir, B. (1970). Reproduction in female wild guinea pigs. *J. Reprod. Fert.* **23**, 393–409.

Sansone, M., and Bovet, D. (1969). Effects of amphetamine on the decrement of performance in avoidance conditioning of guinea pigs. *Psychopharmacologia* **16**, 234–239.

Sansone, M., and Bovet, D. (1970). Avoidance learning by guinea pigs. *Quart. J. Exp. Psychol.* **22**, 458–461.

Schiffman, H. R. (1970). Evidence for sensory dominance: Reactions to apparent depth in rabbits, cats, and rodents. *J. Comp. Physiol. Psychol.* **71**, 38–41.

Sedláček, J., Hlaváčková, V., and Švehlová, M. (1964). New findings on the formation of the temporary connection in the prenatal and perinatal period in the guinea pig. *Physiol. Bohemoslov.* **13**, 268–273.

Seward, G. H. (1940). Studies on the reproductive activites of the guinea pig II. The role of hunger in filial behavior. *J. Comp. Psychol.* **29**, 25–41.

Seward, J. P., and Seward, G. H. (1940). Studies on the reproductive activities of the guinea pig I. Factors in maternal behavior. *J. Comp. Psychol.* **29**, 1–25.

Sherrick, C., and Bilger, R. (1959). Auditory sensitivity of the guinea pig to low-frequency tones. *Percept. Mot. Skill* **9**, 339–344.

Shipley, W. U. (1963). The demonstration in the domestic guinea pig of a process resembling classical imprinting. *Anim. Behav.* **11**, 470–474.

Sluckin, W. (1968). Imprinting in guinea pigs. *Nature (London)* **220**, 1148.

Sluckin, W., and Fullerton, C. (1969). Attachments of infant guinea pigs. *Psychon. Sci.* **17**, 179–180.

Smith, K. U. (1938). Behavior of decorticate guinea pigs. *J. Comp. Psychol.* **18**, 433–447.

Srimal, R. C., and Dhawan, B. N. (1970). An analysis of methyphenidate induced gnawing in guinea pigs. *Psychopharmacologia* **18**, 99–107.

Stainsbury, R. S. (1970). Hippocampal activity during natural behavior in the guinea pig. *Physiol. & Behav.* **5**, 317–324.

Stark, K. A. (1963). Effects of early and prolonged experience with bitter water on its preferableness to guinea pigs. *Diss. Abstr.* **24**, 859–860.

Stern, J. (1971). Litter size and weight gain of neonatal guinea pigs. *Psychol. Rep.* **28**, 981–982.

Stern, J., and Hoffman, B. (1970). Effects of social isolation until adulthood on maternal behavior in guinea pigs. *Psychon. Sci.* **21**, 15–16.

Stern, J., and Siepierski, L. (1971). Spreading cortical depression and the maternal behavior of guinea pigs. *Psychon. Sci.* **25**, 301–302.

Stockard, C. R., and Papanicolaou, G. (1919). The vaginal closure membrane, copulation, and the vaginal plug in the guinea-pig, with further considerations of the oestrus rhythm. *Biol. Bull.* **37**, 222–245.

Tindal, J. S., Knaggs, G. B., and Turvey, A. (1968). Preferential release of oxytocin from the neurohypophysis after electrical stimulation of the afferent path of the milk-ejection reflex in the brain of the guinea-pig. *J. Endocrinol.* **40**, 205–214.

Tobach, E. and Gold, P. S. (1966). Behavior of the guinea pig in the open-field situation. *Psychol. Rep.* **18**, 415–425.

von Kunkel, P., and Kunkel, I. (1964). Beitrag zur ethologie des haus meerschweinchens *Cavia aperea* f. *porcellus* (L.). *Z. Tierpsychol.* **21**, 602–641.

Warren, R. and Pfaffman, C. (1959). Early experience and taste aversion. *J. Comp. Physiol. Psychol.* **52**, 263–266.

Webster, C. D. and Walsh, M. (1968). Acquisition of stimulus control of bar-press avoidance behavior with guinea pigs. *Psychon. Sci.* **11**, 17–18.

Webster, C. D., Brimer, C. J., and Evonic, I. (1965). Factors affecting intersession facilitation of avoidance learning in guinea-pigs. *Psychon. Sci.* **3**, 291–292.

Wolff, P. C., Burnstein, D. D., Flory, R. K., and Malory, J. (1966). Stimulus discrimination through intracranial reinforcement. *Percept. Mot. Skill* **22**, 891–895.

Young, W. C. (1969). Psychobiology of sexual behavior in the guinea pig. *Advan. Study. Behav.* **2**, 1–110.

Zucker, I. (1966). Facilitatory and inhibitory effects of progesterone on sexual responses of spayed guinea pigs. *J. Comp. Physiol. Psychol.* **62**, 376–381.

Zucker, I. (1968). Biphasic effects of progesterone on sexual receptivity in the female guinea pig. *J. Comp. Physiol. Psychol.* **65**, 472–478.

Chapter 6

Anatomy

James E. Breazile and Esther M. Brown

I. INTRODUCTION

This discussion of gross and microscopic anatomy of the guinea pig (*Cavia porcellus*) was based upon gross dissection of 10 guinea pigs, euthanatized and perfused with 10% buffered neutral formalin to retain conformation and topographical relationships of internal organs. Six additional animals were similarly perfused prior to preparation of histological materials. The anatomical discussions of this chapter presuppose a general knowledge of mammalian gross anatomy and histology. A detailed gross anatomy of the guinea pig by Ballard (1937) served as the basis for anatomical discussions. As no general histological work concerning the guinea pig is available, materials prepared in the authors laboratories serve as the primary basis for descriptive material.

Detailed descriptions of osteology, myology, and neurology are not presented, but a general description of these systems is provided.

In this chapter, terminology recommended by the International Committee on Veterinary Anatomical Nomenclature has been adopted wherever possible, thus directional terms, cranial—toward the head, caudal—toward the tail, dorsal—toward the vertebral surface, and ventral—toward the abdominal surface, are utilized. For description of structures in the head, rostral—toward the nose—is used in place of cranial.

II. OSTEOLOGY

The number of bones of the skeleton varies with age. A number of separate bones in immature animals become fused in adults. The *skeleton* is comprised of two parts; the *axial*: the skull, hyoid apparatus, vertebrae, ribs and sternum; and *appendicular*: the pectoral and pelvic girdles, and pectoral and pelvic limbs.

A. Axial Skeleton

The skull is elongated rostrocaudally, with prominent zygomatic arches, a deep pterygopalatine fossae and large orbits (Landry, 1959). The orbit is incomplete dorsally, being completed by the orbital ligament. The infraorbital canal is short and markedly large. The dorsal surface of the skull is gently curved rostrocaudally and relatively smooth, with the exception of low temporal lines which extend from the external occipital protuberance to the orbital crest of each side, and a lacrimal tubercle on the rostral margin of the orbit. The ventral surface of the skull is characterized by small, paired, slitlike, palatine fissures, prominent tympanic bullae, and large rounded foramen lacerae. The dental formula of the adult guinea pig is

$$I\frac{1}{1}, C\frac{0}{0}, P\frac{1}{1}, \text{and } M\frac{3}{3}$$

The maxillary dental arcades form a distinct V, with the apex directed rostrally. The absence of canine teeth result in a spatius diastema between the premolar and incisor teeth. The cheek teeth are hypsodont in type and the incisors are chisel-like in shape. Roots of the maxillary premolars and molars incline laterally within the alveoli, while those of the mandible incline medially within their respective alveoli.

The hyoid bone is an irregular U-shaped bone composed of a transverse basihyoid (body) and rostral and caudal cornua. The rostral cornu is composed of a short slender epihyoid, an elongated stylohyoid and a short terminal tympanohyoid which is attached to the mastoid process of the skull by the tympanohyoid cartilage. The caudal cornu is a short, stout process and articulates with the thryoid cartilage of the larynx.

The mandibles are united at the rostral midline by a mandibular symphysis. The body of the mandible bears the teeth, and the ramus gives rise to an angular and a condyloid process. The body bears a single alveolus rostrally for the incisor tooth and four large alveoli for the premolar and molar teeth. A small mental foramen is present just below the alveolus of the premolar tooth. The lateral surface of the ramus of the mandible is roughened for the insertion of the masseter muscle. The mandibular foramen pierces the medial surface of the ramus ventral to the alveolus of the last molar tooth. The medial pterygoid muscle inserts into a fossa on the medial surface of the mandible.

The vertebral column is comprised of 32 to 36 vertebrae. The vertebral formula is C_7, T_{13-14}, L_6, S_{2-3}, C_{4-6}. The sternum has six segments; the presternum, manubrium, 3 sternebrae, and a xyphoid process. The first 6 pair of ribs articulate with the sternum, the remainder are asternal. There are 13 or 14 pair of ribs in the guinea pig, the last one or two are cartilaginous. The first pair bears a small uncinate process near the middle of its caudal margin. Ribs 7 through 9 contribute to the costal arch. Ten through 14 are floating ribs.

B. Appendicular Skeleton

The pectoral girdle is comprised of the scapulae and the small cylindrical clavicle. The clavicle, a vestigial bone, attaches laterally to the small coracoid process of the scapula and medially to the manubrium of the sternum. The scapula is a thin triangular bone with a well-developed scapular spine bearing both an acromion and a metacromion.

The pelvic girdle is comprised of paired os coxae, which articulate craniolaterally with the transverse processes of the sacrum. The os coxae are comprised of the ilium, ischium, and pubis bones and in the immature animal, the acetabular bone. The latter fuses with the other three bones to form the acetabulum as the animal matures. Complete fusion of individual components of the os coxae occurs around 2 weeks of age. The os coxae of each side are joined in the midline at the symphysis pelvis. The symphysis is comprised of both symphysis pubis and symphysis ischii, and may be ossified in old males, but generally remains fibrocartilage throughout the life of the animal. At about 2 weeks prior to parturition a degeneration of the pelvic symphysis occurs in the female resulting in complete destruction by the time of parturition (Todd, 1923). Palpation of the separation can be utilized for estimation of the time of parturition.

The bones of the forelimb are the humerus, ulna, eight carpal bones (radial, ulnar, and accessory in the proximal row, and first, second, third, fourth, and fifth carpals in the distal row), four metacarpal bones, and three phalanges for digits one, two and three, with only two phalanges associated with digit four. There are nine sesamoid bones in the forelimb; a small sesamoid becomes fused with the accessory carpal bone with age, two sesamoids are located on the palmar surface of the metacarpophalangeal articulations. There are no sesamoid bones associated with the remaining phalangeal articulations.

The pelvic limb is comprised of the femur, tibia, fibula,

seven tarsal bones (tibial, fibular, central, first, second, third, and fourth tarsal bones), three metatarsals (second, third, and fourth), and three digits, each with three phalanges. There are eight sesamoids in the pelvic limb; the patella, a tarsal sesamoid at the proximal extremity of the third metatarsal which articulates with this bone and fibular tarsal bone, and two sesamoids at each metatarsophalangeal articulation. As in the forelimb, there are no digital sesamoids beyond those at the metatarso-phalangeal articulation. The third phalanx of both forelimb and pelvic limb digits supports a heavy, strongly curved claw.

III. MUSCULAR SYSTEM

The muscular system of the guinea pig is well defined with exception of the cutaneous muscles. Particularly, those of the head where they tend to fuse, making identification of individual muscles difficult. The masticatory muscles are well developed, particularly the masseter and digastricus muscles, reflecting the gnawing behavior of these animals and mastication by grinding rather than shearing. The pterygoid and temporalis muscles are relatively small. The muscles of the limbs are modified to account for the number of digits, but are easily delineated.

IV. CARDIOVASCULAR SYSTEM

(Potter *et al.*, 1958; Shively and Stump, 1974; Morin, 1965; Favre, 1967)

The four-chambered heart lies in the pericardial sac within the mediastinum. The atria are thin walled and are separated from the ventricles by the coronary sulcus which contains the right and left coronary arteries and veins. Superficially, the atria are separated on their ventral surface by the pulmonary artery and dorsally by the aorta. The cranial and caudal vena cavae enter the right atrium and the pulmonary veins enter the left atrium. The atria are separated internally by the interatrial septum, which bears a small fossa ovale on its right side. The auricular portion of the atria contain well-developed pectinate muscles arising from the terminal crest of the atrium. The right atrioventricular ostium is guarded by the right atrioventricular valves. These valves are comprised of three large cusps and several small cusps, all are attached at their base to the cartilaginous skeleton of the heart. The free edges of the cusps are attached to the papillary muscles of the ventricle by chordae tendinae. The left atrioventricular valve is comprised of two large cusps with several smaller accessory cusps and is similarly attached to the cartilaginous skeleton of the heart and the papillary muscles of the left ventricle.

The pulmonary artery arising from the conus arteriosus of the right ventricle and the aorta arising from the left ventricle are guarded by the pulmonary and aortic valves, respectively. These valves are comprised of three cusps each. The cusps are unattached at their free border, but their base is attached to the connective tissue skeleton of the heart. The ventricles are separated by a thick interventricular septum. The lumen of the right ventricle usually contains a single septomarginal trabeculum (moderator band). The left ventricle more often is lacking such a trabeculum.

The heart is comprised of three layers, an external mesothelial layer, the epicardium, a thick myocardium, and an inner layer of mesothelium, the endocardium. The heart receives its blood supply from the right and left coronary arteries which arise from the right and left aortic sinuses. These are dilatations of the aorta, behind the cusps of the aortic valves, so that coronary blood flow is not interrupted with opening of the valve. Blood is drained from the heart through the right and left coronary veins which unite to form the coronary sinus. The coronary sinus empties into the right atrium near the opening of the caudal vena cava.

Blood supply to the lungs is provided by the pulmonary and bronchoesophageal arteries. Pulmonary veins drain blood from the lungs to the left atrium. Three groups of pulmonary veins drain blood from the lung; a dorsal group drains the cranial and middle lobes of the right lung, a group on the left side drains the cranial and middle lobes of the left lung, and a group on the right side drains the caudal lobes of both lungs and the accessory lobe of the right lung.

The dorsal aorta distributes blood from the heart to all other organs. It arises from the left ventricle at the level of the third rib and curves dorsally to the left over the cranial surface of the heart and passes caudally below the bodies of the vertebrae. The ascending aorta gives rise to the right and left coronary, brachiocephalic and left subclavian arteries. The brachiocephalic trunk in turn gives rise to the right and left common carotid arteries and continues as the right subclavian artery. The distribution of these arteries follows the general pattern of those of other mammals. A bronchoesophageal artery arises from the right subclavian, the right internal thoracic arteries or the brachiocephalic trunk and passes caudally into the mediastinum where it bifurcates into right and left bronchial arteries (Shively and Stump, 1974). The abdominal aorta gives rise to a celiacomesenteric artery. In some guinea pigs as many as three pairs of renal arteries are present; however, a single pair is most common. The male testicular and the female ovarian arteries arise from the aorta and are distributed to the testis and epididymis of the male or the ovary of the female. The oviduct and uterus of the female are supplied by the uterine artery, a branch of the internal iliac, and the ovarian artery (Del Campo and Ginther, 1972). The remaining aortic distribution is similar to that of other mammalian species.

The venous system for the most part follow the general course of the arteries. The veins are less muscular and consequently thinner than the arteries and within the appendages and head occupy a more superficial position than do the major arteries.

The cranial and caudal vena cava provide the primary routes for drainage of systemic blood back to the right atrium of the heart. The cranial vena cava drains blood from the head, neck, and forelimbs. This vein enters the craniodorsal surface of the right atrium. Near its entrance into the atrium the vein receives the azygous vein which drains the walls of the thoracic cavity. The cranial vena cava is formed by the junction of the right and left brachiocephalic trunks which are in turn formed by the union of the internal and external jugular veins with the subclavian veins of the forelimbs.

The caudal vena cava is the chief vessel by which blood from caudal regions of the body is returned to the heart. The caudal vena cava enters the caudodorsal surface of the right atrium. The large vessel passes caudally from the heart through the thoracic cavity penetrating the diaphragm near its middle as the hiatus vena cava. On the abdominal side of the diaphragm the caudal vena cava receives the phrenic veins from the diaphragm, which may unite to form a common trunk prior to joining the vena cava, but more often are found in three groups, two entering the lateral surface and one the ventral surface of the vena cava. Immediately caudal to the diaphragm, the caudal vena cava receives three hepatic veins from the liver. Caudal to this level, the vena cava is located ventrally and to the right of the aorta, but gradually assumes a laterodorsal position within the lumbar and sacral regions where it receives the iliac veins from the pelvic limbs. In its course through the abdomen, the caudal vena cava receives the renal veins, right genital vein (uteroovarian in female, Del Campo and Ginther, 1972; testicular in male), and seven pairs of lumbar veins from the abdominal wall. The external iliac veins drain blood from the pelvic limbs, and the internal iliacs receive blood from the pelvic structures.

The hepatic portal system consists of those veins which are concerned with transport of blood from stomach, spleen, small intestine, and most of the large intestine to the liver. Veins from these organs converge to form the hepatic portal vein. Within the substance of the liver, the hepatic portal blood enters the hepatic sinusoids where it is mixed with arterial blood from the hepatic artery. Blood is then drained from the hepatic sinusoids through the hepatic venous system into the caudal vena cava. The hepatic portal vein is formed immediately caudal to the liver by the convergence of the gastroduodenal, gastropancreaticosplenic, pancreaticoduodenal, and cranial and caudal mesenteric veins.

The lymphatic system is comprised of a number of lymph nodes of varing size distributed throughout the body (Hashiba, 1917; Hadek, 1951) and their associated lymphatic vessels. The major lymphatics are the right and left tracheal lymph ducts draining the head, the thoracic duct draining the caudal portion of the animal, and the mediastinal ducts draining the peritoneal, pleural, and pericardial cavities. The thoracic duct originates within the lumbar region, where it lies immediately dorsal to the aorta. The duct in this region is large and may be divided into two or three channels. It is referred to as the cisterna chyli. The cysterna chyli receives lymph from the pelvic limbs, the lumbar axial musculature, the body wall of the abdomen, and all the pelvic and abdominal visera. The thoracic duct passes into the thoracic cavity and maintains its position dorsal to the aorta as it passes through the aortic hiatus. Near the cranial thoracic inlet, the duct is joined by the tracheal duct of the left side of the neck, just prior to its entry into the external jugular vein. The right tracheal duct enters the right external jugular vein independently.

The most commonly dissectable lymph nodes of the guinea pig are the maxillary lymph node of the head, which lies just caudal to the masseter muscle; cranial cervical lymph nodes at the level of the thyroid gland; cubital lymph nodes in the flexor surface of the elbow; caudal superficial cervical lymph nodes beneath the cleidobrachialis muscle at the level of the shoulder; axillary nodes within the axilla; caudal deep cervical lymph nodes at the thoracic inlet; cranial, middle, and caudal mediastinal lymph nodes within the mediastinum; mesenteric lymph nodes of the small and large intestine; one particularly large mesenteric node occurs near the central portion of the mesentery; iliac lymph node near the bifurcation of the aorta; superficial inguinal nodes near the external inguinal ring; and popliteal nodes in the popliteal fossa. Other glands are recognizable in animals in which glandular enlargement is a reflection of a pathological condition.

The parathymic lymph nodes located within the cervical region which serve to drain lymph from the thymus have been of considerable interest from the standpoint of investigations of the interrelationships between the thymus and lymph nodes in immune mechanisms.

A. Spleen

The spleen is suspended along the dorsolateral portion of the fundus of the stomach by the gastroleinal ligament (Morin, 1965). The spleen which is broader in its proportion than that of rabbits and other rodents is approximately 26 mm in length and 13 millimeters at its greatest width. Its caudal tip lies dorsal to a portion of the pancreas. The dorsal surface of the spleen is convex, its concave ventral surface fits caplike over the dorsolateral surface of the stomach. The general position of the spleen varies with fullness of the stomach.

The spleen is enclosed by a thin capsule comprised of collagenous connective tissue. From the internal surface of the capsule a network of trabeculae subdivide the organ into many communicating compartments. Many of the capsular trabeculae are comprised predominantly of smooth muscle; however, little smooth muscle is seen in the capsule itself. The tissue enclosed by the capsule comprises the splenic pulp. Most of the pulp is red due to the presence of blood and is designated red pulp. Red pulp is comprised of elongated thin-walled splenic sinuses separated by thin partitions, the splenic cords. Lymphatic nodules comprise the white pulp. White pulp comprised of lymphatic tissue ensheathing small arteries makes up the bulk of the organ.

There are no sheathed arterioles in the spleen and the arterioles ramify in the red pulp as a well-defined system of short straight vessels known as penicillial arteries. These arteries empty into the sinuses of the spleen, which are in turn drained by capillary venules, leading to collecting veins. The storage capacity of this spleen is largely a function of the venous sinuses.

B. Thymus

The thymus is a transitory structure, present in the immature animal and gradually involutes as the animal matures. In mature specimens, the thymus may be completely gone or may persist as a small remnant within the cranial mediastinum. In immature animals, it is a compressed lobulated gland enclosed within the precardial mediastinum and extending into the neck where it surrounds the trachea ventrally and laterally. Barnes (1972) reported that the thymus is present as a pair of distinctly ovoid masses located entirely in the cervical region. This is in contrast to Gordon (1974) who divided the organ into a cervical thymus and a mediastinal thymus. The guinea pig has been a popular experimental animal for immunological studies because the cervical thymus is easily removed without extensive surgery.

Thymic corpuscles (Hassal's corpuscles) are organizations of epithelial cells within the thymus. In these structures the epithelial cells are tightly associated with each other to form a corpuscular structure. The epithelial cells in the center of the corpuscle may exhibit signs of degeneration. The epithelial cells at the periphery of the corpuscle are continuous with those forming the reticulum.

The thymus is enclosed by a thin capsule of dense connective tissue which usually contains numerous macrophages, plasma cells, fat cells, mast cells, and granular leukocytes. Connective tissue trabeculae arise from the inner surface of the capsule to separate the lobules of the thymus.

There appear to be no afferent lymphatic vessels to the thymus. Several efferent vessels leave the medulla and drain into the mediastinal lymph nodes. With age, the vessels become less prominent and the thymic tissue is replaced primarily with fat.

V. SKIN AND DERIVATIVES

The body surface is for the most part covered with coarse hair, with hairless regions around the external opening of respiratory, digestive, and urogenital systems. The two mammary glands, located within the inguinal region are also hairless around the nipples.

The epidermis for the most part is thin in the guinea pig, being somewhat thicker on the foot pads, muzzle, nipples, and around the external genital and anal orifices. Toward the epidermal surface, the dermis is organized into vascular papillae which project into the overlying epidermis, particularly in hairless skin. In hairy skin, dermal papillae are less frequently seen, but dermal ridges are prevalent.

A. Hair

Hair of the guinea pig is characteristically coarse, with a fine undercoat. Tactile hairs are seen on the lateral surface of the nose where they form five or six rows. Two tactile hairs are generally present as a superciliary tuft dorsal to the medial canthus of the eye, two just caudal to the lateral canthus of the eye and a variable number on the dorsolateral surface of the face. These are typical sinus hairs. The general hair coat of the guinea pig is characterized by complex hair beds, which are comprised of large guard hairs surrounded by an undercoat of fine hairs. Each hair emerges from independent follicles, but the follicles occur in clusters, with several (3–7) small follicles surrounding a large follicle. Each hair follicle has an associated sebaceous gland, but sudoriferous glands are apparently absent. The hair on the ears and within the external ear canal are fine hairs with no large coarse guard hairs.

Sebaceous glands are particularly abundant along the dorsal surface of the animal and around the anal orifice. The circumanal region contains a large accumulation of sebaceous glands. Anal sacs are present as bilateral diverticula from the mucocutaneous junction of the anus. This sac is surrounded by large sebaceous glands which secrete into it.

B. Mammary Glands

The mammary glands are inguinal in position in the guinea pig. There is a single pair of glands, which are somewhat elongated and finely lobulated. The glands open through a number of small ducts into a single large papillary duct which opens to the exterior. There are two teats, one on each side of the midline craniomedial to the thigh. In the pigmented animals, the papillae are generally darkly pigmented and hairless or covered with fine hairs.

VI. GASTROINTESTINAL SYSTEM

The oral orifice is triangular in shape. The lips are rounded and covered with short fine hair. The two halves of the upper lip are separated in the midline by a well-defined philtrum. The edge of the upper lip is rolled inward forming a broad flattened buccal pad covered with short fine hair. About the middle of the diastema the buccal pad is separated from an oval area which is covered with relatively long bristles. The lower lip is relatively short and is attached to the incisive gingiva by a frenulum.

The rostral portion of the oral cavity is nearly completely separated from the caudal region by the premolar teeth. The molar region of the oral cavity increases in width caudally, then continues as a funnel-shaped cavity into the pharynx.

The hard palate is roughly triangular in shape, with a well-developed incisive papilla behind the incisor teeth. The soft palate is a very flexible membranous structure extending caudal from the hard palate.

The tongue is a relatively large organ extending from the rostroventral portion of the pharynx to the symphysis of the mandible. The rostral one-third of the tongue is free, the remaining is attached to the floor of the oral cavity. A distinct lingual frenulum is not always present. The dorsal surface is separated into two distinct regions; a caudal raised portion on which the fungiform papillae are large and almost erect, and rostral portion on which small filiform papillae are identified.

Rostrodorsally, the pharynx communicates with the nasopharynx and rostroventrally it communicates with the oropharynx. The nasopharynx and oropharynx are separated by the soft palate. The walls of the oropharynx are smooth with the exception of a series of lateral folds representing the pharyngeal tonsils.

The esophagus opens into the caudodorsal portion of the pharynx and passes caudoventrally over the dorsal surface of the larynx. The esophagus occupies a position on the dorsal surface of the trachea somewhat displaced to the left near the thoracic inlet. The esophagus passes through the thoracic cavity within the mediastinum, perforates the diaphragm at the esophageal hiatus, extends through the esophageal notch of the liver dorsal to the caudal vena cava, and enters the stomach. The esophagus lies near the right half of the lesser curvature of the stomach and joins the stomach obliquely at the cardiac orifice.

The stomach lies in the left cranial portion of the abdominal cavity in contact with the caudal surface of the liver (Morin, 1965). The long axis extends transversely across the abdominal cavity. The greater curvature extends caudoventrally and the lesser curvature craniodorsally. The esophagus enters the stomach slightly to the right of the center of the lesser curvature so that a large fundus extends to the right and dorsal to the cardia. The inner surface of the stomach is smooth with the exception of the pyloric region which is characterized by a number of longitudinal rugae. The gastric mucosa does not exhibit a keratinized portion.

The small intestine is a series of coils occupying the right half of the abdominal cavity and measuring about 125 cm in length. There are no external landmarks which allow a separation of the small intestine into the duodenum, jejunum, and ileum, but the topography of the small intestine contributes to such a delineation.

The mucosal surface of the small intestine characteristically has villi throughout. The common bile duct enters the duodenum only about a centimeter caudal to the pylorus.

The ileum enters a small compartment of the cecum, which in turn communicates through a wide opening with the remaining cecum and colon. The walls of the ileum project slightly into the cavity of the cecum to form the ileocecal papilla.

The cecum is one of the most characteristic features of the intestinal tract. It is a large thin-walled sack bearing numerous lateral pouches. It assumes a semicircular form occupying the left side of the abdominal cavity. There are three taenia coli, which pass along the lesser curvature and dorsal and ventral surfaces, respectively. The walls of the cecum are thin and smooth except for ridgelike folds and Peyer's patches. The cecum communicates with the colon through the cecocolic orifice located about 7 mm caudal to the ileocecal orifice. The taenia coli of the guinea pig has served as a favorite source of smooth muscle for physiologists as the muscle fibers are linearly arranged and a large sample of smooth muscle cells can be obtained without appreciable damage prior to study.

The colon passes cranially along the left margin of the cecum, as the ascending colon forms a tight loop and passes dorsal to the duodenum near the pylorus, where it bends caudally as the descending colon near the median plane of the abdomen. The colon is continued caudally to the anal opening. The rectum is the terminal segment of the large intestine and is not sharply delineated from the colon except for an increase in diameter.

A. Liver

The liver lies within the cranial portion of the abdominal cavity, closely applied to the diaphragm (Morin, 1965). It is comprised of six lobes; right lateral, right medial, left lateral, left medial, caudate, and quadrate. The right medial lobe is separated from the caudate and quadrate lobes by the esophageal notch impression dorsally and the gallbladder ventrally. The caudate and quadrate lobes are separated from the left medial lobe by the esophageal impression dorsally and the round ligament of the liver ventrally. The gallbladder is well developed and drained by the cystic duct. The cystic duct is joined by several hepatic bile ducts to form the common bile duct. The common bile duct is in turn joined by the pancreatic duct prior to its opening into the duodenum, 3–4 mm caudal to the pyloric extremity of the duodenum. A unique ampullary swelling in the common bile duct is cut off by a sphincter action after filling and then empties into the duodenum.

B. Pancreas

The pancreas is a triangular gland, with its apex directed caudally, it consists of three lobes, each separated into a number of minor lobules. The pancreas lies in contact with the descending duodenum and extends to the left dorsal to the spleen. The exocrine secretions of the pancreas are collected by a number of ducts from the various lobules, which form a single pancreatic duct.

There are four pairs of salivary glands in the guinea pig: parotid, mandibular, sublingual, and molar. The parotid lies in the triangle formed by the axial muscles of the neck and the caudal ramus of the mandible. The parotid duct passes across the lateral to the first molar tooth. The mandibular gland is oval in form and lies ventral to the caudal margin of the parotid gland. The two mandibular glands of each side contact each other in the ventral midline. The mandibular duct passes rostrally parallel to the mandible and enters the oral cavity proper on the sublingual papilla. The sublingual gland is divided into two portions, a monostomatic portion which is similar in appearance and lies adjacent to the mandibular gland and a polystomatic portion which lies beneath the sublingual fold in the floor of the oral cavity. The sublingual duct of the monostomatic portion lies medial to the mandibular duct and opens in this position upon the sublingual caruncle. The polystomatic portion is drained by many ducts into the oral cavity proper. The molar gland is located between the oribicularis oris muscle and the mucosa of the lower lip. It opens into the oral cavity through a number of small ducts opposite the upper molar teeth.

C. Microscopic Structure of Gastrointestinal System

The esophagus is lined with stratified squamous epithelium which is keratinized. The muscularis of the proximal portion of the esophagus is comprised of striated muscle, but the distal portion is comprised of smooth muscle. The stomach cannot be readily separated into its glandular regions by gross examination. There is no portion of the stomach which is nonglandular in contrast to that of other rodents. The stomach glands are simple branched tubules, with several short straight glands opening into each gastric pit. There are three types of glands present; cardiac, pyloric and fundic, the fundic gland being prevalent. Fundic glands contain mucous cells, chief cells and parietal cells. Cardiac glands are comprised of columnar cells without secretory granules in their cytoplasm. Pyloric glands are characterized by deep gastric pits and short glandular portions, which are comprised primarily of mucus-secreting cells. There is a gradual transition from one gland type to another.

The small intestine is characterized by cylindrical or leaflike villi, which are tall in the duodenum and jejunum and short in the ileum. Short tubular intestinal glands open between bases of villi. Duodenal glands are present throughout the duodenum; these glands lie within the submucosa of the intestine and are comprised of mucus-secreting cells. Lymph nodules and Peyer's patches are within the lamina propria and submucosa of the small intestine. These structures become more numerous toward the distal extremity of the small intestine. A characteristic feature of the lamina propria of villi of both the small and large intestine is the accumulation of hemosiderin, providing a pseudohemosiderosis in the normal animal.

The mucosa of the cecum and colon contains columnar epithelium with many goblet cells. Short simple tubular glands extend to the anus. The muscularis extends along the entire large intestine and cecum, but is best developed in the caudal extremity of the large intestine. Anal sacs are well developed in the guinea pig. They are surrounded by very large sebaceous glands which empty into its lumen. Perianal sebaceous glands are also numerous.

The liver of the guinea pig histologically is similar to that of other animals. The hepatic lobules are not well delineated by connective tissue, but tend to blend into each other. Septa between hepatic lobules are only evident around interlobular branches of the hepatic artery, portal vein and bile ducts.

The mucosa of the gallbladder is covered with cuboidal epithelium overyling a thin lamina propria. There is a thin muscular layer covered with adventitia and serosa. The common bile duct is lined with cuboidal cells which become columnar at the point where the duct penetrates the duodenal wall. Small mucus-secreting glands are found within the lamina propria of the gallbladder and the duct which secrete into the lumen.

The histology of the pancreas is similar to that of other species. The islets of Langerhans are distributed throughout all portions of the organ. The highest concentration, however, is within the splenic (right) portion, with intermediate concentrations within the body and lowest concentrations within the duodenal portion (Bensley, 1911).

VII. RESPIRATORY SYSTEM

The external nares and nasal passageways are typical of mammals the nasopharynx is relatively short and contains on its dorsolateral walls the small openings of the auditory tubes. The pharynx is relatively smooth on its internal surface, with the exception of irregularities produced by underlying lymph nodules or tonsils found in both the nasopharynx and oropharynx. The stratified squamous epithelium of the skin continues into the external nasal orifices and covers the vestibules of the nasal passageways. This changes abruptly within the nasal cavity to pseudostratified columnar ciliated epithelium with many goblet cells. The caudodorsal portion of the nasal cavity is lined with olfactory epithelium which contains specialized receptor organs for olfaction. At the caudal portion of the dorsal surface of the soft palate, the epithelium becomes abruptly stratified squamous and is continuous with that of the oropharynx and pharynx proper. The lamina propria of the nasal cavities and pharynx contains numerous glands with short ducts which open onto the surface.

The larynx is comprised of five cartilaginous elements: epiglottis, thyroid, cricoid, and the paired arytenoid cartilages. These articulate with each other and with the hyoid apparatus in the typical mammalian fashion. There is no laryngeal ventricle in the guinea pig and the vocal folds are small and appear poorly developed. The trachea contains 35–40 cartilaginous rings and bifurcates into two primary bronchi at the level of the third rib. The right lung is comprised of four lobes: cranial, middle, caudal, and accessory. The left lung is comprised of three lobes: cranial, middle, and caudal.

The pseudostratified columnar ciliated epithelium of the upper respiratory system continues through the pharynx, larynx, trachea, and bronchi. At about the third bronchial division, the epithelium becomes columnar in shape, maintains its ciliated form, and exhibits a decrease in goblet cells. The submucosa of the larynx, trachea, and bronchi contain simple, branched, coiled, tubuloacinar, mucous, and serous glands referred to as laryngeal, tracheal, and bronchial glands, respectively. The bronchi continue to divide within the lung to form terminal bronchioles; these terminate in respiratory bronchioles, which in turn open into alveolar ducts. An alveolar duct is in communication with several aveolar sacs, each sac being comprised of several alveoli.

VIII. REPRODUCTIVE SYSTEM

A. Male (Guiard, 1962)

The male reproductive system is comprised of testes, epididymis, ductus deferens, urethra, vesicular glands, prostate, coagulating glands, and bulbourethral glands (Rauther, 1903; Marshall, 1910).

The testis is supported by a mesorchium which passes from its medial surface to the kidney. The epididymis is closely associated with the testis and is easily divided into three portions: head, body, and tail. The head and body are ordinarily covered by a large fat body. The epididymis lies along the dorsolateral margin of the testis. The tail gives rise to a slender ductus deferens. The two ductus deferentes lie adjacent to each other on the dorsal surface of the initial portion of the urethra, and enter the urethra in common with the duct of the vesicular gland to form a short ejaculatory duct opening (Warnock, 1923) on each side of the colliculus seminalis.

The large vesicular glands are long (10 cm), coiled, tubular structures and extend cranially ventral to the ureter (Warnock, 1923). The glands contain a single cavity lined with simple columnar epithelium. The secretory material fills the lumen of the gland with a semisolid mass, causing difficulty in the preparation of histological materials.

The coagulating glands are located close to the base of the vesicular glands. Each gland gives rise to a small slender duct which enters the urethra, other small ducts may enter the caudal surface of the vesicular gland or its duct. The mucosa of the coagulating glands is organized into longitudinal folds which project into the lumen. The epithelium is comprised of columnar cells. The ducts are lined with low columnar epithelium. The secretory material, when mixed with vesicular gland secretions, may result in a concretion which is very difficult to section for histological examination.

The prostate is located caudal to the base of the vesicular and coagulating glands. The prostate is comprised of two ventral and two dorsal lobes. Each ventral lobe empties into the urethra by a single duct, the dorsal lobes empty into the urethra through numerous small ducts. The internal structure of the dorsal lobes of the prostate is similar to that of the coagulating glands. The glandular tubules of the ventral prostate are lined with low columnar cells; the secretion is somewhat acidophilic and tends to form globular masses.

The bulbourethral glands are located on the lateral surfaces of the urethra near the ischial arch. These glands are oval and paired, communicating with the urethra with a slender duct which enters the lateral surface of the urethra. In some instances, the duct enters the dorsal surface of the urethra. The tubules and alveoli of the glands are lined with columnar epithelium, while the ducts are lined with cuboidal epithelium.

Caudal to the ischial arch, the penis extends cranially for about 10 mm, then extends caudally 25 to 30 mm to terminate. The glans penis is cylindrical and is covered primarily by keratinized scales which are arranged in a definite pattern. The glans tapers distally so that the urethral opening is slightly ventral to the tip of the penis. The distal extremity of the penis contains an os penis which is flattened dorsoventrally at both extremities but is narrow in the middle. Caudoventral to the urethral opening is a pouch which contains two horny styles. This pouch is everted during erection so that the styles project externally. In the nonerect state the glans penis lies within the prepuce, which is characterized by an epithelium containing small mucous glands.

B. Female

The reproductive organs of the female consist of the ovaries, oviducts, uterus, and vagina. The ovaries lie within the abdominal cavity caudal and lateral to the kidneys, where they are supported by a short mesovarium. Each ovary is 6 to 8 mm in length, 4 to 5 mm in diameter. Corpora lutea are produced at each 16- to 17- day cycle. Although fading after the thirteenth day, the corpora lutea are grossly visible as pink structures in the ovary. The oviducts lie in close contact with the dorsolateral surface of the ovary within the wall of the ovarian bursa. The oviduct joins the uterine horn caudal to the ovary, by passing obliquely through the uterine wall. The oviduct can be divided into 3 portions; an infundibular portion, near the ovary, an isthmus portion, and an intramural portion which penetrates the uterine wall. The uterine horns are suspended by the broad ligaments from the dorsolateral abdominal wall. The uterine body is about 12 mm in length and about 10 mm in diameter, decreasing in size from cranial to caudal. The body appears to be as much as 45 mm in length due to a well-developed intercornual ligament. The uterine horns are joined at the cervices and a single os cervicis opens to the vagina. The cervix is characterized by a series of small mucosal ridges which extend caudomedially from its lateral walls to converge at the ventral midline. The cervix is about 25 mm long and is about 14 mm in diameter cranially and 5 mm in diameter at its caudal extremity. The vagina is smaller in outside diameter than the cervix and has thinner walls. The vagina lies on the caudal portion of the pelvic floor and curves ventrally around the caudal margin of the ischial arch where it opens to the exterior at the vaginal orifice. Unlike murid and sciurid rodents all hystricomorph rodents except the coypu have a vaginal closure membrane perforate only at estrus and parturition (Weir, 1967). The clitoris is located within a shallow fossa in the floor of the caudal portion of the vagina. The urethral orifice is seen on the caudal surface of the clitoral fossa.

Microscopically, the female reproductive tract is typical of that of other mammals. The ovary is divided into a cortex and medulla and is covered by a thin capsule. The oviduct has long fibria on its abdominal opening which are covered by ciliated columnar epithelium. The isthmus of the oviduct is covered by a pseudostratified and low columnar epithelium with an occasional ciliated cell. The intramural portion of the oviduct is lined with a simple columnar epithelium. The lamina propria consists of a thin layer of connective tissue and the muscularis of circularly arranged smooth muscle.

The epithelium of the uterus is elevated into folds that are well supplied by blood vessels and nerves. The epithelium is simple columnar and is organized into branched tubular glands projecting into the underlying lamina propria which is comprised of reticular tissue. The myometrium consists of inner circular and outer longitudinal layers of smooth muscle separated by a highly vascular layer of loose connective tissue.

The caudal portion of the body of the uterus, the cervix, and the vaginal canal are lined with stratified squamous epithlium that is continuous through the vaginal orifice with that of the skin.

IX. URINARY SYSTEM

The urinary system is similar in both sexes, with variations in regard to the external openings which correspond to alterations in the associated reproductive systems.

The kidneys are the organs of urine production and are the principal excretory organ of the body. The kidneys are paired and are located on each side of the dorsal midline within the abdomen. Both kidneys are retroperitoneal and do not have mesenteries. The kidneys are somewhat bean shaped with the hilus directed medially. They are slightly flattened dorsally and strongly convex ventrally. The left kidney is located somewhat caudal to the right with the cranial extremity of the left on a transverse plane through the caudal pole of the right.

The kidney is comprised of definitive cortex and medulla. The cortex is characterized by glomeruli and tortuous tubules and the medulla by relatively straight tubules. The straight tubules give the medulla a somewhat striated appearance. The renal pelvis of the kidney is somewhat large and characterized by a single longitudinal renal papilla with lateral calyces.

The ureter is continuous with the renal pelvis and is somewhat enlarged at its origin. The ureter passes from the hilus of the kidney along the dorsolateral body wall to the urinary bladder. The ureters pass dorsal to the ductus deferens as they enter the urinary bladder. The epithelium of the ureter is similar to that covering the renal papilla and lining the ducts of the larger collecting tubules of the kidney. It is a transitional epithelium overlying a fibrous lamina propria and inner circular and outer longitudinal smooth muscle layers. The mucosa of the ureter is generally in longitudinal folds.

The urinary bladder is a relatively large saclike structure with relatively thin walls. It is triangular in shape with the apex directed caudally. The bladder is maintained by two lateral ligaments and a single ventral ligament. The caudal portion of the urinary bladder is continued as the urethra which passes into the penis of the male or to the external urethral orifice in the female. The external urethral orifice in the female is generally along the ventral edge of the clitoral fossa, but occasionally opens independently below the vulva.

The bladder is lined by transitional epithelium which becomes thin when the bladder is distended. It contains a fibrous lamina propria and well-developed muscularis. The urethral mucosa is longitudinally folded with transitional epithelium covering its surface. Near the external orifice of the urethra, the epithelium becomes stratified squamous.

X. ADRENAL GLANDS

The adrenal gland is associated with the craniomedial surface of each kidney. Each gland is roughly triangular and is bilobed with the lateral lobe being larger than the medial. The caudal surface is slightly concave, capping the medial surface of the kidney.

XI. APPENDIX: ORGAN WEIGHTS

Table I
Organ Weights of 900-gm Guinea Pig

Organ	Grams
Ligaments and skeleton	64.0
Musculature	320.0
Brain	4.3
Spinal cord	14.5
Eyes	1.25
Hypophysis	0.022
Thyroid gland	0.134
Adrenal glands	0.725
Lung	5.0
Stomach and intestines (with contents)	120.0
Stomach (empty)	0.42
Intestine (empty)	28.0
Pancreas	2.5
Liver	42.5
Kidneys	6.12
Urinary bladder	4.25
Testes	4.30
Epididymis	0.66
Ovaries	0.192

REFERENCES

Ballard, O. T. (1937). The gross anatomy of *Cavia cobaya* with a comparative study of another hystricomorph rodent; *Erethizon dorsatus,* Ph.D. Thesis, University of Kansas, Lawrence.

Barnes, R. D. (1972). Unpublished Autotutorial. "Special Anatomy of Laboratory Mammals." University of California, Davis.

Bessesen, A. N., Jr., and Carlson, H. A. (1922–1923). Postnatal growth in weight of the body and the various organs in the guinea pig. *Amer. J. Anat.* **91,** 483–521.

Bensley, R. R. (1911). Studies of the pancreas of the guinea pig. *Amer. J. Anat.* **12,** 297–398.

Del Campo, C. H., and Ginther, O. J. (1972). Vascular anatomy of the uterus and ovaries and the unilateral luteolytic effect of the uterus: Guinea pigs, rats, hamsters and rabbits. *Amer. J. Res.* **33,** 2561–2578.

Favre, P. (1967). Contribution à l'étude du système artériel du Cobaye (abdomen, bassin, membre pelvien). D.V.M. Thesis, Ecole Nationale Veterinaire d'Alfort, France.

Guiard, C. H. (1962). Anatomie de l'appariel genital mâle du Cobaye. D.V.M. Thesis pour le Doctorat Veterinaire, Ecole Nationale Veterinaire d'Alfort, France.

Hadek, R. (1951). The lymph nodes of the guinea-pig. *Brit. Vet. J.* **107,** 487–890.

Hashiba, G. T. (1917). The lymphatics system of the guinea pig. *Anat. Rec.* **12,** 331–356.

Landry, S. O., Jr. (1959). The interrelationships of the new and old world hystricomorph rodents. *Univ. Calif., Berkeley, Publ. Zool.* **56,** 1–117.

Marshall, F. H. A. (1910). "The Physiology of Reproduction." Longmans, Green, New York.

Morin, G. (1965). Anatomie descriptive et topographique des organes postdiaphragmatiques du Cobaye. D.V.M. Thesis, Ecole Nationale Veterinaire d'Alfort, France.

Potter, G. E., Jones, W. D. C., and Hermann, C. L. (1958). The circulatory system of the guinea pig. *Bios* **29,** 3–13.

Rauther, M. (1903). Uber den genitalapparat einiger Nager u Insektivoren inbesondere die accessorischen genitaldrusen derselben. *Jena. Z. Naturwiss.* **30.**

Shively, M. J., and Stump, J. E. (1974). The systemic arterial pattern of the guinea pig: The head, thorax and thoracic limb. *Amer. J. Anat.* **139,** 269–284.

Todd, T. W. (1923). The pubic symphysis of the guinea pig in relation to pregnancy and parturition. *Amer. J. Anat.* **31,** 345–357.

Warnock, A. W. (1923). The anatomy of the seminal vesicles of the guinea-pig *Cavia cobaya. Anat. Rec.* **25,** 275–287.

Weir, B. J. (1967). The care and management of laboratory hystricomorph rodents. *Lab. Anim.* **1,** 95–104.

Note added in proof: A comprehensive study of the gross anatomy of the guinea pig was published during the final stages of preparation for publication. "Anatomy of the Guinea Pig" by G. Cooper and A. L. Schiller, Harvard University Press, Cambridge, 1975 should be utilized for a more detailed presentation of the guinea pig anatomy.

Chapter 7

Physiology

Dudley B. Sisk

I. INTRODUCTION

This chapter is a comprehensive literature review of three of the more intensively reported areas of guinea pig physiology: hematological, cardiovascular, and reproductive. Studies of normal parameters and facets of function in the guinea pig are largely piecemeal. There are relatively few reports which have as their principal goal the elucidation of physiological norms for the guinea pig. Most available normative data are ancillary to disease-oriented studies. This review brings together potentially useful information from a comparative view, especially relative to the guinea pig as a model for human disease.

II. HEMATOLOGY

A. Introduction

The guinea pig has been used extensively in hematological studies; consequently, there is considerable data on cellular elements, physiological properties, and biochemical characteristics of circulating blood and bone marrow. One of the difficulties in compiling a bank of hematological data is individual variation with age, diet, or physiological state (Long, 1961). Encouragingly, Griffiths and Rieke (1969) found no significant difference in blood and bone marrow of unrelated strains, Dunkin–Hartley and Bahndorf, suggesting either strain may be useful for quantitative hematological experiments. A comprehensive review of the literature on guinea pig hematology prior to 1926 was published by Scarborough (1931).

B. Oxygen Transport

1. Erythrocyte (RBC)

a. RBC Numbers. RBC numbers in the circulating blood of guinea pigs are presented in Table I. After examining the data from several laboratory rodents, Zeman and Wilber (1965a) concluded that erythrocyte and hemoglobin values for the guinea pig and the rabbit are similar. Values for rats, mice, and hamsters are noticeably higher. Ostwald and Shannon (1964) demonstrated no significant differences between sexes of guinea pigs. Constable (1963) reported increased RBC counts from birth to 600 gm, 4.89×10^6 to $5.81 \times 10^6/mm^3$, with a small decrease to $4.61 \times 10^6/mm^3$ at 200 gm of body weight. Lucarelli *et al.* (1968) described a sharp decrease during the first 20 days of life, from $5.29 \times 10^6/mm^3$ at birth to $3.76 \times 10^6/mm^3$ at 20 days of age, followed by an increase to $4.36 \times 10^6/mm^3$ at adulthood (Table II). Nevertheless, the maturing guinea pig had relatively little variation in RBC count compared to a twofold increase between birth and 250 gm in the rat. Constable (1963) reported the rat (50 gm) and guinea pig (200 gm) to have a physiological erythrocytopenia at weaning.

Reticulocyte counts are presented in Tables II and III. Lucarelli *et al.* (1968) concluded that reticulocytes are generally more numerous in the circulating blood of immature than mature guinea pigs. Maturation of the guinea pig erythron is discussed in Section I, F, 4, b.

b. Packed Cell Volume (PCV). PCV of the guinea pig ranges from 37.0 to 48.0% (Baumann *et al.*, 1971; Griffiths and Rieke, 1969; Kutscher, 1968; Coldman and Good, 1967; Osmond and Everett, 1965). Ostwald and Shannon (1964) reported 48.0 and 45.0% for the male and the female, respectively. Lucarelli *et al.* (1968) reported that at birth the guinea pig has a higher [48.0 (± 1.0 SE)] PCV than the adult [37 (± 0.9 SE)]. During the first three weeks PCV decreases, then between the twentieth and thirtieth day of life erythrocyte production associated with reticulocytosis increases (Table II).

Table I
Erythrocyte Count (cells $\times 10^6/mm^3$) of Circulating Blood in the Guinea Pig

No. of animals	Mean ± SE or range	Conditions described	Reference
50	4.98 ± 0.090	No description of animals	Baranski (1971)
26	4.60 ± 0.039	♂, Dunkin–Hartley, approx. 400 gm	Griffiths and Rieke (1969)
10	4.60 ± 0.110	♂, Bahndorf strain, approx. 400 gm	Griffiths and Rieke (1969)
56	4.36 ± 0.082	Adult	Lucarelli *et al.* (1968)
20	4.90 – 5.80	Range only, 250–400 gm	Bonciu *et al.* (1967)
145	4.74 ± 0.057	♂ and ♀, Hartley, 400–650 gm	Burns and deLannoy (1966)
52	6.23 ± 0.076	♂, inbred mongrel, 350–800 gm	Zeman and Wilber (1965a)
9	5.83 ± 0.080	♂, Dunkin–Hartley, 385–594 gm	Osmond and Everett (1965)
33	4.72 ± 0.046	♂, Dunkin–Hartley, approx. 400 gm	Moffatt *et al.* (1964)
5	5.40 ± 0.140	♂, 225–290 gm	Ostwalt and Shannon (1964)
5	5.55 ± 1.110	♀, 225–290 gm	Ostwalt and Shannon (1964)
105	4.89[a]	♂, albino, at birth	Constable (1963)
105	4.61[a]	♂, albino, approx. 200 gm	Constable (1963)
105	5.81[a]	♂, albino, approx. 600 gm	Constable (1963)
104	5.13[a]	♂ and ♀, long hair hybrid, 1–1820 days	Fand and Gordon (1957)
53	5.00[a]	♂, 300–570 gm, "variation up to ± 0.4"	Bilbey and Nicol (1955)
48	5.63 (4.40–6.70)	Adult, approx. 500 gm	Innes *et al.* (1949)
47	5.20[a]	♂ and ♀, 268–640 gm	Sawitsky and Meyer (1948)
9	5.06 (4.70–5.25)	Counts followed for 18–21 days	King and Lucas (1941)
4	5.70 (5.40–6.10)	No description of animals	Wintrobe (1933)

[a]No statistics reported.

Table II
Age Variation in Peripheral Blood Values of the Guinea Pig[a]

No. of animals	Age (days)	Hematocrit (PCV)	Hemoglobin	RBC	Reticulocytes (%)	MCV[b]	MCHC[c]
22	1	48 ± 1	14± 0.2	529 ± 20	3.3 ± 0.5	91 ± 3.3	29 ± 0.5
9	3	48 ± 2.5	13 ± 0.6	504 ± 29	3.0 ± 0.6	95 ± 1.7	27 ± 0.5
10	5	39 ± 1.3	13 ± 0.5	445 ± 16	1.4 ± 0.1	88 ± 3.5	33 ± 1.3
11	10	35 ± 0.9	12 ± 0.5	447 ± 19	1.7 ± 0.6	78 ± 1.7	34 ± 0.8
5	15	35 ± 0.9	13 ± 0.7	432 ± 20	1.6 ± 0.3	81 ± 2	37 ± 1.7
7	20	34 ± 0.6	11 ± 0.3	376 ± 14	6.4 ± 2	90 ± 2.6	32 ± 1
5	30	38 ± 0.8	11 ± 0.3	417 ± 7.2	4.8 ± 1	91 ± 1.7	29 ± 0
56	Adult	37 ± 0.9	11 ± 0.6	436 ± 8.2	2.3 ± 0.3	85 ± 1.3	30 ± 0.3

[a]Mean ± SE; from Lucarelli *et al.* (1968).
[b]MCV, mean corpuscular volume.
[c]MCHC, mean corpuscular hemoglobin concentration.

Table III
Reticulocyte Count[a] of Circulating Blood

No. of animals	Mean ± SE or range	Condition described	Reference
11	2.0 (0.9–5.0)	% of RBC, no description of animal	Bethlenfalvay (1972)
56	101.1 ± 13	Adult	Lucarelli *et al.* (1968)
33	59.0 ± 2.96	♂, Dunkin–Hartley, approx. 400 gm	Moffatt *et al.* (1964)
48	67.5 (5.6–168.9)	Adult, approx. 500 gm	Innes *et al.* (1949)

[a] Cells × $10^3/mm^3$ or percent of RBC.

Constable (1963) reported a similar decrease in PCV up to 3 weeks of age, however at 600 gm, the PCV had increased to near birth levels.

c. Dimensions. Banerjee (1966) reported mean RBC lengths of 8.27 μm (± 0.09 SE) and 8.22 μm (± 0.09 SE) for the male and female guinea pig, respectively. Using Pearson's coefficient of variation, they showed that the length of both the male and female RBC's is more variable than in seven other species studied. Reports of the mean RBC diameter include Burnett (1904), 7.5 μm; Scarborough (1931) (average of 8 authors), 7.1 μm; and Ponder (1948), 7.1 μm.

d. RBC Mass. This was estimated by Edmondson and Wyburn (1963) to range from an average of 19.5 ml/kg of body weight for adult animal to 22.3 ml/kg of body weight for young animals. Reported mean corpuscular volumes ranged from 70.3 (Osmond and Everett, 1965) to 85.0 μm^3 (Wintrobe, 1933; Lucarelli *et al.*, 1968).

e. Life Span. Life span of circulating RBC's was studied by several estimation procedures and reported values and conditions of determination varied considerably. Best estimates put the life span between 60 and 80 days (Edmondson and Wyburn, 1963; Grönroos, 1960). Yamanaka *et al.* (1967) suggested values reported by Everett and Yoffey (1959) and Smith and McKinley (1962) are inconclusive because of theoretical problems and wide confidence intervals, respectively.

2. Hemoglobin

a. Average Hemoglobin Concentrations. Concentrations range from 11.0 to 15.2 gm/100 ml of blood. Hemoglobin concentrations followed a trend similar to hematocrit values from birth to maturity (Constable, 1963). An average value at birth of 13.2 gm/100 ml decreased to 11.0 gm/100 ml at about 200 gm of body weight, then increased to about 16 gm/100 ml at 600 gm of body weight. Results reported by Lucarelli *et al.* (1968) differed; there was a gradual decrease in hemoglobin concentration from birth to adulthood (Table II). Reported *mean corpuscular hemoglobin concentration* (MCHC) values average 30.5% (Table IV).

Rodkey *et al.* (1972), applying a codilution technique with endogenous carbon monoxide production determinations, calculated total body hemoglobin to be 8.6 (± 1.00 SD) gm per kilogram.

Neither the amino acid sequence nor tertiary structure of guinea pig hemoglobin has been reported. Based on comparative studies, Bunn (1971) concluded that there are the usual 146 amino acids in the β chain.

Table IV
Whole Blood and Corpuscular Hemoglobin Concentrations in the Guinea Pig

No. of animals	Mean ± SE or range	Conditions described	Reference
		Hemoglobin (gm/100 ml whole blood)	
10	14.4 ± 0.28	♂, cardiac blood, ether anesthetized	Baumann *et al.* (1971)
12	12.8 ± 0.22	♂, Hartley, 400–600 gm, anesthetized	Schaefer *et al.* (1970)
56	11.0 ± 0.6	Adult	Lucarelli *et al.* (1968)
20	94–104%	Sahli method, 250–400 gm	Bonciu *et al.* (1967)
27	12.5 ± 0.298	♂, inbred mongrel, 350–800 gm, anesthetized	Zeman and Wilbur (1965a)
33	100.0 ± 0.59%	♂, Haldane method, approx. 400 gm	Moffatt *et al.* (1964)
53	81%	♂, Sahli method, 300–570 gm	Bilbey and Nicol (1955)
48	15.2 (13.6–17.9)	Adult, approx. 500 gm	Innes *et al.* (1949)
47	14.2	♂ and ♀, 268–640 gm	Sawitsky and Meyer (1948)
4	14.5 (13.6–15.7)	No description of animals	Wintrobe (1933)
		Mean corpuscular hemoglobin concentration (%)	
12	31.5 ± 0.59	♂, Hartley, 400–600 gm	Schaefer *et al.* (1970)
56	30.0 ± 0.30	Adult	Lucarelli *et al.* (1968)
4	30 (29–31)	No description of animals	Wintrobe (1933)

b. Affinity for Oxygen. Hemoglobin of the rat, rabbit, dog, horse, man, and guinea pig has a relatively high affinity for oxygen reflecting a higher level of 2,3-diphosphoglycerate (2,3-DPG) in the erythrocytes. These species apparently require high levels of 2,3-DPG as a cofactor to sufficiently lower oxygen affinity for physiological oxygen unloading. In contrast the cat and ruminants have low levels of RBC organic phosphate and, consequently, a decreased hemoglobin affinity for oxygen (Bunn, 1971). Bartels (1964) demonstrated a positive correlation between animal size and hemoglobin affinity for oxygen (Fig. 1). The P_{50} (mmHg) ranges from 26.9 to 27.8 and the oxygen capacity of guinea pig hemoglobin ranges from 16.8 to 18.5 ml O_2/100 ml blood (Schaefer *et al.*, 1970; Baumann *et al.*, 1971).

Hemoglobin of the guinea pig, rat, mouse, hamster, and gerbil is remarkably resistant to oxidation by nitrites to methemoglobin. In contrast hemoglobin of the dog, rabbit, monkey, and man is very susceptible to nitrite oxidation. The difference

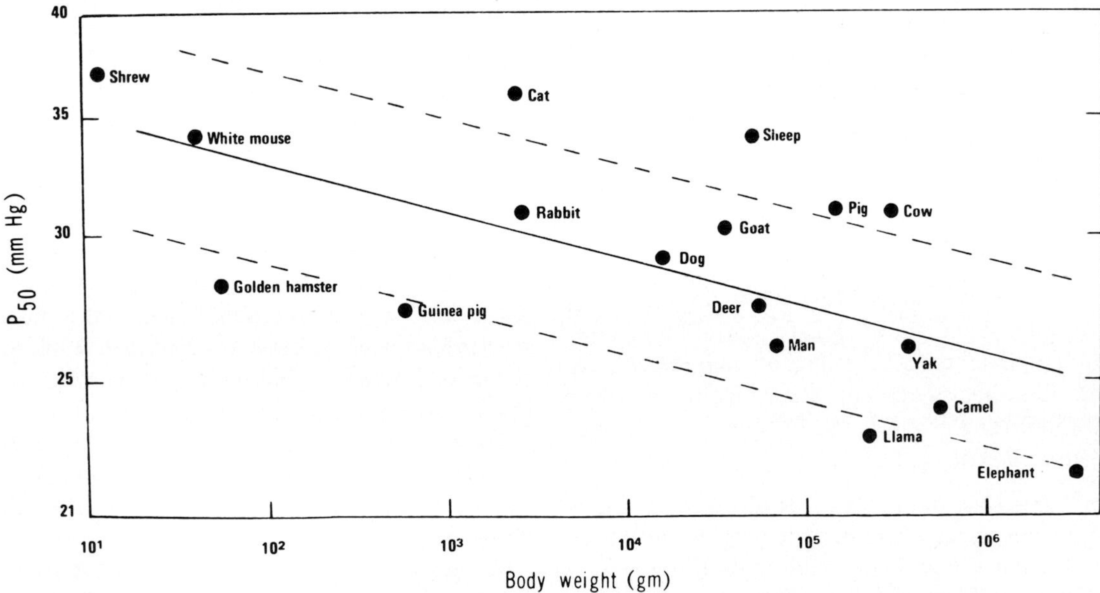

Fig. 1. Half-saturation oxygen tension (P_{50}) as a function of body weight. All animals' blood corrected to pH 7.4 and 37°C. P_{50} = oxygen tension at which 50% hemoglobin is oxyhemoglobin (from Bartels, 1964).

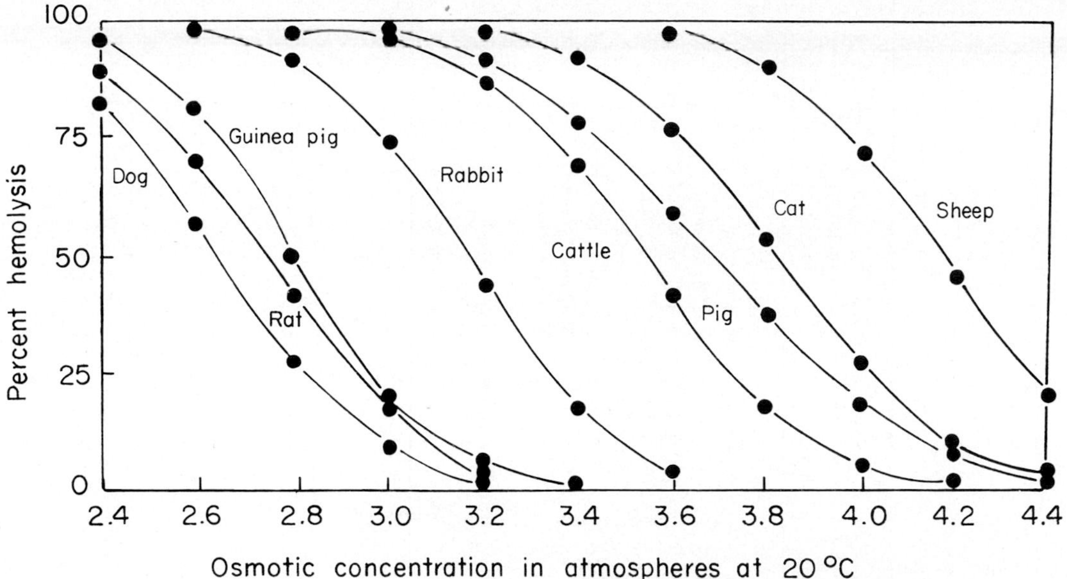

Fig. 2. Mean osmotic hemolysis curves for mammalian erythrocytes in hypotonic solutions of sodium chloride. Conditions: fully oxygenated whole blood; dilution 1:21; temperature 20°C. One atmosphere = 0.127 gm NaCl/100 ml (from Coldman *et al.,* 1969).

may reflect enhanced RBC metabolic activity serving to more readily reduce methemoglobin in the former species (Bethlenfalvay, 1972).

C. Other Erythrocyte Data

1. Fragility

Guinea pig erythrocytes rank with those of the rat and dog, being less fragile in electrolyte solutions than those of the ruminant, cat, pig, or rabbit (Fig. 2). NaCl concentrations causing initial and complete hemolysis are 0.450 and 0.330 gm/100 ml, respectively (Kato, 1941), and according to Coldman *et al.*, 1969, 0.406 gm/100 ml and 0.305 gm/100 ml, respectively.

The guinea pig develops acute hemolytic anemia in response to excess dietary cholesterol, a unique response compared to cardiovascular lesions which develop in most experimental animals. This species variability has been attributed to differences in RBC lipid composition affecting cell membrane stability (Nelson, 1967; Ostwald *et al.*, 1970).

2. Erythrocyte Sedimentation Rate (ESR)

The guinea pig ESR ranks intermediate among common laboratory animals, being greater than the mouse, rat, and ruminants and less than the rabbit, chicken, dog, pig, man, cat, and horse (Richter, 1966). ESR averages for the guinea pig range from 1.06 to 1.20 mm in 60 minutes (Nicolle and Simons, 1939; Richter, 1966).

D. Leukocytes

1. Enumeration and Differentiation

Reported average leukocyte numbers range from 4.09 to 10.6 × $10^3/mm^3$ of blood (Table V). Zeman and Wilber (1965a) found variability in differential counts in guinea pigs making comparison with other species difficult. The majority of guinea pig leukocytes are lymphocytes, whereas neutrophils predominate in adult human blood. Otherwise, cytology of guinea pig peripheral blood is remarkably similar to that of man (Innes *et al.*, 1949). Dineen and Adams (1970) presented evidence that blood lymphocyte concentration stays fairly constant as the animal grows and blood volume increases. However, others demonstrated an increase in blood lymphocyte concentration (Fig. 3).

2. Kurloff Cells

Kurloff cells are unique mononuclear leukocytes containing round or ovoid inclusions (called Kurloff bodies) from 1 μm to 8 μm in diameter. They were first described by Kurloff (1889) and Foà and Carbonne (1889). Kurloff cells most nearly resemble lymphocytes, yet recent studies leave their true classification uncertain (Berendsen and Telford, 1966; Christensen *et al.*, 1970; Revell *et al.*, 1971; Simmons, 1967). Although some Kurloff cells originate in the thymus, most workers consider the spleen as their principle origin (Christensen *et al.*, 1970; Ernström and Sandberg, 1971; Ranløv *et al.*, 1970). The inclusion material is a mucopolysaccharide substance (Dean and Muir, 1970; Marshall and Swettenham, 1959), apparently

Table V
Total Leukocytes and Differential Counts of the Guinea Pig[a]

No. of animals	Total leukocytes ($\times 10^3/mm^3$)	No. of animals	Differential counts (%)					Conditions described	Reference[b]
			Neutrophils	Lymphocytes	Monocytes	Eosinophils	Basophils		
7	9.81	7	53.8	41.5	2.1	2.0	0.4	♂, 480–630 gm[c]	7
20	(4.50–6.00)	20	(28.0–36.0)	(56.0–65.0)	(4.0–6.0)	(0.0–2.0)	(0.0–1.0)	250–400 gm	3
41	8.03 ± 0.382	54	27.2 ± 1.76	71.3 ± 1.81	0.9 ± 0.13	0.3 ± 0.06	0.1 ± 0.03	♂, 350–800 gm	12
53	9.10 (5.00–15.00)	53	32.1 (16.0–44.0)	64.0 (55.0–81.0)	3.1 (0.0–7.0)	0.6 (0.0–3.0)	0.2 (0.0–2.0)	♂, 300–570 gm	2
48	10.60 (5.00–15.00)	48	44.7 (20.0–76.0)	47.6 (21.0–74.0)	5.2 (1.0–12.0)	1.2 (0.0–4.0)	1.3 (0.0–5.0)	Approx. 500 gm	9
5	6.51 ± 0.707	5	48.2 ±6.05	50.8 ± 6.50[d]	–	1.1 ± 0.00	0.3 ± 0.20	♂, 6–7 weeks[e]	10
26	4.80 ± 0.275	26	31.3 ± 2.04	6.46 ± 4.89	–	–	–	♂, approx. 400 gm[e]	8
10	5.50 ± 0.378	10	32.7 ± 3.47	61.8 ± 4.57	–	–	–	♂, approx. 400 gm[f]	8
50	10.39 ± 0.560	50	–	47.6 ± 2.98	–	–	–	No description	1
10	4.09 ± 0.248	10	–	–	–	0.0156 ± 0.0025	0.0014 ± 0.0004	362–452 gm[e]	6
8	7.63 ± 0.365	8	–	–	–	0.0044 ± 0.0010	0.0012 ± 0.0004	Mixed strain	5
25	7.69 (4.60–10.30)	–	–	–	–	–	–	400 gm	11
146	7.65 ± 0.189	–	–	–	–	–	–	♂ and ♀, 400–650 gm[e]	4

[a]Mean ± standard error; ranges are set in parentheses.
[b]Reference:

(1) Baranski, 1971
(2) Bilbey and Nicol, 1955
(3) Bonciu *et al.*, 1967
(4) Burns and deLannoy, 1966
(5) Chan, 1965
(6) Chan, 1968
(7) Dineen and Adams, 1970
(8) Griffiths and Rieke, 1969
(9) Innes *et al.*, 1949
(10) Sibley and Hudson, 1970
(11) Zawisza-Zenkteler, 1963
(12) Zeman and Wilber, 1965a

[c]Heston strain.
[d]Includes monocytes and unclassifieds.
[e]Dunkin–Hartley strain.
[f]Bahndorf strain.

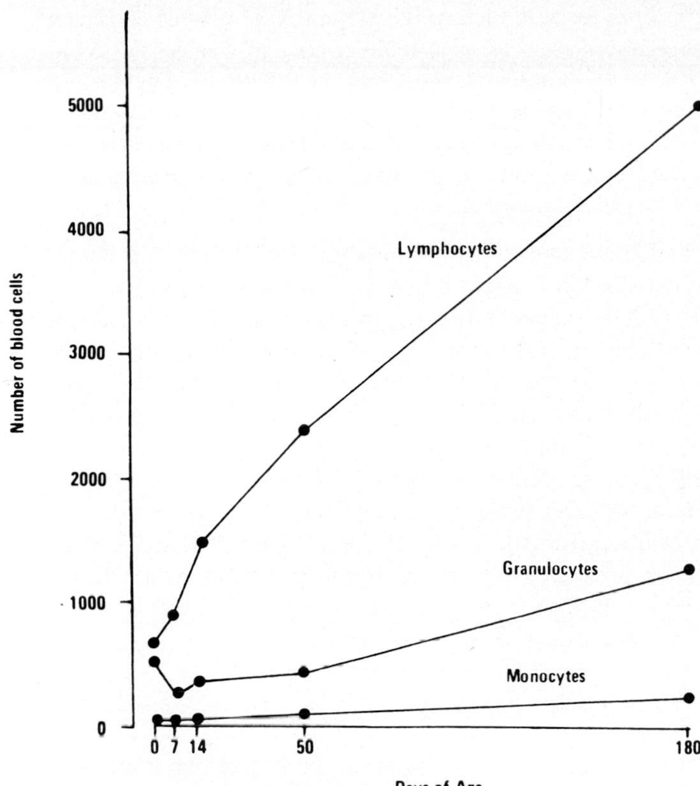

Fig. 3. Number of lymphocytes, granulocytes, and monocytes per cubic millimeter of blood in guinea pigs at different ages after sham operation at birth (after Ernström and Larsson, 1966).

secreted by the cell per se (Berendsen and Telford, 1966; Revell *et al.*, 1971).

The number of Kurloff cells in the spleen and circulation increase markedly during pregnancy or exogenous estrogen treatment in either sex (Ledingham, 1940). They apparently migrate preferentially to the placental labyrinth in pregnant guinea pigs (Revell *et al.*, 1971). The Kurloff cell may constitute a physiological barrier separating fetal antigens from immunologically competent maternal cells; thus, protecting the embryo from sensitized lymphocytes and IgM molecules (Marshall *et al.*, 1971).

As expected, numbers of circulating Kurloff cells vary considerably. They are rare in the fetus and neonate (Smith, 1947). Zeman and Wilber (1965a) reported 0.24% (± 0.57 SE) of leukocytes were Kurloff cells in adult male guinea pigs. The numbers circulating in the female depends on the stage of the estrous cycle.

3. Physiological Data

a. Alkaline Phosphatase. Among animals (guinea pig, rabbit, mouse, rat, hamster, dog, and man) studied by Kaplow (1969), only man and guinea pig had alkaline phosphatase activity in both lymphocytes and granulocytes.

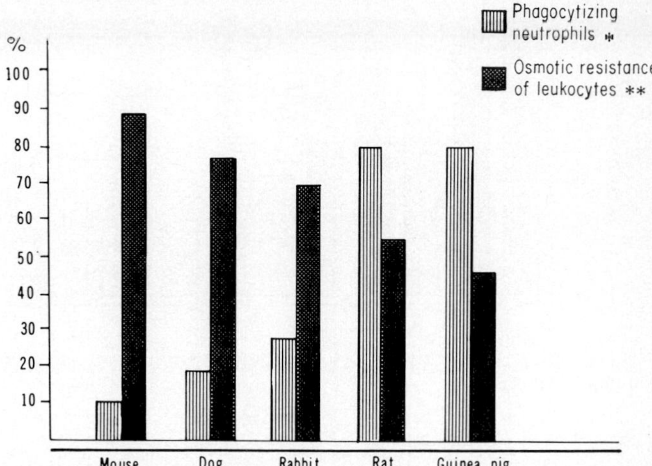

Fig. 4. Relationship between phagocytic activity and osmotic resistance of leukocytes in five species. *,Percent of neutrophils with phagocytic activity. **,Percent decrease in the leukocyte count after 30 minutes exposure to hypotonic (0.2%) NaCl solution at room temperature (from Fiala and Viktora, 1970).

b. Osmotic Resistance and Phagocytic Activity. Leukocytes of guinea pigs and human infants had the greatest resistance to osmotic lysis of several species (Fiala *et al.*, 1966). Mouse and dog leukocytes were most susceptible. Phagocytic activity of neutrophilic leukocytes of various species was inversely related to osmotic resistance (Fig. 4; Fiala and Viktora, 1970).

E. Lymphomyeloid Complex (LMC)

The physiological nature of the LMC is very complex and poorly understood. The guinea pig has been used extensively to elucidate LMC function; consequently, considerable basic physiological data have accrued. The guinea pig is particularly suited for studies of the LMC for the following reasons. (1) Unlike many species which, compared to human infants, are very immature at birth, the neonatal guinea pig possesses a very mature LMC (Ernström, 1970). (2) Hormonally and immunologically the guinea pig more nearly resembles man than do rats or mice (Bellanti *et al.*, 1965; Shewell and Long, 1956). (3) The cervical thymus of the guinea pig is easily accessible to surgical and measurement procedures without grossly modifying the animal through intrathoracic intervention (Ernström, 1970).

1. Lymphocyte Production

Yoffey (1960) reported the lymphocyte output of various organs of the standard "400-gm" Dunkin–Hartley guinea pig

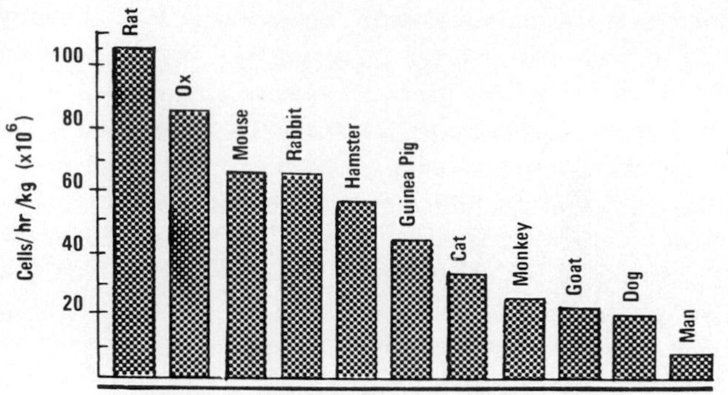

Fig. 5. Thoracic duct lymphocyte output of various mammals (from Reinhardt, 1964).

(cells × 10^6/day): mesenteric nodes, 600; cervical nodes, 264; thymus, 470; and spleen, 336. Reinhardt (1964) summarized lymphocyte production in several species (Fig. 5).

Thoracic duct lymphocyte output, measured at approximately 373 × 10^6 cells/day, is often used as an index of total lymphocyte production. Yoffey (1956) cautioned against use of this assumption because (1) the duct drains the abdominal area almost exclusively; (2) the head, neck, limbs, and thorax have alternate drainage routes, and (3) lymphocytes may enter the blood directly, not by way of lymphatics. Nevertheless, based on the above total daily lymphocyte production and a calculated total circulating lymphocyte population of 91 × 10^6 for a 272-gm guinea pig, it was estimated that the daily replacement factor for lymphocytes is at least 4.1. The daily replacement rate is inversely related to animal size: rat, 5.0 to 6.0; rabbit, 5.0; cat, 0.5 to 3.5; dog, 2.0; and man, 1.0. Thus, daily lymphocyte production in the guinea pig is markedly greater than in man (Yoffey, 1956). For further information on the lymphocyte see Section I, F, 4, a.

2. Thymus Production of Lymphocytes

The guinea pig thymus is a major contributor of circulating lymphocytes. The output of small lymphocytes from the thymus is sufficient to exchange circulating small lymphocytes 3.7 times per day (Ernström and Larsson, 1967). The following routes and fates of thymocytes (small lymphocytes of thymic origin) have been suggested.

a. In Situ Degeneration. Sainte-Marie and Peng (1971a) demonstrated, with [^{3}H]thymidine labeling, that large numbers of newly formed thymocytes migrate into large thymic cysts and degenerate. Jolly (1923) established the existence of thymic medullary cysts associated with Hassal's corpuscles. The cyst-forming phenomenon is negligible in rats and mice. The atypical *in situ* degeneration phenomenon of the guinea pig should be recognized when using studies of the lymphomyeloid complex.

b. Lymphatic Emigration. Kotani *et al.* (1966) considered lymphatic vessels to be a main route for transfer of thymocytes to the general circulation of the guinea pig. They demonstrated an extensive efferent lymphatic network around the thymic artery and suggested that pulsation of the artery enhanced lymph flow. In contrast, most species possess no, or few, thymic lymphatics.

c. Venous Emigration. Ernström *et al.* (1965) first demonstrated absolute venous emigration of thymocytes by comparing cellular concentration of thymus vein blood and carotid artery blood. Thirty percent of all small lymphocytes produced in the guinea pig thymus are released into the thymic vein (Ernström and Sandberg, 1970). The role of medullary vessels in thymocyte export was questioned by Kotani *et al.* (1966). Sainte-Marie and Peng (1971b) noted guinea pig thymic medullary venules are less developed and have fewer diapedizing cells than those of the rat. Thymic production and release of small lymphocytes has been reviewed by Ernström (1963), Larsson (1966a,b), Ernström and Larsson (1967, 1969), and Ernström and Sandberg (1970).

3. Other Thymic Physiology

Most thymic tissue of 12-month-old guinea pigs is involuted and contains fat deposits (Ernström and Larsson, 1970). Thymectomy has a less dramatic effect in guinea pigs than in mice or rats, due to the guinea pigs more mature lymphomyeloid system at birth. Thymectomy, however, reduces lymphoid organ weights, produces lymphopenia (Ernström, 1965b; Ernström and Larsson, 1966), and reduces output of thoracic duct lymphocytes (Reinhardt and Yoffey, 1956).

Administration of moderate doses of thyroxine causes lymphatic hyperplasia without increase in thymic weight in the guinea pig, while large doses cause thymic involution (Ernström, 1965a; Ernström and Gyllensten, 1959; Gyllensten, 1953).

The guinea pig, ferret, monkey, and man are considered corticosteroid-resistant species because treatment with steroids does not markedly affect thymic physiology or peripheral lymphocyte count. The hamster, mouse, rabbit, and rat have a dramatic decrease in thymic weight and peripheral lymphocyte counts consequent to steroid therapy (Calman, 1972).

Thymic blood flow increases as the gland enlarges with age. However, flow in microliters per minute per milligram thymic weight remains nearly constant from birth to 6 months of age (Ernström and Larsson, 1970).

F. Bone Marrow

The guinea pig has been used extensively in studies of bone marrow physiology because: (1) its marrow is similar to that of man (Epstein and Tompkins, 1943; Innes *et al.*, 1949), (2) its marrow is easily dispersed giving uniform cell suspensions (Yoffey, 1956), and (3) its cells stain well and are more easily identified than those of the rat (Yoffey, 1966). According to Yoffey and Courtice (1970), the most complete quantitative information on bone marrow thus far available was derived from studies of guinea pigs.

1. Marrow Volume and Distribution

Critical studies of bone marrow require data on marrow volume, content, and distribution. Hudson (1958) established bone marrow volumes of guinea pigs and found a linear relationship to the logarithm of body weight. Mean total marrow volume of 400-gm guinea pigs was 7.014 (± 0.348 SD) ml. Marrow was distributed: 19.5%, skull; 31.5%, trunk; and 48.9%, limbs. Apparently the guinea pig skull contained a considerably higher percentage of the total bone marrow than did the skull of adult man or rabbit; for the limbs the reverse was true. The mean red marrow volume for the "400-gm" guinea pig was 6.249 (± 0.446 SD) ml; approximately 89% of the total marrow volume. Total marrow volume approximated 2.5% of body weight in the 1-week-old animal, whereas in the adult it formed only 1%. Figure 6 is a graph of the relationship of total marrow volume to body weight.

2. Marrow Blood Volume

Using a ^{59}Fe-labeled red cell dilution technique, coupled with liquid nitrogen freezing, Osmond and Everett (1965) estimated the mean volumes of whole blood and circulating RBC's in bone marrow and other organs. The relative vascularity of bone marrow exceeded that of thymus and lymph node, but was considerably less than that of the spleen. Further, the mean blood content per gram of femoral marrow was higher than that of humeral or tibial marrow. Using bone marrow volume data from Hudson (1958), these workers estimated the total blood volume of the marrow of a "400-gm" guinea pig to be 0.41 ml or 1.72% of the whole body blood volume. Bone marrow contained approximately 2.0% of the whole body circulating red cell mass.

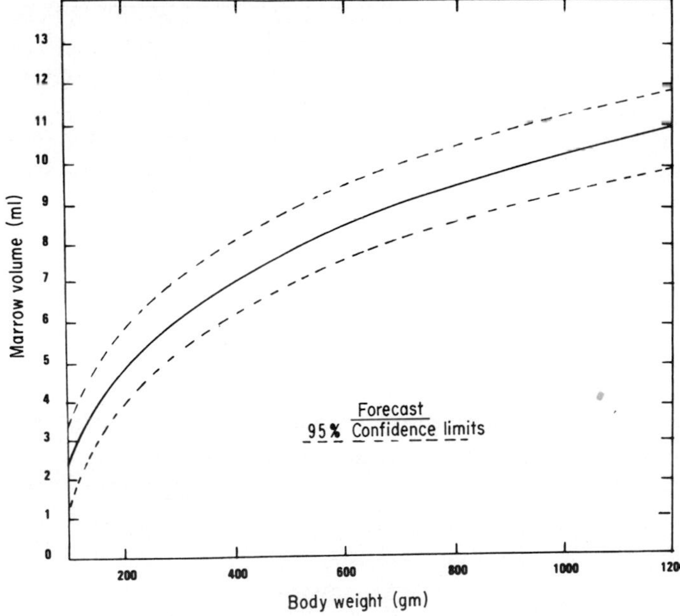

Fig. 6. Forecast of marrow volume for guinea pigs of known body weight, based on 120 observations (from Yoffey 1958; after Hudson, 1958).

3. Myelogram

It is difficult to present a typical myelogram for the guinea pig because of variations in terminology and methods of classification. Hudson *et al.* (1963) reported myelograms of 25 "400-gm" male Dunkin–Hartley guinea pigs. There was no significant difference between myelograms of Dunkin–Hartley and Bahndorf strains (Griffiths and Rieke, 1969). Baranski (1971) reported the following percentages for the principal cell catagories of guinea pig bone marrow: erythroblasts, 26.7%; myeloid, 63.3%; lymphocytes, 4.6%; and reticulum cells, 5.4%. The myeloid:erythroid ratio ranges from 1.5:1 (Harris *et al.*, 1954) to 1.9:1 (Dineen and Adams, 1970). The cellularity of bone marrow from large guinea pigs was significantly less than that of smaller animals (Hudson, 1959).

4. Hematopoiesis

The hematopoietic centers of the newborn guinea pig are rather mature and resemble the human infant more so than those of the rat neonate (Lucarelli and Butturini, 1967). As in the human neonate the primitive undifferentiated syncytial-type cell is not seen in bone marrow of newborn guinea pigs (Lucarelli *et al.*, 1968).

a. Lymphocytes. Guinea pig bone marrow contains large numbers of small lymphocytes scattered throughout the marrow rather than clumped in nodules (Yoffey, 1956). Marrow of the 1- to 2-day-old guinea pig is predominantly lymphocytic, changing to an essentially erythrogenic function in the 3- to 38-day-old animal (Fand and Gordon, 1957). In the standard "400-gm" guinea pig the lymphocytes and transitional cells make up about one-third of the total nucleated cells in bone marrow (Yoffey and Courtice, 1970). Yoffey (1956) calculated that marrow storage of lymphocytes is about eight times the daily output.

Based on life-span studies, the bone marrow lymphocytes of the guinea pig are quite heterogenous. Most of the small lymphocyte population is maintained in a dynamic steady state with an average turnover time of 3 days or less (Osmond and Everett, 1964). This turnover rate compares closely with that of the rat, but is substantially more rapid than in the dog and man. Rosse (1971) demonstrated, through [^{3}H] thymidine labeling, that about 14% of the small lymphocytes have a slow turnover rate and represent a population distinct from rapid turnover small lymphocytes. Seven percent of the marrow lymphocytes survive at least 4 weeks. Such long-lived lymphocytes have not been demonstrated in the bone marrow of the rat (Rosse, 1971).

Yoshida and Osmond (1971) demonstrated that large lymphocytes (transitional cells) of the guinea pig bone marrow are capable of sustaining the population of small lymphocytes and may represent the principal precusor for small lymphocytes.

b. Erythropoiesis. Bone marrow of the guinea pig, unlike that of the rat, is actively erythropoietic at birth. Lucarelli and Butturini (1967) reported that relative erythrocytosis with normocytes can be seen in the newborn guinea pig. They also demonstrated that the response of the neonate guinea pig erythron to stimuli is similar to that of the adult, e.g., depression of erythropoiesis following starvation or bilateral nephrectomy. Such response in the rat is delayed until after the nineteenth day of life.

Compared to man, the guinea pig has a more rapid maturation cycle for nucleated red cells and a considerably shorter life for mature cells (Yoffey, 1958; see Section B,1,e). Erythropoietic activity reaches a peak at maturity in the guinea pig, then gradually diminishes as the animal approaches senility. Long bone marrow from senile animals contains only 58% of the erythroid cell numbers counted in mature guinea pigs. Since the peripheral blood concentration of RBC's did not diminish, it was suggested that erythropoiesis must shift to the flat bones in older guinea pigs (Fand and Gordon, 1957).

Early theories attributed the source of iron for fetal development to maternal erythrocyte hemolysis in the placenta. More recent work has demonstrated that maternal plasma is an adequate source for transferrin (Vosburgh and Flexner, 1950). Placental transfer of iron is an active process dependent on cellular metabolism in the guinea pig. Active transfer of iron across the placenta and high fetal plasma iron-binding capacity creates a higher concentration of iron on the fetal side of the placenta than the maternal side (Wong and Morgan, 1973). Contrary to the human, rat, and rabbit fetus near term, guinea pig fetal plasma has a significantly greater iron-binding capacity than maternal plasma. This difference is possibly related to the high degree of maturity of the newborn guinea pig compared to the newborn of the other species. With regard to transferrin synthesis, it has been suggested the guinea pig fetus, near term, corresponds in maturity with the 6- to 12-month-old human infant (Wong and Morgan, 1973).

Iron is believed to be supplied to the erythroblast of man and guinea pig by a process called rhopheocytosis (micropinocytosis). Tanaka (1970) demonstrated, through electron microscopy, that the process of moving ferritin-laden vesicles across the erythroblast wall is probably bidirectional in the guinea pig and nonexistent in rats and rabbits. Tanaka and Brecher (1971) suggested that the guinea pig may be a suitable model for study of ferritin uptake.

c. Granulocytes. Fand and Gordon (1957) demonstrated an absolute increase in numbers of marrow eosinophils with advancing age in the guinea pig. They cautioned that commensal parasitism may be a contributory factor. Granulocytes increased with age, thus, increasing the myeloid:erythroid ratio.

G. Platelets and Blood Coagulation

1. Platelets

a. Platelet Numbers. In guinea pig peripheral blood platelet numbers range from 3.4×10^5 to $10.0 \times 10^5/\text{mm}^3$ with a mean of about $650{,}000/\text{mm}^3$ (Table VI).

b. Aggregation. According to Mills (1970), the physiology of platelet aggregation is quite variable among species. Although a good model for study of human platelets has not been found, Mills suggested that those of the baboon, cat, and guinea pig are functionally more similar to human platelets than are those of the rabbit, rat, dog, or larger domestic animals.

Adenosine diphosphate (ADP) is the only physiological substance known to directly stimulate platelet aggregation. Adenosine will inhibit aggregation of human, rabbit, and pig platelets. However, in guinea pig platelets, which are particularly responsive to the aggregation effect of ADP, there is no adenosine inhibition of ADP-induced aggregation. In most species, ADP is believed to be released from platelets through an interaction with epinephrine, 5-hydroxytryptamine (5-HT), or other chemicals. In the guinea pig, however, neither epinephrine nor 5-HT stimulates aggregation and it is suggested that ADP may act directly as the aggregating substance (Constantine, 1966).

Table VI
Platelet Counts ($\times 10^5/\text{mm}^3$) in the Guinea Pig

No. of animals	Mean[a]	Conditions described	Reference
80	6.2 ± 0.12	♂ and ♀, 400–600 gm	Hurt and Krigman (1970)
8	4.9 ± 0.39	♂, 250 gm	Barkhan and Howard (1959)
53	7.1 (5.4–10.0)	♂, 300–570 gm	Bilbey and Micol (1955)
8	6.4 (3.4–8.6)	No description	Ledingham and Bedson (1915)

[a]Means are given with ± SE or with range set in parentheses.

c. Nucleotides. Chemical and ultrastructural analysis of isolated storage organelles of guinea pig platelets indicated that adenosine triphosphate (ATP) content is about equal to that found in rabbit platelets, but that it is stored without major amounts of 5-HT. The 5-HT/ATP quotient of the guinea pig platelet was 0.06 compared to 2.7 in the rabbit. (Da Prada *et al.*, 1971).

Mills and Thomas (1969) found that both guinea pig and rabbit platelets contained significantly less ADP than human platelets. A comparative study of nucleotide content of human, guinea pig, and rabbit platelets was conducted by Goetz *et al.* (1971). Results of this study indicated that the nucleotide content of platelets in the guinea pig resemble those of man more so than those of the rabbit.

Table VII
Levels of Selected Procoagulants and Platelets from Guinea Pigs[a]

	No. of animals	Mean	Range	SD
Platelets ($mm^3 \times 10^3$)	80	616	415–920	±104
Factor VIII (U/100 ml)	67	102	63–142	±38
Partial thromboplastin (sec)	65	44	40–49	±2
One-stage prothrombin (sec)	60	25.2	43.5–28.0	±1.5
Two-stage prothrombin (Iowa units)	44	193	106–243	±29
Euglobulin lysis (min)	46	88	30–300	±55
Fibrinogen (mg/100 ml)	42	387	263–572	±90
Factor V (U/100 ml)	14	82	55–105	±19
Factor IX (U/100 ml)	14	104	67–141	±21

[a]Hurt and Krigman (1970).

2. Blood Coagulation

a. Procoagulants. With respect to procoagulants, guinea pig blood differs in several ways from that of other species. Guinea pig plasma is about one-half as rich in prothrombin as that of the rat and dog. Along with man, the guinea pig has a very long prothrombin conversion time (4 minutes) which may be related to the incidence of a number of different hematological diseases in these species (Warner *et al.*, 1939). Chenkin *et al.* (1959) reported a one-stage prothrombin time range of 32 to 45 seconds, which represents a considerably lower prothrombin activity than man. They suggested that the guinea pig may be useful in studying mechanisms involved in coumarin anticoagulation action. The guinea pig had the longest prothrombin time of several species studied (rabbit, dog, rat, hamster, pony, goat, cat, and man) (Hwang and Wosilait, 1970). The guinea pig had the least Factor VII (proconvertin) and was among the three lowest species in Factor V (proaccelerin) levels. Chenkin and Weiner (1965) also reported low levels of Factor VII in the normal guinea pig.

Astrup *et al.* (1970) reported a complete absence of tissue thromboplastin activity in the lungs of guinea pigs. The lungs of most species are rich in thromboplastin. Few tissues are low in thromboplastin, e.g., human synovial membranes and heart valves. According to Astrup, such thromboplastin distribution, concomitant with low fibrinolytic activity, places the guinea pigs in a class by itself. It should be noted that their methods used human plasma and that Quick (1936) found extracts of guinea pig brain and lung enhanced coagulation of guinea pig blood, although they had little effect on blood of other species. Thromboplastin of guinea pig lung may require a unique plasma cofactor to initiate significant coagulation. The atypical coagulation behavior of guinea pig blood may involve a balanced combination between (1) a near complete lack of Factor VII, retarding extrinsic coagulation, (2) an excess of Factor XI (plasma thromboplastin antecedent), enhancing the intrinsic coagulation system, and (3) a definite lack of tissue thromboplastin, unneeded in view of low Factor VII levels. Perhaps low levels of tissue thromboplastin provide a teleological explanation for the higher levels of Factor XI which would enhance the intrinsic coagulation system of the guinea pig (Astrup *et al.*, 1970).

Hurt and Krigman (1970) conducted a critical analysis of the procoagulants in the guinea pig (Table VII). Dodds and Pickering (1972) have also reported normative data on coagulation in the guinea pig.

b. Fibrinolysin System. The fibrinolytic system of the guinea pig differs considerably from the fibrinolytic system of plasma of other laboratory animals and man (Gryglewski *et al.*, 1968). Proactivator A and B have been identified for the human being, but Takada *et al.* (1969) were unable to demonstrate significant amounts of either A or B in guinea pig plasma. Latallo *et al.* (1959) reported that spontaneous activation of plasmin in dilute guinea pig serum at pH 5.3 is a highly specific trait of the specie. They suggest that a plasmin–antiplasmin complex may be a chief component of the guinea pig fibrinolytic system. Compared to most species, the mature guinea pig has very low levels of plasminogen activator in its lungs (Astrup *et al.*, 1970). The changes in pulmonary plasminogen activator activity in the developing guinea pig are presented in Fig. 7. Ambrus *et al.* (1965) theorized that the preterm increase in pulmonary plasminogen activator represents a physiological protective mechanism intended to eliminate pulmonary fibrin deposits which may occur following the initial pulmonary expansion and hemodynamic readjustments at birth.

Compared to the human being, the guinea pig (and ox, rabbit, and cat) has low tissue levels of plasminogen (Albrechtsen, 1957). Lieberman (1959) found the lungs of rabbit and guinea pig to be totally deficient in plasminogen activity while the rat had readily demonstrable levels.

Reduced proteolytic potential of the guinea pig lung may

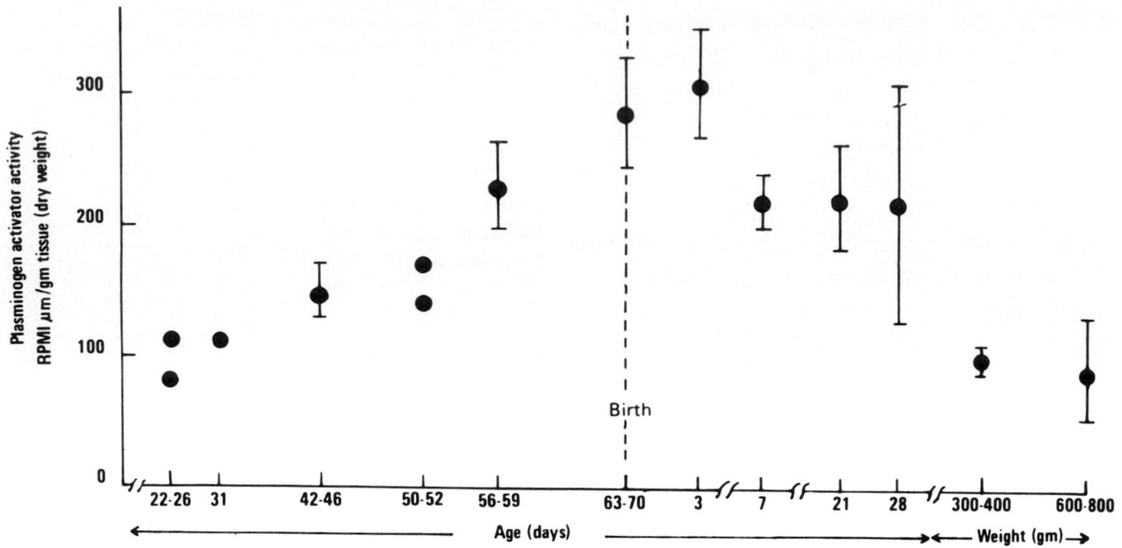

Fig. 7. Development of pulmonary plasminogen activator activity (PAA) in guinea pigs. RPMI units—see Ambrus *et al.* (1960) for explanation. (From Ambrus *et al.*, 1965.)

explain its greater resistance, compared to the rat, to alveolar proteinosis after exposure to silica dusts (Gross and deTreville, 1968). The absence of thromboplastin in the guinea pig lung and low plasminogen activator make it unlikely that the effects of tissue repair in the guinea pig lung would simulate the human respiratory distress syndrome (Astrup *et al.*, 1970).

c. Coagulopathy Model. The guinea pig, bearing an intracerebrally transplanted glioblastoma multiforme (HC 305) tumor, is an ideal model for study of the effects of neoplasm on the clotting mechanism. Transplanted animals usually survive 35 to 55 days, and alterations in intravascular coagulation and primary fibrinogenolysis begin to appear during the last 2 weeks (Hurt *et al.*, 1970).

III. CARDIOVASCULAR SYSTEM

A. Blood Distribution

1. Plasma and Blood Volumes

Guinea pig plasma and blood volumes are approximately 3.88 and 6.96 ml per 100 gm of body weight, respectively (Table VIII). Constable (1963) used Evans Blue (T-1824) dye to determine that plasma and blood volumes vary considerably with body weight of growing guinea pigs (Fig. 8). Plasma volume was highest at birth (5.73% of body weight) and decreased steadily to 3.0% at 900 gm of body weight. Blood volume followed a similar pattern, decreasing from 11.5% to 5.86% during the same period.

Table VIII
Plasma and Blood Volume of the Guinea Pig[a]

No. of animals	Plasma volume (ml/100 gm body weight)	Blood volume (ml/100 gm body weight)	Conditions described	Reference
13	4.39 ± 0.29	7.42 ± 0.27	♂, Hartley, 350–600 gm, ^{51}Cr-labeled RBC's, [^{125}I] albumin	Baker and Schaefer (1969)
10	3.82 ± 0.01	5.72 ± 0.02	♂, 860 gm, Evans blue (T-1824)	Kutscher (1968)
6	4.22 ± 0.06	7.81 ± 0.26	♂, 505–602 gm, ^{131}I-labeled serum protein, fasted 30 hours	Bocci and Viti (1965)
3	4.15 ± 0.39	6.89 ± 0.34	♂, 505–602 gm, ^{131}I-labeled serum protein, fed	Bocci and Viti (1965)
10	3.31 ± 0.07	–	♂, English Short Hair, 1073 ± 20 gm, [^{131}I] albumin	Edmondson and Wyburn (1963)
10	3.59± 0.07	–	♀, English Short Hair, 929 ± 18 gm, [^{131}I] albumin	Edmondson and Wyburn (1963)
18	–	7.20 ± 0.07	♂, Mill Hill strain, 250–750 gm, Evans blue (T-1824)	Ancill (1956)
13	3.94 ± 0.37	7.53 ± 0.20	♂, 414–543 gm, [^{131}I] globulin	Masouredis and Melcher (1951)
18	–	6.40 ± 0.12	270–480 gm, vital red	Went and Drinker (1929)

[a]Mean ± SE.

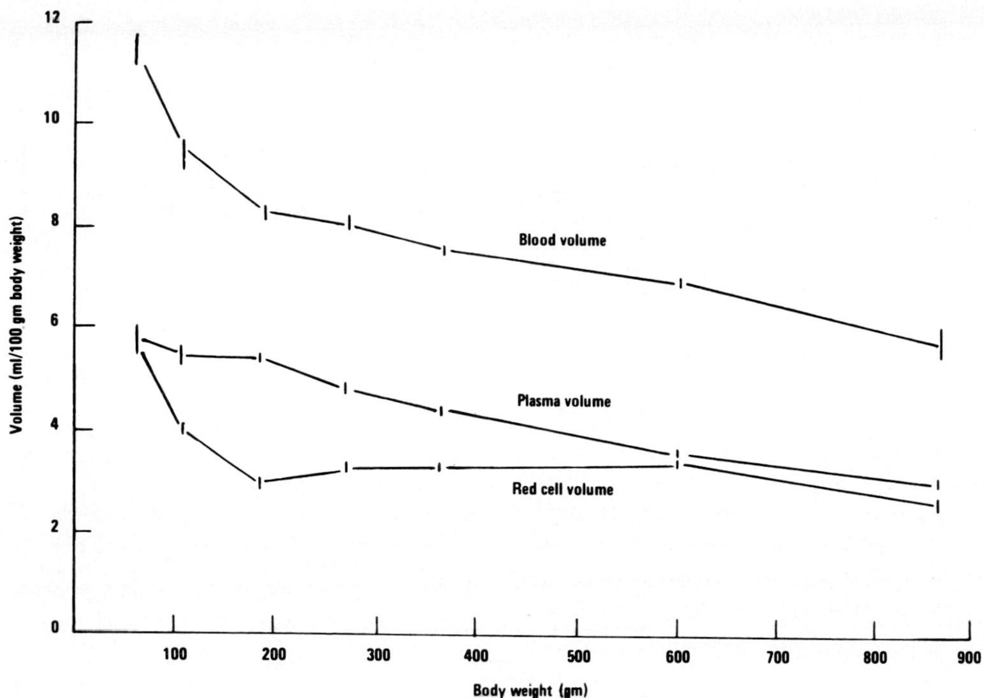

Fig. 8. Mean blood volumes, plasma volumes, and red cell volumes of guinea pigs expressed as a percentage of body weight. The height of each symbol indicates the standard error of the mean. Each graph in this figure represents the results of 105 experiments (from Constable, 1963).

2. Blood Content and Mean Plasma Volume of Organs and Tissues

Bosse and Wassermann (1970) determined the blood content and mean plasma volume of various organs and tissues of the guinea pig (Table IX). Measurements were made using ^{131}I-labeled human plasma albumin.

B. Heart Rate and Blood Pressure

1. Heart Rate

Mikisková and Mikiska (1968) constructed a normogram of heart rate values in the normal, restrained male guinea pig. Female and young animals also fit the normogram which can

Table IX
Blood Content of Guinea Pig Tissues

Tissue	Mean blood content (% of wet wt, ± SE, n = 9)	Tissue	Mean plasma content (ml/100 gm of wet wt)
Cerebrum, left side	1.98 ± 0.11	Brain	1.15
Cerebellum, left side	2.75 ± 0.18	Liver	8.6
Medulla oblongata	3.02 ± 0.21	Kidney	11.5
Spinal cord	2.45 ± 0.22	Lungs	12.0
Sciatic nerve	2.17 ± 0.24	Atrium	9.1
Fat tissue (mesenteric)	1.54 ± 0.11	Ventricle	5.4
Diaphragm	3.79 ± 0.18	Diaphragm	2.2
Ileum	4.22 ± 0.27	Intestine	2.4
Ventricle	9.33 ± 0.32	Spleen	6.8
Atrium	15.79 ± 0.70		
Liver	14.88 ± 0.76		
Kidney	19.84 ± 1.06		
Adrenals	11.35 ± 0.46		
Lungs	20.69 ± 2.98		
Spleen	11.68 ± 0.44		

[a]After Bosse and Wassermann (1970).

be derived by the following equation: log (heart rate) = 0.47 log (weight) + 1.226. A marked cardiac arrhythmia was found in less than 5% of restrained guinea pigs. More rarely there were randomly occurring ventricular extrasystoles.

Fara and Catlett (1971) used an implanted telemetry device to record the electrocardiogram (EKG) of 28 free-ranging, 463- to 544-gm guinea pigs. They recorded a mean rate of 275.5 beats per minute as a normal resting heart rate. A range of 229 to 319 beats per minute demonstrated wide individual variation. They also reported that the guinea pig, while often appearing quiescent, is keenly aware of environmental changes as reflected in heart rate fluctuations. Introduction of a rat into a guinea pig cage caused a distinct bradycardia (25% less than resting rate) which could be blocked with atropine.

Eklund *et al.* (1972) reported that the heart rate was significantly ($P < 0.001$) slower in summer than winter. Dawe and Morrison (1955) found a direct relationship between the duration of the cardiac cycle (R–R interval) and body weight (W) in small mammals. They demonstrated that the following relationships exist in anesthetized and unanesthetized animals, respectively:

$$\text{R–R} = 0.052\ W^{0.22} \quad \text{and} \quad \text{R–R} = 0.047\ W^{0.25}$$

Adolph (1971) characterized the ontogeny of heart rate control in the fetal guinea pig. Other reports of heart rate in the guinea pig are presented in Table X.

2. Blood Pressure

Spitzer and Edelmann (1971) reported that the mean carotid artery pressure increased gradually from 41 mm Hg at 1 day of age to 61 mm Hg at 49 days of age. They further noted that there was less than a 10% decrease in arterial pressure consequent to anesthetization (thiobarbituric acid). Marshall and Hanna (1956) measured the end pressure of the carotid artery in eight, 200- to 1000-gm, Hartley strain guinea pigs under ether, pentobarbital, or procaine anesthesia. They reported the following averages (mm Hg): systolic, 76.7; diastolic, 46.8; and calculated mean, 57.2. They further found that only rarely did the arterial pressure exceed 100 mm Hg and systole lasted for a longer unit of time than reported for other small animals. Reid (1958) commented that perhaps the guinea pig heart was capable of more rapid filling and aortic outflow than has been described in other small animals. A typical carotid artery pressure curve is shown in Fig. 9.

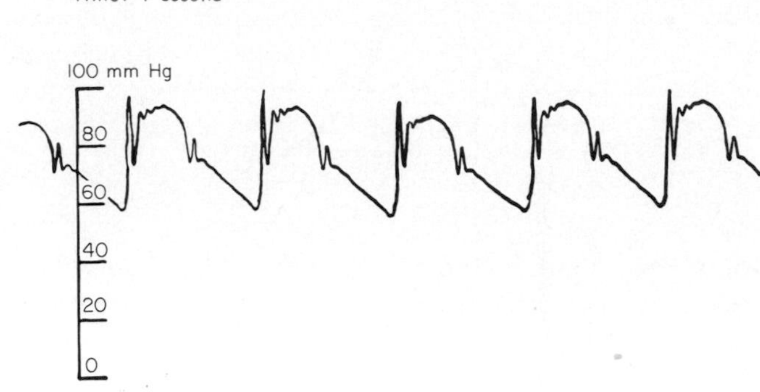

Fig. 9. Record of carotid pressures of a Hartley strain guinea pig weighing about 1000 gm under procaine anesthesia, conscious, and turned to the prone position 2 minutes previously. Mean blood pressure = 68 mm Hg, systolic = 88–94, diastolic = 55–58, pulse rate = 260/minute, respiration=64/minute, cardiac cycle=0.232 second, diastole=0.118 second, systole = 49% of cycle, late diastole rate of decent = 179 mm/second (from Marshall and Hanna, 1956).

Right ventricular pressure was measured in 49 adult (700–1000 gm) mixed sex guinea pigs by Lynch *et al.* (1967). Immediately after cannulation, under pentobarbital anesthesia they recorded a mean pressure of 13.4 (±4.6 SD) mm Hg.

C. Electrocardiogram (EKG)

Unlike other small laboratory rodents such as mice, rats, and hamsters, the EKG wave-form of the guinea pig is very similar to human EKG tracings (Mikisková and Mikiska, 1968; Petelenz, 1971). Because of the generally quiescent attitude of the

Table X
Heart Rate of the Guinea Pig

No. of animals	Beats/minute (mean ± SD or range)	Conditions described	Reference
38	260 ± 40	370–590 gm, anesthetized	Petelenz (1971)
8	260	200–1000 gm. Hartley, anesthetized	Marshall and Hanna (1956)
10	240–310	Conscious, standing unrestrained	Farmer and Levy (1968)
34	335 ± 33.3	♂, 300–500 gm, restrained	Zeman and Wilber (1965b)
7	260 ± 11	♀, 822–1055 gm, unrestrained	Richtarik *et al.* (1965)
	230–300	300–750 gm	Altman and Dittmer (1964)
	269 (225–312)	234 gm, anesthetized	Altman and Dittmer (1964)
10	260 ± 30	593 ± 166 gm, anesthetized	Lombard (1952)
45	301 ± 80.5	♂, restrained, supine	O'Bryant *et al.* (1949)

guinea pig, it has been possible to get continuous, stable EKG tracings while the animal stands unrestrained on plate electrodes. Such success is not usually found with other common laboratory animals (Farmer and Levy, 1968). Reported values for various components of the EKG are presented in Table XI.

1. P Wave

The P wave is most distinct in Lead II and has a very stable duration (Petelenz, 1971). Pratt (1938) and Lombard (1952), using standard leads, found the P wave is usually positive in deflection.

2. QRS Complex

Mikisková and Mikiska (1968) reported that the QRS complex was usually diphasic and can be designated "R–S" type, the first deflection being of higher voltage in most leads. In the extremity leads, the polarity of deflections generally corresponded to the standard position of the heart axis in the human EKG. Typical EKG tracings of three orthogonal leads with measured components are presented in Fig. 10.

3. T Wave

The T wave of the guinea pig EKG was shown to be distinct from the QRS complex as in man (Lombard, 1952). It was often negative in lead I and always positive in leads II and III

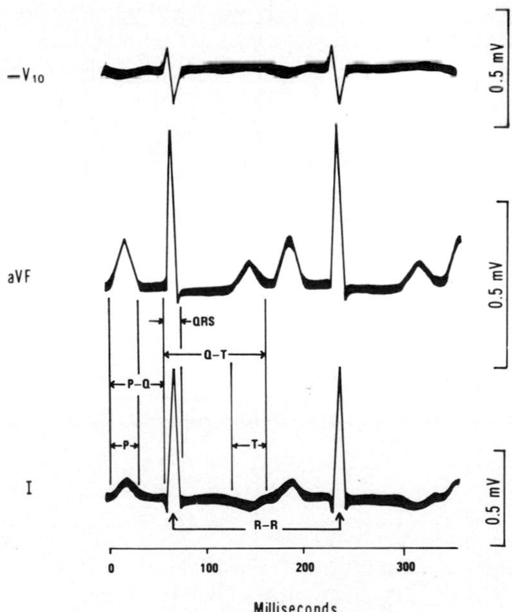

Fig. 10. Three orthogonal leads of a normal electrocardiogram of the guinea pig (age, 2 to 4 months; body weight, 400 to 650 gm). $-V_{10}$ signifies opposite polarity to conventional V_{10} lead. Heart rate [mean (± SD) beats /minute] = 346 + 27.4. Time relations [mean (± SD) msec]: P = 30 ± 3.0, P–Q = 56 ± 4.2, QRS = 17 ± 2.2, Q–T = 107 ± 6.2, T = 35 ± 3.6, R–R = 173 ± 13.7 (after Mikisková, 1971).

(Pratt, 1938). Its voltage was small, not exceeding 0.1 mV in 90% of animals tested. The maximal recorded deflection was 0.2 mV (Petelenz, 1971). The T wave has been shown to sometimes be diphasic, the first phase being of opposite polarity to the R wave. The S–T interval in the guinea pig EKG is distinct and at least 0.05 seconds in duration. An outstanding feature is that it deviates no more than 0.05 mV from an isoelectric position (Mikisková and Mikiska, 1968). Lepeschkin (1965) compared species and reported that "the section Hystricognathi, which includes Hystricoidea (porcupines) and Cavioidea (guinea pig and agouti), shows a slightly longer Q–aT interval than that of the Carnivora, with a tendency to peaking of T wave." He reports this also applies to the suborder Duplicidentata or Lagomorphae, which includes the rabbit.

4. Electrical Axis

Pratt (1938) reported a range of 0° to +76° for the mean electrical axis of the heart in the restrained, standing guinea pig. Eighty percent of his recordings were between +20° and +60°; 50% between +30° and +45°. Using anesthetized animals, Petelenz (1971) recorded a mean QRS vector direction of +20° to +80° (maximum deviation was −20° to +115°).

5. Seasonal Variation

The seasonal variation in time components of the guinea pig EKG was investigated by Eklund *et al.* (1972). They found no major differences between P–R and QRS durations, but shorter Q–T durations were recorded during the winter when heart rate was significantly ($P < 0.001$) more rapid.

D. Heart Sounds

Luisada *et al.* (1944) studied heart sounds in several laboratory and domestic animals including the guinea pig. The first heart sound in the guinea pig follows immediately after the R wave and consists of 1 or 2 slow vibrations followed by 3 or 4 quick vibrations of great magnitude. It lasts about 0.03 seconds. Sometimes it is preceded by a fourth heart sound due to atrial contraction. The second heart sound lasts from 0.02 to 0.03 seconds and consists of 2 or 3 quick vibrations of less magnitude than the first sound. No third heart sound was detected. Graphic comparison of the EKG and heart sounds of the guinea pig is presented in Fig. 11.

E. Other Studies

The guinea pig atria is frequently used for physiological and pharmacological studies of action potential, contraction strength, and their interrelationships (Fozzard and Sleator, 1967; Sleator *et al.*, 1964).

Table XI
Time Components of the Guinea Pig Electrocardiogram

	References						
	Petelenz (1971)	Farmer and Levy (1968)	Richtarik *et al.* (1965)	Zeman and Wilber (1965b)	Lombard (1952)	O'Bryant *et al.* (1949)	Pratt (1938)
No. of animals	38	10	7	34	10	45	57
Body weight (gm)	370–590	–	822–1055	300-500	593 ± 166	–	–
Heart rate (beats/min)	260 ±40	240–310	261 (214–311)	335 ± 33.3	–	301	327 (232–400)
R–R interval (sec)	–	0.18	–	0.181 ± 0.0188	0.065 ± 0.005	–	0.183 (0.162–0.288)
P–R interval (sec)	–	0.07	–	0.054 ± 0.0059	–	0.072	–
P–Q interval (sec)	0.060 ± 0.005	–	0.055 (0.044–0.068)	–	–	–	0.036 (0.024–0.055)
Q–T interval (sec)	0.130 ± 0.015	0.11	0.116 (0.106–0.144)	0.1077 ± 0.0132	–	–	–
S–T interval (sec)	–	–	0.078 (0.006–0.098)	0.083 ± 0.0193	0.033 ± 0.001	–	0.059 (0.041–0.084)
QRS duration (sec)	0.030	0.02	0.038 (0.033–0.046)	0.024 ± 0.004	–	–	0.013 (0.008–0.021)
P wave duration (sec)	–	–	0.022 (0.015–0.028)	0.030 ± 0.0048	–	–	0.016 (0.008–0.025)
T wave duration (sec)	0.050 ± 0.009	–	0.040 (0.035–0.050)	0.035 ± 0.0048	–	–	0.022 (0.013–0.034)
QRS amplitude (mV)	1.5 ± 0.4	–	–	–	–	0.665	–
Lead I	–	0.6	–	–	–	–	–
Lead II	–	0.4	–	–	–	–	–
T_2 amplitude (mV)	–	–	–	–	–	0.062	–
Conditions	Ether anesthetized	Conscious, standing, unrestrained	Conscious standing, unrestrained	Conscious, prone, restrained	Anesthetized, upright	Conscious, supine, restrained	Conscious upright, restrained

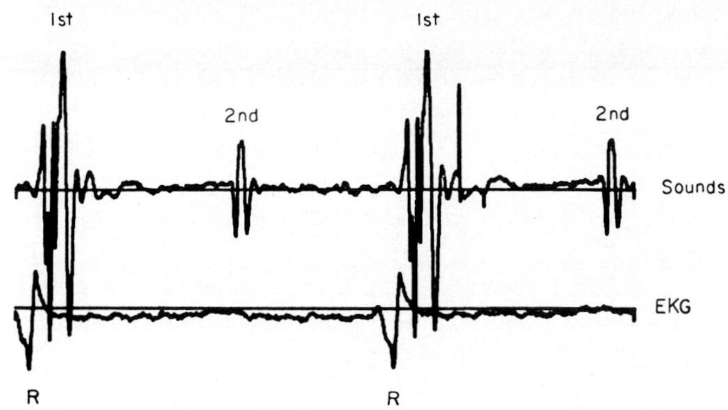

Fig. 11. Guinea pig heart sounds showing the relationship in time with the EKG (from Wilton-Davies, 1972).

The role of surrounding oxygen tension in contraction of smooth muscle and closure of the ductus arteriosus was first studied in the newborn guinea pig (Kennedy and Clark, 1942). Subsequently, the newborn guinea pig has been commonly used in studies of this physiological phenomena (Fay and Jöbsis, 1972; Gillman and Burton, 1966; Ikeda *et al.*, 1973). Within 24 to 72 hours after birth, the duct no longer will dilate in response to hypoxia and will remain "irreversibly" closed thereafter (Fay and Cooke, 1972).

Östman and Sjöstrand (1971) found that heavy physical training with cardiac hypertrophy caused an increase in catacholamine levels in the heart of the guinea pig.

IV. REPRODUCTIVE SYSTEM

A. Introduction

The guinea pig is particularly well suited for studies in reproductive physiology because of easy handling, distinct signs of estrus, and behavior related fairly distinctly to physical changes in the reproductive tract (Young *et al.*, 1935). Of all the small laboratory mammals, the guinea pig reproductive system most resembles man in that it has a long cycle, ovulates spontaneously, and has an actively secreting corpus luteum (Reed and Hounslow, 1971). Under laboratory conditions, domestic guinea pigs are polyestrous, nonseasonal breeders, although slight seasonal variations in reproductive performance have been reported (Rowlands, 1949; Stockard and Papanicolaou, 1917; Wright, 1960).

B. Puberty (Female)

The female guinea pig does not exhibit its first heat until after 30 days of age. Young *et al.* (1939) observed 617 females through 2102 cycles over a 2- year period and recorded a mean age at first heat of 67.8 (± 21.5 SD) days (range = 33 to 134 days). The average age of first rupture of the vaginal membrane was slightly younger: 58.2 days (range = 33 to 111 days). Mills and Reed (1971) reported that the body weight at puberty is a more constant parameter than age and suggested that there may be an interaction between hypothalamic centers controlling body weight and puberty.

C. Estrous Cycle

1. Length of Estrous Cycle

Stockard and Papanicolaou (1917), in their now classic study, recorded a mean estrous cycle length in the guinea pig of 15.73 days (range = 15 to 17 days). They detected a slight seasonal variation in the cycle length: October, 15.50 days; January, 16.14 days. Young *et al.* (1935) cited a mean of 16 days and 6 hours with a range of 13 to 21.5 days and a 6.1% variability. They found that the range was much less for any one animal at a given age and that sterile mating did not affect the length of the cycle. The average length of the first two cycles of the guinea pig are shorter than the subsequent cycles (Young *et al.*, 1939). Ishii (1920) reported the length of the various stages of the estrous cycle to be: proestrus, 1 to 1.5 days, except the first heat of breeding life was preceded by a proestrus of 3 to 8 days; estrus, 9 to 11 hours; metestrus, 2.5 to 3 days; and total length of estrous cycle, 15 to 16.5 days.

2. Proestrus

Signs of proestrus include increased activity and often vigorous running pursuit of cage mates. The female may begin a swaying motion of the hindquarters, while uttering a distinct gutteral sound. Females are more active than are the males and mounting behavior may occur as long as 53 hours before estrus. Vigorous mounting activity, however, is only seen in the 10 hours immediately preceding estrus (Young *et al.*, 1935). Mills and Reed (1971) reported that in the young adolescent female there is a period just before the vaginal membrane ruptures for the first time, when the nipples increase rapidly in size and vascularity and the external genitalia become swollen. This period ranged from 0 to 6 days, but if two of these three signs were observed in an animal, the vaginal membrane would rupture in 3 to 4 days.

3. Estrus (Heat)

a. Onset of Estrus. The onset of estrus and its duration can be easily detected by external signs in the guinea pig. Most dependable is the copulatory reflex (lordosis or opisthotonus).* This consists of an arching and straightening of the

*See Chapter 5 for further information on behavior during the estrous cycle.

back and the elevation of the entire posterior region with dilation of the pudendum (Young *et al.*, 1935). The vaginal smear is also a fairly accurate guide to the onset of estrus (see Section IV, C,5).

The onset of the estrus period in the guinea pig is correlated with the light/dark sequence of environmental illumination (Donovan and Lockhart, 1972b). Dempsey *et al.* (1934) reported that estrous activity is twice as prominent between 6 PM and 6 AM as between 6 AM and 6 PM. They found that the animals lost this diurnal rhythm if they were continuously maintained in darkness. The light/dark ratio did not affect the basic reproduction rhythm; duration of estrus, length of the estrous cycle, fertility, and vaginal smear were unaffected by changes in environmental light exposure. It has been noted that if one examines guinea pig sows between 8 PM and 8 AM from October 15 to December 15 he should find approximately 75% in estrus (Young *et al.*, 1935).

The intensity of estrous behavior is always greatest at the beginning of estrus and diminishes gradually as the end approaches (Young *et al.*, 1935). Donovan and Kopriva (1965) noted a tendency for the estrous cycle of guinea pigs caged together to become synchronous. Their findings were not supported by the work of Harned and Casida (1972). Occasionally, guinea pigs display a split estrus (Young *et al.*, 1935).

b. Vaginal Membrane. Except during estrus and parturition, the vagina of the guinea pig is sealed with an epithelial membrane. Opening of the membrane precedes estrus, but its timing is too variable to be used in accurately establishing the onset of estrus (Harned and Casida, 1972). The vaginal membrane is open for 2.3 ± 0.1 days during estrus in the mature sow. During the first cycles, however, the length of opening is prolonged: first cycle, 11.2 ± 1.0 days; second cycle, 5 days. Closure of the vaginal membrane does not occur until after ovulation (Ford and Young, 1953).

c. Length of Estrus. Stockard and Papanicolaou (1917) considered the estrous period to be about 24 hours based on distinct characteristics of the vaginal fluids. Their determinations did not emphasize receptivity to the male and breeding activity. Subsequently, Young *et al.* (1935) used sexual receptivity as a guide in studying 592 cycles and established the length to be 8.21 ± 0.07 hours (range = 1–18 hours). Ishii (1920) reported a 6- to 11-hour period of sexual receptivity in 90% of animals observed.

d. Time of Ovulation. Ovulation occurs approximately 10 hours following the onset of estrus and usually within 1.5 to 2 hours of the end of estrus (Blandau and Young, 1939; Myers *et al.*, 1936; Young *et al.*, 1935).

With respect to opening and closure of the vaginal membrane, Mills and Reed (1971) found that ovulation did not occur in any animals before the first day the vagina showed signs of opening. Reed and Hounslow (1971) confirmed this and noted that ovulation usually takes place after the vagina had been open for more than 1 day. Autopsying animals at various stages of estrus, they found that 50% of the animals had ovulated on the morning after the vagina had been fully open for 1 day. Ovulation had always (12 of 12 animals) occurred in animals killed as the vagina was beginning to close. Ford and Young (1953) noted that ovulation was delayed in young females; 50% having ovulated 48 hours postvaginal opening vs. 78.6% of adults having ovulated 48 hours after opening.

Stockard and Papanicolaou (1917) established the time of ovulation with respect to the vaginal smear characteristics (see Section IV, C,5).

e. Postpartum and Newborn Estrus. Postpartum estrus with ovulation is the rule in the guinea pig, with ovulation occurring 12 to 15 hours postpartum (Labhsetwar and Diamond, 1970; Rowlands, 1956). The length of postpartum estrus is short, 3.5 hours vs. 8.6 hours recorded for nonpostparturient females. Boling *et al.* (1939) reported that it occurred in 50 of 74 females observed. The postpartum estrus occurred within 10 hours of parturition; usually within 2 hours. Due to the short estrus, the sows usually mate only once. Bruce and Parkes (1948) estimate that 74% of pregnancies in monogamous pairs are from postpartum matings.

Boling *et al.* (1939) reported that newborn guinea pigs of both sexes exhibit estrus signs of lordosis almost immediately after birth. The response was greatest at the onset, diminished with time, and was slightly longer in the female (2.8 hours) than in the male (2.4 hours). These workers noted that the reflex was present even in the young of sows ovariectomized on the fiftieth and fifty-fifth day of gestation. The ontogeny of this behavior was studied by Beach (1966).

4. Ovarian Activity and Hormonal Control

a. Follicle Development. About the fourth day of the estrous cycle, the follicle population from which ovulating follicles will ultimately develop is distinguishable. Some of these will become atretic, others will continue to mature. If the corpus luteum is removed immediately after estrus or ovulation, some of the advanced follicles at that time will be triggered to mature and the estrous cycle will be shortened to 11 days (Dempsey, 1937). Normally, growth and maturing of follicles is at a slow, steady rate until the beginning of estrus at which time there is at least a ninefold acceleration in follicular growth which culminates in ovulation about the end of estrus. The only gross ovarian change associated with the onset of estrus is the preovulatory swelling of follicles, assumed to be consequent to rising levels of luteotropic hormone (Hermreck and Greenwald, 1964; Myers *et al.*, 1936).

Labhsetwar and Diamond (1970) recorded no significant change in the numbers of follicles in the ovaries during the estrous cycle (101 ± 9 SE). There was, however, a significant ($P < 0.01$) decrease to 67 (± 5 SE) during pregnancy and the immediate postpartum period (Fig. 12). Large follicles (> 700 μm in diameter) were found only during the proestrus period

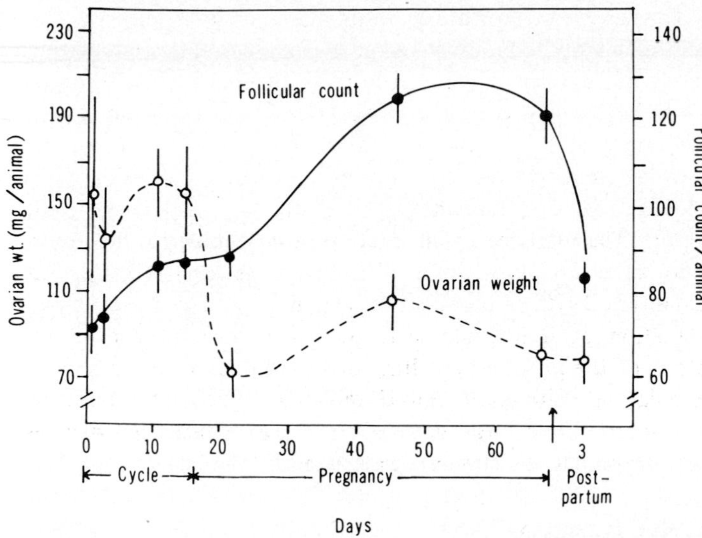

Fig. 12. Changes in ovarian weight and follicular count in cyclic, pregnant, and postpartum guinea pigs. Bar at each point denotes mean ± SE. Arrow on abscissa corresponds to day of parturition (after Labhsetwar and Diamond, 1970).

and after day 65 of gestation. There was no significant change in ovarian weights during the estrous cycle (Fig. 12).

Williams (1956) described the atretic follicle of the guinea pig: "...atretic follicles show initially a pyknosis of the nucleus, and disintegration of the granulosa cells bordering the antrum. The granulosa layers rapidly degenerate and, as the follicle shrinks, the inner thecal cells proliferate and take on a fibrolytic appearance. Meanwhile the ovum also degenerates and finally only the theca retains its structure—it remains unaffected by the fibrolytic tissue, so that thecal nodules persist giving the interstitual tissue a nodular appearance before merging into general uniform interstitial tissue." Loeb (1906) also studied the properties of atretic follicles. This meticulous work examined the ovaries of 30 guinea pigs at 28 intervals between 6 to 127 hours postcoitus.

b. Ovulation. The number of follicles reaching maturity and ovulating was reported at 3.34 (± 0.41 SE). These were evenly divided between the two ovaries. However, when an animal was unilaterally ovariectomized on day 1 of the cycle the remaining ovary assumed the full production of follicles (3.71 ± 0.37 SE). Unilateral ovariectomy did not affect the cycle length (Hermreck and Greenwald, 1964). In another study, Young *et al.* (1938) found that the number of ova ovulated was related to the aggressiveness of the estrous behavior. Animals with a very active estrus produced an average of 3.48 ova while animals with a rather quiescent estrous period produced only 2.63 ova.

The mature follicle protrudes above the convexity of the ovary, bulging the tunica albuginea. After rupture a small crater forms over which germinal epithelium is reestablished in 48 to 72 hours. Both the granulosa and the theca interna contribute to the developing luteal tissue which forms a narrow band at 3 to 4 days, enclosing a central cavity (Rowlands, 1956).

Reed and Hounslow (1971) studied the endocrine relationships involved in follicular maturation, ovulation, and luteinization. They concluded that in a normally cycling guinea pig, about 13 days after ovulation, when the level of progesterone in the corpus luteum is decreasing and the follicles are reaching maturity, there is an increase in follicle stimulating hormone (FSH) secretion. This increase in FSH stimulates theca interna cell activity, probably promoting estrogen synthesis by the developing follicle. This estrogen production, together with the basal levels of luteinizing hormone (LH), apparently facilitates the increase in follicle cell size and the ultimate ripening of one to two follicles. These ripe follicles remain in a state of ovulation readiness for approximately 2 days as the anterior pituitary accumulates and releases a surge of LH adequate to effect ovulation. Four to five days must elapse between the decrease in plasma progesterone, consequent to corpus luetum regression, and follicular rupture (Donovan and Lockhart, 1972a). It is during this state of ovulation readiness that a single dose of exogenous LH can induce ovulation in the proestrus guinea pig. Likewise, ovulation can be regularly induced by a single injection of gonadotropins in immature guinea pigs showing external signs of hormonal activity, e.g., increased vascularity and growth of nipples and external genitalia (Mills and Reed, 1971).

c. Corpus Luteum of the Estrous Cycle. The number of corpora lutea (CL) in the guinea pig varies from cycle to cycle. Nineteen pairs of ovaries examined through two cycles had an average of 3.5 CL, yet only 9 of 19 had the same number of CL on both cycles (Reed and Hounslow, 1971). Fewer CL are present in ovaries of young guinea pigs compared to adults. Ford and Young (1953) counted an average of 2.17 ± 0.15 CL in young animals, a number which was significantly less than the average of 3.50 ± 0.18 CL counted in adults. They also found significantly less volume in the CL of young [156 (± 56) × 10^6 μm^3] compared to adult [444 (±45) × 10^6 μm^3] animals when measured within 48 hours after vaginal membrane rupture. The difference in CL volume was not significant by 96 hours after membrane rupture: young, 702 (± 102) × 10^6 μm^3 vs. adult, 887 (± 75) × 10^6 μm^3. In the normal estrous cycle, the CL grows to a volume of 2 mm^3 (2000 × 10^6 μm^3) by the ninth to tenth postovulatory day then begins to regress (Heat *et al.*, 1967; Hermreck and Greenwald, 1964; Labhsetwar and Diamond, 1970; Rowlands, 1956). Sterile mating does not inhibit regression, but hysterectomy before day 11 results in persistence of the CL for at least 50 days (Loeb, 1932; Rowlands, 1956).

Challis *et al.* (1971) reported that plasma progesterone levels increased rapidly after ovulation, reaching a maximum of 2.8 ± 0.33 ng/ml by day 5. As the CL began to regress the plasma progesterone levels decreased and were less than 0.5 ng/ml by day 12. These workers calculated the maximum production rate of progesterone to be 0.26 mg/day. Illingworth *et al.*

(1970) determined the metabolic clearance rate of the normal guinea pig during the estrous cycle to be rather stable at 112.8 (±7 SE) liters of plasma/day/kg.

Exogenous progesterone (2.5 mg/animal/day) modifies the estrous cycle length depending on when the animals are treated (Woody *et al.*, 1967). If treated from day 0 to day 3 the CL volume is reduced and the cycle is shortened from 16.3 days to 14.8 days. Treatment later in the cycle leads to cycle lengthening (Ginther, 1969). Five milligrams per day from day 2 to day 5 or day 4 to day 7 had no effect on cycle length (Bland and Donovan, 1970). One-tenth (0.1) mg of progesterone absorbed daily resulted in normal cycling in the guinea pig with inhibition of ovulation. This treatment regime was complicated by gross enlargement and pathological changes in the uterus (Deanesly, 1968).

The CL of cyclic guinea pigs grow by hypertrophy and hyperplasia of luteal cells between day 3 and 10 of the cycle and start to regress by day 10 to 12. Regression is gradual, being completed by day 16 of the cycle.

Except for the role of LH in conversion of the ovulated ovarian follicle to a luteal body, there does not appear to be any two species that control the luteal phase of their cycle in identical fashion (Greep, 1971). In nonpregnant guinea pigs, pituitary support of the CL is needed only in the first 2 to 3 days of the estrous cycle (Aldred *et al.*, 1961; Heap *et al.*, 1967). A hormonal complex rather than a single hormonal factor is considered to be responsible for the luteotropic effect in the guinea pig. Neither LH (Deanesly, 1966) nor prolactin (Rowlands, 1962) alone is responsible for growth and maintenance of the CL. Choudary and Greenwald (1968) have presented evidence that FSH is luteotropic in the guinea pig and they suggest that it may act synergistically with other hypophyseal gonadotropins in maintaining the CL.

Donovan (1967) presented evidence that the life span of the guinea pig CL is determined by a luteolytic factor produced by the ipsilateral uterine horn. This work supported the earlier studies by Loeb (1932), demonstrating that normal luteal regression was delayed by hysterectomy, and the work of Oxenreider and Day (1967) which showed that severance of the uterine artery and vein prevented the regression of the CL in the ipsilateral ovary of the guinea pig.

The exact nature of the luteolytic factor is uncertain. Blatchley and Donovan (1969) demonstrated that exogenous prostaglandin $F_{2\alpha}$ ($PGF_{2\alpha}$) was luteolytic in hysterectomized guinea pigs. Blatchley *et al.* (1972) later reported that endogenous $PGF_{2\alpha}$ levels in the uteroovarian vein were related to changes in luteal function and dependent on intact uteri and that estrogen treatment stimulates uterine secretion of $PGF_{2\alpha}$ (Blatchley *et al.*, 1971). An attempt to block the luteolytic effect of $PGF_{2\alpha}$ by treating cycling guinea pigs with indomethacin (blocker of $PGF_{2\alpha}$ synthesis) was not successful, thus failing to support the hypothesis of $PGF_{2\alpha}$ as the luteolytic factor in the guinea pig (Marley, 1972).

The study of hormonal influence on the release of the uterine luteolytic factor is currently focused on low circulating levels of estrogen which can initiate luteolysis when administered before day 6 of the cycle (Bland and Donovan, 1970; Choudary and Greenwald, 1968). The route of action of estrogen may be via the pituitary, possibly inhibiting FSH required for luteal maintenance (Choudary and Greenwald, 1969). The presence of an intact pituitary enhances the luteolytic effect of low doses (10 μg) of estrogen (Bland and Donovan, 1970). Luteolysis is accompanied by a precocious ovulation, no doubt related to the release of the progesterone block of the pituitary resulting in an LH surge into the general circulation (Choudary and Greenwald, 1968). It should be pointed out that large doses ($>$ 0.1 mg) of estrogen can be luteotrophic in the guinea pig (Rowlands, 1962).

5. Vaginal Smear

The vaginal smear has been determined to be a better indicator of the onset of estrus than vaginal opening (Harned and Casida, 1972). The classic work of Stockard and Papanicolaou (1917), who used the guinea pig to establish that the composition of vaginal fluids changes with the various stages of the rodent estrous cycle, provides a sound foundation for discussion of vaginal smear changes in the guinea pig. They described four stages of the 24-hour "sexual activity" period based on microscopic changes observed in the vaginal smear. The first stage was longest, lasting at least 6 to 12 hours. Large amounts of mucous fluid containing masses of pyknotic squamous cells dominated the smear, with a few elongate, cornified cells without nuclei appearing late in stage one and early in stage two. Stage two lasted only 2 to 4 hours and the smear fluid was of cheeselike consistency with an enormous number of cells, mostly of more healthy squamous architecture. Stage three lasted 4 to 6 hours and there was liquefaction of the cheesy mass. Epithelial cells were less numerous and polymorphonuclear leukocytes had infiltrated in the thin fluid discharge. The fourth stage was the shortest (1 to 2 hours) and not consistently present in all individuals. It was characterized by varying numbers of red blood cells accompanying large numbers of leukocytes and desquamated epithelial cells. Young (1937) regarded the fourth stage as artifactual and suggested it be disregarded.

Donovan and Lockart (1972b) reported that smears taken after first opening of the vaginal membrane contain epithelial cells, cornified cells and leukocytes (proestrus). But as estrus approached the number of leukocytes diminished and numerous brightly stained rounded cornified cells entered the discharge. The end of estrus was evidenced by a marked return of leukocytes to the vaginal smear. Stockard and Papanicolaou (1917) established that ovulation is most nearly coincident with return of leukocytes to the vaginal smear. Although Young (1937) disputed the relationship between vaginal smear character and ovulation time, Donovan and Lockhart (1972b) confirmed that the influx of leukocytes into the vaginal smear occurs around the time of ovulation. The influx of leukocytes tends to take place during or soon after the dark period (see Section IV, C,3,a).

Hematoxylin-staining granules appear in the cytoplasm of superficial cells of the vaginal mucosa during proestrus in the guinea pig. Although the cause or function of the inclusions is not known, it is suggested that they are the result of lysomal involvement in a degenerating cell. Gibb (1969) suggested that the guinea pig is an ideal subject and experimental model in which to study the appearance of hematoxylin-staining granules.

D. Fertilization and Implantation

1. Ovum Passage and Viability

Ovulated ova progress to midway through the fallopian tube in 3 to 4 hours where they remain for as long as 30 hours. During the next 50 hours, they progress through the remainder of the tube and, if fertilized, enter the uterus 72 hours or so after ovulation in the 8- to 12-cell stage of development (Hunter *et al.*, 1969; Squier, 1932). The ovum remains capable of being fertilized and undergoing normal development for only a very short time after ovulation. Aging effects are first noted 8 hours after ovulation and normal development is usual only in ova fertilized within 20 hours of ovulation. Beyond 32 hours apparently no development whatsoever is possible (Blandau and Young, 1939). These workers found that as time of fertilization was delayed there was (1) increase in numbers of sterile inseminations, (2) decrease in average litter size, (3) decrease in number of normal pregnancies, and (4) increase in number of abortions.

2. Fertilization and Artificial Insemination

The exact time of fertilization has not been determined in the guinea pig. Some estimates are between 6 and 15 hours postcoitus while the ovum is located in the midportion of the fallopian tubes. Blandau (1949) estimated that fertilization occurs 1 to 2 hours postcoitus. A very high proportion of ovulated ova undergo fertilization under natural conditions of mating with proven males (Hunter *et al.*, 1969). This high fertilization rate seems particularly important in view of the relatively small number of ova ovulated (3.4, range 1 to 5) and the rather long gestation period (68 days). Hunter *et al.* (1969), in contrast to Austin and Walton (1960), reported the penetration of the vitellus by more than one sperm to be very rare; dispermy was recorded in only 1.8% of 169 penetrated ova examined.

Even though the female will not mate after the end of heat, postestrus artificial insemination is very practical (Myers *et al.*, 1936). Rowlands (1957) reported that postestrous intraperitoneal insemination of semen was as equally successful as natural mating during estrus. A high conception rate was noted 0 to 16 hours postestrus. In fact, all 17 animals inseminated with 5.0×10^7 spermatoza between 0 and 8 hours postestrus conceived. Insemination via intraperitoneal cavity was of little success 18 or more hours postestrus.

3. Implantation

Previous to implantation, embryo mortality is low; Hunter *et al.* (1969) reported only one of 53 embryos to be degenerating by day 6 postovulation. Implantation occurs 6 to 7.5 days postcoitus (Blandau, 1949; Deanesly, 1960b). At this time (3 to 9 days postovulation) the uterus is sensitive to the decidual reaction (Loeb, 1932).

Ovariectomy on day 2 postcoitus will result in implantation failure unless exogenous progesterone is administered. However, implantation is not affected by excision of the ovaries on day 3 to 7 postcoitus. Embryos of guinea pigs ovariectomized at the later time develop normally until day 11 to 14 when they may regress; exogenous progesterone can prevent regression (Deanesly, 1960b). Ovariectomy in other rodents prevents normal implantation. The only other species reported to implant after ovariectomy is the armadillo and then only subsequent to a long delay (Buchanan *et al.*, 1956).

E. Gestation

The guinea pig has a rather long gestation period, the duration of which is inversely related to the number of fetuses carried (Table XII). Rowlands (1949) and Labhsetwar and Diamond (1970) reported mean gestation period lengths of 68.0 days (range = 59 to 72 days) and 68 (± 2 SE) days, respectively. Such long gestation periods make the guinea pig particularly valuable for investigations of teratogenesis and

Table XII
The Relationship between Litter Size and Gestation Length[a]

No. in litter at birth	No. of litters	Gestation length (mean ±SD)
1	37	70.5 ± 1.1
2	216	69.5 ± 1.4
3	427	68.8 ± 1.6
4	276	68.2 ± 1.6
5	63	67.4 ± 1.7
6	8	66.8 ± 1.5

[a]From Goy *et al.* (1957).

provides an excellent opportunity for study of deleterious factors which act differentially with respect to the stage of pregnancy as do many noxious agents in man (Goy *et al.*, 1957).

Workers in prenatal physiology use two methods of estimating the gestional age of the fetus. Perhaps the most accurate procedure is to use guinea pigs bred during the postpartum estrus which occurs within 10 hours of parturition (see Section IV,C,3,e). Alternatively, the meticulous developmental studies of Draper (1920) have served as a standard for estimation of fetal age.

1. Ovaries during Pregnancy

The guinea pig was the first species, excluding man, in which it was shown that pregnancy could be normally completed in the absence of both ovaries (Herrick, 1928). Other laboratory animals (rat, mouse, rabbit) abort, making the guinea pig particularily valuable as a model for study of the endocrine control of human pregnancy. Normally, the corpus luteum of pregnancy continues to grow until day 18 or 20, and remains functional throughout pregnancy. However, pregnancy can in some cases be successfully completed subsequent to bilateral ovariectomy as early as day 21. This capability probably reflects the supportive function of the placenta which begins its endocrine activity as early as day 15 (Deanesly, 1960a).

Ovarian weights begin to increase during the second and third trimester (Fig. 12) consequent to the onset of follicular activity. Although actual numbers of follicles are markedly decreasing [from a prepregnancy average of 101 (± 9 SE) to 67 (± 5 SE) during pregnancy] due to atresia, a few follicles are concomitantly maturing to diameters greater than 700 μm by day 66 of gestation. These follicles are destined to ovulate immediately postpartum (Labhsetwar and Diamond, 1970). Spontaneous ovulation during pregnancy probably does not occur (Rowlands, 1956).

2. Hormones of Pregnancy

a. Progesterone. Studies by Challis *et al.* (1971) demonstrated that plasma progesterone levels begin to increase rapidly after day 15 postcoitus. Levels peaked at 329 ± 14 ng/ml during days 30 to 45, followed by a decrease to less than 200 ng/ml between days 45 to 60. A significant increase in concentration was recorded during the days just preceding parturition (Fig. 13). The midgestational decrease in plasma progesterone may be due to the change-over from ovary to placenta as the principal producers of progesterone. The mean wet weight of placentae is significantly correlated (Fig. 13) with progesterone values and during the last two weeks of pregnancy, there are no differences between the plasma progesterone levels of intact vs. ovariectomized guinea pigs (Heap and Deanesly, 1966). Production rate of progesterone, during the last two trimesters, has been estimated by Challis *et al.* (1971) to be 1.24±0.3 mg/day. This represents a fivefold increase over production rates during the luteal phase of the cycle (0.26 mg/day).

The dynamic regulation of the fluctuations in plasma progesterone levels during various phases of reproductive activity appears to be multifaceted in guinea pigs. Besides variations in the progesterone production rate by ovaries and placentae, there are changes in the *metabolic clearance rate* (MCR) of progesterone which makes possible elevations in the plasma levels independent of production per se. Illingworth *et al.* (1970) determined the MCR of normal cycling guinea pigs to be 112.8 (±7.0 SE) liters/day/kg. In pregnant animals (day 15 to 20), the MCR decreased sharply to 8.3 ± 0.8 liters/day/kg. This modification in the kinetics of metabolism is related to the increased production of a *progesterone-binding globulin* (PBG) during pregnancy. The existence of a PBG as a molecular entity independent of *cortisol-binding globulin* (CBG) is apparently unique to the guinea pig and another hystricomorph rodent, the coypu (Diamond *et al.*, 1969; Illingworth and Heap, 1971; Milgrom *et al.*, 1970). PBG has been recently

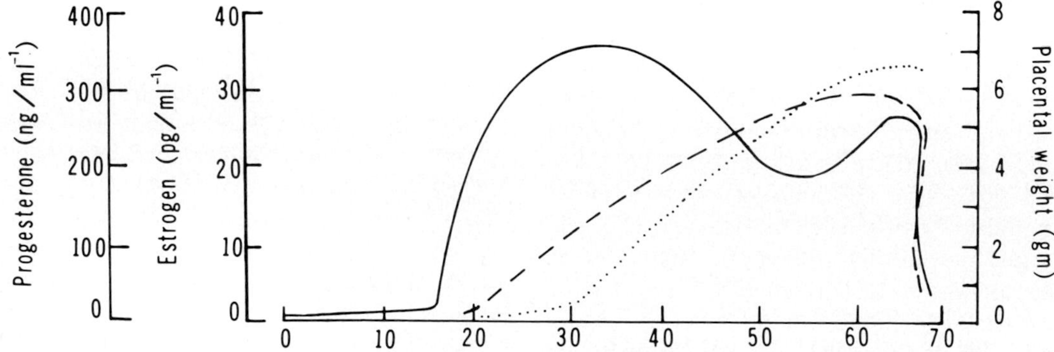

Fig. 13. Circulating hormone levels and placental weight during pregnancy in the guinea pig. Solid line = progesterone; dashed line = estrogens; dotted line = placental weights (from Bedford *et al.*, 1972; after Challis *et al.*, 1971, and Heap and Deanesly, 1966).

purified and characterized by Milgrom *et al.* (1973). Separate binding proteins for cortisol and progesterone makes the guinea pig a useful animal for study of progesterone physiology (Faber *et al.*, 1972; Westphal, 1971). The possible role of these binding globulins in protecting the fetus and the maternal CNS from masculinization by exogenous androgens is discussed by Diamond *et al.* (1969).

Midpregnancy opening of the vaginal membrane is not uncommon and may be related to the surge in progesterone and the increase in relaxin production at this time (Jagiello, 1965; Zarrow, 1947).

b. Estrogen. The estrogens of guinea pig plasma have been tentatively identified as estriol, 16α-epiestriol, 16-keto-17β-estradiol, 17α- and 17β-estradiol, and an estrone-like compound. Ovarian estrogens were identified as 17α- and 17β-estradiol, 16α-epiestriol, and the estrone-like compound (Church and Eleftheriou, 1966). Challis *et al.* (1971) reported that estrone accounted for 35 to 45% and 17β-estradiol for less than 10% of the total plasma unconjugated estrogens.

Detectable levels of unconjugated estrogen begin to appear in the plasma about day 20 of pregnancy. Challis *et al.* (1971) reported that estrogen levels increased from 12.8 ± 1.95 pg/ml at days 31 to 35 to peak values of 31.05 ± 5.21 pg/ml by days 56 to 60. Deanesly (1960b) attributes the continuing increase in mucification and thickening of the vaginal mucosa during the third and fourth weeks of pregnancy to developing placental estrogen production. After parturition, the estrogens decreased precipitously to undetectable values (< 5 pg/ml) within 2 days (Fig. 13). The progesterone to estrogen ratio decreased from high values in early pregnancy to very low values by day 50. There was no apparent correlation between the number of fetuses and plasma steriod concentrations.

Challis *et al.* (1971) estimated the MCR of 17β-estradiol to be 80–100 liters/day in the guinea pig. From these studies, they calculated the maximum production rate of 17β-estradiol to be about 0.4 mg/day at day 17, increasing to 2.6 mg/day in late pregnancy.

Bϕrjesson and Stϕa (1970) studied the urinary metabolites of [^{14}C]17β-estradiol and found that about 50% of the injected radioactivity is accounted for in the urine, 90% of which is excreted within the first 24 hours. Estrone glucuronoside and 17β-estradiol-3-glucuronoside comprised 74 and 16%, respectively, of the total radioactivity excreted in the urine. Other identifiable metabolites were estrone sulfate (about 4.4%) and 17β-estradiol-3-sulfate (about 2.0%).

3. Myometrial Activity

Evidence suggests that progesterone is not the regulator of myometrial activity in the guinea pig (Porter, 1970, 1971b; Schofield, 1964; Zarrow *et al.*, 1963). During the luteal phase of the estrous cycle, myometrial activity is more pronounced than during the estrous phase. Weak myometrial contractions are present and the uterus is responsive to oxytocin throughout pregnancy; the gravid horn is less active than the nongravid uterine horn. Unlike the rabbit, but similar to the human being, progesterone will not block uterine contractions nor prolong gestation in the guinea pig (Porter, 1971b).

Porter (1971a) demonstrated that intramuscular injections of relaxin caused inhibition of uterine activity in the guinea pig. Subsequent crosscirculation experiments between pregnant and nonpregnant animals led to the conclusion that relaxin or a relaxin-like substance is the major myometrial regulating factor in the guinea pig. Relaxin regulation was achieved by a frequency modulation of the intrauterine pressure cycles (as opposed to an amplitude modulation as seen in the rabbit consequent to progesterone treatment) (Porter, 1972).

Relaxin is first detectable in the blood of the guinea pig on day 21 and reaches peak levels (0.5 guinea pig units/ml serum) on day 28. These levels are maintained until day 63 at which time the concentration starts to wane, precipitously decreasing at parturition (Zarrow, 1947).

4. Placenta

Three characteristics of the guinea pig make it particularly useful in the study of placental physiology: (1) The placenta has many morphological features in common with the human placenta, (2) gestation period is long enough to permit easy differentiation between various stages of development, and (3) fetuses are large enough in the last trimester for easy blood collection (Fuchs, 1957; Hill and Young, 1973).

a. Type and Structure. According to the Grosser system of classification, the guinea pig has a hemochorial placenta with fetal trophoblasts in direct contact with the maternal bloodstream. Although the guinea pig is joined in this classification by such mammals as the rat, mouse, hamster, rabbit, chipmunk, armadillo, and human being, there are distinct variations within the group. The guinea pig placenta is further classified as *labyrinthine hemomonochorial*, having but a single trophoblast layer present. In the labyrinth, the maternal blood circulates in a meshwork of trophoblastic septa carrying fetal capillaries. Electron microscopy reveals that the trophoblast forms a continuous syncytial layer varying greatly in thickness and having microvilli on both the free and basal surface. The large microvilli projecting from the trophoblast into the maternal blood spaces form areas in which the flow of plasma might be slowed (Enders, 1965; Ferguson and Christie, 1967). The hypothesized role of Kurloff cells in the protection of these fetal tissues so intimately associated with maternal antibody defense mechanisms was described in Section III, D, 2 of this chapter.

b. Placental Transfer. The viseral yolk sac of the guinea pig is the major route of maternal–fetal transfer for antitoxin, antibodies, and serum proteins, while the chorioallantoic placenta (trophoblast) is an important barrier to the maternal–fetal passage of proteins (King and Enders, 1971). Barnes (1959) demonstrated that antitoxins can be transferred by the yolk sac and vitelline vessels. *Brucella abortus* antibodies can be transferred to the fetus as early as day 45 of gestation with peak transfer taking place in the last week of pregnancy. Vitelline vessels are the major site of entry of antibodies into the fetal circulation early in gestation, with the fetal gut assuming a larger role in later stages. The longer gestation period is held responsible for the advanced absorptive capabilities of the guinea pig fetal gut (Leissring and Anderson, 1961).

Placental gas exchange was studied by Bartels *et al.* (1967). Oxygen tensions were 10 mm Hg higher in the guinea pig fetus arterial blood than in the uterine vein. Compared to rabbits and goats, the guinea pig placenta appeared to be more efficient in oxygen exchange, perhaps consequent to a hypothesized countercurrent or a multivillous flow system in the guinea pig placental structure.

Electrical potentials across the placenta and fetal/maternal electrolyte concentrations have been studied in the guinea pig by Mellor (1969) and Štulc *et al.* (1972). Electrical gradients of −18 mV (±4 SD) and −21.4 mV (± 5.6 SD) were recorded by these workers, respectively (fetus electronegative with respect to dam). These gradients contrast with those seen in man and rabbit (0 mV) and rat (+15 mV). Electrolyte concentration (mEq/liter ±SD) in maternal plasma and amniotic fluid in the last half of gestation were recorded as $[Na^+] = 145 \pm 4$, $[Cl^-] = 97 \pm 2$ and $[Na^+] = 134 \pm 8$, $[Cl^-] = 140 \pm 15$, respectively (Mellor, 1969).

Other recent studies of placental transfer in the guinea pig include: iron, Wong and Morgan (1973); amino acids, Butt and Wilson (1968), Dancis *et al.* (1968); fatty acids, Hershfield and Nemeth (1968); thyroid hormones, London *et al.* (1963); electrolytes, Foreman and Segal (1972).

c. Blood Supply. Umbilical artery blood flow was measured to average 64 ml/kg fetal weight/minute (range = 45 to 108 ml). Blood flow (b) in liters per day was related to the fetal weight (w) in grams as follows: $b = -0.589 \pm 0.104\ w$ (Shepherd and Whelan, 1951). Comparable results (86 ml/kg/minute) were more recently recorded by Bartels *et al.* (1967). It has been calculated that 1.28 (± 0.38 SD) liters of blood flows through the umbilical artery for each gram of guinea pig fetal growth; less than one-fourth the volume required for a gram of sheep fetal growth (Greenfield *et al.*, 1951).

The principal resistance to blood flow in the hemochorial placenta of the guinea pig lies in the arteries outside the placenta. At a central arterial pressure of 65 (± 5 SD) torr, the preplacental arterial pressure was 12 (± 3 SD) torr (Moll and Kunzel, 1973).

Fuchs (1952) studied the blood volume of the guinea pig placenta. Average blood volume (milliliters/gram of placenta) during various stages of gestation are shown in the following tabulation.

Maternal vessels			Fetal vessels		
Day of gestation	Litter size (no. fetuses)	ml/gm	Day of gestation	Litter size (no. fetuses)	ml/gm
38	2	0.102	60	3	0.226
41	3	0.117	61	4	0.197
44	4	0.102	62	4	0.182
51	4	0.163	66	3	0.193
54	3	0.146			
57	4	0.242			
64	3	0.197			
65	3	0.222			

Fuchs also noted that the total conceptus weight may equal as much as 30% of the total maternal body weight.

F. Parturition

1. Onset and Delivery

The stimulus for the onset of parturition in the guinea pig is not known. Unlike other species, progesterone is not the principal regulator of myometrial activity and there is no precipitous withdrawal of progesterone just before parturition. Challis *et al.* (1971) suggested that there may be change in the local concentration of readily available progesterone or in the progesterone–estrogen quotient before the onset of parturition activity.

Subsequent to increased production of relaxin (see Section IV, E, 3), the symphysis pubis begins to relax in the last half of gestation becoming so separated (7 to 8 mm) that the two halves of the pelvis can be freely and independently manipulated, thus making possible an increased diameter of the birth canal (Hisaw, 1926; Hisaw *et al.*, 1944). Some workers feel that young breeding females should be bred at their first heat to facilitate adequate separation of the pubis during subsequent deliveries. The pubis remains separated for approximately 5 to 7 days and returns to normal within 24 hours postpartum (Ishii, 1920).

Rowlands (1949) reported that parturition is very infrequent during the day; however, Boling *et al.* (1939) found a random distribution throughout the 24 hours in their colony. Parturition normally lasts from 10 to 30 minutes with an average interval between deliveries of 7.4 minutes (range = 1 to 16 minutes).

Rogers (1951) studied some 388 breeding females through 2368 litters and recorded an average age of the dam at first delivery to be 175 days (range = 93 to 420). One female had her seventeenth litter at 2173 days of age.

2. Litter Size (Number of Young)

Based on the reported variations from different laboratories, one surmises that the average litter size at birth varies with such parameters as strain of guinea pig, management practices, etc. [Bruce and Parkes (1948), 3.8; Rogers (1951), 2.3; Haines (1931), 2.6 (82.8% were 2,3, or 4); Dunkin *et al.* (1930), 3.0]. Dunkin *et al.* (1930) noted that fertility was diminished in the January to March quarter and litter size was down to 2.65. The reported distribution of litter size within several colonies is presented in Table XIII.

Litter size is dependent on number of follicles ovulating, percentage implantation, and percentage surviving early death and absorption, all of which are influenced by genetic factors of the dam and fetus, and through the condition of the dam by external environment. Environmental conditions from year to year seem to markedly affect fecundity, viability, and growth. However, the recent advent of controlled environment animal quarters may reduce the influence of this variable. The larger the dam the larger the litter. There also appears to be a positive correlation between the interval since the preceding gestation and litter size (Wright, 1960). In a colony of heterogenous females, Goy *et al.* (1957) reported that the length of gestation was inversely related to litter size (Table XII).

3. Fetal and Neonate Viability, Size, and Growth

The single factor most related to number of stillbirths and early neonate growth rate is size of litter, which in turn affects gestation length. Haines (1931), reporting on nearly 12,000 litters, noted that as the litter size increased, stillbirths and neonate mortality increased. Goy *et al.* (1957) found that the number of premature deaths (abortions) were not related to litter size; whereas, stillbirth incidence was highly associated with size of litter. Hoar *et al.* (1957) considered vaginal bleeding to be indicative of resorption of one or more fetuses or abortion of the litter. Optimal viability occurs when the conceptus contains two fetuses. Pregnancies with 3 or 4 fetuses are only slightly less successful (Wright, 1960).

From day 62 through 74 of pregnancy, when most of the young are delivered alive, the probability of death depends on the day of birth; lowest incidence of mortality being among litters born on day 69 (Fig. 14). Goy *et al.* (1957) further noted that a litter has only one chance in 1000 of containing some living young if delivered more than 3 standard deviations below (abortion) or above (stillbirth) the colony mean gestation length. The incidence of abortion and stillbirth varied between strains in the colony of Goy and associates (see following tabulation).

Strain	Abortions	Stillbirths
Genetically heterogenous	8.3% in 277 litters	24.0% in 254 litters
Strain 13	21.2% in 53 litters	45.2% in 42 litters

In each case the strain 13 litters had highly significant ($P < 0.001$) greater mortality.

Rowlands (1949) reported a 95% live birth delivery in his colony and commented that the main cause of death at birth was asphyxia from fetal membranes. Wright (1960) states that the dam will occasionally chew on dead fetuses, but evidently because they are large (up to 25% of dam weight) at birth with mature hair and skin, fetalphagia is not seen in the guinea pig.

Fetal weight in grams (w) as a function of gestation age in days (t) can be expressed by the formula: $w\,0.333 = 0.09\,(t - 16)$ (Huggett and Widdas, 1951). In small litters (1 to 5 fetuses) fetal weight appears to increase with increasing length of gestation, but weight decreases in larger litters (McKeown and MacMahon, 1956). In a study of 1032 young from 292

Table XIII
Percentage of Litters in Each Litter Size at Birth in the Guinea Pig as Reported by Four Sources

Litter size (no. of young in litter)	Bruce and Parkes (1948)[a]	Dunkin *et al.* (1930)[b]	Goy *et al.* (1957)[c]	McKeown and MacMahon (1956)[d]
1	6	4.5	3.6	5.2
2	13	23.1	21.0	8.7
3	26	45.5	41.5	18.2
4	25	22.4	26.8	31.5
5	17	4.0	6.1	22.5
6	5	0.5	<1.0	11.7
7	7	0	0	2.2
8	<1	0	0	0

[a]Mill Hill colony strain; 324 litters.
[b]Dunkin–Hartley colony strain; 404 litters.
[c]Genetically heterogenous colony; 1027 litters.
[d]Mill Hill colony strain; 276 litters.

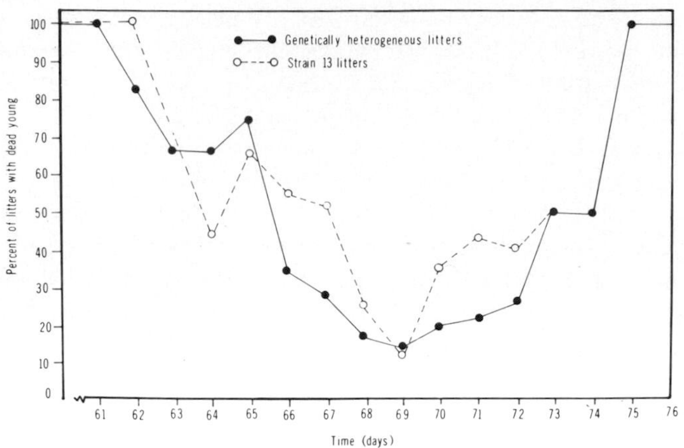

Fig. 14. Percent of guinea pig litters containing dead individuals on the different days of parturition (from Goy *et al.*, 1957).

litters (559 males, 473 females), the mean weight at birth was 93.4 gm and at 28 days of age was 227.1 gm (293% gain). There did not appear to be a sex difference. Birth weights and 28-day weights were related inversely to litter size (Table XIV); however, young from large litters grew more rapidly (in relation to their birth rates) than did young from small litters. Dunkin *et al.* (1930) reported the average birth weight in 1209 young from their albino stock to be 81.2 (± 0.36 SE) gm. They also recorded an inverse relationship between litter size and birth weight.

G. Postpartum Physiology

As the guinea pig nears the end of gestation, a few follicles are maturing to a preovulatory size (> 700 μm in diameter). Three days postpartum most ovaries contain fresh corpora lutea (CL) (see Section IV, C, 3, e). Thus, shortly after parturition there exists two generations of CL: new CL and rapidly regressing CL which at times can be stimulated into renewed function as the animal moves into the next gestation period. A similar situation exists in the domestic cat (Rowlands, 1956, as discussed by E.C. Amoroso). Challis *et al.* (1971) measured serum progesterone levels in nonpregnant and delivered guinea pigs up to 10 days postpartum and could find no difference, concluding that regressing CL do not produce appreciable amounts of progesterone.

Table XIV
Weight of Offspring at Birth and at 28 Days as Related to Litter Size[a]

No. in litter at birth	No. of offspring ♂	No. of offspring ♀	Mean weight at birth (gm) ♂	Mean weight at birth (gm) ♀	Mean weight at 28 days (gm) ♂	Mean weight at 28 days (gm) ♀	Weight gain % ♂	Weight gain % ♀
1	6	9	130.1	128.2	347.7	316.4	267	247
2	32	40	112.8	111.5	298.9	284.6	265	255
3	108	86	101.0	101.4	283.3	275.3	280	271
4	218	172	96.0	91.4	280.9	269.9	293	295
5	128	112	90.3	84.9	278.5	271.0	308	319
6	62	52	82.4	80.8	273.8	263.9	332	327
Average			95.7	93.2	281.8	272.6	294	292

[a]From McKeown and MacMahon (1956).

H. Lactation

Subsequent to the postpartum estrus, the estrous cycle continues normally regardless of whether the sow is lactating or not (Ishii, 1920). The guinea pig neonate, born in an advanced state of maturity, is not as dependent upon the mammary glands as are other mammals. Linzell (1971) mammectomized six virginal guinea pigs which bred successfully for 3 years, delivering from 7 to 15 litters. Fifty percent of the young survived without milk, provoking the thought that perhaps the placenta is teleologically replacing the mammary gland in *Cavia porcellus*. Nonetheless, Ishii (1920) suggested that to avoid weak, runty individuals with a high mortality rate, young should not be weaned before 15 to 20 days of age.

1. Lactation Curve and Milk Collection

Mepham and Beck (1973) studied lactation of 850- to 1100-gm Dunkin–Hartley sows in their second and third lactation. They used a timed-nursing method of milk yield determination in litters of 2 to 4 pups. Milk secretion in the nursing guinea pig sow increased rapidly the first 5 days postpartum. Peak milk yield reached 65 gm/day on days 5 through 8, then production diminished to agalactia by days 18 to 23 (Fig. 15). Productivity (milk yield) varied with litter size, strain, body weight, and parity of the sow. These workers recorded two distinct types of lactation curves in their study of five sows: (1) those (3 sows) whose yields peaked near 70 gm/day on days 5 to 8 then drastically declined to about 28 gm/day on day 9, recovering briefly to yield 44 gm/day on day 12, and (2) those (2 sows) whose yield was rather constant near 50 gm/day through the peak lactation period (day 4 to 12). No satisfactory explanation could be offered for these differences in lactation curves.

The rate of pup growth (weight gain) was directly related to the milk yield of the dam, and the sows with the larger litters gave the best milk yield (as discussed by Linzell, 1972). Also illustrated was the nutritional demand of lactation on the sows; they lost 54 to 163 gm of body weight over the 17-day experiment.

Collection of milk samples for chemical analysis does not yield large volumes; 5 to 10 gm can usually be harvested at a milking (Hamosh and Scow, 1971; Houston and Kon, 1939). Nelson *et al.* (1951) used a vacuum pump device (10–11 inches of mercury, 25 pulsations/minute) to collect milk for composition studies. Two milkings per day yielded from 3.64 to 18.71 gm of milk with peak productivity on day 3 of lactation. They noted that sows ceased to lactate if the young were removed for longer than 24 hours. Hesselberg and Loeb (1937) studied the histology of the lactating and regressing mammary gland and noted that retrogressive changes begin to appear after 3 weeks of lactation or shortly after the pups are weaned.

2. Composition of Milk

a. General. Nelson *et al.* (1951) reported the composition of guinea pig milk to be that shown in the following tabulation.

Water (%)	83.56	Solids (%)	16.44
Calories/100 gm	77	Fat (%)	3.92
Lactose (%)	3.02	Ash (%)	0.82
Protein (%)	8.10	Casein (%)	6.62
Whey protein (%)	1.48	Iodine no.	79.5
Saponification no.	196		

They also reported the amino acid and vitamin content. Mepham and Beck (1973) reported milk lactose to be 4.65 ± 0.3% and protein to be 6.9 ± 0.2% of which 79% was casein. Baker *et al.* (1963) reported total protein ($N \times 6.38$) to be 8.93%. Using paper electrophoresis, they demonstrated an α- and β-casein representing 23.3 and 48.1%, respectively, of milk casein. Their milk samples contained 4.0% fat of which 8.4% was linolenic with only a trace of linoleic. Brew and Campbell (1967) studied the whey protein and found α-lactalbumin (MW = 15,800; N-terminal = lysine; C-terminal = glutamine) to be the major protein component with significant amounts of blood serum albumin also present. No β-lactoglobulin was detected. These workers also listed the amino acid composition of the major protein of guinea pig milk. Mepham and Beck (1973) noted that the protein concentration increased in the last half of lactation while the lactose concentration tended to decline (Fig. 15).

b. Electrolytes. The fluxations in milk [Na^+] and [K^+] with stage of lactation are presented in Fig. 15. Note that milk [Na^+] increased throughout lactation while [K^+] decreased. Linzell and Peaker (1971) studied the water Na^+, K^+, and Cl^- content of fresh mammary gland tissue from lactating guinea pigs. Values (mean ± SE) were water content (ml/100 gm tissue) = 75.7 ± 0.6; Na^+ (mEq/kg tissue) = 38.6 ± 2.2; K^+ (mEq/kg tissue) = 71.8 ± 2.6 and Cl^- (mEq/kg tissue) = 47.9 ± 4.1. Calculated intracellular concentration (mEq/liter intracellular water) were Na^+ = 41.7; K^+ = 115.2; and Cl^- = 66.5.

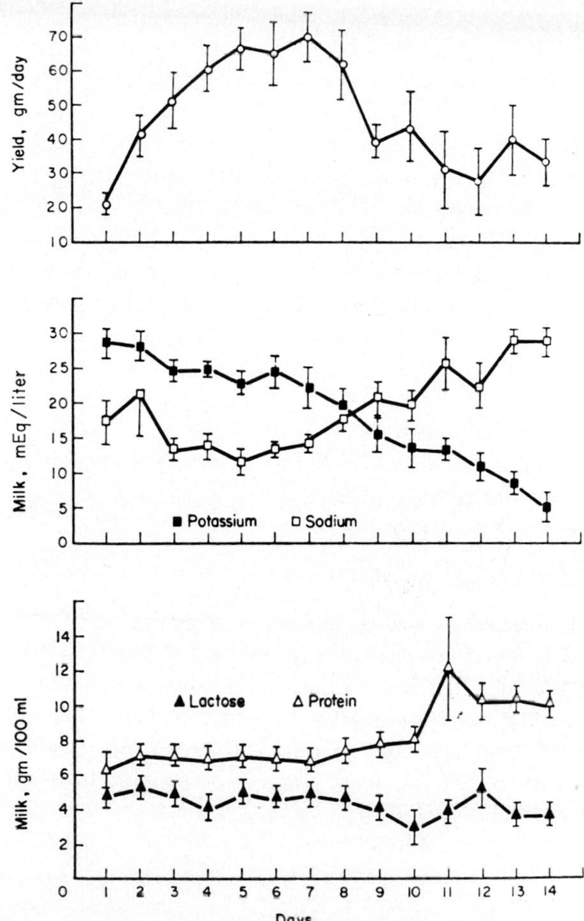

Fig. 15. Mean data (±SE) for milk yield and milk concentrations of Na^+, K^+, lactose, and protein ($N \times 6.38$) through first 2 weeks of lactation in five guinea pig sows (from Mepham and Beck, 1973).

c. Fatty Acids (FA). Unlike most other land animals, guinea pig milk does not contain significant amounts of short chain FA; butyric acid has not been detected (Smith *et al.*, 1968; Strong and Dils, 1972). Whereas short chain FA represent about 65% of rabbit milk FA, only about 0.1% of guinea pig milk FA contain less than 14 carbon atoms, making the guinea pig more nearly like the dog and man in this respect (Breckenridge and Kuksis, 1967). The FA chain lengths of adipose tissue in the guinea pig, rabbit, rat, and mouse are quite similar (16.9–17.4 carbons); however, the average milk FA chain length varies considerably: rabbit, 11.7; rat, 14.2; mouse, 15.3; and guinea pig, 17.2. Only about 40% of guinea pig milk FA are unsaturated; whereas, rabbit and rat milk FA are 80% unsaturated and mouse milk FA are 60% unsaturated (Smith *et al.*, 1968).

d. Lipoprotein Lipase. Lipoprotein lipase activity is high in the mammary gland milk of lactating guinea pigs (Hamosh and Scow, 1971; Robinson, 1963). Lipase activity in the gland tissue increases rapidly just before parturition and may reach 100 times that of pregnancy. Lipase is probably localized in the gland epithelial cells and its level remains elevated for the duration of lactation. The extremely high levels found in guinea pig milk (up to 500 times that of rat milk) suggests that the mammary gland epithelial cells may rupture during milk secretion in the guinea pig, but not in the rat which has high tissue lipase but low milk lipase activity (Hamosh and Scow, 1971). Other evidence suggesting that milk secretion in the guinea pig is of the apocrine type was presented by Wooding (1971), who demonstrated that the ultrastructure of the mammary gland epithelial cell wall was essentially the same as that of the milk fat globule membrane.

3. Miscellaneous (Lactation)

a. Assay System for Oxytocin. The guinea pig is particularly suited as a biological assay system for oxytocin. Its milk secretion apparatus is ten times as sensitive as the rabbit's and its teats are easily cannulated due to the single large glactophore of each teat canal (Tindal and Yokoyama, 1962). The milk ejection reflex pathway has been studied in detail by Tindal and Knaggs (1971).

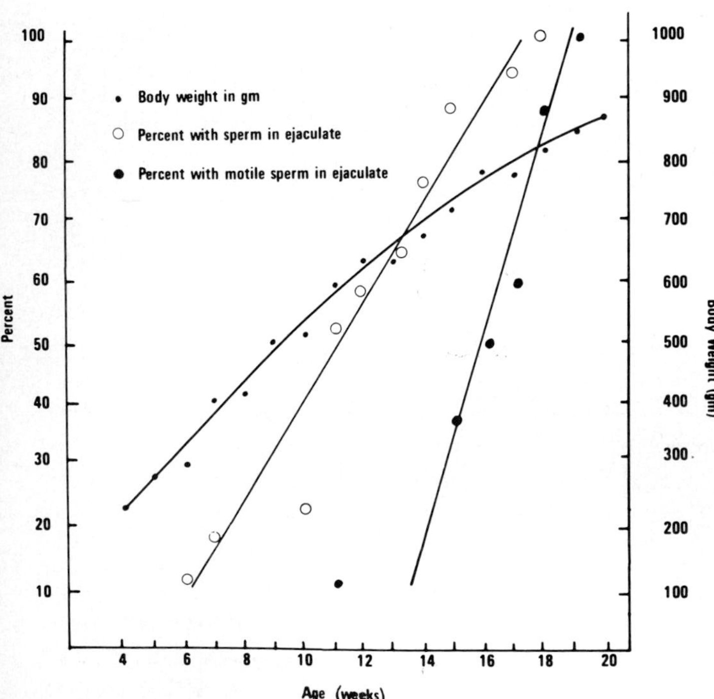

Fig. 16. Sperm production in the guinea pig in relation to age (from Freund, 1962).

b. Leukocyte Counts. In guinea pig milk leukocyte counts are quite high (50% of samples studied counted greater than 500,000/ml) and variable between animals (range 10,000 to 6,000,000). Gupta *et al.* (1971) suggested that these high counts may be related to the "stagnation" of milk consequent to no nursing for 6 to 10 hours presampling.

c. Immunization. Local immunization of the mammary gland of the pregnant guinea pig just previous to parturition elicited a local production of antibodies. These were mostly IgA, with levels in the milk reaching concentrations 10 to 25 times those found in the serum. IgG antibodies were but one-fifth as concentrated in the milk as in the serum. The guinea pig could be useful as an experimental animal for studies on local immunity in the mammary gland (McDowell, 1973).

d. Mammary Gland Weights. Mammary gland weights were found to correlate with body weight; animals over 750 gm body weight have average lactating gland weights of 24 gm (Linzell and Peaker, 1971).

e. Milk pH. Values range from 6.7 to 7.0 (Hamosh and Scow, 1971).

I. Male Reproduction

1. Puberty and Sexual Maturity

Age at puberty in the male has often been cited to be about 70 days (Reid, 1958; Sayles, 1939). This was based on the "uniform appearance" of sperm in the electroejaculate by that age. More recently, Freund (1962) placed puberty in a strain of English guinea pigs at 18 weeks of age. He defined puberty as the earliest age at which semen containing motile spermatozoa may be collected by electroejaculation. In this study, age at puberty ranged from 11 to 19 weeks. Freund differentiated between puberty and sexual maturity on the basis that although the reproductive organs may be functionally operative and secondary sex characteristics developed (puberty), adult concentrations of motile sperm often do not materialize until later (Fig. 16).

Sexual maturity is related to the secretion of androgens. Riss *et al.* (1955) reported a rise in plasma testosterone to coincide with the onset of sex behavior in the male guinea pig (3–4 weeks of age). Posterior mounting, the first component of male sexual behavior, has been reported to have a median appearance at 30.8 days (Gerall, 1963). Recently, Resko (1970) measured plasma androgen levels in the developing guinea pig. He reported a surge in plasma testosterone at approximately 30 days of age and found that androgen levels decreased rapidly following castration, even though sexual behavior persisted for several weeks.

2. Ejaculation, Semen Collection, and Volume

Ejaculation in the sexually rested guinea pig usually occurs during the first or second intromission and is followed by a refractory period during which he usually cannot be induced to copulate again for at least an hour. Earlier return to copulatory activity is sometimes effected by introducing a new female in estrus (Grunt and Young, 1952).

Transection of the spinal cord between T_{12} and L_1 in the guinea pig is followed in 1 to 7 minutes by rhythmic movements in the anogenital region, leading to erection and ejaculation. The ejaculation phase of this response is blocked by abdominal sympathectomy or severence of the two hypogastric nerves (Bacq, 1931).

The electroejaculatory methods of Moore and Gallagher (1930) were effective in collecting semen but the treatment was rather harsh: "despite the severity of the shock, the animal recovers within five minutes, and one-half hour later is essentially normal." About 2% of their subjects died from the stimulation and in the hands of other investigators ejaculation was often accompanied by apnea, generalized tonic muscular contractions, and eversion of the anal mucosa (Freund, 1969; Sayles, 1939). The procedure applied approximately 33 V, 60 cycle (ac) through a subcutaneous electrode on the dorsum of the neck and an electrode inserted into the guinea pig's mouth. Their protocol consisted of three 10-second stimulations at 1 minute intervals. Using this technique they collected 1.5 to 3 gm of semen weekly, most of which was seminal vesicle secretion. They found no seasonal variation in amount of ejaculate.

Freund (1958, 1969) developed a more precise and less traumatic electroejaculation method using lumbar and rectal electrodes. The stimulus was delivered as a square-wave, 25V, 1000 cycle (ac) current with an automatic 3-second "on period" and 12-second "off period." An average of 5 impulses were required and an average ejaculate volume of 0.5 ml (range = 0.1 to 1.2 ml) was collected biweekly.

Collection with the artificial vagina has not been possible and the volume of guinea pig ejaculate under normal coital circumstances is not known.

3. Semen Characteristics

a. Vaginal Plug. The portion of the male ejaculate secreted by the seminal vesicles coagulates almost instantaneously on emission and during copulation forms the *bouchon vaginal*, a rigid plug, filling the lumen of the vagina and cervix. Such a plug seems to be a general characteristic of the class Rodentia and was first described in the guinea pig in 1847 by Leuckart (from Stockard and Papanicolaou, 1919). Coagulation is greatly enhanced by an enzyme secreted by the anterior lobe of the prostate. The plug apparently prevents the outflow of sperm from the uterus after coagulation. It is enveloped in a mass of flat epithelial cells which evidently exfoliate from the vaginal wall. This "cast" of epithelial cells sheds, is fragmented, and expelled late in estrus, whether or not copulation takes place. The vaginal plug falls out of the vagina a few hours after its formation (Stockard and Papanicolaou, 1919).

Freund (1958) found that semen collected by electroejaculation was often ejaculated in plug form, having coagulated in the urethra. The coagulum did not spontaneously liquefy after 6 hours at 39°C. Such semen samples are difficult to study and liquefication can be effected and maintained for up to 6 hours with 0.1% chymotrypsin phosphate.

b. Rouleau Formation. Guinea pig spermatozoa cohere in rouleau formation in the epididymis prior to ejaculation and for varying periods of time following ejaculation into the female tract (Simeone and Young, 1931; Martan and Shepherd, 1973). Three to five minutes postcopulation, single cells and rouleaux of spermatozoa are found in the vagina, cervix, and uterus, but were absent from the oviduct until 15 minutes or more postcopulation. The number of single spermatozoan increased while the number of rouleaux decreased during the 24-hour postcopulation period. Whereas rouleau formation and dissociation occurs entirely in the male tract of other mammals, the environment of the female tract appears to be requisite for complete dissociation of rouleaux in the guinea pig. Martan and Shepherd (1973) suggested that rouleau formation may be important in protecting spermatozoa from polymorphonuclear cell phagocytosis and in facilitating the maturation process.

c. Capacitation. In vivo capacitation has not been studied in the guinea pig. Yanagimachi (1972), in reporting the first successful *in vitro* fertilization of guinea pig ova, suggested the optimal time for capacitation may be 8 to 10 hours and certainly no less than 2 hours.

d. Sperm Motility and Morphology. Compared to man and the bull, there is an unusual swimming pattern exhibited by guinea pig spermatozoa. Movement is curvilinear and characterized by an irregular forward progression. The frequent "head-to-head" rouleau formation often makes motility rating difficult.

There is a very high percentage of morphologically normal spermatozoa in the guinea pig semen sample, supporting the histological impression that spermatogenesis in the rodent is a more precise and well-ordered process than in man.

The semen data shown in the tabulation on p. 92 were collected from 29 animals by Freund (1969).

e. Seminal Fluid Toxic Principle. Freund and Thompson (1957) and Freund *et al.* (1958) discovered a toxic principle in the seminal fluid of the guinea pig which produced urination, defecation, salivation, and death when injected intramuscularly in the rabbit and guinea pig. Weil *et al.* (1964) named the principle *cobayin* and found it to be extremely toxic on

No. of specimens	870
Mean body weight (gm)	875
Ejaculate volume (ml)	0.5
Sperm conc. (× 10^6/ml)	41.782
Sperm conc. (× 10^6/ejaculate)	13.376
Motility (%)	66
No. of motile sperm (× 10^6/ejaculate)	9.268
Normal morphology (%)	95
Mean fructose conc. (mg/100 ml)	101 (54–152)

intraperitoneal injection in rabbits causing signs within minutes, including agitation, flushing of ears, dyspnea, diarrhea, and weakness with death occurring in 0.5 to 20 hours. The mouse, rat, and dog were less susceptible, while the guinea pig was resistant to the toxic effects. The only other known seminal fluid with toxic properties is that of the bat, *Myotis lucifugus* (Hunter *et al.*, 1971).

f. Antigens and Autoantigens. A review of the many investigations of the antigens and autoantigens of the guinea pig testis and testicular sperm is provided by Shulman (1971). Little is known of the immunological properties of ejaculated spermatozoa (Hekman and Shulman, 1971; Maruta and Moyer, 1967). This dearth of information has been attributed to the difficulty in obtaining an ejaculated semen sample and the toxic principle, *cobayin* found in guinea pig seminal plasma.

4. Vas Deferens

Huković (1961) first described the isolated vas deferens with its hypogastric nerve as an easy to prepare, durable preparation which gives quick, strong, and uniform contractions to nerve stimulation without significant spontaneous activity. The unique suitability of this preparation to neural decentralization and *in vitro* studies has been confirmed by Westfall (1970). There are innumerable reports of the use of this preparation in the literature, the majority of which deal with studies of autonomic pharmacology.

An *in vivo* preparation of both the vas deferens and the seminal vesicles has been described by Saxena (1970). In spite of its extensive use in physiological and pharmacology research, the precise characterization of innervation to the guinea pig vas deferens is disputed (Furness and Iwayama, 1972; Gosling and Dixon, 1972).

REFERENCES

Adolph, E. F. (1971). Ontogeny of heart-rate controls in hamster, rat and guinea pig. *Amer. J. Physiol.* **220**, 1896–1902.

Albrechtsen O. K. (1957). The fibrinolytic activity of animal tissues. *Acta Physiol.* **39**, 284–290.

Aldred, J. P., Sammelwitz, P. H., and Nalbandov, A. V. (1961). Mechanism of formation of corpora lutea in guinea pigs. *J. Reprod. Fert.* **2**, 394–399.

Altman, P. L., and Dittmer, D. S., eds. (1964). "Biology Data Book." Fed. Amer. Soc. Exp. Biol., Washington, D. C.

Ambrus, C. M., Weintraub, D. H., Niswander, K. R., and Ambrus, J. L. (1965). Studies on hyaline membrane disease. II. The ontogeny of the fibrinolysin system. *Pediatrics* **35**, 91–96.

Ambrus, J. L., Ambrus, C. M., Sokal, J. E., Markus, G., Back, N., Stutzman, L., Razis, D., Ross, C. A., Smith, B. H., Rekate, A. C., Collins, G. L., Kline, D. L., and Fishman, J. B. (1960). Clinical pharmacology of various types of fibrinolytic enzyme preparations. *Amer. J. Cardiol.* **6**, 462–475.

Ancill, R. J. (1956). The blood volume of the normal guinea-pig. *J. Physiol. (London)* **132**, 469–475.

Astrup, T., Glas, P., and Kok, P. (1970). Thromboplastic and fibrinolytic activity in lungs of some mammals. *Lab. Invest.* **22**, 381–386.

Austin, C. R., and Walton, A. (1960). Fertilisation. *In* "Marshall's Physiology of Reproduction" (A. S. Parkes, ed.), 3rd ed., Vol. 1, Part 2, Chapter 10. Longmans, Green, New York.

Bacq, Z. M. (1931). Impotence of the male rodent after sympathetic denervation of the genital organs. *Amer. J. Physiol.* **96**, 321–330.

Baker, B. E., Bertok, E. I., and Symes, A. L. (1963). The protein and lipid constitution of guinea pig milk. *Can. J. Zool.* **41**, 1041–1044.

Baker, G. T., and Schaefer, K. E. (1969). Effect of chronic hypercapnia on blood volume, plasma volume, and red cell volume. *U. S. Nav. Submar. Med. Cent., Rep.* No. 604.

Banerjee, V. (1966). Relative variation in some vertebrate erythrocytes. *Naturwissenschaften* **53**, 233–234.

Baranski, S. (1971). Effect of chronic microwave irradiation on the blood forming system of guinea pigs and rabbits. *Aerosp. Med.* **42**, 1196–1199.

Barkhan, P., and Howard, A. N. (1959). Some blood coagulation studies in normal and scrobutic guinea pigs. *Brit. J. Nutr.* **13**, 389–400.

Barnes, J. M. (1959). Antitoxin transfer from mother to fetus in the guinea-pig. *J. Pathol. Bacteriol.* **77**, 371–380.

Bartels, H. (1964). Comparative physiology of oxygen transport in mammals. *Lancet* **2**, 599–604.

Bartels, H., Yassin, D. E., and Reinhardt, W. (1967). Comparative studies of placental gas exchange in guinea pigs, rabbits, and goats. *Resp. Physiol.* **2**, 149–162.

Baumann, R., Bauer, C., and Bartels, H. (1971). Influence of chronic and acute hypoxia on oxygen affinity and RBC 2,3-diphosphoglycerate of rats and guinea pigs. *Resp. Physiol.* **11**, 135–144.

Beach, F. A. (1966). Ontogeny of "coitus-related" reflexes in the female guinea pig. *Proc. Nat. Acad. Sci. U. S.* **56**, 526–533.

Bedford, C. A., Challis, J. R. G., Harrison, F. A., and Heap, R. B. (1972). The role of estrogens and progesterone in the onset of parturition in various species. *J. Reprod. Fert., Suppl.* **16**, 1–23.

Bellanti, J. A., Russ, S. B., Holmes, G. E., and Buescher, E. L. (1965). The nature of antibodies following experimental arbovirus infection in guinea pigs. *J. Immunol.* **94**, 1–11.

Berendsen, P. B., and Telford, I. R. (1966). A light and electron microscopic study of Kurloff bodies in the blood and spleen of the guinea pig. *Anat. Rec.* **156**, 107–118.

Bethlenfalvay, N. C. (1972). Cytologic demonstration of methemoglobin and carboxyhemoglobin in certain vertebrates. *Amer. J. Vet. Res.* **33**, 1017–1022.

Bilbey, D. L. J., and Nicol, T. (1955). Normal blood picture of the guinea pig. *Nature (London)* **176**, 1218.

Bland, K. P., and Donovan, B. T. (1970). Oestrogen and progesterone and the function of the corpora lutea in the guinea-pig. *J. Endocrinol.* **47**, 225–230.

Blandau, R. J. (1949). Observations on implantation of the guinea pig ovum. *Anat. Rec.* **103**, 19–47.

Blandau, R. J., and Young, W. C. (1939). The effects of delayed fertilization on the development of the guinea pig ovum. *Amer. J. Anat.* **64**, 303–330.

Blatchley, F. R., and Donovan, B. T. (1969). Luteolytic effect of prostaglandin in the guinea pig. *Nature (London)* **221**, 1065–1066.

Blatchley, F. R., Donovan, B. T., Poyser, N. L., Horton, E. W., Thompson, C. J., and Los, M. (1971). Identification of prostaglandin $F_{2\alpha}$ in the utero-ovarian blood of guinea-pig after treatment with oestrogen. *Nature (London)* **230**, 243–244.

Blatchley, F. R., Donovan, B. T., Horton, E. W., and Poyser, N. L. (1972). The release of prostaglandins and progestin into the utero-ovarian venous blood of guinea-pigs during oestrous cycle and following oestrogen treatment. *J. Physiol. (London)* **223**, 69–88.

Bocci, V., and Viti, A. (1965). Organ plasma volume of normal rat and guinea-pig. *Arch. Fisiol.* **63**, 85–98.

Boling, J. L., Blandau, R. J., Wilson, J. G., and Young, W. C. (1939). Post-parturitional heat response of newborn and adult guinea pigs. Data on parturition. *Proc. Soc. Exp. Biol. Med.* **42**, 128–132.

Bonciu, C., Bonciu, O., Dincoulesco, M., and Petrovici, M. (1967). Recherches sur les constantes hématologicques et sur la température normale chez les cobayes d'élévage. *Arch. Roum. Pathol. Exp. Microbiol.* **26**, 337–344.

Bφrjesson, B., and Stφa, K. F. (1970). Metabolism of 17β-oestradiol in the guinea-pig. *Abst., Int. Cong. Horm. Steroids, 3rd, 1970* Int. Congr. Ser. No. 210, pp. 232–233.

Bosse, J.-A., and Wassermann, O. (1970). On the blood content of guinea-pig tissues. *Pharmacology* **4**, 273–277.

Breckenridge, W. C., and Kuksis, A. (1967). Molecular weight distributions of milk fat triglycerides from seven species. *J. Lipid Res.* **8**, 473–478.

Brew, K., and Campbell, P. N. (1967). The characterization of the whey proteins of guinea-pig milk. *Biochem. J.* **102**, 258–264.

Bruce, H. M., and Parkes, A. S. (1948). Feeding and breeding of laboratory animals. *J. Hyg.* **46**, 434–437.

Buchanan, G. D., Enders, A. C., and Talmage, R. V. (1956). Implantation in armadillos ovarectomized during the period of delayed implantation. *J. Endocrinol.* **14**, 121–128.

Bunn, H. F. (1971). Differences in the interaction of 2,3-diphosphoglycerate with certain mammalian hemoglobins. *Science* **172**, 1049–1050.

Burnett, S. H. (1904). A study of the blood of normal guinea-pigs. *J. Med. Res.* **11**, 537–551.

Burns, K. F., and deLannoy, C. W. (1966). Compendium of normal blood values of laboratory animals, with indication of variations. I. Random-sexed populations of small animals. *Toxicol. Appl. Pharmacol.* **8**, 429–437.

Butt, J. H., and Wilson, T. H. (1968). Development of sugar and amino acid transport by intestine and yolk sac of the guinea pig. *Amer. J. Physiol.* **215**, 1468–1477.

Calman, H. N. (1972). Corticosteroids and lymphoid cells. *N. Engl. J. Med.* **287**, 388–397.

Challis, J. R. G., Heap, R. B., and Illingworth, D. V. (1971). Concentrations of oestrogen and progesterone in the plasma of non-pregnant, pregnant and lactating guinea-pigs. *J. Endocrinol.* **51**, 333–345.

Chan, B. S. T. (1965). Quantitative changes in the basophil cells of guinea-pig bone marrow following the administration of *Ascaris* body fluid. *Immunology* **8**, 566–577.

Chan, B. S. T. (1968). Quantitative changes in the basophil cells of guinea-pig bone marrow following the administration of desiccated *Ascaris* ova. *Immunology* **14**, 99–106.

Chenkin, T., and Weiner, M. (1965). A comparison of some human clotting abnormalities with the clotting pattern of normal guinea pigs. *Exp. Med. Surg.* **23**, 398–405.

Chenkin, T., Dayton, P. G., Weisberg, L. G., and Weiner, M. (1959). Effect of starvation, acenocoumarin, and vitamin K on the coagulation pattern of the guinea pig. *Exp. Med. Surg.* **17**, 219–226.

Choudary, J. B., and Greenwald, G. S. (1968). Luteolytic effect of oestrogen on the corpora lutea of the cyclic guinea-pig. *J. Reprod. Fert.* **16**, 333–341.

Choudary, J. B., and Greenwald, G. S. (1969). Reversal by gonadotrophins of the luteolytic effect of oestrogen in the cyclic guinea-pig. *J. Reprod. Fert.* **19**, 503–510.

Christensen, H. E., Wanstrup, J., and Ranlφv, P. (1970). The cytology of the Foà-Kurloff reticular cells of the guinea pig. *Acta Pathol. Microbiol. Scand., Suppl.* **212**, 15–24.

Church, R. L., and Eleftheriou, B. E. (1966). Tentative identification of plasma, ovarian and placental oestrogens in the guinea-pig. *J. Reprod. Fert.* **12**, 369–372.

Coldman, M. F., and Good, W. (1967). The distribution of sodium, potassium and glucose in the blood of some mammals. *Comp. Biochem. Physiol.* **21**, 201–206.

Coldman, M. F., Gent, M., and Good, W. (1969). The osmotic fragility of mammalian erythrocytes in hypotonic solutions of sodium chloride. *Comp. Biochem. Physiol.* **31**, 605–609.

Constable, B. J. (1963). Changes in blood volume and blood picture during the life of the rat and guinea-pig from birth to maturity. *J. Physiol. (London)* **167**, 229–238.

Constantine, J. W. (1966). Aggregation of guinea-pig platelets by adenosine diphosphate. *Nature (London)* **210**, 162–164.

Dancis, J., Money, W. L., Springer, D., and Levitz, M. (1968). Transport of amino acids by placenta. *Amer. J. Obstet. Gynecol.* **101**, 820–829.

Da Prada, M., Pletscher, A., and Tranzer, J. P. (1971). Storage of ATP and 5-hydroxytryptamine in blood platelets of guinea-pigs. *J. Physiol. (London)* **217**, 679–688.

Dawe, A. R., and Morrison, P. R. (1955). Interspecific influence of body weight on electrocardiographic time components in small mammals. *Amer. J. Physiol.* **183**, 608.

Dean, M. F., and Muir, H. (1970). The characterization of a protein-polysaccharide isolated from Kurloff cells of the guinea pig. *Biochem. J.* **118**, 783–790.

Deanesly, R. (1960a). Endocrine activity of the early placenta of the guinea-pig. *J. Endocrinol.* **21**, 235–239.

Deanesly, R. (1960b). Implantation and early pregnancy in ovariectomized guinea-pigs. *J. Reprod. Fert.* **1**, 242–248.

Deanesly, R. (1966). The effects of purified sheep luteinizing hormone on the guinea-pig ovary. *J. Reprod. Fert.* **11**, 303–305.

Deanesly, R. (1968). The effects of progesterone, testosterone and ergocornine on non-pregnant and pregnant guinea-pigs. *J. Reprod. Fert.* **16**, 271–281.

Dempsey, E. W. (1937). Follicular growth rate and ovulation after various experimental procedures in the guinea pig. *Amer. J. Physiol.* **120**, 126–132.

Dempsey, E. W., Myers, H. I., Young, W. C., and Jennison, D. B. (1934). Absence of light and the reproductive cycle in the guinea pig. *Amer. J. Physiol.* **109**, 307–311.

Diamond, M., Rust, N., and Westphal, U. (1969). High-affinity binding of progesterone, testosterone and cortisol in normal and androgen-treated guinea pigs during various reproductive stages: Relationship to masculinization. *Endocrinology* **84**, 1143–1151.

Dineen, J. K., and Adams, D. B. (1970). The effect of long-term lymphatic drainage on the lympho-myeloid system in the guinea-pig. *Immunology* **19**, 11–30.

Dodds, W. J., and Pickering, R. J. (1972). The effect of cobra venom factor on hemostasis in guinea pigs. *Blood* **40**, 400–411.

Donovan, B. T. (1967). The existence of a luteolytic hormone in the uterus of the guinea-pig. *In* "Reproduction in the Female Mammal"

(G. E. Lamming and E. C. Amorosa, eds.), pp. 317–335. Butterworth, London.

Donovan, B. T., and Kopriva, P. C. (1965). Effect of removal or stimulation of the olfactory bulbs on the estrous cycle of the guinea pig. *Endocrinology* 77, 213–217.

Donovan, B. T., and Lockhart, A. N. (1972a). Gonadal hormones and the control of ovulation in the guinea-pig. *J. Endocrinol.* **55**, 599–607.

Donovan, B. T., and Lockhart, A. N. (1972b). Light and the timing of ovulation in the guinea-pig. *J. Reprod. Fert.* **30**, 207–211.

Draper, R. L. (1920). The prenatal growth of the guinea-pig. *Anat. Rec.* **18**, 369–392.

Dunkin, G. W., Hartley, P., Lewis-Faning, E., and Russell, W. T. (1930). A comparative biometric study of albino and coloured guinea-pigs from the point of view of their suitability for experimental use. *J. Hyg.* **30**, 311–330.

Edmondson, P. W., and Wyburn, J. R. (1963). The erythrocyte life-span, red cell mass and plasma volume of normal guinea-pigs as determined by the use of ^{51}chromium, ^{32}phosphorus labelled di-iso-propyl fluorophosphonate and ^{131}iodine labelled human serum albumin. *Brit. J. Exp. Pathol.* **44**, 72–80.

Eklund, B., Senturia, J. B., and Johansson, B. W. (1972). Electrocardiogram. *Acta Physiol. Scand., Suppl.* **380**, 28–30.

Enders, A. C. (1965). A comparative study of the fine structure of the trophoblast in several hemochorial placentas. *Amer. J. Anat.* **116**, 29–68.

Epstein, R. D., and Tompkins, E. H. (1943). A comparison of techniques for the differential counting of bone marrow cells (guinea pig). *Amer. J. Med. Sci.* **206**, 249–260.

Ernström, U. (1963). Thyroxine-induced changes in cell composition of lymph node tissue, spleen and thymus. *Acta Pathol. Microbiol. Scand.* **59**, 145–155.

Ernström, U. (1965a). Influence of the thymus on thyroxin-induced lymphatic hyperplasia in young guinea-pigs. I. Treatment with thyroxin one month after thymectomy. *Acta Pathol. Microbiol. Scand.* **64**, 83–89.

Ernström, U. (1965b). Influence of neonatal thymectomy on the lymphatic system and on its reaction to exogenous thyroxin in guinea-pigs. *Acta Pathol. Microbiol. Scand.* **65**, 192–202.

Ernström, U. (1970). Hormonal influences on thymic release of lymphocytes into the blood. *Ciba Found. Study Group* **36**, 53–65.

Ernström, U., and Gyllensten, L. (1959). The histologic picture in thyroxin-induced lymphatic hyperplasia. *Acta Pathol. Microbiol. Scand.* **47**, 243–255.

Ernström, U., and Larsson, B. (1966). Changes in circulating lymphocyte populations in growing guinea-pigs. *Acta Pathol. Microbiol. Scand.* **67**, 267–275.

Ernström, U., and Larsson, B. (1967). Export and import of lymphocytes in the thymus during steroid-induced involution and regeneration. *Acta Pathol. Microbiol. Scand.* **70**, 371–384.

Ernström, U., and Larsson, B. (1969). Thymic export of lymphocytes 3 days after labelling with tritiated thymidine. *Nature (London)* **222**, 279–280.

Ernström, U., and Larsson, B. (1970). Determination of thymic blood flow in guinea-pigs of different ages. *Acta Pathol. Microbiol. Scand., Sect. A* **78**, 366–367.

Ernström, U., and Sandberg, G. (1970). Quantitative relationship between release and intrathymic death of lymphocytes. *Acta Pathol. Microbiol. Scand., Sect. A* **78**, 362–363.

Ernström, U., and Sandberg, G. (1971). On the origin of Foà-Kurloff cells. *Scand. J. Haematol.* **8**, 380–391.

Ernström, U., Gyllensten, L., and Larsson, B. (1965). Venous output of lymphocytes from the thymus. *Nature (London)* **207**, 540–541.

Everett, N. B., and Yoffey, J. M. (1959). Life of guinea pig circulating erythrocyte and its relation to erythrocyte population of bone marrow. *Proc. Soc. Exp. Biol. Med.* **101**, 318–319.

Faber, L. E., Sandmann, M. L., and Stavely, H. E. (1972). Progesterone binding in uterine cytosols of the guinea pig. *J. Biol. Chem.* **247**, 8000–8004.

Fand, I., and Gordon, A. S. (1957). A quantitative study of the bone marrow in the guinea pig throughout life. *J. Morphol.* **100**, 473–507.

Fara, J. W., and Catlett, R. H. (1971). Cardiac response and social behavior in the guinea-pig (*Cavia porcellus*). *Anim. Behav.* **19**, 514–523.

Farmer, J. B., and Levy, G. P. (1968). A simple method for recording the electrocardiogram and heart rate from conscious animals. *Brit. J. Pharmacol. Chemother.* **32**, 193–200.

Fay, F. S., and Cooke, P. H. (1972). Guinea pig ductus arteriosis. II. Irreversible closure after birth. *Amer. J. Physiol.* **222**, 841–849.

Fay, F. S., and Jöbsis, F. F. (1972). Guinea pig ductus arteriosus. III. Light absorption changes during response to O_2. *Amer. J. Physiol.* **223**, 588–595.

Ferguson, M. M., and Christie, G. A. (1967). Distribution of hydroxysteroid dehydrogenases in the placentae and foetal membranes of various mammals. *J. Endocrinol.* **38**, 291–306.

Fiala, J., and Viktora, L. (1970). Comparative study of the phagocytic activity of the leucocytes of some laboratory animals. *Physiol. Bohemoslov.* **19**, 447–450.

Fiala, J., Viktora, L., and Urbánková, J. (1966). Osmotic resistance of leucocytes of some laboratory animals. *Physiol. Bohemoslov.* **15**, 281–284.

Foà, P., and Carbone, T. (1889). Beiträge zur histologie und physiopathologie der milz der säugethiere. *Beitr. Pathol. Anat. Allg. Pathol.* **5**, 227–252.

Ford, D. H., and Young, W. C. (1953). Duration of the first cyclic vaginal openings in maturing guinea pigs and related ovarian conditions. *Anat. Rec.* **115**, 495–503.

Foreman, P., and Segal, M. B. (1972). The effect of pH on the selective permeability of the guinea-pig amnion to monovalent ions. *J. Physiol. (London)* **226**, 92P–93P.

Fozzard, H. A., and Sleator, W. (1967). Membrane ionic conductances during rest and activity in guinea pig atrial muscle. *Amer. J. Physiol.* **212**, 945–952.

Freund, M. (1958). Collection and liquefaction of guinea pig semen. *Proc. Soc. Exp. Biol. Med.* **98**, 538–540.

Freund, M. (1962). Initiation and development of semen production in the guinea pig. *Fert. Steril.* **13**, 190–201.

Freund, M. (1969). Interrelationships among the characteristics of guinea-pig semen collected by electro-ejaculation. *J. Reprod. Fert.* **19**, 393–403.

Freund, J., and Thompson, G. E. (1957). Toxic effects of fluid from the coagulating gland of the guinea pig. *Proc. Soc. Exp. Biol. Med.* **94**, 350–351.

Freund, J., Miles, A. A., Mill, P. J., and Wilhelm, D. L. (1958). Vascular permeability factors in the secretion of the guinea pig coagulating gland. *Nature (London)* **182**, 174–175.

Fuchs, F. (1952). The red cell volume of the maternal and foetal vessels of the guinea pig placenta. *Acta Physiol. Scand.* **28**, 162–171.

Fuchs, F. (1957). "Studies on the Passage of Phosphate between Mother and Foetus in the Guinea Pig." Munksgaard, Copenhagen.

Furness, J. B., and Iwayama, T. (1972). The arrangement and identification of axons innervating the vas deferens of the guinea-pig. *J. Anat.* **113**, 179–196.

Gerall, A. A. (1963). The effect of prenatal and postnatal injections of testosterone propionate on prepubertal male guinea pig sex behavior. *J. Comp. Physiol. Psychol.* **56**, 92–95.

Gibb, D. G. A. (1969). The histochemistry of hematoxylin staining granules (HSG) in the vaginal epithelium of the proestrus guinea pig. *Acta Cytol.* **13**, 89–93.

Gillman, R. G., and Burton, A. C. (1966). Constriction of the neonatal aorta by raised oxygen tension. *Circ. Res.* **19**, 755–765.

Ginther, O. J. (1969). Length of estrous cycle and size of corpus luteum in guinea pigs and sheep treated with progesterone at different days of the estrous cycle. *Amer. J. Vet. Res.* **30**, 1975–1978.

Goetz, U., Da Prada, M., and Pletscher, A. (1971). Adenine-, guanine- and uridine-5′- phosphonucleotides in blood platelets and storage organelles of various species. *J. Pharmacol. Exp. Ther.* **178**, 210–215.

Gosling, J. A., and Dixon, J. S. (1972). Differences in the manner of autonomic innervation of the muscle layers of the guinea-pig ductus deferens. *J. Anat.* **112**, 81–91.

Goy, R. W., Hoar, R. M., and Young, W. C. (1957). Length of gestation in the guinea pig with data on the frequency and time of abortion and stillbirth. *Anat. Rec.* **128**, 747–757.

Greenfield, A. D. M., Shepherd, J. T., and Whelan, R. F. (1951). The relationship between the blood flow in the umbilical cord and the rate of foetal growth in the sheep and guinea-pig. *J. Physiol. (London)* **115**, 158–162.

Greep, R. O. (1971). Regulation of luteal cell function. *Proc. Int. Congr. Horm. Steroids, 3rd, 1970* Int. Congr. Ser. No. 219, pp. 670–679.

Griffiths, D. A., and Rieke, W. O. (1969). A comparison of quantitative hematological value in two strains of guinea pig. *Exp. Hematol.* **18**, 36–39.

Grönroos, P. (1960). The life span of guinea pig red cells estimated by use of $Na_2{}^{51}CrO_4$. *Aust. J. Sci.* **23**, 195–196.

Gross, P., and deTreville, R. T. P. (1968). Alveolar proteinosis–its experimental production in rodents. *Arch. Pathol.* **86**, 255–261.

Grunt, J. A., and Young, W. C. (1952). Psychological modification of fatigue following orgasm (ejaculation) in the male guinea pig. *J. Comp. Physiol. Psychol.* **45**, 508–510.

Gryglewski, R. Y., Gaertner, H., and Durek, B. (1968). Influence of flufenamic acid on thrombolysis of human and animal plasma *in vitro. Diss. Pharm. Pharmacol.* **20**, 467–477.

Gupta, B. N., Langham, R. F., and Conner, G. H. (1971). The leukocytic component of guinea pig milk. *Lab. Anim. Sci.* **21**, 911–912.

Gyllensten, L. (1953). Influence of thymus and thyroid on the postnatal growth of the lymphatic tissue in guinea pigs. *Acta Anat., Suppl.* **18**, 1–163.

Haines, G. (1931). A statistical study of the relation between various expressions of fertility and vigor in the guinea pig. *J. Agr. Res.* **42**, 123–164.

Hamosh, M., and Scow, R. O. (1971). Lipoprotein lipase activity in guinea pig and rat milk. *Biochim. Biophys. Acta* **231**, 283–289.

Harned, M. A., and Casida, L. E. (1972). Failure to obtain group synchrony of estrus in the guinea pig. *J. Mammal.* **53**, 223–225.

Harris, R. S., Herdan, G., Ancill, R. J., and Yoffey, J. M. (1954). A quantitative comparison of the nucleated cells in the right and left humeral bone marrow of the guinea pig. *Blood* **9**, 374–378.

Heap, R. B., and Deanesly, R. (1966). Progesterone in systemic blood and placentae of intact and ovariectomized pregnant guinea-pigs. *J. Endocrinol.* **34**, 417–423.

Heap, R. B., Perry, J. S., and Rowlands, I. W. (1967). Corpus luteum function in the guinea-pig; arterial and luteal progesterone levels, and the effects of hysterectomy and hypophysectomy. *J. Reprod. Fert.* **13**, 537–553.

Hekman, A., and Shulman, S. (1971). Antibodies to spermatozoa. III. Responses in rabbits and guinea-pigs to immunization with guinea-pig sperm cells. *Clin. Exp. Immunol.* **9**, 147–160.

Hermreck, A. S., and Greenwald, G. S. (1964). The effect of unilateral ovariectomy on follicular maturation in the guinea pig. *Anat. Rec.* **148**, 171–176.

Herrick, E. H. (1928). The duration of pregnancy in guinea-pigs after removal and also after transplantation of the ovaries. *Anat. Rec.* **39**, 193–200.

Hershfield, M. S., and Nemeth, A. M. (1968). Placental transport of free palmitic and linoleic acids in the guinea pig. *J. Lipid Res.* **9**, 460–468.

Hesselberg, C., and Loeb, L. (1937). The structure of the secreting and retrogressing mammary gland in the guinea pig. *Anat. Rec.* **68**, 103–112.

Hill, P. M. M., and Young, M. (1973). Use of the guinea-pig foetal placenta, perfused *in situ*, as a model to study the placental transfer of pharmacological substances. *Brit. J. Pharmacol.* **47**, 655–656.

Hisaw, F. L. (1926). Experimental relaxation of the pubic ligament of the guinea pig. *Proc. Soc. Exp. Biol. Med.* **23**, 661–663.

Hisaw, F. L., Zarrow, M. X., Money, W. L., Talmage, R. V. N., and Abramowitz, A. A. (1944). Importance of the female reproductive tract in the formation of relaxin. *Endocrinology* **34**, 122–134.

Hoar, R. M., Goy, R. W., and Young, W. C. (1957). Loci of action of thyroid hormone on reproduction in the female guinea pig. *Endocrinology* **60**, 337–346.

Houston, J., and Kon, S. K. (1939). Vitamins in rat's and in guinea-pig's milk. *Biochem. J.* **33**, 1655–1659.

Hudson, G. (1958). Bone marrow volume in guinea-pigs. *J. Anat.* **92**, 150–161.

Hudson, G. (1959). Marrow cellularity in different regions of the guinea-pig's skeleton. *Acta Haematol.* **22**, 380–384.

Hudson, G., Osmond, D. G., and Roylance, P. J. (1963). Cell-populations in the bone marrow of the normal guinea-pig. *Acta Anat.* **53**, 234–239.

Huggett, A. St.G., and Widdas, W. F. (1951). The relationship between mammalian foetal weight and conception age. *J. Physiol. (London)* **114**, 306–317.

Huković, S. (1961). Responses of the isolated sympathetic nerve-ductus deferens preparation of the guinea-pig. *Brit. J. Pharmacol. Chemother.* **16**, 188–194.

Hunter, A. G., Barker, L. D. S., Johnson, W. L., Fahning, M. L., and Schultz, R. H. (1971). Antigenicity, toxicity and cross-reactions of male bat (*Myotis lucifugus*) reproductive organs. *J. Reprod. Fert.* **24**, 171–177.

Hunter, R. H. F., Hunt, D. M., and Chang, M. C. (1969). Temporal and cytological aspects of fertilization and early development in the guinea pig, *Cavia porcellus. Anat. Rec.* **165**, 411–430.

Hurt, J. P., and Krigman, M. R. (1970). Selected procoagulants in the guinea pig. *Amer. J. Physiol.* **218**, 832–837.

Hurt, J. P., Odom, M. H., Perlmutt, L., and Krigman, M. R. (1970). Blood clotting changes in guinea pigs with a heterologous intracranial neoplasm. *Lab. Invest.* **23**, 179–183.

Hwang, S. W., and Wosilait, W. D. (1970). Comparative and developmental studies on blood coagulation. *Comp. Biochem. Physiol.* **37**, 595–599.

Ikeda, M., Rubinstein, E. H., and Sonnenschein, R. R. (1973). Development of the oxygen induced contractions in the ductus arteriosus of the guinea-pig. *Experientia* **29**, 445–446.

Illingworth, D. V., and Heap, R. B. (1971). A decrease in the metabolic clearance rate of progesterone in the coypu during pregnancy. *J. Reprod. Fert.* **27**, 492–494.

Illingworth, D. V., Heap, R. B., and Perry, J. S. (1970). Changes in the metabolic clearance rate of progesterone in the guinea-pig. *J. Endocrinol.* **48**, 409–417.

Innes, J., Innes, E. M., and Moore, C. V. (1949). The hematologic changes induced in guinea pigs by the prolonged administration of pteroyl glutamic acid antagonists. *J. Lab. Clin. Med.* **34**, 883–901.

Ishii, O. (1920). Observations on the sexual cycle of the guinea pig. *Biol. Bull.* **38**, 237–250.

Jagiello, G. (1965). Effects of selected hormones on the closed vaginal membrane of the ovariectomized guinea pig. *Proc. Soc. Exp. Biol. Med.* **118**, 412–414.

Jolly, J. (1923). "Traité technique d' hématologie." Maloine, Paris.

Kaplow, L. S. (1969). Alkaline phosphatase activity in peripheral blood lymphocytes. *Arch. Pathol.* **88**, 69–72.

Kato, K. (1941). A single and accurate microfragility test for measuring erythrocyte resistance. *J. Lab. Clin. Med.* **26**, 703–713.

Kennedy, J. A., and Clark, S. L. (1942). Observations on the physiological reactions of the ductus arteriosus. *Amer. J. Physiol.* **136**, 140–147.

King, B. F., and Enders, A. C. (1971). Protein absorption by the guinea pig chorioallantoic placenta. *Amer. J. Anat.* **130**, 409–430.

King, E. S., and Lucas, M. (1941). A study of the blood cells of normal guinea pigs. *J. Lab. Clin. Med.* **26**, 1364–1365.

Kotani, M., Seike, K., Yamashita, A., and Horii, I. (1966). Lymphatic drainage of thymocytes to the circulation in the guinea pig. *Blood* **27**, 511–520.

Kurloff, M. G. (1889). Blood cells in splenectomized animals after one year of life. *Vrach. Delo.* **10**, 515–518 and 538–543.

Kutscher, C. (1968). Plasma volume change during water-deprivation in gerbils, hamsters, guinea pigs and rats. *Comp. Biochem. Physiol.* **25**, 929–936.

Labhsetwar, A. P., and Diamond, M. (1970). Ovarian changes in the guinea pig during various reproductive stages and steroid treatments. *Biol. Reprod.* **2**, 53–57.

Larsson, B. (1966a). A quantitative estimation of the venous output of lymphocytes from the thymus in guinea-pigs. *Acta Pathol. Microbiol. Scand.* **67**, 586–587.

Larsson, B. (1966b). Venous output of ^{3}H-thymidine-labelled lymphocytes from the thymus. *Acta Pathol. Microbiol. Scand.* **68**, 622–624.

Latallo, Z., Niewiarowski, S., and Copley, A. L. (1959). Fibrinolytic system of guinea pig serum. *Amer. J. Physiol.* **196**, 775–778.

Ledingham, J. C. G. (1940). Sex hormones and the Fòa-Kurloff cell. *J. Pathol. Bacteriol.* **50**, 201–219.

Ledingham, J. C. G., and Bedson, S. P. (1915). Experimental purpura. *Lancet* **1**, 311–316.

Leissring, J. C., and Anderson, J. W. (1961). The transfer of serum proteins from mother to young in the guinea pig. I. Prenatal rates and routes. *Amer. J. Anat.* **109**, 149–155.

Lepeschkin, E. (1965). The configuration of the T wave and the ventricular action potential in different species of mammals. *Ann. N. Y. Acad. Sci.* **127**, 170–178.

Lieberman, J. (1959). Clinical syndromes associated with deficient lung fibrinolytic activity. I. A new count of hyaline-membrane disease. *N. Engl. J. Med.* **260**, 619–626.

Linzell, J. L. (1971). The role of the mammary glands in reproduction. *Res. Reprod.* **3**, 2–3.

Linzell, J. L. (1972). Milk yield, energy loss in milk, and mammary gland weight in different species. *Dairy Sci. Abstr.* **34**, 351–360.

Linzell, J. L., and Peaker, M. (1971). Intracellular concentrations of sodium, potassium and chloride in the lactating mammary gland and their relation to the secretory mechanism. *J. Physiol. (London)* **216**, 683–700.

Loeb, L. (1906). The formation of the corpus luteum in the guinea-pig. *J. Amer. Med. Ass.* **46**, 416–423.

Loeb, L. (1932). Some mechanisms in the sexual cycle of the guinea pig. *Aust. J. Exp. Biol. Med. Sci.* **9**, 141–158.

Lombard, E. A. (1952). Electrocardiograms of small mammals. *Amer. J. Physiol.* **171**, 189–193.

London, W. T., Money, W. L., and Rawson, R. W. (1963). Placental transport of I^{131}-labeled thyroxine and triiodothyronine in the guinea pig. *Endocrinology* **73**, 205–209.

Long, C. (1961). "Biochemists' Handbook." Spon, London.

Lucarelli, G., and Butturini, U. (1967). The control of foetal and neonatal erythropoiesis. *Proc. Roy. Soc. Med.* **60**, 1036–1037.

Lucarelli, G., Porcellini, A., Carnevali, C., Carmena, A., and Stohlman, F. (1968). Fetal and neonatal erythropoiesis. *Ann. N. Y. Acad. Sci.* **149**, 544–559.

Luisada, A., Weisz, L., and Hantman, H. W. (194). A comparative study of electrocardiogram and heart sounds in common and domestic mammals. *Cardiologia* **8**, 63–84.

Lynch, V. deP., Clemente, E., and Carson, S. (1967). Effect of mescaline on cardiopulmonary dynamics. Method for determination of right ventricular pressure in the guinea pig. *J. Pharm. Sci.* **56**, 477–483.

McDowell, G. H. (1973). Local antigenic stimulation of guinea-pig mammary gland. *Aust. J. Exp. Biol. Med. Sci.* **51**, 237–245.

McKeown, T., and MacMahon, B. (1956). The influence of litter size and litter order on length of gestation and early postnatal growth in the guinea-pig. *J. Endocrinol.* **13**, 195–200.

Marley, P. B. (1972). An attempt to inhibit the uterine luteolysin in the guinea-pig. *J. Physiol. (London)* **222**, 169P–170P.

Marshall, A. H. E., and Swettenham, K. V. (1959). The formation of mucoprotein-sulphated mucopolysaccharide complex in the lymphoid tissue of the pregnant guinea-pig. *J. Anat.* **93**, 348–353.

Marshall, A. H. E., Swettenham, K. V., Vernon-Roberts, B., and Revell, P. A. (1971). Studies on the function of the Kurloff cell. *Int. Arch. Allergy Appl. Immunol.* **40**, 137–152.

Marshall, L. H., and Hanna, C. H. (1956). Direct measurement of arterial blood pressure in the guinea pig. *Proc. Soc. Exp. Biol. Med.* **92**, 31–32.

Martan, J., and Shepherd, B. A. (1973). Spermatozoa in rouleaux in the female guinea pig genital tract. *Anat. Rec.* **175**, 625–630.

Maruta, H., and Moyer, D. L. (1967). Immunologic studies of the antigens of guinea pig semen. *Fert. Steril.* **18**, 649–658.

Masouredis, S. P., and Melcher, L. R. (1951). Blood, plasma and "globulin" space of guinea pigs determined with I^{131} rabbit globulin. *Proc. Soc. Exp. Biol. Med.* **78**, 264–266.

Mellor, D. J. (1969). Potential differences between mother and foetus at different gestational ages in the rat, rabbit and guinea-pig. *J. Physiol. (London)* **204**, 395–405.

Mepham, T. B., and Beck, N. F. G. (1973). Variation in the yield and composition of milk throughout lacation in the guinea pig (*Cavia porcellus*). *Comp. Biochem. Physiol. A* **45**, 273–281.

Mikisková, H. (1971). Quantitative estimation of the action of narcotic agents by some electrophysiological methods. (In Czech.) Doctoral Dissertation, Institute of Hygiene and Epidemiology, Prague.

Mikisková, H., and Mikiska, A. (1968). Some electrophysiological methods for studying the action of narcotic agents in animals, with special reference to industrial solvents: A review. *Brit. J. Ind. Med.* **25**, 81–105.

Milgrom, E., Atger, M., and Baulieu, E. E. (1970). Progesterone binding plasma protein(PBP). *Nature (London)* **228**, 1205–1206.

Milgrom, E., Allouch, P., Atger, M., and Baulieu, E. E. (1973). Progesterone-binding plasma protein of pregnant guinea pig. Purification and characterization. *J. Biol. Chem.* **248**, 1106–1114.

Mills, D. C. B. (1970). Platelet aggregation and platelet nucleotide concentration in different species. *Symp. Zool. Soc. London* **27**, 99–107.

Mills, D. C. B., and Thomas, D. P. (1969). Blood platelet nucleotides in man and other species. *Nature (London)* **222**, 991–992.

Mills, P. G., and Reed, M. (1971). The onset of first oestrus in the guinea-pig and the effects of gonadotrophins and oestradiol in the immature animal. *J. Endocrinol.* **50**, 329–337.

Moffatt, D. J., Rosse, C., Sutherland, I. H., and Yoffey, J. M. (1964). Studies on hypoxia. I. The response of the bone marrow to primary hypoxia. *Acta Anat.* **58**, 26–36.

Moll, W., and Künzel, W. (1973). The blood pressure in arteries entering the placentae of guinea pigs, rats, rabbits, and sheep. *Pfluegers Arch.* **338**, 125–131.

Moore, C. R., and Gallagher, R. T. (1930). Seminal-vesicle and prostate function as a testis-hormone indicator; the electric ejaculation test. *Amer. J. Anat.* **45**, 39–69.

Myers, H. I., Young, W. C., and Dempsey, E. W. (1936). Graafian follicle development throughout the reproductive cycle in the guinea pig, with special reference to changes during oestrus (sexual receptivity). *Anat. Rec.* **65**, 381–402.

Nelson, G. J. (1967). Lipid composition of erythrocytes in various mammalian species. *Biochim. Biophys. Acta* **14**, 221–232.

Nelson, W. L., Kaye, A., Moore, M., Williams, H. H., and Herrington, B. L. (1951). Milking techniques and composition of guinea pig milk. *J. Nutr.* **44**, 585–594.

Nicolle, P., and Simons, H. (1939). L'épreuve de la vitesse de sédimentation des hématies chez le cobaye normal. *Sang* **13**, 401–415.

O'Bryant, J. W., Packchanian, A., Reimer, G. W., and Vadheim, R. H. (1949). An apparatus for studying electrocardiographic changes in small animals. *Tex. Rep. Biol. Med.* **7**, 661–670.

Östman, I., and Sjöstrand, N. O. (1971). Effect of heavy physical training on the catecholamine content of the heart and adrenals of the guinea-pig. *Experientia* **27**, 270–271.

Osmond, D. G., and Everett, N. B. (1964). Radioautographic studies of bone marrow lymphocytes *in vivo* and in diffusion chamber cultures. *Blood* **23**, 1–17.

Osmond, D. G., and Everett, N. B. (1965). Bone marrow blood volume and total red cell mass of the guinea-pig as determined by ^{59}Fe-erythrocyte dilution and liquid nitrogen freezing. *Quart. J. Exp. Physiol. Cog. Med. Sci.* **50**, 1–14.

Ostwald, R., and Shannon, A. (1964). Composition of tissue lipids and anaemia of guinea pigs in response to dietary cholesterol. *Biochem. J.* **91**, 146–154.

Ostwald, R., Yamanaka, W., and Light, M. (1970). The phospholipids of liver, plasma, and red cells in normal and cholesterol-fed anemic guinea pigs. *Proc. Soc. Exp. Biol. Med.* **134**, 814–820.

Oxenreider, S. L., and Day, B. N. (1967). Regression of copora lutea in unilaterally pregnant guinea-pigs. *J. Endocrinol.* **38**, 279–289.

Petelenz, T. (1971). Electrocardiogram of the guinea-pig. *Acta Physiol. Pol.* **22**, 113–121.

Ponder, E. (1948). "Hemolysis and Related Phenomena." Grune & Stratton, New York.

Porter, D. G. (1970). The failure of progesterone to affect the myometrial activity in the guinea-pig. *J. Endocrinol.* **46**, 425–434.

Porter, D. G. (1971a). The action of relaxin on myometrial activity in the guinea-pig *in vivo. J. Reprod. Fert.* **26**, 251–253.

Porter, D. G. (1971b). Quantitative changes in myometrial activity in the guinea-pig during pregnancy. *J. Reprod. Fert.* **27**, 219–226.

Porter, D. G. (1972). Myometrium of the pregnant guinea-pig: The probable importance of relaxin. *Biol. Reprod.* **7**, 458–464.

Pratt, C. L. G. (1938). The electrocardiogram of the guinea-pig. *J. Physiol. (London)* **92**, 268–272.

Quick, A. J. (1936). On various properties of thromboplastin (aqueous tissue extracts). *Amer. J. Physiol.* **114**, 282–296.

Ranløv, P., Christensen, H. E., and Wanstrup, J. (1970). Effects of thymectomy upon the formation of Foá-Kurloff cells in the guinea pig. *Acta Pathol. Microbiol. Scand., Sect. B* **78**, 330–332.

Reed, M., and Hounslow, W. F. (1971). Induction of ovulation in the guinea-pig. *J. Endocrinol.* **49**, 203–211.

Reid, M. E. (1958). "The Guinea Pig in Research." Human Factors Research Bureau, Inc., Washington, D. C.

Reinhardt, W. O. (1964). Some factors influencing the thoracic-duct output of lymphocytes. *Ann. N. Y. Acad. Sci.* **113**, 844–866.

Reinhardt, W. O., and Yoffey, J. M. (1956). Thoracic duct lymph and lymphocytes in the guinea pig. *Amer. J. Physiol.* **187**, 493–500.

Resko, J. A. (1970). Androgens in systemic plasma of male guinea pigs during development and after castration in adulthood. *Endocrinology* **86**, 1444–1447.

Revell, P. A., Vernon-Roberts, B., and Gray A. (1971). The distribution and ultrastructure of the Kurloff cell in the guinea-pig. *J. Anat.* **109**, 187–199.

Richtarik, A., Woolsey, T. A., and Valdivia, E. (1965). Method for recording ECG's in unanesthetized guinea pigs. *J. Appl. Physiol.* **20**, 1091–1093.

Richter, W. (1966). Relative aggregation tendency of erythrocytes from man and various animal species. *Acta Chir. Scand.* **132**, 601–612.

Riss, W., Valenstein, E. S., Sinks, J., and Young, W. C. (1955). Development of sexual behavior in male guinea pigs from genetically different stocks under controlled conditions of androgen treatment and caging. *Endocrinology* **57**, 139–146.

Robinson, D. S. (1963). Changes in the lipolytic activity of the guinea pig mammary gland at parturition. *J. Lipid Res.* **4**, 21–23.

Rodkey, F. L., Collison, H. A., and O'Neal, J. D. (1972). Carbon monoxide and methane production in rats, guinea pigs, and germ-free rats. *J. Appl. Physiol.* **33**, 256–260.

Rogers, J. B. (1951). The aging process in the guinea pig. *J. Gerontol.* **6**, 13–16.

Rosse, C. (1971). Lymphocyte production and life-span in the bone marrow of the guinea pig. *Blood* **38**, 372–377.

Rowlands, I. W. (1949). Postpartum breeding in the guinea-pig. *J. Hyg.* **47**, 281–287.

Rowlands, I. W. (1956). The corpus luteum of the guinea pig. *Ciba Found. Colloq. Ageing* **2**, 69–85.

Rowlands, I. W. (1957). Insemination of the guinea-pig by intraperitoneal injection. *J. Endocrinol.* **16**, 98–106.

Rowlands, I. W. (1962). The effect of oestrogens, prolactin and hypophysectomy on the corpora lutea and vagina of hysterectomized guinea-pigs. *J. Endocrinol.* **24**, 105–112.

Sainte-Marie, G., and Peng, F. S. (1971a). Death of thymocytes in the guinea pig thymus. *Rev. Eur. Etud. Clin. Biol.* **16**, 800–804.

Sainte-Marie, G., and Peng, F. S. (1971b). Emigration of thymocytes from the thymus. A review and study of the problem. *Rev. Can. Biol.* **30**, 51–78.

Sawitsky, A., and Meyer, L. M., (1948). Bone marrow of normal guinea pigs. *Blood* **3**, 1050–1054.

Saxena, P. R. (1970). Effect of some drugs on the responses of the vas deferens and seminal vesicle to hypogastric nerve stimulation in guinea-pig *in vivo. Pharmacology* **3**, 220–228.

Sayles, E. D. (1939). Postnatal development of reproductive system in male guinea pigs and its relation to testis hormone secretion. *Physiol. Zool.* **12**, 256–267.

Scarborough, R. A. (1931). The blood picture of normal laboratory animals. *Yale J. Biol. Med.* **3**, 169–179.

Schaefer, K. E., Messier, A. A., and Morgan, C. C. (1970). Displacement of oxygen dissociation curves and red cell cation exchange in chronic hypercapnia. *Resp. Physiol.* **10**, 299–312.

Schofield, B. M. (1964). Myometrical activity in the pregnant guinea-pig. *J. Endocrinol.* **30**, 347–354.

Shepherd, J. T., and Whelan, R. F. (1951). The blood flow in the umbilical cord of the foetal guinea-pig. *J. Physiol. (London)* **115**, 150–157.

Shewell, J., and Long, D. A. (1956). A species difference with regard to the effect of cortisone acetate on body weight, γ-globulin and circulating antitoxin levels. *J. Hyg.* **54**, 452–460.

Shulman, S. (1971). Antigenicity and autoimmunity in sexual reproduction. A review. *Clin. Exp. Immunol.* 9, 267–288.

Sibley, Y. D. L., and Hudson, G. (1970). Eosinophil leukocytes and recovery from severe hypoxia. *Acta Haematol.* **43**, 31–39.

Simeone, F. A., and Young, W. C. (1931). A study of the function of the epididymis. IV. The fate of non-ejaculated spermatozoa in the genital tract of the male guinea-pig. *J. Exp. Biol.* 8, 163–175.

Simmons, V. P. (1967). Diverse diseases, globulins, plasma cells, Russell bodies, Foà-Kurloff bodies, and the thymus. A unifying concept. *Wis. Med. J.* **66**, 349–364.

Sleator, W., Furchgott, R. F., de Gubareff, T., and Krespi, V. (1964). Action potentials of guinea pig atria under conditions which alter contraction. *Amer. J. Physiol.* **206**, 270–282.

Smith, E. (1947). Certain characteristics of the leukocytes of guinea pig blood with particular reference to the Kurloff body. *Blood, Suppl.* **1**, 125–141.

Smith, L. H., and McKinley, T. W. (1962). Erythrocyte survival in guinea pigs. *Proc. Soc. Exp. Biol. Med.* **111**, 768–771.

Smith, S., Watts, R., and Dils, R. (1968). Quantitative gas-liquid chromatographic analysis of rodent milk triglycerides. *J. Lipid Res.* **9**, 52–57.

Spitzer, A., and Edelmann, C. M. (1971). Maturational changes in pressure gradients for glomerular filtration. *Amer. J. Physiol.* **221**, 1431–1435.

Squier, R. R. (1932). The living egg and early stages of its development in the guinea-pig. *Contrib. Embryol. Carnegie Inst.* **23**, 225–250.

Stockard, C. R., and Papanicolaou, G. N. (1917). The existence of a typical oestrous cycle in the guinea-pig–with a study of its histological and physiological changes. *Amer. J. Anat.* **22**, 225–283.

Stockard, C. R., and Papanicolaou, G. N. (1919). The vaginal closure membrane, copulation, and the vaginal plug in the guinea-pig, with further considerations of the oestrous rhythm. *Biol. Bull.* **37**, 222–245.

Strong, C. R., and Dils, R. (1972). Fatty acids synthesized by mammary gland slices from lactating guinea pig and rabbit. *Comp. Biochem. Physiol. B* **43**, 643–652.

Štulc, J. J., Rietveld, W. J., Soeteman, D. W., and Versprille, A. (1972). The transplacental potential difference in guinea-pigs. *Biol. Neonatorum* **21**, 130–147.

Takada, Y., Takada, A., and Ambrus, J. L. (1969). Comparative study of proactivators of the fibrinolysin system in three mammalian species. *Thromb. Diath. Haemorrh.* **21**, 594–603.

Tanaka, Y. (1970). Bi-directional transport of ferritin in guinea pig erythroblasts *in vitro. Blood* **35**, 793–803.

Tanaka, Y., and Brecher, G. (1971). Effect of surface digestion and metabolic inhibitors on appearance of ferritin in guinea pig erythroblasts *in vitro:* Evidences for the production of apoferritin in the erythroblast cell membrane. *Blood* **37**, 211–219.

Tindal, J. S., and Knaggs, G. S. (1971). Determination of the detailed hypothalamic route of the milk-ejection reflex in guinea-pig. *J. Endocrinol.* **50**, 135–152.

Tindal, J. S., and Yokoyama, A. (1962). Assay of oxytocin by the milk-ejection response in the anesthetized lactating guinea pig. *Endocrinology* **71**, 196–202.

Vosburgh, G. J., and Flexner, L. B. (1950). Maternal plasma as a source of iron for the fetal guinea pig. *Amer. J. Physiol.* **161**, 202–211.

Warner, E. D., Brinkhous, K. M., and Smith, H. P. (1939). Plasma prothrombin levels in various vertebrates. *Amer. J. Physiol.* **125**, 296–300.

Weil, A. J., Roberts, C. O., and Dube, A. (1964). Cobayin: a poisonous principle in the guinea pig's seminal plasma. *Proc. Soc. Exp. Biol. Med.* **117**, 896–898.

Went, S., and Drinker, C. K. (1929). A micromethod for the determination of the absolute blood volume, with data upon the blood volume of the guinea pig, white rat, rabbit and cat. *Amer. J. Physiol.* 88, 468–478.

Westfall, D. P. (1970). Nonspecific supersensitivity of the guinea-pig vas deferens produced by decentralization and reserpine treatment. *Brit. J. Pharmacol.* **39**, 110–120.

Westphal, U. (1971). Characteristics of steroid-protein interactions, including results on a progesterone-binding globulin. *Proc. Int. Congr. Horm. Steroids, 3rd, 1970* Int. Congr. Ser. No. 219, pp. 410–419.

Williams, P. C. (1956). The history and fate of redundant follicles. *Ciba Found. Colloq. Ageing* **2**, 59–68.

Wilton-Davies, C. C. (1972). Computer-assisted monitoring of ECG's and heart sounds. *Med. Electron. Biol. Eng.* **10**, 153–162.

Wintrobe, M. M. (1933). Variations in the size and hemoglobin content of erythrocytes in the blood of various vertebrates. *Folia Haematol. (Leipzig)* **51**, 32–49.

Wong, C. T., and Morgan, E. H. (1973). Placental transfer of iron in the guinea pig. *Quart. J. Exp. Physiol. Cog. Med. Sci.* **58**, 47–58.

Wooding, F. B. P. (1971). The mechanism of secretion of the milk fat globule. *J. Cell Sci.* **9**, 805–821.

Woody, C. O., First, N. L., and Pope, A. L. (1967). Effect of exogenous progesterone on estrous cycle length. *J. Anim. Sci.* **26**, 139–141.

Wright, S. (1960). The genetics of vital characters of the guinea pig. *J. Cell. Comp. Physiol.* **56**, Suppl. 1, 123–151.

Yamanaka, W., Winchell, H. S., and Ostwald, R. (1967). Erythrokinetics in dietary hypercholesteremia of guinea pigs. *Amer. J. Physiol.* **213**, 1278–1284.

Yanagimachi, R. (1972). Fertilization of guinea pig eggs *in vitro. Anat. Rec.* **174**, 9–13.

Yoffey, J. M. (1956). The mobilization and turnover times of cell populations in blood and blood-forming tissue. *J. Histochem. Cytochem.* **4**, 516–530.

Yoffey, J. M. (1958). Cellular equilibria in blood and blood-forming tissues. *Brookhaven Symp. Biol.* **10**, 1–30.

Yoffey, J. M. (1969). "Quantitative Cellular Haematology," p. 10. Thomas, Springfield, Illinois.

Yoffey, J. M. (1966). "Bone Marrow Reactions," p. 1. Arnold, London.

Yoffey, J. M., and Courtice, F. C., eds. (1970). "Lymphatics, Lymph, and Lymphomyeloid Complex." Academic Press, New York.

Yoshida, Y., and Osmond, D. G. (1971). Identity and proliferation of small lymphocyte precursors in cultures of lymphocyte-rich fractions of guinea pig bone marrow. *Blood* **37**, 73–86.

Young, W. C. (1937). The vaginal smear picture, sexual receptivity and the time of ovulation in the guinea pig. *Anat. Rec.* **67**, 305–325.

Young, W. C., Dempsey, E. W., and Myers, H. I. (1935). Cyclic reproductive behavior in the female guinea pig. *J. Comp. Physiol. Psychol.* **19**, 313–335.

Young, W. C., Dempsey, E. W., Myers, H. I., and Hagquist, C. W. (1938). The ovarian condition of sexual behavior in the female guinea pig. *Amer. J. Anat.* **63**, 457–487.

Young, W. C., Dempsey, E. W., Hagquist, C. W., and Boling, J. L. (1939). Sexual behavior and sexual receptivity in the female guinea pig. *J. Comp. Physiol. Psychol.* **27**, 49–68.

Zarrow, M. X. (1947). Relaxin content of blood, urine and other tissues of pregnant and postpartum guinea pigs. *Proc. Soc. Exp. Biol. Med.* **66**, 488–491.

Zarrow, M. X., Anderson, N. C., and Callantine, M. R. (1963). Failure of progestogens to prolong pregnancy in the guinea pig. *Nature (London)* **198**, 690–692.

Zawisza-Zenkteler, W. (1963). A comparative study of the glycogen content of leukocytes in human beings and in laboratory animals. *Arch. Immunol. Ther. Exp.* **11**, 210–216.

Zeman, F. J., and Wilber, C. G. (1965a). Hematology in the normal male guinea pig. *Life Sci.* **4**, 871–883.

Zeman, F. J., and Wilber, C. G. (1965b). Some characteristics of the guinea pig electrocardiogram. *Life Sci.* **4**, 2269–2274.

Chapter 8

Genetics

Michael F. W. Festing

I. INTRODUCTION

Studies of guinea pig genetics have been conducted in two distinct phases. The first phase included the period from 1900 to the early 1960's. It was largely concerned with the genetic analysis of visible characters, such as coat color and texture, and studies of the effects of inbreeding. This work was initiated by W. E. Castle (1905) and continued by Sewall Wright (1915, 1963) and his students in a distinguished series of studies. The findings had far-reaching implications and made fundamental contributions to genetic theory, particularly to the theory of inbreeding, genic interaction, and the genetic basis of threshold characters.

The second phase of guinea pig genetics started in the early 1960's and is continuing today. This phase, concerned with the analysis of biochemical, physiological, and immunological characters, creates a better understanding of fundamental mammalian biology. In contrast to earlier work, these studies are conducted by specialists in disciplines other than genetics. It seems doubtful whether the guinea pig will make any important contribution to theoretical genetics in the future, even though it will undoubtedly make important contributions to other biological disciplines.

One disturbing trend is the lack of conservation of potentially useful genetic material. Many mutants described here are no longer obtainable and others are scattered throughout the world. Unfortunately, there is no center in the world devoted to research on this important species, where genetic materials could be preserved. Closely associated with this problem is the use of a narrow range of genetic types in research. Much research is conducted with only two inbred strains, strains 2 and 13, and the widely distributed "Dunkin–Hartley" outbred stock. Fortunately, a wide range of stocks is maintained by guinea pig fanciers which will be available for research workers at any time.

II. SINGLE GENE CHARACTERS

All the characters in this section are presumed to have a single gene mode of inheritance, though in some cases the exact mode of inheritance is not yet established.

A. Pigmentation

1. Introduction

Probably more is known about the genetics of pigmentation in guinea pigs than in any other rodent species, including the mouse. Early work by Castle (1905, 1908, 1912, 1913, 1916) was followed by many distinguished papers by Wright (quoted extensively in this section) covering six decades. A recent and comprehensive summary of genetics of pigmentation in mammals (Searle, 1968) lists twelve loci that influence coat color in guinea pigs. Robinson (1970a) considered loci, *A, B, C, E, P, S*, and *Si* homologous in the guinea pig and mouse. In addition to descriptions of individual genetic loci, there have been extensive studies of interaction between color genes. These studies will only be reviewed briefly after a description of individual loci, since the results are extremely complex and beyond the scope of this review.

2. Individual Loci

a. Agouti (A) Locus. This locus controls the distribution of eumelanin (brown or black pigment) and phaeomelanin (yellow or reddish pigment) both in individual hairs and in the coat. Hairs in the wild type agouti coat have a terminal or subterminal yellow band (phaeomelanin), the rest of the hair being black or brown with eumelanin. In guinea pigs three alleles are recognized:

A (light-bellied agouti *Cavia porcellus* wild type). Animals of this type have yellow bellies usually with some black, so the allele is analogous to A^w in mice. Hairs of the back are black with a yellow band. The width of the yellow band is quite variable and, when it is narrow, black may invade the belly region (Wright, 1917b). The width of the yellow band can also be modified by other genes, particularly *p* and e^p.

A^r (ticked-bellied agouti *Cavia rufescens* wild type). This allele was discovered by Detlefsen (1914) when a wild Brazilian cavy, *C. rufescens*, was crossed with the domestic guinea pig. *Cavia rufescens* does not differ very markedly from the agouti guinea pig, but hybrids are different. However, the expression of the ticked-bellied agouti gene varies and clearly depends on the presence of modifying genes (Searle, 1968; Wright, 1917b). The allele A^r is probably homologous to the agouti wild type in mice.

a (nonagouti). This mutation eliminates the phaeomelanin band; therefore, hairs are uniformly black.

b. Brown (B) Locus. *B* ("wild type") in which eumelanin is black. *b* ("brown") a single mutation to brown which affects the coat, skin, and eyes. This mutation changes the color of eumelanin from black to brown. When combined with the agouti phenotype the cinnamon-agouti coat color results (Castle, 1908).

c. Color (Albino) Locus (C). A series of mutants at this locus reduce the amount of pigment. The effect is more severe on the yellow phaeomelanin than on eumelanin. Thus, the red-eyed dilute gene eliminates all phaeomelanin but not eumelanin (cf. the chinchilla gene in other species). Some lower alleles in the series also have a heat-labile product, leading to pigment formation only at the cooler extremities such as feet and ears.

These alleles have been intensively studied by Wright (1915, 1916, 1925), particularly in relation to interactions with other loci. Wolff (1955) studied the heat lability of various combinations of albino alleles. He reported that the pigment is heat labile in "albinos" of genotype E-c^ac^aP- and in most intermediate combinations of the *c* locus, but not in the wild type.

The phenotypes of four albino alleles in order of dominance are as follows:

C (wild-type with full color). The most highly pigmented condition and also the most familiar. This condition includes guinea pigs that have intense black or intense orange-yellow ("red") pigmentation, or both, in the fur. Examples are blacks, reds, golden agoutis, and black-and-red tortoiseshells of fanciers. All of these have black eyes.

c^d (light dilution). In these animals, black is reduced to a sepia-brown similar to human brown hair, known very inappropriately as "blue." Red is reduced to yellow or cream. Eye color remains black. Thus, there are blues, creams, silver agoutis, and blue-and-cream tortoiseshells in place of the four types mentioned above.

c^r (red-eyed dilution). The third condition is not so familiar as the others. It appeared at the Bussey Institution in descendants of three guinea pigs brought from Peru in 1911 (Castle, 1912). Among these, black is reduced to sepia (or "blue"), indistinguishable from the "blue" of the dilutes. Red is reduced to white. No yellow pigment has been found in guinea pigs with this allelomorph. A most striking feature is the glowing red of the eyes, easily distinguishable from black eyes of intense and dilute guinea pigs as well as from pink eyes of albinos. A deficiency of pigment in both retina and iris causes this condition to be known as red-eye. With the red-eye factor, the blacks, reds, golden agoutis, and black-and-red tortoiseshells become red-eyed blues, red-eyed whites, red-eyed silver agoutis, and red-eyed blue-and-white tortoiseshells, respectively.

c^a. In the acromelanic albino condition black is absent from the coat except in patches on the nose, ears, and feet, and occasionally some sootiness on the back. Nose, ears, and feet are generally the most highly pigmented regions in the dilute and red-eyed conditions. Acromelanic albinos have no yellow hairs. The eyes are pink, due to the lack of pigment in the iris and retina. Blacks and golden agoutis are replaced by sooty albinos; reds, by clear albinos; and the black-and-red tortoiseshells, by albinos in which nose, feet, and ears are sooty or white, depending on the location of the spots.

c^k ("dark dilution"). This condition is similar to c^d except it has slightly more black/brown pigment.

The effects of combining various albino alleles in various ways is shown diagrammatically in Fig. 1 (from Wright, 1925). Various combinations of alleles have been graded according to the amount of eumelanin and phaeomelanin present in the coat. Classification was carried out by comparison with a series of standard skins.

It is interesting to note that the normal "albino" laboratory guinea pig (e.g., the Dunkin–Hartley strain) has the genotype eec^ac^a.

d. Extension (E) Locus. Alleles at this locus either extend or diminish the amount of eumelanin in the guinea pig.

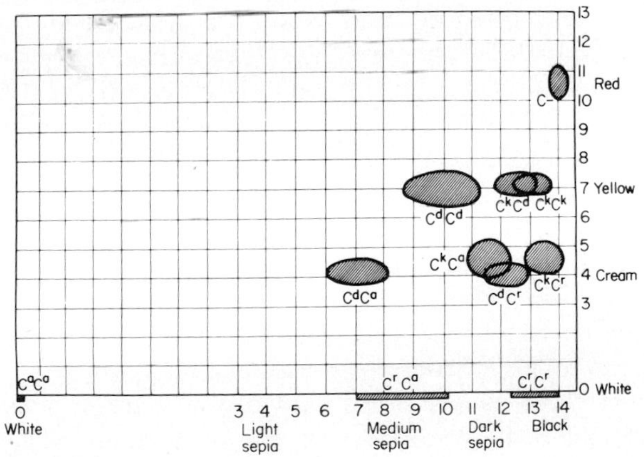

Fig. 1. The grades of intensity with respect to both sepia and yellow, of the albino series compounds of guinea pigs. The shaded areas extend horizontally to a distance above and below the mean equal to the standard deviation with respect to grade of sepia, and extend vertically the corresponding amount with respect to grade of yellow. This range includes about 68% of the individuals. The area should thus include about 47% of them (redrawn from Wright, 1925).

E (extension wild type).

e^p (partial extension, tortoiseshell). This allele was first described by Ibsen (1916). Homozygotes have a brindled or tortoiseshell pattern, a mixture of black and yellow areas with black predominating. There is, however, great variability in the pattern so that individuals can approach the wild type. e^p is only incompletely dominant over the next allele in the series e, and the heterozygote e^pe is also very variable, overlapping the homozygous e^pe^p, though there is usually more yellow in the coat of the latter.

e (yellow/orange). Animals of this genotype have a uniform color due to the presence of phaeomelanin.

The e^p allele and the spotting locus S interact. In spotted animals of the genotype sse^pe^p agouti and yellow areas tend to separate out to give areas of black and yellow on a white background. This leads, when the animals are also aa, to the tricolored pattern of both inbred strains 2 and 13, and common in fancy stocks (Wright and Chase, 1936). The proportion and positions of the three colors vary depending on both genetic modifying factors and environmental influences. This is considered in more detail in relation to the S locus.

e. Pink-eyed Dilution (P) Locus. Genes at this locus alter the shape and distribution of pigment granules in hair. In contrast with the C locus p only affects eumelanin and not phaeomelanin. The following alleles at this locus are known:

P (wild type, with full color).

p^r (ruby-eye). This allelomorph was first described by Iljin (1926) (see Gregory, 1928). Apparently it has little or no effect on hair pigmentation but causes a reddish gleam in the pupil of the eye.

p. This allele was first described by Castle (1912). It causes a pink eye similar to the albino gene and a marked dilution of the black and chocolate pigments of the coat (eumelanin), but has little effect on the red/yellow pigment (phaeomelanin). Gregory (1928) studied the mutant p in relation to other mutations affecting eye color, including "sm" (salmon eye), and the previously described mutants a and b. No linkages were found. Wright (1927) combined mutant p with all albino alleles both in the presence and absence of mutant b. All animals were scored for color, which was less intense than when the normal allele P was present.

f. Fading (F) Locus. A single mutation is known at this locus, designated f. (F is the full colored wild type.) In the homozygous state it reduces phaeomelanin in much the same way as the dark dilution c^k, but unlike the latter there is an increasing dilution with age (Searle, 1968). The mutant has no effect on eumelanin. Wright (1927) described the origin of this mutation, which was present in one of the control lines of his inbreeding experiment, though not recognized until crosses were made with animals that possessed various albino alleles. He bred animals of various genotypes in which f was combined with different albino alleles, as well as with *b* and *p*. In the presence of *pp*, *f* eliminates eumelanin as well as phaeomelanin, consequently, animals of the genotype *C-ffpp* are pale cream. The mutant *pp* alone causes a marked reduction in eumelanin. Although in most cases the heterozygotes (*Ff*) are indistinguishable from the homozygous (*FF*) littermates, more extensive studies in which a numerical score is given to the coat color intensities shows that in some combinations there is incomplete dominance.

g. White Spotting (S) Locus. Spotting is common among pet and fancy guinea pigs and is present in strains 2 and 13. There have been many studies of the inheritance of spotting, but the most authoritative one is that of Wright and Chase (1936). They studied the extent and variation of spotting in a number of outbred and inbred strains and their crosses and backcrosses. The following conclusions were reached:

1. There is a major pair of alleles *S, s* in which *S* (tending toward self, i.e., not spotted) is usually incompletely dominant over *s* (tending toward white). The presence of this pair of alleles was confirmed by backcrossing of "self" animals onto an inbred spotted strain for eleven generations. The persistence of a bimodal distribution of degree of spotting can only be attributed to the transmission of an undilutable unit (*s*).

2. There are many modifying genes with individually small effects which are additive on a suitably transformed scale. These can shift the median grade of spotting in *ss* animals from about 10% to about 97% white while the median grade of white in *Ss* animals can be shifted from self color to about 30% white. Finally, a little white may appear in *SS* animals with an extreme array of white modifiers.

3. There is an enormous amount of nonhereditary variation, not common for the most part even to littermates. This individual variation can range from a trace of white to 100% white in an inbred strain with a median grade of spotting near 50%. In a typical outbred stock homozygous for *ss*, about 58% of the variation can be attributed to nongenetic causes, of which only 6% is common to littermates.

4. There is a slight sex effect, with females having slightly more white than males in all strains. This effect accounted for about 2–3% of the total variation.

The effects of spotting in relation to the tricolor pattern was studied by Chase (1939a). His results agreed with those of Wright and Chase (1936) but he reported that there are also minor differences in the localization of the patterns which are hereditary. Correlation studies in two inbred strains indicated that nonhereditary factors involved in the spotting act locally rather than on the animal as a whole. Chase (1939b) studied the interactions between loci *E* and *S*. Guinea pigs in which the spotting pattern (*Ss* or *ss*) is combined with the tortoiseshell genotype (e^pe^p or e^pe) have a tricolor pattern. If a very high grade of spotting is present the spots tend to be either black or red, with very little brindled, and in some cases the animals are white-black or white-red bicolored rather than tricolored. The relationship between the *S* and *E* locus was also studied by Wright (1923).

h. Grizzled (Gr) Locus. The gene "grizzled" (*gr*) causes a progressive type of silvering which appears only after the first pelage. White hairs appear first on the posterior back, but later become sprinkled over the entire back, head, and belly mixed among hairs of the color determined by the rest of the genotype. The gene (*gr*) is inherited as an incompletely recessive autosomal gene (Wright, 1947; Lambert, 1935).

i. Silvering (Si) Locus. The gene causing silvering is similar to that in the mouse and rat in that it causes a mixture of hairs which are either fully pigmented, partly pigmented, or not pigmented at all. The genetics of silvering were studied by Wright (1947), who distinguished several different types of silvering controlled by different loci. The most common "stationary silvering" controlled by the *Si* locus was described by Wright (1947) as follows:

> . . . The common silvering of the guinea-pig varies enormously in degree and character. In its weakest development there are merely a few light or white hairs, usually on the mammary region of the belly. In higher grades, the belly (thorax and abdomen) may be more or less uniformly silvered or there may be irregularly distributed blotches of white within silvered areas. Extensive silvering of the belly is correlated with the occurrence of patches of silvering on the sides and middle of the back. More rarely, slight silvering of the back occurs without silvering of the belly. In the highest grades, the belly becomes almost white, usually sprinkled here and there with dark hairs or blotches, and the back becomes strongly silvered. The head and feet show little or no silvering even in the highest grade, as in roan horses. Red hairs are more conspicuously diluted in silvered areas than are black ones. It is sometimes difficult to decide whether a tortoiseshell with apparently dilute yellow hairs, intermingled with intense black, but no white, is to be considered a low grade silver or not. Silvered self reds and yellows are also difficult to classify unless the silvering is strong.

The silvering depends mainly on a single incompletely recessive gene (*si*), but varies continuously over a wide range due to modifying factors and environmental variation.

The mode of inheritance was confirmed by Wright (1959a) who not only noted a bimodal distribution of silvering in the second backcross of self to a high grade silver, but also showed that expression of the gene is strongly modified by additive factors which resulted in regression of offspring on midparent reaching as much as 0.40.

Silvering interacts with diminished, as noted in the description of the *Dm* locus.

j. Diminished (Dm) Locus. The mutant "diminished" (*dm*) causes extra dilution of color with the lower albino genotypes, but has no effect in the presence of *C* (Wright, 1959b).

Diminished usually interacts with silvering so that the combination *sisidmdm* is entirely white except for one or two small spots of pale color on the cheeks in about 50% of cases. With *C* these spots are strongly silvered. Diminished animals have a higher mortality rate at birth than normal littermates. Males are sterile, with testes weighing about 25% of normal. Spermatogenesis is completely absent and cannot be induced by testosterone propionate, pituitary implants, or gonadotropin. About 50% of females are also sterile. Hemoglobin concentration is about 75% of normal. Searle (1968) suggested that this syndrome may be comparable to the anemia in the black-eyed whites of *W* and *Sl* series in mice.

k. Whitish or White-tipped (W) Locus. This locus is not to be confused with the *W* locus in the mouse (Searle, 1968). The locus was described by Ibsen (1932) and Ibsen and Goertzen (1951a). An incompletely dominant gene (*W*) causes whitening or extreme paling of hair several millimeters below its tip. The animal must carry *C* for *W* to be expressed. Red hair *eeCC* is entirely unaffected by *W*. The expression of *W* can also be affected by modifying factors.

l. Salmon-eye (Sm) Locus. The mutation "salmon-eye" (*sm*) limits pigmentation of the eye to a circular region around the pupillary margin of the iris. This ring of pigment may vary widely in density and width. Black, yellow, and chocolate pigments of the coat are not materially affected (Gregory, 1928).

m. Roan (Ro) Locus. This mutant was described by Ibsen and Goertzen (1951b), but Wright (1959a) considered it identical to si.

n. Dilution at Base of Hairs (di). According to Searle (1968) this mutation was described by Ibsen (1932) but is not recognized by other workers.

o. Roan Spotting and Anophthalmos Locus (Rs). A mutation causing uneven silvering with white hairs on the back, sides, and belly, with a white blaze and dark red eyes was described by Whiteway (1973). This appeared to be inherited as an autosomal dominant, with the above description referring to the heterozygote *Rsrs*.

More recently, matings between heterozygotes have produced putative homozygotes which are white with unpigmented skin and are anophthalmic or microphthalmic (Whiteway and Robinson, 1975). The mutation may be homologous to anophthalmic white found in the hamster, chinchilla, and the mouse.

3. Other Pigmentation Studies

Most early studies on guinea pig pigmentation were descriptive. Results of crossing guinea pigs of various colors could be predicted without much insight into the mode of gene action. However, studies by Wright on the interaction between genes and the biochemical nature of gene action were fundamental stepping stones to modern quantitative genetics and evolutionary theories on the one hand, and to biochemical and physiological genetics on the other. Provine (1971) gives an historical account of the way in which Wright's studies (largely on guinea pigs) influenced theoretical population genetics. Although in many ways the guinea pig is a difficult animal to work with due to its relatively poor reproductive performance and large size, studies of coat color genetics may have been a fortunate historic choice, since it bridged very neatly the qualitative studies of pure Mendelian genetics and the quantitative studies of population and quantitative genetics. Also, control of pigmentation is clearly determined by biochemical and physiological mechanisms, enabling Wright as early as 1917 (1917a) to advance the "one gene, one enzyme" hypothesis in his classic series of papers on color inheritance in mammals. According to Peters (1959), "this paper lays the foundation for the field of biochemical or physiological genetics, and in fact remains as the basic source of information and the starting point of modern investigation." Other important contributions to physiological and biochemical genetics include Wright (1941) on "the physiology of the gene" and Wright (1942) on "the physiological genetics of coat colour of the guinea-pig." Other physiological studies of coat color include Billingham and Medawar (1947a,b, 1948), and Billingham and Silvers (1970), who examined the effects of transplanting pigmented skin to white areas and vice versa. Biochemical studies of pigmentation include Foster (1952) on tyrosinase and Ginsburg (1944) and Russell (1939) on dopa oxidase.

4. Genic Interaction

A number of complex studies on genic interaction have important implications in quantitative genetics. The general method was to synthesize a wide range of genotypes and study the intensity of the main types of pigment either by reference to a graded series of skins or by the use of reflectometer readings. In some cases colorimetric determinations of hair samples were also used. Wright (1959c) compared these three methods in a paper that is in many ways typical of this type of study. Wright (1959d) also used reflectometer readings to give quantitative scores to different genotypes. Reflectometer readings were made with different filters. It was then possible to quantify intensity of pigmentation and of different qualities, depending on the presence of different pigments. It was possible to show that different loci interact with each other on a quantitative scale, showing the importance of epistasis in quantitative inheritance.

Postnatal changes in intensity of coat color in different genotypes and residual variability in intensity of coat color at birth were examined by Wright (1960a,b). Both papers are elegant examples of the way in which color can be expressed quantitatively so mathematical methods can be used to analyze the mode of gene action. Many studies on genic interaction were summarized by Wright (1963). He gives a very brief conclusion, which cannot really do justice to such a complex series of studies, but is nevertheless worth quoting:

> . . . It may be seen that the products of the color factors enter into a rather complicated pattern of interactions before formation of the final products: sepia, brown, or yellow pigment granules. The pattern resembles somewhat the branching chains of reactions worked out for gene-controlled metabolic reactions in microorganisms. Some of the steps may indeed be of similar nature, since most of the factors probably act in the nuclei of the pigment cells themselves as demonstrated in mice by Reed and Henderson. Others, however, probably act from adjacent epidermal cells as already noted. The difference between adult male and female dingy browns is probably under endocrine control. Some seem to be concerned directly with the pigment process but others undoubtedly affect pigment merely because of effects on the vitality or metabolic efficiency of the pigment cells.

B. Pelage Variation

a. Rough (R), Rough Modifier (M), and Rough Eye (Re) Loci. In wild guinea pigs and smooth haired varieties of domesticated animals, hairs are directed posteriorly over the body toward the toes on the feet and legs and toward the margins of the ears. Hairs above and below the eyes diverge slightly. There may be a slight whorl on the lower lip and very slight whorls on the throat, which are difficult to recognize except in newly born, short haired young. There are various degrees of "roughness" dependent on four major genes (*R, M, Re,* and *St*), though there is considerable residual genetic and environmental variation.

The dominant gene *R* (*rough*) is necessary for any "roughness" of the familiar sort, e.g., the rosette pattern of Abyssinian guinea pigs. The action of this gene is modified by the incompletely dominant gene *M* and by *Re*.

A third gene influencing hair direction is the dominant gene *Star*, discussed separately below. Wild guinea pigs apparently have the genotype *rrMMstst* (the status of *Re* is unknown). The following combinations of *R* and *M* have been described by Wright (1949a):

> *R-MM*. Like the smooth type except for irregularities on the feet, especially the hind feet. Occasionally *R-Mm* may grade into this type.
>
> *R-Mm*. A crest present along the middorsal line, but no rosettes on sides, heads, or belly. Sometimes *R-MM* may appear like this. *R-Mm* (but not *R-MM*) also grades into types with the dorsal crest and a single major divergent rosette on each (or one) side of the back.
>
> *R-mm*. At least two pairs of divergent rosettes, anterior and posterior, on the back, well-developed head rosettes, and rosettes or partings on the belly. There may be additional small rosettes.

Dominance of *R* seems to be complete. However, in animals of the *R-mm* type the number and pattern of rosettes varies. This is partly inherited (regression of offspring on midparent being +0.47). Wright (1963) isolated one of these modifiers *Re* (*rough eye*), which acted on the rosettes surrounding the eye. In some cases rosettes were asymmetrical, occurring more frequently on the right side.

b. Star (St) Locus. The completely dominant mutation Star (*St*) is responsible for a uniform, very flat rosette on the forehead which is not associated with roughness of the feet or any other part of the coat. The hair radiates from the center without any rotation (Wright, 1949b). This gene also tends to cause a white forehead spot in front of the center of the rosette, though this is inhibited by *R*. (Bock, 1950).

Interactions among *St, R* and *M* have been described by Wright (1950, 1963). They are mutually inhibitive rather than being additive as might be expected. Animals of type *rrSt-* have 99.6% single flat forehead rosettes. About 19% of animals of genotype *R-MMSt-* have the forehead rosette of star reduced to two weak ones. At the other extreme, animals of genotype *R-mmSt-*, which might be expected to have a strong and well-developed rosette as a result of combining Star with well-expressed rough, in fact, have only a slight irregularity of hair direction on the forehead. Likewise, the action of *St* inhibits the action of *R-mm*, though in this case *St* no longer shows complete dominance.

c. Sticky Haired (sth). A mutation "sticky" appeared spontaneously in stock maintained in the Department of Pathology, Cambridge (Herbertson *et al.*, 1959). Affected young were identified at birth by their unkempt, ruffled, and grubby appearance. The coat felt sticky, as though resin had been rubbed into it, and was also wavy. The gene symbol *sth* is proposed for this mutant, since *St* has already been used for Star.

Breeding tests showed that the condition was inherited as a fully penetrant autosomal recessive gene having little or no effect on fertility or viability.

Histological examination of the skin and hair showed no abnormality. However, Sudan III and IV test for lipids on hairs was positive. The stickiness could be removed by lipid solvents but not water. Although no structural defect of sebaceous glands could be detected, the results of further studies suggested the condition was caused by an abnormal sebaceous secretion.

d. Fuzzy (Fz). An autosomal dominant mutation named "fuzzy" was recorded by Garber (1953). It occurred spontaneously among stock segregating for both color and hair direction. Fuzzy guinea pigs could be identified at birth by their curly vibrissae. The fuzzy coat became apparent within 2 or 3 days and became more pronounced with age.

e. Long Hair (l). The genetics of long hair was studied by Castle (1905). Apparently no more recent studies have been published. The coat of the short-haired animal reaches maximum length (about 4 cm) at about 1 month of age and is then gradually shed and replaced with new hairs. In long-haired animals the coat is not shed and continues to grow so that it is 5 to 7 cm at 2 months and 6 to 9 cm at 3 months. The coat may begin to shed at about this time so that the length does not exceed about 8 cm or it may continue to grow to 14 to 16 cm or more at 6 to 7 months. The hair produced in this way is uniform in width in contrast with tapered normal hair.

Castle considered that hair length did not conform to a continuous series but tended to be grouped about mean maximum lengths as follows:

1. 8 cm, double the normal coat length and attained at about 3 months of age
2. 12 cm, three times normal length and not attained until over 5 months old
3. 16 cm, four times normal, and not attained until 7 months of age

Long hair is inherited as an autosomal recessive character since crosses to short-coated animals produce short-coated young, though the hair is usually softer than normal. Crosses between two long-haired animals differing in length of hair shows dominance of the shorter type. This observation, together with anomalous segregations with a surplus of long-coated animals in the backcross to long-haired parents suggests that hair length may not be inherited as a single gene character. It seems probable that there are one or two major genes and possibly a number of modifiers. Clearly, inheritance of hair length should be investigated in more detail.

The Peruvian breed of guinea pigs has not only the long hair gene, but also "rough," so that they have two hip rosettes that throw the hair forward over the animal's head. Rough and long hair are not linked and the smooth coated long-haired type can be segregated out. The fanciers name for this type is "sheltie" in the United Kingdom and "angora" in the United States.

C. Immunogenetics

1. Introduction

In spite of its general importance as a laboratory animal and its widespread use in studying delayed hypersensitivity, relatively little is known about the immunogenetics of the guinea pig. Prior to 1960 there were very few papers on the subject. Loeb and Wright (1927) studied tissue transplantation in five inbred strains developed by Wright (1922b). They reported that after 17 to 25 generations of consecutive brother × sister mating strain 2 was virtually histocompatible, while in strain 13 graft acceptance was prolonged, but not indefinitely. Bauer (1958) noted that after about 50 generations both strains were fully histocompatible, but interstrain grafts were uniformly rejected on about the eighth day. Scheibel (1943) showed by selective inbreeding that the ability to produce diphtheria antitoxin was inherited. She selected two lines, one of which was a poor and the other a good antitoxin producer. However, no studies of the mode of inheritance of ability to produce antitoxin were undertaken. A general enhancement of immunological competence, as a result of acclimatization to a cold environment, which could apparently be passed on to subsequent generations was demonstrated by Szemere *et al.* (1960).

2. Transplantation Antigens

Little is known about the histocompatibility genes of the guinea pig, though it is likely that there will be some important advances in the next few years. Bauer (1960) extended his studies to show that strain 2 and strain 13 differ at not less than 4 to 6 histocompatibility loci as estimated from graft survival in F_2 segregating generations. Similar studies in mice by Barnes and Krohn (1957) indicated at least 14 different loci controlling skin graft rejection. Bauer considered that the relatively low number of loci estimated from his studies was a reflection of a fairly close relationship between strain 2 and strain 13 rather than a species difference. Wright (1922a) recorded that both strains were developed from the same random bred colony.

Further transplantation studies have been done by Aron *et al.* (1964) and Rebel and Marescaux (1965), though neither of these give much additional information on transplantation genetics. Billingham and Silvers (1965) studied the possible occurrence of maternally induced tolerance. They grafted strain 2 skin to reciprocal backcrosses of (2 × 13) F_1 × 13 and examined the survival of grafts when the F_1 hybrid was the female or male parent. If maternal tolerance had occurred the grafts would have survived longer if the F_1 was the female parent than if it was the male. This was not the case and they concluded that maternal tolerance is rare in guinea pigs.

The chemical nature of transplantation antigens was studied by Kahn and Reisfield (1968). Water-soluble antigens were liberated from guinea pig spleens and lungs by sonification and purified by gel filtration and by discontinuous electrophoresis on acrylamide gel. Chemical analysis of the antigen produced by strains 2 and 13 revealed significant differences in their content of serine, alanine, leucine, isoleucine, and valine. These data suggest that transplantation antigens have allotypic specificities related to protein structure.

More recently work on immune response genes, discussed in greater detail below, together with use of cytotoxic techniques (Brummerstadt and Franks, 1970), suggests that there is a major histocompatibility locus analogous to the *H-2* locus in the mouse, which is closely linked to or identified with the immune response locus (Martin *et al.*, 1970; Ellman *et al.*,

1970c; Bluestein *et al.*, 1971a–d). The relationship between the *Ir-1* and *H-2* locus of the mouse has been studied by McDevitt *et al.* (1972). The fine structure of the H-2 complex, which includes the *Ir-1* locus is currently being studied intensively and there are likely to be important advances in this field in the near future.

3. The *GPL-A* Locus

Further evidence that guinea pigs have a major histocompatibility locus with multiple alleles, similar to the *H-2* locus in mice, is given by DeWeck *et al.* (1970) and Sato and DeWeck (1972). They cross-immunized random pairs of animals in a colony of random bred white Himalayan spotted guinea pigs. These had been kept as a closed colony for about 25 years. The antigen consisted of lymphocytes suspended in saline or Freund's adjuvant. A lymphocytotoxic test was used to type each animal. Two major antisera were produced which recognized different lymphocyte antigens and these were named A and B. Further cross-immunizations revealed two further antigens–C and D.

Analysis of the results suggested that the B, C, and D antigens were allelic genes of the same locus, since they were never all present together. There was also some cross reactivity between A and D antigens since all D positive were also A positive. Anti-D-antisera could only be raised in A-positive animals lacking the D antigen. Altogether a total of 7 lymphocyte phenotypes were observed as follows: ABC, ABD, AC, ACD, AD, B, and BC. The following phenotypes were not observed: A, AB, BCD, BD, CD, C, and D.

Skin grafting was carried out between pairs of typed animals (DeWeck *et al.*, 1971). Graft survival averaged 17.4 days in matched pairs compared with 12.4 days in unmatched pairs and 12.7 days in randomly grafted animals of unknown phenotype. Thus, guinea pig isoantigens detected by lymphocytotoxic antisera appear to be transplantation antigens. DeWeck *et al.* (1971) named this histocompatibility locus the *GPL-A* locus.

Both strain 2 and 13 are $GPL\text{-}A^B$ which is rather surprising since graft rejection is rapid between these two strains. However, it is probable that further studies will refine and clarify the situation, in which case, it may be found that strain 2 and 13 do in fact differ either at the *GPL-A* locus, or at other important transplantation loci. More recently De Weck and Geczy (1975) renamed the *A, B,* and *C* alleles as *B.1, B.2,* and *B.3,* respectively, and have stated that the *GPL-A* locus is probably homologous to the *H-2D* or *H-2K* locus in mice.

4. Immune Response Genes and the GPIr-1 Locus

Extensive studies of genetic control of the immune response to synthetic antigens in guinea pigs have been reviewed by Green (1970), Milstein and Munro (1970), and McDevitt and Benacerraf (1969). Early work on delayed hypersensitivity (defined as "an immunologically specific inflammatory reaction, which takes some hours to reach a maximum, occurring in the absence of demonstrable antibody of the conventional type") using simple protein antigens has been reviewed by Gell and Benacerraf (1961). However, it was Kantor *et al.* (1963) who first showed that the response to 2,4-dinitrophenyl poly-L-lysine (DNP-PLL), 2,4-dinitrophenyl glutamic acid lysine copolymer (DNP-GL), or GL alone is under genetic control. Responder animals immunized with DPN-PLL or DNP-GL produce large amounts of anti-DNP antibodies and develop delayed hypersensitivity to these compounds. It is proposed here that the immune response locus of which the *PLL* gene is one allele should be named the *GPIr-1* locus.

Further studies revealed that the *PLL* gene is inherited as an autosomal fully dominant gene. All inbred strain 13 guinea pigs are nonresponders, and all strain 2 are responders. Random bred strains usually segregate for the two alleles (Benacerraf *et al.*, 1967; Ellman *et al.*, 1970a; McDevitt and Benacerraf, 1969; Milstein and Munro, 1970; Paul *et al.*, 1968).

The immunological properties of the *PLL* gene have also been extensively studied; e.g., Ben-Efraim and Liacopoulos (1969) studied the competitive effect of DNP-PLL in responder and nonresponder guinea pigs and Foerster *et al.* (1969) and Green *et al.* (1967b) studied the passive transfer of responsiveness to DNP-PLL and DNP-GL.

Green *et al.* (1966, 1969) studied the effect of various minor alterations of the antigen and also adjuvants on the immune response to DNP-PLL and DNP-GL. They found that high levels of *Mycobacterium butyricum* adjuvant could induce a few strain 13 (nonresponder) guinea pigs to produce low levels of antibody against DNP-PLL, but not DNP-GL. They concluded that in nonresponder guinea pigs the positively charged DNP-PLL molecule behaves as a hapten and that mycobacterial antigens can act as an immunological carrier or "Schlepper" molecule when present in large amounts.

The induction of tolerance and stimulation of cells *in vitro* was studied by Green *et al.* (1968). They concluded that the function of the PLL gene product is to act at an early crucial step in the immune mechanism to form an antigen–inducer complex. The specificity of this early step may be much lower than that of the antibody which is eventually produced.

Other immunological aspects of the PLL gene have been studied by Green *et al.* (1967a), Lamelin *et al.* (1968), Lamm *et al.* (1968), Levine (1969), Levine and Benacerraf (1964, 1965), Levine *et al.* (1963a,b), Oppenheim *et al.* (1967), Selaway *et al.* (1971), Yoshida *et al.* (1970) and Paul *et al.* (1966).

5. Other Alleles at the *GPIr-1* Locus

Two additional immune response genes named *GA* and *GT* were reported by Bluestein *et al.* (1971a). They found that the immune response to the linear polypeptide antigens poly-*d*-(L-glutamic acid 60%, L-alanine 40%), (GA) and poly-*d*-(L-glutamic acid 50%, L-tyrosine 50%), (GT) was under genetic control.

All inbred strain 2 guinea pigs were responders to GA giving significant serum antibody levels and delayed hypersensitivity. However, strain 2 would not respond to GT. The converse situation was observed in strain 13 guinea pigs. All F_1 hybrids of strains 2 × 13 were found to be responders to both antigens. It was concluded that the response to both these antigens was governed by autosomal dominant genes. A variable percentage of random bred guinea pigs responded depending on the strain and source.

The response to GAT (poly-*d*-glutamic acid 60%, L-alanine 30%, L-tyrosine 10%) was also studied but did not appear to be under simple genetic control in the guinea pig strains investigated.

The relationship between the *GA, GT,* and *PLL* genes was then studied by Bluestein *et al.* (1971b) in random bred Hartley guinea pigs. They found that in most animals PLL responders were also GA responders, though there were a few individuals responding to GA or PLL alone, showing that the genes are not identical but are "linked" in some way. In contrast, the *GT* gene is apparently inherited as an allele or pseudo-allele of *GA* and *PLL* since all GA responders were PLL nonresponders, thus, "the ability to respond to GA segregates away from the ability to respond to GT."

Further studies (Ellman *et al.*, 1970c, 1971a; Martin *et al.*, 1970; Bluestein *et al.*, 1971c,d) have related the immune response genes PLL, *GA*, and *GT* to the major histocompatibility (*GPL-A*) locus. The general findings can be summarized in the words of Bluestein *et al.* (1971c):

> . . . as more genetically controlled immune responses are being identified, it is becoming increasingly clear that the linkage between specific immune response genes and histocompatibility loci is a general phenomenon. Further, it is apparent that within a species immune response genes tend to be grouped together on the same chromosome. Thus, McDevitt and Chinitz (1969) have demonstrated the existence of a genetic locus in mice, the Ir-1 locus, which is made up of at least three immune response genes, each of which is linked to a different H-2 allele.
>
> The significance of the observations is not yet clear. The possibility must be entertained that immune response genes may determine histocompatibility specificities. There is no evidence that rules this out. Among the 92 random bred guinea pigs tested for concurrences of PLL responsiveness and the presence of a major strain 2 histocompatibility specificity, the two characteristics have *always* occurred together. Thus, the PLL gene is either part of or *very* closely linked to the locus coding for the major strain 2 histocompatibility antigens.

At this stage it seems possible, therefore, that the immune response genes *PLL, GA,* and *GT* are part of a complex locus (including the *GPL-A* and *GPIr-1* loci) with multiple alleles controlling both immune responses and histocompatibility antigens, though there may also be other loci involved in both the immune response and transplantation antigens.

6. Other Immune Response Genes

Green and Benacerraf (1971) studied the response to limiting doses of bovine serum albumin (BSA) and human albumin (HSA), and its relation to the *PLL* gene. They found that responsiveness to these antigens was not dependent on the presence of the *PLL* gene, since although all strain 2 guinea pigs were PLL positive and good HSA responders, in some random bred strains the two were separated. They also considered it highly likely that ability to respond to HSA and BSA was controlled by the same gene.

Arquilla and Finn (1963, 1965) studied the genetic control of combining sites of insulin antibodies produced by guinea pigs, and found that segregation in the F_2 generation of crosses between strain 2 and strain 13 was consistent with a 2 or more loci hypothesis rather than with a single locus with multiple alleles.

Ellman *et al.* (1971c) studied the immune response to hydralazine. Hartley and strain 13 guinea pigs were able to mount a vigorous immune response to the drug, but strain 2 animals were "low or nonresponders." Six strain 2 × 13 F_1 animals were all "responders" and of ten backcross animals five were responders and five nonresponders. These results are compatible with an autosomal dominant mode of inheritance, though the numbers are too small to give complete confidence in this interpretation. Four of 10 backcross animals were tested for presence of strain 13 histocompatibility antigen using a cytotoxic test. It was concluded that there was no correlation between the histocompatibility antigen and the ability to respond to hydralazine, suggesting that the immune response to hydralazine is independent of the *GPIr-1* locus.

The immunological response of 5 strains or breeds of guinea pigs to dextran was studied by Battisto *et al.* (1968). Highly purified dextran with a molecular weight of 20 to 50 million emulsified in Freund's adjuvant was injected intramuscularly and into the foot pads. After 3 weeks each animal received an intradermal injection of 125 μg of the same dextran in saline. The sites were observed hourly for 6 hours and again at 24 and 48 hours. A delayed type cutaneous reaction was observed, but was confined mostly to the Abyssinian breed. Circulating antibody to dextran was detected by the passive cutaneous anaphylaxis reaction.

7. Delayed Hypersensitivity and the S^{hy} Locus

Battisto (1960) found delayed-type skin reactions among guinea pigs inoculated for the first time with serum from other guinea pigs. For example, among 12 Rockefeller Institute stock animals, three individuals developed skin erythema after injection of 0.1 ml serum diluted 1:3 in saline. First noticeable after 8 to 10 hours, they were maximal at 18 to 24 hours, and lasted several days. The remaining 9 animals showed no significant skin reaction, but 8 of these were capable of evoking the response in the first three animals. Studies with other stocks revealed 3 types of animals: (a) Dermally reactive animals, the sera of which did not evoke skin reactions. (b) Dermally nonreactive animals possessing sera capable of evoking reactions in others. (c) Individuals with neither positive attributes.

The mode of inheritance of the serum factor was investigated by Battisto (1961a,b, 1963).

It was concluded that the serum factor is controlled by an autosomal dominant gene designed S^{Hy}. Absence of the factor (i.e., the recessive gene) was designated S^{hy} (Battisto, 1963). A number of strains of guinea pigs was characterized on the basis of whether they fell into groups a, b, or c above (Battisto, 1964).

Further studies (Lieberman *et al.*, 1964) showed that the serum factor is inactivated by boiling, but not by heating whole serum at 56°C for 30 minutes or by repeated freezing and thawing and is unrelated to permeability substances that evoke immediate type dermal reactions. The factor was found to be elutable from starch gels following electrophoresis of whole serum. About one-third of the factor applied was recovered from the area that lies ahead of the slow α-globulins and behind the fast α-globulins. The serum factor containing fraction had about 0.5% of the protein content of whole serum. The starch gel-eluted fraction travelled to the β-globulin zone using electrophoresis on paper strips.

Further immunological studies of the serum factor have been carried out by Battisto (1968) and Follett and Battisto (1968).

8. Anaphylaxis

Although the guinea pig has been widely used in the study of anaphylaxis, the mode of inheritance has not been studied in much detail. Stone *et al.* (1964) found important strain differences in the acute bronchospasm phase of anaphylactic shock. Strain 2 animals were much more resistant than strain 13. This difference was not due to a difference in sensitivity to histamine since the intravenous minimum lethal dose was about the same for both strains (i.e., about 0.3 mg/kg), nor were any strain differences noted in the sequestration of antibody in lungs, intestines, spleen, skin, liver, or muscle. There were, however, important strain differences in the histamine content of various tissues. The lungs of Hartley strain guinea pigs had three times as much histamine as animals of strain 2.

In vitro studies of histamine release from the lungs during bronchospasm again revealed important strain differences with up to 86 μg from Hartley and 2.0 μg from strain 2 animals. Not only were there strain differences in the histamine content of the lungs but there were also important strain differences in histamine release.

There have been at least two selection experiments to try to develop strains sensitive and insensitive to anaphylaxis. One of these has resulted in the development of 5 partly inbred strains, though the results have not yet been fully reported. The lines were developed by selection for sensitivity to ovalbumin by repeated inhalations of aerosolized aqueous ovalbumin containing 5 mg ovalbumin per milliliter (Lundberg, 1972).

Resistant and susceptible lines were developed by brother × sister mating. At generation F_{15}, nearly 100% of line IMM/1 animals had an extremely strong anaphylactic reaction to low doses of ovalbumin with good antibody production. In the resistant line IMM/2 most animals had no anaphylactic reaction and did not produce measurable antibodies against ovalbumin. Animals of this strain were less resistant to infection than those of strain IMM/1.

Takino *et al.* (1971) developed two lines of guinea pigs sensitive and insensitive to chemical mediators and anaphylaxis. Intensity of bronchospasm on inhalation of 2.5% aqueous histamine solution was the selection criterion. Due to high mortality histamine was later replaced by acetylcholine. The lines were developed by brother × sister inbreeding.

By the tenth generation sensitive animals took an average of 109 ± 20 seconds before collapsing as a result of inhaling acetylcholine, whereas resistant animals all remained standing for more than 5 minutes. The sensitive line was also much more sensitive to histamine, serotonin, pilocarpine, and bradykinin. A number of other differences were noted.

It was concluded that increased sensitivity was due to localized heightened reactivity of the bronchial walls, since there was no increased sensitivity of the salivary glands, cardiovascular system, intestinal tract, or skin. Increased sensitivity to acetylcholine and pilocarpine was associated with an increased sensitivity to all drugs having a parasympathomimetic action.

D. Biochemical Genetics

1. Introduction

The biochemical genetics of vertebrates, excluding man, have been reviewed by Lush (1966, 1970). Recently several additional biochemical polymorphisms have been described.

a. Allotypic marker $GP\gamma_2$–1. Although little work has been done on allotypic markers of guinea pig immunoglobulins, Kelus (1969) reported a single polymorphism of this type which he named $GP\gamma_2$–*1*. Only small numbers of animals were used and no breeding studies were carried out, but it was concluded that such studies may reveal a great variety of protein polymorphisms.

b. Complement Deficiencies. The genetics of complement deficiencies in man and laboratory animals has been reviewed by Alper and Rosen (1971). In guinea pigs two complement deficiencies and one possible polymorphism have been reported, but unfortunately one of these (a possible C3 deficiency) has been lost.

i. C2 polymorphism. Colten *et al.* (1970) used the technique of electrofocusing to show that C2 of guinea pigs may be polymorphic. Human C2 has an isoelectric point of 5.6, but guinea pig serum was bimodal with peaks at 5.6 and 5.2 in six animals and unimodal at 5.6 in two animals. No genetic studies have been reported.

ii. "C3 complement deficiency." A deficiency of "the third component of complement" was reported by Moore (1919) which was the subject of a number of studies before it was lost (e.g., Hyde, 1923, 1924a,b,c, 1927, 1932). As the mutant has now been lost it is difficult to discover the exact nature of this deficiency in modern terminology, but Alper and Rosen (1971) considered these animals to have been deficient in C3, since enhancement of phagocytosis and probably of local anaphylotoxin generation was impaired. "C3 deficient" guinea pigs made antibody but their serum lacked opsonic activity. Heat-inactivated human or normal guinea pig serum restored hemolytic complement activity. Serum previously treated with cobra venom, yeast, or bacteria did not. The complement deficient serum had only about 1% of the hemolytic activity of normal guinea pig serum.

Hyde (1932) suggested that the condition is inherited as a simple Mendelian recessive gene. There was some controversy over whether complement deficient guinea pigs were as vigorous as normals. Moore (1919) claimed that the deficient animals were more susceptible to an enteric infection and were also more sensitive to low temperatures. Hyde (1932), however, considered that under normal conditions deficient animals were as vigorous as nondeficient ones. When exposed to "a natural infection which, on three different occasions swept through and almost depleted a colony of 500 animals" there was no difference in susceptibility among deficient and nondeficient animals.

iii. C4 complement deficiency. Ellman *et al.* (1970b), and Ellman (1970) reported a C4 complement deficiency in the NIH multipurpose guinea pig stock. In trying to produce guinea pig immunoglobin allotype antiserum animals were immunized with heat-killed *Proteus* and strain 2 guinea pig antibodies to *Proteus* in Freund's adjuvant. One month following immunization, one recipient had precipitating antibodies that reacted by Ouchterlony analysis with serum of other guinea pigs from several different strains and breeds.

Further analysis showed that this animal was totally deficient in C4 and was producing an antiserum specific to guinea pig C4. Further screening of the colony revealed that about 2% of the animals were deficient in C4. Both normal guinea pig serum and partially purified C4 restored the hemolytic activity of the serum of a nonantibody-producing C4-deficient animal. C4 could be titrated by adding a dilution of partially purified C4 to serum of this guinea pig. Thus, there was no evidence of a C4 inhibitor. Crosses between C4-deficient and normal animals produced heterozygous young with an intermediate C4 level as determined by titration of C4. Further crosses gave results consistent with a simple Mendelian interpretation. Although Ellman (1970) concluded that the C4 deficiency was inherited as "a simple autosomal recessive trait," it would be more correct to state that it has a simple "partially dominant" mode of inheritance in view of the intermediate levels of C4 activity found in heterozygotes (Serra, 1966).

Extensive studies of *in vivo* immune responses of C4-deficient animals have been reported by Ellman *et al.* (1971b). They found that most immunological reactions studied were normal. These included contact and delayed hypersensitivity, passive cutaneous anaphylaxis, Arthus and passive Arthus reactions, and foreign body-induced exudative response. The normal Arthus reaction was unexpected since guinea pigs depleted of complement by cobra venom failed to show this reaction. The most probable explanation for the normal Arthus response is that there is an alternative pathway in the complement sequence. Antibody production in two out of three antigens tested was impared as was the immune clearance of guinea pig erythrocytes sensitized with rabbit antibodies. C4 complement-deficient animals were studied *in vitro* by Frank *et al.* (1971). These studies lend support to the hypothesis that there is an alternative pathway for activation of late acting complement components.

c. Carbonic Anhydrase. In a comparative study of carbonic anhydrase isozymes in a number of different animal species, Funakoshi and Deutsch (1971) noted individual differences in the starch gel electrophoretograms of six guinea pigs. According to their nomenclature human erythrocytes contain A, B, and C forms of this enzyme whereas individual guinea pigs had A and D or B and D but not A, B, and D forms. Carbonic anhydrase has been shown to exist in two primary isozymic forms in erythrocytes of a number of species (Carter, 1972). The low activity form is designated CAI (or CAB) and the high activity form as CAII (or CAC). Carter and Festing (1972) found strain differences in the expression of the *CAII* locus. The partially inbred strains OM3 and R9 were both homozygous for the allele $CAII^B$ while strain B (again partially inbred) was homozygous for an alternative allele $CAII^A$. Carter (1972) studied crosses between *C. procellus* and *C. apera*. Both species had a low and a high activity form of the enzyme, though the activities differed substantially between the two species. Hybrids expressed both parental forms. Data from the F_2 generation suggested that the *CAI* and *CAII* loci are linked in these species.

d. Cortisol Hydroxylation. The mode of inheritance of the ability to form hydroxylated derivatives of cortisol was studied by Burstein *et al.* (1965). There were extremely large differences between strains 2 and 13 in 2α-hydroxycortisol production following ACTH administration. The F_1 hybrid showed intermediate levels. Segregation in the F_2 generation was consistent with a Mendelian interpretation provided account was taken of the distribution in the F_1 generation. However, it seems likely that the character is controlled by more than one gene. The observed strain difference has been studied in more detail by Burstein (1971).

e. Hypocatalasemia (Ca). Catalase is a protein mainly contained in erythrocytes and is extremely active in breaking down hydrogen peroxide. Radev (1960) discovered a polymorphism for catalase activity in an unnamed guinea pig stock. Normal guinea pigs had a catalase index (the quantity of H_2O_2 decomposed by 1 ml of blood) of about 9.7 (161 animals tested); whereas, hypocatalasemia animals had an index of only about 0.2 to 0.4. Crosses between hypocatalasemia and normals gave the following results:

Normal 10.96 ± 0.24
F_1 10.34 ± 0.26

Hypocatalasemic (hypocat.) young were produced in the ratio of 11 hypocat. to 39 normal in F_2 generation, and in the ratio of 43 normal to 37 hypocat. in the backcross of F_1 to hypocat animals. These results are consistent with a Mendelian autosomal recessive gene mode of inheritance.

Hypocatalasemic guinea pigs also have a low catalase activity level in their tissues, but there was no indication of whether viability is in any way reduced. It is not known whether this is a common polymorphism in guinea pigs and no subsequent studies can be traced. The gene symbol *ca* is proposed for the condition.

f. Phosphoglucomutase (PGM). Carter and Festing (1972) studied a number of different enzyme systems by starch gel or cellulose acetate electrophoresis. No polymorphisms were found for phosphoglucose isomerase, phosphogluconate dehydrogenase, or glucose-6-phosphate dehydrogenase, but PGM was found to be polymorphic, though PGM_2 and PGM_3 showed no variation. The partially inbred strain OM3 was homozygous (14 animals tested) for the allele PGM_1^1 while strain R9 was homozygous for the alternative allele PGM_1^2 (8 animals tested) and strain B was segregating for both alleles. The observed segregation in strain B was unexpected since skin grafts show that the strain is virtually homozygous for most of the strong histocompatibility loci and 17 generations of brother × sister inbreeding have been recorded. Polymorphism for PGM in several hystrichomorph rodents was recorded by Carter *et al.* (1972).

E. Miscellaneous Conditions

a. Polydactyl (Px) Locus. A mutation causing a tendency to have extra toes in the heterozygous condition and a polydactylous monster which usually dies *in utero* in the homozygous condition was described by Wright (1934a, 1935). Guinea pigs normally have four toes on the front feet and three on the hind feet. However, extra toes are quite common and lines breeding true for this characteristic have been developed. These lines differ from normals by multiple factors (see Section III,A,1) and the condition is therefore inherited differently from the Px mutation.

A guinea pig with vestiges of atavistic little toes, thumbs, and one big toe appeared in normal stock. Breeding experiments within this stock indicated a semidominant mutation (Wright, 1934a). Among heterozygotes 54% had both thumb and little toe on one or both sides, 20% thumbs only, 8% little toes only, and only 18% were normal. However, these incidences depended strongly upon the genetic background. When the *Px* gene was crossed into a strain having a high incidence of atavistic polydactyly almost 100% of the heterozygotes had extra digits. Other pleiotropic effects of the *Px* gene in the heterozygous state were noted. Birth weight was about 7% higher than in the normals and the preweaning mortality was also slightly higher. Several heterozygotes also had flexures of the feet which persisted throughout life.

A detailed analysis of the interactions between the *Px* gene and the multiple factors causing atavistic polydactyly was also given by Wright (1934b, 1935). Details of the abnormalities found in the homozygotes are given in the Section III,A,1 on "congenital abnormalities."

b. Dominant Waltzing (Wz) Locus. At least two independent mutants causing "waltzing" or circling behavior have been reported in guinea pigs. One of these was designated W by Ernstson (1970) but as W has already been used for the mutant "Whitish" by Ibsen (1932) it is proposed here that the symbol Wz should be used instead.

According to Anonymous (1969) typical animals show a structurally normal hearing apparatus at birth, but shortly thereafter, the hair cells of Corti's organ begin to disappear, followed by a gradual atrophy and disappearance of the other cellular elements of the organ. Cochlear neurons atrophy more slowly with some persisting for more than 2 years. The condition is described in greater detail by Ernstson (1971a,b).

The Wz mutation occurred spontaneously in stock maintained by the National Institutes of Health in 1953. Genetics of the condition are described by Ernstson (1970). Crosses between waltzers and normals gave live offspring in the ratio of approximately one normal to one waltzing. Crosses of waltzing × waltzing gave live offspring conforming well to a 2:1 ratio of waltzing to normals. In this case there was extremely high perinatal mortality which probably included all the homozygous Wz/Wz animals, though no obvious abnormalities could be found. It was concluded that the condition is inherited as an autosomal dominant gene with full penetrance which is lethal soon after birth in the homozygous condition.

c. Recessive Waltzing (wtz) Locus. A mutation causing "waltzing similar to that found in Japanese waltzing mice" was reported by Ibsen and Risty (1929). Breeding tests suggested that the condition was inherited as an autosomal recessive mutation though in one case a cross to an inbred strain gave anomalous results.

The waltzing condition was studied in more detail by Lurie (1941) who found that affected guinea pigs not only tended to run in circles but were deaf. The circling began soon after birth and became more pronounced with age. There was also a tendency to throw the head backward with head tremors. The animals did not respond to external sounds, except when they could feel vibration of the air or the cage.

Histological examination showed degeneration of the organ of Corti. It started with the external followed by the internal hair cells. The cochlear nerve and spiral ganglia cells degenerated at a much later period. The stria vascularis also showed definite degenerative changes. No other abnormalities were detected.

It is not known whether the two waltzing mutations reported here are related though from the descriptions they appear to be rather similar apart from the dominant mode of inheritance in one case and recessive mode in the other.

F. Summary of Mutant Genes and Linkage

1. Mutants

A summary of the identifiable single gene mutations known in the guinea pig is given in Table I.

2. Linkage

Although there have been a number of linkage studies in guinea pigs, no new data have been reported since Wright (1959a). However, Robinson (1970b) summarized these early studies and concluded that only two linkages are firmly established to date (see Fig. 2). These are between the mutants si (silvering) and m (rough modifier), with a recombination value of about 22%, and between R (rough) and Px (Polydactyly), with a recombination value of about 46%.

Few of the more recently discovered biochemical or immunological mutants have been used in linkage studies but there is some evidence that the *GPL-A* and *GPIr-1* loci are closely linked (Shevach *et al.*, 1972). (See Immunogenetics, Section II, C.)

Table I
Summary of Established Mutants of Guinea Pigs

Gene effect[a]	Gene symbol	Name
1	*A*	Light- or yellow-bellied agouti
1	A^r	Ticked-bellied agouti
1	*a*	Non-agouti
1	*b*	Brown
9	*C4*	C4 complement deficiency
1	c^k	Dark dilution
1	c^d	Light dilution
1	c^r	Red-eyed dilution
1	c^a	Albinism or Himalayan
9	*CAII*	Carbonic anhydrase
9	*ca*	Hypocatalasemia
1	*di*	Dilution at base of hairs
1	*dm*	Diminished
1	e^r	Partial extension
1	*e*	Yellow
10	*GPIr-1*	Immune response locus, includes *PLL, GT, GA* alleles
10	*GPL-A*	Main histocompatibility locus (several alleles)
2	*Fz*	Fuzzy
1	*f*	Fading yellow
2	*gr*	Grizzled
2	*l*	Long hair
2	*M*	Rough modifier
1	p^r	Ruby eye
1	*p*	Pink-eyed dilution
9	*PGM*	Phosphoglucomutase
3	*Px*	Polydactyly
2	*R*	Rough
2	*Re*	Rough eye (modifier of rough)
1	*Rs*	Roan spotting and anophlthalmos
1	*s*	White spotting
10	S^{Hy}	Serum factor–hypersensitivity
1	*si*	Silvering
1	*sm*	Salmon eye
2	*St*	Star
2	*sth*	Sticky haired
1	*W*	Whitish or white tipped
6	*wtz*	Recessive waltzing
6	*Wz*	Dominant waltzing

[a]Gene effect codes (as used in *Mouse News Letter*): 1, pigmentation; 2, hair direction and texture; 3, skeleton; 4, tail; 5, eye; 6, ear and circling behavior; 7, neuromuscular; 8, blood, endocrine, internal defects, dwarfs, sterility; 9, enzymes; 10, antigens, disease resistance, etc.; 11, miscellaneous.

III. QUANTITATIVE GENETICS

All the characters in this section are presumed to have a multifactorial mode of inheritance, though in some cases this is not entirely established.

A. Threshold Characters

1. Congenital Abnormalities

A large number of congenital abnormalities were described by Wright (1934a, 1960c) among the 76,000 to 120,000 young produced in order to study inbreeding, coat color, and factor interaction. The abnormalities were described below

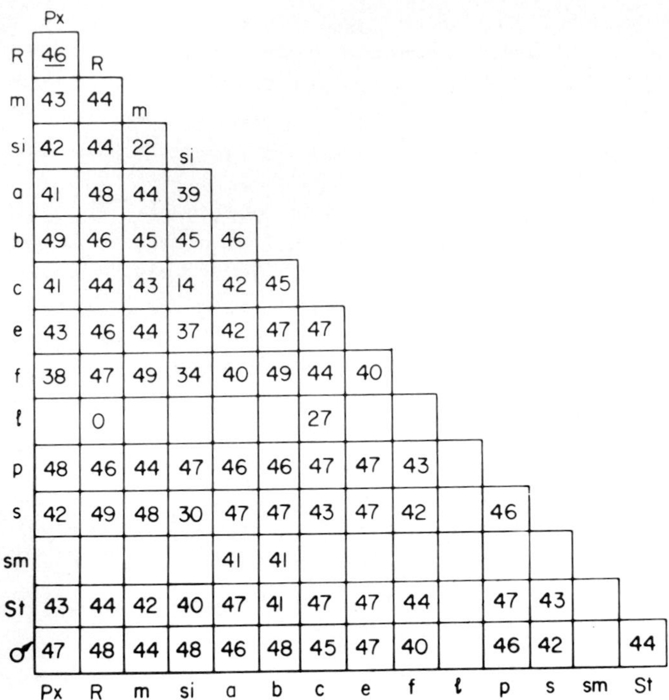

	Px	R	m	si	a	b	c	e	f	ℓ	p	s	sm	St
R	46													
m	43	44												
si	42	44	22											
a	41	48	44	39										
b	49	46	45	45	46									
c	41	44	43	14	42	45								
e	43	46	44	37	42	47	47							
f	38	47	49	34	40	49	44	40						
ℓ		0					27							
p	48	46	44	47	46	46	47	47	43					
s	42	49	48	30	47	47	43	47	42		46			
sm					41	41								
St	43	44	42	40	47	41	47	47	44		47	43		
♂	47	48	44	48	46	48	45	47	40		46	42		44

Fig. 2. Summary of linkage studies in the guinea pig (Robinson, 1970b). Figures shown are the closest linkage compatible with the data, except in the two cases of linkage so far discovered (i.e., *R–Px* and *si–M*) in which the figures give the average recombination percentage.

and most are presumed to have a multifactorial threshold mode of inheritance.

a. Otocephaly and Cyclopia. In this condition the mandible and ventral approximation of the ears were absent (agnathia) and this was usually associated with cyclopia. The condition varied in severity from mere shortness of the mandible to complete absence of mandible, maxilla, nose, eyes, all of the brain in front of the medulla, and most of the skull. A more detailed description is given by Wright and Wagner (1934) and Wright (1934b). The condition was rare in the general colony (0.04%) but in some sublines of strain 13 it reached 28%. Although the condition was clearly genetic, it could not be attributed to simple mendelian inheritance and it was concluded that it was due to "The conjunction of a hereditary tendency of this sort with unfavourable conditions." This type of inheritance will be described simply as threshold inheritance in the rest of this section.

b. Cruciate Double Monsters. There are only 3 recorded cases of cruciate double monsters. They consisted of double monsters joined at the chest with the head or heads at right angles to the bodies (Wright, 1960c). Two of the three cases had strain 13 ancestry. Presumably it has a threshold mode of inheritance.

c. Anotia. The anotia defect superficially resembled the otocephalic monsters but differed in that the eye defect was bilateral microphthalmia rather than cyclopia, together with a complete absence of the inner, middle, and external ears. Several were found in a subline of strain 2.

d. Polydactylous Monsters. Polydactylous monsters result from matings in which both parents are of the type Px/px (see Atavistic Polydactyly, Section III,A,2,b). About 89% of homozygous polydactylous young die before birth, usually at about the twenty-sixth day of gestation. The remaining 8% reach full term as monsters with the following defects: the spinal column has a C-shaped instead of an S-shaped flexure; they have excessive subcutaneous fat; there is a shortening of all parts of the limbs, except the upper arm; the tibia is missing, and the hind limbs are rotated; the feet are of double width with 7 to 12 digits; there are many abnormalities of the head region including hydrocephaly or exencephaly, microphthalmia, cleft palate, and cleft lip. The circulatory and reproductive systems are normal. The embryology of the condition has been reported by Scott (1937, 1938). It is interesting that the heterozygote Px/px often has an extra digit depending on genetic background.

e. The Chunky Monster. A total of 26 (0.03%) chunky monsters were described (Wright, 1960c). Body length was about two-thirds of normal but body weight was normal. There were conspicuous abnormalities of the legs and often a ventral flexure of the feet. It is inherited as a threshold character.

f. Flexure of the Feet. A total of 50 animals had ventral flexure of the feet sometimes associated with torsion of the legs. Five also had other abnormalities. It was concluded that the condition was caused largely by an unfavorable intrauterine environment with little or no genetic involvement.

g. Abnormal Digits. A number of animals with abnormal digits, not associated with atavistic polydactyly, were recorded. It was concluded that there was no direct evidence that heredity played a role in their production.

h. Miscellaneous Defects. There were a few cases of exencephaly, hydrocephaly, harelip, missing incisors, short ears, umbilical hernia, and one case of spina bifida. The mode of inheritance of these defects was not determined.

2. Other Conditions

a. Anophthalmos and Microphthalmia. Inherited anophthalmos was reported by Komich (1971). It occurred spontaneously in a random bred colony of "The English Variety" when a normal appearing sow gave birth to one male and one female with bilateral anophthalmos and one female with unilateral anophthalmos. All three had white coats. These three individuals were used to found a colony by "selective line breeding." Bilateral anophthalmosis was produced in 146 offspring. Matings between bilaterally affected individuals produced 82.3% bilaterally anophthalmic young and a further 15.9% of young with various eye abnormalities. Only two individuals (1.8%) had apparently normal eyes. Unfortunately, no crosses were made to normal animals and it is not clear exactly how the condition is inherited, although the author notes that a report of such studies is in preparation.

Extensive anatomical studies of the anophthalmic animals revealed that the optic tracts, chiasma, and optic nerves were absent. There was hypoplasia of the lateral geniculate bodies.

Lambert and Shrigley (1933) described an inherited microphthalmos and dryness of the cornea. Eaton (1937) reported on microphthalmos, opaque lens, and rotation of the axis of ocular bulbs. A total of 43 affected young (26%) were produced, but mating of affected animals was not possible since most of them did not survive to maturity.

Wright (1960c) reported 145 cases of microphthalmia among 76,000 guinea pigs (0.19%). Sixteen animals had other defects, which suggests a common developmental error. There was a marked excess of females with microphthalmia. Although there were strain differences in the incidence of defects, the mode of inheritance was not studied in detail. Anophthalmos is also associated with the roan spotting locus, *Rs*.

b. Atavistic Polydactyly. Although the guinea pig normally has three toes on the hind foot, the occurrence of an extra digit is relatively common. Castle (1906) first studied the condition and by selective breeding was able to develop a strain (strain D) with 100% of animals having a perfect fourth toe. Inheritance of the condition was also studied by Stockard (1927, 1930) and Wright (1934b,c) who showed that a polygenic threshold model was the best explanation of inheritance of the condition.

Reciprocal crosses were made between strain 2 and strain D. All 146 F_1 young were normal. In the F_2 generation 19.3% were polydactylous, a proportion that was statistically not significantly different from 25%. In the backcross of the F_1 to strain D the proportion of the young with polydactyly did not differ significantly from 50%. This suggested an autosomal recessive mode of inheritance. However, this interpretation completely broke down when crosses were made between the segregants of the F_2 generation. It became clear that many genes were involved in inheritance of the condition. A formula was developed for estimating the number of factors contributing to the condition:

$$n = \frac{D^2}{8(\sigma^2_{F_2} - \sigma^2_P)}$$

Where n is the minimum number of factors influencing the condition, D is the difference between parental means, and $\sigma^2_{F_2}$ and σ^2_P are the variances in the F_2 and parental generations, respectively. The various statistics were calculated from the data by transforming the percentages observed to a threshold model with an underlying normal distribution, shown in Fig. 3 (Wright, 1963). Using the formula, it was estimated that strain D and strain 2 differed by about 3 to 4 factors (assuming each factor had equal magnitude).

Crosses between strain 32 and D (not shown in Fig. 3) gave results closely similar to those quoted above, but crosses involving strain 13 were different, indicating that although strain 13 is entirely normal in the number of digits, it lies closer to the threshold. This can also be seen in Fig. 3. Estimates showed that strain 13 differed from strain D in at least two and more probably three factors. Strain 35 lies even closer to the threshold than strain 13, so that most of the F_1 progeny of 35 × D had four toes.

This work has been discussed in some detail since it represents the classic analysis of a polygenically determined threshold character of a type which is probably very common in the inheritance of susceptibility to disease.

c. Spermatogenic Hypoplasia. An inherited spermatogenic hypoplasia associated with a "red-eyed chocolate" color was reported by Jakway and Young (1958). The condition appeared spontaneously in a colony being maintained to study mating behavior. Affected animals had a chocolate (or sometimes red) coat color and the eyes lacked pigmentation. The

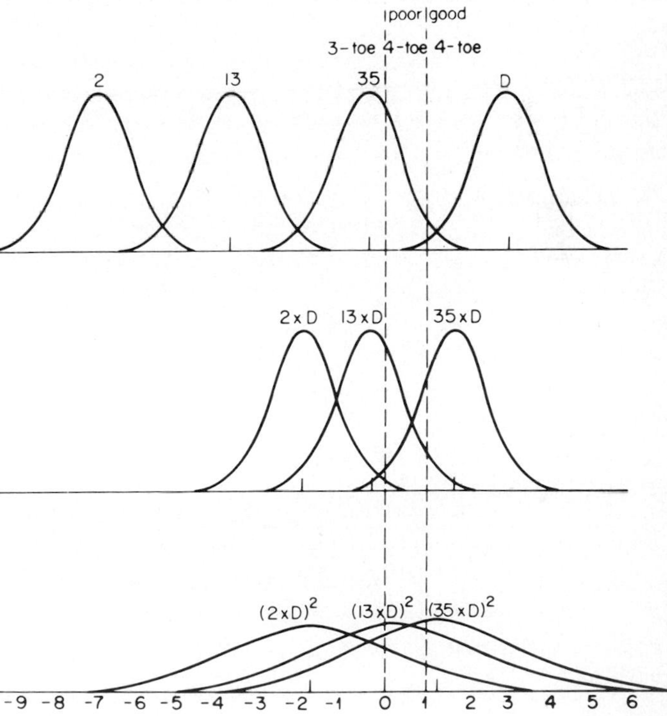

Fig. 3. Theoretical distribution of factors determining development of the small toe on an underlying physiology scale in relation to thresholds for any small toe and for perfect development, in four inbred strains, in F_1 and F_2 of crosses of one (D) with the other three (from Wright, 1963).

animals appeared so vigorous and healthy that a number of them were selected for breeding purposes before it became apparent that they carried any defect.

Fertility in females was normal but 19 out of 86 (22%) of the red-eyed chocolate (or occasionally red) males were sterile and a further eight or nine were subfertile. Fertility in the nonchocolate males from the same stock was normal. Histological examination revealed that the defect ranged from germinal aplasia in most seminiferous tubules to a slightly subnormal state in which the germinal epithelium appeared normal but spermatazoa in the epididymides were distributed abnormally. An estimated 30 to 50% of males were affected. The authors considered that the condition resembled germinal aplasia and spermatogenic arrest in man, though the latter conditions are not associated with pigmentation defects in the eye.

B. Inbreeding

There have been two large-scale long-term experiments on inbreeding in guinea pigs. Undoubtedly, the best documented is the experiment started by G. M. Rommel, the chief of the Animal Husbandry Division of the U. S. Bureau of Animal Industry in 1906. The main findings of this experiment have been recorded by Wright (1922a,b,c). The origin of the stock used in these experiments is obscure, but they were traceable to 1894 as a closed colony consisting of many varieties. Some new stock was introduced in 1894 but a severe outbreak of disease in 1897 reduced the colony from over 700 to 54 animals. Most of the subsequent work was done on the progeny of this small group of survivors.

In 1906 the stock was divided into 42 families and single pair brother × sister mating was initiated. However, only 23 families were eventually started, the rest being lost for various reasons. By 1915 only 18 families were left and in 1917 all but five of the inbred strains were terminated. These were strains 2, 13, 32, 35, and 39. A noninbred control strain was started in 1911.

Many different characteristics were studied including age at sexual maturity, fertility, growth rate, mortality of the young, resistance to tuberculosis, sex ratio, coat colors, and the production of monstrosities. Analysis of some results was complicated by important environmental effects. For example, there was a marked seasonal influence on litter size. However, the general results were clear cut and have been confirmed in other species and in guinea pigs by Mehner (1956). All aspects of reproductive performance declined as a result of inbreeding. Thus the total number of young weaned per breeding female per year declined from about 12 in 1906 to about 7 to 9 in 1917 to 1928. At the same time, the families became differentiated with coat color and reproductive performance becoming stabilized (Wright and Eaton, 1929), though there were changes in ranking as inbreeding progressed in the latter case. Although there were few monstrosities produced, these tended to be characteristic of the strain (see Congenital Abnormalities, Section III,A,1). Similar findings were reported by Mehner (1956), whose experiment lasted for 27 years.

The genetic material produced in Rommel's and Wright's inbreeding experiment was used in a large number of subsequent studies, which contributed substantially both to theoretical population genetics (Provine, 1971) and to an understanding of the mode of gene action in controlling factors such as coat color. Many of these studies have been quoted in other sections of this chapter. Wright (1960c) gave an extensive discussion of the effects of inbreeding on growth and reproductive performance. The need to quantify the degree of inbreeding in these guinea pig strains led Wright (1922d) to formulate the coefficient of inbreeding F, which is widely used in quantitative genetics. Similarly, the need to quantify the relative importance of environment and heredity in determining the spotted pattern in inbred guinea pigs led Wright (1920) to define what is now termed the "heritability" of the character (actually Wright defined the square root of the heritability and called it h, so that heritability is now always symbolized as h^2). Both the inbreeding coefficient and heritability are now widely used in quantitative genetics. A list of inbred strains of guinea pigs is published annually in *Guinea-Pig Newsletter* (M.R.C. Laboratory Animals Centre, Carshalton, Surrey).

C. Growth and Body Composition

1. Growth

There have been several studies on the inheritance of growth rate in guinea pigs (Eaton, 1932; Haines, 1931; McPhee and Eaton, 1931). Wright (1960c) carried out a detailed analysis of factors influencing 33-day weight using the method of path coefficients. In general, these studies indicated that growth rate is highly inherited, though birth weight, weaning weight, and 33-day weight are also dependent on other factors such as litter size and perinatal mortality. Dillard *et al.* (1972) analyzed the heritability and genetic correlations between various growth parameters, a study particularly valuable for investigators interested in developing larger or smaller strains and for animal breeders interested in developing the guinea pig as a meat animal. They examined two noninbred populations consisting of 1192 progeny of 86 sires in line 1 and 473 progeny of 28 sires in line 2. Average litter size at birth was 2.93 ± 0.04 and 3.00 ± 0.06 young in the two lines, respectively. Birth weights were adjusted by covariance for litter size. Heritability estimates for various traits are given in Table II and phenotypic and genetic correlations between the traits were also calculated. The general conclusion was that heritability of

Table II

Heritability Estimates for Weights and Rates of Gain in Two Lines of Guinea Pigs[a]

	Line 1	Line 2	Pooled data
Birth weight	0.15 ± 0.12	0.51 ± 0.26	0.25 ± 0.11
Weaning weight	0.41 ± 0.15	0.75 ± 0.31	0.49 ± 0.13
91-day weight	0.50 ± 0.15	0.49 ± 0.23	0.52 ± 0.13
Gain birth to weaning	0.40 ± 0.14	0.67 ± 0.27	0.46 ± 0.13
Gain weaning to 91-day	0.27 ± 0.12	0.08 ± 0.13	0.25 ± 0.10
Gain birth to 91-day	0.48 ± 0.15	0.37 ± 0.19	0.48 ± 0.12

[a]Values are h^2 ± SE.

most of the traits associated with growth was relatively high, offering good scope for improving growth rate by selection. The correlation between weaning weight and 91-day weight was so high (0.86) that selection for improved weaning weight should be relatively effective in increasing 91-day weight.

Prenatal growth was studied by Ibsen (1928) though this did not include a genetic analysis.

2. Organ Weights

Although the mode of inheritance of organ weights has not been studied, a comparison of inbred strain 2 and 13 showed statistically significant differences in absolute organ weights between the two strains (Table III) (Strandskov, 1939). All animals were over a year old when weights were recorded. The animals were maintained in unmated groups of six with both strains being kept in the same environment as far as possible. Probably the most interesting differences were the relatively greater weights of the kidney, adrenal, and spleen in strain 2 compared with strain 13 guinea pigs.

3. Skeleton

Some studies of skeletal dimensions in crosses between various races of domestic guinea pigs and *Cavia cutleri* were reported by Castle (1916).

D. Reproduction

There does not appear to have been recent studies on inheritance of reproductive performance in guinea pigs though Wright (1960c) reanalyzed some of the results of his earlier studies on the effect of inbreeding (Wright, 1922a,b,c). The details of his findings are too complex to discuss in any detail

Table III

Some Organ Weights in Strain 2 and 13 Guinea Pigs[a, b]

Organ	Weight (gm) ± SD			
	Strain 2 ♂♂	Strain 2 ♀♀	Strain 13 ♂♂	Strain 13 ♀♀
Body	802 ± 65	780 ± 69	1044 ± 69	940 ± 99
Liver	25.37 ± 2.9	29.21 ± 4.83	33.7 ± 3.89	35.5 ± 8.50
Lungs[c]	5.21 ± 0.97	5.18 ± 1.22	7.23 ± 0.94	7.44 ± 0.88
Heart	2.12 ± 0.28	2.07 ± 0.27	2.42 ± 0.33	2.26 ± 0.23
Thyroid[d]	0.061 ± 0.013	0.058 ± 0.007	0.078 ± 0.017	0.074 ± 0.924
Kidney[d]	2.94 ± 0.56	2.79 ± 0.38	2.57 ± 0.24	2.33 ± 0.15
Adrenal[d]	0.402 ± 0.13	0.394 ± 0.110	0.310 ± 0.050	0.284 ± 0.041
Spleen	0.78 ± 0.12	1.03 ± 0.27	0.73 ± 0.07	0.93 ± 0.16

[a]After Strandskov (1939).
[b]N = 20 in all cases.
[c]Weight of both lungs.
[d]Weight of left organ only.

Table IV
Summary of Karyological Investigations of the Guinea Pig[a]

Defined autosomal groups	No. of metacentrics			No. of acrocentrics			Sex chromosomes[b]		References
	Large	Medium	Small	Large	Medium	Small	X	Y	
–	0	1	0	1	14	15	Lm	Sa	Awa *et al.* (1959)
3	1	7	0	1	9	13	Lm	Sa	Ohno *et al.* (1961)
–	1	10	3	1	0	16	Lm	Sa	Watson *et al.* (1966)
4	1	7	1	3	9	10	Mm	Sa	Dobrijanov and Goljdman (1967)
4	0	12	0	2	10	7	Mm	Sa	Cohen and Pinsky (1966)
4	0	10	0	1	13	7	Lm	–	Jagiello (1969)

[a]After Robinson (1971).
[b]L = large; M = medium; m = metacentric; a = acrocentric (acrocentric embraces subtelocentric and telocentric elements); S = small.

as they include a complete path coefficient analysis of factors influencing 33-day weight, including birth weight, postnatal growth, conception age at birth, interval between litters, litter size, perinatal mortality, and residual factors. In general, the analysis is in agreement with other studies on the effects of inbreeding mentioned previously.

IV. CYTOGENETICS

Early studies of the chromosome complement of the guinea pig were summarized by Makino (1947) who showed that the diploid chromosome number was $2N = 64$, with an XX-Xy sex determining mechanism. More recent studies have been summarized by Robinson (1971) who points out that it is difficult to characterize the chromosomes of the guinea pig due to the large number of small elements. A summary of several recent findings was given by Robinson and is reproduced in Table IV. The lack of general agreement emphasizes the difficulty of working with guinea pig chromosomes.

More recently, Blanchi and Ayres (1971) used the cytological DNA denaturation–renaturation technique to study the distribution of heterochromatin. Their findings were similar to those of Cohen and Pinsky (1966). Only four autosomal pairs (labeled 1–4) could be identified with accuracy. Pairs 1 and 2 were large acrocentrics and pairs 3 and 4 were medium submetacentrics. Remaining autosomes had a subterminal or terminal kinetochore position and formed a continuous series which decreased in size without noticeable gaps. Only three animals were examined but there appeared to be a polymorphism with respect to the size of one of the X chromosomes in the two females. Although morphologically indistinguishable the Y chromosome could easily be identified using this staining technique. The distribution of heterochromatin in pair 21 was described. Unfortunately, no breeding tests were performed to determine whether this type of polymorphism is truly inherited.

Chromosome polymorphisms have also been reported by Cohen and Pinsky (1966), Fernandez and Spotorno (1968), and Manna and Talukdor (1964). The apparent prevalence of such polymorphisms could be worthy of further investigation.

REFERENCES

Alper, C. A., and Rosen, F. S. (1971). Genetic aspects of the complement system. *Advan. Immunol.* **14**, 251–290.

Aron, M., Marescaux, J., and Rebel, A. (1964). Role of racial factors in the duration of pituitary gland heterografts in the guinea-pig. *C.R. Soc. Biol.* **158**, 190–192.

Arquilla, E. R., and Finn, J. (1963). Genetic differences in antibody production to determinant groups on insulin. *Science* **142**, 400–401.

Arquilla, E. R., and Finn, J. (1965). Genetic control of combining sites of insulin antibodies produced by guinea-pigs. *J. Exp. Med.* **122**, 771–784.

Anonymous. (1969). "Laboratory Aids Branch Services." Publication of the National Institutes of Health, Division of Research Services.

Awa, A., Sasaki, M., and Takayama, S. (1959). An *in vitro* study of the somatic chromosomes in several mammals. *Jap. J. Zool.* **12**, 257–265.

Barnes, A. D., and Krohn, P. L. (1957). The estimation of the number of histocompatibility genes controlling the successful transplantation of normal skin in mice. *Proc. Roy. Soc. Ser. B* **146**, 505–526.

Battisto, J. R. (1960). Natural occurrence of delayed-type iso-hypersensitiveness. *Nature (London)* **187**, 69–71.

Battisto, J. R. (1961a). An erythematous disease of adult guinea-pigs following transplantation of homologous lymphoid cells. *Proc. Soc. Exp. Biol. Med.* **106**, 725–727.

Battisto, J. R. (1961b). Natural delayed iso-hypersensitivity among inbred guinea-pigs. *Fed. Proc., Fed. Amer. Soc. Exp. Biol.* **20**, 258.

Battisto, J. R. (1963). Genetic control of a guinea-pig serum factor toward which natural delayed iso-hypersensitivity occurs. *Nature (London)* **198**, 598–599.

Battisto, J. R. (1964). Polymorphism of serum factors detected by naturally occurring delayed-type iso-hypersensitivity. *Proc. Int. Congr. Anim. Reprod. and Artif. Insem., 5th, 1964.* Vol. 11, pp. 245–249.

Battisto, J. R. (1968). Spontaneous delayed iso-hypersensitivity in guinea-pigs. *J. Immunol.* **101**, 743–752.

Battisto, J. R. Chiapetta, G., and Hixon, R. (1968). Immunologic responses of guinea-pigs to dextran. *J. Immunol.* **101**, 203–209.

Bauer, J. A. (1958). Histocompatibility in inbred strains of guinea-pigs. *Ann. N.Y. Acad. Sci.* **73**, 663–672.

Bauer, J. A. (1960). Genetics of skin transplantation and an estimate of the number of histocompatibility genes in inbred guinea-pigs. *Ann. N.Y. Acad. Sci.* **87**, 78–92.

Benacerraf, B., Green, I., and Paul, W. E. (1967). The immune response of guinea-pigs to hapten-poly-L-lysine conjugates as an example of the genetic control of the recognition of antigenicity. *Cold Spring Harbor Symp. Quant. Biol.* **32**, 569–575.

Ben-Efraim, S., and Liacopolos, P. (1969). The competitive effect of DNP-poly-L-lysine in responder and non responder guinea-pigs. *Immunology* **16**, 573–580.

Billingham, R. E., and Medawar, P. B. (1947a) The "cytogenetics" of black and white guinea-pig skin. *Nature (London)* **159**, 115–117.

Billingham, R. E., and Medawar, P. B. (1947b). Role of dendritic cells in the infective colour transformation of guinea-pig skin. *Nature (London)* **160**, 61–62.

Billingham, R. E., and Medawar, P. B. (1948). Pigment spread and cell heredity in guinea pig-skins. *Heredity* **2**, 29–47.

Billingham, R. E., and Silvers, W. K. (1965). Re-investigation of the possible occurrence of matnerally induced tolerance in guinea-pigs. *J. Exp. Zool.* **160**, 221–224.

Billingham, R. E., and Silvers, W. K. (1970). Studies on the migratory behavior of melanocytes in guinea-pig skin. *J. Exp. Med.* **131**, 101–117.

Bianchi, N. O., and Ayres, J. (1971). Polymorphic patterns of heterochromatin distribution in guinea-pig chromosomes. *Chromosoma* **34**, 254–260.

Bluestein, H. G., Green, I., and Benacerraf, B. (1971a). Specific immune response genes of the guinea-pig. I. Dominant genetic control of responsiveness to copolymers of L-glutamic acid and L-alanine and L-glutamic acid and L-tyrosine. *J. Exp. Med.* **134**, 458–470.

Bluestein, H. G., Green, I., and Benacerraf, B. (1971b). Specific immune response genes of the guinea-pig. II. Relationship between the poly-L-lysine gene and the genes controlling immune responsiveness to copolymers of L-glutamic acid and L-alanine and L-glutamic acid and L-tyrosine in random bred Hartley guinea-pigs. *J. Exp. Med.* **134**, 471–481.

Bluestein, H. G., Ellman, L., Green, I., and Benacerraf, B. (1971c). Specific immune response genes of the guinea-pig. III. Linkage of the GA and GT immune response genes to histocompatibility genotypes in inbred guinea-pigs. *J. Exp. Med.* **134**, 1529–1537.

Bluestein, H. G., Green, I., and Benacerraf, B. (1971d). Specific immune response genes of the guinea-pig. IV. Demonstration in randombred guinea-pigs that responsiveness to a copolymer of L-glutamic acid and L-tyrosine is predicated upon the possession of a distinct stain 13 histocompatibility specificity. *J. Exp. Med.* **134**, 1538–1544.

Bock, F. C. (1950). White spotting in the guinea-pig due to a gene (star) which alters hair direction. Ph.D. Thesis, University of Chicago Library.

Brummerstadt, E., and Franks, D. (1970). Guinea-pig alloantigens studied by a cytotoxic test with lymphocytes. *Transplantation* **10**, 137–140.

Burstein, S. (1971). Effect of ions on the enzymatic cortisol 2- and 6-hydroxylase activities of the liver and adrenal preparations from two guinea-pig genotypes. *Endocrinology* **89**, 928–931.

Burstein, S., Bharnani, B. R., and Kimball, H. L. (1965). Genetic aspects of cortisol hydroxylation in guinea-pigs; urinary excretion and production rates of cortisol and 2α-hydroxycortisol. *Endocrinology* **76**, 753–761.

Carter, N. D. (1972). Carbonic anhydrase in *Cavia apera, Cavia porcellus* and their hybrids. *Comp. Biochem. Physiol. B* **43**, 743–747.

Carter, N. D., and Festing, M. F. W. (1972). Erythrocyte enzyme and protein variation in three guinea-pig strains. *Guinea-Pig Newslett.* **6**, 12–16.

Carter, N. D., Hill, M. R., and Weir, B. J. (1972). Genetic variation of phosphoglucose isomerase in some hystricomorph rodents. *Biochem. Genet.* **6**, 147–156.

Castle, W. E. (1905). Heredity of coat characters in guinea-pigs and rabbits. *Carnegie Inst. Wash. Publ.* **23**, 1–78.

Castle, W. E. (1906). The origin of a polydactylous race of guinea-pigs. *Carnegie Inst. Wash. Publ.* **49**, 17.

Castle, W. E. (1908). A new colour variety of the guinea-pig. *Science* **28**, 250–252.

Castle, W. E. (1912). On the origin of a pink-eyed guinea-pig with a coloured coat. *Science* **35**, 508–510.

Castle, W. E. (1913). Reversion in guinea-pigs and its explanation. *Carnegie Inst. Wash. Publ.* **179**, 1–10.

Castle, W. E. (1916). Studies of inheritance in guinea-pigs and rabbits. An expedition to the home of the guinea-pig and some breeding experiments with material there obtained. *Carnegie Inst. Wash. Publ.* **231**, 3–55.

Chase, H. B. (1939a). Studies on the tricolour pattern of the guinea-pig. I. The relations between different areas of the coat in respect of the prime colour. *Genetics* **24**, 610–621.

Chase, H. B. (1939b). Studies on the tricolour pattern of the guinea-pig. II. The distribution of black and yellow as affected by white spotting and by imperfect dominance in the tortoiseshell series of alleles. *Genetics* **24**, 622–643.

Cohen, M. M., and Pinsky, L. (1966). Autosomal polymorphism via a translocation in the guinea-pig, *Cavia porcellus. Cytogenetics* **5**, 120–132.

Colten, H. R., Borsos, T., and Rapp, H. J. (1970). Isoelectric foccusing of human and guinea-pig C2: Polymorphism of guinea-pig C2. *Immunology* **18**, 467–472.

Detlefsen, J. A. (1914). Genetic studies on a cavy species cross. *Carnegie Inst. Wash. Publ.* **205**, 1–134.

De Weck, A. L., Polak, L., Sato, W., and Frey, J. R. (1970). Determination of histocompatibility antigens by leucocyte typing in outbred guinea-pigs and effect of matching on skin graft survival. *Guinea-Pig Newslett.* **2**, 34–37.

De Weck, A. L., Polak, L., Sato, W., and Frey, J. R. (1971). Determination of histocompatibility antigens by leucocyte typing in outbred guinea-pigs and effect of matching on skin graft survival. *Transplant. Proc.* **3**, 192–194.

De Weck, A. L., and Geczy, A. F. (1975). Histocompatibility antigens of the guinea-pig. *Guinea-Pig Newslett.* **9**, 9–12.

Dillard, E. U., Vaccaro, R., Lozano, J., and Robison, O. W. (1972). Phenotypic and genetic parameters for growth in guinea-pigs. *J. Anim. Sci.* **34**, 193–194.

Dobrijanov, D. S., and Goljdman, I. L. (1967). The normal karyotype of the guinea-pig. *Tsitol. Genet.* **1**, 78–82.

Eaton, O. N. (1932). Correlation of heredity and other factors affecting growth in guinea-pigs. *U.S., Dep. Agr., Tech. Bull.* **279**.

Eaton, O. N. (1937). A hereditary eye defect in guinea-pigs. *J. Hered.* **28**, 353–358.

Ellman, L. (1970). Guinea-pigs deficient in the fourth component of complement. *Guinea Pig Newslett.* **2**, 19–20.

Ellman, L., Green, I., and Benacerraf, B. (1970a). Effect of gene dose on the immune response to a 2,4-dinitrophenyl glutamic acid lysine copolymer. *Nature (London)* **227**, 1140–1141.

Ellman, L., Green, I., and Frank, M. (1970b). Genetically controlled total deficiency of the fourth component of complement in the guinea-pig. *Science* **170,** 74–75.

Ellman, L., Green, I., Martin, W. J., and Benacerraf, B. (1970c). Linkage between the poly-L-lysine gene and the locus controlling the major histocompatibility antigens in strain 2 guinea-pigs. *Proc. Nat. Acad. Sci. U.S.* **66,** 322–328.

Ellman, L., Green, I., and Benacerraf, B. (1971a). The PLL gene and histocompatibility genotype in inbred and random bred guinea-pigs. *J. Immunol.* **107,** 382–388.

Ellman, L., Green, I., Judge, F., and Frank, M. M. (1971b). *In vivo* studies in C4-deficient guinea-pigs. *J. Exp. Med.* **134,** 162–175.

Ellman, L., Inman, J., and Green, I. (1971c). Strain differences in the immune response to hydralazine in inbred guinea-pigs. *Clin. Exp. Immunol.* **9,** 927–937.

Ernstson, S. (1970). Heredity in a strain of the waltzing guinea-pig. *Acta Oto-Laryngol.* **69,** 358–362.

Ernstson, S. (1971a). Cochlear morphology in a strain of the waltzing guinea-pig. *Acta Oto-Laryngol.* **71,** 469–482.

Ernstson, S. (1971b). Vestibular physiology in a strain of the waltzing guinea-pig. *Acta Oto-Laryngol.* **72,** 303–309.

Fernandez, R., and Spotorno, A. (1968). Heteromorphism in the chromosome pair No. 1 of *Cavia porcellus* L. *Arch. Biol. Med. Exp.* **5,** 81–85.

Foerster, J., Green, I., Lamelin, J. P., and Benacerraf, B. (1969). Transfer of responsiveness to hapten conjugates of poly-L-lysine and of a copolymer of L-glutamic acid and L-lysine to lethally irradiated non responder guinea-pigs by bone marrow or lymph node and spleen cells from responder guinea-pigs. *J. Exp. Med.* **130,** 1107–1122.

Follett, D. A., and Battisto, J. R. (1968). Iso-antibodies to a β globulin that detects spontaneous delayed iso-hypersensitivity in guinea-pigs. *J. Immunol.* **101,** 753–763.

Foster, M. (1952). Manometic and histochemical demonstrations of tyrosinase in foetal guinea-pig skin. *Proc. Soc. Exp. Biol. Med.* **79,** 713–715.

Frank, M. M., May, J., Gaither, T., and Ellman, L. (1971). *In vitro* studies of complement function in sera of C4-deficient guinea-pigs. *J. Exp. Med.* **134,** 176–187.

Funakoshi, S., and Deutsch, H. F. (1971). Animal carbonic anhydrase isoenzymes. *Comp. Biochem. Physiol. B* **39,** 489–498.

Garber, E. D. (1953). Fuzzy, a dominant mutation in the guinea-pigs. *J. Hered.* **44,** 232.

Gell, P. G. H., and Benacerraf, B. (1961). Delayed hypersensitivity to simple protein antigens. *Advan. Immunol.* **1,** 319–341.

Ginsburg, B. (1944). The effects of the major genes controlling coat colour in the guinea-pig on the dopa oxidase activity of skin extracts. *Genetics* **29,** 176–198.

Green, I. (1970). Genetic control of immune responses in guinea-pigs. *Guinea-Pig Newslett.* **2,** 40–47.

Green, I., and Benacerraf, B. (1971). Genetic control of immune responsiveness to limiting doses of proteins and hapten protein conjugates in guinea-pigs. *J. Immunol.* **107,** 374–381.

Green, I., Paul, W. E., and Benacerraf, B. (1966). The behavior of hapten-poly-L-lysine conjugates as complete antigens in genetic responder and as haptens in non responder guinea-pigs. *J. Exp. Med.* **123,** 859–879.

Green, I., Vassalli, P., and Benacerraf, B. (1967a). Cellular localization of anti-DNP-PLL and anticonveyor albumin antibodies in genetic non responder guinea-pigs immunized with DNP-PLL albumin complexes. *J. Exp. Med.* **125,** 527–536.

Green, I., Paul, W. E., and Benacerraf, B. (1967b). A study of the passive transfer of delayed hypersensitivity to DNP-poly-L-lysine and DNP-GL in responder and non responder guinea-pigs. *J. Exp. Med.* **126,** 959–967.

Green, I., Paul, W. E., Benacerraf, B. (1968). Hapten carrier relationships in the DNP-PLL foreign albumin complex system: Induction of tolerance and stimulation of cells *in vitro*. *J. Exp. Med.* **127,** 43–53.

Green, I., Benacerraf, B., and Stone, S. H. (1969). The effect of the amount of mycobacterial adjuvants on the immune response of strain 2, strain 13, and Hartley strain guinea-pigs to DNP-PLL and DNP-GL. *J. Immunol.* **103,** 403–412.

Gregory, P. W. (1928). A histological description of pigment distribution in the eyes of guinea-pigs of various genetic types. *J. Morphol. Physiol.* **47,** 227–258.

Gregory, R. A. (1946). Some new genetic types of eyes in the guinea-pig. *J. Exp. Zool.* **52,** 159–181.

Haines, G. (1931). A statistical study of the relation between various expressions of fertility and vigor in the guinea-pig. *J. Agr. Res.* **42,** 123–164.

Herbertson, B. M., Skinner, M. E., and Tatchell, J. A. H. (1959). Sticky, a new mutant in the guinea-pig. *J. Genet.* **56,** 315–324.

Hyde, R. R. (1923). Complement deficient guinea-pig serum. *J. Immunol.* **8,** 267–289.

Hyde, R. R. (1924a). The activation of complement-deficient guinea-pig serum with heated sera. *Amer. J. Hyg.* **4,** 62–64.

Hyde, R. R. (1924b). Complement deficient guinea-pig serum and supersensitized corpuscles. *Amer. J. Hyg.* **4,** 65–67.

Hyde, R. R. (1924c). Corpuscle counts on normal and complement deficient guinea-pigs. *Amer. J. Hyg.* **4,** 169–187.

Hyde, R. R. (1927). The complement deficient guinea-pig. A study of an inherited biochemical structure in relation to a toxic immune body. *Amer. J. Hyg.* **7,** 619–626.

Hyde, R. R. (1932). The complement deficient guinea-pig. A study of an inheritable factor in immunity. *Amer. J. Hyg.* **15,** 824–836.

Ibsen, H. L. (1916). Tricolour inheritance. I. The tricolor series in guinea-pigs. *Genetics* **1,** 287–309.

Ibsen, H. L. (1928). Prenatal growth in guinea-pigs with special reference to environmental factors affecting weight. *J. Exp. Zool.* **51,** 51–91.

Ibsen, H. L. (1932). Modifying factors in guinea-pigs. *Proc. Int. Congr. Genet., 6th, 1932* Vol. 2; pp. 97–101.

Ibsen, H. L., and Goertzen, B. L. (1951a). Whitish, a modifier of chocolate and black hairs in the guinea-pig. *J. Hered.* **42,** 231–236.

Ibsen, H. L., and Goertzen, B. L. (1951b). Roan, a modifier of pigmented hairs in guinea-pigs. *J. Hered.* **42,** 267–269.

Ibsen, H. L., and Risty, K. T. (1929). A new character in guinea-pigs, Waltzing. *Anat. Rec.* **44,** 294 (abstr).

Iljin, N. A. (1926). Ruby eye in animals and its heredity. *Trans. Lab. Exp. Biol. Zoopark, Moscow* **1,** 1–23.

Jagiello, G. M. (1969). Some cytologic aspects of meiosis in female guinea-pigs. *Chromosoma* **27,** 95–101.

Jakway, J. S., and Young, W. C. (1958). An inherited spermatopenic hypoplasia in the guinea-pig. *Fert. Steril.* **9,** 533–544.

Kahn, B. D., and Resifield, R. A. (1968). Differences in the amino acid compositions of allogeneic guinea-pig transplantation antigens. *J. Immunol.* **101,** 237–241.

Kantor, F. S., Ojeda, A., and Benacerraf, B. (1963). Studies on artificial antigens. I. Antigenicity of DNP-poly-lysine and DNP copolymers of lysine and glutamic acid in guinea-pigs. *J. Exp. Med.* **117,** 55.

Kelus, A. S. (1969). Allotypic marker GP_{α_2}-1 of guinea-pig immunoglobins. *Nature (London)* **223,** 398–399.

Komich, R. J. (1971). Anophthalmos. An inherited trait in a new stock of guinea-pigs. *Amer. J. Vet. Res.* **32,** 2099–2105.

Lambert, W. V. (1935). Silver guinea-pigs. *J. Hered.* **26,** 279–283.

Lambert, W. V., and Shrigley, E. W. (1933). An inherited eye defect in the guinea-pig. *Proc. Iowa Acad. Sci.* **40,** 227–230.

Lamelin, J. P., Paul, W. E., and Benacerraf, B. (1968). The immune response of randomly-bred Hartley strain guinea-pigs to 2:4-dinitrophenyl conjugates of a polymer of L-glutamic acid and L-lysine. *J. Immunol.* **100,** 1058–1061.

Lamm, M. E., Lisowska-Bernstein, B., Green, I., and Benacerraf, B. (1968). Peptide mapping study of anti-DNP-PLL antibodies produced by guinea-pigs with and without the PLL gene. *Proc. Soc. Exp. Biol. Med.* **127,** 1139–1141.

Levine, B. B. (1969). Studies on the polylysine immune responder gene: The rank order of immunogenecity of dinitrophenyl conjugates of basic homopolyamino acids in guinea-pigs. *J. Immunol.* **103,** 931–1142.

Levine, B. B., and Benacerraf, B. (1964). Studies on antigenicity. The relationship between *in vivo* and *in vitro* enzymatic degradability of hapten polylysine conjugates and their antigenicities in guinea-pigs. *J. Exp. Med.* **120,** 995–965.

Levine, B. B., and Benacerraf, B. (1965). Genetic control in guinea-pigs of the immune response to conjugates of haptens and poly-L-lysine. *Science* **147,** 517–518.

Levine, B. B., Ojeda, A., and Benacerraf, B. (1963a). Basis for the antigenicity of hapten-poly-L-lysine conjugates in random-bred guinea-pigs. *Nature (London)* **200,** 544–546.

Levine, B. B., Ojeda, A., and Benacerraf, B. (1963b). Studies on artificial antigens. III. The genetic control of the immune response to hapten-poly-L-lysine conugates in guinea-pigs. *J. Exp. Med.* **118,** 953–957.

Lieberman, G., Edelstein, G., Davies, I. M., Datta, S. P., and Battisto, J. R. (1964). Studies on the guinea-pig serum factor that detects naturally occurring delayed iso hypersensitivity. *Ann. N. Y. Acad. Sci.* **121,** 490–493.

Loeb, L., and Wright, S. (1927). Transplantation and individuality differentials in inbred families of guinea-pigs. *Amer. J. Pathol.* **3,** 251.

Lundberg, L. (1972). "Announcement." *Guinea-Pig News Lett.* **6,** 21.

Lurie, M. H. (1941). The Waltzing (circling) guinea-pig. *Ann. Otol.* **50,** 113–128.

Lush, I. E. (1966). "The Biochemical Genetics of Vertebrates Except Man." North-Holland Publ., Amsterdam.

Lush, I. E. (1970). The extent of biochemical variation in mammalian populations. *Symp. Zool. Soc. London* **26,** 43–71.

McDevitt, H. O., and Benacerraf, B. (1969). Genetic control of specific immune responses. *Advan. Immunol.* **11,** 31–74.

McDevitt, H. O., and Chinitz, A. (1969). Genetic control of the antibody response relationship between immune response and histocompatibility (H-2) type. *Science* **164,** 1207–1208.

McDevitt, H. O., Deak, B. D., Schreffler, D. F., Klein, J., Stimpfling, J. H., and Snell, G. D. (1972). Genetic control of the immune response. Mapping of the *Ir-1* locus. *J. Exp. Med.* **135,** 1259–1278.

McPhee, N. C., and Eaton, O. N. (1931). Genetic growth differentiation in guinea-pigs. *U. S. Dep. Agr., Tech. Bull.* **222.**

Makino, S. (1947). Notes on the chromosomes of four species of small mammals. *J. Fac. Sci., Hokkaido Univ.* **9,** 345–357.

Manna, G. K., and Talukdor, M. (1964). Chromosomal polymorphism in the guinea-pig. *Cavia porcellus. Experientia* **20,** 324–325.

Martin, W. J., Ellman, L., Green, I., and Benacerraf, B. (1970). Histocompatibility type and immune responsiveness in random bred Hartley strain guinea-pigs. *J. Exp. Med.* **132,** 1259–1266.

Mehner, A. (1956). Results of a long term inbreeding experiment. Z. Tierzücht. *Züchtungsbiologie* **66,** 149–172.

Milstein, C., and Munro, R. J. (1970). The genetic basis of antibody specificity. *Annu. Rev. Microbiol.* **24,** 335–358.

Moore, W. D. (1919). Complementary and opsonic functions in their relation to immunity. A study of the serum of guinea-pigs naturally deficient in complement. *J. Immunol.* **4,** 425–441.

Ohno, S., Weiler, C., and Stenius, C. (1961). A dormant nucleolus organiser in the guinea-pig, *Cavia cobaya. Exp. Cell Res.* **25:** 498–503.

Oppenheim, J. J., Wolstencroft, R. A., and Gell, P. G. H. (1967). Delayed hypersensitivity in the guinea-pig to a protein-hapten conjugate and its relationship to in vitro transformation of lymph node, spleen, thymus and peripheral blood lymphocytes. *Immunology* **12,** 89–102.

Paul, W. E., Siskind, G. W., and Benacerraf, B. (1966). Studies on the effect of the carrier molecule on antihapten antibody synthesis. II. Carrier specificity of anti-2,4 dintrophenyl-poly-L-lysine antibodies. *J. Exp. Med.* **123,** 689–705.

Paul, W. E., Green, I., and Benacerraf, B. (1968). Genetic control of the immune response to hapten poly-L-lysine conjugates. *J. Reticuloendothel. Soc.* **5,** 282–283.

Peters, J. A., ed. (1959). Classic Papers in Genetics. Prentice-Hall, Englewood Cliffs, New Jersey.

Provine, W. B. (1971). "The Origins of Theoretical Population Genetics." Univ. of Chicago Press, Chicago, Illinois.

Radev, T. (1960). Inheritance of hypocotalasaemia in guinea-pigs. *J. Genet.* **57,** 169–172.

Rebel, A., and Marescaux, J. (1965). The role of genetic factors in the success of homografts in the guinea-pig. *C. R. Soc. Biol.* **159,** 1416–1419.

Robinson, R. (1970a). Homologous mutants in mammalian coat colour variation. *London* **26,** 251–269.

Robinson, R. (1970b). A review of genetic linkage in the guinea pig. *Ann. Genet. Select. Anim.* **2,** 241–248.

Robinson R. (1971). Guinea-pig chromosomes. *Guinea-Pig Newslett.* **4,** 15–18.

Russell, W. L. (1939). Investigation of the physiological genetics of hair and skin colour in the guinea-pig by means of the dopa reaction. *Genetics* **24,** 645–667.

Sato, W., and De Weck, A. L. (1972). Leucocyte typing in guinea-pigs. *Z. Immunstaetsforsch. Exp. Klin. Immunol.* **144,** 49–62.

Scheibel, I. F. (1943). Hereditary differences in the capacity of guinea-pigs for the production of diptheria antitoxin. *Acta Pathol. Microbiol. Scand.* **20,** 464–559.

Scott, J. P. (1937). The embryology of the guinea-pig. III. The development of the polydactylous monster. A case of growth accelerated at a particular period by a semidominant gene. *J. Exp. Zool.* **77,** 123–157.

Scott, J. P. (1938). The embryology of the guinea-pig. II. The polydactylous monster. A new teras produced by the genes *Px Px.* J. *Morphol.* **62,** 299–321.

Searle, A. G. (1968). "Comparative Genetics of Coat Colour in Mammals." Academic Press, New York.

Selaway, H., Green, I., and Benacerraf, B. (1971). Specificity of tolerance to antigens the immune response to which is controlled by the PLL gene. *J. Immunol.* **106,** 276–278.

Serra, J. A. (1966). "Modern Genetics," Vol. 2, Academic Press, New York.

Shevach, E. M., Paul, W. E., and Green, I. (1972). Histocompatibility-linked immune response gene function in guinea-pigs. *J. Exp. Med.* **136,** 1207–1221.

Stockard, C. R. (1927). Extra toes in the guinea-pig. An atavistic condition, and its genetic significance. *Anat. Rec.* **35,** 24.

Stockard, C. R. (1930). The presence of a factorial basis for characters lost in evolution: The atavistic reappearance of digits in mammals. *J. Anat.* **45**, 345–377.

Stone, S. H., Lacopoulos, P., Liacopoulos-Briot, M., Neven, T., and Halpern, B. N. (1964). Histamine differences in amount available for release in lungs of guinea-pig susceptible and resistant to acute anaphylaxis. *Science* **146**, 1061–1062.

Strandskov, H. H. (1939). Inheritance of internal organ differences in guinea-pigs. *Genetics* **24**, 722–727.

Szemere, C. Y., Bodi, A., and Csik, L. (1960). Immune biology of guinea-pigs acclimated to cold. III. Inheritance of natural immunity. *Acta Biol. (Budapest)* **10**, 363–371.

Takino, Y., Sugahava, K., and Horino, I. (1971). Two lines of guinea pigs sensitive and non sensitive to chemical mediators and anaphylaxis. *J. Allergy* **47**, 247–261.

Watson, E. D., Blumenthal, H. T., and Hutton, W. E. (1966). A method for the culture of leucocytes of the guinea-pig (*Cavia cobaya*) with karyotype analysis. *Cytogenetics* **5**, 179–185.

Whiteway, C. (1973). A new dominant spotting and silvering factor in the guinea-pig. *Heredity* **31**: 123–125.

Whiteway, C., and Robinson, R. (1975). Anophthalmic white and microphthalmic white in the cavy. *Guinea-Pig Newslett.* **9**(in press).

Wolff, G. L. (1955). The effects of environmental temperature on coat colour in diverse genotypes of guinea-pig. *Genetics* **40**, 90–106.

Wright, S. (1915). The albino series of allelomorphs in guinea-pigs. *Amer. Natur.* **49**, 140–147.

Wright, S. (1916). An intensive study of the inheritance of colour and of other coat characters in guinea-pigs with especial reference to graded variations. *Carnegie Inst. Wash. Publ.* **241**, 59–121.

Wright, S. (1917a). Color inheritance in mammals. *J. Hered.* **8**, 224–235.

Wright, S. (1917b). Colour inheritance in mammals. V. The guinea-pig. *J. Hered.* **8**, 476–480.

Wright, S. (1920). The relative importance of heredity and environment in determining the piebald pattern of guinea-pigs. *Proc. Nat. Acad. Sci. U.S.* **6**, 320–332.

Wright, S. (1922a). The effects of inbreeding and cross breeding on guinea-pigs. I. Decline in vigor. *U.S. Dep. Agr. Bull.* **1090**, 1–36.

Wright, S. (1922b). The effects of inbreeding and cross breeding on guinea-pigs. II. Differentiation among inbred families. *U.S. Dep. Agr. Bull.* **1090**, 37–63.

Wright, S. (1922c). The effects of inbreeding and cross breeding on guinea-pigs. III. Crosses between highly inbred families. *U.S. Dep. Agr. Bull.* **1121**, 1–61.

Wright, S. (1922d). Coefficients of inbreeding and relationship. *Amer. Natur.* **56**, 330–338.

Wright, S. (1923). The relation between piebald and tortoiseshell colour patterns in guinea-pigs. *Anat. Rec.* **26**, 393.

Wright, S. (1925). The factors of the albino series of guinea-pigs and their interaction effects on black and yellow pigmentation. *Genetics* **10**, 223–260.

Wright, S. (1927). The effects in combination of the major color factors of the guinea-pig. *Genetics* **12**, 530–569.

Wright, S. (1934a). Polydactylous guinea-pigs. Two types respectively heterozygous and homozygous in the same mutant gene. *J. Hered.* **25**, 359–362.

Wright, S. (1934b). Genetics of abnormal growth in the guinea-pig. *Cold Spring Harbors Symp. Quant. Biol.* **2**, 137–147.

Wright, S. (1934c). The results of cross between inbred strains of guinea-pigs differing in number of digits. *Genetics* **19**, 537–551.

Wright, S. (1935). A mutation of the guinea-pig tending to restore the pentadactyl foot when heterozygous, producing a monstrosity when homozygous. *Genetics* **20**, 84–107.

Wright, S. (1941). The physiology of the gene. *Physiol. Rev.* **21**: 487–527.

Wright, S. (1942). The physiological genetics of coat colour of the guinea-pig. *Biol. Symp.* **6**, 337–355.

Wright, S. (1947). On the genetics of several types of silvering in the guinea-pig. *Genetics* **32**, 115–141.

Wright, S. (1949a). On the genetics of hair direction in the guinea-pig. I. Variability in the patterns found in combination of the *R* and *M* loci. *J. Exp. Zool.* **112**, 303–323.

Wright, S. (1949b). On the genetics of hair direction in the guinea-pig. II. Evidence for a new dominant gene, star and tests for linkage with eleven other loci. *J. Exp. Zool.* **112**, 325–340.

Wright, S. (1950). On the genetics of hair direction in the guinea-pig. III. Interactions between the process due to the loci *R* and *St. J. Exp. Zool.* **113**, 53–63.

Wright, S. (1959a). On the genetics of silvering in the guinea-pig with special reference to interaction and linkage. *Genetics* **44**, 387–405.

Wright, S. (1959b). Silvering (si) and diminution (dm) of coat colour of the guinea-pig, and male sterility of the white or near white combination of these. *Genetics* **44**, 563–590

Wright, S. (1959c). A quantitative study of variations in intensity of genotypes of the guinea-pig at birth. *Genetics* **44**, 1001–1026.

Wright, S. (1959d). Qualitative differences among colours of the guinea-pig due to diverse genotypes. *J. Exp. Zool.* **142**, 75–113.

Wright, S. (1960a). The residual variability in intensity of coat colour at birth in a guinea-pig colony. *Genetics* **45**, 583–612.

Wright, S. (1960b). Postnatal changes in the intensity of coat colour in diverse genotypes of the guinea-pig. *Genetics* **45**, 1503–1529.

Wright, S. (1960c). The genetics of vital characters in the guinea-pig. *J. Cell. Comp. Physiol* **56**, 123–151.

Wright, S. (1963). Genic interaction. *In* "Methodology in Mammalian Genetics" (W. J. Burdette, ed.), Holden-Day, San Francisco, California. p. 159–192.

Wright, S., and Chase, H. B. (1936). On the genetics of the spotted pattern of the guinea-pig. *Genetics* **21**, 758–787.

Wright, S., and Eaton, O. N. (1929). The persistence of differentiation among inbred families of guinea-pigs. *U.S. Dep. Agr. Tech. Bull.* **103.**

Wright, S., and Wagner, K. (1934). Types of subnormal development of the head from inbred strains of guinea pigs and their bearing on the classification and interpretation of vertebrate monsters. *Amer. J. Anat.* **54**, 383–447.

Yoshida, T., Paul, W. E., and Benacerraf, B. (1970). Genetic control of the specificity of anti-DNP antibodies. I. Differences in the specificity of anti-DNP antibody produced by mammalian species. *J. Immunol.* **105**, 306–313.

Chapter 9

Bacterial, Mycoplasma, and Rickettsial Diseases

James R. Ganaway

I. INTRODUCTION

Perhaps there was a time when the guinea pig was the preferred species in the laboratory and, as such, came to be known as "the experimental animal." Remnants of this idea linger today in the minds of the laity who commonly refer to the guinea pig in this context even though they may possess little if any knowledge about guinea pigs per se. If one could correlate the number of an animal species used in research with the number of reports about the natural diseases of that species, the period of popularity for the guinea pig would then encompass the last decade of the nineteenth century and the first quarter or so of the twentieth century. Many bacteria were discovered during the 1880's as causes of human and animal diseases. A logical sequence was the study of these bacteria in a laboratory animal. The guinea pig must have served a noble purpose, for Meyer (1928) stated, "The guinea pig is probably more frequently used for bacteriological studies than any other animal since it is particularly susceptible to infections with human and animal pathogenic microorganisms." A recent survey (Institute of Laboratory Animal Resources News, 1972), however, shows that guinea pigs account for less than 2% of the rodents used in research. Obviously, this figure does not reflect upon the relative importance of this species, but it may have a bearing upon the paucity of reports in the recent literature regarding the subject at hand, and it may have influenced a recent point of view (Lane-Petter and Porter, 1963), namely, that guinea pigs are subject to comparatively few diseases. Some historical insight is provided by Paterson (1962) who points out that the problem of disease in guinea pigs in the United Kingdom is not as formidable today as it was in the 1930's and 1940's. It is not likely that such an improvement in the health status of guinea pig colonies was influenced by the use of antibiotics. Rather, it is probably due to a combination of several factors: (1) improved husbandry, including sanitation and the exclusion of feral rodents, birds, and insects from the colony; (2) better control of the environment with emphasis on temperature and humidity; (3) a more adequate diet, especially vitamin C requirement; and (4) an increased surveillance for disease conditions through diagnostic laboratory support of colonies. The point is that apparent good health of guinea pigs available to the researcher is not incompatible with their known susceptibility to a variety of infectious agents.

Indeed, there is a distinct trend toward the production of pathogen-free guinea pigs, a product of germfree and barrier room technology. This type of guinea pig is more economical to produce than the diseased counterpart and is a better tool for the researcher because the complicating effect of intercurrent disease is minimized or eliminated. Proper use of such guinea pigs, however, requires adequate caging that will ensure their continued pathogen-free status during experimentation.

It will become apparent that our knowledge of naturally occurring bacterial, mycoplasmal, and rickettsial diseases of the guinea pig is quite deficient. This problem increases in magnitude when sick or dying guinea pigs are part of a valuable research project. The all too common recommendation—"Destroy all animals, clean up the room, and start anew with *clean* animals"—is a painful ultimatum which leaves much to be desired, particularly from the researcher's point of view.

There is a need for caution in interpreting the often detailed clinical and pathological descriptions provided by early investigators. For example, complete pelletized ration for guinea pigs is a fairly recent development. Green leafy vegetables, excellent sources of vitamin C, were not available for extended periods during winter months, and it is therefore reasonable to assume that many reported disease conditions were complicated with scurvy. Second, many bacterial diseases were endemic in colonies and mixed infections were reported frequently. And finally, taxonomy of infectious agents has been changed frequently. For example, at least 11 genera have been used with the species name "pseudotuberculosis," and 15 taxons have been used to designate the presently recognized bacterium, *Yersinia pseudotuberculosis.*

Bacterial diseases will be presented from the standpoint of etiology and in order of their relative frequency of having been reported in the literature.* Minimal treatment will be given to characterization of etiological agents as this information is available in standard textbooks.

II. BACTERIAL INFECTIONS

A. *Salmonella*

Salmonellosis is, by far, the most frequently reported bacterial disease of the guinea pig. From the first record of its occurrence in 1885 (Eberth, cited by Nelson and Smith, 1927) to the present, there has been no lull in the profuse stream of reports. Attributable factors are (1) the spontaneous disease occurs worldwide and few stocks of guinea pigs have escaped its ravaging effect; (2) there is still no known effective means of eradicating the disease in a colony once the infection becomes established; and (3) the disease provides an excellent model of a similar disease of man, typhoid fever.

The serotypes recovered most frequently from guinea pigs are *S. typhimurium* and *S. enteritidis;* less often encountered are *S. dublin, S. limete, S. bledgam, S. moscow, S. amersfoort, S. marashino, S. glostrup, S. nagoya, S. poona,* and *S. weltevreden.* The organisms are gram-negative, usually motile, nonsporeforming, and grow readily on artifical culture media; they usually produce acid and gas from glucose but not from lactose. When present in the blood or parenchymatous organs, isolation is relatively simple as pure cultures are usually obtained. Selective culture media that suppress nonpathogens are necessary when attempting recovery from feces. In addition to biochemical testing, salmonella are differentiated by means of appropriate typing antisera.

Salmonellosis affects guinea pigs of all ages, strains, and both sexes. In a production colony earliest and heaviest losses occur in dams about the time of parturition and in young recently weaned stock. The incubation period is 5–7 days. Epizootics are encountered most frequently during winter months.

Ingestion of contaminated food, especially fresh green leafy vegetables, such as kale, is considered to be the most likely method of introducing and spreading infection in a colony.

*Only selected references have been cited in the text.

Loose leaves are easily contaminated by feces of wild rodents, birds, or farm animals. Interestingly, Moore (1957) has shown that the conjunctival route is far more sensitive than the oral route; a 50% spleen infective dose was 10^2 organisms by the conjunctival route while it was 10^8 organisms by the oral route. Kent *et al.* (1966) and Takeuchi and Sprinz (1967) pretreated guinea pigs with opium and fasted them to show that intestinal motility is a decisive factor in invasion of intestinal epithelium by *S. typhimurium*. The following factors appear to affect the frequency and course of salmonellosis (Edington, 1929; Kent *et al.*, 1966): *Salmonella* species or strain, host species or strain, dose of *Salmonella,* route of administration, age, sex of host, antibiotic treatment, metabolic and nutritional deficiencies, and presence of other diseases. Recovered guinea pigs may become carriers and shed the bacilli intermittently and unpredictably in their feces. A series of papers (Nelson, 1927a,b; 1928a,b; Nelson and Smith, 1927) describe the epizootic and ensuing endemic nature of this infection in a colony of guinea pigs.

Salmonellosis is a zoonosis which needs no elaboration. *Salmonella typhimurium* is the most common serotype recovered from both human and nonhuman sources (Steele, 1969). Fish *et al.* (1968) recorded an incident in which 500 guinea pigs died in 30 days during which time all three members of the owner's family suffered from an acute febrile illness. The same phage type of *S. enteritidis* was isolated from each of the three persons and from the guinea pigs.

In a colony, the first clinical sign is usually an increased mortality. The infection spreads rapidly. Close examination of the colony may reveal some guinea pigs that fail to eat or respond to sound and some which lack a smooth coat and bright eye. Diarrhea is not usually seen. Conjunctivitis is reported as a frequent sign by some authors (Moore, 1957; Pandalai, 1934). As the epizootic gains momentum, young guinea pigs die suddenly without prior signs of illness. Heaviest losses occur in the young and in dams at parturition. Abortion is observed frequently. A mortality rate of 50% is commonly encountered and may reach 100% (Petrie and O'Brien, 1910).

In acute cases, one may see no lesions at necropsy. Splenomegaly is usually seen in subacute and chronic infections. Edington (1929) observed spleens as large as 21 gm.* Minute white foci and/or yellowish-white nodules up to several millimeters in diameter may occur in the spleen and liver. The mesenteric lymph nodes may be enlarged and contain similar nodules. Nodules may also occur in the lung, pleura, peritoneum, and in the wall of the uterus. Rupture of the nodules may result in purulent pleuritis, peritonitis, and pericarditis.

Histopathologically, the picture is one of bacterial invasion, histiocytosis, necrosis, and abscess formation. Kent *et al.* (1966) described the nodules as typhoid-like granulomatous lesions. Small central areas of necrosis are surrounded by histiocytes. Focal accumulations of polymorphonuclear leukocytes and histiocytes are present in the lymphoid patches of the ileum and jejunum. In chronic cases the nodules increase in size and abscesses form. In the small intestine the abscesses rupture to the lumen and form ulcers.

Diagnosis is dependent upon the isolation of *Salmonella* spp. Though culture of blood is satisfactory in acute cases, the spleen is the organ of choice for routine isolation procedures at necropsy.

A philosophy that suggests that the "normal" laboratory animal is one which represents survival of the fittest is untenable; thus, "control" of salmonellosis in a colony is not of concern. Vaccines may be effective in controlling losses but they do not prevent infection. Furthermore, infection with one serotype does not prevent infection with other serotypes. Antibiotics have been helpful in controlling losses but they, likewise, do not eliminate the infection. Thus, it seems that prevention is the only tenable approach. This poses a problem since so many species of mammals are potential carriers. Although guinea pigs relish green foods this feeding practice is hazardous. A better approach would be to feed a complete pelletized diet to a closed colony housed to exclude wild rodents, birds, and other vermin.

Paterson (1962) and Lane-Petter and Porter (1963) believe that epizootics can be prevented by early detection, either by cultural isolation procedures or by palpation of enlarged mesenteric lymph nodes of weanlings whereby the infected dam can be detected, then killing all guinea pigs in close proximity, sanitizing the area, etc. This approach may have merit if the source of infection is focal such as an infected guinea pig newly introduced into the colony. Culture of selected tissue from every guinea pig that dies in a colony would no doubt help detect early infection in the colony. However, most reports indicate that when increased mortality is obvious and a chronic case is recognized at necropsy, the infection may be widespread and well established in the colony. In such case, there seems to be no alternative but to destroy the colony, sanitize the premises, and restock with *Salmonella*-free guinea pigs.

B. *Streptococcus*

Streptococcosis of guinea pigs, like salmonellosis, was recognized in the late 1800's and has since been observed by numerous investigators as a major cause of morbidity and mortality.

Lancefield (1933) provided a systematic approach to the classification of streptococci which are grouped serologically. Several investigators (Karel *et al.*, 1941; Paterson, 1962, 1967; Valee *et al.*, 1969; Fraunfelter *et al.*, 1971) have since classi-

*A normal spleen of an adult guinea pig weighs about 1.4 gm.

fied their isolants from guinea pigs as β-hemolytic *Streptococcus,* Lancefield Group C. Failure to speciate their isolants leaves some doubt but, according to the latest classification schema (Deibel and Seeley, 1974), they probably were *Streptococcus zooepidemicus.* Rae (1936) provided an excellent historical account of spontaneous disease in guinea pigs caused by this type of organism. *Streptococcus pneumoniae* remains ungrouped according to the Lancefield classification. Holman (1916–1917) provided an excellent review of the early literature on pneumococcal infection of guinea pigs. The first report of this disease in guinea pigs in the United States was provided by Homburger *et al.* (1945). α-Hemolytic streptococci have been isolated from the milk and mammary tissue of guinea pigs with mastitis (Gupta *et al.,* 1970). The heterogeneity of this genus is exemplified by the recognition of over 60 serological type-specific strains of Lancefield Group A, β-hemolytic *Streptococcus* (Ginsburg, 1972). Infections due to Lancefield Group C *Streptococcus* are apparently far more prevalent in guinea pigs than are pneumococcal infections. Hence, these two major types of streptococcal infection will be dealt with in this order.

Lancefield Group C streptococcal infections of guinea pigs occur worldwide and affect all ages and both sexes. For unknown reasons, a greater frequency of infection occurs in females (Hardenbergh, 1926). Fraunfelter *et al.* (1971) observed a difference in strain susceptibility. Spontaneous cases occurred in strain 2 guinea pigs while none occurred in strain 13 guinea pigs similarly caged in the same room.

The most likely means of spread of infection in a colony remains unknown. Several routes have been suggested; the digestive tract wherein the oral mucosa is abraded by rough food; the respiratory tract by droplet spread of nasopharyngeal secretions; abrasions in the skin such as from fight wounds or bites; the female genital tract, especially at parturition; and the conjunctiva. According to Boxmeyer (1907), the infection follows the lymphatics. He observed that when a culture of *Streptococcus* was rubbed into abraided skin the regional lymph nodes became affected.

The public health significance of Lancefield Group C, β-hemolytic streptococcal infections in guinea pigs remains obscure. Although these organisms are found primarily in lower animals, they have also been isolated from man.

Several forms of Lancefield Group C streptococcal disease have been noted in guinea pigs. The most commonly recognized form is the chronic condition called "lumps" by Boxmeyer (1907) or cervical lymphadenitis by numerous subsequent workers. Affected guinea pigs usually remain in good flesh and show no other sign of illness. Lymph nodes in other parts of the body are less frequently involved. Affected nodes gradually increase in size up to several centimeters in diameter. Surgical drainage or spontaneous rupture to the skin surface is followed by healing with granulation tissue. The septicemic form may occur in epizootics with high mortality. Experimentally, the incubation period is 3–12 days depending upon the route of inoculation (Rae, 1936). Seastone (1939) suggests a 1- to 2-week incubation period following contact transmission.

At necropsy, enlarged lymph nodes contain well-encapsulated abscesses filled with thick, nonodorous, yellowish-white pus. In terminal cases, a variety of suppurative processes may be seen including pneumonia, otitis media, pleuritis, peritonitis, pericarditis, myocarditis and myocardial degeneration, chronic nephritis, arthritis, and cellulitis. Abscesses may be found in various organs.

A detailed histopathological description of the formation of streptococcal abscesses was presented by Boxmeyer (1907) and Rae (1936). The lymph node is eventually destroyed and replaced by the abscess. At the periphery, chains of gram-positive cocci are readily demonstrated.

Diagnosis depends upon isolation of streptococci which are readily obtained from pus of chronic abscesses or heart blood in acute septicemic disease. On blood agar, β-hemolytic colonies of streptococci are surrounded by a clear zone of hemolysis. Chains of gram-positive cocci are seen in stained smears. They are grouped serologically.

Inability to ascertain the source of infection and portal of entry into the guinea pig presents a problem in prevention. Lane-Petter and Porter (1963) feel that the disease is not very contagious. Paterson (1967) suggests that palpation for swollen lymph nodes and culling is useful. Others (Boxmeyer, 1907; Parsons and Hyde, 1928) have found that intensive culling may control spread of the disease but fails to eradicate the disease. Sulfonamides are bacteriostatic for streptococci but drug resistance develops with prolonged use. Antibiotic treatment of chronically infected guinea pigs with well-encapsulated abscesses is futile. Diaz and Soave (1973), however, reported successful treatment of 10 guinea pigs with enlarged lymph nodes following daily intramuscular injections of Loridine (Cephaloridine, Eli Lilly) for 2 weeks. In any event recovery follows spontaneous rupture through skin or surgical incision and drainage of abscesses. Vaccines have failed (Seastone, 1939) probably because immunity to streptococcal infections is type specific. Moen (1936) demonstrated a skin test as a means of detecting carriers but this procedure apparently has not been repeated. A reddened, edematous, indurated swelling, 10–40 mm in diameter, appeared within 24 hours after intradermal inoculation with a bacterial extract if the guinea pig was infected. This gradually subsided after several days leaving a central area of necrosis. Normal guinea pigs were nonreactive. Using this procedure, he selected a herd of guinea pigs that remained free of infection for 15 months.

Streptococcus pneumoniae is a lancet-shaped, gram-positive coccus usually arranged in pairs or short chains. It is distinguished from the viridans streptococci by its bile solubility.

Seventy-five or more types of pneumococci are differentiated according to their capsular polysaccharide content. Protective antibodies are type specific for the polysaccharide. Types IV and XIX cause disease in guinea pigs.

Greatest losses have been noted during the winter months. Predisposing factors include stress of pregnancy, sudden or prolonged changes in temperature, shipment, dietary deficiencies, concurrent infections, poor husbandry, and experimental procedures.

Apparently normal guinea pigs may carry virulent pneumococci in the upper respiratory passages. Neufeld and Etinger-Tulczynska (1932) found a 55% carrier rate which persisted for months in a sample of 329 guinea pigs. Other animal species which harbor pneumococci include rats, monkeys, and man. Between 40 and 70% of all normal human beings are carriers of pneumococci of which many types are potentially virulent. Due to the high carrier rate of pneumococci in both man and guinea pigs, it may be difficult to assess the ease with which pneumococci are transmitted between these species.

Affected guinea pigs sit quietly, fail to eat, and have ruffled fur. They may have a wet nose and show dyspnea. Pregnant dams may abort dead fetuses. Death is likely to be the first sign noted. At necropsy, a variety of pyogenic processes occur such as fibrinopurulent pleuritis, pericarditis, peritonitis, lung consolidation with abscesses, otitis media, endometritis, and suppurative meningitis. The essential lesion in the lung is marked edema of alveolar walls and filling of alveoli with fibrinous exudate which contains polymorphonuclear leukocytes and erythrocytes. Pneumococci in large numbers are readily demonstrated on direct smears and in stained tissue sections throughout the lesions.

Diagnosis is based upon isolation of pneumococci which are typed with specific antisera. "Quellung," or capsular swelling, occurs when pneumococci are mixed with a homologous antibody type. Methylene blue is incorporated into the mixture which is then examined under the oil-emersion lens. In a positive reaction, the capsule swells, is refractile, and its border is sharply delimited from surrounding medium.

Pneumococcal infection apparently does not present a problem in the well-cared for guinea pig production colony. Limited use of bacterins to control epizootics have not shown promise (Neufield and Etinger-Tulczynska, 1932; Petrie, 1933). Sulfadiazine appears to control the epizootic but does not eliminate carriers (Homburger *et al.*, 1945). Similar results were obtained with oral tetracycline treatment (Wagner and Owens, 1970).

C. *Yersinia*

One of the earliest recognized bacterial diseases of the guinea pig was caused by *Yersinia pseudotuberculosis.* As the species name implies, differentiation between this disease and experimentally induced tuberculosis in guinea pigs was a major problem near the turn of the century. The guinea pig was also used for isolation of plague bacillus, *Yersinia pestis,* closely related serologically to *Y. pseudotuberculosis.* The disease appears to be common in Europe but uncommon in the United States. Bishop (1932) provided an excellent review of the literature and described an epizootic in a guinea pig colony.

Yersinia pseudotuberculosis is a gram-negative, nonsporeforming, pleomorphic rod which seldom takes the bipolar stain in contrast to *Y. pestis.* It is one of the few pathogenic bacteria which does not grow optimally at 37°C. Though growth occurs at 37°C, the bacteria are nonmotile, dissociation is accelerated, and virulence is decreased. Smooth motile forms develop best at temperatures between 20° and 30°C. It is fairly stable, surviving 60°C for 3 hours in saline.

Epizootics tend to occur during the winter months. Other predisposing factors are apparently not recognized. Both sexes and all ages are affected. Indeed, guinea pigs are one of the more susceptible animals in which natural infections occur. Susceptible animals include turkeys, rabbits, mice, hares, cats, chickens, pigeons, swans, canaries, sparrows, blackbirds, monkeys, sheep, swine, horses, lions, foxes, goats, and doubtless other untested animals. The ubiquity of this bacterium in nature is further suggested by its recovery from dust, soil, water, fodder, and milk.

Infection is probably acquired by ingestion of contaminated food or through skin lacerations resulting from fighting or biting. Recovered guinea pigs may become carriers which shed organisms in feces. A selective medium (Morris, 1958) for isolation of *Y. pseudotuberculosis* from guinea pig feces was used by Paterson and Cook (1963) to show that infected wood pigeons contaminated green food fed to guinea pigs. The result was an explosive epizootic during which more than 1000 guinea pigs died.

Yersinia pseudotuberculosis is infectious for man (Finlayson and Fagundes, 1971; Topping *et al.*, 1938; Snyder and Vogel, 1943; Moss and Battle, 1941). The septicemic form may be fatal. Infection in man may be more common than the literature indicates (Wetzler and Hubbert, 1968). Forty-three cases of mesenteric adenitis, resembling acute or subacute appendicitis, have been recognized in Great Britain since 1967 (Anonymous, 1972).

Three types of clinical disease are recognized in guinea pigs: (1) acute septicemic form which is rapidly fatal in 24–48 hours; (2) classic pseudotuberculosis, a chronic infection which results in emaciation, diarrhea, and death in 3–4 weeks; and (3) nonfatal infection wherein the lesions are confined to lymph nodes of the head and neck. Haughton and Minkin (1966) suggest a latent form of the disease can exist in apparently healthy guinea pigs.

Experimentally, the disease may be produced in guinea pigs by feeding, inhalation, or parenteral injection. Inoculation of pure cultures is fatal in 15–45 days. Necropsy reveals nodules throughout the body including the regional lymph nodes, spleen, liver, lung, and bone marrow. When bacilli are ingested, nodules occur in the wall of the ileum and cecum, mesenteric lymph nodes, and omentum. The grayish-white spherical nodules vary from pinpoint to 2–3 cm in diameter and contain creamy or caseous pus. The nodules represent focal necrosis and contain coagulated cells, granular debris, and polymorphonuclear leukocytes. They may be surrounded by foamy macrophages but rarely by epithelioid cells. Giant cells are absent. Blood vessels plugged with bacterial emboli may be seen within the necrotic mass. In chronic cases, fibroblast and epithelial cell proliferation is marked. Some nodules may become granulomatous but do not calcify. Bacilli are readily demonstrated in sections of nodules or smears of pus.

Diagnosis depends upon isolation of *Y. pseudotuberculosis* which is readily cultured from abscesses or from blood in acute septicemic cases.

The paucity of reports of this disease in guinea pigs in the United States suggests that present preventive measures are adequate, the disease is rare, or is not being recognized. Cook (1953–1954) and Paterson (1967) feel that pseudotuberculosis in a colony can be controlled by routinely palpating for enlarged mesenteric lymph nodes in weanling guinea pigs. The dam of infected young is then removed from the colony because the disease is apparently spread from the dam to her offspring with ease. Thal (1962) cited several reports that indicate that immunity to pseudotuberculosis and plague is of a cellular nature. His studies showed that oral pretreatment of guinea pigs with an avirulent strain of *Y. pseudotuberculosis* protected them from subsequent lethal challenge with a virulent strain. The avirulent strain, however, was recovered from feces 11 days after oral dosing and from mesenteric lymph nodes after 18 days. Thus vaccination may protect from otherwise lethal challenge but may not prevent the carrier state and subsequent spread of infection in a colony. Prevention appears to be the only tenable approach. The premises, especially food, should be protected from contamination by excreta of wild birds and rodents.

D. *Bordetella*

Bordetella bronchiseptica infection was recognized around the turn of the century as a cause of epizootic respiratory disease of guinea pigs associated with high mortality. The descriptive account of Theobald Smith (1913–1914) is particularly noteworthy. Few reports appeared in the literature until Ganaway *et al.* (1965) proposed the use of a vaccine to prevent losses associated with acute disease in a large guinea pig colony. Since that time, epizootics of *B. bronchiseptica* pneumonia in guinea pigs have been reported in Europe (Woode and McLeod, 1967; Nikkels and Mullink, 1971), Japan (Nakagawa *et al.*, 1969b), and the United States (unpublished communications).

Bordetella bronchiseptica is one of three species in this genus; *B. pertussis* and *B. parapertussis,* both of which cause whooping cough or pertussis in man, are the other two members. *Bordetella bronchiseptica* causes acute respiratory disease in a variety of birds and other animals including dogs, cats, rats, rabbits, swine, horses, turkeys, monkeys, and man. It is a motile, nonspore-forming, short, gram-negative rod or coccobacillus. Differences in strains of *B. bronchiseptica* have not been observed. Any fresh isolant from guinea pigs can be used in serodiagnosis (Nakagawa *et al.*, 1969a).

All ages and both sexes are susceptible but the greatest morbidity and mortality occur in young guinea pigs. Stressful events such as transporting, crowding, unfavorable climatic conditions, inadequate diet, pregnancy, other intercurrent diseases, or experimental influences may trigger the onset of acute fatal pneumonia. Sporadic deaths occur throughout the year in colonies where the disease is enzootic but highest losses have been noted during winter months. The incubation period is 5 to 7 days.

Infection in a colony is maintained by carriers which may exceed 20% of normal appearing guinea pigs (Nakagawa *et al.*, 1969a). Close contact is apparently necessary for spread of the infection from animal to animal (Woode and McLeod, 1967).

Though *B. bronchiseptica* apparently does not cause epidemic disease in man, it can cause a whooping cough syndrome similar to that caused by *B. pertussis* or *parapertussis* (Lautrop and Lacey, 1960). The ease or frequency with which *B. bronchiseptica* is transmitted from guinea pigs to man or vice versa is unknown.

There are no clinical signs which typify *B. bronchiseptica* infection. Inappetence, insensitivity to sound, and dyspnea may be seen in the 24-hour period preceding death.

At necropsy of terminal cases, various degrees of lung consolidation and tracheitis are seen. The skin and hair surrounding the external nares may be moistened and encrusted with a blood-tinged mucous or mucopurulent exudate. The trachea may contain frothy blood-tinged exudate. A clear to slightly yellow serous fluid may be seen in the thoracic cavity. Portions of the lung are dark red, reddish-brown, or gray and firm. Areas of consolidation are often patchy and follow the bronchus and its branches.

Histologically, there is marked purulent bronchitis; the lumen is filled with polymorphonuclear leukocytes, mucus, and remnants of desquamated bronchiolar epithelium. The exudate may extend to terminal bronchioles. Neutrophils and edema are seen in bronchiolar walls and in peribronchiolar and perivascular connective tissue. Alveolar walls are prominent due to hyperemia of the capillaries. In late stages a fibrinous bronchopneumonia occurs; the bronchi contain protein-rich masses, many neutrophils, and phagocytes and a fine network of fibrin occurs in the alveoli.

Diagnosis depends upon isolation and identification of *B. bronchiseptica* which is present throughout the respiratory tract and frequently in the middle ears. Isolation in pure culture is readily obtained by incubating exudate from the lower trachea or bronchial lumen on blood agar. Growth is slow. Colonies, hardly visible at 24 hours, reach maximum size at 72 hours and appear as half-embedded pearls usually surrounded by a zone of hemolysis. Biochemical tests and agglutination by known immune serum establish the identity of isolants.

Guinea pigs that harbor *B. bronchiseptica* in the nasal cavity and trachea are a source of infection for other guinea pigs and are unsatisfactory subjects for research. To detect carriers, Winsser (1960), Woode and McLeod (1967), and Nakagawa *et al.* (1969a) advocated nasal swabs. For this purpose, MacConkey's agar is preferable to blood agar (Woode and McLeod, 1967; Nakagawa *et al.*, 1969a). Nakagawa *et al.* (1969b) thus attempted to rid their colony of *B. bronchiseptica* infection by repeatedly screening for carriers. They were unsuccessful, however, and subsequently found that this procedure failed to detect 10–20% of carriers. Thus, it appears that the carrier state can be detected with greater accuracy at necropsy.

Ganaway *et al.* (1965) found that a single intramuscular injection of a formalin-killed bacterin emulsified with Freund's incomplete adjuvant administered to each of the breeders in a large guinea pig colony resulted in the stimulation of high levels of circulating antibody, in the range of 1:4096 to 1:8192, which persisted for at least 7 months. By comparison, the serum from recovered cases and carriers irregularly (60–80% of the cases) contained low levels of antibody in the range of 1:20 to 1:160. No further deaths due to *B. bronchiseptica* have been noted in the strain 13 colony at the National Institutes of Health, Bethesda, Maryland, where the vaccine has been in use since 1964. Study of a small number of animals suggested that the carrier state had been eliminated. Nikkels and Mullink (1971) have confirmed these findings and have further shown that prolonged use of the bacterin does, indeed, eradicate the organism from the colony. Further confirmation and extension of these findings was recently provided by Nakagawa *et al.* (1974). They suggested that merthiolate was superior to formalin as an inactivating agent and that a single injection resulted in immunity of too short a duration to last for an anticipated 18 to 24 months which is necessary under breeding colony conditions. However, their results were based upon experimental rather than natural challenge or exposure. Furthermore, since a single injection results in eradication of the carrier state in the vaccinated guinea pig, it is doubtful whether the heightened immune state resulting from multiple injections is necessary or desirable (considering the time and effort required) unless the breeding colony is not maintained as a closed colony.

An aspect of *B. bronchiseptica* infection needing further study is uterine infection. Smith (1913–1914) occasionally cultured the bacillus from uteri containing dead embryos. Sinha and Sleight (1968) isolated *B. bronchiseptica* from a guinea pig with bilateral pyosalpinx. Thus *B. bronchiseptica* infection might also be associated with stillbirths, abortion, and infertility.

E. *Klebsiella*

Klebsiella pneumoniae is a nonmotile, nonspore-forming, gram-negative bacillus. One of the enteric bacteria, it is found in the intestinal tract of about 5% of apparently normal human subjects and accounts for less than 3% of all bacterial pneumonias of man. The susceptibility of guinea pigs to primary *K. pneumoniae* infection is unclear. The disease is infrequently encountered. Perkins (1900–1901) described an epizootic in which 25 guinea pigs from a colony of unstated size died of acute disease. At necropsy, there was seropurulent peritonitis and gaseous emphysema of the liver, spleen, and kidneys. *Klebsiella* organisms were isolated, usually in pure culture, from heart blood, liver, spleen, and peritoneal exudate. The disease was reproduced in guinea pigs given a broth culture intraperitoneally. Histopathologically there was congestion with fibrin thrombi in the blood vessels, cloudy swelling, and coagulation necrosis of the liver; congestion and emphysema of the spleen; and congestion, cloudy swelling, and granular degeneration of epithelial cells of the convoluted tubules of the kidney. Bacteria were seen in blood vessels of these organs.

Branch (1927) isolated *Klebsiella* spp. from 56 of 114 guinea pigs which died during an epizootic. However, the guinea pigs were used in tuberculosis research and numerous other pathogenic bacteria were isolated also. Associated lesions were pneumonia, otitis media, pleuritis, pericarditis, peritonitis, metritis, and skin abscesses.

Dennig and Eidmann (1960) reported that *Klebsiella* infection was responsible for death of 200 guinea pigs in a colony of unstated size. The disease affected both sexes, young and old. Sixteen animals were studied: 7 died without clinical signs or lesions and *Klebsiella* could not be isolated from heart blood, spleen, or lung but was isolated from cerebrospinal fluid of 2 animals; 6 refused food for 2–3 days, showed dyspnea, became comatose, and died; and 3 older guinea pigs became cachectic over 2 weeks and died. At necropsy, there was a serofibrinous exudate in the pleural cavity, pericardial sac, and peritoneal cavity. There was consolidation of the lungs, hyperplasia of the spleen, and catarrh and hemorrhage in the large and small intestine. The disease was reproduced in guinea pigs given a broth cultures intraperitoneally and *Klebsiella* spp. was recovered from heart blood, spleen, and lung.

F. *Pasteurella*

Pasteurella multocida inhabits the upper respiratory passages of a variety of apparently healthy birds and animals, including man. When stressed, a hemorrhagic septicemia may ensue. The disease does not appear to be common in guinea pigs. The literature indicates that early investigators were overzealous in their diagnosis of pseudotuberculosis, any disease which might be confused with tuberculosis. Thus the common usage of the terms pasteurellosis and pseudotuberculosis by these workers leaves some doubt as to the prevalence of spontaneous *P. multocida* infection.

Pasteurella multocida is a small nonmotile, nonsporeforming, gram-negative rod or coccobacillus which fails to grow on MacConkey's agar. The organism is stained evenly with aniline dyes in a smear from an actively growing culture but appears as a bipolar rod in animal tissue or fluids.

Wright (1936) suggested that this infection can cause epizootic disease in a guinea pig colony. Approximately 600 guinea pigs died over a period of 1 year of an acute disease without showing other clinical signs. At necropsy, lung consolidation and fibrinopurulent serositis of the pericardium, pleura, and peritoneum were seen. A histopathological description was not reported. Broth cultures were uniformly fatal in 24–72 hours when given subcutaneously to guinea pigs, rats, mice, chickens, or pigeons. Diagnosis rests upon isolation and identification of the bacterium.

G. *Pseudomonas*

Natural infection of guinea pigs with *Pseudomonas* appears to be rare. Scherago (1936) isolated a new species, *P. caviae,* from each of 16 young guinea pigs that died approximately 2 weeks after receipt from a local dealer. Though Koch's postulates were fulfilled, the procedure used to establish this criterion may have been too drastic in that young guinea pigs (100–200 gm) died in less than 24 hours when given a large dose either intravenously, intraperitoneally, or subcutaneously. Apparently the disease has not been seen by others. Interestingly, he fed oats and alfalfa. As the spontaneous disease occurred in March it may have been complicated by scurvy.

Bostrum *et al.* (1969) reported two cases of pulmonary botryomycosis in guinea pigs due to *P. aeruginosa.* They died during an undescribed epizootic in a conventional guinea pig colony. At necropsy, the lungs were consolidated. Microscopically, a severe, focal, necrotizing, suppurative bronchopneumonia was seen. Numerous atypical "sulfur granules," 15–40 μm in diameter, containing gram-negative bacteria were scattered throughout the pneumonic areas. *Pseudomonas aeruginosa* was isolated from the lung of 1 guinea pig and from the drinking water.

H. *Staphylococcus*

Markham and Markham (1966) found β-hemolytic staphylococci in the nasal passages of 23 of 55 apparently healthy guinea pigs. The phage type, which tended to be species specific, and the carrier rate remained remarkably stable over a 3-year observation period.

Taylor *et al.* (1971) isolated coagulase positive staphylococci from guinea pigs with chronic pododermatitis. The volar surface of the enlarged forefeet was encrusted with hemorrhagic, necrotic tissue. Progressive severity of the foot lesions was paralleled by increased amounts of amyloid in the liver, spleen, adrenal glands, and pancreatic islets. Caging of the guinea pigs on rusty wire floors which were infrequently cleaned was believed to be a predisposing factor. Gupta *et al.* (1972) found similar foot lesions in 3 guinea pigs which also had osteoarthritis. Hemolytic *S. aureus* was isolated from two of the affected joints. Senility and trauma were suggested as predisposing factors.

While studying the cause of death in a colony of 170 specific pathogen-free guinea pigs, Blackmore and Francis (1970) noted 4 instances of staphylococcal infection; 2 died with purulent pneumonia, 1 with purulent mastitis, and 1 had conjunctivitis. The coagulase-positive staphylococci were typable using human phage types. Thus guinea pigs in cesarean-derived barrier-maintained colonies might acquire potentially pathogenic staphylococci from attendants.

I. *Corynebacterium*

Spontaneous corynebacterial infections of guinea pigs appear to be rare. *Corynebacterium pyogenes* (Mlinac and Hajsig, 1958) was isolated from a guinea pig with a fatal septicemic disease. A broth culture was pathogenic for other guinea pigs when given intraperitoneally but was without effect when given either orally or intranasally. Passage in broth or in guinea pigs resulted in reduced virulence.

During an epizootic of highly fatal streptococcal (β-hemolytic, Lancefield Group C) disease in a guinea pig colony, Vallée *et al.* (1969) recovered a strain of *C. kutcheri* from the lung of a guinea pig. Experimentally, a broth culture was more virulent for mice than for guinea pigs. The subcutaneous or intraperitoneal inoculation of guinea pigs resulted in the formation of small abscesses at the site of inoculation or in the abdominal cavity, respectively. No effect was noted when large doses were given intranasally. When given intravenously (30×10^6 organisms), guinea pigs died in 48 hours and *C. kutcheri* was recovered from the blood and kidneys.

J. *Streptobacillus*

Streptobacillus moniliformis has been isolated from guinea pigs with cervical adenitis (Klineberger, 1939) and from localized chronic abscesses (Smith, 1941) which contained thick creamy or caseous pus. According to Smith (1941), the abscesses either regressed or broke to the skin surface. Isolations from pus were obtained on an enriched medium containing 30% horse serum. Guinea pigs inoculated subcutaneously with a broth culture developed local abscesses which regressed. The disease is believed to be of low contagiousness and easily controlled by culling affected guinea pigs (Lane-Petter and Porter, 1963) and by providing good quality hay and bedding (Paterson, 1962). Though the source of infection remains unknown, the colony should be protected from intrusion by wild rats which carry *S. moniliformis* in their nasal and oral cavities.

K. *Clostridium*

Clostridium perfringens infection in conventionally raised guinea pigs is not a problem, but Madden *et al.* (1970) have shown that when germfree guinea pigs were removed from the isolator, they invariably died within 2–10 days with an acute enterotoxemia syndrome. *Clostridium perfringens,* type E, was cultured from their blood. When cultures were fed to germfree guinea pigs, they died similarly while conventionally raised guinea pigs given the same culture remained unaffected.

L. *Leptospira*

Leptospirosis has been frequently observed in wild guinea pigs in Argentina and Brazil (Blood *et al.,* 1963a,b). It is rare in laboratory guinea pigs. *Leptospira icterohemorrhagica* was isolated from 1 of 12 guinea pigs that died after receipt from a dealer (Mason, 1937). At necropsy, jaundice was marked, petechial hemorrhages were seen in the skin, fascia, and muscles and ecchymosis in the lung. Though the source of the infection was not established, the dealer related that rats had gained entry to his colony and killed some guinea pigs about 10 days before shipment to the investigator.

M. *Mycobacterium*

Spontaneous tuberculosis in guinea pigs is rare despite the fact that they are highly susceptible. Natural infection with the bovine and human strains have been recorded (Adams, 1953; Mitscherlich, 1958). The source of the infections were unknown but believed to be from contact with human cases.

N. *Brucella*

Spontaneous brucellosis in guinea pigs apparently has not been reported in the United States. It is not likely to occur in the closed colony where a complete pasteurized diet is fed. As guinea pigs are very susceptible to *Brucella* infection experimentally, the natural infection would be expected to occur if guinea pigs are fed improperly treated animal by products from infected animals, especially cattle, goats, and swine. Such a source of infection is probably responsible for the natural infections due to *B. abortus, B. melitensis,* and *B. suis* which have been encountered (three papers cited by Mitscherlich, 1958; Szukiewicz and Prazmo, 1971). In the report of Szukiewicz and Prazmo (1971), marked testicular and joint swelling was noted in a male guinea pig from a colony of unstated size approximately 3 months after the guinea pigs were received from a private vendor. An infected female guinea pig was detected by agglutination tests and *B. suis* was isolated from small abscesses in the liver and pancreas. The authors felt the female was infected when received from the vendor and the male became infected by coitus.

O. *Escherichia*

Infections with *E. coli* apparently do not occur in the well-managed guinea pig colony. *Escherichia coli* is not a major component of the normal intestinal flora of guinea pigs (Crecelius and Rettger, 1943; Roine and Elvehjem, 1950; Pallaske and Krahnert, 1958). With poor husbandry, overcrowding, and high humidity, coliforms may become the predominant flora (Pallaske and Krahnert, 1958). As a result, a fatal syndrome characterized by wasting for 4 to 9 days, diarrhea, rough hair coat, and subnormal temperature may occur, especially in weanlings. As increasing numbers of guinea pigs die, the clinical course is more brief, presumably due to increased virulence of *E. coli.* At necropsy, the intestine is distended and contains yellow fluid and gas, excessive peritoneal fluid is present, the spleen is slightly enlarged, and small grayish-white necrotic foci may be seen in the liver. Isolation is readily obtained by culture of peritoneal fluid, intestinal lymph nodes, spleen, liver, or blood. Treatment has not been a consideration.

P. *Listeria*

Brief mention of infection with *L. monocytogenes* is made in view of the single reference found in the literature (Seeligek, 1955, cited by Pallaske and Krahnert, 1958). The spontaneous infection was seen concurrently in guinea pigs and rabbits maintained at the same laboratory. As guinea pigs are very susceptible to *L. monocytogenes* infection experimentally, this disease should be considered in the differential diagnosis of monocytic leukocytosis, conjunctivitis, focal necrosis of internal organs, abortions and stillbirths, and meningitis. Of note is the ability of this bacterium to grow in soil at 4°C which may account for its widespread occurrence in nature. It has a wide host range causing disease in birds and many mammals including man.

III. MYCOPLASMAL INFECTIONS

The role of mycoplasmas in disease of guinea pigs is uncertain. Freundt (1968) in a review, alluded to the uncertain identity of previous *Mycoplasma*-like isolations from the nasopharynx and cervical abscesses of guinea pigs (Klineberger, 1939; Findlay *et al.*, 1940), and noted the unknown extent to which mycoplasma organisms have been looked for. Hill *et al.* (1969; Hill, 1971a,b,c) isolated mycoplasmas from the vagina, uterus, brain, and nasopharynx of guinea pigs. None of the isolates was related to known murine mycoplasmas. A suggested new species, *Mycoplasma caviae,* was isolated (Hill, 1971d) from the nasopharynx and vagina of 10% of 232 apparently normal guinea pigs. In contrast, Juhr and Obi (1970) isolated *M. pulmonis* from the uterus of each of 80 guinea pigs examined. Stalheim and Matthews (1975) recently conducted a survey of 108 mature female guinea pigs to determine the extent of mycoplasma infection. Of 39 isolations obtained from the nose (31 isolations) and vagina (eight isolations), 23 were *Acholeplasmas,* seven were *M. caviae,* and nine remained unidentified. Their role in disease remains unknown.

IV. RICKETTSIAL INFECTIONS

Bozeman *et al.* (1968) compared four strains of rickettsia-like agents recovered from guinea pigs; two were their own isolants, one was received from Jackson *et al.* (1952), and one from Tatlock (1944). The source of the agents remains unknown. In each instance, they were isolated from guinea pigs previously inoculated with material from human patients suffering with unknown febrile disease. It was not possible, however, to link the agents with human disease. Attempts to isolate similar agents or to demonstrate antibody in sera from other guinea pigs were not successful. The four isolants remain distinct though related serologically and are unrelated to known rickettsia.

Inoculated guinea pigs developed fever which persisted for 7 days. They lost weight, became lethargic, and died during the second week. At necropsy, there was enlargement of the spleen and lymph nodes and a marked peritonitis. Purple bacilli in the cytoplasm of mononuclear cells were readily demonstrated in Giemsa-stained smears of spleen. The agents killed the embryo of hen's eggs in 2–6 days postinoculation and titers of 10^7 ELD_{50} were obtained. The agents were sensitive to terramycin and streptomycin when tested in embryonated eggs. They were stable for 7 days at 35°C. Bozeman *et al.* (1968) suggested that the agents were probably present in the guinea pigs as latent infections.

V. SUMMARY AND CONCLUDING REMARKS

Guinea pigs are susceptible to a wide variety of bacterial diseases. At least 19 genera of bacteria, mycoplasma, and rickettsia-like agents have been recovered from laboratory guinea pigs with spontaneous disease. Infections due to *Salmonella* spp., *Bordetella bronschseptica, Streptococcus* (Lancefield Group C), and *Yersinia pseudotuberculosis* are the most frequently reported causes of epizootic disease and are often associated with high mortality in the guinea pig colony. Less frequently reported causes of epizootic disease are infections due to *Streptococcus pneumoniae, Klebsiella pneumoniae, Pasteurella multocida,* and *Pseudomonas* spp. Once these organisms are introduced into the colony and the epizootic subsides, carriers persist resulting in enzootic disease. Predisposing factors that contribute to the severity of the morbidity and mortality due to these infections in the guinea pig colony are: faulty husbandry practices such as poor sanitation, overcrowding and mixing of animal species in the same room; improper ventilation and temperature and humidity control; inadequate diet, especially vitamic C intake; transporting the guinea pigs; and experimental procedures. Though the use of antibiotics which selectively inhibit or destroy gram-positive intestinal flora of guinea pigs is to be avoided (Farrer *et al.*, 1966), the selective use of broad-spectrum antibiotics may have merit in the laboratory. Such substances may also be used in the production colony to suppress losses, but this procedure may become expensive and probably will not eliminate the agent from the colony. Once established in the colony, *B. bronchiseptica* appears to be the only bacterial disease of guinea pigs which can be eradicated by the use of a bacterin. As for other bacterial pathogens, "an ounce of prevention is worth a pound of cure," for destruction of the colony and starting anew with noninfected stock appears to be the best alternative in most cases.

SELECTED REFERENCES

Adams, M. O. (1953). Natural infection of the guinea pig with the human type of tubercle bacillus. *Mon. Bull. Min. Health Pub. Health Lab. Ser.* **12,** 146–148.

Anonymous (1972). *Pasteurella* and *Yersinia* infections. *In* "Morbidity and Mortality Weekly Report," Vol. 21, pp. 146–147. Center for Disease Control, Atlanta, Georgia.

Bishop, L. M. (1932). Study of an outbreak of pseudotuberculosis in guinea pigs (cavies) due to *B. pseudotuberculosis rodentium. Cornell Vet.* **22,** 1–9.

Blackmore, D. K., and Francis, R. A. (1970). The apparent transmission of staphylococci of human origin to laboratory animals. *J. Comp. Pathol.* **80,** 645–651.

Blood, B. D., Czyfres, B., and Moya, V. (1963a). Natural *Leptospira pamona* infections in the pampas cavy. *Pub. Health Rep.* **78,** 537–542.

Blood, B. D., Czyfres, B., and Moya, V. (1963b). Infection caused by *Leptospira pamoma* in pampas guinea pigs (*Cavia pamparum*). I. Existence in a natural population. *Bull. Pan. Amer. Sanit. Bur.* **54,** 603–609.

Bostrum, R. E., Huckins, J. G., Kroe, D. J., Lawson, N. S., Martin, J. E., Ferrell, J. F., and Whitney, R. A., Jr. (1969). Atypical fatal pulmonary botryomycosis in two guinea pigs due to *Pseudomonas aeruginosa. J. Amer. Vet. Med. Ass.* **155,** 1195–1199.

Boxmeyer, C. H. (1907). Epizootic lymphadenitis. A new disease of guinea pigs. *J. Infec. Dis.* **4,** 657–664.

Bozeman, R. M., Humphries, J. W., and Campbell, J. M. (1968). A new group of rickettsia-like agents recovered from guinea pigs. *Acta Virol. (Prague)* **12,** 87–93.

Branch, A. (1927). Spontaneous infections of guinea pigs. Pneumococcus, Friedlander bacillus and pseudotuberculosis (*Eberthella caviae*). *J. Infec. Dis.* **40,** 533–548.

Cook, R. (1953–1954). Diseases of guinea pigs. *J. Anim. Tech. Ass.* **4,** 71–74.

Crecelius, H. G., and Rettger, L. F. (1943). The intestinal flora of the guinea pig. *J. Bacteriol.* **46,** 1–13.

Deibel, R. H. and Seeley, H. W. Jr. (1974). Streptococcaceae. *In* "Bergey's Manual of Determinative Bacteriology" 8th edition (R. E. Buchanan and N. E. Gibbons, eds.), pp. 490–498. The Williams and Wilkins Co., Baltimore, Maryland.

Dennig, H. K., and Eidmann, E. (1960). Klebsielleninfektionen bein meerschweinchen. *Berlin. Tieraerztl. Wochenschr.* **73,** 273–274.

Diaz, J., and Soave, O. A. (1973). Cephaloridine treatment of cervical lymphadenitis in guinea pigs. *Lab. Anim. Dig.* **8,** 60–62.

Edington, J. W. (1929). Endemic infection of guinea-pigs with *B. aertryche* (Mutton). *J. Comp. Pathol. Ther.* **42,** 258–268.

Farrer, W. E., Kent, T. H., and Elliott, V. B. (1966). Lethal gram-negative bacterial superinfection in guinea pigs given bacitracin. *J. Bacteriol.* **92,** 496–501.

Findlay, G. M., Mackenzie, R. D., and MacCallum, F. O. (1940). Chemotherapeutic experiments on pleuropneumonia-like organisms in rodents. *Brit. J. Exp. Pathol.* **21,** 13–22.

Finlayson, N. B., and Fagundes, B. (1971). *Pasteurella pseudotuberculosis* infection: Three cases in the United States. *Amer. J. Clin. Pathol.* **55,** 24–29.

Fish, N. A., Fletch, A. L., and Butler, W. E. (1968). Family outbreak of salmonellosis due to contact with guinea pigs. *Can. Med. Ass. J.* **99,** 418–420.

Fraunfelter, F. C., Schmidt, R. E., Beattie, R. J., and Garner, F. M. (1971). Lancefield type C streptococcal infections in strain 2 guinea pigs. *Lab. Anim.* **5,** 1–13.

Freundt, E. A. (1968). Mycoplasma infections in laboratory rodents. *Z. Versuchstierk.* **10,** 17–26.

Ganaway, J. R., Allen, A. M., and McPherson, C. W. (1965). Prevention of acute *Bordetella bronchiseptica* pneumonia in a guinea pig colony. *Lab. Anim. Care* **15,** 156–162.

Ginsburg, I. (1972). Mechanisms of cell and tissue injury induced by group A streptococci: Relation to poststreptococcal sequelae. *J. Infec. Dis.* **126,** 419–456.

Gupta, B. N., Langham, R. F., and Conner, G. H. (1970). Mastitis in guinea pigs. *Amer. J. Vet. Res.* **31,** 1703–1707.

Gupta, B. N., Conner, G. H., and Meyer, D. B. (1972). Osteoarthritis in guinea pigs. *Lab. Anim. Sci.* **22,** 362–368.

Hardenbergh, J. G. (1926). Epidemic lymphadenitis with formation of abscesses in guinea pigs due to infection with hemolytic streptococcus. *J. Lab. Clin. Med.* **12,** 119–129.

Haughton, L. J., and Minkin, P. (1966). Some aspects of pseudotuberculosis among a small colony of guinea pigs. *J. Inst. Anim. Technicians* **17,** 37–40.

Hill, A. (1971a). *Mycoplasma caviae:* A new species. *J. Gen. Microbiol.* **65,** 109–113.

Hill, A. (1971b). The isolation of two further species of mycoplasma from guinea pigs. *Vet. Rec.* **89,** 225.

Hill, A. (1971c). Accidental infection of man with mycoplasma caviae. *Brit. Med. J.* **2,** 711–712.

Hill, A. (1971d). Incidence of mycoplasma infection in guinea pigs. *Nature (London)* **232,** 560.

Hill, A., Blackmore, D. K., and Francis, R. A. (1969). The isolation of mycoplasmas from guinea pigs (*Cavia porcellus*). *Vet Rec.* **85,** 291–292.

Holman, W. L. (1916–1917). Spontaneous infection in the guinea pig. *J. Med. Res.* **35,** 151–185.

Homburger, F., Wilcox, C., Barnes, M. W., and Finland, M. (1945). An epizootic of pneumococcus type 19, infections in guinea pigs. *Science* **102,** 449–450.

Institute of Laboratory Animal Resources News. (1972). "Annual Survey of Animals Used for Research Purposes during Calendar Year 1971" (R. H. Yager and C. B. Frank, eds.), Vol. 16. Nat. Res. Counc., Washington, D. C.

Jackson, E. B., Crocker, T. T., and Smadel, J. E. (1952). Studies on the rickettsia-like agents probably isolated from guinea pigs. *Bacteriol. Proc.* p. 119.

Juhr, N. C., and Obi, S. (1970). Uterus infection in guinea pigs. *Z. Versuchstierk.* **12,** 383–387.

Karel, L., Grubb, T. C., and Chapman, C. W. (1941). The treatment of group C streptococcus infection in guinea pigs with vitamin C and sulfanilamide. *J. Infec. Dis.* **69,** 125–130.

Kent, T. H., Formal, S. B., and LaBrec, E. H. (1966). Acute enteritis due to *Salmonella typhimurium* in opium-treated guinea pigs. *Arch. Pathol.* **81,** 501–508.

Klineberger, E. (1939). Studies on the pleuropneumonia-like organisms: Bacteriological features and serological relationships of strains from various sources. *J. Pathol. Bacteriol.* **49,** 451–452.

Lancefield, R. C. (1933). A serological differentiation of human and other groups of hemolytic streptococci. *J. Exp. Med.* **57,** 571–595.

Lane-Petter, W., and Porter, G. (1963). Guinea pigs. *In* "Animals for Research" (W. Lane-Petter, ed.), pp. 287–321. Academic Press, New York.

Lautrop, H., and Lacey, B. W. (1960). Laboratory diagnosis of whooping-cough or bordetella infections. *Bull. W. H. O.* **23,** 15–35.

Madden, D. L., Horton, R. E., and McCullough, N. B. (1970). Spontaneous infection in ex-germfree guinea pigs due to *Clostridium perfringens. Lab. Anim. Care* **20,** 454–455.

Markham, N. P., and Markham, J. G. (1966). Staphylococci in man and animals. Distribution and characteristics of strains. *J. Comp. Pathol.* **76,** 49–56.

Mason, N. (1937). Leptospiral jaundice occurring naturally in guinea pigs. *Lancet* **232,** 564–565.

Meyer, K. F. (1928). Communicable diseases of laboratory animals. *In* "The Newer Knowledge of Bacteriology and Immunology" (E. O. Jordan and I. S. Falk, eds.), pp. 607–638. Univ. of Chicago Press, Chicago, Illinois.

Mitscherlich, E. (1958). Serologische Diagnostik der Spontanerkrankungen der Kleinen Laboratoriumstiere. *In* "Pathologie de Laboratoriumstiere" (P. Cohrs, R. Jaffé, and H. Meessen, eds.), Vol. II, pp. 240–249. Springer-Verlag, Berlin and New York.

Mlinac, F., and Hajsig, M. (1958). *Corynebacterium pyogenes* U Zamarceta. (*Corynebacterium pyogenes* in guinea pigs.) *Vet. Arh.* **28,** 43–48.

Moen, J. K. (1936). A skin test for detecting group C hemolytic streptococcal infection causing epizootic lymphadenitis in guinea pigs. *J. Exp. Med.* **64,** 553–558.

Moore, B. (1957). Observations pointing to the conjunctiva as a portal of entry in salmonella infection of guinea pigs. *J. Hyg.* **55,** 414–433.

Morris, E. J. (1958). Selective media for some *Pasteurella* species. *J. Gen. Microbiol.* **19,** 305–311.

Moss, E. S., and Battle, J. D., Jr. (1941). Human infection with *Pasteurella pseudotuberculosis rodentium* of Pfeiffer. *Amer. J. Clin. Pathol.* **11,** 677–699.

Nakagawa, M., Muto, T., Nakano, T., Yoda, H., Ando, K., Isobe, Y., and Imaizumi, K. (1969a). Some observations on diagnosis of *Bordetella bronchiseptica* infection in guinea pigs. *Exp. Anim.* **18,** 105–116.

Nakagawa, M., Yoda, H., Yasa, T., Sugisaki, M., Haruzono, S., and Nakano, T. (1969b). Epizootiological survey and control of *Bordetella bronchiseptica* infection in guinea pigs. *Exp. Anim.* **18,** 117–122.

Nakagawa, M., Yoda, H., Muto, T., and Imaizumi, K. (1974). Prophylaxis of *Bordetella bronchiseptica* infection in guinea pigs by vaccination. *Jap. J. Vet. Sci.* **36,** 33–42.

Nelson, J. B. (1927a). The biological characters of a mucoid variant of *Bacillus paratyphi* from guinea pigs. *J. Exp. Med.* **45,** 379–389.

Nelson, J. B. (1927b). Studies on a paratyphoid infection in guinea pigs. III. A second type of salmonella naturally appearing in the endemic stage. *J. Exp. Med.* **46,** 541–548.

Nelson, J. B., and Smith, T. (1927). Studies on a paratyphoid infection in guinea pigs. I. Report of a natural outbreak of paratyphoid in a guinea pig population. *J. Exp. Med.* **45,** 353–363.

Nelson, J. B. (1928a). Studies on a paratyphoid infection in guinea pigs. IV. The course of a second type of salmonella infection naturally appearing in the endemic stage. *J. Exp. Med.* **47,** 207–217.

Nelson, J. B. (1928b). Studies on a paratyphoid infection in guinea pigs. V. The incidence of carriers during the endemic stage. *J. Exp. Med.* **48,** 647–658.

Neufeld, F., and Etinger-Tulczynska, R. (1932). Utersuchungen über die pneumokokkenseuche des meerschweinchens. *Z. Hyg. Infektionskr.* **114,** 324–346.

Nikkels, R. J., and Mullink, J. W. M. A. (1971). *Bordetella bronchiseptica* pneumonia in guinea pigs. Description of the disease and elimination by vaccination. *Z. Versuchstierk.* **13,** 105–111.

Pallaske, G., and Krahnert, R. (1958). Durch bakterin und pflanzliche parasiten hervorgerufene infektionskrankheiten. *In* "Pathologie der Laboratoriumstiere" (P. Cohrs, R. Jaffé, and H. Meessen, eds.), Vol. II, pp. 1–53. Springer-Verlag, Berlin and New York.

Pandalai, N. G. (1934). An epizootic affecting laboratory-bred guinea pigs. *Indian J. Med. Res.* **21,** 625–626.

Parsons, E. I., and Hyde, R. R. (1928). Spontaneous streptococcus infections in guinea pigs. *Amer. J. Hyg.* **8,** 356–385.

Paterson, J. S. (1962). Guinea-pig disease. *In* "The Problems of Laboratory Animal Disease" (R. J. C. Harris, ed.), pp. 169–184. Academic Press, New York.

Paterson, J. S. (1967). The guinea pig or cavy. *In* "The UFAW Handbook on the Care and Management of Laboratory Animals" (UFAW, ed.), 3rd ed., pp. 241–287. Williams & Wilkins, Baltimore, Maryland.

Paterson, J. S., and Cook, R. (1963). A method for the recovery of *Pasteurella pseudotuberculosis* from feces. *J. Pathol. Bacteriol.* **85,** 241–242.

Perkins, R. G. (1900–1901). Report of a laboratory epizootic among guinea pigs associated with gaseous emphysema of the liver, spleen and kidneys due to *Bacillus mucosus capsulatus. J. Exp. Med.* **5,** 389–396.

Petrie, G. F. (1933). Pneumococcal disease of the guinea pig. *Vet. J.* **89,** 25–30.

Petrie, G. F., and O'Brien, R. A. (1910). A guinea pig epizootic with an organism of the food-poisoning group but probably caused by a filter passer. *J. Hyg.* **10,** 287–305.

Rae, M. V. (1936). Epizootic streptococcic myocarditis in guinea pigs. *J. Infec. Dis.* **59,** 236–241.

Roine, P., and Elvehjem, C. A. (1950). Significance of the intestinal flora in nutrition of the guinea pig. *Proc. Soc. Exp. Biol. Med.* **73,** 308–310.

Scherago, M. (1936). An epizootic septicemia of young guinea pigs caused by *Pseudomas caviae.* n. sp. *J. Bacteriol.* **31,** 83.

Seastone, C. V. (1939). Hemolytic streptococcus lymphadenitis in guinea pigs. *J. Exp. Med.* **70,** 347–359.

Sinha, D. P., and Sleight, S. D. (1968). Bilateral pyosalpinx in a guinea pig. *J. Amer. Vet. Med. Ass.* **153,** 830–831.

Smith, W. (1941). Cervical abscesses of guinea pigs. *J. Pathol. Bacteriol.* **53,** 29–37.

Smith, T. (1913–1914). Some bacteriological and environmental factors in the pneumonias of lower animals with special reference to the guinea-pig. *J. Med. Res.* **29,** 291–323.

Snyder, G. A. C., and Vogel, N. J. (1943). Human infection by *Pasteurella pseudotuberculosis. Northwest Med.* **42,** 14–15.

Stalheim, O. H. V. and Matthews, P. J. (1975). Mycoplasmosis in specific-pathogen-free and conventional guinea pigs. *Lab. Anim. Sci.* **25,** 70–73.

Steele, J. H. (1969). The epidemiology and control of the zoonoses. *In* "The Theory and Practice of Public Health" (W. Hobsen, ed.), pp. 220–251. Oxford Univ. Press, London and New York.

Szukiewicz, Z., and Prazmo, Z. (1971). Przypadek brucelozy u świnek morskich. (A case of brucellosis in guinea pigs.) *Med. Wet.* **27,** 12–13.

Takeuchi, A., and Sprinz, H. (1967). Electron microscopic studies of experimental salmonella infection in the preconditioned guinea pig. II. Response of the intestinal mucosa to the invasion by *Salmonella typhimurium. Amer. J. Pathol.* **51,** 137–161.

Tatlock, H. (1944). A rickettsia-like organism recovered from guinea pigs. *Proc. Soc. Exp. Biol. Med.* **57,** 95–99.

Taylor, J. L., Wagner, J. E., Owens, D. R., and Stuhlman, R. A. (1971). Chronic pododermatitis in guinea pigs. *Lab. Anim. Sci.* **21**, 944–945.

Thal, E. (1962). Oral immunization of guinea pigs with avirulent *Pasteurella pseudotuberculosis. Nature (London)* **194**, 490–491.

Topping, N. H., Watts, C. E., and Lillie, R. D. (1938). A case of human infection with *B. pseudotuberculosis rodentium. Pub. Health Rep.* **53**, 1340–1352.

Vallée, A., Guillon, J. C., and Cayeux, P. (1969). Isolement d'une souche de *Corynebacterium kutcheri* chez un cobaye. (Isolation of a strain of *Corynebacterium kutcheri* in a guinea pig.) *Bull. Acad. Vet. Fr.* [N.S.] **42**, 797–800.

Wagner, J. E., and Owens, D. R. (1970). Type XIX *Streptococcus pneumonia* (*Diplococcus pneumoniae*) infections in guinea pigs. *Proc. 21st Meet. Amer. Ass. Lab. Anim. Sci.* Abstr. No. 71.

Wetzler, T. F., and Hubbert, W. T. (1968). *Pasteurella pseudotuberculosis* in North America. *In* "International Symposium on Pseudotuberculosis" (R. H. Regamey *et al.*, eds.), pp. 33–44. Karger, Basel.

Winsser, J. (1960). A study of *Bordetella bronchiseptica. Proc. Anim. Care Panel* **10**, 87–104.

Woode, G. N., and McLeod, N. (1967). Control of acute *Bordetella bronchiseptica* pneumonia in a guinea pig colony. *Lab. Anim.* **1**, 91–94.

Wright, J. (1936). An epidemic of *Pasteurella* infection in guinea pig stock. *J. Pathol. Bacteriol.* **42**, 209–212.

RELATED REFERENCES

Alkis, N. (1966). *Salmonella typhimurium* infection in a guinea-pig population. *Turk. Hij. Tecr. Biyol. Derg.* **26**, 147–150.

Angrist, A., and Mollov, M. (1948). Morphologic studies of the intestine in salmonella infection in guinea pigs and mice. *Amer. J. Med. Sci.* **215**, 149–157.

Asakawa, Y., Endo, M., and Tajima, Y. (1954a). Salmonellosis in guinea pigs. I. An epizootic outbreak caused by *S. marashino. Jap. J. Med. Sci. Biol.* **7**, 461–465.

Asakawa, Y., Sakaguchi, G., and Tajima, Y. (1954b). Salmonellosis in guinea pigs. II. An epizootic outbreak caused by *S. enteritidis* and some other additional species of salmonella associated with hemolytic streptococcus. *Jap. J. Med. Sci. Biol.* **7**, 467–471.

Bainbridge, F. A., and O'Brien, R. A. (1911–1912). An epizootic in guinea pigs in which *B. enteritidis* (Gaertner) was present. *J. Pathol. Bacteriol.* **16**, 145.

Beattie, W. W. (1931). An epizootic produced by a hemolytic streptococcus in laboratory guinea pigs with abscess formation. *J. Pathol. Bacteriol.* **34**, 453–458.

Beck, O., and Coffee, W. B. (1943). Observations on *Salmonella typhimurium. J. Bacteriol.* **45**, 200.

Beer, J. (1960). Über das vorkommen und über die rolle von *Bordetella* (*B.*) *bronchiseptica* bei lungenerkrankungen einiger haus-und laboratoriumstiere. (Incidence and role of *Bord. bronchiseptica* in lung disease of some domestic and laboratory animals.) *Zentralbl. Bakteriol., Parasitenk., Infektionskr. Hyg., Abt. I: Orig.* **177**, 208–214.

Binaghi, R. (1897). Ueber einen streptococcus capsulatus. *Zentralbl. Bakteriol., Parasitenk., Infektionskr., Abt. 1* **22**, 273–279.

Binato, G., and Corrado, A. (1960). Antibiotic therapy of pseudotuberculosis in guinea pigs. *Nuova Vet.* **36**, 239–242.

Bjotvedt, G. (1964). The nature and variety of diseases of laboratory animals. *Vet. Scope* **9**, 14–22.

Bronson, R. T., May, B. D., and Ruebner, B. H. (1972). An outbreak of infection by *Yersinia pseudotuberculosis* in nonhuman primates. *Amer. J. Pathol.* **69**, 289–308.

Buhles, W. C., Jr. (1969). Airborne staphylococcic contamination in experimental procedures on laboratory animals. *Lab. Anim. Care* **19**, 465–469.

Busson, B. (1921). Die erreger der hamorrhagischen septikamie. *Zentrablat. Bakteriol., Parasitenk., Infektionskr. Abt. 1: Orig.* **86**, 101–118.

Colusi, A. D. (1962). Streptococcal infections with concomitant pseudotuberculosis in guinea pigs. *Gac. Vet.* **24**, 489–498.

Corrado, A. (1963). Streptococcal cervical lymphadenitis in guinea pigs. *Nuova Vet.* **39**, 162–166.

Cotchin, E. (1944). A natural case of tuberculosis in a guinea pig. *Vet. Rec.* **56**, 437.

Cunningham, J. S. (1929). Epizootic lymphadenitis in guinea pigs due to an encapsulated mucoid hemolytic streptococcus. *J. Infec. Dis.* **45**, 474–484.

Czaplicki, S., and Chandlee, G. C. (1965). Incidence, identification and pathogenesis of a gram negative microorganism found in guinea pigs. *Bacteriol. Proc.* **p.52.**

Czaplicki, S., Chandlee, G., and Fukui, G. M. (1965). Incidence, identification and pathogenesis of a *Bord. bronchiseptica* in guinea pigs. *Proc. 16th Annu. Meet. Anim. Care Panel* Abstr. No. 43.

Dean, D. J., and Duell, C. (1963). Diets without green food for guinea pigs. *Lab. Anim. Care* **13**, 191–196.

Duthrie, R. C., and Mitchell, C. A. (1931). *Salmonella enteritidis* infection in guinea pigs and rabbits. *J. Amer. Vet. Med. Ass.* **78**, 27–41.

Edwards, P. R., Bruner, D. W., and Moran, A. B. (1948). Further studies on the occurrence and distribution of salmonella types in the United States. *J. Infec. Dis.* **83**, 220–231.

Feldman, W. H. (1929). Multiple focal splenitis of guinea pigs. *Amer. J. Pathol.* **5**, 371–376.

Ferry, N. S. (1914). Bacteriology and control of the acute infections of laboratory animals. *J. Pathol. Bacteriol.* **18**, 445–455.

Filion, P. R., Coultier, S., Vranchen, E. R., and Bernier, G. (1967). Infection respiratoire du dindonneau causée par un microbe apparenté au *Bordetella bronchiseptica. Can. J. Comp. Med.* **31**, 129–134.

Florey, H. W. (1933). Observations on the functions of mucus and the early stages of bacterial invasion of the intestinal mucosa. *J. Pathol. Bacteriol.* **37**, 283–289.

Friedlander, R. D., and Hertert, L. D. (1929). Virulence of *B. paratyphosus* B (aertryche) in guinea pigs. *J. Infec. Dis.* **44**, 481–488.

Fujisaki, Y. (1961). [On experiments with the infection with *Salmonella typhimurium* in whooping cough vaccine-inoculated animals (mice, guinea pigs).] *Jap. J. Bacteriol.* **16**, 391–402.

Genov, I. (1961). Pseudotuberculosis in rabbits and guinea pigs. *Izv. Tsent. Vet. Inst. Zarazni. Parazit. Bolesti* **2**, 257–268.

Gheorghiu, I. (1922). Infection a pneumocoques chez le cobaye, vaccination antipneumococcique. *C. R. Soc. Biol.* **11**, 39–40.

Gheorgiu, I. (1926). Note sur les caractéres dún micro-organisme, appartenant au group des *Salmonellae* provenant de rats et de cobayes atteints d'une maladie épizootique. (Properties of microorganisms belonging to salmonella group, obtained from rats and guinea pigs affected with epizootic disease.) *Ann. Inst. Pasteur, Paris* **40**, 447–449.

Ghosh, G. K., and Chatterjie, A. (1960). Salmonellosis in guinea pigs, rabbits and pigeons. *Indian Vet. J.* **37**, 144–148.

Gibbons, N. E. (1929). *Hemophilus* sp. and *Neisseria* sp. in skin abscesses in rabbits and guinea pigs. *J. Infec. Dis.* **45**, 288–292.

Glenny, A. T., and Allen, K. (1921). A guinea pig epizootic associated with dietary deficiency. *Lancet* **201**, 1109.

Goodpasture, E. W. (1937). Concerning the pathogenesis of typhoid fever. *Amer. J. Pathol.* **13**, 175–186.

Griffin, C. A. (1955). Bacterial diseases of common laboratory animals. *Proc. Anim. Care Panel* **6**, 92–112.

Gunn, F. D. (1928). Bacillus of paratyphoid-enteritidis group causing fatal disease in guinea pigs. *Bull. Buffalo Gen. Hosp.* **6**, 17–21.

Gupta, B. N., Carter, G. R., Langham, R. F., and Conner, G. H. (1972). Bacteriologic examination of guinea-pig mammary gland: Preliminary report. *J. Dairy Sci.* **55**, 867–870.

Gupta, B. R., and Rao, S. B. (1969). Some outbreaks of salmonellosis in guinea pigs. *Indian Vet. J.* **46**, 1102–1103.

Habermann, R. T., and Williams, F. P., Jr. (1958). Salmonellosis in laboratory animals. *J. Nat. Cancer Inst.* **20**, 933–948.

Hartwigk, H. (1949). Über eine streptokokken infektion beim meerschwienchen. (Streptococcus infection of guinea pigs.) *Zentralbl. Bakteriol., Parasitenk., Infekionskr. Hyg., Abt. 1: Orig.* **154**, 8–11.

Hertert, L. D., and Meyer, K. F. (1929). Cutaneous immunization against the streptococcus of guinea-pig lymphadenitis. *J. Infec. Dis.* **44**, 489–494.

Hibbs, C. M. (1969). Immunologic response of guinea pigs to *Salmonella typhimurium* bacterin. *Cornell Vet.* **59**, 35–40.

Horie, K., Fujisaki, Y., Irisawa, J., Okazaki, S., and Usuba, I. (1960a). Some aspects of diseases of small laboratory animals. I. Isolation of *Bordetella bronchiseptica* from the lung of guinea pigs. *Jap. Bull. Exp. Anim.* **9**, 35–40.

Horie, K., Okazaki, S., Fujisaki, Y., Irisawa, J., Shimazaki, Y., and Kamel, T. (1960b). Some aspects of disease in small laboratory animals. 2. Isolation of salmonella like organisms from the mesenteric lymph node of guinea pigs. *Jap. Bull. Exp. Anim.* **9**, 93.

Horton, R. E., Madden, D. L. and McCullough, N. B. (1970). Pathogenicity of *Clostridium perfringens* for germ-free guinea pigs after oral ingestion. *Appl. Microbiol.* **19**, 314–316.

Howell, K. M., and Schultz, O. T. (1922). An epizootic among guinea pigs due to a paratyphoid *B. bacillus. J. Infec. Dis.* **30**, 516–535.

Imaizumi, K. (1961). Streptococcal infection of guinea pigs. *J. Jap. Vet. Med. Ass.* **22**, 307.

Imaizumi, K., Tanaka, T., and Tajima, Y. (1956). Hemolytic streptococcosis of guinea pigs. I. Pattern of occurrence and its control measures. *Jap. J. Vet. Sci.* **17**, 19.

Imaizumi, K., Arai, T., and Tajima, Y. (1959). Haemolytic streptococcosis of guinea pigs. IV. Hemolytic streptococcal flora of guinea pigs. (In Japanese.) *Jap. J. Vet. Sci.* **21**, 307–315.

Jayaraman, M. S., Krishnan, R., and Sethumadhavan, V. (1964). An outbreak of salmonellosis in guinea pigs due to *Salmonella weltevreden. Indian Vet. J.* **41**, 675–681.

Joubert, L., Bonnal, J., and Oudor, J. (1962). Outbreak of pseudotuberculosis in laboratory guinea pigs: Diagnosis by the chlortetracycline test. *Rev. Serv. Biol. Vet. Armes (Fr.)* **15**, 10–13.

Katijar, R. D. (1952). Pseudomoniasis in guinea pigs. *Indian Vet. J.* **28**, 443–445.

Kaura, Y. K., and Singh, I. P. (1968). Prevalence of salmonella in some of the common wild lizards, birds and rodents. *Indian J. Med. Res.* **56**, 1174–1179.

Kent, T. H., Formal, S. B., LaBrec, E. H., and Takeuchi, A. (1967). Diffuse enteritis due to *Salmonella typhimurium* in opium-treated guinea pigs. *Fed. Proc., Fed. Amer. Soc. Exp. Biol.* **25**, 456–457.

Keyhani, M., and Naghshineh, R. (1974). Spontaneous epizootic of pneumococcus infection in guinea pigs. *Lab. Anim.* **8**, 47–49.

Kjar, T. (1934). Jahreszeitliche schwankungen verschiedener spontaninfektionen des Meerschweinchens. (Seasonal fluctuations in several spontaneous infections of guinea pigs.) *Z. Immunitaetsforsch. Exp. Ther.* **81**, 511–518.

Krumwiede, C., Jr., Valentine, E., and Kohn, L. A. (1918–1919). Studies on the paratyphoid-enteritidis group. VI. The separation of a distinct paratyphoid group among strains of rodent origin. *J. Med. Res.* **39**, 449–460.

Kunz, L. L., and Hutton, G. M. (1971). Diseases of the laboratory guinea pig. *Vet. Scope* **16**, 12–20.

McGuire, E. A., Young, V. R., Newberne, P. M., and Payne, B. J. (1968). Effects of *Salmonella typhimurium* infection. *Arch. Pathol.* **86**, 60–68.

Maassen, W. (1951). Über die durch streptokokken der C-gruppe hero-orgerufene lymphadenitis purulenta oposthemotosa der meerschweinchen. (Purulent lymphadenitis of guinea pigs caused by streptococcus group C.) *Arch. Hyg. Bakteriol.* **135**, 57–65.

Matejovska, D., and Kral, J. (1968). Salmonella surveillance in Czeckoslovakia. II. The occurrence of salmonella serotypes in veterinary material in the years 1963–64. *J. Hyg., Epidemiol., Microbiol., Immunol.* **12**, 192–200.

Matejovska, D., and Kral, J. (1970). Salmonella surveillance in Czeckoslovakia. IV. The occurrence of salmonella serotypes in veterinary material in the year 1965. *J. Hyg., Epidemiol., Microbiol., Immunol.* **14**, 110–118.

Maternowska, I. (1931). Beobachtungen uber eine Meerschweinchen-paratyphusepidemie (*Paratyphus cavium*). *Z. Infectionskr. Haustiere* **38**, 50–63.

Megrail, E., and Hoyt, R. N. (1929). Epizootic lymphadenitis in guinea pigs. *J. Infec. Dis.* **44**, 243–249.

Menges, R. W., and Galton, M. M. (1961). Direct cultural methods for the isolation of leptospires from experimentally infected guinea pigs. *Amer. J. Vet. Res.* **22**, 1085–1092.

Meyer, K. F., and Batchelder, A. P. (1926). Selective mediums in the diagnosis of rodent plague. *J. Infec. Dis.* **39**, 370–385.

Meyer, K. F., and Eddie, B. (1952). Disease problems in guinea pigs. *Proc. Anim. Care Panel* **3**, 23–39.

Morse, E. V., Roberstad, G. W., Wipf, L., and Glattli, H. R. (1952). A study of the pathogenicity of *Corynebacterium pyogenes* for laboratory white mice, hamsters, and rabbits. *Cornell Vet.* **42**, 368–379.

Nabb, D. P., and O'Dell, B. L. (1964). Influence of dietary factors upon *Salmonella typhimurium* infection in the guinea pig. *J. Nutr.* **84**, 191–199.

Nakagawa, M., Muto, T., Yoda, H., Nakano, T., and Imaizumi, K. (1971). Experimental *Bordetella bronchiseptica* infection in guinea pigs. *Jap. J. Vet. Sci.* **33**, 53–60.

Nakamura, Y. (1941). An epizootic outbreak of septicemia in guinea pigs due to *Salmonella moscow.* (In Japanese.) *Dojinkai Igaku Zasshi* **15**, 599–613.

Nakase, Y. (1957). Studies on *Hemophilus bronchisepticus.* I. The antigenic structures of *H. bronchisepitcus* from guinea pigs. *Kitasato Arch. Exp. Med.* **30**, 57–72.

Nedjalkov, S., Dragonov, M., and Pejtschev, B. (1966). Guinea pig diseases caused by *Cl. perfringens* Type A. (In German.) *Arch. Exp. Veterinaermed.* **20**, 323–325.

Nishimura, T. (1942). Die infection durch die salmonella-gruppe bei den verschiedenen kleintieren in Hokkaido. (In Japanese, summary in German.) *Jap. J. Vet. Sci.* **4**, 649–662.

O'Dell, B. L., Nabb, D. P., Garner, G. B., and Regan, W. O. (1961). A salmonellosis resistance factor for the guinea pig. *Proc. Soc. Exp. Biol. Med.* **108**, 512–514.

Ohder, H. (1969). Microbiological problems in experimental animal breeding. (In German.) *Bibl. Microbiol.* **7**, 42–53.

Okamoto, T. (1926). Epidemiologische beobachtungen an mause und meerschweinchen. (In German.) *Klin. Wochenschr.* **5**, 795–796.

Olitzki, A. L., and Godinger, D. (1965). Accumulation of a soluble antigen in the peritoneal fluid of guinea pigs infected with *Salmonella typhi. J. Infec. Dis.* **115,** 303–311.

Paget, G. E. (1954). Exudative hepatitis in guinea pigs. *J. Pathol. Bacteriol.* **67,** 393–400.

Paterson, J. S., and Cook, R. (1955). Naturally occurring *Salmonella limete* infection in guinea pigs. *J. Pathol. Bacteriol.* **70,** 242–245.

Pestana de Castro, A. F., Santa Rosa, C. A., and Troise, C. (1961a). The wild guinea pig (*Cavia aperea ayarea*) as reservoir of *Leptospira ioterohaemorrhagica* in Brazil. *Biologica* **27,** 207–209.

Pestana de Castro, A. F., Santa Rosa, C. A., and Troise, C. (1961b). Wild guinea pig (*Cavia aperea*) as reservoir of leptospirosis in Brazil. *Arq. Inst. Biol. (Sao Paulo)* **28,** 219–224.

Pivnick, H., Stuart, P. F., and Walcroft, M. (1966). Establishment of a salmonella-free guinea pig colony. *Can. J. Comp. Med. Vet. Sci.* **30,** 279–281.

Porter, G., and Lane-Petter, W. (1962). Common diseases in guinea pigs. *In* "Notes for Breeders of Common Laboratory Animals" (G. Porter and W. Lane-Petter, eds.), pp. 25–27. Academic Press, London and New York.

Rabstein, M. M. (1958). The practical establishment and maintenance of salmonella-free mouse colonies. *Proc. Anim. Care Panel* **8,** 67–74.

Raebiger, H. (1923). "Das Meerschweinchen: Seine Zucht, Haltung, Und Krankheiten." von Schlaper, Hannover.

Rake, G. (1938). Active immunity against an intestinal and a respiratory infection. *Amer. J. Hyg.* **28,** 377–389.

Ramisse (1961). *Haemophilus bronchisepticus* bronchopneumonia in a guinea pig colony. *Rev. Med. Vet.* **112,** 118–120.

Ratcliffe, H. L. (1945). Infectious diseases of laboratory animals. *Ann. N. Y. Acad. Sci.* **46,** 77–96.

Ray, J. P., and Mallick, B. B. (1970). Public health significance of salmonella infections in laboratory animals. *Indian Vet. J.* **47,** 1033–1037.

Richter, G. W., and Kress, Y. (1967). Electron microscopy of a strain of *Bordetella bronchiseptica. J. Bacteriol.* **94,** 1216–1224.

Roine, P., Raito, A., and Vartiovaara, U. (1953). *Listeria* infection in the guinea pig caused by feeding with aureomycin. *Nature (London)* **172,** 767.

Roth, H. (1934). Zur bakteriologie und pathologie der fibrinösen serositis der meerschwinchen. *Bacterium caviarum pericarditis,* n. sp. *Acta Pathol. Microbiol. Scand.* **11,** 335–360.

Sakazaki, R. (1952). Distribution of salmonella in north Mie Perfecture. IV. Investigation into horses, cattle, swine, dogs, fowls, rats, guinea pigs and mice. (In Japanese.) *Jap. J. Vet. Sci.* **14,** 11–27.

Sakazaki, R., and Yamada, C. (1951). Studies on the SS agar and the comparative examination with this media for the isolation of salmonella from animals. (In Japanese.) *Jap. J. Vet. Sci.* **13,** 349–350.

Scherago, M. (1937). An epizootic septicemia of young guinea pigs caused by *Pseudomonas caviae.* N. Sp. *J. Infec. Dis.* **60,** 245–250.

Seastone, C. V. (1937). The effect of sulfanilimide (para-aminobenzenesulfonamide) on group "C" hemolytic streptococcus infections. *J. Immunol.* **33,** 403–406.

Sikinami, L., and Hosokawa, H. (1942). The isolation of *Salmonella blegdam* from live-stock breeder and guinea pigs. *Nippon Densembyo Gakkai Zasshi* **16,** 694–697.

Simeone, D. H., and Arambuell, H. G. (1967). Enzootic de Cobayos (*Cavia cabaya*) debida a *Salmonella typhimurium.* (Outbreak of *Salmonella typhimurium* infection in a guinea pig breeding unit). *Rev. Med. Vet.* **48,** 113–122.

Simon, H. J. (1963). Epidemiology and pathogenicity of staphylococcal infection. I. An experimentally induced attenuated staphylococcal infection in guinea pigs and its modification by tetracycline. *J. Exp. Med.* **118,** 149–164.

Smith, H. W. (1965). The development of the flora of the alimentary tract in young animals. *J. Pathol. Bacteriol.* **90,** 495–513.

Smith, H. W., and Halls, S. (1966). The immunity produced by a rough *Salmonella dublin* variant against *Salmonella typhimurium* and *Salmonella cholerasuis* infection in guinea-pigs. *J. Hyg.* **64,** 357–359.

Smith, T., and Nelson, J. B. (1927). Studies on a paratyphoid infection in guinea pigs. II. Factors involved in the transition from epidemic to endemic phase. *J. Exp. Med.* **45,** 365–377.

Smith, T., and Stewart, J. R. (1896–1897). Spontaneous pseudo -tuberculosis in a guinea pig, and the bacillus causing it. *J. Boston Soc. Med. Sci.* **1,** 12–17.

Somasundararao, G., and Surendron, N. S. (1971). A short note on salmonellosis in laboratory animals. *Indian Vet. J.* **48,** 336–337.

Splino, M., Peychl, L., Kyntera, F., and Kotrlik, J. (1969). Isolation of *Pasteurella pseudotuberculosis* from inguinal lymph nodes. *Zenbralbl. Bakteriol., Parasitenk., Infektionskr. Orig.* **211,** 360–364.

Takeuchi, A. (1967). Electron microscopic studies of experimental salmonella infection. I. Penetration into the intestinal epithelium by *Salmonella typhimurium. Amer. J. Pathol.* **50,** 109–136.

Tartakowsky, M. G. (1897–1898). Pneumonie contagieuse des cobayes. *Arch. Sci. Biol., St. Petersbourg* **6,** 255–284.

TenBroeck, C. (1920). A group of paratyphoid bacilli from animals closely resembling those found in man. *J. Exp. Med.* **32,** 19–31.

Thomas, B. G. H. (1924). Occurrence of organisms of the enteritidis paratyphoid B group in guinea pigs. *J. Infec. Dis.* **35,** 407–422.

Torres, C., Pacheco, G., and Cardoso, R. (1949). Streptococcal epizootic in guinea pigs. *Mem. Inst. Oswaldo Cruz* **47,** 701–706.

Treacher, J. H., and Burton, J. A. G. (1913–1914). Infective abortion in guinea pigs. *J. Pathol. Bacteriol.* **18,** 440–441.

Treacher, J. H., and Burton, J. A. G. (1915–1916). Infective abortion in guinea pigs. *J. Pathol. Bacteriol.* **20,** 14–20.

Trum, B. F., and Roultedge, J. K. (1967). Common disease problems in laboratory animals. *J. Amer. Vet. Med. Ass.* **151,** 1886–1896.

Uchida, Y. (1926). Experimentelle infecktionen von mäusen und meerschwinchen parenteral und den naturlichen eingangspforten aus. III. Versuche an meerschwinchen mit milzbranderregern, bacillen der hemerrhagischen septicämie und anderen pathogenen bakterien. *Z. Hyg. Infectionskr.* **106,** 281–307.

van Loghem, J. J. (1944–1945). The classification of the plague-bacillus. *Antonie van Leeuwenhoek; J. Microbiol. Serol.* **10,** 15.

Verma, N. S., and Sharma, S. P. (1969). Salmonellosis in laboratory animals. *Indian Vet. J.* **46,** 1101–1102.

Walker, E. L., and Sweeney, M. A. (1932). Some infections simulating experimental typhus in guinea pigs. *Amer. J. Trop. Med. Hyg.* **12,** 217–222.

Wherry, W. B. (1908). Experiments on the use of *Bacillus pestis-caviae* as a rat virus. *J. Infec. Dis.* **5,** 519–533.

Wren, W. B., and Twiehaus, M. J. (1968). Studies on the etiology, pathology, and control of cervical lymphadenitis in guinea pigs. *Proc. Anim. Lab. Med.* Abstr. No. 157.

Zydeck, F. A., Bennett, R. R., and Langham, R. F. (1970). Subacute pericarditis in a guinea pig caused by *Diplococcus pneumoniae. J. Amer. Vet. Med. Ass.* **157,** 1945–1947.

Chapter 10

Viral and Chlamydial Diseases

G. L. Van Hoosier, Jr., and L. R. Robinette

I. INTRODUCTION

The separation of virus infections of the guinea pig among those which occur naturally and those which are primarily experimental is necessary, although naturally occurring infections may also be induced experimentally. Viruses used in experimental studies may have other species as natural hosts but some viruses could conceivably infect normal guinea pigs under laboratory conditions where the agent is being used.

The authors acknowledge the aid of Dr. John C. Parker of Microbiological Associates for data on the occurrence of antibodies in guinea pigs to various rodent viruses. This information has not been previously published because parallel virus isolation studies were not performed. Therefore, one cannot be certain that the antibodies assayed were due to infection with the agent used as antigen in the serological test. Infection with distinct but antigenetically related agents or the occurrence of nonspecific inhibitors are possible alternative explanations for the results obtained. After reviewing the serological results, it was felt that the advantages of the contribution of otherwise unavailable information on the subject outweighed the disadvantages of the limitations of the data.

Methods for the control and prevention of virus infections in guinea pigs or other laboratory animals are limited and, for the most part, similar regardless of the agent. For these reasons, the topic is included in this section, except to the extent that the procedures may be different for specific viruses or for cases in which a particular technique should have special emphasis. Procurement of disease-free animals and isolation and examination of guinea pigs upon arrival are always indicated. Animals with clinical signs of disease must be quarantined to control spread of infections. Filter caps to cover cages and adoption of rigorous procedures to prevent cross-contamination between cages during cleaning procedures has been found effective in controlling or eliminating virus infections in mice and should be effective in guinea pigs.

Naturally Occurring Virus and Psittacosis-Lymphogranuloma-Trachoma Group Infections

These viruses are listed in Table I with information on their prevalence, significance, classification, and nucleic acid type.

Table I

Naturally Occurring Virus Infections of the Guinea Pig

Agent/disease	Prevalence[a]	Significance: Morbidity and mortality	Model	Complication	Genus or group	Nucleic Acid
Poliovirus	++ (16%)	X		X	*Enterovirus*	
Reovirus type 3 (Reo-3)	+ (4%)			X	*Reovirus*	
Pneumonia virus mice (PVM)	++ (23%)			X	*Paramyxovirus*	
Simian virus 5 (SV5)	++ (25%)			X	*Paramyxovirus*	RNA
Sendai virus	++ (9%)	X		X	*Paramyxovirus*	
Leukemia (type C virus)	?	X	X		*Leukovirus*	
Lymphocytic choriomeningitis	+	X		X	*Arenavirus*	
Cytomegalovirus (salivary gland virus)	++	X	X	X	*Herpesvirus*	
Guinea pig herpes-like viruses (GPHLV)	+		X	X	*Herpesvirus*	DNA
Guinea pig pox-like virus (GPPLV)	+	X		X	*Poxvirus*	
Guinea pig inclusion conjunctivitis virus (GPIC)	+	X	X	X	Psittacosis group (PLT)	RNA and DNA
Myositis	+	X	X	X	Unclassified	Unclassified
Wasting disease	+	X		X	Unclassified	Unclassified
Highly fatal disease	+	X		X	Unclassified	Unclassified
Hepatoenteritis	+	X		X	Unclassified	Unclassified
Virus pneumonia	+	X		X	Unclassified	Unclassified

[a]Prevalence: Percent of approximately 200 guinea pigs with antibodies in studies of J.C. Parker (personal communication, 1972). + Uncommon; ++ common; ? unknown.

In regard to prevalence, infections were considered uncommon if the percent of guinea pigs with antibodies was less than 5% and if only a single or occasional report appeared in the literature. Designations under the column entitled significance refer to whether the agent is a potential cause of illness and death in a colony, whether it is potentially a good model for a similar disease in other animals including man, or whether it is significant as a complication of other types of experiments with guinea pigs.

In studies by J. C. Parker (personal communication, 1972), 200 guinea pig sera tested from 16 different colonies had no detectable antibodies to these following agents: K virus, polyoma virus, minute virus of mice, rat virus, H-1 virus, vaccinia, mouse adenovirus, mouse hepatitis virus, and lymphocytic choriomeningitis virus.

II. RNA VIRUSES

A. Enteroviruses: Poliovirus

1. General

The enteroviruses are small relatively stable RNA viruses varying in size between 17 and 28 nm. Members include polioviruses, rhinoviruses, and the etiological agent of foot and mouth disease. The basis for the inclusion of this group in this chapter is somewhat tenuous but relates to the serological data of J. C. Parker (personal communication, 1972) and early reports by Rohrer on a disease he called guinea pig lameness and a similar disease described by Gasperi and Sangiorgi, called guinea pig pest (Rohrer *et al.*, 1958).

Determination of the specific etiology will require additional investigation. Rohrer isolated a filterable agent from the brain, spinal cord, and lymph nodes of affected animals. In serological studies by Parker, guinea pig sera reacted positively when the GD-VII strain of mouse polio was used as antigen, suggesting common antigens although the similarities of any biological properties remain to be determined.

Forty-five of 197 (23%) guinea pig sera had antibodies in the hemagglutination-inhibition (HAI)-test with murine poliovirus antigen. Description of clinical disease associated with poliovirus infection has not been recently reported. It appears that disease, in contrast to infection, is rare. Its significance therefore is either as a cause of morbidity and mortality or as a potential complication for other types of animal experimentation.

No information is available on the epizootiology and it is doubtful if there is any potential public health hazard as the murine polioviruses are not infectious for man.

2. Clinical Signs

Affected animals were pyrexic with progressive development of flaccid paralysis and loss of weight within an incubation period of 9 to 23 days. The duration of the condition was 1 to 2 weeks (Rohrer *et al.*, 1958).

3. Pathology

Microscopic changes were those of a meningomyeloencephalitis with degenerative and inflammatory changes of neurons. Sites of the central nervous system affected included the lumbar region of the spinal cord and the medulla oblongata (Rohrer *et al.*, 1958).

4. Diagnosis

A presumptive diagnosis may be made based upon characteristic signs of flaccid paralysis of one or more extremities and lesions of degeneration or necrosis in anterior horn cells of the spinal cord. A definitive diagnosis would depend upon isolation and characterization of the virus. Procedures similar to those described for murine and human polioviruses would be indicated.

B. Reoviruses: Reovirus Type 3

Reoviruses are ubiquitous and infect a variety of birds and animals, including laboratory rodents. They are approximately 70 nm in size, relatively stable, and produce hemagglutins which permit the use of the HAI test for detection of antibodies. Serological evidence of infection is common in mice although their association with disease, e.g., enteritis or encephalitis, is uncommon.

In the studies of J. C. Parker (personal communication, 1972), 8 of 188 sera had HAI antibodies to reovirus type 3 at a dilution of 1:20 or greater. The percent of animals with antibodies is relatively low as compared to mice (Parker *et al.*, 1966), and problems of interpretation of serological data are particularly noteworthy with these agents. Accordingly, these observations mainly suggest the possibility of infection with reovirus 3 in guinea pigs. Other aspects of the infection in rodents including signs of the disease and procedures for the diagnosis of infection are described by Calisher and Rowe (1966).

C. Paramyxoviruses: Sendai Virus, Simian Virus 5, and Pneumonia Virus of Mice

This group of agents is commonly associated with highly contagious respiratory disease in various mammalian species, e.g., parainfluenza 5 in cattle and distemper in dogs. They are relatively labile and 100–300 nm in diameter.

Pneumonia virus of mice (PVM) is a common enzootic infection of laboratory mice (Tennant *et al.*, 1966). Antibodies have also been demonstrated in hamsters and rats. The agent can be isolated from animals without apparent disease although serial passage by intranasal inoculation of mice under ether anesthesia results in an interstitial pneumonia. J. C. Parker (personal communication, 1972) detected antibodies in approximately 23% of 197 guinea pig sera tested. Its significance in guinea pigs other than as a nuisance to other types of experiments remains to be determined.

Simian virus 5 (SV5) was initially isolated from monkey kidney cell cultures. Included with it in the parainfluenza 5 group of agents are isolates from humans and dogs (Wilner, 1969). These strains are antigenically identical by serological tests. Which species serves as the natural host and reservoir for these agents is unknown. Whether infection is associated with disease or not is undetermined at this time. Antibodies to SV5 have been detected in sera from Syrian hamsters and guinea pigs although there have been no attempts to isolate the agent (Van Hoosier *et al.*, 1970; J. C. Parker, personal communication, 1972). Forty-nine of 196 guinea pig sera tested had HAI antibodies to SV5 (J. C. Parker, personal communication, 1972). The significance of these observations remains to be determined although the presence of the antibodies suggest that the agent is present and could potentially interfere with experiments in guinea pigs.

Sendai virus (parainfluenza 1) was reported to be isolated from children with respiratory disease in Japan and subsequently the agent was found to be indigenous in mouse colonies in both Japan and the United States (Fukumi *et al.*, 1962; Parker *et al.*, 1964). Antibodies have also been detected in rats and hamsters (Tennant *et al.*, 1966). Overt clinical disease in rodents is usually associated with various types of stress (Robinson *et al.*, 1969). Nine percent or 18 of 199 guinea pig sera tested had antibodies to Sendai virus antigen in the HAI test, and on one occasion, Sendai virus was isolated from guinea pigs in a colony associated with mice (J. C. Parker, personal communication, 1972). These observations suggest that this agent may at times cause disease or interfere with animal experimentation in guinea pigs as in other rodents.

Serological reactivity between guinea pig sera and other agents of the parainfluenza group may interfere with the use of guinea pig serum as a source of complement and suggests the existence of other viruses of this group indigenous to guinea pigs (Chanock *et al.*, 1958; K. D. Quist, personal communication, 1973).

D. Leukoviruses

1. General

Viruses associated with malignancies of the hematopoietic system have been isolated from chickens, mice, hamsters, cats, and other species. The mature virus particles are commonly designated as type B or C depending on whether the electron dense nucleoid is located eccentrically or centrally, respectively.

a. History. Congdon and Lorenz (1954) described ten cases of spontaneous lymphatic leukemia, and two lines, L2B and L2C, were established by serial transplantation in strain 2 inbred guinea pigs.

Reports on the incidence of cavian leukemia vary but was found to be 3.3% in one study (Congdon and Lorenz, 1954). The impression that guinea pigs have a lower incidence may be attributable to the relatively short life span of experimental animals and the failure to carefully examine blood and bone marrow at necropsy (Ediger and Rabstein, 1958; Opler, 1971).

b. Etiology. By electron microscopy, particles similar to type C virus particles of mice have been observed in tissues of leukemic guinea pigs (Fig. 1) (Nadel *et al.*, 1967; Opler, 1967c). The particles range from 800 to 1000 Å in diameter and appear in the area of the nuclear envelope and cisternae of the endoplasmic reticulum (Ioachim and Berwick, 1969; Feldman and Gross, 1970). The immature particle has a dense inner shell and a thick granular outer coat with a dense, spherical, centrally located nucleoid giving it a double membrane doughnut appearance. Particles form by budding from the membrane of the endoplasmic reticulum. Immature par-

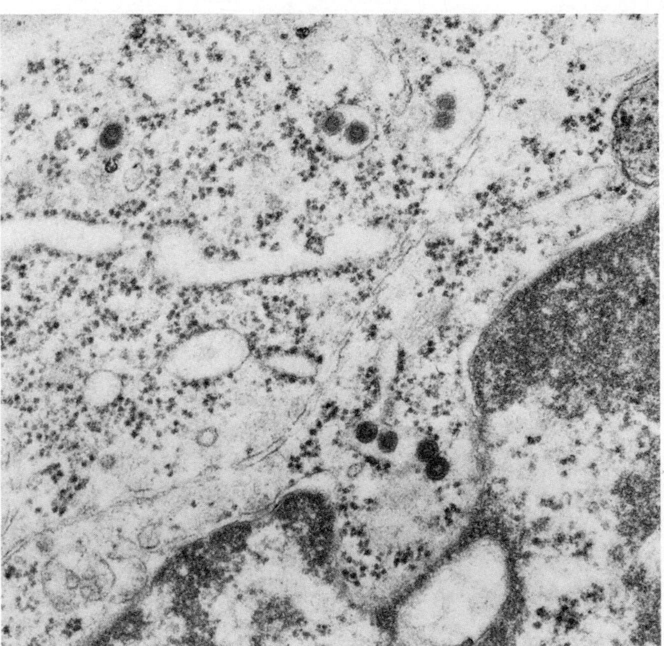

Fig. 1. Guinea pig leukemia virus particles in an infiltrating leukemic cell in the ovary of a leukemic guinea pig; magnification 44,000×. Electron micrograph prepared by D. G. Feldman and L. Gross, Cancer Research Unit, Veterans Administration Hospital, Bronx, New York.

ticles were within cisternae of endoplasmic reticulum and rarely in intercellular spaces. Mature particles were only in intercellular spaces (Feldman and Gross, 1970). With respect to size, number of particles generally observed, structure of the nucleoid, and cellular site of maturation, there are differences between the guinea pig agent and those commonly observed in the mouse, rat, and cat (Gross and Feldman, 1970).

Infectivity of the leukemia agent can be preserved by freezing at -90° C for 5 months. It can be destroyed by ultraviolet light, X-rays, and incubation at 56°C for 30 minutes. It is resistant to trypsin but sensitive to ether, acetone, sodium deoxycholate, and formalin (Opler, 1967c).

The etiological relationship between the type C particles of guinea pigs and cavian leukemia requires further investigation and clarification (Feldman and Gross, 1970; Ioachim and Berwick, 1969). Noteworthy in this regard are reports of virus particles in tissues of normal guinea pigs (Ma *et al.*, 1969) and observations on guinea pig herpesviruses (Section II, A, 2).

c. Significance. Cavian leukemia may prove to be a useful animal homologue for the disease in humans. Similarities between the two include a rapidly fulminating course with lymphocyte counts of 100,000 to 250,000/mm^3, frequent infiltration of practically all organ systems, origin from bone marrow, and response to therapeutic agents (Opler, 1971).

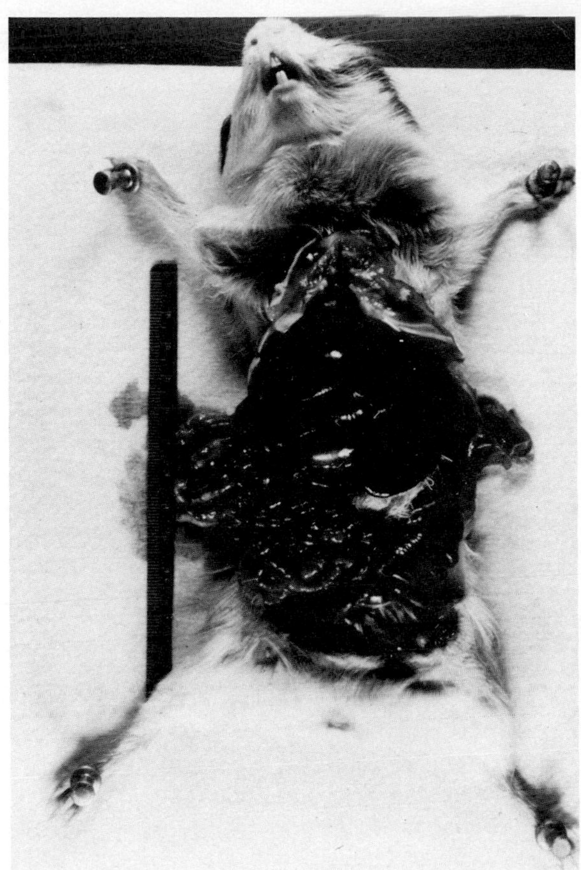

Fig. 2. Guinea pig leukemia: Organs *in situ.* (Contributed by and with the permission of Stanley R. Opler.)

2. Signs and Pathology

a. The Natural Disease. Initial signs may be similar to those of any serious illness, i.e., ruffling of the hair, pale mucous membranes, sluggishness, and dull eyes. Greatly enlarged peripheral and mesenteric lymph nodes may be present before death (Ediger and Rabstein, 1968; Congdon and Lorenz, 1954; Opler, 1971). White blood cell counts may range from 25,000 to 250,000/mm^3. There may be thrombocytopenia. Leukemic cells usually resemble lymphoblasts (Congdon and Lorenz, 1954; Opler, 1971; Ioachim and Berwick, 1969; Feldman and Gross, 1970). On necropsy, grossly enlarged lymph nodes, splenomegaly, and hepatomegaly are usually present. Microscopically, lymphoblastic cells may infiltrate many tissues, especially perivascularly. The spleen, cervical and mesenteric lymph nodes, Peyer's patches, and bone marrow are all heavily invaded if not entirely replaced with leukemic cells (Ioachim and Berwick, 1969; Opler, 1967a).

b. The Experimental Disease. Serial transplantation with neoplastic spleen cells suspensions of L2C leukemia results in an incubation period of 2 to 3 weeks with 100% morbidity and mortality (Fig. 2) (Opler, 1967b; Ioachim and Berwick, 1969). Small firm subcutaneous tumors develop at the site of inoculation, gradually increase in size, and in 7 to 10 days result in generalized leukemia. Within 5 to 10 days peripheral blood counts of 250,000 to 500,000 WBC/mm^3 of primitive stem cells (Fig. 3) are seen accompanied by an anemia (Gross *et al.*, 1970; Ioachim and Berwick, 1969).

Leukemia can be transmitted by inoculation of cell suspension, plasma pellets and by oral feeding of leukemic spleen suspensions (Opler, 1968a,b,c; Gross *et al.*, 1970). Transplacental transmission from leukemic-susceptible mother to fetus has been reported (Jungeblut and Kodza, 1962a). Transmission with cell-free filtrates has met with failure by many investigators (Gross *et al.*, 1970; Feldman and Gross, 1970; Sarma *et al.*, 1969), although Opler (1967c) has reported successful transmission with filtered and differentially centrifuged material. The very short latency period, the narrow and specific strain susceptibility, and the inability to infect other than strain 2 or F_1 hybrids usually indicates transmission by cell graft (Gross *et al.*, 1970). Chromosomal studies of the present L2C leukemia indicate blast cells are of the female karyotype. The original leukemia arose in a strain 2 female implying that present lines are all transplantations of the original tumor (Sarma *et al.*, 1969).

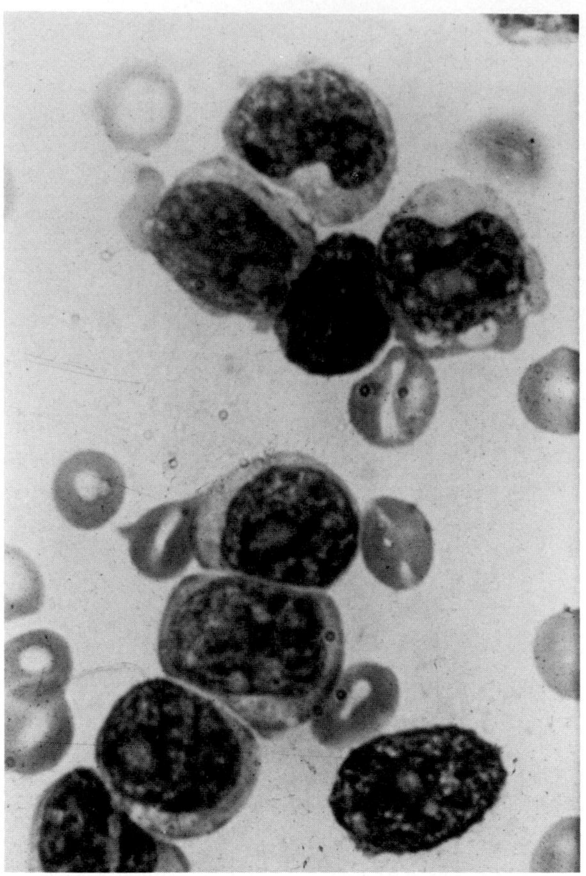

Fig. 3. Guinea pig leukemia: Lymphoblasts in peripheral blood. (Contributed by and with the permission of Stanley R. Opler.)

E. Arenaviruses: Lymphocytic Choriomeningitis

1. General

a. History. This taxonomic group was recently established for several morphologically and serologically related agents including lymphocytic choriomeningitis and arboviruses of the Tacaribe group.

Lymphocytic choriomeningitis (LCM) occurs as a natural disease in the guinea pig. Other species naturally susceptible are mice, chinchillas, cotton rats, foxes, dogs, monkeys, and man. Experimental infections have been induced in the rabbit, hamster, ferret, dog, and horse. Cattle, pigs, cats, and chickens are not susceptible (Maurer, 1964).

Most of the literature on LCM is concerned with the disease in mice. Wild mice and chronically infected mouse colonies are the usual reservoirs of LCM and represent a twofold threat of disease: (1) as a masked latent contaminant in other virus systems; and (2) as a public health hazard because LCM is transmissible to man and can cause a rare fatal infection (Hotchin, 1971; Maurer, 1964).

Various agents isolated from or in the guinea pig may in retrospect have been LCM. These include Durand's virus (Durand, 1940), the agent associated with respiratory disease described by Lepine *et al.*, in 1943 (refer to Section V, D, Virus Pneumonia), African epidemic icterus virus (Pellissier and Lumaret, 1948; Pellissier, 1949, 1953; S. S. Cross, J. A. Morris, and J. C. Parker, personal communication, 1973), and Pellissier's virus (Pellissier *et al.*, 1950).

b. Etiology. LCM virus is a lipoprotein-enveloped RNA virus, approximately 50 nm in diameter and is relatively heat labile since 56°C for 20 minutes inactivates it (Hotchin, 1971; Wilsnack, 1966). Multiple discrete electron-dense bodies within the virion give it a unique appearance. LCM virus, the Machupo-Tacaribe group and Lassa virus have been placed in a new group called the arenaviruses based on their identical appearance and other findings (Hotchin, 1971).

Strains of LCM virus differ in their pathogenicity and tissue tropism but there is only one antigenic type. It is inactivated by ultraviolet light and 0.05% formalin but remains viable when frozen or in the lyophilized state. It is insensitive to 0.5% phenol solutions. Virus is present in all tissues and fluids of infected animals but liver has proved to be the most desirable organ for virus detection by immunofluorescence (Wilsnak, 1966; Maurer, 1964; Hotchin, 1971).

c. Incidence and Significance. There are numerous examples of LCM virus as a significant contaminant of experimental results. The first report of LCM (Armstrong and Lillie, 1934) was as a contaminant of their investigation of St. Louis encephalitis. Since then it has been reported in association with canine distemper, mycoplasma, rabies virus, murine poliovirus, lymphosarcoma, Ehrlich carcinoma, and *Toxoplasma gondii* (Hotchin, 1971). There are several examples in which LCM virus was found to contaminate leukemias. Experimental infection of guinea pigs with LCM virus significantly prolonged the life of animals bearing transplantable leukemia L2B/N and L2C (Hotchin, 1971; Jungeblut and Kodza, 1962b). LCM virus infection apparently functions as an interference system with the leukemia agent rather than as an oncolytic agent (Jungeblut and Kodza, 1962b).

d. Public Health Aspects. Human infection can result from contact with LCM infected animals or infective tissue culture material (Hotchin, 1971). Transmission occurs readily by direct contact via the conjunctiva, respiratory tract, digestive tract, or through the intact skin. Blood-sucking insects have been shown to transmit the disease (Maurer, 1964). Human infections with LCM vary in severity from inapparent to a rare fatal systemic response. One survey revealed 12% of 2000 randomly selected human serum samples had neutralizing antibody with no associated history of clinical illness (Maurer, 1964). The most common form of the disease in man is a mild influenza-like illness sometimes with meningitis, rarely with encephalitis, myocarditis, parotitis, orchitis, pneumonia, and very rarely as a fatal, severe, nonsuppurative lymphocytic meningoencephalomyelitis (Hotchin, 1971; Maurer, 1964).

2. Signs and Pathology

Little information is available on the clinical signs in the guinea pig although they are well described for the mouse. Some controversy exists over the question of whether a persistent latent infection can exist in species other than the mouse. In the mouse there are three basic reactions to the LCM virus: (1) clinical LCM and death; (2) clinical signs may or may not be present and immunity develops; or (3) a chronic infection with transient or life-long viremia and resistance to challenge with homologous virus without the development of humoral antibody. Reactions are age related with the first two being most likely with exposure 48 hours postpartum and the third following *in utero* exposure. Signs of disease are attributable to the host's response rather than viral replication (Wilsnack, 1966).

LCM in guinea pigs is a neurological syndrome with signs of meningitis and hind leg paralysis (Jungeblut and Kodza, 1962b). Gross lesions may be minimal although viral pneumonia, pulmonary edema, pleural exudate, fatty liver, and enlarged spleen may be noted. Microscopically, lymphocytic infiltration predominates in the meninges especially at the base of the brain, choroid plexus, and ependyma (Maurer, 1964). There is a marked lymphocytic infiltrate in liver, adrenals, kidneys, and lungs (Hotchin, 1971).

3. Diagnosis

The simplest method of demonstrating LCM virus is to inoculate tissue suspensions from affected animals into groups of LCM-free mice by the intracranial route. Occurrence of typical clonic convulsions after 6 to 10 days is suggestive of LCM. Convulsions may be initiated in the sick mouse by picking it up by the tail and twirling it. The diagnosis can be confirmed by giving the same inocula to mice previously immunized against LCM; these mice will not exhibit convulsions or death. Mice can be inoculated via the foot pad (FP) with suspected material; gross edema of FP in the next 7 to 14 days is suggestive of LCM (Hotchin, 1971). Parenteral inoculation of suspect materials in LCM-free guinea pigs generally result in death if virus is present.

4. Control and Prevention

Since wild mice are considered natural reservoirs of infection, all attempts at control must be directed toward isolating the laboratory animal colony from contact with wild rodents. Feed, bedding material, and water must be from noncontaminated sources. Insects and external parasites must be eliminated from the colony since ticks, mosquitoes, bedbugs, fleas, *Trichinella spiralis*, nematodes, flies, and body lice have been implicated in transmissions of LCM (Hotchin, 1971).

Dogs and monkeys have been the source of infection to other laboratory animal species. Therefore, separation of colonies by species, especially mice, is recommended. Laboratory workers should be aware of the fact that not only airborne transmission is possible but also that urine of infected laboratory animals may contain virus (Maurer, 1964).

III. DNA VIRUSES

A. Herpesviruses

1. Cytomegalovirus (Salivary Gland Virus)

a. General. i. History. Jackson (1920) first described cytoplasmic and intranuclear inclusion bodies in the ductal epithelium of guinea pig salivary gland. She regarded them as an intracellular stage of a protozoan parasite, most probably a coccidium. Cole and Kuttner (1926) reported the cause of the inclusions as a filterable virus. Since that time several species of animals including man, mice, and guinea pigs have been found to have their own cytomegaloviruses (CMV) or salivary gland viruses as they were first called. In the last 15 years much interest and research has been manifested in the human cytomegalovirus infections. Guinea pig CMV bears some similarity to human CMV suggesting that it may be an appropriate model for the human infection (Smith, 1959).

ii. Comparative aspects. In recent years considerable effort has been spent unraveling the causal relationship of human CMV with a myriad of clinical illnesses (Weller, 1971a,b). In cases of intrauterine infection, encephalitis may occur in the infant with various degrees of central nervous system damage. The disease in 2- to 4-month-old infants has diverse clinical manifestations referable to the localization of the viral infection, e.g., interstitial pneumonitis or enteritis.

Recently a CMV respiratory disease was recognized in renal allograft recipients on immunosuppressive therapy, and infection has been causally associated with either spontaneous or posttransfusion mononucleosis. Other possible CMV entities in man include autoimmune hemolytic anemia, hepatitis, pancreatitis, polioneuritis, and myocarditis.

iii. Etiology. Cytomegaloviruses are relatively labile to ether, heat, freezing and thawing, and prolonged storage at $-70°C$. Viral replication is associated with intranuclear inclusion bodies and the agents may persist in infected hosts for long periods of time (Smith, 1959; Weller, 1971a,b). Most cytomegaloviruses are relatively species specific as attempts to transmit the guinea pig CMV to rabbits, rats, cats, chickens, pigeons, dogs, mice, hamsters, and rhesus monkeys have been unsuccessful (Cook, 1958).

Initial isolation of the agents in tissue culture is difficult but after several serial transfers, isolates apparently adapt and *in vitro* propagation becomes easier (Weller, 1971a).

iv. Incidence. The infection in guinea pigs is assumed to be widespread in affected colonies; 70 to 80% of guinea pigs 6 months of age and older may have typical inclusions in their salivary glands (Cook, 1958). In the natural disease no clinical signs or gross lesions have been associated with the infection (Cook, 1958). The question remains whether or not this persistent latent virus infection may have an association with an unrecognized clinical illness.

v. Epizootiology. While developing a complement fixation test for the guinea pig cytomegalovirus, Hartley *et al.* (1957) found that most commercially available complement contained high titers of antibody to the virus. Serological surveys of several guinea pig colonies established age and incidence of infection. Maternal antibody was present in guinea pigs 4 weeks of age and younger; infection evidently took place after 5 months of age.

b. Signs and Pathology. The typical microscopic lesions of guinea pig CMV are eosinophilic intranuclear and rarely intracytoplasmic inclusion bodies in ductal epithelium of salivary glands (Fig. 4) of epithelium of proximal and distal convoluted tubules of the kidney (Cook, 1958; Smith and Jones, 1968). In salivary glands affected cells may be enlarged up to four times normal size and may bulge into the lumen of the duct. Kidney cells do not appear to be greatly enlarged (Cook, 1958). In the human disease exfoliative cytology of saliva and urine sediments has been used as a diagnostic aid (Weller, 1971b). Intranuclear inclusions vary in size and may be kidney shaped. They are usually surrounded by a clear halo and chromatin is marginated against the nuclear membrane (Cook, 1958). Cytoplasmic inclusions appear as round masses of clumped basophilic granules and are best seen in Giemsa-stained sections. There may be mononuclear cell infiltrates in affected areas (Cook, 1958).

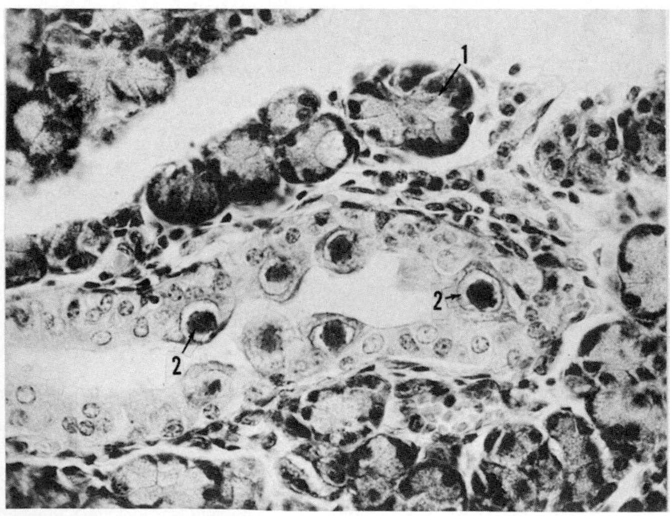

Fig. 4. Cytomegalovirus inclusion bodies in the duct cells for the salivary glands of the guinea pig. 1, Salivary acinar epithelium; 2, intranuclear inclusions in epithelium of a duct. (From J. C. Jones, "Veterinary Pathology," 1968, with permission.)

As a result of experimental inoculation of virus into susceptible guinea pigs by most routes, the microscopic lesions are similar to those of the natural disease except that the site of inoculation becomes infiltrated by mononuclear cells some of which contain inclusion bodies (Cook, 1958). Subsequent to intracerebral inoculation, a meningitis develops with fever, weakness, uncoordination, and convulsive movements; the animals become moribund within 5 to 6 days (Hartley *et al.*, 1957). Rarely is there encephalomyelitis (Cook, 1958), but marked mononuclear meningitis occurs throughout the spinal cord. Typical inclusions are seen in the mononuclear cells (Hartley *et al.*, 1957; Cook, 1958; Smith, 1959).

Pappenheimer and Slanetz (1942) reported on a generalized visceral disease in a small group of guinea pigs on nutritional experiments. Clinical signs were gradual weight loss, inappetence, lethargy, and dullness. At necropsy characteristic intranuclear inclusions were in several organs. Although they were unable to transmit the disease to other guinea pigs, their description resembles that of generalized CMV infection in other species.

2. Guinea Pig Herpes-Like Viruses (GPHLV)

a. General. i. History. A herpes-like virus of guinea pigs (GPHLV) was first isolated by Hsiung and Kaplow (1969b) during a general study on latent virus infections in laboratory animals. GPHLV was detected in degenerating kidney cell cultures from both leukemic and nonleukemic strain 2 guinea pigs (Fig. 5). Since then it has been isolated from tissues of other strains of guinea pig (Hsiung and Kaplow, 1969a; Hsiung *et al.*, 1971; Bhatt *et al.*, 1971).

ii. Etiology. The Hsiung–Kaplow herpes virus of GPHLV is different from the cytomegalovirus of guinea pigs although they are morphologically similar herpesviruses (Hsiung *et al.*, 1971; Lam and Hsiung, 1971a,b). As seen by light microscopy, large Feulgen-positive intranuclear inclusions indicate the virus contains DNA (Hsiung and Kaplow, 1969b). Electron microscopically, cells of degenerated tissue cultures had numerous single membrane-bound immature particles with or without electron-dense cores in the nuclear matrix. Double membrane-

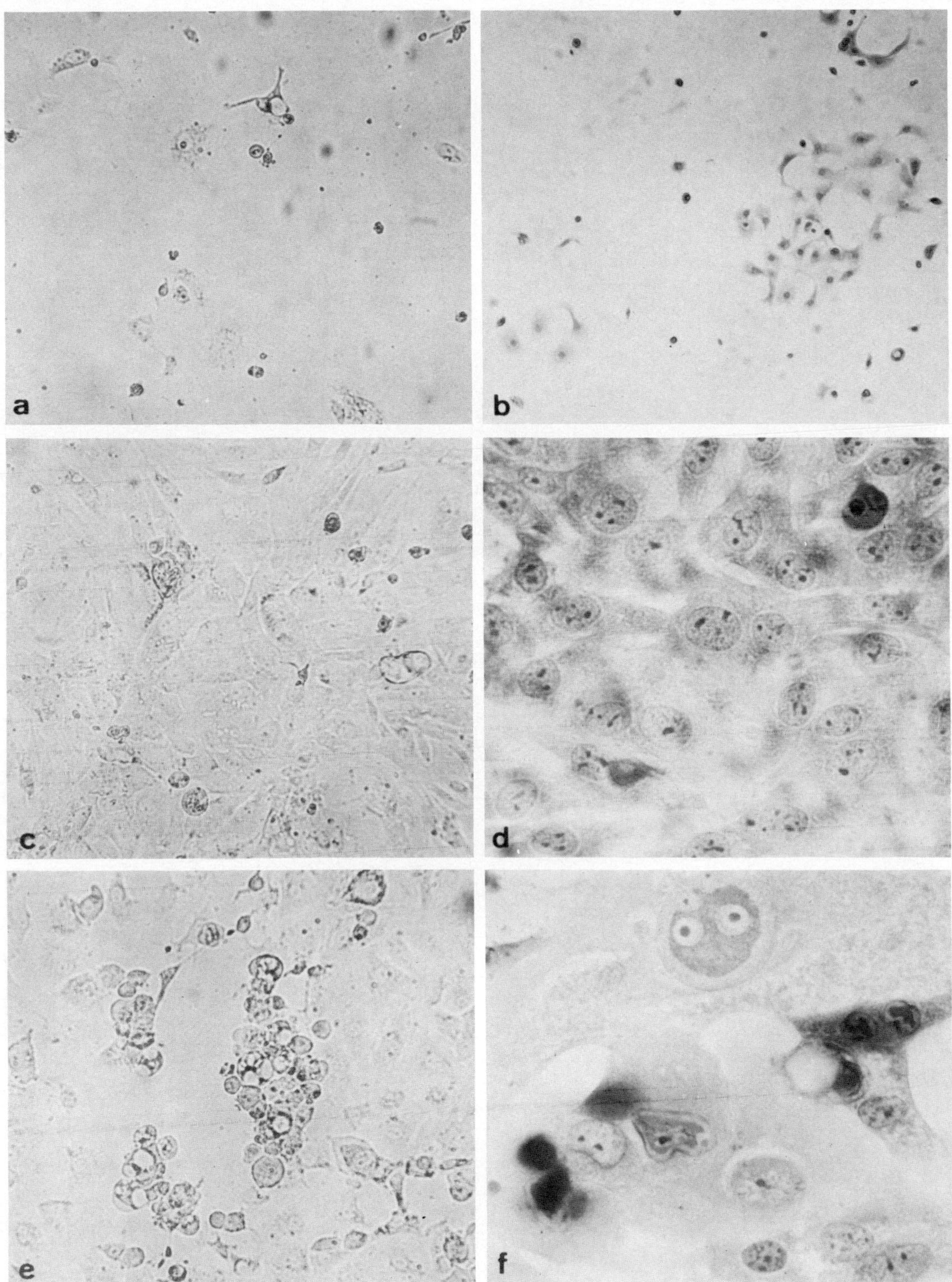

Fig. 5. Photomicrographs of kidney cell cultures infected with a herpes-like virus of guinea pigs. (From Hsiung and Kaplow, *J. Virol.* 1969b, with permission of G. D. Hsiung.)

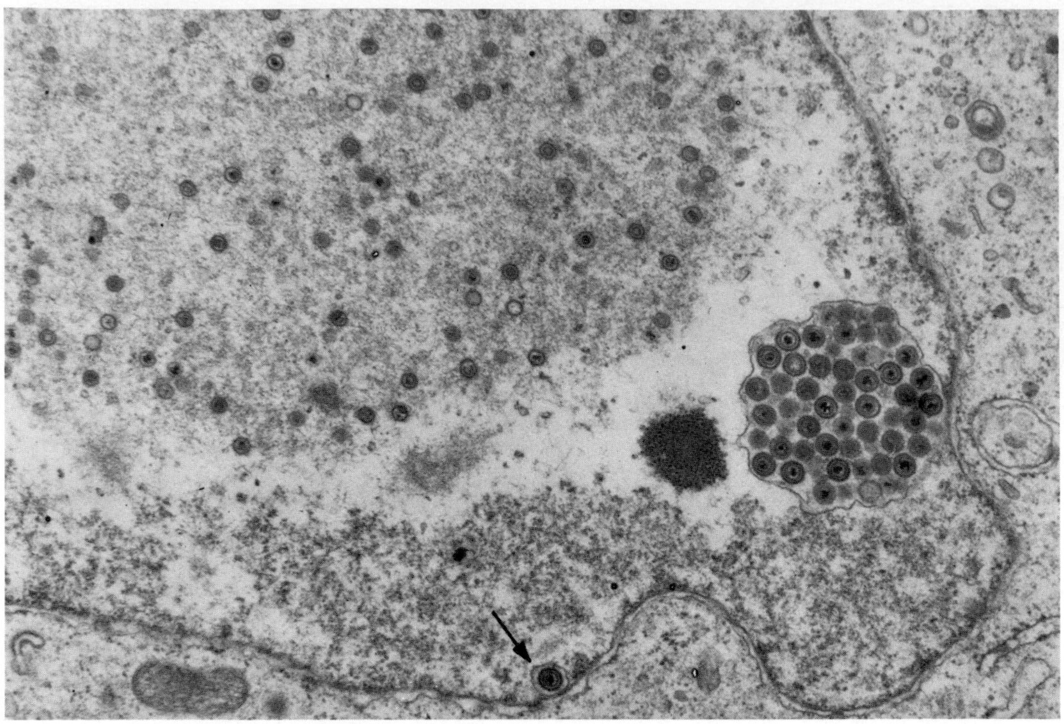

Fig. 6. Electron micrograph of a herpes-like virus of guinea pigs. (From Hsiung and Kaplow, *J. Virol.,* 1969b, with permission of G. D. Hsiung.)

bound mature particles closely packed within a vesicle were also in the nuclei (Fig. 6). The particles ranged in diameter from 100 to 160 nm. The virus is ether sensitive and has an icosahedral capsid.

iii. Significance. GPHLV may be a suitable model for persistent virus infection or virus-induced neoplastic disease (Lam and Hsiung, 1971a; Nayak, 1971). Since both type C virus particles and the herpesvirus-type DNA agent have been found in strain 2 leukemic guinea pigs the possible interaction of these viruses and their association with neoplasia poses intriguing questions of current interest. The possible analogies with the Epstein–Barr virus in Burkitt's lymphoma (Robbins, 1967), lymphoma in some New World monkeys, and Marek's disease of chickens are noteworthy because of the involvement of herpesviruses in each system.

b. Signs and Pathology. Guinea pigs or mice experimentally infected with GPHLV had no evidence of acute or chronic disease although the virus could be recovered easily later (Hsiung *et al.,* 1971; Booss and Hsiung, 1971). At no time were intranuclear inclusions observed in any tissue taken directly from experimentally or naturally infected guinea pigs or intracerebrally inoculated mice. Intranuclear inclusions were seen only in degenerated tissue culture cells. A morphologically similar agent has been isolated from the inner ear of guinea pigs (Craft and Hilding, 1968).

B. Poxviruses

Guinea Pig Pox-Like Virus (GPPLV)

The guinea pig has not been associated with a disease characterized by classic pox lesions. However, there is one report of pox-type virus particles from guinea pigs (Hampton *et al.,* 1968). Several 8-month-old guinea pigs spontaneously developed a fibrovascular proliferation in the thigh muscles up to six times normal size of the thigh. Tissue from these growths grew readily in tissue culture, and Giemsa-stained cells had basophilic and eosinophilic cytoplasmic inclusion bodies. By electron microscopy, large particles resembling pox viruses were observed (Hampton *et al.,* 1968).

IV. AGENTS OF PSITTACOSIS-LGV-TRACHOMA GROUP (BEDSONIAE, CHLAMYDIAE)

A. Guinea Pig Inclusion Conjunctivitis Virus (Figs. 7, 8)

1. General

a. History. During the course of an experiment to determine if a vitamin-deficient diet would render guinea pigs susceptible to trachoma virus, conjunctivitis occurred among

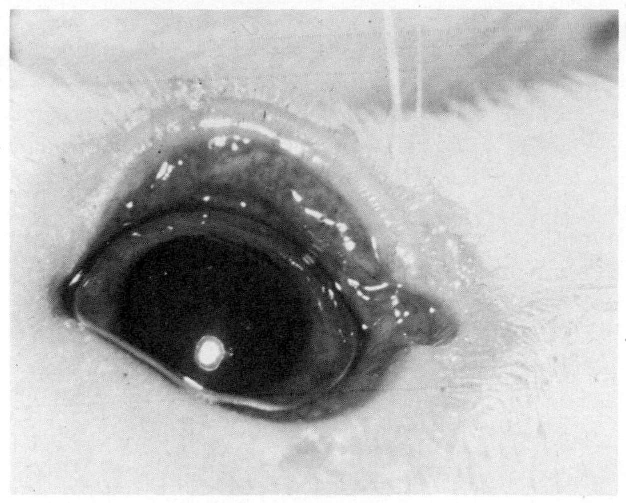

Fig. 7. Hyperemia and chemosis of conjunctiva associated with experimentally induced inclusion keratoconjunctivitis in an adult guinea pig 7 days after inoculation. (From Kazdan *et al.*, *Amer. J. Opthalmol.*, 1967, with permission of Dr. Kazdan.)

normal as well as vitamin-deficient guinea pigs (Murray, 1964). Conjunctival scrapings from affected animals revealed intracytoplasmic inclusions indistinguishable from those produced by trachoma and inclusion conjunctivitis (GPIC) virus and identified it as a member of the psittacosis-lymphogranuloma-trachoma (PLT) group (Murray, 1964). Also noteworthy in regard to this group of agents is the report by Storz (1964) in which a member of the PLT family was isolated from seven guinea pigs which died within a few days after birth.

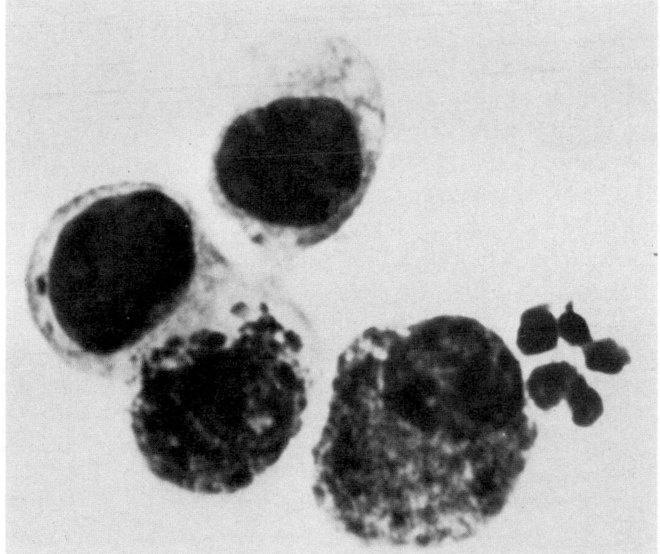

Fig. 8. Conjunctival scraping from a 15-day-old guinea pig with guinea pig inclusion conjunctivitis. Note intracytoplasmic inclusion bodies. Magnification 320×. (From Kazdan *et al.*, *Amer. J. Opthalmol.*, 1967, with permission of Dr. Kazdan.)

b. Etiology. Gordon characterized the GPIC virus as a member of subgroup B of the PLT group which contains other avian and mammalian PLT viruses whereas trachoma and human inclusion conjunctivitis (TRIC agents) viruses are placed in subgroup A (Gordon *et al.,* 1966). The agent forms an irregular rather than compact inclusion in cell culture, is negative to tests for glycogen in its inclusions from conjunctival smears, and is not susceptible to sulfadiazine. It resembles the TRIC agents in the type of infection caused and its host specificity (Murray, 1964; Gordon *et al.*, 1966).

c. Significance and Incidence. The disease in guinea pigs may provide a model for the human diseases of trachoma and inclusion conjunctivitis (Kazdan *et al.,* 1967). Trachoma has replaced small pox as the world's leading cause of blindness. Over 400 million people are afflicted worldwide with this ancient disease. Over a period of months or years trachoma causes pannus formation, corneal ulceration, and scarring leading to partial or complete blindness (Smith *et al.,* 1968). Inclusion conjunctivitis is a mild and usually self-limiting disease of newborns. It may be epidemic in adults usually following accidental contamination of unchlorinated swimming pools. The reservoir of infection is the cervical canal of certain females who are themselves asymptomatic.

d. Epizootiology. The GPIC agent is apparently enzootic in some herds and not in others. Since the signs of infection are so mild they are likely to be overlooked unless special observations are made.

2. Clinical Signs

About half of infected guinea pigs (by positive conjunctival smears) had no signs. The other half had slight redness of the lid margins and very few had a thick exudate that caused the eyelids to adhere. No studies have been done in which the eyelids were everted in examination for signs of conjunctivitis (Murray, 1964).

The disease usually occured in 1- to 3-week-old guinea pigs and was completely eliminated by 28 days after onset as determined by cytological examinations (Kazdan *et al.*, 1967; Murray, 1964). Subconjunctival steroids failed to reactivate infections (Kazdan *et al.,* 1967).

3. Pathology

Numerous initial and elementary bodies were seen forming cytoplasmic inclusions in epithelial cells from conjunctival scrapings stained with Giemsa. There were a few intracytoplasmic initial bodies and a lymphocytic infiltrate in the earliest stages of infection. Later, there was an intense heterophilic response and many inclusions. The heterophilic response was seen only in animals with inclusion conjunctivitis in spite of heavy bacterial flora (Kazdan *et al.*, 1967).

4. Diagnosis

Diagnosis and differential diagnosis can be made on the basis of typical cytoplasmic inclusion bodies on Giemsa-stained conjunctival scrapings. Following experimental inoculation of guinea pigs inclusions were present from the fifteenth hour to the seventeenth day postinfection (Murray, 1964). Complement fixation (CF) tests on serum from naturally infected animals do not show significant titers. There is little correlation between antibody titers and ability to resist reinfection.

V. DISEASES OF THE GUINEA PIG OF POSSIBLE VIRAL ETIOLOGY

A. Myositis

A myositis of guinea pigs was described by Saunders (1958). About a week after arrival, a group of newly purchased animals had swelling and pain in the large muscles of the hind legs. The hind legs were kept flexed and the guinea pigs dragged themselves around by their forelegs. After 3 or 4 days the front legs were involved, their appetites diminished and 3 or 4 days after that they died, apparently of inanition.

The gross lesions in the early stages of disease were ecchymotic hemorrhages in affected muscles and edema of surrounding tissue. Later, muscles of the forelimbs, abdomen, and thorax were similarly involved (Saunders, 1958). Microscopically, hemorrhage and edema of skeletal muscles were most prominent. An inflammatory infiltrate of neutrophils, lymphocytes, and macrophages was present around muscle fibers. Peripheral nerves seemed unaffected even in areas of severe myositis. No inclusion bodies or lesions were observed in other organs except three animals which had focal lymphocytic infiltration in the adrenal medulla (Saunders, 1958). No etiological agent was isolated. Attempts to identify bacteria, protozoa, and fungi by culture and staining were unsuccessful. There was one successful attempt at reproducing the disease with extracts of frozen muscle but subsequent attempts failed. First passage in egg embryos resulted in death of the embryo but the agent, if present, could not be passed further (Saunders, 1958).

Several other diseases will cause paralysis in guinea pigs. These include the spontaneous virus infection described by Rohrer *et al.* (1958), experimental infections with lymphocytic choriomeningitis and salivary gland virus, toxoplasmosis, and Pellissier's virus. Myositis can be differentiated from these by its lack of meningoencephalitis. The prominent swellings of the legs help distinguish myositis clinically from vitamin E deficiency and scurvy.

The animals with myositis were probably not truly paralyzed. More likely the pain caused by the inflammation made them unwilling to use their legs (Saunders, 1958). Myopathy in guinea pigs has also been observed by investigators in England (Webb, 1970; D. K. Blackmore, personal communication, 1972), although the similarities, if any, to the entity described by Saunders are uncertain.

Myositis in guinea pigs may be worthy of further investigation as a model for muscle diseases. Some investigators believe that chronic polymyositis of man may be due to a slow virus infection with a chronic clinical course; electron micrographs have shown myxovirus-like intranuclear inclusions in nuclei of affected muscles in man (Sato *et al.*, 1971).

B. Wasting Disease

A highly fatal epizootic among a colony of guinea pigs was reported by Pirtle and McKee (1951). The guinea pigs were used by a diagnostic laboratory for tuberculosis testing. The guinea pigs first became sluggish and unresponsive. Their hair was shaggy and shed easily. Weight loss and emaciation followed. The wet hair was in the ventral cervical region and was attributed to nausea and vomiting. Death occurred within 6 days of onset of signs. At autopsy, few gross lesions were noted except a marked absence of subcutaneous fat and a slight amount of hemorrhage in the meninges. Five percent of the animals had secondary bacterial pneumonia from which α-hemolytic streptococcus was isolated. Microscopically lesions were confined to the central nervous system and consisted of degenerative changes in the neurons of the hippocampal gyrus. Less often there was demyelination of the posterolateral columns of the spinal cord and patchy degeneration of anterior born neurons.

Attempts to infect mice and chicken embryos failed. Guinea pigs infected with sterile milk, human serum, and other materials showed almost identical incubation periods and infection rates as those inoculated with material from infected guinea pigs. This raised the possibility that the act of inoculation was stimulating a latent infection rather than transferring an infectious agent.

The prevalence of this entity is difficult to assess since subsequent reports on the disease have not appeared in the literature. Accordingly, the significance of wasting disease is uncertain at this time.

C. Highly Fatal Disease

Ten Broeck and Nelson (1938) reported an infection of guinea pigs which caused a febrile response in naturally infected animals but was highly fatal when animals were infected experimentally. Organ suspensions from these febrile animals when inoculated subcutaneously, intraperitoneally, and intranasally caused a fever within 2 to 5 days which persisted for 5 days. White blood cell counts ranged from 3000 to 5000 cells while red blood cell counts were normal. The animals died about 2 weeks postinoculation. Autopsy revealed no gross lesions except loss of subcutaneous fat. The agent passed through Berkefeld N and Berkefeld W filters and grew on the chorioallantoic membrane of chicken eggs. A portion of injected white mice died and rabbits showed transient fever. No histological studies were reported (Ten Broeck and Nelson, 1938).

D. Hepatoenteritis

There is one report in the literature by Marcos (cited in Rohrer *et al.*, 1958) in 1933 of a hepatoenteritis affecting guinea pigs. Affected guinea pigs were first observed to want to hide; subsequently, a rough hair coat and rapid weight loss were observed. A severe diarrhea, weakness, and death followed. On necropsy, the intestinal tract was inflamed and hyperemic, the liver was blackened, and the gallbladder was distended. Some cases also had gastritis and peritonitis. The agent, suspected to be a virus, passed through Seitz filters. When inoculated subcutaneously it caused death in 5 to 6 days. Rabbits, rats, pigeons, and chickens failed to show any signs after inoculation (Rohrer *et al.*, 1958).

E. Virus Pneumonia

Lepine *et al.* (1943) reported the isolation of a filterable agent from guinea pigs with pneumonia. Guinea pigs were the only susceptible laboratory animal. When inoculated by the subcutaneous as well as intracranial route a fatal disease developed. Fevers of 40°–41°C (104°–105.8°F) were recorded 5 days after inoculation. Death occurred 9 to 10 days postinoculation following rapid emaciation. Gross lesions consisted of reddened and consolidated lungs. Microscopic examination revealed an interstitial pneumonia, edema of alveolar walls, fibrin, desquamating alveolar epithelium, and an extensive exudate. Consolidation was not complete since air-filled alveoli existed throughout inflamed areas. Subsequent studies have shown that the agent involved was probably lymphocytic choriomeningitis (Blanc *et al.*, 1951; Blanc, 1952; refer to Section II, E).

Pneumonia attributed to virus(es) is reported to be fairly common with a morbidity and mortality rate of 80 to 100% in affected colonies. Infection is apparently transmitted by inhalation or direct contact and has an incubation period of a week. Diagnosis is based on the history of rapid spread through a colony, congestion and consolidation of viral pneumonitis at autopsy, and ability to culture an agent in embryonated eggs (Kunz and Hutton, 1971).

VI. EXPERIMENTAL VIRUS INFECTIONS OF THE GUINEA PIG

Listed in Table II are selected experimental virus infections of the guinea pig. As mentioned previously, the natural host for these agents is some animal other than the guinea pig.

Guinea pigs have been used experimentally with these viruses for a variety of reasons, including: differential diagnostic purposes, e.g., foot and mouth disease and vesicular stomatitis; preparation of specific immune sera, e.g., the arbovirus group; as an experimental model for the disease in other animals or

Table II
Experimentally Induced Viral, PLT, and Rickettsial Infections of the Guinea Pig

Virus	Reference
A. RNA viruses	
1. Enteroviruses	
a. Poliovirus	Sandow, 1969
b. Coxsackie virus	Gaudin *et al.*, 1971
c. Encephalomyocarditis virus	Craighead, 1965
d. Foot and mouth disease	Platt, 1958
2. Rhabdoviruses	
a. Vesicular stomatitis	Myers and Hanson, 1962
b. Marburg virus	Simpson *et al.*, 1968
c. Rabies	Soave, 1964
3. Orthomyxoviruses	
Influenza A	Merchant and Packer, 1967
4. Arboviruses	
a. Group A (alphaviruses)	
1. Venezuelan equine encephalitis	Kissling and Chamberlain, 1967
2. Chikungunya virus	Bedekar and Pavri, 1969
b. Group B	
1. St. Louis encephalitis	Merchant and Packer, 1967
2. Wesselsborn	Merchant and Packer, 1967
c. Miscellaneous	
1. Junin virus (Argentinian hemorrhagic fever)	Kierszenbaum *et al.*, 1970
2. Tacaribe	Coto *et al.*, 1967
B. DNA viruses	
1. Polyomavirus	
Polyoma	Eddy *et al.*, 1960
2. Herpesviruses	
a. Herpes simplex	Harper and Sommerville, 1965
b. B virus	Merchant and Packer, 1967
c. Pseudorabies	Merchant and Packer, 1967
d. Equine rhinopneumonitis	Merchant and Packer, 1967
e. Epstein–Barr virus	Grace, 1970
3. Poxviruses	
Cow pox	Downie, 1939
C. PLT group agents (Bedsoniae, Chlamydiae)	
1. Trachoma agent	Jawetz and Thygeson, 1965
2. Psittacosis	Rivers and Berry, 1931
3. Others	Parker and Younger, 1963

man, e.g., Marburg virus; and for the evaluation of viral vaccines.

ACKNOWLEDGMENT

The excellent secretarial and bibliographic assistance of Mrs. Margaret Ferro in the preparation of this chapter is gratefully acknowledged.

REFERENCES

Armstrong, C., and Lillie, R. D. (1934). Experimental lymphocytic choriomeningitis of monkeys and mice produced by a virus encountered in studies of the 1933 St. Louis encephalitis epidemic. *Pub. Health Rep.* **49,** 1019–1027.

Bedekar, S. D., and Pavri, K. M. (1969). Studies with chikungunya virus. I. Susceptibility of birds and small mammals. *Indian J. Med. Res.* **57,** 1181–1192.

Bhatt, P. N., Percy, D. H., Craft, J. L., and Jonas, A. M. (1971). Isolation and characterization of a herpeslike (Hsiung-Kaplow) virus from guinea pigs. *J. Infec. Dis.* **123,** 178–189.

Blanc, G. (1952). Pneumopathie du cobaye et L.C.M. *Sem. Hop.* **28,** 3805–3810.

Blanc, G., Bruneau, J., Delage, B., and Poitrot, R. (1951). Etude comparative de virus de choriomeningite lymphocytaire d'origine humaine (W. E. Armstrong) et animale (pneumonopathie du cobaye). *Bull. Acad. Nat. Med., Paris* **[3]** 135, 520.

Booss, J., and Hsiung, G. D. (1971). Herpes-like virus of the guinea pig: Propagation in brain tissue of guinea pigs and mice. *J. Infec. Dis.* **123,** 284–291.

Calisher, C. H., and Rowe, W. P. (1966). Mouse hepatitis, Reo-3, and the Theiler viruses. *Nat. Cancer Inst., Monogr.* **20,** 67–75.

Chanock, R. M., Parrott, R. H., Cook, K., Andrews, B. E., Bell, J. A., Reighelderfer, T., Kapikian, A. Z., Mastrota, F. M., and Huebner, R. J. (1958). Newly recognized myxoviruses from children with respiratory disease. *N. Engl. J. Med.* **258,** 207–213.

Cole, R., and Kuttner, A. G. (1926). A filterable virus present in the submaxillary glands of guinea pigs. *J. Exp. Med.* **44,** 855–874.

Congdon, C. C., and Lorenz, E. (1954). Leukemia in guinea-pigs. *Amer. J. Pathol.* **30,** 337–359.

Cook, J. E. (1958). Salivary-gland virus disease of guinea pigs. *J. Nat. Cancer Inst.* **20,** 905–909.

Coto, C. E., Rey, E., and Parodi, A. S. (1967). Tacaribe virus infection of guinea-pig. Virus distribution, appearance of antibodies and immunity against Junin virus infection. *Arch. Gesamte Virusforsch.* **20,** 81–86.

Craft, J. L., and Hilding, D. A. (1968). Virus-like particles in the spiral ganglion of the guinea pig cochlea. *Science* **162,** 1485–1487.

Craighead, J. E. (1965). Necrosis of the pancreas, parotid and lachrymal glands associated with encephalomyocarditis virus infection. *Nature (London)* **207,** 1268–1269.

Downie, A. W. (1939). A study of the lesions produced experimentally by cowpox virus. *J. Pathol. Bacteriol.* **48,** 361–379.

Durand, P. (1940). Virus filtrant pathogène pour l'homme et les animaux de laboratoire et à affinitis meningée et pulmonaire. *Arch. Inst. Pasteur Tunis* **29,** 179.

Eddy, B. E., Borman, G. S., Kirschstein, R. L., and Touchette, R. H. (1960). Neoplasia in guinea-pigs infected with S.E. polyoma virus. *J. Infec. Dis.* **107,** 361–368.

Ediger, R. D., and Rabstein, M. M. (1968). Spontaneous leukemia in a Hartley strain guinea pig. *J. Amer. Vet. Med. Ass.* **153,** 954–956.

Feldman, D. G., and Gross, L. (1970). Electron microscope study of the guinea pig leukemia virus. *Cancer Res.* **30,** 2702–2711.

Fukumi, H., Mizutani, H., Takeuchi, Y., Tajima, Y., Imaizumi, K., Tanaka, T., and Kanake, J. (1962). Studies on Sendai virus infection in laboratory mice. *Jap. J. Med. Sci. Biol.* **15,** 153–163.

Gaudin, E. G., Bringuier, J. P., Brigaud, M., Terraillon, J., and Sohier, R. (1971). Immunologic response of 3 animal species (guinea pigs, hamster, mice) to different coxsackievirus A.I. Comparative study of complement fixing antibodies. *Ann. Inst. Pasteur, Paris* **120,** 228–242.

Gordon, F. B., Weiss, E., Quan, A. L., and Dressler, H. R. (1966). Observations on guinea pig inclusion conjunctivitis agent. *J. Infec. Dis.* **116,** 203–207.

Grace, J. T., Jr. (1970). Studies of Epstein-Barr virus. *Ann. N. Y. Acad. Sci.* **174,** 946–966.

Gross, L., and Feldman, D. G. (1970). Comparative study of the morphology and distribution of virus particles causing leukemia and lymphosarcoma in mice, rats, cats, and guinea pigs. *Arch. Geschwulstforsch.* **36,** 1–9.

Gross, L., Dreyfuss, Y., Ehrenreich, T., and Moore, L. A. (1970). Experimental studies on lukemia in guinea pigs. *Acta Haematol.* **43,** 193–209.

Hampton, E. G., Bruce, M., and Jackson, F. L. (1968). Virus-like particles in a fibrovascular growth in guinea pigs. *J. Gen. Virol.* **2,** 205–206.

Harper, I. A., and Sommerville, R. G. (1965). Herpetic keratitis produced in the guinea pig by a new, standardized technique. *Arch. Ophthalmol.* **[N.S.] 73,** 552–554.

Hartley, J. W., Rowe, W. P., and Huebner, R. J. (1957). Serial propagation of the guinea pig salivary gland virus in tissue culture. *Proc. Soc. Exp. Biol. Med.* **96,** 281–285.

Hotchin, J. (1971). The contamination of laboratory animals with lymphocytic choriomeningitis. *Amer. J. Pathol.* **64,** 747–769.

Hsiung, G. D., and Kaplow, L. S. (1969a). The association of herpeslike virus and guinea pig leukemia. *In* "Comparative Leukemia Research 1969" (R. M. Dutcher, ed.), pp. 578–583, Karger, Basel.

Hsiung, G. D., Kaplow, L. S. (1969b). Herpeslike virus isolated from spontaneously degenerated tissue culture derived from leukemia-susceptible guinea pigs. *J. Virol.* **3,** 355–357.

Hsiung, G. D., Kaplow, L. S., and Booss, J. (1971). Herpesvirus infection of guinea pigs. I. Isolation, characterization and pathogenicity. *Amer. J. Epidemiol.* **93,** 298–307.

Ioachim, H. L., and Berwick, L. (1969). Leukemia of guinea pigs. *In* "Comparative Leukemia Research 1969" (R. M. Dutcher, ed.), pp. 566–573. Karger, Basel.

Jackson, L. (1920). An intracellular protozoan parasite of the ducts of the salivary glands of the guinea pig. *J. Infec. Dis.* **26,** 347–351.

Jawetz, E., and Thygeson, P. (1965). Trachoma and inclusion conjunctivitis agents. *In* "Viral and Rickettsial Infections of Man" (F. L. Horsfall, Jr. and I. Tamm, eds.), 4th ed., pp. 1042–1058. Lippincott, Philadelphia, Pennsylvania.

Jungeblut, C. W., and Kodza, H. (1962a). Studies of leukemia L2C in guinea pigs. *Arch. Gesamte Virusforsch.* **12,** 537–551.

Jungeblut, C. W., and Kodza, H. (1962b). Interference between lymphocytic choriomeningitis virus and the leukemia transmitting agent of leukemia L2C in guinea pigs. *Arch. Gesamte Virusforsch.* **12,** 552–560.

Kazdan, J. J., Schachter, J., and Okumoto, M. A. (1967). Inclusion conjunctivitis in the guinea pig. *Amer. J. Ophthalmol.* **64,** 116–124.

Kierszenbaum, F., Budzko, D. B., and Parodi, A. S. (1970). Alterations in the enzymatic activity of plasma of guinea pigs infected with Junin virus. *Arch. Gesamte Virusforsch.* **30,** 217–223.

Kissling, R. E., and Chamberlain, R. W. (1967). Venezuelan equine encephalitis. *Advan. Vet. Sci.* **11,** 65–84.

Kunz, L. L., and Hutton, G. M. (1971). Diseases of the laboratory guinea pig. *Vet. Scope* **16,** 12–20.

Lam, K. M., and Hsiung, G. D. (1971a). Herpesvirus infection of guinea pigs. II. Transplacental transmission. *Amer. J. Epidemiol.* **93,** 308–313.

Lam, K. M., and Hsiung, G. D. (1971b). Further studies on the mode of transmission of herpes-like virus in guinea pigs. *Proc. Soc. Exp. Biol. Med.* **138,** 422–426.

Lepine, P., Sautter, V., and Lamy, R. (1943). C. R. Soc. Biol. **137,** 317–318 (as described by Rohrer *et al.,* 1958).

Ma, B. I., Swartzendruber, D. C., and Murphy, W. H. (1969). Detection of virus-like particles in germinal centers of normal guinea pigs. *Proc. Soc. Exp. Biol. Med.* **130,** 586–590.

Maurer, F. D. (1964). Lymphocytic choriomeningitis. *Lab. Anim. Care* **14,** 415–419.

Merchant, I. A., and Packer, R. A. (1967). *In* "Veterinary Bacteriology and Virology," pp. 610–731. Iowa State Univ. Press, Ames.

Murray, E. S. (1964). Guinea pig inclusion conjunctivitis virus. I. Isolation and identification as a member of the psittacosis-lymphogranuloma-trachoma group. *J. Infec. Dis.* **114,** 1–12.

Myers, M. L., and Hanson, R. P. (1962). Studies on the response of rabbits and guinea pigs to inoculations with vesicular stomatitis virus. *Amer. J. Vet. Res.* **23,** 1078–1080.

Nadel, E., Banfield, W., Burstein, S., and Tousimis, A. J. (1967). Virus particles associated with strain 2 guinea pig leukemia (L2C/N-B). *J. Nat. Cancer Inst.* **38,** 979–982.

Nayak, D. P. (1971). Isolation and characterization of a herpesvirus from leukemic guinea pigs. *J. Virol.* **8,** 579–588.

Opler, S. R. (1967a). Pathology of cavian viral leukemia. *Amer. J. Pathol.* **51,** 1135–1151.

Opler, S. R. (1967b). Observations on a new virus associated with guinea pig leukemia: Preliminary note. *J. Nat. Cancer Inst.* **38,** 797–800.

Opler, S. R. (1967c). Animal model of viral oncogenesis. *Nature (London)* **215,** 184.

Opler, S. R. (1968a). "Davian Leukemia: A Hematologic and Autopsy Study," Symposium on Myeloproliferative Disorders of Animals and Man, (Richland, Washington), pp. 340–345. U. S. At. Energy Comm., Washington, D.C.

Opler, S. R. (1968b). Transmission of viral induced cavian leukemia by the oral route. *Oncology* **22,** 273–280.

Opler, S. R. (1968c). New oncogenic virus producing acute lymphatic leukemia in guinea pigs. *Proc. Int. Symp. Comp. Leuk. Res., 3rd, 1967* pp. 81–88.

Opler, S. R. (1971). Defining the role of the guinea pig in cancer research: A new model for leukemia and cancer immunology studies. *In* "Defining the Laboratory Animal," pp. 435–449. Nat. Acad. Sci., Washington, D.C.

Pappenheimer, A. M., and Slanetz, C. A. (1942). A generalized visceral disease of guinea pigs, associated with intranuclear inclusions. *J. Exp. Med.* **76,** 299–306.

Parker, H. D., and Younger, R. L. (1963). The distribution of some psittacosis-lymphogranuloma group viruses in experimentally infected pregnant guinea pigs. *Amer. J. Vet. Res.* **24,** 367–370.

Parker, J. C., Tennant, R. W., and Ward, T. G., and Rowe, W. P. (1964). Enzootic Sendai virus infections in mouse breeder colonies within the United States. *Science* **146,** 936–938.

Parker, J. C., Tennant, R. W., and Ward, T. G. (1966). Prevalence of viruses in mouse colonies. *Nat. Cancer Inst., Monogr.* **20,** 25–36.

Pellissier, A. (1949). Isolement d'un ultravirus dans un foyer d'ictère épidémique sevissant en Oubangui (A.E.F.) 2^{e}note: Etude expérimentale. *Bull. Soc. Pathol. Exot.* **42** (5–6), 197–209.

Pellissier, A. (1953). Culture sur oeuf embryonné et identification immunologique du virus de L'ietere épidémique d'A.E.F. *Ann. Inst. Pasteur, Paris* **85,** 492–496.

Pellissier, A., and Lumaret, R. (1948). Sur un ultravirus isolé dans un foyer d'ictère épidémique sevissant en Oubangui. *Ann. Inst. Pasteur, Paris* **74,** 507.

Pellissier, A., Ceccaldi, J., and Arnoult, H. (1950). Isolement d'un virus de cobaye a brazzaville. *Ann. Inst. Pasteur, Paris* **79,** 200–202.

Pirtle, E. C., and McKee, A. P. (1951). An epizootic of unknown etiology in guinea pigs. *Proc. Soc. Exp. Biol. Med.* **77,** 425–429.

Platt, H. (1958). Observations on the pathology of experimental foot and mouth disease in adult guinea pigs. *J. Pathol. Bacteriol.* **76,** 119–131.

Rivers, T. M., and Berry, G. P. (1931). Psittacosis. III. Experimentally induced infections in rabbits and guinea pigs. *J. Exp. Med.* **54,** 119–128.

Robbins, S. M. (1967). Lymphosarcoma. *In* "Pathology," p. 671. Saunders, Philadelphia, Pennsylvania.

Robinson, T. W. E., Cureton, R. J. R., and Heath, R. B. (1969). The effect of cyclophosphamide on Sendai virus infection of mice. *J. Med. Microbiol.* **2,** 137–145.

Rohrer, H., Kotshe, W., Hoffman, G., and Fisher, K. (1958). Virusbedingte Krankheiten. *In* "Pathologie der Laboratoriumsteire" (P. Cohrs, R. Jaffe, and H. Meessen, eds.), Vol. II, pp. 104–111. Springer-Verlag, Berlin and New York.

Sandow, J. (1969). The influence of the first antigenic stimulus upon further immunizability, guinea-pig experiments with poliomyelitis virus vaccines. *Zentralbl. Bakteriol., Parasitenk., Infektionskr. Hyg., Abt.1: M.-H., Orig.* **209,** 389–406.

Sarma, P. S., Ueberhorst, P. J., Zeve, V., Whang-Peng, J., and Huebner, R. J. (1969). L2C/NB guinea pig leukemia: Failure to demonstrate transmissible leukemogenic virus. *In* "Comparative Leukemia Research 1969" (R. M. Dutcher, ed.), pp. 574–577. Karger, Basel.

Sato, T., Walker, D. L., Peters, H. A., Reese, H. H., and Chou, S. M. (1971). Chronic polymyositis and myxovirus-like inclusions. *Arch. Neurol. (Chicago)* **24,** 409–418.

Saunders, L. Z. (1958). Myositis in guinea pigs. *J. Nat. Cancer Inst.* **20,** 899–903.

Simpson, D. I. H., Zlotnik, I., and Rutter, D. A. (1968). Vervet monkey disease. Experimental infection of guinea-pigs and monkeys with the causative agent. *Brit. J. Exp. Pathol.* **49,** 458–464.

Smith, D. T., Conant, N. F., and Willett, H. P. (1968). The Chlamydiaceae. *In* "Zinsser Microbiology," pp. 876–881. Appleton, New York.

Smith, H. A., and Jones, T. C. (1968). Diseases caused by viruses. *In* "Veterinary Pathology," p. 321. Lea & Febiger, Philadelphia, Pennsylvania.

Smith, M. G. (1959). The salivary gland viruses of man and animals (cytomegalic inclusion disease). *Progr. Med. Virol.* **2,** 171–202.

Soave, O. A. (1964). Reactivation of rabies virus in a guinea pig due to stress of crowding. *Amer. J. Vet. Res.* **25,** 268–269.

Storz, J. (1964). Naturally occurring PLT infection in guinea pigs. *Zentralbl. Bakteriol., Parasitenk., Infektionsk. Hyg., Abt. 1: M.-H., Orig.* **193,** 432–446.

Ten Broeck, C., and Nelson, J. B. (1938). A highly fatal disease of guinea pigs. *Proc. Soc. Exp. Biol. Med.* **39**, 572–573.

Tennant, R. W., Parker, J. C., and Ward, T. G. (1966). Respiratory virus infections of mice. *Nat. Cancer Inst., Monogr.* **20**, 93–104.

Van Hoosier, G. L., Jr., Stenback, W. A., Parker, J. C., Burke, J. G., and Trentin, J. J. (1970). The effects of cesarean derivation and foster nursing procedures on enzootic viruses of the LSH strain of inbred hamsters. *Lab. Anim. Care* **20**, 232–237.

Webb, J. N. (1970). Naturally occurring myopathy in guinea-pigs. *J. Pathol.* **100**, 155–159.

Weller, T. H. (1971a). The cytomegaloviruses: Ubiquitous agents with protean clinical manifestations (part one). *N. Engl. J. Med.* **285**, 203–214.

Weller, T. H. (1971b). The cytomegaloviruses: Ubiquitous agents with protean clinical manifestations (part two). *N. Engl. J. Med.* **285**, 267–274.

Wilner, B. I. (1969). "Classification of the Major Groups of Human and Other Animal Viruses." Burgess, Minneapolis, Minnesota.

Wilsnack, R. E. (1966). Lymphocytic choriomeningitis. *Nat. Cancer Inst., Monogr.* **20**, 77–92.

Chapter 11

Mycoses

Ronald F. Sprouse

I. INTRODUCTION

Survey of reported spontaneously occurring fungal diseases of *Cavia porcellus* indicates that the vast majority are dermatophytoses. This is especially true of the guinea pig in its confined role as a laboratory tool. However, even though most spontaneously occurring mycotic diseases of the guinea pig are of low incidence, experimentally induced mycoses have been of paramount importance in elucidation of the pathogenesis and pathognomonic sequela of the spontaneous disease processes in man and other animals. If one contemplates the possible variation in host response and other parameters such as route of inoculation, dose, virulence, etc., guarded extrapolation of results from experimentally induced mycotic infections in the guinea pig to other host species certainly is warranted. The reward often is a workable model for subsequent therapeutic evaluations, *in vivo* and *in vitro* immunological evaluations, and epidemiological studies.

II. SYSTEMIC MYCOSES

Review of the literature indicates only sporadic reports of "spontaneously occurring systemic mycoses," including the yeast diseases, in guinea pigs. The following text will attempt to summarize the initial report of those few that have been documented and provide a synopsis of current knowledge for both spontaneously occurring or experimentally induced diseases.

A. Coccidioidomycosis

As a spontaneously occurring disease of the guinea pig, coccidioidomycosis does not appear to have been reported. This is incomprehensible when one considers that the etiological agent, *Coccidioides immitis,* is common to soils of the Gran Chaco region of South America (Posadas, 1892) and the guinea pig normally inhabits this region (Starrett, 1967).

Evidence presented by Giltner (1918) indicates the guinea pig is highly susceptible to experimental coccidioidal infection. Rosenthal and Elmore (1950) observed that 10 of 13 noninfected guinea pigs housed with experimentally infected cage mates developed spontaneous disease after 46 to 175 days of contact. These investigators demonstrated spherules by microscopic examination of wet mounts prepared from pulmonary lesions that developed in noninoculated cage mates. One could rationalize that the tissue phase (spherule–endospore) of the fungus was excreted by the infected cage mates into the bedding and reverted to the mycelial phase with subsequent production of infectious arthrospores. These mycelial elements, in turn, were inhaled into alveoli of the noninfected animals, reestablished the tissue phase, and developed focal lesions, completing the infectious cycle as undoubtedly occurs in nature.

Data supporting the foregoing hypothesis in conjunction with evidence presented by Giltner (1918) strongly suggest the existence of spontaneously occurring coccidioidomycosis in the guinea pig. Extreme caution, at any rate, should be exercised in using the guinea pig as a model for experimentally induced coccidioidomycosis, lest one obtain erroneous results and more importantly inadvertently expose laboratory personnel.

B. Histoplasmosis

Correa and Pacheco (1967) observed an epizootic outbreak of histoplasmosis in a laboratory colony of guinea pigs at the School of Medicine, Botucatu, San Paulo, Brazil. The etiological agent, *Histoplasma capsulatum,* previously was isolated from Brazilian soil (Silva, 1956). It was speculated that the animal colony was exposed to the fungus through grass used for food and bedding. Correa and Pacheco (1967) described two clinical forms of the disease. Adult animals generally presented chronic disease with progressive emaciation and lameness of the hind limbs. Animals 3 months or less in age exhibited ruffled fur, pronounced dorsal curvature, catarrhal conjunctivitis, and usually expired within 2 to 4 weeks after the onset of signs. Principle lesions, at necropsy, were ulcerative gastritis, hemorrhagic and catarrhal enteritis, splenomegaly, and mesenteric lymphadenectasis. Occasionally, lesions were observed in the liver, lungs, mediastinal lymph nodes, and other organs.

Other investigators have observed analogous progression of histoplasmosis and similar lesions in experimentally infected guinea pigs. Larsh (1960) infected animals via inhalation with 10^2 to 10^3 viable mycelial particles of *H. capsulatum* and followed the disease progression. Sprouse (1969) in similar experiments infected animals with comparable concentrations of viable cells intraperitoneally. Both investigators observed lesions similar to those initially reported for spontaneously occurring histoplasmosis in the guinea pig.

C. North American Blastomycosis and South American Blastomycosis

Neither North American blastomycosis nor South American blastomycosis (paracoccidioidomycosis) has been reported in the guinea pig. The former, caused by *Blastomyces dermatitidis,* appears to be endemic for the eastern half of the United States and the southern part of Canada (Menges *et al.*, 1965). Isolated cases of human disease have been reported from Central America (Ajello, 1967) and certainly raises the possibility for spontaneously occurring North American blastomycosis in the guinea pig. *Blastomyces dermatitidis* has been isolated from soil (Denton *et al.*, 1961). However, its elusive existence in nature remains to be totally elucidated and possibly accounts for the low incidence of the disease.

The guinea pig appears to be highly susceptible to experimental infection with *B. dermatitidis* via almost any route of inoculation. Intraperitoneal inoculation of approximately 10^4 viable mycelial particles generally results in chronic progressive disease characterized by granulomata in the abdominal viscera and testes (R. F. Sprouse, unpublished data; Robinson and Schell, 1951). Lymphadenitis, analogous to streptococcal lymphadenitis (Corrado, 1963) with enlargement of tracheobronchial and mediastinal lymph nodes, is common in guinea pigs experimentally infected with *B. dermatitidis.* Cutaneous lesions, although rarely observed in experimentally induced blastomycosis of the guinea pig, appear to indicate the latter phases of dissemination, analogous to cutaneous blastomycosis in the canine (Jungerman and Swartzman, 1972), and contrary to most human infections (Wilson and Plunkett, 1967).

Batista *et al.* (1962) isolated *Paracoccidioides brasiliensis,* the etiological agent of South American blastomycosis, from Brazilian soil. However, some investigators doubt a natural soil habitat and speculate that soil functions only as an intermediate, while some plant provides the natural host in a highly complex life cycle. Analyses of reported human cases, at any rate, indicated predominance of the disease in Brazil, Argentina, and Venezuela and only occasional reports in other South and Central American countries (Wilson and Plunkett, 1967). The portal(s) of entry remains vague. Current opinion favors impregnation into mucous membranes of the mouth and nose rather than inhalation, as with most other systemic mycoses. One again would presuppose spontaneous infection of the guinea pig which is native to most areas endemic for *P. brasiliensis.* However, specific reports have not been documented.

D. Aspergillosis

Survey of the literature also fails to document spontaneously occurring aspergillosis in the guinea pig. This, indeed, is surprising in light of the perpetual exposure of guinea pig colonies to aspergilli conidia from food products and bedding. This probably indicates a low host susceptibility and emphasizes the opportunistic nature of *Aspergillus* infections.

Numerous reports indicate the guinea pig is subject to aflatoxicosis (Newberne and Butler, 1969; Brook, 1966) and consequently provides a model for experimental studies. Analysis of these reports suggests that the liver is predisposed to develop characteristic lesions which result from marked inhibition of nucleoprotein and protein synthesis, analogous to aflatoxicosis in the rat (Wogan, 1968).

E. Cryptococcosis

Spontaneously occurring cryptococcosis in the guinea pig, a result of *Cryptococcus neoformans,* was reported by Dezest (1953). Freeman and Weidman (1923) published a more detailed report describing experimental cryptococcosis. These investigators infected guinea pigs intranasally and observed rapid progression of the disease. They also demonstrated lesions and encapsulated yeast cells in the meninges within 3 weeks postinoculation. The specific mode of metastasis from the nasal cavity to the meninges remains obscure. Semerak (Wilson and Plunkett, 1967) suggested that infection can spread directly to the meninges from the nasopharynx. However, it would seem more plausible that metastasis is from a pulmonary focus in light of the frequent occurrence of concurrent pulmonary lesions.

F. Candidiasis

Spontaneously occurring candidiasis in the guinea pig has been reported (Flores *et al.,* 1948). The etiological agent, *Candida albicans,* is a normal inhabitant of the mucous membranes and intestinal mucosa of man, many other animals, and avian species. The fungus is uniquely dimorphic, propagating primarily by a blastogenic yeast phase when there are suitable concentrations of reduced carbohydrate and molecular oxygen available and reverting to a hyphal–pseudohyphal type of growth when the opposite environment occurs. This possibly explains the filamentous type tissue invasion seen microscopically. The microorganism is opportunistic and reverts to the latter invasive form only when the host has been subjected to some predisposing condition such as prolonged antibiotic therapy, especially tetracycline, steroid, or other immunosuppressive therapy, prolonged radiation therapy or concomitant disease.

Radaelli (1924) inoculated guinea pigs by many different routes and observed that once *C. albicans* gained entrance to the circulation it formed occlusive capillary emboli and subsequent infarction. In larger blood vessels, thrombi were formed in which the microorganism developed and eventually penetrated the vessel wall with invasion of surrounding tissue. Clinical forms of candidiasis are multiform and depend on a variety of predisposing conditions.

III. DERMATOPHYTOSIS

Dermatophytoses are among the most common spontaneously occurring diseases in the guinea pig. The remaining text is devoted to these diseases, their incidence, pathogenesis, epidemiology, diagnosis, and prevention control. A variety of parameters contribute to the incidence of dermatophytic disease including genetic predisposition, age, sex, nutrition, and environmental conditions. Dermatophytic disease in the guinea pig has devastated many breeding programs or experiments to the economic loss and disappointment of individuals involved.

The type of guinea pig selected usually depends on the purpose for which the animal is to be used. A fairly wide range of genetic variability such as found in the mongrel types may be desirable. On the other hand, inbred strains are superior to random bred animals in their uniformity of response to external stimuli. Consequently, a significant difference between experimental and control groups usually can be demonstrated with fewer animals at considerable savings to the investigator (Porter, 1967). However, "inbred animals" are more responsive to stress and probably more susceptible to dermatophytic infection.

Age appears to be related to incidence of dermatophytoses with demonstrable lesions occurring predominantly in the young (Georg, 1959). Whether this results from immunoincompetency, underdevelopment of the endocrine system, or malnutrition remains unclear. Male animals reach sexual maturity in about 10 to 12 weeks and the female as early as 4 to 6 weeks. The suggested, though not documented, higher incidence of disease in the sexually immature male would support the endocrine theory. To my knowledge there have been no discrete susceptibility studies correlated to either sexuality or the 15- to 17-day estrous cycle of the female guinea pig. It has been our experience that experimentally induced cutaneous lesions, occur in less than 50% of animals regardless of age or sex. This and observations by others (Alteras and Evolceanu, 1966) would cause one to question the use of guinea pigs for experimental studies of the dermatophytoses.

Less than half of the approximately 24 dermatophytes are

either geophilic (soil loving) or zoophilic, i.e., have their natural habitat on some animal host other than man and then infect man only transitionally. The remaining species are anthropophilic, generally favoring human keratinized tissue as a natural habitat and only rarely have been reported as transitional to other hosts. Thus host susceptibility plays an extremely important role in the dermatophytoses. Zoonotic transmission, though limited, is significant especially for the zoophilic agents. When transitional infection does occur, lesions that may be more or less benign for the natural zoophilic host often are highly inflammatory for the transitional host. Thus, it is important that the clinician have at hand the specific etiology in any ringworm infection. Generally, lesions caused by *Microsporum* species respond readily to therapy, while *Trichophyton* infections are less responsive and the prognosis is considerably more reserved.

Collectively these fungi generally fall into two taxonomic groups: the genus *Microsporum* and the genus *Trichophyton.* The former contains some eight species and the latter roughly sixteen (Table I). Historically, many species have had several different names. Relatively few of these 24 species have been implicated in spontaneously occurring dermatophytoses of the guinea pig. Specific references to these few reports also are indicated in Table I.

Table I
Species in the Genera *Microsporum* and *Trichophyton*

Genus Species	Reported host	Reported guinea pig disease (ref.)
Microsporum	Man, monkey, dog	Vogel and Timpe, 1957
audouinii	Cat, dog, man, monkey,	Dvorak and Otcenasek, 1964
canis	horse, rabbit, swine	
cookei	Man	Dvorak and Otcenasek, 1964
distortum	Man, monkey,	
	dog, horse, pig	Dvorak and Otcenasek, 1964
gypseum	Most species	Evolceanu *et al.,* 1963
nanum	Swine, man	
vanbreuseghemii	Man, dog, squirrel	
ferrugineum	Man	
Trichophyton		
equinum	Horse, dog	Negroni, 1932
mentagrophytes	Most species	Dvorak and Otcenasek, 1964
rubrum	Man, dog, cattle	Reported
tonsurans	Man	
violaceum	Man (calf??)	Reported
gallinae	Bird, man	
megninii	Man	Dvorak and Otcenasek, 1964
schoenleinii	Man, dog, cat, mouse	
verrucosum	Man, cattle, dog, goat, sheep, horse	
concentricum	Man	
simii	Man, money, bird, dog	
gourvilii	Man	
soudanense	Man	
yaqundei	Man	
georgii	Soil	

This is a rather unique group of microorganisms in that all are able to solublize the highly insoluble protein keratin. All are strict aerobes, basically saprophytic, and can survive the reduced environment of the deeper tissue layers for only a short time. With rare exception, dermatophytes invade only the keratinized zone of the epithelium including hair. The fungus invades the epidermis by mycelial or hyphal extention and also grows in a similar fashion on any suitable cultural medium. Epidermal scrapings or epilated hair immersed in 10 to 40% KOH solution often can provide a rapid provisional diagnosis. Hyphae and various stages of fragmented hyphal elements called arthrospores are all that can be demonstrated by this technique. Many provisional diagnoses of demodectic or sarcoptic mange have been proved erroneous by this technique and vice versa. Any provisional diagnosis should always be substantiated by cultural procedures. Several adequate cultural media can be prepared *de novo* or obtained commercially. Most laboratories prefer to use some modification of Sabouraud's dextrose agar with Chloromycetin and cycloheximide added to inhibit growth of bacteria and nonpathogenic fungi, respectively. In recent years DTM or Dermatophytes Test Medium (Taplin *et al.,* 1969) has come into wide use. It is more selective for dermatophytes in clinical specimens and growth is easily interpreted. However, it must be used with reservation since some nonpathogenic fungi will produce the alkaline condition necessary to activate the phenol red indicator. Consistently successful cultural examination of clinical specimens requires analysis of gross and microscopic fungal characteristics. The most commonly used microscopic method is bright field examination of wet mounts prepared from cultures isolated from properly collected clinical specimens. Reliable analysis presumes some basic understanding of the morphological and physiological characteristics of the etiological agents.

Dermatophytes reproduce *in vitro* predominantly by asexual conidial or spore formation. Classically, two types of conidia referred to as macronidia and microconidia are produced. Recognition of these various conidial types or their unique arrangements is requisite to identification of the pathogen. Figure 1 illustrates large macronidia produced by *Microsporum canis,* a very common cause of feline and canine ringworm. These structures are large (100 × 25 μm), thick walled, and produced in abundance by this species. The peripheral wall is spiny or echinulate and has 6 to 10 cross-walls or septa.

Figure 2A shows similar structures found with less frequency in the *Trichophyton* species. In contrast to *Microsporum canis* these cells are smaller, thin walled, smooth, and pencil shaped rather than fusiform. Since macroconidia are not profusely produced by any *Trichophyton* species, one must rely heavily on the gross appearance of the culture and the arrangement of teardrop-shaped small cells or microconidia for identification. *Trichophyton mentagrophytes,* the usual cause of spontaneous

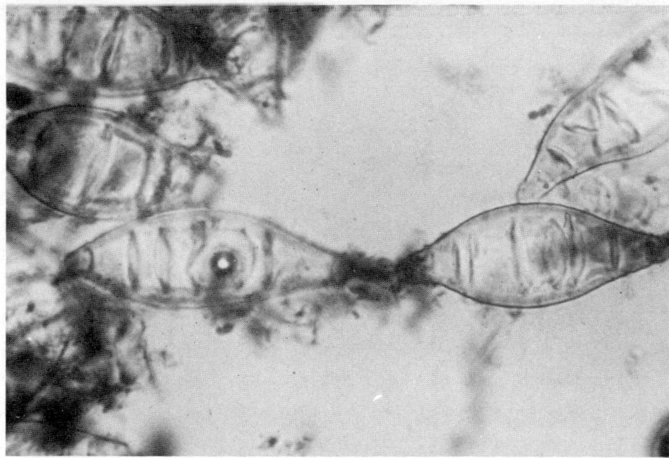

Fig. 1. Microconidia produced in abundance by *M. canis.*

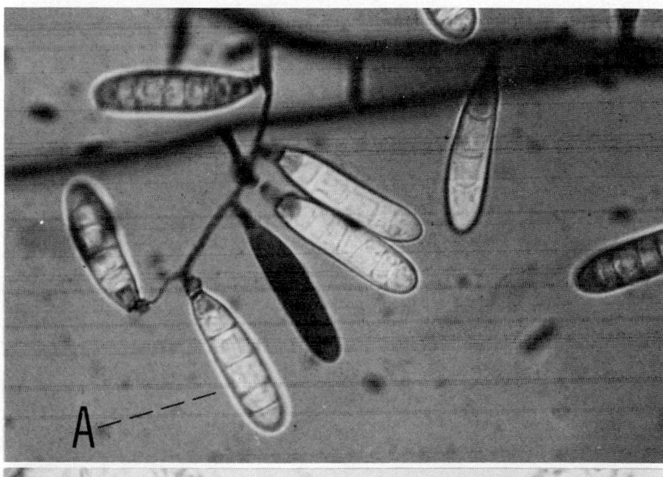

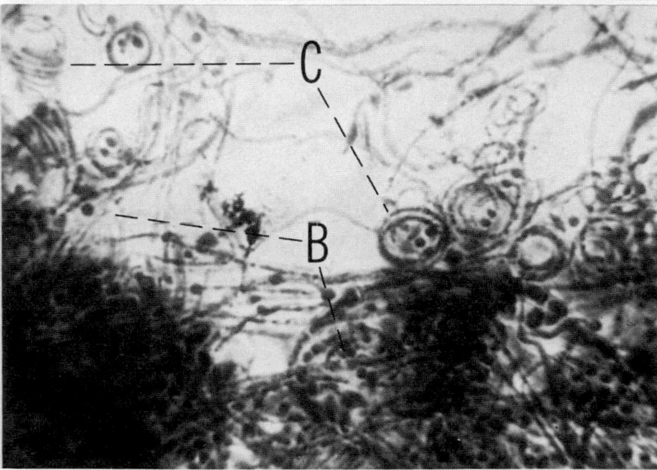

Fig. 2. Microscopic characteristics produced by *T. mentagrophytes:* (A) macroconidia; (B) microconidia; and (C) spiral hyphae.

ringworm in the guinea pig, has two somewhat unique characteristics; the microconidia are irregular in size and have a grape-like arrangement (Fig. 2B) and bizarre structures such as spiral hyphae frequently are demonstrable in cultures, especially on primary isolation from clinical specimens (Fig. 2C). The conidial characteristics for both genera are depicted in Table II. These are general comparisons, ascertained at the generic level and certainly there are exceptions. Table III lists some idiosyncrasies for various species of *Microsporum* and *Trichophyton.* They may be bizarre structures such as spiral hyphae or antler hyphae, chains of chlamydospores, a characteristic colonial morphology, or in some instances a unique biochemical requirement.

Thus far conformational diagnosis of dermatophytoses has been based primarily on microscopic identification of characteristics of cultural isolates. These unique microorganisms grow relatively slowly, requiring 10 to 20 days for characteristic sporulation. Often an immediate provisional diagnosis must be made and appropriate therapy initiated. Discrete examination of lesions, use of the Wood's lamp (ultraviolet), and potassium hydroxide wet mount examination of properly obtained clinical specimens often aid in clinical diagnosis. Table IV summarizes the host range and some pathological features of the four more commonly encountered species in animals.

Trichophyton mentagrophytes, next to *M. canis,* is the most commonly encountered dermatophyte in animals and almost invariably the cause of epizootic ringworm in the guinea pig. The skin and hair are involved with consistent patchy alopecia and Wood's lamp examination usually results in no appreciable fluorescence. Lesions often start on the tip of the nose and then spread to areas above or below the eyes, forehead, and the ears. Lesions may develop later over the posterior portion of the back (Fig. 3). The limbs and dorsal areas usually remain free of true invasion.

Clinically apparent lesions usually appear hyperkeratotic (scaly) in their simplest form or may have superimposed vesicules and bullae at the serpiginous erythematous borders. Deep tissues suppurate and form boggy lesions called kerions (Fig. 4). Secondary bacterial infection most probably accounts for conversion of vesicles and pustules to abscesses. The fungus extends through the follicular orifice, penetrates the hair cuticle, and solubilizes the hard keratin of the shaft which results in loosening from the hair papilla. The hair either falls out or is broken off causing patchy baldness and folliculitis. When severe inflammation or kerion occurs, tufts of hair often can be lifted from the center of the boggy, cercinate lesion. Debris invariably adheres to the base of the hair tuft (Fig. 5) and consists of tissue exudate, hyphae, and arthrospores and usually provides an excellent specimen for laboratory examination. However, with the more common noninflammatous lesion the hair papilla itself usually is not destroyed and thus regeneration of the hair shaft can occur assuming regression of the

Table II
Conidial Characteristics for the Genera *Microsporum* and *Trichophyton*

	Macroconidia					Microconidia				
Genus	Occurrence	Size	Shape	Septa	Cell wall	Occurrence	Size (μm)	Shape	Cell wall	Arrangement
Microsporum	Many	Large (100 × 25 μm)	Fusiform	3–15	Thick echinulate (exception: *gypseum, nanum*)	Few	2–5	Spherical pyriform	Smooth	Singly
Trichophyton	Few	Medium (20–50 × 4–8 μm)	Pencil-shaped	Many	Thin smooth	Many	3–8	Spherical clavate pyriform	Smooth	Single clusters

Table III
Unique Characteristic(s) of Species in the Genera *Microsporum* and *Trichophyton*

	Unique characteristics		
Genus species	Colonial	Microscopic	Biochemical
Microsporum			
canis	Lemon-colored peripheria and reverse	Macroconidia	
gypseum	Gypsum powder surface	Macroconidia	
audouinii	Reddish-brown reverse	Chlamydospores, no macroconidia	
nanum		2-Celled macroconidia	
distortum		Distorted macroconidia	
cookei	Confined red pigment		
Trichophyton			
mentagrophytes	Mahogany reverse pigment	Clusters–microconidia	
equinum	Yellow reverse pigment		Requires nicotinic acid
rubrum	Confined red pigment	Singular microconidia	
verrucosum			Requires thiamine and inositol
violaceum	Violet pigment		Requires thimine
gallinae	Diffusable red pigment		
megninii	Confined red pigment		Requires L-histidine
schoenleinii		Antler hyphae	
tonsurans	Powdery, tan surface	Singular microconidia	
soudanense	Apricot-colored		

Table IV
Host Preference and Pathological Characteristics of Commonly Encountered Dermatophytes

Genus species	Host preference	Tissue preference	Hair invasion	Wood's lamp examination	Lesions
Microsporum					
canis	Common: cat, dog Occasional: horse Rare: rodents	Skin and hair	Mosaic, small-spored (2–5μm–ectothrix at hair base	Yellow-green fluorescence	Scattered lesions with cercinate, dry scaly center and inflamed borders originating on head. Patchy alopecia
gypseum	Occasional: cat, dog, horse, rodents	Skin and hair	Large-spored (5–8μm) ectothrix on hair surface	Weak or no fluorescence	Often single lesion or localized group of coalesced lesions with serpiginous, crusted boarders. Rare highly inflamed lesions occurring anywhere on body with limited boggy alopecia
Trichophyton					
rubrum	Occasional: dog Rare: cattle, rodents	Skin, hair, and nails	Large-spored (5–8μm) endothrix, when hair is invaded	No fluorescence	Single or rare scattered lesions. Cercinate regular lesion usually occurring on head. Occasional high inflamed erythematous deep lesion with invasion of hard keratin and papillary layer
mentagrophytes	Common: cat, dog, rabbit, rodents Occasional: cattle, horse Rare: pig	Skin and hair	Large-spored (5–10μm) ectothrix	No fluorescence	Scattered lesions originating at nose, eyes, ears, spreading over head to trunk. Serpiginous, scaly, or pustular lesions with elevated inflamed borders. Consistent patchy alopecia

fungus. Fungal byproducts often diffuse into the vascularized tissue and are deposited as antigens in distal parts of the skin. The resulting allergic reactions termed ID's or dermatophytids usually are more pronounced on the dorsal trunk and on the undersides of the limbs. These lesions are sterile, contain a clear liquid, and represent an immediate type I skin reaction.

This is somewhat analogous to the skin test reactivity to trichophytin in human dermatophytoses. Analysis of data obtained from human beings indicates that 40% of patients with active trichophyton disease show immediate type I skin test reactions and 71% type IV delayed hypersensitivity as compared to 19% and 38% for respective control groups (Woods and Cruickshank, 1962). Strongly positive delayed type IV reactions generally are associated with deep inflammatory lesions in the patient (Neves, 1962). Our experience indicates that skin testing of trichophyton-infected guinea pigs with

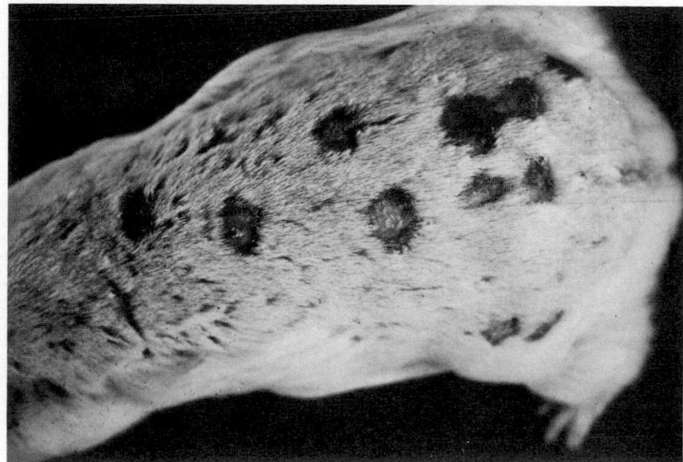

Fig. 3. Generalized trichophytosis in the guinea pig.

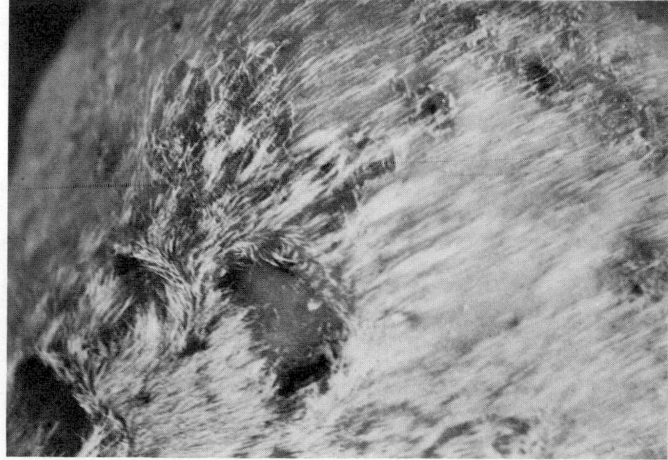

Fig. 4. Kerion lesion in the guinea pig.

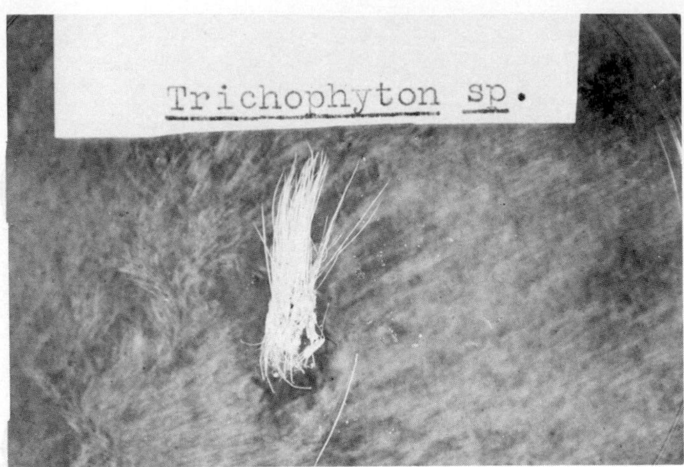

Fig. 5. Hair tuft with adherent debris resulting from trichophytosis.

autogenously prepared antigens routinely elicits the type IV delayed reaction associated with severe inflammation. Trichophytin is a mycelial growth filtrate usually administered in its crudest antigenic form. Chemical studies have shown that antigenically active components are galactomannan peptides, probably from the cell wall of the fungus (Barker *et al.*, 1962). Immunofluorescence studies in man have failed to demonstrate circulating antibodies in the sera of patients with active trichophyton disease. This probably explains the present unavailability of an effective vaccine for either human or animal disease. Thus, prophylaxis essentially depends on prevention or control via administration of appropriate antibiotics or chemotherapeutic agents.

IV. THERAPY

Systemic mycoses are most often treated with amphotercin B, a conjugated heptene produced by *Streptomyces nodosus* (Gold *et al.*, 1956). This antibiotic usually is administered systemically and is toxic for many host species. Its fungistatic action is exhibited through complexing lipids in the fungal cell membrane, thus rendering it permeable to crucial proteins and nucleoproteins.

Examination of the "Physician's Desk Reference" (Huff, 1973) indicates some 100 compounds or composite of compounds are available for treatment of dermatophytoses. Some examples of the more commonly used agents are the aromatic acids and alcohols (benzoic acid, salicylic acid, phenol, resorcinol, cresols), saturated and unsaturated fatty acids (propionic acid, caprylic acid, undecylenic acid), idodine mixtures, triacetate derivatives, and tolnaftate. The mode of action is multifaceted and generally results from some combination of keratolysis, inhibition of keratogenesis, induction of inflammation, fungistasis, or fungicidal action. Treatment generally is limited to topical application and efficacy for many of these agents is questionable. The use of most of these agents has been superceded by the advent of griseofulvin.

Gentles (1958, 1960) and Gentles *et al.* (1959) observed that the oral administration of a metabolic byproduct of *Penicillium griseofulvum*, termed griseofulvin, caused regression of dermatophytic lesions in guinea pigs. The antibiotic was quick to gain acceptance by the medical profession and with the development of a microcrystalline form in recent years has become economically feasible for use in veterinary medicine. The drug is administered orally (15 mg/kg body weight per day for 14 to 28 days) and exhibits low toxicity. It appears to have its principle mode of action through complexing the lipoidial moiety in the fungal cell membrane thus allowing leakage of crucial proteins and nucleoproteins through the cell wall. Peak plasma levels are reached in 3 to 4 hours and absorption across the intestinal mucosa is enhanced by ingestion of divided doses of griseofulvin in conjunction with a high fat diet (Crounse, 1961).

REFERENCES

Ajello, L. (1967). Comparative ecology of respiratory mycotic disease agents. *Bacteriol. Rev.* **31,** 6–24.

Alteras, I., and Evolceanu, R. (1966). Is the guinea pig the best animal for the experimental inoculation of dermatophytes in Bucharest, Romania. *Dermato-Venerologia* **4,** 33–337.

Barker, S. A., Cruickshank, C. N. D., Morris, J. H., and Woods, S. R. (1962). The isolation of trichophytin glycopeptide and its structure in relation to the immediate and delayed reactions. *Immunology* **5,** 627–632.

Batista, A. C., Shome, S. K., and Santos, M. D. (1962). Pathogenicity of *Paracoccicioices brasiliensis* isolated from soils. *Publ. Inst. Micol. Univ. Recite (Brasil)* **373,** 27.

Brook, P. J. (1966). Fungus toxins affecting mammals. *Annu. Rev. Phytopathol.* **4,** 171–194.

Corrado, A. (1963). Streptococcal cervical lymphadenitis in guinea pigs. *Nuova Vet.* **39,** 162–166.

Correa, W. M., and Pacheco, A. C. (1967). Naturally occurring histoplasmosis in guinea pigs. *Can. J. Comp. Med.* **31,** 203–206.

Crounse, R. G. (1961). Human pharmacology of griseofulvin: The effect of fat intake on gastrointestinal absorption. *J. Invest. Dermatol.* **37,** 529.

Denton, J. F., McDonough, E. S., Ajello, L., and Ausherman, R. J. (1961). Isolation of *Blastomyces dermatitidis* from the soil. *Science* **133,** 1126.

Dezest, G. (1953). Torulase spontanée chez le cabaye b. (Spontaneous cryptococcosis in the guinea pig.) *Ann. Inst. Pasteur, Paris* **85,** 131–133.

Dvorak, J., and Otcenasek, M. (1964). Geophilic, zoophilic and anthropophilic dermatophytes. *Mycopathol. Mycol. Appl.* **23,** 294–296.

Evolceanu, R., Alteras, I., and Stoian, M. (1963). Considerations of the morphology, pathogenicity and geophilic nature of *Microsporum nanum*. *Mycopathologia* **19**, 24–36.

Flores, D. F., Brncic, C. H., and Brncic, J. D. (1948). Moniliasis renal espontanea en cuy (*Cavia cabaya*) accion patogena experimental. (Spontaneous renal moniliasis in guinea pig.) *Agr. Tec. (Santiago de Chile)* **8**, 87–111.

Freeman, W., and Weidman, F. D. (1923). Cystic blastomycosis of the cerebral gray matter caused by *Torula histolytica* (Stoddard and Culter). *Arch. Neurol. Psychiat.* **9**, 589–603.

Gentles, J. C. (1958). Experimental ringworm in guinea pigs: Oral treatment with griseofulvin. *Nature (London)* **182**, 476.

Gentles, J. C. (1960). Report on animal experiments with griseofulvin. *Arch. Dermatol.* **81**, 703.

Gentles, J. C., Barnes, M. J., and Fantes, K. H. (1959). Presence of griseofulvin in hair of guinea pig after oral administration. *Nature (London)* **183**, 256.

Georg, L. (1959). "Animal Ringworm in Public Health Diagnosis and Nature." U. S. Dept. of Health, Education, and Welfare Public Health Services, Bureau of State Services, Communicable Disease Center.

Giltner, C. T. (1918). Occurrence of coccidioidal granuloma (oidiomycosis) in cattle. *J. Agr. Res.* **14**, 533–542.

Gold, W., Stout, H. A., Pagano, J. F., and Donorick, R. (1956). Amphotericins A and B: Antifungal antibiotics produced by streptomycete I *in vitro* studies. *Antibiot. Annu.* **56**, 579–586.

Huff, B., ed. (1973). "Physician's Desk Reference." Medical Economic Co., Oradell, New York.

Jungerman, P. F., and Schwartzman, R. M. (1972). "Veterinary Medical Mycology." Lea & Febiger, Philadelphia, Pennsylvania.

Larsh, H. W. (1960). Natural and experimental epidemiology of histoplasmosis. *Ann. N. Y. Acad. Sci.* **89**, 78–90.

Menges, R. W., Furcolow, M. L., Selby, L. A., Ellis, H. R., and Haberman, R. T. (1965). Clinical and epidemiologic studies on seventy-nine canine Blastomycosis cases in Arkansas. *Amer. J. Epidemiol.* **81**, 164–179.

Negroni, D. (1932). *Trichophyton laticolor* cultivado en dos casos de Tina espontanea de la cabaya. *Rev. Soc. Argent. Biol.* **8**, 709.

Neves, H. (1962). Trichophytin reaction in natural and experimental dermatophytosis and in tuberculosis. *Sabouraudia* **1**, 197–202.

Newberne, P. M., and Butler, W. H. (1969). Acute and chronic effects of aflatoxin on the liver of domestic and laboratory animals. *Cancer Res.* **29**, 236–250.

Porter, G. (1967). Assessman of environmental influence on the biological response of the animal. *In* "Husbandry of Laboratory Animals" (M. L. Conalty, ed.), pp. 29–42. Academic Press, New York.

Posados, A. (1892). Ensaye anatomapatologico sobre una neoplasia considerado como micosis fungoidea. *Ann. Circ. Med. Argent.* **15**, 8.

Redaelli, P. (1924). Experimental moniliasis. *J. Trop. Med. Hyg.* **27**, 211.

Robinson, V. B., and Schell, F. G. (1951). Blastomycosis in a dog: A case report. *Amer. Vet.* **32**, 555–558.

Rosenthal, S. R., and Elmore, F. H. (1950). III. Infection in guinea pigs by contact with diseased animals. *Amer. Rev. Tuberc.* **61**, 106–115.

Silva, M. E. (1956). Isolamento do Histoplasma capsulatum do solo em zona endemica de Calazar na Bahia. *Bol. Fund. Goncalo Moniz* **10**, 118.

Sprouse, R. F. (1969). Purification of histoplasmin purified derivative. *Amer. Rev. Resp. Dis.* **100**, 685–689.

Starrett, A. (1967). *In* "Recent Mammals of the World—A Synopsis of Families" (S. Anderson and J. K. Jones, Jr., eds.), pp. 260–263. Ronald Press, New York.

Taplin, D., Zaias, N., Rebell, G., and Blank, H. (1969). Isolation and recognition of dermatophytes on a new medium (DTM). *Arch. Dermatol.* **99**, 203–209.

Vogel, R. A., and Timpe, A. (1957). Spontaneous *Microsporum audouinii* infection in a guinea pig. *J. Invest. Dermatol.* **28**, 311–312.

Wilson, J. W., and Plunkett, O. A. (1967). "The Fungous Diseases of Man." Univ. of California Press, Berkeley.

Wogan, G. N. (1968). Biochemical responses to aflatoxins. *Cancer Res.* **28**, 2282–2287.

Woods, S. R., and Cruickshank, C. N. D. (1962). The relation between trichophytin sensitivity and fungal infections. *Brit. J. Dermatol.* **74**, 329–336.

Chapter 12

Protozoan Parasites

John M. Vetterling

I. INTRODUCTION

Protozoan parasites of guinea pigs have often been reviewed in reference texts on laboratory animals. Steinmetz and Lerche (1923) in Raebiger's work "Das Meerschweinchen" included sections on trichomoniasis and coccidiosis that comprised only seven small pages. Most recently, "Parasites of Laboratory Animals" by Flynn (1973) has 116 pages devoted to parasitic protozoa. In the intervening fifty years, publications on protozoa of laboratory animals ranged from simple pamphlets (Habermann *et al.*, 1954) to monographs (Nie, 1950) and comprehensive works (Frenkel, 1971). In the present review, the "Index Catalogue of Medical and Veterinary Zoology" was used to obtain most of the references, many of which were not cited by previous reviewers. References are included through spring of 1975.

Initially, this chapter was to be entitled "Protozoan Diseases" as have similar chapters in other publications, but protozoan inhabitants of guinea pigs rarely cause disease and a chapter so restricted would exclude many protozoa so the more comprehensive title, "Protozoan Parasites," was chosen. The term "parasite" is used in the broad sense to include any organism living in another, whether or not it causes harm (Levine, 1973).

Our knowledge of guinea pig protozoa has developed as a result of: (1) the interference of these protozoa with experimental studies of other organisms, as occurred with *Toxoplasma gondii* and *Cryptosporidium wrairi;* (2) the appearance of a spontaneous disease, as occurred with *Eimeria caviae;* and (3) the interest of protozoologists who, out of scientific curiosity, have compiled the long list of protozoa known to parasitize the guinea pig cecum. Because in recent years researchers have often used laboratory guinea pigs relatively free of disease, it is not surprising that the participation of protozoa in experiments is rarely suspected. However, all except gnotobiotic animals have a veritable microcosm of protozoa that we are to examine here. Although protozoa may not commonly invalidate experimental results, they may occasionally do so. Certain latent infections may give rise to disease in hosts whose resistance is altered by starvation, nutritional variations, radiation, and immunosuppressant agents, among other factors. Of particular interest are the cecal protozoa because microflora in the cecum of other rodents have been shown to affect the biological response of the host. Because the laboratory animal veterinarian most likely will be using this chapter, the material is presented in a manner intended to facilitate differential diagnosis. The protozoa are discussed according to the organ system or part of the body most generally involved, and thus are under two main categories, parenteral and alimentary infections.

The material is presented for each protozoan in the following order: historical review, description, location in host, prevalence and geographical distribution, pathology, clinical signs, diagnosis, methods of cultivation, and control and prevention. However, when little or nothing is known about a protozoan in a subject area, that subject is deleted or combined in another section for conciseness and brevity.

II. PARENTERAL INFECTIONS

A. Blood Infections

Four blood protozoa have been reported from guinea pigs: *Babesia tropicus, Leucocytozoon caviae, Trypanosoma brucei,* and *Trypanosoma cruzi,* but the first three have been reported only once. All four of these parasites require an invertebrate vector for natural transmission. Therefore, infections occur only in endemic regions. With prohibition of outdoor rearing and use of vermin-proof facilities there should be no blood infections.

1. *Babesia tropicus* Lingard and Jennings, 1904

Bhatia (1938) reported that Lingard and Jennings (1904) found a piroplasm in the blood of guinea pigs in India, but careful examination of the latter report revealed that the guinea pigs had been inoculated with blood from infected horses and cattle. Therefore, *Babesia tropicus* cannot be considered a valid species from the guinea pig (*Cavia porcella*).

2. *Leucocytozoon caviae* Fraser, 1908

Fraser (1908) reported a *Leucocytozoon* in guinea pig blood in the Malay states. He gave no description and since the leucocytozoa are blood parasites of birds, it seems more reasonable to suppose he found a hepatozoan, since these parasites are common in rodents (Levine, 1973).

3. *Trypanosoma brucei* Plimmer and Bradford, 1899

Mettam (1932) reported *Trypanosoma brucei* in blood smears from two of six guinea pigs. This is the only report of a natural infection of trypanosomes in guinea pigs from Africa, even though guinea pigs are good experimental hosts for trypanosomes.

4. *Trypanosoma cruzi* Chagas, 1909 (Synonym: *Schizotrypanum cruzi*)

All reports of *Trypanosoma cruzi* infections in guinea pigs have originated in South America (Dias, 1956; Barretto *et al.*, 1966; Ferriolli Filho and Barretto, 1966). Because South America is the natural habitat of the domestic guinea pig, with both vectors and wild guinea pigs (*Cavia aperea*) (Barretto *et al.*, 1966), this is expected. However, all reports of spontaneous *T. cruzi* infections were in domestic guinea pigs used for human consumption and not laboratory animals (Herrer, 1964).

B. Cutaneous Infections

Only one protozoan, *Leishmania enriettii,* reportedly infects skin. However, *Besnoitia* is found subcutaneously in wild rodents and should be considered as a potential finding at necropsy.

Leishmania enriettii Muniz and Medina, 1948

a. Historical Review. A leishmania of laboratory guinea pigs was first reported by Medina (1946) in Brazil. Muniz and Medina (1948a,b), after comparison with other species of *Leishmania,* described and named it *Leishmania enriettii.* It is unique among leishmanias of mammals in its recorded host specificity. Muniz and Medina (1948a,b) failed to establish the parasite in human volunteers, monkeys (*Macaca mulatta*), golden hamsters, puppies, rats, mice, or wild guinea pigs. Interestingly, Muniz and Medina failed to infect the wild guinea pig which, according to some, is indistinguishable from the domesticated guinea pig. Yet 100% of the latter, from both Brazil and the United States, were infected successfully. Because of the ease with which it is transmitted and the lack of infectivity to man, *L. enriettii* has become a choice organism for experimental studies of cutaneous leishmaniasis.

b. Description. The amastigote (leishmania form) is nearly always ellipsoidal, 3.0–7.0 by 2.0–3.0 μm (5.2 × 2.5 μm)*; it is much larger than the other species of *Leishmania.* The nucleus and kinetoplast are ordinarily visible in stained preparations. A trace of 1–3 internal fibrils (the rudimentary flagellum) can be seen, which is distinctive for this species (Muniz and Medina, 1948a,b). The promastigote (leptomonad form) develops in culture and presumably in the invertebrate host. It measures 8–10 by 3–4 μm, with a 10- to 14-μm flagellum. Bray *et al.* (1969) described the ultrastructure of this leishmania.

Although the natural vector is unknown, Hertig and McConnell (1963) infected the sandfly, *Phlebotomus gomezi.* Adler and Halff (1955) suggested the vector might not be a biting fly but an invertebrate that infects itself by feeding on depilated unbroken skin rather than on ulcerated lesions.

c. Location in Host. *Leishmania enriettii* causes ulceration of the skin, especially on the feet, ears, nose, and genitalia (Figs. 1 and 2). Muniz and Medina (1948a,b) considered *L. enriettii* to cause only cutaneous lesions in guinea pigs, and they attributed lesions on the extremities and external genitalia to mechanical transfer by scratching. However, Tôrres *et al.* (1948a,b) found that intraperitoneal injection of parasites caused pathological changes, including granulomas in the epididymis and tunica vaginalis. Paraense (1952a,b) and Guimarães (1952) found amastigote forms in the nasal mucosa of guinea pigs inoculated intraperitoneally with large doses of parasites. Paraense (1953) saw parasites in lymph nodes near the site of intradermal inoculation as well as in the bone marrow of the carpals and tarsals. He considered that parasites spread via the bloodstream. Adler and Halff (1955) obtained metastases to the nares, right ear, forelimbs and hind limbs, back, and perianal region for 70 days to 3 months after subcutaneous injection into the left ear (Fig. 3). It is noteworthy that *L. enriettii* has not been found in the spleen of even heavily infected guinea pigs.

*Whenever possible, measurements are expressed as the range of length and width with the mean in parentheses.

d. Prevalence and Geographical Distribution. *Leishmania enriettii* is restricted to South America. Spontaneous infections have been reported only twice (Medina, 1946; Coutinho, 1951). Strangely, it is purportedly endemic in Brazil, yet the native wild guinea pig is not susceptible.

e. Pathology. Little is known about the pathogenesis of natural transmission. When inoculated intradermally into the ear of the guinea pig, *L. enriettii* produces a local infection from which parasites are conveyed by the lymph stream to a parotid lymph node where parasites are arrested and destroyed. Metastases to extremities are via the blood (Medina, 1947a). The leishmanias drain into regional lymph nodes shortly after the development of metastatic foci; the nodes undergo hyperplasia and contain parasites long before the metastatic lesion becomes clinically patent. Metastases in the feet may involve the bone marrow, and extremely heavy infections are sometimes confined exclusively to the marrow (Paraense, 1953).

f. Clinical Signs. Severe cutaneous lesions are grossly visible.

g. Diagnosis. The parasite can be found in Giemsa-stained scrapings of the lesions. However, Adler and Halff (1955) showed that parasites can be found in "normal skin." Therefore, if an investigator is intensely interested in leishmania-free guinea pigs, he should examine skin biopsies and teased subcutis. While not in the literature, diagnosis by cultivation would seem to be in order.

h. Methods of Cultivation. *Leishmania enriettii* is readily cultivated in a number of media including NNN medium (Levine, 1973). The parasite multiplies in the promastigote form and grows best at temperatures below 30°C (Greenblatt and Glaser, 1965). Guinea pigs can be inoculated with the organisms grown in culture; however, prolonged cultivation between animal passages may destroy the ability of the parasite to infect guinea pigs.

C. Kidney Infections

Toxoplasma gondii and *Encephalitozoon cuniculi* may be found in the kidneys, but because they cause a generalized infection, they will be discussed later (Sections II, E, 1 and 3). The coccidium *Klossiella cobayae* has been reported from other tissues but is predominantly a kidney parasite.

Klossiella cobayae Seidelin, 1914 (Synonym: *Klossia caviae*)

a. Historical Review. The first record of a coccidium in the kidneys of the guinea pig was made by Pianese (1901). Seidelin (1914) observed a similar parasite in Nigeria. In Seidelin's opinion it differed from *Klossiella muris* (Smith and Johnson,

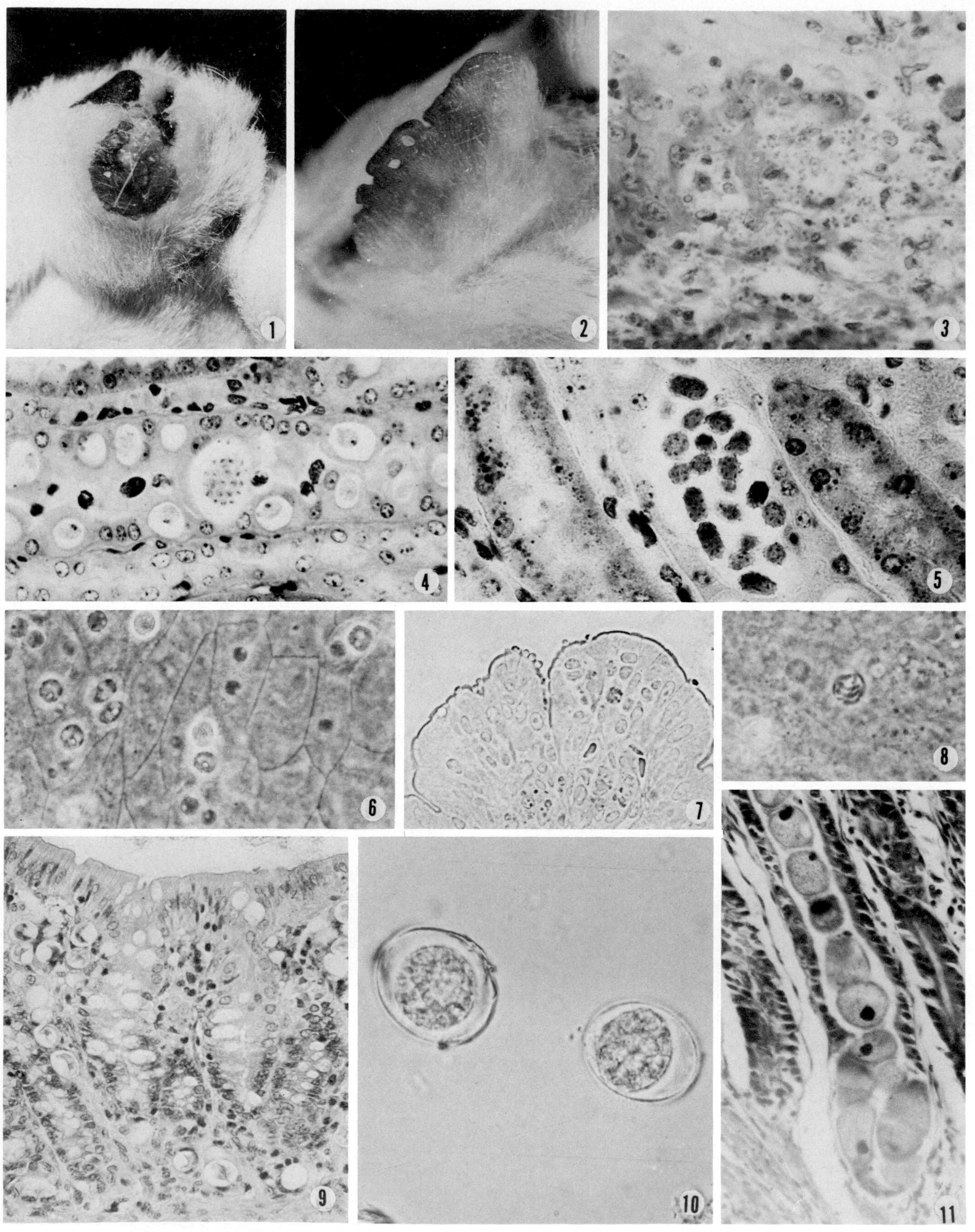

1902) in the number of organisms (sporoblasts) produced, therefore he established a new species, *Klossiella cobayae.* Pearce (1916) reported the parasite in guinea pigs from Pennsylvania and New Jersey. Sangiorgi (1916), not aware of Seidelin's work, described a coccidian parasite of guinea pig kidneys and named it *Klossia caviae.* The first complete account of the life cycle was given by Wenyon (1926) when he related the unpublished observations of Stevenson. That account is still considered valid (Levine and Ivens, 1965). Alves de Souza (1931) reported the infection of a wild guinea pig in Brazil. All other reports have concerned infections in domestic guinea pigs. Krenn's (1936) paper on infections in mice and guinea pigs was the last of *K. cobayae* until 1952, when periodic reports began to appear in European journals (Maržan, 1952; Reichenow, 1953; Bonciu *et al.*, 1957; Cossel, 1958; Stojanov and Cvetanov, 1965; Bonciu and Petrovici, 1966; Hofman and Hänichen, (1970).

b. Description. First generation schizonts of *K. cobayae* are in endothelial cells of glomerular capillaries and supposedly in other organs (Fig. 4). Schizonts reach 2–7 μm diameter and cause the host cell to bulge into the capillary lumen. Mature schizonts contain eight to twelve merozoites measuring 2 × 1 μm. They are released into the blood when the host cell ruptures. Some merozoites invade other endothelial cells where schizogony is presumably repeated, while others move into the proximal convoluted tubules and initiate second generation schizogony. These schizonts are large, contain approximately 100 merozoites, and greatly enlarge the epithelial cell nearly filling the lumen of the tubule. When merozoites are released by rupture of the host cell, they migrate down the tubules to the thick limb of Henle's loop and enter epithelial cells. These merozoites begin the gametogonous stages. According to Stevenson, two merozoites associate in syzygy and one becomes much larger than the other; the smaller one is the microgametocyte; the larger, the macrogamete. The microgametocyte divides once to form two microgametes, one of which fertilizes the macrogamete. Stevenson (in Wenyon, 1926) observed that sometimes there are two or three microgametocytes associated with a macrogamete. On the other hand, Vetterling and Thompson (1972) found a large microgametocyte in *K. equi* that produced about ten microgametes. These migrated to the macrogamete, where up to five were found in the parasitophorous vacuole. I have observed similar stages in kidney sections from guinea pigs. Therefore, this facet of the life cycle of *K. cobayae* is open to further investigation.

Once the macrogamete is fertilized, the resultant zygote undergoes sporogony. The sporont grows to 30–40 μm and produces 30 or more sporoblasts, each of which becomes a sporocyst (Fig. 5). According to Stevenson (in Wenyon, 1926), it is doubtful whether a true oocyst wall is formed around the developing sporocysts, but Reichenow (1953) considered that an oocyst wall exists. My observations agree with those of Stevenson. What Reichenow considered to be the "oocyst wall" is the host cell membrane. After formation of the sporocyst membrane, about 30 sporozoites develop within each sporocyst. When the host cell membrane ruptures, sporulated sporocysts flow down the kidney tubules and pass in the urine. Once they infect a new host, the sporozoites apparently excyst in the gut lumen, pass through the mucosa, and enter the capillary or lymphatic system where they invade endothelial cells. Some sporozoites reach the glomeruli and the cycle begins anew.

c. Location in Host. The stages most readily identifiable and most frequently seen are the gametogonous and sporogonous cycle in the epithelium of the loops of Henle. The schizogonous stages are found in epithelial cells of proximal convoluted tubules and glomerular endothelium. These latter stages are seen infrequently.

According to Stevenson (in Wenyon, 1926), Twort and Twort (1932), and Bonnc (1925), schizogonous stages of *K. cobayae* and *K. muris* are found in endothelial cells of blood vessels, lung, spleen, and other organs; but Otto (1957) failed to find them outside the kidneys. Because these stages somewhat resemble *Encephalitozoon* and *Toxoplasma,* any stages found outside the kidneys should be examined carefully.

d. Prevalence and Geographical Distribution. Most reports are not recent and have not given sufficient data from which to derive prevalence figures. Seidelin (1914) reported 20% of 20 guinea pigs infected in Nigeria. Pearce (1916) found 20% of

Figs. 1 and 2. Lesions of *Leishmania enriettii* in scrotum and ear of a guinea pig. (Photographs, courtesy of Dr. E. J. L. Soulsby.)

Fig. 3. Section of ear lesion with numerous amastigote stages in tissue. Hematoxylin and eosin. ×400. (Slide, courtesy of Dr. E. J. L. Soulsby.)

Fig. 4. Stages of *Klossiella cobayae* in kidney tubules. Single nucleated gametocytes and budding sporont. Hematoxylin and eosin. ×400.

Fig. 5. Sporocysts of *Klossiella cobayae.* Hematoxylin and eosin. ×1000.

Fig. 6. Surface of ileal mucosa with numerous stages of *Cryptosporidium wrairi.* Phase contrast microscopy. ×1000. (Courtesy of *The Journal of Protozoology*.)

Fig. 7. Section through epon embedded ileal mucosa. Stages of *Cryptosporidium wrairi* perched along surface of epithelial cells. Phase contrast microscopy. ×400.

Fig. 8. First generation schizont with 8 merozoites on surface of epithelial cell. Phase contrast microscopy. ×1000. (Courtesy of *The Journal of Protozoology*.)

Fig. 9. Section through colon infected with *Eimeria caviae.* Oocysts and macrogametes in mucosa. Hematoxylin and eosin. ×400.

Fig. 10., Unsporulated oocysts of *Eimeria caviae* in scraping of cecal mucosa. ×400.

Fig. 11. *Balantidium caviae* in cecal crypt. Note the absence of tissue invasion. Hematoxylin and eosin. ×400.

60 guinea pigs infected in Pennsylvania and New Jersey. The most complete and thorough report to date concerns a study of 976 guinea pigs in Romania (Bonciu *et al.*, 1957). They found *K. cobayae* in an average of 60.5% of the adult animals (13 to 65% in different groups) and in 17% of old animals. The youngest animals found infected were 3 weeks old. They reported a seasonal fluctuation, 91% in the summer and 43% in the winter.

Klossiella cobayae is presumably cosmopolitan in distribution; it has been found in Nigeria (Seidelin, 1914), Italy (Pianese, 1901; Sangiorgi, 1916), England (Stevenson, in Wenyon, 1926), Romania (Bonciu *et al.*, 1957), Brazil (Alves de Souza, 1931), Germany (Hofman and Hänichen, 1970), and the United States in Pennsylvania and New Jersey (Pearce, 1916), Illinois (Levine and Morrill, in Levine, 1973), and Missouri (J. E. Wagner and J. L. Taylor, personal communication).

e. Pathology. According to Pearce (1916), kidney lesions due to *K. cobayae* are slight, consisting of an irregular accumulation of inflammatory and fibroblastic cells. Conversely, Bonciu *et al.* (1957) reported nearly all of the kidneys examined had a subacute nephritis with degenerative lesions. However, these may not have been caused by *K. cobayae.* Tubules may appear to be obstructed by masses of sporocysts and degenerative cells. Cossel (1958) described the microscopic appearance of infected kidneys.

f. Clinical Signs. Klossiella cobayae apparently causes no clinical signs. However, guinea pigs with signs of kidney dysfunction should be examined for this parasite.

g. Diagnosis. Heavily infected kidneys may have an irregular surface with gray mottling, but in most cases gross lesions are not apparent. Finding distinctive stages in tissue sections examined microscopically is the only reliable means of diagnosis. Schizogonic stages must be differentiated from *Toxoplasma* and *Encephalitozoon.*

Sporocysts should be demonstrable in urine, but reports of such findings are sketchy and leave some doubt as to the practicability of this technique. There are, at present, no reliable means to diagnose the infection in living animals.

h. Control and Prevention. Because infections with *K. cobayae* cannot yet be diagnosed reliably in living guinea pigs, treatment has not been investigated. However, sulfonamides may be effective.

The best way to control *Klossiella* is to prevent urine contamination of guinea pig facilities.

D. Lung Infections

Only *Pneumocystis carinii* has been reported from the lungs of guinea pigs. It is now generally considered to be a fungus but was thought to be a protozoan for many years. For this reason, it is discussed in this chapter.

Pneumocystis carinii Delanoë and Delanoë, 1912

Historical Review. Pneumocystis was observed for the first time by Chagas (1909) in the lungs of a guinea pig infected experimentally with *Trypanosoma cruzi.* Chagas later (1911) found it in the lungs of a human who had died from acute Chagas' disease. Carini and Maciel (1915) found the organisms in rats infected with *Trypanosoma lewisi* and in guinea pigs. Each thought the cysts were a part of the trypanosome life cycle. Delanoë and Delanoë (1912) found the cysts in rats free of the concurrent trypanosome infection and described the parasite as *Pneumocystis carinii.* This parasite is regarded as a protozoan by some (Campbell, 1972; Frenkel, 1971) and as a fungus or yeast by others (Vavra and Kučera, 1970). I tend to agree with the latter authors. Transmission of *Pneumocystis* from one species to another has never been proved. The complement fixing antibodies against organisms from humans and from rats are specific (Goetz, 1960; Frenkel *et al.*, 1966). There are also differences in size of the cysts; those from rats are smaller than those from rabbits. Nevertheless, the same name, *P. carinii,* is used for organisms from all hosts. The infection in guinea pigs is among the least known. Kučera *et al.* (1971) have reviewed the spontaneous hosts of *P. carinii.* A review of the disease in humans is found in Marcial-Rojas (1971). The reader is referred to Pakes (1974) or Frenkel (1971) for a description, pathology, and diagnosis.

E. Generalized Infections

Three protozoa can cause generalized infections during their acute state: *Toxoplasma gondii, Sarcocystis caviae,* and *Encephalitozoon cuniculi.* However, during the chronic stage, their cysts are usually found in more specific locations, particularly the brain and heart.

1. *Toxoplasma gondii* Nicolle and Manceaux, 1909

a. Historical Review. The first report of a spontaneous *Toxoplasma* infection in guinea pigs was by Carini and Migliano (1916) in Brazil. They named it *Toxoplasma caviae.* However, after a review of 24 described species and cross-transmission studies, Mesnil (1918) concluded that the only valid species was *Toxoplasma gondii.*

Toxoplasma has typically appeared spontaneously in animals inoculated with various agents. Mooser (1929) and de la Barrera and Riva (1927, 1928) found *Toxoplasma* in guinea pigs used for transmission of typhus. In studies with rabies virus, Nicolau (1932a,b, 1933) encountered spontaneous infections of *Toxoplasma* and *Klossiella cobayae.* Sabin and Olitsky

(1937) inoculated brains of two guinea pigs suspected of viral infection into mice, which succumbed to toxoplasmosis. They pointed out the consistent association of filterable viruses and *Toxoplasma*, and that unless filtrations or careful histological checks were made, it would be possible to transmit *Toxoplasma* in series and thus mistake the signs and lesions for those of neurotropic viruses. Markham (1937) had a similar experience but obtained histological evidence of the presence of *Toxoplasma*. However, he misidentified *Klossiella cobayae* in the kidneys as *Toxoplasma*. Through the 1930's, 1940's, 1950's, and 1960's, sporadic reports of spontaneous *Toxoplasma* infections in guinea pigs appeared (Boisseau and Nodenot, 1936; Mariani, 1941; Perrin, 1943b; Kean and Grocott, 1945; de Rodaniche and de Pinzon, 1949; Varela *et al.*, 1953; Orio *et al.*, 1958; Kulasiri, 1962; Berengo *et al.*, 1967; Bérard-Badier *et al.*, 1968).

b. Description. *Toxoplasma gondii* has recently been shown to have a typical coccidian life cycle in the intestine of felines and to produce oocysts similar to those of the "small race" of *Isospora bigemina*. The tissue stages in mammals, birds, and reptiles are asexual developmental stages in an intermediate host, which are then transmitted to the definitive host, the cat, by carnivorism (Hutchison *et al.*, 1970; Sheffield and Melton, 1970; Frenkel *et al.*, 1970; Dubey *et al.*, 1970; Overdulve, 1970; Witte and Piekarski, 1970; Weiland and Kühn, 1970). The only stages found spontaneously in guinea pigs are asexual tissue stages, i.e., proliferative and cystic forms. To clarify terminological confusion, Frenkel (1973) introduced two new terms, "tachyzoites" for the rapidly multiplying forms of acute infection (previously referred to as trophozoites, pseudocysts, or proliferative forms) and "bradyzoites" for the slowly multiplying encysted forms characteristic of chronic infections (previously called merozoites, zoites, or cyst forms). Hoare (1972) has also suggested terms for these stages, endozoites and cystizoites, respectively. Frenkel's terminology will be used here.

Tachyzoites are crescentic or banana shaped, with one end pointed and the other rounded, and are 4–8 by 2–4 μm. Once intracellular, they assume an ovoid shape and undergo endodyogony, whereby two daughter organisms develop within the parent organism. This development may be rapid, so that 8–30 tachyzoites are found in a single cell.

Bradyzoites are the same size and shape as tachyzoites but contain large polysaccharide granules, multiply slowly, and are more resistant to peptic digestion (Jacobs *et al.*, 1960; Frenkel, 1973). From ten to several hundred bradyzoites are found within a 1 μm cyst wall. These intracellular cysts are characteristic of chronic infection. They are ellipsoidal (50 × 100 μm) in cardiac and skeletal muscle and spherical (30–100 μm diameter) in brain, eye, and other organs. Cysts may persist for months and have been recorded 5 years after experimental infection of guinea pigs (Lainson, 1959).

Acute *Toxoplasma* infections, parasitemia, and chronic infection of the uterus may result in infection of the fetus *in utero*. Bérard-Badier *et al.* (1968) reported abortion in experimentally infected guinea pigs.

c. Location in Host. Tachyzoites can be found in nearly every organ in acute infections, but bradyzoites are usually seen in the brain, heart, and skeletal muscles (Frenkel, 1973). Rommel and Breuning (1967) observed *Toxoplasma* in the milk of acutely infected guinea pigs.

d. Prevalence and Geographical Distribution. Spontaneous *Toxoplasma* infections in guinea pigs have been reported from Argentina (de la Barrera and Riva, 1928), Brazil (Carini and Migliano, 1916), Panama (Kean and Grocott, 1945; de Rodaniche and de Pinzon, 1949), Mexico (Mooser, 1929; Varela *et al.*, 1953), the United States (Mooser, 1929; Sabin and Olitsky, 1937; Markham, 1937; Perrin, 1943b; Miller and Feldman, 1953), France (Nicolau, 1932a), The Netherlands (Makstenieks and Verlinde, 1957), Italy (Mariani, 1941; Berengo *et al.*, 1967), Brazzaville (Boisseau and Nodenot, 1936; Orio *et al.*, 1958), and Sri Lanka (Kulasiri, 1962).

No accurate figures on the prevalence of *Toxoplasma* infections in guinea pigs are available. Since 1940, some reports have included prevalance data: Perrin (1943b) reported 12% of 17 and 5% of 275 guinea pigs infected; Kean and Grocott (1945), 8% of 60; de Rodaniche and de Pinzon (1949), 37% of 8; Orio *et al.* (1958), 23% of 31; Miller and Feldman (1953), 27% of 51; and Makstenieks and Verlinde (1957), 33% of 174. Spontaneous infections are rare in laboratory guinea pigs in the United States, but infections continue to be found in pets and zoo animals (Frenkel, 1973).

e. Pathology. In laboratory guinea pigs, spontaneous *Toxoplasma* infections result from either injection of material contaminated with zoites or ingestion of material contaminated with oocysts from cats. The number of zoites acquired and the route of infection determines the severity of infection. Injection of *Toxoplasma* may result in acute fatal pneumonia and hepatitis. Such findings were vividly reported by Mooser (1929) who, during investigations of murine typhus, injected guinea pigs with tissue homogenates from rats. More severe lesions are seen in other laboratory animals that have been studied more thoroughly (Frenkel, 1971; Pakes, 1974). Asymptomatic chronic infections are usually detected by finding cysts in the myocardium (Kean and Grocott, 1945), or brain (Perrin, 1943b). Unless preexperimental sera are available, it may be impossible to determine whether the cysts arose from natural infection or from the results of experimentation.

f. Clinical Signs. Nearly all spontaneous *Toxoplasma* infections are asymptomatic, and infections are usually discovered through animal inoculations or examination of sections of heart muscle and brain.

g. Diagnosis. Diagnosis of *Toxoplasma* infections in guinea pigs is based ideally on a combination of animal inoculation, morphological identification, and consistent serological changes. Mice or hamsters are preferable for intraperitoneal inoculation of tissue homogenates (Frenkel, in Davis, 1973). Identification of zoites in smears of peritoneal exudate and in sections of tissues are necessary. *Toxoplasma* are differentiated from other protozoa by differential staining (Pakes, 1974). Several serological tests are available for diagnosing *Toxoplasma* infections: complement fixation, hemagglutination, latex agglutination, toxoplasmin skin test, indirect fluorescent antibody, and dye test. The latter two are the simplest and results are reliable. Both tests are specific for *Toxoplasma gondii* (Soltys and Woo, 1972; Frenkel, 1973; Levine, 1973). Serological tests should be repeated several times for each animal.

h. Methods of Cultivation. Toxoplasma gondii can be cultivated as tachyzoites in cell culture (Frenkel, in Davis, 1973; Doran, 1973).

i. Control and Prevention. Some sulfonamides (sulfadiazine, sulfamethazine), sulfones (4,4′-diaminodiphenylsulfone), tetracyclines (chlortetracycline most active, oxytetracycline intermediate, and tetracycline least active), and dihydro-*s*-triazines (1,2-dihydrotriazine) as well as spiramycin and pyrimethamine inhibit both tachyzoites and bradyzoites in mice. The most effective chemotherapy is the combined use of sulfadiazine and pyrimethamine, which are synergistic (Eyles, 1963). Frenkel (1971) recommends a dosage of 60 ppm of soluble sulfadiazine in drinking water or 60 ppm of sulfadiazine with 30 ppm pyrimethamine in the food, or both. If multiplication of the parasite is inhibited severely, the development of immunity may be insufficient for protection, and the guinea pigs may die from toxoplasmosis when the treatment is terminated. Established infection is rarely eradicated even by combined therapy. Unless the guinea pigs are particularly valuable for one reason or another, the soundest approach would be to destroy all animals that show a positive dye test titer.

Toxoplasma is transmitted by cannibalism, by oocysts, and, occasionally, transplacentally. The use of commercially prepared food and the prevention of cannibalism should eliminate the spread of *Toxoplasma* in laboratory guinea pigs. Cats should not be permitted to come in contact with guinea pig colonies because cat feces can be a source of infection. Oocysts are resistant to most disinfectants, and high temperatures (60°C) are needed to kill them. If *Toxoplasma* has been introduced into a colony, transplacental transmission can be obviated by breeding only seronegative guinea pigs.

Nematode and cestode eggs have been reported as carriers of *Toxoplasma* to guinea pigs, but this was refuted by Rommel *et al.* (1968). Flies, cockroaches, earthworms, and probably coprophagous invertebrates can be transport hosts for *Toxoplasma* (Wallace, 1971; Frenkel *et al.*, 1970).

Infections of humans from accidental aspiration, inhalation of spray, needle puncture, and contamination of cuts with tissue stages has been reported sporadically (Rawal, 1959; Neu, 1967), but the danger is slight if the accident is noticed and prompt treatment is begun. Disinfection of cuts with 70% ethanol or common disinfectants is effective. Several investigators who had worked safely with the tissue stages of *Toxoplasma* for many years became infected soon after beginning to work with infected cat feces (Frenkel, 1973; H. G. Sheffield, personal communication).

2. *Sarcocystis caviae* de Almeida, 1928

a. Historical Review. Like many parasites of guinea pigs, *Sarcocystis caviae* was first reported in Brazil. de Almeida (1928) found the parasite in the heart muscle of a guinea pig inoculated with a culture of "Blastomycose," thus a long period of confusion between *Sarcocystis* and fungi was begun. Few of the subsequent reports of *Sarcocystis* in guinea pigs are documented and in many cases the reported infection appears to have been with *Toxoplasma* (Kean and Grocott, 1945). The incidence of *Sarcocystis* has dwindled with refinement of husbandry techniques. Recently, however, Muir (Frenkel, 1973) found *Sarcocystis* in a colony of guinea pigs in Malaysia that had been fed natural food substances, particularly fresh greens.

b. Description. Sarcocystis forms cysts, also known as Miescher's tubules in muscles. These cysts are visible grossly as whitish streaks arranged lengthwise in muscles. Cysts are filled with small organisms called by many names, e.g., spores, trophozoites, Rainey's corpuscles, banana-shaped organisms, zoites. The term zoite will be used. Mature zoites, 4.5 × 1.0 μm, are sausage or banana shaped. Electron microscopic studies of *Besnoitia, Eimeria, Frenkelia, Isospora, Sarcocystis,* and *Toxoplasma* have demonstrated their close relationship (Scholtyseck *et al.*, 1973).

A great deal has been written concerning the life cycle of *Sarcocystis* species and we are nearing the goal of understanding its life cycle and transmission. *Sarcocystis,* like *Toxoplasma,* is a tissue stage of an "isosporan-like" coccidian of carnivores, (Rommel *et al.,* 1972; Heydorn and Rommel, 1972; Rommel and Heydorn, 1972; Wallace, 1973). Rommel and colleagues fed *Sarcocystis*-infected muscle from sheep, cattle, and pigs to cats, dogs, and man and showed that *Sarcocystis tenella* from sheep produced oocysts in cats; *Sarcocystis fusiformis* from cattle produced sporocysts and oocysts in cats, dogs, and man; and *Sarcocystis miescheriana* from pigs produced sporocysts and oocysts in man. Wallace (1973) fed "isosporan-like" oocysts from cats to mice and obtained *Sarcocystis muris* cysts in the mouse muscles. Then he fed these mice to cats and recovered oocysts in the cat feces and thus completed the life cycle. Whether the *Sarcocystis* coccidia will retain this generic name and where *Sarcocystis caviae* will fit has not been resolved.

c. Location in Host. Supposedly, *Sarcocystis* is found only in skeletal and heart muscle. When cysts resembling *Sarcocystis* are found elsewhere, a careful comparison with *Toxoplasma* and *Encephalitozoon* should be made.

d. Pathology. Like *Toxoplasma, Sarcocystis* is not likely to cause damage unless sporocysts or oocysts are ingested, and because *Sarcocystis* has not been transmitted by inoculation of the tissue stages (Frenkel, 1973), the pathogenesis is unknown.

e. Clinical Signs. The infection is asymptomatic. Organisms have been found in histological sections taken for other purposes. Because skeletal and heart muscle is not usually taken for routine examinations, *Sarcocystis* has probably been missed most of the time.

f. Diagnosis. In heavy infections, *Sarcocystis* can be detected by gross examination, but in light infections, tissue sections from leg, diaphragm, masseter, and heart muscle should be examined. Differentiation from *Toxoplasma* may be difficult and depends upon identification of the zoites. When *Toxoplasma* cysts are found in the heart, they should be accompanied by cysts in other organs, especially in the central nervous system, whereas, *Sarcocystis* cysts are found only in muscle.

Serological diagnosis has been attempted with the dye, complement fixation, precipitin, and agglutination tests (Arcay-de-Peraza, 1966; Soltys and Woo, 1972). Antibodies to *Sarcocystis* are different than those to *Toxoplasma* (Frenkel, 1973), but in view of the work of Rommel and colleagues (Rommel *et al.,* 1972; Heydorn and Rommel, 1972; Rommel and Heydorn, 1972), one might question the specificity of *Sarcocystis* antibodies.

g. Methods of Cultivations. Fayer (1970, 1972) obtained development of an avian *Sarcocystis* in avian and mammalian cell cultures. Zoites penetrated a variety of cells and developed into multinucleate stages. In embryonic bovine kidney and trachea cells, unsporulated oocysts formed.

h. Control and Prevention. No treatment is known. Because *Sarcocystis* infections, like those of *Toxoplasma*, are apparently acquired through ingestion of food and water contaminated with oocysts, they can be prevented by sanitation and good management.

3. *Encephalitozoon cuniculi* Levaditi, Nicolau, and Schoen, 1923 (Synonym: *Nosema cuniculi*)

Historical Review. *Encephalitozoon* is a protozoan parasite belonging to the subphylum Microspora that, with the exception of *Encephalitozoon* and *Thelohania,* are parasites of invertebrates. Although some believe the parasite belongs to the genus *Nosema,* the majority believe it belongs in a separate genus, *Encephalitozoon,* based on the work of Shadduck and Pakes (1971) and Sprague and Vernick (1971).

Encephalitozoon was first described by Wright and Craighead (1922) as the etiological agent in a spontaneous paralytic disease of young rabbits. Levaditi *et al.* (1923) named this organism *Encephalitozoon cuniculi.* The parasite was not recognized in guinea pigs until the report of Perrin (1943a). Some years later, Ruge (1951) also reported the infection in guinea pigs. The number of reports is significantly fewer for guinea pigs than for mice or rabbits. Shadduck and Pakes (1971) reviewed encephalitozoonosis in all laboratory animals.

Guinea pigs appear to be resistant to the effects of *E. cuniculi* (Levaditi *et al.,* 1924; Perrin, 1943a; Petri, 1966). Petri (1966) used a very large inoculum of Yoshida ascitic fluid contaminated with *E. cuniculi* spores with no apparent effect on the guinea pigs. Jordan and Mirick (1955) and Perrin (1943a) observed asymptomatic infections in guinea pigs, which were detected only by subinoculation of their organs to mice. Because of the lesser importance of *Encephalitozoon* in guinea pigs, the reader is referred to the review of Pakes (1974) for details.

III. ALIMENTARY INFECTIONS

A. Oral Cavity

Jackson (1920a,b) discovered an intracellular protozoan in guinea pig salivary glands. This parasite was usually found in ducts of serous glands, but occasionally seen in ducts of mucous glands. In several pigs, nearly all ductal and acinar tissue was altered. She found 54% of 48 guinea pigs infected in one group and a similar percentage of infection in another colony, both in Pennsylvania. There were many mononucleated parasites of 3–10 μm diameter and a few multinucleated forms with 30–40 buds. Jackson thought this parasite was a coccidium. Her photomicrographs show an organism remarkably similar to *Klossiella.*

B. Small Intestine

Giardia caviae and *Cryptosporidium wrairi* have been reported from the small intestine. Kofoid *et al.* (1935) reported *Tritrichomonas caviae* in the small intestine but it normally is considered a cecal flagellate and will be discussed later.

1. *Giardia caviae* Hegner, 1923

a. Historical Review. Hegner (1923a,b, 1924a, 1925, 1926c, 1927) endeavored to differentiate various species of *Giardia* in mammals from species found in man. He described the organism in the guinea pig as *G. caviae* (Hegner, 1923a). Other reports of *G. caviae* are indicative of the cosmopolitan distribution of this protozoan (Fantham, 1923; Deschiens, 1926; Gabaldón, 1930; Chang, 1935; Morénas, 1938; Pinto, 1938; Dagert Boyer and Scorza Boyer, 1957; Ray *et al.*, 1961; Corradini and Binato, 1962).

Names given to various species of *Giardia* depend on the reporting author. Traditionally, workers have thought that *Giardia* are highly specific (Hegner, 1926c, 1927, 1930) so different names have been assigned those from different hosts (Ansari, 1951, 1952). Filice (1952) did not find any structural differences between giardias in laboratory rats and those in wild rodents. He found no acceptable documentation of cross-transmission studies between species. He did not discuss all described species of *Giardia,* but he concluded that only two species occur in mammals: *Giardia muris* in the mouse, rat, and hamster; and *Giardia duodenalis* in the rabbit, rat, chinchilla, ground squirrel, deer mouse, pocket mouse, and man and presumably also in the ox, dog, cat, and guinea pig. Successful transfers of *Giardia lamblia* from man to laboratory rats (Hegner, 1930; Armaghan, 1937; Haiba, 1953, 1956) suggest that Filice (1952) may have been correct. However, additional careful cross-transmission studies are needed (Bemrick, 1962). Meanwhile, the use of different specific names for forms in different hosts is convenient, hence, *Giardia caviae.*

b. Description. Giardia caviae is bilaterally symmetrical with a piriform to ellipsoidal body (Fig. 17). The anterior is broadly rounded and the posterior tapers to a blunt point. The dorsal side is convex, whereas the ventral surface is a concave sucking disc. *Giardia caviae* has two anterior vesicular nuclei with large nucleoli, two slender rods or axostyles, four pairs of flagella, and a pair of long darkly staining clawlike bodies. The trophozoites are 8.0–15.0 by 6.5–1.0 μm and divide by bilateral division.

For reasons not yet known, some trophozoites form cysts which are approximately the same size as the trophozoites and have two or four nuclei and a number of fibrillar remnants of trophozoite organelles. Cysts are passed in feces, and susceptible hosts may become infected through fecal contamination.

Giardia lie on the epithelium attached by marginal lips of the sucking disc and use digestive products of the brush border (Solovjev, 1968; Holberton, 1973).

c. Location. Giardia caviae occurs in the anterior small intestine, primarily the duodenum.

d. Prevalence and Geographical Distribution. Wenrich (Nie, 1950) found one case of *Giardia* infection in over 20 years of research with guinea pigs. It is probably of very low prevalence in guinea pigs. *Giardia* has been reported from guinea pigs in Italy (Corradini and Binato, 1962; Castellino and de Carneri, 1964), China (Chang, 1935), India (Ray *et al.*, 1961), and the U.S.S.R. (Zasukhin and Kheisin, 1957).

e. Clinical Signs. Overt clinical signs and pathology have not been reported for guinea pigs infected with *G. caviae.* A mucous, but not bloody, diarrhea has been reported from other infected laboratory rodents.

f. Diagnosis. Giardia caviae infections can be diagnosed rapidly by identifying trophozoites or cysts in fecal smears with phase contrast microscopy. Fixing with Schaudinn's fluid and staining with iron hematoxylin is also satisfactory. Trophozoites and cysts occur in normal fecal pellets, whereas only trophozoites are found in diarrheic feces. Cysts should be concentrated by zinc sulfate flotation because sugar and salt solutions distort them. An even better method to avoid distortion would be flotation on Ficol gradients.

g. Methods of Cultivation. Karapetyan (1962) obtained development of *G. lamblia* in cell cultures inoculated with yeast, and Meyer (1970) has grown *Giardia* from rabbits and chinchilla in axenic cultures.

h. Control and Prevention. Standard sanitary measures should be used to prevent transmission of *Giardia. Giardia lamblia* cysts can be killed with 2 to 5% phenol or Lysol (Červa, 1955). *Giardia* can be removed from the intestine with quinacrine, chloroquine, or aldarsone, or by starvation (Wenrich, 1949; Choquette, 1950). However, more effective drugs used for humans may also be effective in guinea pigs (Levine, 1973). If *Giardia* can be freely transmitted from one host to another, guinea pigs should be examined carefully when a *Giardia* infection is suspected.

2. *Cryptosporidium wrairi,* Vetterling, Jervis, Merrill, and Sprinz, 1971

a. Historical Review. The genus *Cryptosporidium* and the type species, *C. muris,* from the stomach of the laboratory mouse, were described by Tyzzer (1907, 1910). Later, Tyzzer (1912) described *C. parvum* from the ileum of the mouse. He also mentioned cryptosporidia in the chicken and rabbit but gave no details. Jervis *et al.* (1966) observed cryptosporidia in the small intestine of laboratory guinea pigs. It was subsequently described as a new species, *C. wrairi,* based on cross-transmission studies and morphological variations (Vetterling *et al.*, 1971a).

b. Description. No oocysts have been found. Vetterling *et al.* (1971a) concluded that the four-merozoite packet that Tyzzer (1912) called an oocyst was a second generation schizont. Schizonts, which develop from trophozoites, range from 0.9–2.8 μm when immature to 3.4–4.4 μm when mature.

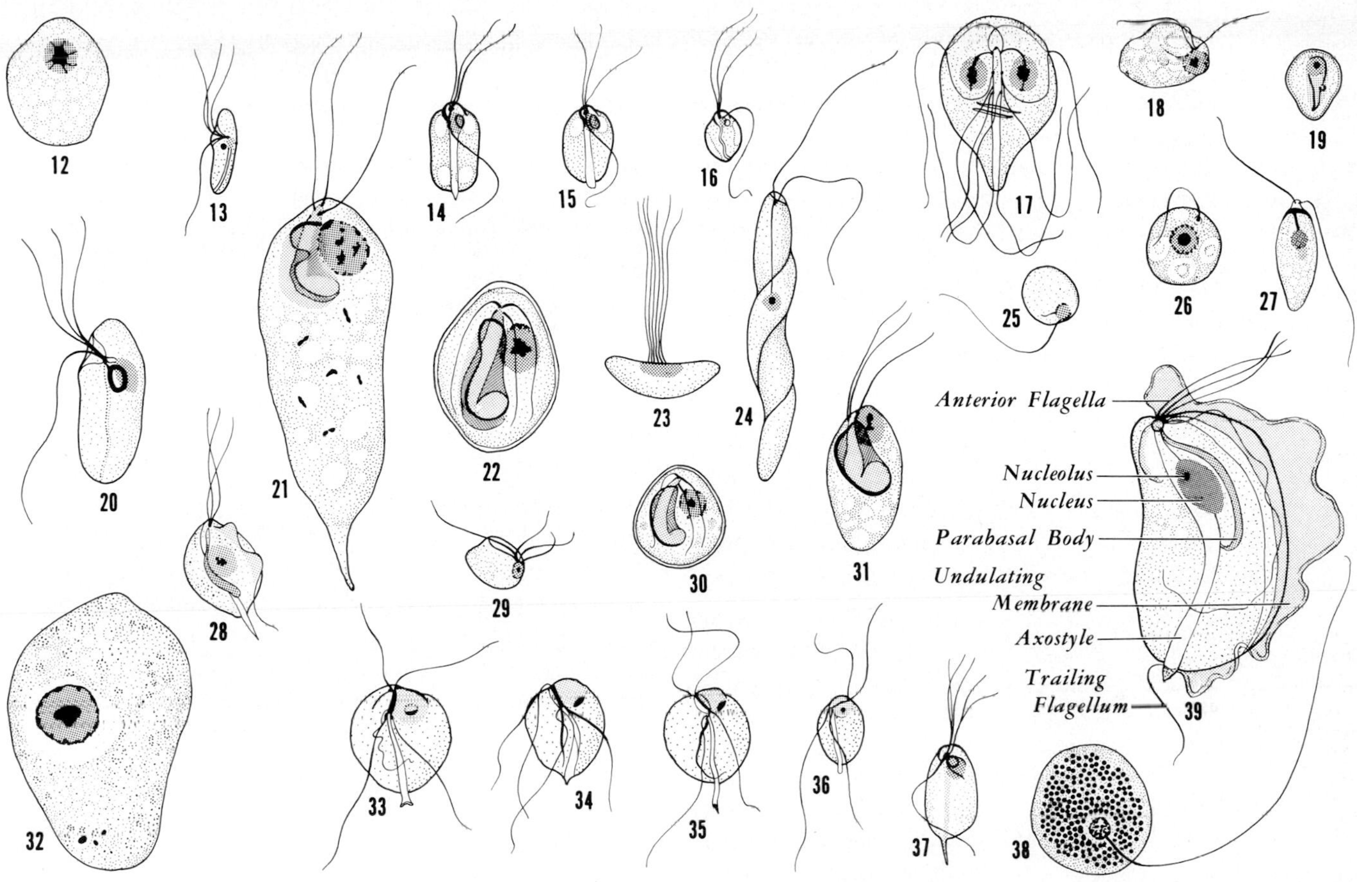

Figs. 12–39. Line drawings of guinea pig flagellates. ×2000.

Fig. 12. *Endolimax caviae* (redrawn from Hegner, 1926b).
Fig. 13. *Chilomitus conexus* (redrawn from Nie, 1950).
Fig. 14. *Monocercomonas caviae* (redrawn from Nie, 1950).
Fig. 15. *Monocercomonas pistillum* (redrawn from Nie, 1950).
Fig. 16. *Monocercomonas minuta* (redrawn from Nie, 1950).
Fig. 17. *Giardia caviae* (redrawn from Hegner, 1923a).
Fig. 18. *Retortamonas caviae* (redrawn from Nie, 1950).
Fig. 19. *Retortamonas caviae* cyst (redrawn from Nie, 1950).
Fig. 20. *Chilomitus caviae* (redrawn from Nie, 1950).
Fig. 21. *Chilomastix intestinalis* (redrawn from Nie, 1948).
Fig. 22. *Chilomastix intestinalis* cyst (redrawn from Nie, 1948).
Fig. 23. *Selenomonas ruminantum* (redrawn from da Fonseca, 1915).
Fig. 24. *Spiromonas augusta* (redrawn from Faust, 1950).
Fig. 25. *Caviomonas mobilis* (redrawn from Nie, 1950).
Fig. 26. *Oikomonas termo* (redrawn from Nie, 1950).
Fig. 27. *Proteromonas brevifilia* (redrawn from Nie, 1950).
Fig. 28. *Tritrichomonas* sp. (redrawn from Nie, 1950).
Fig. 29. *Enteromonas caviae* (redrawn from Nie, 1950).
Fig. 30. *Chilomastix wenrichi* cyst (redrawn from Nie, 1950).
Fig. 31. *Chilomastix wenrichi* (redrawn from Nie, 1950).
Fig. 32. *Entamoeba caviae* (redrawn from Nie, 1950).
Fig. 33. *Monocercomonoides caviae* (redrawn from Nie, 1950).
Fig. 34. *Monocercomonoides quadrifunilis* (redrawn from Nie, 1950).
Fig. 35. *Monocercomonoides wenrichi* (redrawn from Nie, 1950).
Fig. 36. *Monocercomonoides exilis* (redrawn from Nie, 1950).
Fig. 37. *Hexamastix caviae* (redrawn from Nie, 1950).
Fig. 38. *Sphaeromonas communis* (redrawn from da Fonseca, 1915).
Fig. 39. *Tritrichomonas caviae* (redrawn from Nie, 1950).

Granules are occasionally seen in fresh specimens but not in stained preparations (Figs. 6 and 7). The nucleus of the trophozoite divides three times to form eight daughter nuclei. Merozoites in the first generation schizonts are formed around these eight nuclei (Fig. 8). In second generation schizonts, only two divisions take place and four merozoites are formed. The first generation merozoites are vermiform, 3.0–5.0 by 0.4 μm; those of the second generation are slightly shorter. The nucleus is in the posterior part of merozoites of both generations, and no polysaccharide granules are found in the residuum.

Microgametocytes differ little from schizonts except the nuclei of the microgametocytes are smaller and stain more densely once nuclear division begins. They give rise to 12 to 16 microgametes and a large residuum. The microgametes are about 1 by 0.2 μm and have no flagella.

Developing macrogametes measure 4.0–7.0 μm diameter and, unlike schizonts and microgametocytes, have many refractile and polysaccharide granules. The "attachment" organ of Tyzzer (1910, 1912) is found on all stages in smears and sectioned material. However, it is a feeding structure rather than a holdfast structure.

c. Location in Host. Cryptosporidia are more numerous in the anterior ileum and are progressively less numerous posteriorly. The parasites are usually distributed over the entire surface of intestinal villi, being most numerous toward the tips and absent in the crypts. They often are found in large numbers in the irregular depressions that indent the mucosal surface. All forms are seen near the epithelial cell surface within the striated border of epithelial cells. Vetterling *et al.* (1969, 1971b) have shown that although the parasites appear to be extracellular, they are actually within the host cell.

d. Prevalence and Geographical Distribution. This parasite has been reported in the guinea pig colony of the Walter Reed Army Institute of Research, Washington, D.C. Infection rates of 90% were found, but the more usual rate was 30 to 40%. The parasite was found only in young guinea pigs weighing 250 to 300 gm; it has not been observed in animals weighing 1 kg or more; older animals apparently are either naturally resistant or have developed immunity from earlier infections.

e. Clinical Signs. Weight loss has been reported (Jervis *et al.*, 1966).

f. Pathology. Although infection was accompanied by chronic enteritis, it did not produce diarrhea. Infected villi are short, broad, sometimes flattened, and often irregular. Irregularities appear in microvilli and in the cytoplasmic components of infected epithelial cells (Jervis *et al.*, 1966; Takeuchi, 1971; Vetterling *et al.*, 1971b). The lamina propria contains increased numbers of monocytes and eosinophils that transmigrate through the epithelial layer. Lesions, proportional to the degree of infection, are most severe in the terminal ileum and occasionally extend to the upper jejunum. Seven mucosal enzymes studied by Jervis *et al.* (1966) had lower activity in the infected than uninfected ileum.

Starvation of the guinea pigs reduced the number of organisms, which increased and reappeared as trophozoites when feeding was resumed. Consequently, the parasite's nutrition may be closely tied to the host cell's intake of nutrients from the intestinal lumen (Jervis *et al.*, 1966). Reduction of the mucosal surface area and decreased activity of several epithelial enzymes probably lower the absorptive ability of the small intestine and thereby affect the results of experimental studies (Jervis *et al.*, 1966).

g. Diagnosis. Results in identifying cryptosporidia in the mucosa and in studying the various developmental stages are best when fresh mucosal scrapings are examined with phase contrast microscopy. Examination of paraffin-embedded material is less satisfactory, especially when buffered formalin is used as a fixative. Cryptosporidia are frequently diagnosed in intestinal tissues prepared for electron microscopy.

h. Control and Prevention. Infections in guinea pig colonies can be eliminated by addition of 0.2% sulfaquinoxiline or sulfamethazine to the water.

C. Cecum and Colon

By far the greatest number of protozoa that parasitize the guinea pig are found in the cecum and colon. A greater variety of protozoan species are found in the guinea pig than in any other laboratory rodent; however, each species is found in fewer numbers. At least 35 species of protozoa have been described from the guinea pig cecum and colon: one coccidium, two amebas, 22 flagellates, and 10 ciliates. Several flagellates and ciliates have been reported only once. Because they are related to coprophagous free-living forms, some may be opportunistic parasites ingested with fecal material (Watson, 1946); others are definitely parasitic protozoa. Thorough surveys of cecal and colon fauna have not been made. No one has studied the quantitative relationship between cecal fauna and guinea pig physiology. These cecal protozoa, except *Eimeria caviae,* occur in the lumenal contents. They usually feed on bacteria, undigested plant material, starch, and soluble nutrients. Although only *Eimeria caviae* is pathogenic, *Balantidium caviae* may invade the cecal mucosa.

Special procedures to study flagellates and ciliates include protargol silver protein and French silverline staining techniques. Special morphological terms include pelta, costa, and parabasal body. The reader is referred to Levine (1973) for background information.

1. *Eimeria caviae* Sheather, 1924

a. Historical Review. Labbé (1899) noticed coccidial oocysts in intestinal contents of the guinea pig. However, he thought they were a variety of rabbit coccidia. Strada and Traina (1900) reported coccidia in intestinal contents of diarrhetic guinea pigs and found coccidia in nodules on the liver. Bugge and Heinke (1921) described an outbreak of coccidiosis in a colony of guinea pigs. They described oocysts and their sporulation, published photomicrographs of the oocyst, and discussed clinical and pathological results of infection. They showed that the parasite was not the same as that of the rabbit. Later, Sheather (1924) studied an outbreak of coccidiosis in guinea pigs in England. He described the oocyst and partly described the endogenous stages, and transmitted the infection to other guinea pigs with sporulated oocysts. He identified the coccidium as a species of *Eimeria* to which he gave the name *E. caviae*. Subsequently, Alves de Souza (1931) reported *E. caviae* in wild guinea pigs in Brazil and successfully transmitted it to laboratory guinea pigs with sporulated oocysts. Henry (1932) conducted a complete study of the biological, pathological, and immunological aspects of guinea pig coccodiosis; Lapage (1940) published a detailed description of the life cycle, cytological characters of the endogenous stages, and host–parasite relationships; and Ellis and Wright (1961) reported the gross and microscopic lesions in a laboratory outbreak.

During the early days of coccidiosis research, workers used the guinea pig coccidium as a standard for differentiating other species (Lerche, 1921; Dieben, 1924; Gusev, 1934; Yakimov, 1934).

Many reports have reviewed the available information on *E. caviae*. These range from mere lists of the species (Rastegaieff, 1930; Levine and Becker, 1933; Gauget, 1938; Hardcastle, 1943; Zasukhin and Kheisin, 1957) to short evaluations (Steinmetz and Lerche, 1923; Wenyon, 1926; Fritzsche, 1933; Faust, 1950; Levine, 1957; Horton-Smith, 1958) and extensive reviews (Becker, 1934; Levine and Ivens, 1965). Interestingly, the coccidium of guinea pigs has been reviewed more frequently than it has been studied in depth. With the controversy over large and small oocysts (Henry, 1932; Lapage, 1940), the possible existence of a liver coccidium (Strada and Traina, 1900; Kleeberg and Steenken, 1963), and the widespread use of guinea pigs, the lack of anything more than "case reports" since 1940 seems an enigma.

b. Description. Most laboratory animals have a multiplicity of eimerian species but the guinea pig has only one reported species, *Eimeria caviae*.

Oocysts are ellipsoidal and subspherical with a smooth, often brownish wall and no micropyle (Fig. 10). They measure 17–25 by 13–18 μm (19 × 16 μm) (Lapage, 1940). Henry (1932) found oocysts of this size, but also reported smaller oocysts measuring 12.8 μm diameter. Larger oocysts had no polar granule; an oocyst residuum is either present (Lapage, 1940) or absent (Pellérdy, 1965). Sporocysts measure 11–13 by 6–7 μm and contain two sporozoites and a residuum. Sporulation time is temperature dependent and ranges from 2 to 11 days (Bugge and Heinke, 1921; Sheather, 1924; Henry, 1932; Lapage, 1940; Pellérdy, 1965).

Sporozoites penetrate epithelial cells of the mucosa, where schizogony may be detected on the seventh or eighth day after infection (Sheather, 1924; Henry, 1932; Lapage, 1940). Schizonts measure 6–10 μm and produce from fewer than 12 to 32 merozoites. The sickle-shaped merozoites range from 6 to 16 μm in length. Based on the length of time from inoculation to gametocyte formation and the heterogeneity in size and number of merozoites, there is likely more than one schizogonous generation. Microgametocytes are 13–18 μm in diameter and produce about 100 curved microgametes 3 μm long, each with two flagella 6–9 μm long. Macrogametes, averaging 11.5 × 13.5 μm, can be distinguished by spherical granules that coalesce to form the oocyst wall. They stain black with iron hematoxylin, blue with Mayer's haemalum, and are PAS positive. They are also highly refractile with bright field or phase contrast microscopy. The prepatent period is 11–12 days (Henry, 1932; Lapage, 1940).

c. Location in Host. Endogenous stages are in colonic epithelial cells in the crypts of Lieberkühn (Fig. 9). They are predominantly in the proximal part but may extend the full length of the colon, and even into the cecum. Henry (1932) reported a few isolated coccidia in the small intestine of some guinea pigs, but Lapage (1940) did not.

d. Prevalence and Geographical Distribution. Little data exists on the prevalence of *E. caviae* and only relatively old information is available. Bugge and Heinke (1921) found 73% of 180 guinea pigs infected, Henry (1932) found 40.9% of 22 guinea pigs naturally infected, and Yakimov *et al.* (1940) found 45% of 165 infected, of which 42% died. Lapage (1940) examined each guinea pig in his colony over an extended period and found 100% infection. Improved management since these early reports has probably resulted in a much lower prevalence of this coccidium. However, Pellérdy (1965) believes that *E. caviae* occurs very frequently in guinea pigs because oocysts are in the feces of most young animals. Nevertheless, no *E. caviae* were found in guinea pig colonies in Pennsylvania, Illinois, or Maryland (Nie, 1950; Jervis *et al.*, 1966; Vetterling *et al.*, 1971a). Therefore, occurrence of *E. caviae* in guinea pig colonies seems to be sporadic, at least in North America.

The distribution of *E. caviae* is worldwide. It has been reported from England (Sheather, 1924; Lapage, 1940; Porter, 1943; Ellis and Wright, 1961), France (Gauget, 1938; Dollfus, 1961), Italy (Strada and Traina, 1900; Sacchetti, 1903), Germany (Bugge and Heinke, 1921; Steinmetz, 1921), Czechoslovakia (Ryšavý, 1954; Villágiová, 1962), Hungary (Pellérdy, 1965), Poland (Dubienska, 1967), U.S.S.R. (Yakimov, 1934; Yakimov and Gusev, 1935; Zasukhin and Kheisin, 1957; Litvenkova, 1969), North Vietnam (Houdemer, 1938), India (Katiyar, 1953), Brazil (Alves de Souza, 1931), Bolivia and Paraquay (Maciel, 1914), Peru (Arnao Mendoza, 1951), Mexico (Faust, 1950), and the United States (Henry, 1932; Wicktor, 1951; Kleeberg and Steenken, 1963).

e. Pathology. In severe *E. caviae* infections, the wall of the colon is hyperemic, the mucosa has petechial hemorrhages, and grayish-white nodules containing oocysts may occur. Intestinal contents are watery and fetid, occasionally flecked with blood. Usually the intestine and mesentery are edematous.

Microscopically, numerous developmental stages are apparent in epithelial cells. The host cells are destroyed by the coccidia and the epithelium may be sloughed in large patches.

Pathogenicity of *E.caviae* is moderate even in cases of massive infection. However, where poor sanitary conditions prevail, more intense infections may occur, resulting in near epidemic outbreaks of severe coccidiosis among young guinea pigs (Ellis and Wright, 1961). Lack of vitamin C appears to exacerbate the disease (Wicktor, 1951).

f. Clinical Signs. The first sign of the disease is diarrhea. Henry (1932) observed diarrhea between the eleventh and thirteenth day after inoculation, about the time of oocyst discharge. If no reinfection occurs, diarrhea stops after a few days; whereas continuous exposure to sporulated oocysts results in an increase of parasites and aggravation of signs, with occasional fatalities. Mortality may reach 40% (Henry, 1932; Yakimov *et al.*, 1940), but as a rule it is much lower.

g. Diagnosis. Eimeria caviae can be diagnosed by finding oocysts in fecal examinations. However, diarrhea may occur early in the life cycle before oocysts are passed in the feces. Positive diagnosis is ensured by finding intracellular stages or oocysts in lesion scrapings at necropsy. Scrapings of the cecum or colon mixed with a physiological saline solution can be examined microscopically for stages of coccidia. However, for routine examination of colonies, techniques for fecal flotation of oocysts are easiest (Levine, 1973). Because of the long prepatent period, the fecal flotations for oocysts should be repeated every 4 to 5 days for 2 to 3 weeks.

h. Control and Prevention. Eimeria caviae is only moderately pathogenic and occasional outbreaks of coccidiosis do not involve high morbidity. Usually, improved hygiene is sufficient to prevent an epidemic. Occasionally, treatment of animals with anticoccidial drugs is necessary.

There are only three reports of drug treatment of *E. caviae* in guinea pigs (Katiyar, 1953; Ellis and Wright, 1961; Pellérdy, 1965). A 0.2% solution of sulfamethazine or sulfamethylthiazole in water was used to eliminate the infection.

Proper cage design prevents contamination of food and water by feces and prevents accumulation of oocysts. The idea that guinea pigs infect themselves through their coprophagous habits is fallacious. The fecal pellets are generally taken directly from the anus (vent) and any oocysts would not have had time to sporulate. Thus, fecal material should be removed before sporulation can be completed. If coccidiosis is a significant disease in a colony, breeding in wire cages may help to free them of infection.

Heat sterilization has been the only consistently successful way to eliminate oocysts from cages and equipment. However, several attempts have been made to find an effective means of chemical sterilization. Horton-Smith *et al.* (1940) proposed ammonia solution to kill coccidial oocysts, but it has not proved very successful. Methyl bromide as a fumigant against coccidial oocysts was suggested by Andrews *et al.* (1943). Clapham (1950) confirmed that methyl bromide penetrates several inches into soil and is lethal for oocysts; and Long and Burns Brown (1972) showed that methyl bromide fumigation was effective on an experimental basis in ridding animal facilities of poultry coccidia. Therefore, its use in destroying oocysts in contaminated guinea pig facilities should be considered seriously.

2. *Entamoeba caviae* Chatton, 1918 (Synonyms: *Ameba cobayae* [*sic*], *Entamoeba cobayae*)

a. Historical Review. This parasite is frequently referred to as *Entamoeba cobayae* (Walker, 1908), Chatton, 1917. Unfortunately, the organism that Walker called *Ameba cobayae* was not an *Entamoeba* but a free living opportunist, therefore this name cannot be used. Léger (1918), Holmes (1923), Hegner and Taliaferro (1924), von Schuckmann (1926), Wenyon (1926), Faust (1950), and Nie (1950) studied the ameba of guinea pigs but did not use the appropriate name. Wenrich (1946) used the appropriate name, *Entamoeba caviae*, when he reported his unsuccessful attempts to cultivate this *Entamoeba*.

b. Description. Entamoeba caviae resembles *Entamoeba coli* from man (Fig. 32). The trophozoites are 10.5–20.0μm (14.4 μm) in diameter with an eccentric or central nucleolus. The ectoplasm and endoplasm are not clearly differentiated. Although Nie (1950) observed no cysts, both Holmes (1923) and Faust (1950) did. Cysts are rarely found. They measure 11–17 μm (14 μm) in diameter and have eight nuclei when mature. The chromatoidal bodies are broad and short with rounded or squared ends. Holmes (1923) attempted to transmit this ameba to laboratory rats unsuccessfully.

c. Prevalence and Geographical Distribution. Entamoeba caviae is relatively common in laboratory guinea pigs. Nie (1950) found 14% of 84 guinea pigs infected in Pennsylvania and Mudrow-Reichenow (1956) found 46% of 13 in Germany. *Entamoeba caviae* has also been reported from guinea pigs in France (Chatton, 1917, 1918a,b; Léger, 1918), Mexico (Faust, 1950), England (Wenyon, 1926), Venezuela (Gabaldón, 1930), and the United States (Hegner and Taliaferro, 1924; Holmes, 1923; Wenrich, 1946).

d. Diagnosis. Live amebas can be detected in fresh smears in physiological saline solutions with phase contrast microscopy or stained with Lugol's iodine solution. Positive identification should be made from smears fixed in Schaudinn's fixative and stained with Heidenhain's iron hematoxylin. Cysts can be concentrated with zinc sulfate flotation (Levine, 1973).

e. Methods of Cultivation. Entamoeba caviae should be cultivatable in any of the media devised for *Entamoeba histolytica.* Efforts should begin with egg slants (Levine, 1973).

3. *Endolimax caviae* Hegner, 1926

a. Historical Review. Hegner (1926b) found trophozoites of this species, in association with *Entamoeba caviae,* in two guinea pigs. It was subsequently reported by Wenrich (1935), Nie (1950), and Faust (1950). The latter was convinced the parasites he observed were *Endolimax nana* from human feces to which the guinea pigs were exposed, even though *E. caviae* is smaller.

b. Description. Endolimax caviae trophozoites are 4.5–11.0 by 4.5–8.2 μm (7.1 × 5.7 μm). The nucleus is typical of this group of amebas in having a delicate membrane with large central nucleolus and fine interconnecting strands (Fig. 12). No cysts have been observed.

c. Prevalence and Geographical Distribution. Nie (1950) found 18% of 84 guinea pigs infected in Pennsylvania. Interestingly, Wenrich (1946) found only 1 of 13 in a previous examination of this colony. Chang (1935) found 1 of 16 guinea pigs infected in China. This ameba has also been reported from Maryland (Hegner, 1926b), Mexico (Faust, 1950), and the Philippines (Hegner and Chu, 1930).

4. *Tritrichomonas caviae* (Davaine, 1875)* (Synonyms: *Trichomonas caviae, Trichomonas flagelliphora)*

a. Historical Review. Tritrichomonas caviae is one of the largest and most common flagellates of the cecal fauna of the guinea pig (Fig 39). Hence, its morphology and biology have been studied extensively (Davaine, 1875; Grassi, 1879, 1882; Kunstler, 1882, 1896; Galli-Valerio, 1900, 1901, 1904, 1939; Galli-Valerio and Bornand, 1927; Laveran and Mesnil, 1901; Mordivilko, 1908; Kuczynski, 1914, 1918; da Fonseca, 1915, 1916, 1920; Yakimov *et al.,* 1921; de Mello, 1932; de Mello and de Sousa, 1924; Lynch, 1922b, 1924; Hegner, 1924b, 1926a, 1927; Guérin and Pons, 1925; Tanabe, 1925; Andrews, 1926; Wenyon, 1926; Grassé, 1926; da Cunha and Muniz, 1927a; Gabaldón, 1930; Takemura, 1932, 1933; Lopez-Neyra and Suarez Peregrin, 1933; Wang and Nie, 1934; Grassé and Faure, 1935, 1939; Kopperi, 1935; Curasson, 1940; Pereira and de Almeida, 1940, 1943a,b; Morgan, 1943b; Alexeieff, 1946b; Bussolati, 1949; Nie, 1950; Nomura, 1956, 1957; Zasukhin and Kheisin, 1957).

Faust (1921) described a trichomonad in guinea pigs in Peking, China. He proposed it as a new species, *T. flagelliphora.* However, neither Wenyon (1926) nor Nie (1950) found sufficient evidence to separate it from *T. caviae.*

Chatton (1920) concluded that *Monocercomonas caviae* was merely a form of *T. caviae* in which the undulating membrane was missing. Grassé (1926) agreed with Chatton and went further by stating that all the smaller flagellates (*Monocercomonas, Monocercomonoides, Enteromonas,* etc.) were merely developmental stages of *T. caviae.* We now know that these were hasty decisions.

b. Description. Tritrichomonas caviae is piriform, ovoid, or lima bean shaped, measuring 10–22 by 6–11 μm. At the anterior end is a blepharoplast complex from which the flagella arise. *Tritrichomonas caviae* has three anterior flagella that are shorter than the body and a recurrent flagellum that forms the edge or marginal filament of the undulating membrane extending beyond it as the trailing flagellum. A costa, a rod-shaped parabasal body and filaments, and an axostyle are present. The axostyle protrudes from the body but comes to a point shortly after emerging. Two or three chromatic rings surround the axostyle where it emerges from the body. Although Nie (1950) reported the presence of a pelta, Honigberg (1963) pointed out that it was an extension of the axostylar capitulum. The nucleus is large and ellipsoidal and contains a nucleolus. The cytoplasm is filled with granules and vacuoles.

A smaller trichomonad was reported by Nie (1950) from a single guinea pig. The body was fusiform, measuring 8.5–11.0 by 4.5–6.5 μm. He stated that this organism had a pelta, three anterior flagella, an undulating membrane, and a posterior trailing flagellum. Nie (1950) gave it no name, but Flynn (1973) referred to this organism as *Tritrichomonas* sp. (Fig. 28).

Kofoid *et al.* (1935) studied the effect of pH on the distribution of trichomonads in the intestine. *Tritrichomonas caviae* was found in the upper duodenum in 38% of the guinea pigs examined, in the jejunum in 63%, in the lower ileum in 88%, and in the cecum 100%.

c. Prevalence and Geographical Distribution. Wenrich (1946) found *T. caviae* in only 1 of 16 guinea pigs, but Villágiová (1962) found it in 85% of 79 guinea pigs examined in Czechoslovakia, and Faust (1950) found 32% of 41 examined in Louisiana. Strangely, Nie (1950) gave no prevalence data for *T. caviae.* This parasite is cosmopolitan, having been reported from Brazil (da Fonseca, 1915), Venezuela (Gabaldón, 1930), China (Faust, 1921; Chang, 1935), Czechoslovakia (Villágiová, 1962), England (Wenyon, 1926), France

*Because of many similarities, the pathology, clinical signs, diagnosis, methods of cultivation, and control and prevention of flagellates will be discussed after all of them have been described.

(Davaine, 1875; Grassé, 1926; Morénas, 1938), Germany (Galli-Valerio, 1901; Steinmetz and Lerche, 1923; Fritzsche, 1933), the U.S.S.R. (Yakimov *et al.,* 1921; Zasukhin and Kheisin, 1957) and the United States (Wenrich, 1949; Wenrich and Saxe, 1950; Nie, 1950).

In reviewing the taxonomic status of the trichomonads of rodents (but unfortunately not *T. caviae*), Honigberg (Daniel *et al.,* 1971) found little structural difference between the various species and, having considered Saxe's (1954) transfaunation studies, stated that they all appeared to be a single species.

Moreover, *Tetratrichomonas microti,* which has never been reported from guinea pigs, can be transmitted to them (Wenrich and Saxe, 1950; Simitch *et al.,* 1954). Hence, natural transmission of trichomonads from other rodents should be regarded as a potential threat.

5. *Chilomitus caviae* da Fonseca, 1915

6. *Chilomitus conexus* Nie, 1950

a. Historical Review. da Fonseca (1915) observed a protozoan with four flagella in the ceca of both wild and domestic guinea pigs in Brazil for which he created the genus *Chilomitus.* Chalmers and Pekkola (1918) contested the authenticity of this genus and suggested that it was the same as *Tetrachilomastix,* which da Fonseca (1915) had erected for the species from the chicken, *Chilomastix gallinarum.* da Fonseca (1918a,b, 1920) perpetuated this controversy. Nie (1950) asserted that *Tetrachilomastix* was incorrect and Honigberg (1963) supported Nie's conclusions.

b. Description. Chilomitus is an ellipsoidal or bean-shaped flagellate with a convex aboral surface, and it maintains its shape by means of a rigid, well-developed pellicle. Three anterior free flagella and a recurrent flagellum, all slightly longer than the body, originate from blepharoplasts at the bottom of a tunnel-shaped depression of the pellicle on the anterior half of the ventral surface (da Cunha and de Freitas, 1937). Nie (1950) called this depression a cytostome, but he apparently did not observe ingestion. Honigberg (1963) chose to call it a depression pending the results of further studies. The flagella adhere to one another until they are well out of the depression. No pelta is present. No cysts occur in this genus.

Chilomitus caviae (Fig. 20) measures 6.0–14.0 by 3.1–4.6 μm (11.2 × 4.4 μm.) Immediately beneath the blepharoplasts is a large ovoid nucleus containing sparsely scattered chromatin and no nucleolus. On the left ventral side, adjacent to the nucleus, is a ring-shaped parabasal body of about the same size. A rudimentary axostyle represented only by a delicate strand is present. The cytoplasm is filled with a variety of siderophilic bodies.

Chilomitus conexus (Fig. 13) measures 3.8–6.6 by 1.3–1.8 μm (5.2 × 1.7 μm). It has a small, densely staining, siderophilic nucleus. The parabasal body is a small, round, solid body situated to the left of the nucleus. In contrast to *C. caviae, C. conexus* has a well-developed axostyle, which never protrudes from the posterior end. The cytoplasm is frequently filled with siderophilic rods.

c. Prevalence and Geographical Distribution. Nie (1950) found *C. caviae* in 24% of 84 guinea pigs examined in Pennsylvania but found *C. conexus* in only one animal. da Fonseca (1915, 1916, 1918a,b; 1920) gave no figures on prevalence in Brazil, neither did Morénas (1938) in France, Ray and Mitra (1935) in India, nor Villágiová (1962) in Czechoslovakia. Chang (1935) did not find *Chilomitus* in guinea pigs in China.

7. *Hexamastix caviae* Nie, 1950

8. *Hexamastix robustus* Nie, 1950

a. Historical Review. These flagellates were not recognized until 1950, when Nie reported them from the ceca of guinea pigs. Their relative recency of discovery may be due to the polymorphic nature of their flagellar system; depending upon age, maturity, or physiological condition. Nie was able to differentiate these organisms using protargol stain.

b. Description. Hexamastix is piriform with a rounded anterior end. It has a pelta, a conspicuous axostyle extending beyond the body like a spike, and a prominent parabasal body. There are six flagella, five anterior and one recurrent. However, as mentioned above, the number of anterior flagella vary from two to five. Honigberg (1963) relates the number of flagella to the degree of maturity. Nie (1950) assumed it to be a species characteristic. He counted the number of anterior flagella on 100 *H. caviae* and 67 *H. robustus.* The percentages with 2, 3, 4, and 5 anterior flagella were 3, 33, 36, and 28% for *H. caviae* and 3, 15, 51, and 34% for *H. robustus.* Nie (1950) reported a cytostome, but Honigberg (1963) discounts reports of cytostomes in the entire Trichomonadida. No cysts were found.

Hexamastix caviae (Fig. 37) measures 3.8–10.0 by 3.3–4.7 μm (6.5 × 4.0 μm). The anterior flagella vary in length, the longest being 1 to 1½ times the body length. The recurrent flagellum is longer than the anterior flagella. The nucleus is angular and contains a small nucleolus. There are distinct parabasal filaments on each side of the ring-shaped parabasal body. *Hexamastix caviae* swims in the rapid, jerky, erratic fashion of a trichomonad. The pellicle is not as rigid as that of many flagellates, and the organism assumes many body forms. The anterior flagella are usually held together and beat backward as a single stout whip.

Hexamastix robustus differs from *H. caviae* in its (1) larger size, 6.6–13.5 by 3.5–7.5 μm (10.2 × 5.2 μm); (2) round or ovoid nucleus with larger endosome; and (3) indistinct parabasal apparatus. In many specimens no parabasal body is found, and only two very faint parabasal fibrils occur.

c. Prevalence and Geographical Distribution. Nie (1950) reported 11% of 84 guinea pigs infected with *Hexamastix caviae* and 14% with *H. robustus.* Seven percent had double infections. These species have been reported only from Pennsylvania.

9. *Monocercomonas caviae* (Davaine, 1875) (Synonyms: *Monas caviae, Heteromita caviae, Trichomastix caviae, Eutrichomastix aguti*)

10. *Monocercomonas pistillum* Nie, 1950

11. *Monocercomonas minuta* Nie, 1950

a. Historical Review. The first to observe a monocercomonad in the guinea pig was Davaine (1875), who named the organism *Monas caviae.* Grassi (1881) questionably assigned it to the genus *Heteromita,* of which he considered Davaine's *Monas caviae* a synonym. da Fonseca (1915, 1916) reported a flagellate under the name of *Trichomastix caviae* (Grassi, 1881) from guinea pigs in Brazil, but his illustration does not appear to be of the species in question. Nie (1950) suggested that da Fonseca's organism was a species of *Enteromonas.* Meanwhile, Yakimov *et al.* (1921) had reported a monocercomonad in the cecum of guinea pigs in Russia. They referred to it as *M. caviae* var. *rossica,* but no justification for separating this variety is apparent. Morénas (1938) reported this flagellate from France, but what he referred to as *"Monocercomonas"* is *Monocercomonoides,* and *"Eutrichomastix"* is *Monocercomonas.* Fortunately, Nie (1950) clarified the taxonomic status, revised the description of *Monocercomonas caviae,* and identified two additional species, *M. pistillum* and *M. minuta.* Honigberg (1963) discussed the evolutionary and systematic relationships of these flagellates within the order Trichomonadida.

b. Description. Monocercomonads are piriform to ellipsoidal with a rounded anterior end. All have a pelta, an ovoid densely staining nucleus with no nucleolus, a parabasal body, an axostyle, and four flagella. There are three anterior and one recurrent flagella, all 1 to 1½ times the body length. Some reports state that a cytostome is present, but Honigberg (1963) refutes this. Unlike *Chilomitus,* there is no depression of the body from which the flagella arise. No cysts occur. Cysts which have been reported have usually been shown to be from another parasite (Bishop, 1932).

Monocercomonas caviae (Fig. 14) measures 4.4–8.5 by 2.2–4.3 μm (6.0 × 3.1 μm). Living specimens swim in a jerky, erratic but rapid manner, resembling small trichomonads. The axostyle protrudes from the body but comes immediately to a sharp blunt point. The two anterior and two posterior siderophilic balls located around the axostyle are diagnostic for this species.

Monocercomonas pistillum (Fig. 15) is about the same size as *M. caviae,* 4.0–6.5 by 3.0–3.6 μm (5.4 × 3.3 μm). It is similar to *M. caviae* in all respects but two: (1) the axostyle, although it protrudes posteriorly, does not end in a point, but rather in a squarely terminated stump, or is even thickened like the head of a pestle; and (2) only the anterior siderophilic balls are present.

Monocercomonas minuta (Fig. 16) is the smallest of this group, 2.7–6.0 by 2.0–2.7 μm (4.2 × 2.3 μm). It differs from the other two species in that the axostyle is much thinner and does not protrude beyond the body. The siderophilic bodies are distributed along the sides of the organism rather than anteriorly or posteriorly around the axostyle. The flagella are also proportionately longer.

c. Prevalence and Geographical Distribution. Nie (1950) found 35% of 84 guinea pigs infected with *M. caviae,* and 5% of the 84 had a double infection with *M. pistillum. Monocercomonas minuta* was found in 11% of the 84 guinea pigs; 8% or 7 were concurrent with *M. caviae,* but 2 guinea pigs had pure infections. Nie (1950) and Wenrich (1946) reported these flagellates from Pennsylvania; Das Gupta (1936) from India; Morénas (1938) from France; da Fonseca (1915, 1916) from Brazil; and Villágiová (1962) from Czechoslovakia.

12. *Chilomastix intestinalis* Kuczynski, 1914

13. *Chilomastix wenrichi* Nie, 1948

a. Historical Review. Kuczynski (1914) first discovered this parasite in the cecum of a guinea pig. His report was followed by those of da Fonseca (1915, 1916, 1918a,b, 1920) and Leiva (1921). Nie (1948, 1950) restudied these flagellates strengthening the description of *Chilomastix intestinalis* and discovering another species, *C. wenrichi.*

b. Description. These flagellates are piriform, sometimes described as elongate sweet potatoes with rounded anteriors and tapered posteriors that terminate in tail-like processes. The body is rigid with a spiral groove running across the ventral surface in living specimens. This groove is lost during slide preparation. A round vesicular nucleus is located a distance of half its own diameter behind the anterior end. One or two marginal nucleolar masses are present. The most characteristic feature is a large figure 8-shaped cytostome on the ventral side, to the right of the nucleus. It is bordered by two siderophilic fibrils. At the anterior pole of the cytostome are four basal bodies from which the flagella arise. There are three anterior flagella less than one body length and a fourth short flagellum that undulates within the cytostomal cleft. The cytoplasm usually contains vacuoles of varying size and content. Cysts are formed that contain all trophozoite organelles.

Chilomastix intestinalis (Figs. 21 and 22) is large, 8.8–27.9 by 6.6–11.0 μm (19.4 × 8.1 μm). It has a tonguelike process on the right cytostomal lip. Cysts are ellipsoidal or lemon shaped, 9.0–11.0 by 6.6–9.9 μm with a single nucleus.

Chilomastix wenrichi (Figs. 30 and 31) is small, 7.5–12.0 by 4.0–5.0 μm (10.1 × 4.4 μm), and does not have a tonguelike process on the right cytostomal lip.

c. Prevalence and Georgraphical Distribution. In three groups of guinea pigs from Pennsylvania, Nie (1948) found 39% of 28, 50% of 24, and 50% of 4 infected with *C. intestinalis;* he also found 1 of 3 from Massachusetts infected with *C. intestinalis.* He rarely found *C. wenrichi;* only 12% of 59 guinea pigs were infected. Of these, six were mixed infections with *C. intestinalis.* Chang (1935) reported 44% of 16 guinea pigs in China infected with *C. intestinalis.* Other reports are da Fonseca (1915) in Brazil, Gabaldón (1930) in Venezuela, and Fantham (1922) in South Africa.

14. *Retortamonas caviae* (Hegner and Schumaker, 1928) (Synonym: *Embadomonas caviae*)

a. Historical Review. This flagellate was first seen by Wenyon (1926) in the cecum of a guinea pig from Egypt. Subsequently, Hegner and Schumaker (1928) found it in Maryland guinea pigs and described it as *Embadomonas caviae.* Wenrich (1932) showed that the genus was not valid and placed all the species of *Embadomonas* in the genus *Retortamonas.* Bishop (1932, 1934) reported a *Retortamonas* sp. from guinea pigs in England, but Nie (1950) concluded that the flagellates she found were *Monocercomonoides.*

b. Descriptions. Retortamonas caviae (Fig. 18) is usually piriform or fusiform, 4.0–7.0 by 2.4–3.2 μm (5.5 × 2.8 μm) (Hegner and Schumaker, 1928) or 4.4–7.7 by 4.0–4.3 μm (5.6 × 4.1 μm) (Nie, 1950). It has two flagella, one anterior and the other trailing, and a large (but not always conspicuous) cytostome through which the trailing flagellum passes. The cytostome is bound by one or two siderophilic cytostomal fibers. The flagella are usually shorter than the body. The nucleus is vesicular with a round central nucleolus. Aside from food vacuoles, no other organelles are seen.

Piriform to ovoid cysts are formed (Fig. 19). They contain one or two nuclei, and the flagella and cytostomal fibrils are visible. The cysts are 3.4–5.7 by 3.0–4.0 μm (4.2 × 3.5 μm) (Hegner and Schumaker, 1928; Nie, 1950).

c. Prevalence and Geographical Distribution. Hegner and Schumaker (1928) found 27% of 52 guinea pigs infected in Maryland; Nie (1950) found 9.5% of 84 infected in Pennsylvania; and Chang (1935) found 12.5% of 16 infected in China. Villágiová (1962) found *R. caviae* to be the third most common flagellate of guinea pigs in Czechoslovakia; 36.8% of 79 were infected.

15. *Monocercomonoides caviae* (da Cunha and Muniz, 1921) (Synonyms: *Monocercomonas caviae, Monocercomonas hassalli*)

16. *Monocercomonoides quadrifunilis* Nie, 1950

17. *Monocercomonoides wenrichi* Nie, 1950

18. *Monocercomonoides exilis* Nie, 1950

a. Historical Review. Monocercomonoides caviae was discovered by da Cunha and Muniz (1921) in the cecum of guinea pigs in Brazil. They named it *Monocercomonas caviae.* Because this name was already in use, da Cunha and Muniz (1927a) renamed their discovery *Monocercomonas hassalli.* Subsequently, Travis (1932) split the monocercomonads into two groups and created a new genus, *Monocercomonoides.* Hence, the old specific name "caviae" was usable. Nie (1950) described three additional species, *M. quadrifunilis, M. wenrichi,* and *M. exilis.*

b. Description. These flagellates have an anterior nucleus, two pairs of flagella connected by a dense blepharoplastic commissure, a pelta, and an axostyle. Depending upon the species, one to four strandlike, argyrophilic funises are associated with the flagella. The funis is a costalike structure. The species in guinea pigs have neither cytostome nor parabasal body and lack cysts.

Monocercomonoides caviae (Fig. 33) is ovoid to subspherical, 4.0–8.0 by 2.7–6.6 μm. A large nucleus with a large round central nucleolus is located at the anterior end just beneath the surface. Three funises are present.

Monocercomonoides quadrifunilis (Fig. 34) is more piriform, 3.5–13.2 by 3.3–11.0 μm. The nucleus is anterior and has a crescent-shaped marginal nucleolus. As indicated by the name, four funises are intimately associated with the four flagella.

Monocercomonoides wenrichi (Fig. 35) is ovoid to globular, 3.3–11.5 by 3.0–8.4 μm (6.6 × 5.2 μm). The nucleus, like that of *M. quadrifunilis,* is anterior with a marginal nucleolus. A single funis is entangled with the recurrent flagellum.

Monocercomonoides exilis (Fig. 36) varies from rhomboidal to spherical, but piriform individuals, 3.5–8.8 by 2.5–5.5 μm (5.5 × 3.5 μm) are most common. The nucleus is smaller than in the other three species, is not located as far anteriorly, and has a small, round central nucleolus. A single funis is associated with the recurrent flagellum.

c. Prevalence and Geographical Distribution. Nie (1950) found these flagellates to be very common in the guinea pigs he examined from Pennsylvania and Massachusetts; over 46% of 84 guinea pigs were infected. Wenrich (1946) also reported them from guinea pigs in Pennsylvania. da Cunha and Muniz (1921) reported this parasite in Brazil, and Villágiová (1962) reported it in Czechoslovakia.

19. *Enteromonas caviae* Lynch, 1922 (Synonym: *Enteromonas fonsecai*)

a. Historical Review. There has been considerable controversy over the genus *Enteromonas.* It remains a valid genus although its relationship to other flagellates is unknown. Lynch (1922a) described *Enteromonas caviae* from the cecum of the guinea pig. Yakimov (1925a,b) named a similar flagellate from the guinea pig in the U.S.S.R., *Enteromonas fonsecai,* and Morénas (1938) adopted this name for parasites he found in 35 guinea pigs in France. However, Nie (1950) did not find sufficient evidence to justify separating this species and synonymized it with *Enteromonas caviae.*

b. Description. The body is spherical to piriform, 3.0–5.5 by 2.3–4.4 μm (4.0 × 3.0 μm) (Fig. 29). There are three anterior flagella shorter than the body, one of which may be difficult to see, and a fourth longer recurrent flagellum running along the flattened portion of the body surface and extending a short distance past the end of the body. A strandlike "funis" of uncertain affinity arises from the blepharoplast and extends beneath the body surface to near the point where the recurrent flagellum becomes free. The nucleus is anterior, vesicular, and may or may not contain a nucleolus. No cytostome is present. Cysts are ovoid and contain four nuclei when mature.

c. Prevalence and Geographical Distribution. This species, although of uncertain taxonomic position, seems to be quite prevalent. Nie (1950) found it in 6% of 84 guinea pigs in Pennsylvania, and Villágiová (1962) found it in 14% of 79 guinea pigs in Czechoslovakia.

20. *Proteromonas brevifilia* Alexeieff, 1946

a. Historical Review. While studying trichomonads from guinea pigs, Alexeieff (1946a) discovered a different parasite, *Proteromonas brevifilia.* Proteromonads are rarely found in mammals; they usually parasitize reptiles and amphibians.

b. Description. The body is spindle shaped, 4.5–9.0 by 1.6–4 μm (6.8 × 3.2 μm) (Fig. 27). The anterior end contains two basal bodies from which arise one anteriorly projecting and one free trailing flagellum. The flagella are 1 to 1½ times the body length. The anucleolar vesicular nucleus is situated in the anterior half of the body. Immediately adjacent to the nucleus is a paranuclear body the same size as the nucleus. Unlike the parabasal body of trichomonads this organelle is not argyrophilic. A rhizoplast runs through the cytoplasm from the centrosome on the nuclear membrane to the basal bodies, and a perirhizoplastic ring, which is thought to be the true parabasal body, encircles it. No cysts are known.

c. Prevalence and Geographical Distribution. Alexeieff (1946a) found 1 of 70 guinea pigs infected in France, and Nie (1950) found 3 of 56 infected in the United States. Villágiová (1962) rarely found it in 79 guinea pigs in Czechoslovakia.

21. *Spiromonas augusta* (Dujardin, 1841)

a. Historical Review. Only Faust (1950) has reported *Spiromonas augusta* in guinea pigs. He found 63% of 41 guinea pigs infected. Spiromonads are usually inhabitants of stagnant freshwater.

b. Description. *Spiromonas augusta* (Fig. 24) is elongate, oval, and flattened with a counterclockwise spiral of the body forming up to 1½ twists. It typically measures 20 by 4 μm. It has a small, round nucleus with a large nucleolus near the midpoint of the body. An axoneme or rhizoplast extends from the nucleus to the blepharoplast, from which two flagella arise and pass through an anterior terminal cytostome. The flagella are shorter than the body. Cysts were reported by Wenyon (1926), but not by Faust (1950).

22. *Caviomonas mobilis* Nie, 1950

a. Historical Review. Nie (1950) described this as a new species. He found it in 11% of 56 guinea pigs in colonies from Pennsylvania and Massachusetts.

b. Description. *Caviomonas mobilis* (Fig. 25) is a small, ovoid, often elongate carrot-shaped flagellate, 2.2–6.6 by 2.0–3.3 μm (4.2 × 2.9 μm). The anterior is rounded, the posterior tapered and frequently pointed. A single long flagellum, 2 to 3 times the body length, originates near the vesicular nucleus. The nucleus contains no nucleolus. Opposite the origin of the flagellum, a bandlike peristyle arises near the nuclear membrane and extends posteriorly along the periphery of the body surface. Cytostome and contractile vacuoles are absent. No cysts have been found.

23. *Oikomonas termo* Ehrenberg, 1838

a. *Historical Review.* Little is known about *Oikomonas termo.* Yakimov *et al.* (1921) and Morénas (1938) reported it from the feces of guinea pigs in the U.S.S.R. and France, respectively. Other members of the genus are common free-living protozoa, hence, *O. termo* may be a coprozoic opportunist.

b. Description. This flagellate is usually spherical or ovoid, 3–7 by 3–5 μm, with a flagellum running posteriorly the length of the body from a basal body near the anterior surface (Fig. 26). *Oikomonas termo* swims in a jerky manner. The centrally located nucleus has a large nucleolus. The cytoplasm is filled with small, darkly staining granules. Cysts have not been found in guinea pig infections.

24. *Sphaeromonas communis* Liebetanz, 1910

a. Historical Review. Sphaeromonas communis was found in guinea pig feces by da Fonseca in Brazil (1915, 1916). Subsequently, in the U.S.S.R. Yakimov *et al.* (1921) described a species called *S. rossica* from guinea pig feces. The description of *S. rossica* is so brief and unsatisfactory that it cannot be separated from *S. communis.* These parasites closely resemble *Oikomonas* and may be synonymous. Several species have been named, all parasitic.

b. Description. The body is spherical to ellipsoidal, 3–14 μm in diameter (Fig. 38). A single long flagellum, 3 to 5 times the body length, arises from near the nuclear membrane. No other organelles except many darkly staining granules occur.

25. *Selenomonas ruminantium* (Certes, 1889) (Synonyms: *Ancyromonas ruminantium, Selenomastix ruminantium, Selenomonas palpitans*)

a. Historical Review. da Fonseca (1915a,b) and da Cunha (1915) identified this species in the ceca of guinea pigs in Brazil. Simons (1922) reported a different species, *Selenomonas palpitans,* in Germany, but his description probably does not warrant a new species. Kofoid *et al.* (1935) and Faust (1950) found *S. ruminantum* in North America.

b. Description. This flagellate is unique in that the body is kidney or crescent shaped with a tuft of flagella arising from the center of the concave side (Fig. 23). A dense nucleus is in the same area. The body measures 6.8–9.1 by 1.8–2.3 μm.

c. Pathology. Cecal flagellates are usually nonpathogenic. Wenyon (1926) reported that *Tritrichomonas caviae* caused ulceration of the cecum and colon with tissue invasion. Kofoid *et al.* (1935) inferred that *T. caviae* was slightly pathogenic in the small intestine where it ingested red blood cells but not in the cecum or colon.

d. Diagnosis. Differential diagnosis of cecal flagellates is very difficult for the untrained person. For each cecal specimen, smears should be fixed in Schaudinn's fluid and stained with iron hematoxylin, and additional smears fixed in Bouin's or Holland's fluid and stained with protargol silver protein. Fresh smears, smears mixed with nickel sulfate or methylcellulose, and smears fixed in the vapors of 2% osmium tetroxide should be examined with phase contrast microscopy. As seen in the description above, identification of many flagellates is based on siderophilic and argyrophilic structures, so good preparations of both kinds of stains are essential. Honigberg and Goldman (1968) developed a fluorescent antibody technique to identify flagellates from other animals, but none has been perfected for guinea pig flagellates.

e. Methods of Cultivation. The simplest approach to cultivating flagellates is similar to that of Wenrich (1946), in which various nutrients (liver infusion, dried serum, dried egg, gastric mucin, or starch) are added to a balanced salt solution. The cecal contents are inoculated into the medium. The culture is either examined and transferred periodically or the nutrients and water are replaced. By this method, Wenrich (1946) maintained *Retortomonas caviae* and *Monocercomonoides caviae* in culture up to 204 days.

Several specialized media have been devised for culturing trichomonads but are also suitable for other enteric flagellates. Among them are CPLM (cysteine-peptone-liver-maltose-serum), BGPS (beef extract-glucose-peptone-serum), Diamond's trypticase-yeast extract maltose-cysteine-serum, thioglycollate broth beef serum, and skim milk with antibiotics media (Levine, 1973). In addition, egg slants and ameba media can be used. Hibler *et al.* (1960) found that trichomonads from swine died off during passage in other media and devised a cecal extract-serum medium containing *Pseudomonas aeruginosa.* They were able to keep the cultures indefinitely in this medium.

To obtain flagellates for cultivation, cecal contents are diluted 1/5 with physiological saline, strained through cheesecloth, and centrifuged at 100 *g* for 5 minutes to remove particles heavier than the flagellates. The supernatant fluid, which contains most of the flagellates, is centrifuged at 1500 to 2500 *g* for 10 to 15 minutes, depending upon the species of flagellate, and the sediment is then used to prepare smears and inoculate cultures. Immediately before inoculation into the medium, 1000 units/ml of penicillin and 1 mg/ml of streptomycin can be added. Alternatively, the flagellates can be incubated in a solution of antibiotics before inoculation into the culture medium. The flagellates should be observed before and after addition of the antibiotics because some of the lesser studied species may be more susceptible than trichomonads to antibiotics. If the use of antibiotics is to be avoided, the rapidly swimming, active flagellates can be isolated by passage through a U tube.

Clone cultures can be prepared on agar plates or in Burri tubes as described by Samuels (1962). Honigberg *et al.* (1964) and Kulda and Honigberg (1969) grew several trichomonad species in cell culture to assay their relative pathogenicity.

f. Control and Prevention. Apparently, those flagellates which produce cysts are transmitted by fecal contamination, but transmission of noncystic forms is not completely understood. Cesarean-derived guinea pigs are free of flagellates (Calhoon and Matthews, 1964).

26. *Balantidium caviae* Neiva, da Cunha and Travassos, 1914

a. Historical Review. Neiva *et al.* (1914) were the first to report the large ciliate *Balantidium caviae*. Several other reports followed (Abe, 1927; Hegner, 1926a, 1927, 1934; Rees, 1927; Scott, 1927). Scott (1927) gave a detailed report on the general morphology, division, and conjugation of *B. caviae*. However, since she concluded that *B. caviae* was the same as *Balantidium coli* from swine, a controversy was started. Faust (1950), Nie (1950), Krascheninnikow (1959), and Krascheninnikow and Wenrich (1958) found morphologically distinct species in each of the two hosts. Krascheninnikow and Jeska (1961) confirmed the morphological observations by demonstrating immunological differences between *B. caviae* and *B. coli*. Moreover, Nie (1950) noted the failure of Hegner (1926a, 1927, 1934) and Rees (1927) to cross-infect guinea pigs with *B. coli* from pigs. However, Levine (1973) tentatively synonymized *B. caviae* with *B. coli* on the basis that Westphal (1957) had found that guinea pigs could readily be infected with *B. coli*. Unfortunately, after Levine's (1973) book had gone to press, Westphal (1971) reported that he was able to infect both mice and guinea pigs with *B. coli*, but could not infect mice with *B. caviae*. Moreover, he supplied additional morphological characters to differentiate the two species. From my own work with these organisms (unpublished), *B. coli* and *B. caviae* are two distinct species.

b. Description. *Balantidium caviae* is ovoid or ellipsoid, 55–115 by 45–73 μm (92 $\times$ 65 μm). As in all ciliates, each organism has a macronucleus and micronucleus. *Balantidium caviae* has a small, thick, ovoid to ellipsoid macronucleus, whereas *B. coli* has a longer, dumbbell-shaped macronucleus (Westphal, 1971). A single contractile vacuole and cytoproct are terminal. A "mouth" is located subterminally and has variously been called a cytostome or peristome. However, these terms are not applicable because by definition (Corliss, 1959), the "mouth" is a vestibulum. The cilia of the vestibulum are specialized to the extent that they are longer than the body cilia and have a continuous rhythmic beat that draws food through the vestibulum to the true cytostome or cytopharynx. The surface of the body is covered with slightly oblique, longitudinal rows of cilia. The number of ciliary rows (kineties) varies (Krascheninnikow, 1959; Krascheninnikow and Wenrich, 1958). Paulin and Krascheninnikow (1973) reported on ultrastructural aspects.

Cysts are occasionally found in the large intestine and feces. These cysts are spherical to ovoid, 40–50 μm (45 μm) in diameter. The cyst wall is fairly thick and is yellow-brownish; the macronucleus is visible.

c. Location in Host. *Balantidium caviae* is found in the lumen of the cecum (Fig. 11) and colon and it occasionally enters the mucosa.

d. Prevalence and Geographical Distribution. Faust (1950) found 55% of 42 guinea pigs infected in Louisiana. Chang (1935) found no balantidia in the 16 guinea pigs he examined in China. *Balantidium caviae* has been reported from Brazil (Neiva *et al.*, 1914), Czechoslovakia (Freund, 1933), India (Krishnan, 1968), and California, Maryland, Pennsylvania, and Louisiana (Hegner, 1926a, 1927; Rees, 1927; Scott, 1927; Kofoid *et al.*, 1935; Nelson, 1935; Faust, 1950; Nie, 1950; Krascheninnikow, 1959; Krascheninnikow and Wenrich, 1958).

e. Pathology. *Balantidium caviae* is ordinarily nonpathogenic, living in the nondescript ingesta. It does not seem able to penetrate the intact mucosa. Tremendous numbers of balantidia may be found in the lumen of a cecum with normal mucosa. However, if another organism or condition initiates a lesion, *B. caviae* may become a secondary invader. Krishnan (1968) reported a case in which the balantidia not only invaded the mucosa, but also were found in the blood vessels of the lamina propria and in local lymph nodules. Many of the balantidia had ingested red blood cells and mononuclear cells. Krishnan (1968) concluded that this invasion of the gut wall by *B. caviae* was the result of a *Salmonella* infection.

f. Diagnosis. *Balantidium caviae* is usually detected in histological sections after postmortem examination. Diagnosis of tissue invasion should be predicated on the report of Scott (1927), who found that balantidia would move to the intestinal wall and penetrate the tissue within 3 to 4 hours after death. Hence, necropsy reports should include the length of time between death and examination.

Balantidia can also be seen by preparing fresh smears from the cecum or the colon. These large ciliates can be seen with only the aid of a dissecting microscope. Smears of cecal contents or feces can also be fixed in Schaudinn's fixative and stained with iron hematoxylin or stained with Lugol's iodine. Cysts can be obtained from fecal pellets by means of zinc sulfate flotation.

g. Methods of Cultivation. *Balantidium caviae* can be cultivated in a number of media: Levine's modification of Rees' Ringer's serum-starch medium, Ringer's egg serum slants, and Balamuth's ameba medium (Levine, 1973). Tempelis and Lysenko (1957) used an agar slant with Balamuth's egg yolk infusion plus rice starch, 500 units/ml of streptomycin, and 250 units/ml of penicillin for *B. coli*. My experience has shown that *B. caviae* does not grow as well in culture as *B. coli* (unpublished).

The filters or purificators designed by Krascheninnikow (1958a,b; Krascheninnikow and Tiesler, 1959) are good for separating balantidia from cecal debris for study or inoculation into culture. The purificators also work well and aid in keeping bacterial growth down if antibiotics are not used.

h. Control and Prevention. No drug treatment has been reported for *B. caviae* infections. Carbarsone has been the drug most commonly used for *B. coli* in man, but chlortetracycline and oxytetracycline have been found more effective. Sanitary measures designed to prevent ingestion of cysts or feces should be effective. Calhoon and Matthews (1964) found no balantidia in cesarian-derived guinea pigs.

27. *Cyathodinium conicum* da Cunha, 1914 (Synonyms: *Cyathodinium vesiculosum, Cyathodinioides vesiculosus, Cyathodinioides pentagonium, Cyathodinioides scotti*)

28. *Cyathodinium piriforme* da Cunha, 1914 (Synonyms: *Cyathodinium sphaericum, Cyathodinioides piriformis, Cyathodinioides breve, Cyathodinioides intermedius, Cyathodinioides parvus*)

29. *Cyathodinium cunhai* (Hasselmann, 1918) (Synonyms: *Cyathodinium piriforme* Type B, *Enterophrya piriforme, Enterophrya piriformis*)

30. *Cyathodinium chagasi* da Cunha and de Freitas, 1936

a. Historical Review. Ten species of *Cyathodinium* have been described from wild and domestic guinea pigs. da Cunha (1914) described *C. conicum* and *C. vesiculosum* from the wild guinea pig (*Cavia aperea*) and *C. piriforme* from both the wild and the domestic guinea pig (*Cavia porcella*) in Brazil. Hasselmann (1918; 1924) found another ciliate in Brazilian guinea pigs, which he called *Enterophrya piriforme,* but gave only a brief description without illustrations. Lucas (1932a,b) studied these ciliates in great detail, especially cell division and subsequent reorganization in *C. piriforme.* She also found another ciliate; but because she could not find dividing stages, she concluded that it was a stage of *C. piriforme* and identified the two as types A and B. Nie (1950) showed that type A was *C. piriforme* and type B was *C. cunhai.* Ritchey (1953) confirmed Nie's conclusion. Kopperi (1935) found *C. conicum* and a supposedly new species, *C. sphaericum*, in a guinea pig in Finland. da Cunha and de Freitas (1936a,b) added a fifth species, *C. chagasi*. They also created a new genus, *Cyathodinioides*, for *C. piriforme*, based mainly on the large mouth. In a later monograph, da Cunha and de Freitas (1940) added five more species to the *Cyathodinioides: C. scotti, C. pentagonium, C. breve, C. intermedius*, and *C. parvus*, all from the wild guinea pig. Nie (1950) thought the large mouth was insufficient criteria for a separate genus and eliminated it. He also synonymized *C. intermedius* with *C. piriforme* and gave *Enterophrya piriforme* the new name *C. cunhai* because the previous name was a homonym. Paulin (unpublished) believes there are only four valid species of *Cyathodinium* in guinea pigs: *C. conicum, C. piriforme, C. cunhai*, and *C. chagasi*. Of these, only *C. chagasi* has not yet been reported from the domestic guinea pig.

The taxonomic position of these protozoa has been uncertain (Corliss, 1961). In a series of studies Paulin (1967, 1968, 1969, 1973; Paulin and Corliss, 1964, 1969) uncovered characteristics indicating that the cyathodinia are neotenic "larval" stages of a suctorian protozoan.

b. Description . *Cyathodinium piriforme* (Fig. 42) is piriform with the posterior end drawn out into a caudal tip and measures 10.0–35.5 by 8.8–24.4 μm (Nie, 1950) with a mean of 29.2 × 20.3 μm (Paulin and Corliss, 1969). The anterior ventral two-thirds of the organism has a depression. Nine rows of somatic cilia are arranged around the depression. Two rows completely encircle the organism; the other seven originate on the left lip of the depression and terminate along the inside of the right wall. The left lip of the ventral depression has 9 to 14 rodlike endosprits that have a buttonlike appearance after staining. The posterior one-half of the body is naked. The ventral depression is not a mouth, and no cytostome or cytopharynx are found in any cyathodinia. The depression appears to serve as a scoop to direct prey organisms onto the endosprits. The endosprits contain missile-like bodies called haptocysts. Their function is to immobilize the prey and cause it to adhere to the endosprit. Paulin and Corliss (1969) believe that the haptocysts contain cytolytic enzymes that digest the prey organism so that it can be absorbed. Each ciliate has a contractile vacuole but no cytoproct. Nie (1950) reported cysts 7.0–24.0 by 12.0–17.0 μm (21.8 × 16.3 μm) in one of 84 guinea pigs, Paulin and Corliss (1964, 1969) found no cysts.

Cyathodinium cunhai (Fig. 41) is also piriform, tapering anteriorly with its widest point across the posterior one-third. It is smaller than *C. piriforme* 10.2–35.5 by 8.0–22.0 μm (Nie, 1950) with a mean of 19.0 × 14.0 μm (Paulin and Corliss, 1969). A small unciliated slit like depression occurs along the anterior ventral one-third of the organism. Of twelve rows of somatic cilia, nine are arranged in semicircles about the ventral depression and three completely encircle the body. A row of about nine endosprits is found along the left margin of the ventral depression. There is a contractile vacuole but no cytoproct. No cysts have been identified.

Cyathodinium conicum (Fig. 40) is cone shaped and is the largest species in the genus, 50.0–80.0 by 20.0–30.0 μm (Faust, 1950) with a mean of 65.0 × 25.0 μm (J. J. Paulin, unpublished). Its ventral depression is proportionally smaller than that of *C. cunhai,* extending only one-fourth the body length. No one has studied this organism recently and details on ciliary rows are unknown.

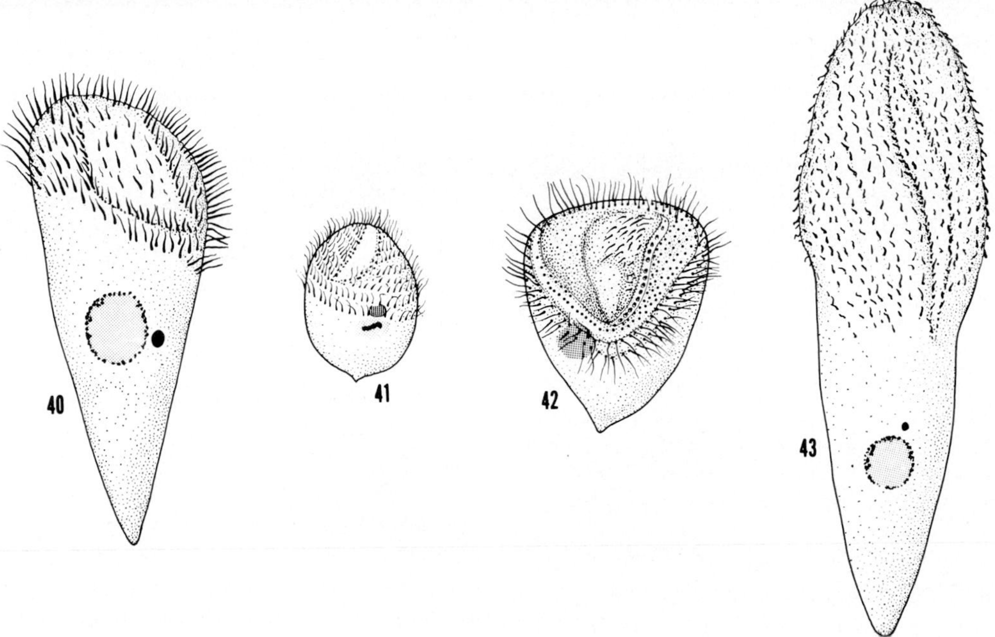

Figs. 40–43. Line drawings of guinea pig ciliates. ×1000.

Fig. 40. *Cyathodinium conicum* (redrawn from da Cunha, 1914).
Fig. 41. *Cyathodinium cunhai* (redrawn from Nie, 1950).
Fig. 42. *Cyathodinium piriforme* (redrawn from Nie, 1950).
Fig. 43. *Enterophrya elongata* (redrawn from da Cunha and de Freitas, 1940).

Cyathodinium chagasi is also cone shaped, 53.7 × 21.9 μm (J. J. Paulin, unpublished). The anterior ventral depression occupies one-fourth of the body. This species is even less well known than *C. conicum*.

c. Location in Host. They are found in the lumen of the cecum and colon.

d. Prevalence and Geographical Distribution. Fantham (1925) reported *Cyathodinium conicum* in two guinea pigs from South Africa. Lucas (1932a,b) found cyathodinia in 78% of 56 adults and 32% of 59 juveniles in Pennsylvania. Chang (1935) found *C. piriforme* in 31% of 16 guinea pigs in China.In their first report, Paulin and Corliss (1964) found 15% of 20 guinea pigs infected with *C. piriforme.* In their second report (1969), 12.9% of 101 guinea pigs had *C. piriforme,* 3.9% had *C. cunhai,* and 3 guinea pigs harbored both species.

e. Diagnosis. Cyathodinia can be detected in fresh smears examined with phase contrast microscopy or smears stained with Chatton–Lwoff silver impregnation (Corliss, 1953) or protargol silver protein (Honigberg and Davenport, 1954).

f. Control and Prevention. Presumably, if cysts do occur, sanitary methods would help prevent the spread. Calhoon and Matthews (1964) found no cyathodinia in cesarean-derived guinea pigs.

31. *Nyctotherus multisporiferus* Walker, 1909

Walker (1909) reported isolating a new ciliate from the intestinal tract of a guinea pig in Massachusetts and cultivating it in an artificial medium. The ciliate supposedly multiplied by a process Walker (1909) called "sporulation." Nie (1950) questioned the validity of this report after examining the figures. Having done the same, I concur with Nie (1950).

32. *Blepharosphaera caviae* Kopperi, 1935

This ciliate was described by Kopperi (1935) from eight of the guinea pigs he examined in Finland. *Blepharosphaera caviae* is spherical, completely covered with longitudinal rows of cilia, and measures 32–50 μm (40 μm) in diameter. A cytostome and macronucleus are found at the anterior end. The cilia around the cytostome are longer than the body cilia. A single contractile vacuole is present.

After examining Kopperi's drawing and description, it appears that he had *Balantidium* rather than *Blepharosphaera* because the latter has cilia only on the anterior three-fourths of the body and in a caudal tuft.

33. *Kopperia intestinale* (Kopperi, 1935) *nomen novum* (Synonym: *Malacosoma intestinale*)

Kopperi (1935) noticed another ciliate for which he erected a new genus and species, *Malacosoma intestinale*. However, as Nie (1950) pointed out, the generic name *Malacosoma* has been used for tent caterpillars (a homonym) so this ciliate is renamed for Kopperi.

The body is egg shaped, 30–50 by 17–30 μm (40 × 25 μm), with the widest part near the anterior end. The entire body is covered with longitudinal rows of long cilia (6–10 μm). Around the cytoproct, longer cilia form a caudal tuft. A "mouth" is situated on the anterior ventral side. The anteriorly located macronucleus is spherical or ovoid, 6–10 μm and is accompanied by a micronucleus. A single contractile vacuole is situated near the anterior end.

34. *Protocaviella acuminata* (da Cunha, 1914) (Synonym: *Paraisotricha acuminata*)

Another ciliate found by Kopperi (1935) in the cecum of the guinea pig was similar to *Paraisotricha acuminata* described by da Cunha (1914) from the cecum of the capybara (*Hydrochoerus capybara*) in Brazil. Kopperi (1935) noted that the ciliates in both guinea pig and capybara lacked the tuft of long cilia on the dorsal wall of the "mouth" found in species of *Paraisotricha* and that there was a row of long cilia on the right lip of the "mouth." Moreover, the macronucleus was usually spherical and always in the anterior end of the body instead of in the middle as in *Paraisotricha*. From these differences, he concluded that the ciliate from the capybara and guinea pig did not belong to *Paraisotricha* and created a new genus, *Protocaviella.*

Protocaviella acuminata has a rigid body with a broader anterior end and measures 30–40 by 12–15 μm. The body is slightly flattened laterally; the dorsal side is convex, and the ventral, concave. The organism has dense longitudinal rows of short somatic cilia. The right lip of the ventral "mouth" has a row of long cilia that beat briskly. The micronucleus is small, spherical, and posterior to the macronucleus. A single contractile vacuole is located near the posterior cytoproct.

Kofoid *et al.* (1935) reported a ciliate resembling *Paraisotricha* in guinea pigs in California which was probably *Protocaviella*.

35. *Enterophrya elongata* Hasselmann, 1918

Hasselmann (1918) described two ciliates, *Enterophrya elongata* and *E. piriforme,* from the cecum of the wild guinea pig of Brazil. da Cunha and Muniz (1927b) reported similar ciliates from the capybara and domestic guinea pig; but like Hasselmann (1918), they gave no illustrations. Kopperi (1935) found a ciliate that he identified as *E. elongata* in the domestic guinea pig and several other rodents, but his description and figures are different from Hasselmann's. da Cunha and de Freitas (1940) gave a good illustration of Hasselman's *E. piriforme* that, as explained previously, is *Cyathodinium cunhai.*

The description of *E. elongata* is incomplete. The body is spindle shaped, 15–35 by 3.5 μm (Fig. 43). Cilia cover the body and no cytostome is found. The micronucleus is located near the round macronucleus in the middle of the body. A single contractile vacuole is situated in the posterior end.

IV. EXPERIMENTAL USE OF GUINEA PIGS IN PROTOZOAN DISEASE RESEARCH

The guinea pig has been used for research on protozoan diseases because it can be infected with a variety of parasites. However, in many cases, it has been supplanted by the less expensive laboratory mouse and rat. In general, the guinea pig has been retained in only those studies that require its particular immunological characteristics or its susceptibility to a broad spectrum of parasites.

In discussing most of the major protozoan diseases in which guinea pigs are used for experimentation, no effort has been made to include an exhaustive literature search; only a few current references are given from which the reader can obtain other references. However, because *Leishmania enriettii* is a natural parasite of guinea pigs, a bibliography as comprehensive as possible is provided. Reviews of protozoan diseases can be found in the work of Marcial-Rojas (1971).

A. Leishmaniasis

As mentioned previously (Section II,B,1), *Leishmania enriettii* is a good experimental model of human cutaneous leishmaniasis. It has the distinct advantage of not being communicable to man. *Leishmania enriettii* has been used in studies of *in vitro* cultivation (Jackson, 1962, 1963; Jadin and Wery, 1963; Glazunova, 1964a; Gleiberman and Belova, 1964; Mancilla *et al.*, 1965; Greenblatt and Glaser, 1965; Ulrich *et al.*, 1968; Machado, 1969); biochemistry and physiology (Zeledón, 1959, 1960a–f; Mühlpfordt, 1963, 1964; du Buy *et al.*, 1965, 1966; du Buy and Riley, 1967; Greenblatt and Wetzel, 1966; Danforth, 1967; Kallinikova, 1967, 1974; Stewart and Beck, 1967; Chance, 1972); pathology (Guimarães, 1952; Paraense, 1953; Coutinho, 1955b; Morini *et al.*, 1959; Glazunova, 1964b; Heisch *et al.*, 1970; Rezai *et al.*, 1972); immunology (Coutinho, 1954a,b; Kulasiri, 1960; Zeledón and Lizano, 1961, 1962; Demina, 1963a,b; Diomina, 1963; Glazunova, 1965; Kretschmar, 1965; Stewart and Beck, 1967; Benex and Lamy, 1967; Nery-Guimarães *et al.*, 1969; Rezai *et al.*, 1969, 1972; Bryceson, 1970; Bryceson *et al.*, 1970a,b, 1972, 1974;

Bryceson and Turk, 1971; Preston and Dumonde, 1971; Bray and Wilson, 1972; Lemma and Yau, 1973; Weissberger *et al.*, 1973; Radwanski *et al.*, 1974; Doyle *et al.*, 1974); chemotherapy (Medina, 1947a,b; Coutinho, 1951, 1955a; Santos and Perine, 1962; Ercoli and Coelho, 1967); and cryopreservation (Mieth, 1966; Raether and Seidenath, 1969).

The guinea pig is also used in experimentation with species of human *Leishmania* (Abboud *et al.*, 1970; Turk and Bryceson, 1971; Clinton *et al.*, 1972; Wetzel, 1972).

B. Trypanosomiasis

As early as 1904 (Thomas and Linton, 1904), guinea pigs were used as experimental hosts for African trypanosomes. Experimental infections of guinea pigs with 19 species of *Trypanosoma* have been reported. This indicates a broad receptiveness of the guinea pig for trypanosomes (Hsu-Kuo *et al.*, 1970; Fink *et al.*, 1971; Marciacq and Seed, 1970).

C. Amebiasis

In early efforts to develop a laboratory model for human amebiasis, i.e., *Entamoeba histolytica*, Adams (1937) established infections in guinea pigs. Faust (1950), while evaluating *E. histolytica* infections, surveyed intestinal protozoa of the guinea pig and reported means of differentiating them. Most amebiasis work has been directed toward understanding the pathogenesis of infections (Soresco and Panaitesco, 1969; Wittner *et al.*, 1971; Takeuchi and Phillips, 1972) and the effects of bacteria on pathogenicity (Carrera and Faust, 1949; Wittner and Rosenbaum, 1970).

Several "heat-resistant" amebas or ameboflagellates, e.g., *Hartmanella, Naegleria*, have been found to be involved in human disease. The guinea pig can be utilized in research on these parasites (Culbertson *et al.*, 1972).

D. Balantidiosis

Little research has been conducted on human and swine balantidiosis. The guinea pig can serve as an experimental host for studying these diseases (Westphal, 1957, 1971). However, spontaneous infections with *Balantidium caviae* must be considered (Section III,D,26).

E. Trichomoniasis

Guinea pigs have been used to maintain strains and to experiment with venereal trichomoniasis of humans caused by *Trichomonas vaginalis* and of cattle caused by *Tritrichomonas foetus* (Wittfogel, 1935a,b; Lwoff and Nicolau, 1935; Nicolau and Lwoff, 1935; Morgan, 1943a). The hamster has replaced the guinea pig for these purposes.

F. Toxoplasmosis

The use of guinea pigs in toxoplasmosis research (Section II,E,1) has been supplanted by mice in most laboratories.

G. Piroplasmosis and Coccidiosis

Some attempts have been made to adapt piroplasms (*Babesia* and *Theileria*) and coccidia (*Eimeria*) to the guinea pig, but none have been successful (Guilbride, 1963; Holbrook and Frerichs, 1970; Pellérdy and Dürr, 1969).

REFERENCES

Abboud, I. A., Ragab, H. A. A., and Hanna, L. S. (1970). Experimental ocular leishmaniasis. *Brit. J. Ophthalmol.* **54,** 256–262.

Abe, T. (1927). On the classification of *Balantidium* (preliminary report). *Dobutsugaku Zasshi* **39,** 191–196.

Adams, A. R. D. (1937). *E. histolytica* infection of guineapig's colon. *Trans. Roy. Soc. Trop. Med. Hyg.* **31,** 2.

Adler, S., and Halff, L. (1955). Observations on *Leishmania enriettii* Muniz and Medina, 1948. *Ann. Trop. Med. Parasitol.* **49,** 37–41.

Alexeieff, A. (1946a). Notes protistologiques. I. Sur un nouveau *Proteromonas P. brevifilia* Alexeieff. *Arch. Zool. Exp. Gen.* **84,** 150–151.

Alexeieff, A. (1946b). Notes protistologiques. II. Sur quelques particularités de structure des trichomonades. *Arch. Zool. Exp. Gen.* **84,** 151–154.

Alves de Souza, M. (1931). Coccidiose em cobaya. *Rev. Zooteh. Med. Vet.* **17,** 11–14.

Andrews, J. M. (1926). Cultivation of *Trichomonas*, thermal deathpoint, anaerobic conditions, attempts at sterilization. *J. Parasitol.* **12,** 148–157.

Andrews, J. S., Taylor, A. L., and Swanson, L. E. (1943). Fumigation of soil with methyl bromide as a means of destroying infective stages and intermediate hosts of some internal parasites of mammals. *Proc. Helminthol. Soc. Wash.* **10,** 4–6.

Ansari, M. A. R. (1951). Contribution à l'étude du genre *Giardia* Kunstler, 1882 (Mastigophora, Octomitidae). I. Tableau synoptique des espèces connues et de quatre espèces nouvelles. *Ann. Parasitol.* **26,** 477–490.

Ansari, M. A. R. (1952). Contribution à l'étude du genre *Giardia* Kunstler, 1882 (Mastigophora, Octomitidae). I. Tableau synoptique des espèces connues et de quatre espèces nouvelles. *Ann. Parasitol.* **27,** 421–479.

Arcay-de-Peraza, L. (1966). The use of *Sarcocystis tenella* "spores" in a new agglutination test for sarcosporidiosis. *Trans. Roy. Soc. Trop. Med. Hyg.* **60,** 761–765.

Armaghan, V. (1937). Biological studies on the *Giardia* of rats. *Amer. J. Hyg.* **26,** 236–258.

Arnao Mendoza, M. (1951). Parásitos identificados en el Instituto nacional de biologiá animal 1946–1951. *Rev. Inst. Nac. Biol. Anim., Lima* **2,** 76–81.

Barretto, M. P., de Siqueira, A. F., Ferriolli Filho, F., and Carvalheiro, J. R. (1966). Estudos sôbre reservatórios e vectores silvestres do *Trypanosoma cruzi.* XI. Observações sôbre um foco natural da tripanossomose americana no Munícipio de Ribeirão Prêto, São Paulo. *Rev. Inst. Med. Trop. Sao Paulo* **8,** 103–112.

Becker, E. R. (1934). "Coccidia and Coccidiosis of Domesticated, Game and Laboratory Animals and of Man." Collegiate Press, Ames, Iowa.

Bemrick, W. J. (1962). The host specificity of *Giardia* from laboratory strains of *Mus musculus* and *Rattus norvegicus. J. Parasitol.* **48,** 287–290.

Benex, J., and Lamy, L. (1967). Etudes comparées de la sensibilité et de la spécificité d'un antigène leishmanien vis-à-vis de diverses espèces de *Leishmania* et autres protozoaires sanguicoles. *Bull. Soc. Pathol. Exot.* **60,** 506–510.

Bérard-Badier, M., Laugier, M., Louchet, E., and Payan, H. (1968). Le placenta dans la toxoplasmose congénitale aiguë expérimentale du cobaye. *Pathol. Biol.* **16,** 829–835.

Berengo, A., Cavallini-Sampieri, L., Cavallini, F., de Lalla, F., and Bechelli, G. (1967). Ricerche sierologiche sulla diffusione della toxoplasmosi. *Minerva Med.* **58,** 1947–1957.

Bhatia, B. L. (1938). "The Fauna of British India, including Ceylon and Burma. Protozoa: Sporozoa." Taylor & Francis, London.

Bishop, A. (1932). A note upon *Retortamonas rotunda* n. sp., an intestinal flagellate in *Bufo vulgaris. Parasitology* **24,** 233–237.

Bishop, A. (1934). The intestinal protozoa of a muskrat, *Fiber (=Ondatra) zibethica,* with a note upon *Retortamonas* sp. from the guinea pig. *Parasitology* **26,** 578–581.

Boisseau, R., and Nodenot, L. (1936). Un cas de toxoplasmose spontanée du cobaye observé à l'Institut Pasteur de Brazzaville (A.E.F.). *Bull. Soc. Pathol. Exot.* **29,** 135–141.

Bonciu, C., and Petrovici, M. (1966). Essais d'infestations expérimentales avec des *Klossiella* chez les cobayes et les souris. *Arch. Roum. Pathol. Exp. Microbiol.* **25,** 523–532.

Bonciu, C., Clecner, B., Greceanu, A., and Mărgineanu, A. (1957). Contribution à l'étude de l'infection naturelle des cobayes avec des sporozoaires du genre *"Klossiella." Arch. Roum. Pathol. Exp. Microbiol.* **16,** 131–143.

Bonne, C. (1925). *Klossiella muris,* parasite général de souris badigeonnées au goudron. *C. R. Soc. Biol.,* **92,** 1190–1192.

Bray, R. S., and Wilson, V. C. L. C. (1972). Lack of transfer factor in guinea pig leishmaniasis. *Trans. Roy. Soc. Trop. Med. Hyg.* **66,** 955–956.

Bray, R. S., Ellis, D. S., and Bird, R. G. (1969). The fine structure of *Leishmania enriettii. Trans. Roy. Soc. Trop. Med. Hyg.* **63,** 10–11.

Bryceson, A. D. M. (1970). Immunological aspects of clinical leishmaniasis. *Proc. Roy. Soc. Med.* **63,** 1056–1060.

Bryceson, A. D. M., and Turk, J. L. (1971). The effect of prolonged treatment with antilymphocyte serum on the course of infections with BCG and *Leishmania enriettii* in the guinea-pig. *J. Pathol.* **104,** 153–165.

Bryceson, A. D. M., Bray, R. S., Wolstencroft, R. A., and Dumonde, D. C. (1970a). Cell mediated immunity in cutaneous leishmaniasis of the guinea-pig. *Trans. Roy. Soc. Trop. Med. Hyg.* **64,** 472.

Bryceson, A. D. M., Bray, R. S., Wolstencroft, R. A., and Dumonde, D. C. (1970b). Immunity in cutaneous leishmaniasis of the guinea-pig. *Clin. Exp. Immunol.* **7,** 301–341.

Bryceson, A. D. M., Preston, P. M., Bray, R. S., and Dumonde, D. C. (1972). Experimental cutaneous leishmaniasis. II. Effects of immunosuppression and antigenic competition on the course of infection with *Leishmania enriettii* in the guinea-pig. *Clin. Exp. Immunol.* **10,** 305–335.

Bryceson, A. D. M., Bray, R. S., and Dumonde, D. C. (1974). Experimental cutaneous leishmaniasis. IV. Selective suppression of cell-mediated immunity during response of guinea-pigs to infection with *Leishmania enriettii. Clin. Exp. Immunol.* **16,** 189–201.

Bugge, G., and Heinke, P. (1921). Ueber das Vorkommen von Kokzidien beim Meerschweinchen. *Deut. Tieraerztl. Wochenschr.* **29,** 41–42.

Bussolati, C. (1949). Alcune osservazioni su *Trichomonas caviae* Davaine, 1875. *Riv. Parassitol.* **10,** 25–29.

Calhoon, J. R., and Matthews, P. J. (1964). A method for initiating a colony of specific pathogen-free guinea pigs. *Lab. Anim. Care* **14,** 388–394.

Campbell, W. G., Jr. (1972). Ultrastructure of *Pneumocystis* in human lung. *Arch. Pathol.* **93,** 312–324.

Carini, A., and Maciel, J. (1915). Ueber *Pneumocystis carinii. Zentralbl. Bakteriol., Parasitenk., Infektionskr. Hyg., Abt. 1: M.-H. Orig.* **77,** 46–50.

Carini, A., and Migliano, L. (1916). Sur un toxoplasme du cobaye (*Toxoplasma caviae* n. sp.). *Bull. Soc. Pathol. Exot.* **9,** 435–436.

Carrera, G. M., and Faust, E. C. (1949). Susceptibility of the guinea pig to *Endamoeba histolytica* of human origin. *Amer. J. Trop. Med.* **29,** 647–667.

Castellino, S., and de Carneri, I. (1964). Frequenza della giardiasi in vari roditori da laboratorio e attecchimento della giardie dell'Hamster nel Ratto. *Parassitologia* **6,** 55.

Červa, L. (1955). Resistence cyst *Lamblia intestinalis* vůči zevním faktorům. *Cesk. Parazitol.* **2,** 17–21.

Chagas, C. (1909). Nova tripanozomiaze humana. *Mem. Inst. Oswaldo Cruz* **1,** 159–218.

Chagas, C. (1911). Nova entidade morbida do homem. *Mem. Inst. Oswaldo Cruz* **3,** 219–275.

Chalmers, A. J., and Pekkola, W. (1918). *Enteromonas hominis* and *Protetramitus testudinis. J. Trop. Med. Hyg.* **21,** 129–133.

Chance, M. L. (1972). DNA base composition differences between species of *Leishmania. Trans. Roy. Soc. Trop. Med. Hyg.* **66,** 352.

Chang, K. (1935). A general survey of the protozoa parasitic in the digestive tract of Shantung mammals. *Peking Natur. Hist. Bull.* **9,** 151–159.

Chatton, E. (1917). Réalisation expérimentale chez le cobaye l'amibiase intestinale à *Entamoeba dysenteriae. Bull. Soc. Pathol. Exot.* **10,** 794–799.

Chatton, E. (1918a). L'amibiase intestinale expérimentale du cobaye à *Entamoeba dysenteriae.* Ses caractères spéciaux: Localisation caecale, absence de dysenterie, improtantes réactions hyperplasiques. *Arch. Inst. Pasteur Tunis* **10,** 138–157.

Chatton, E. (1918b). Les caractères de l'amibiase intestinale du cobaye à *Entamoeba dysenteriae*: Localisation caecale, absence de dysenterie, importantes réactions hyperplasiques. *Bull. Soc. Pathol. Exot.* **11,** 23–26.

Chatton, E. (1920). Culture indéfinie d'un *Trichomonas* intestinal du cobaye, essais de purification, action morphogène des milieux sur la membrane ondulante. *C. R. Soc. Biol.* **83,** 69–72.

Choquette, L. P. E. (1950). Canine giardiasis and its treatment with atebrin. *Can. J. Comp. Med.* **14,** 230–235.

Clapham, P. A. (1950). On sterilizing land against poultry parasites. *J. Helminthol.* **24,** 137–144.

Clinton, B. A., Palczuk, N. C., and Stauber, L. A. (1972). *Leishmania donovani*; partial characterization of some flagellate cytoplasmic immunogens. *J. Immunol.* **108,** 1570–1577.

Corliss, J. O. (1953). Silver impregnation of ciliated protozoa by the Chatton-Lwoff technic. *Stain Technol.* **28**, 97–100.

Corliss, J. O. (1959). An illustrated key to the higher groups of the ciliated protozoa, with definition of terms. *J. Protozool.* **6**, 265–281.

Corliss, J. O. (1961). "The Ciliated Protozoa: Characterization, Classification, and Guide to the Literature." Pergamon, Oxford.

Corradini, L., and Binato, G. G. (1962). Lambliasi nella cavia. *Vet. Ital.* **13**, 259–266.

Cossel, L. (1958). Nierenbefunde beim meerschweinchen bei klossielleninfektion (*Klossiella cobayae*). *Schweiz. Z. Allg. Pathol. Bakteriol.* **21**, 62–73.

Coutinho, J. O. (1951). Nota sôbre o tratamento da leishmaniose espontânea de cobáia (*Leishmania enriettii* Muniz e Medina, 1948) por antimonial pentavelente "Solustibosan." *Folia Clin. Biol.* **17**, 151–155.

Coutinho, J. O. (1954a). Nota sôbre a imunidade adquirida na leishmaniose da cobáia–*Leishmania enriettii* Muniz e Medina, 1948. *Folia Clin. Biol.* **21**, 15–18.

Coutinho, J. O. (1954b). Observações sôbre a vacinação preventiva com leptomonas mortas na leishmaniose espontânea da cobáia: *Leishmania enriettii. Folia Clin. Biol.* **21**, 321–326.

Coutinho, J. O. (1955a). Nota sôbre o tratamento da leishmaniose da cobáia, *Leishmania enriettii* Muniz e Medina, 1948. *Folia Clin. Biol.* **23**, 37–42.

Coutinho, J. O. (1955b). Contribuição para o estudo da *Leishmania enriettii* Muniz e Medina, 1948–Inoculações experimentais. *Folia Clin. Biol.* **23**, 91–102.

Culbertson, C. G., Ensminger, P. W., and Overton, W. M. (1972). Amebic cellulocutaneous invasion by *Naegleria aerobia* with generalized visceral lesions after subsutaneous inoculation: An experimental study in guinea pigs. *Amer. J. Clin. Pathol.* **57**, 375–386.

Curasson, G. (1940). Trichomonas dans le sang d'un cobaye infecté par *Trypanosoma congolense. Bull. Serv. Zootech. Epizoot. Afr. Occident. Fr.* **3**, 236–237.

da Cunha, A. M. (1914). Sôbre os ciliados intestinais dos mammiferos. *Mem. Inst. Oswaldo Cruz* **6**, 212–216.

da Cunha, A. M. (1915). Sôbre a presença de *Selenomonas* no coecum dos roederes. (Nota prévia.) *Brazil-Med.* **29**, 33.

da Cunha, A. M., and de Freitas, G. (1936a). Division et réorganisation chez les ciliés de la famille des Cyathodiniidae. *C. R. Soc. Biol.* **123**, 436–438.

da Cunha, A. M., and de Freitas, G. (1936b). Division et réorganisation chez les ciliés de la famille des Cyathodiniidae. *C. R. Soc. Biol.* **123**, 711–713.

da Cunha, A. M., and de Freitas, G. (1937). Sur la division des flagellés du genre *Chilomitus. C. R. Soc. Biol.* **125**, 175–176.

da Cunha, A. M., and de Freitas, G. (1940). Ensaio monográfico da familia Cyathodiniidae. *Mem. Inst. Oswaldo Cruz* **35**, 457–494.

da Cunha, A. M., and Muniz, J. (1921). Sôbre flagellados parasitas. I. *Monocercomonas caviae* n. sp. *Brazil-Med.* **35**, 379–380.

da Cunha, A. M., and Muniz, J. (1927a). Sur les flagellés intestinaux; description de trois espèces nouvelles. *C. R. Soc. Biol.* **96**, 496–498.

da Cunha, A. M., and Muniz, J. (1927b). Ciliés parasites de mammifères du Brésil. *C. R. Soc. Biol.* **97**, 825–827.

da Fonseca, O. O. R. (1915). "Estudos sôbre dos Flagellados Parasitos dos Mammiferos do Brazil." Typographia Leuzinger, Rio de Janeiro.

da Fonseca, O. O. R. (1916). Estudos sôbre os flagellados parasitos dos mammiferos do Brazil. *Mem. Inst. Oswaldo Cruz* **8**, 5–40.

da Fonseca, O. O. R. (1918a). Sôbre os flagellados parasitos (7ª nota prévia). *Brazil-Med.* **32**, 113.

da Fonseca, O. O. R. (1918b). Sôbre os flagellados parasitos (8ª nota prévia). *Brazil-Med.* **32**, 241.

da Fonseca, O. O. R. (1920). Estudos sôbre os flagellados parasitos. *Mem. Inst. Oswaldo Cruz* **12**, 51–65.

Dagert Boyer, C., and Scorza Boyer, J. V. (1957). Encuesta sôbre parasitos microscopios de algunos Cricetinae silvestres de Venezuela (ratas silvestres). *Bol. Venez. Lab. Clin.* **2**, 59–67.

Danforth, W. F. (1967). Respiratory metabolism. *Res. Protozool.* **1**, 201–306.

Daniel, W. A., Mattern, C. F. T., and Honigberg, B. M. (1971). Fine structure of the mastigont system in *Tritrichomonas muris* (Grassi). *J. Protozool.* **18**, 575–586.

Das Gupta, B. M. (1936). Observations on the flagellates of the genera *Trichomonas* and *Eutrichomastix. Parasitology* **28**, 195–201.

Davaine, C. (1875). Monadiens. *Dict. Encycl. Sci. Med.* [2] **9**, 115–130.

Davis, L. R. (1973). Techniques. *In* "The Coccidia" (D. M. Hammond and P. L. Long, eds.), pp. 411–458. Univ. Park Press, Baltimore, Maryland.

de Almeida, F. P. (1928). Sôbre um protozoario encontrado no coração de cobayo. *An. Fac. Med. Univ. Sao Paulo* **3**, 65–67.

de la Barrera, J. M., and Riva, A. (1927). *Toxoplasma* del cobayo. *Sem. Med.* **34**, 1427–1428.

de la Barrera, J. M., and Riva, A. (1928). Toxoplasmosis de la cobaya. *Rev. Inst. Bacteriol. Dep. Nac. Hig. (Argent.)* **5**, 470–490.

Delanoë, P., and Delanoë, C. (1912). Sur les rapports des kystes des Carini du poumon des rats avec le *Trypanosoma lewisi. C. R. Acad. Sci.* **155**, 658–660.

de Mello, I. F. (1932). Sur un petit flagellé à caractères fixés, intermédiaires entre les genéres *Trimitus, Eutrichomatix* et *Devescovina. Reun. Soc. Argent. Patol. Reg. Norte* **2**, 907–917.

de Mello, I. F., and de Sousa, J. (1924). Sur la morphologie et les mitoses de *Trichomonas caviae*, avec références spéciales à la complexité de son appariel basal. *Bull. Soc. Port. Sci. Natur.* **9**, 122–126.

Demina, N. A. (1963a). [Transfer of immunity to protozoal infections by maternal heredity.] [Russian text] *Proc. Int. Congr. Trop. Med. Malaria, 7th, 1963* Vol. 2, pp. 395–396.

Demina, N. A. (1963b). Immunity studies in leishmaniasis. *Proc. Int. Congr. Protozool., 1st, 1961* Vol. 1, pp. 545–548.

de Rodaniche, E., and de Pinzon, T. (1949). Spontaneous toxoplasmosis in the guinea-pig in Panama. *J. Parasitol.* **35**, 152–155.

Deschiens, R. E. A. (1926). *Giardia cati* R. Deschiens, 1925, du chat domestique (*Felis domestica*). *Ann. Parasitol.* **4**, 33–48.

Dias, E. (1956). Chagas-Krankheit; Chagas' Disease. *In* "Welt Seuchen Atlas" (E. Rodenwaldt, ed.), Vol. II, pp. 135–140. Falk-Verlag, Hamburg.

Dieben, C. P. A. (1924). "Over de Morphologie en Biologie van het Rattencoccodium *Eimeria nieschulzi* n. sp. en zijne verspreiding in Nederland." Proefschr. Veeartsenijk. Hoogesch., Utrecht.

Diomina, N. A. (1963). Transmissão da imunidade materna aos descendentes nas infeccões por protozoários. *Proc. Int. Congr. Trop. Med. Malaria, 7th, 1963* Vol. 2, pp. 330–331.

Dollfus, R. P. F. (1961). Station expérimentale de parasitologie de Rochelieu (Indre-et Loire). Contribution a la faune parasitaire régionale. A. Protozoaires. *Ann. Parasitol.* **36**, 171–451.

Doran, D. J. (1973). Cultivation of coccidia in avian embryos and cell culture. *In* "The Coccidia" (D. M. Hammond and P. L. Long, eds.), pp. 183–252. Univ. Park Press, Baltimore, Maryland.

Doyle, J. J., Behin, R., Manel, J., and Rowe, D. S. (1974). Antibody-induced movement of membrane components of *Leishmania enriettii. J. Exp. Med.* **139**, 1061–1069.

Dubey, J. P., Miller, N. L., and Frenkel, J. K. (1970). Characterization of the new fecal form of *Toxoplasma gondii*. *J. Parasitol.* **56,** 447–456.

Dubienska, W. (1967). Kokcidiosa u morskich świnek. *Med. Wet.* **23,** 370.

du Buy, H. G., and Riley, F. L. (1967). Hybridization between the nuclear and kinetoplast DNA's of *Leishmania enriettii* and between nuclear and mitochondrial DNA's of mouse liver. *Proc. Nat. Acad. Sci. U.S.* **57**, 790–797.

du Buy, H. G., Mattern, C. F. T., and Riley, F. L. (1965). Isolation and characterization of DNA from kinetoplasts of *Leishmania enriettii. Science* **147**, 754–756.

du Buy, H. G., Mattern, C. F. T., and Riley, F. L. (1966). Comparison of the DNA's obtained from brain nuclei and mitochondria of mice and from the nuclei and kinetoplasts of *Leishmania enriettii. Biochim. Biophys. Acta* **123**, 298–305.

Ellis, P. A., and Wright, A. E. (1961). Coccidiosis in guinea pigs. *J. Clin. Pathol.* **14**, 394–396.

Ercoli, N., and Coelho, M. V. (1967). Problems of drug evaluation in cutaneous leishmaniasis. *Ann. Trop. Med. Parasitol.* **61**, 488–499.

Eyles, D. E. (1963). Chemotherapy of toxoplasmosis. *Exp. Chemother.* **1**, 641–655.

Fantham, H. B. (1922). Some parasitic protozoa found in South Africa. V. *S. Afr. J. Sci.* **19**, 332–339.

Fantham, H. B. (1923). Some parasitic protozoa found in South Africa. VI. *S. Afr. J. Sci.* **20**, 493–500.

Fantham, H. B. (1925). Some parasitic protozoa found in South Africa. VIII. *S. Afr. J. Sci.* **22**, 346–354.

Faust, E. C. (1921). A Study of *Trichomonas* of the guinea-pig from Peking. *Arch. Protistenk* **44**, 115–118.

Faust, E. C. (1950). The intestinal protozoa of the guinea pig. *An. Inst. Biol., Univ. Nac. Auton. Mex.* **20**, 229–250.

Fayer, R. (1970). *Sarcocystis*: Development in cultured avian and mammalian cells. *Science* **168**, 1104–1105.

Fayer, R. (1972). Gametogony of *Sarcocystis* sp. in cell cultures. *Science* **175**, 65–67.

Ferriolli Filho, F., and Barretto, M. P. (1966). Estudos sôbre reservatórios e vectores silvestres do *Trypanosoma cruzi*. XIV. Infecção natural da preá, *Cavia aperea aperea* Erxleben, 1777, por tripanossomo semelhante ao *T. cruzi. Rev. Inst. Med. Trop. Sao Paulo* **8,** 267–276.

Filice, F. P. (1952). Studies on the cytology and life history of a *Giardia* from the laboratory rat. *Univ. Calif. Berkeley, Publ. Zool.* **57**, 53–145.

Fink, E. H., Oerlerich, S., and Zum Felde, I. (1971). Antikörpernachweis und quantitative Bestimmung der Serum-IgM bei der experimentellen Trypanosomiasis des Meerschweinchens. *Z. Tropenmed. Parasitol.* **22**, 343–350.

Flynn, R. J., ed. (1973). "Parasites of Laboratory Animals." Iowa State Univ. Press, Ames.

Fraser, H. (1908). Six-monthly report of the Institute for Medical Research, Kwala Lumpur, Federated Malay States (April to September 1907). *Rep. Advisory Comm. Trop. Dis. Res. Fund, London, 1907* pp. 100–105.

Frenkel, J. K. (1971). Protozoal diseases of laboratory animals. *In* "Pathology of Protozoal and Helminthic Diseases" (R. A. Marcial-Rojas, ed.), pp. 318–369. William & Wilkins, Baltimore, Maryland.

Frenkel, J. K. (1973). Toxoplasmosis: Parasite, life cycle, pathology, and immunology. *In* "The Coccidia" (D. M. Hammond and P. L. Long, eds.), pp. 343–410. Univ. Park Press, Baltimore, Maryland.

Frenkel, J. K., Good, J. T., and Shultz, J. A. (1966). Latent *Pneumocystis* infection of rats, relapse, and chemotherapy. *Lab. Invest.* **15**, 1559–1577.

Frenkel, J. K., Dubey, J. P., and Miller, N. L. (1970). *Toxoplasma gondii* in cats: Fecal stages identified as coccidian oocysts. *Science* **167**, 893–896.

Freund, L. (1933). Parasiten des Meerschweinshens. *Tieraerztl. Rundsch.* **39,** 432.

Fritzsche, K. (1933). Die seuchenartigen Krankheiten des Meerschweinchens. *In* "Das Meerschweinchen" (H. Raebiger, ed.), 2nd edition, pp. 68–92. von Schaper, Hannover.

Gabaldón, A. (1930). Nota histórica sôbre los protozoos señalados en Venezuela. *Gac. Med. Caracas* **37**, 131–140.

Galli-Valerio, B. (1900). Notes de parasitologie. *Zentralbl. Bakteriol., Parasitenk. Infektionskr., Abt. 1:* **27**, 305–309.

Galli-Valerio, B. (1901). La collection de parasites du laboratoire d'hygiène et de parasitologie de l'Université de Lausanne. *Bull. Soc. Vaudoise Sci. Natur.* [*2*] **37**, 343–381.

Galli-Valerio, B. (1904). Notes de parasitologie. *Zentralbl. Bakteriol., Parasitenk. Infektionskr., Abt. 1: Orig.* **35**, 81–91.

Galli-Valerio, B. (1939). Observations sur quelques maladies parasitaires et sur quelques intoxications des animaux domestiques et sauvages. *Schweiz. Arch. Tierheilk.* **81**, 91–108.

Galli-Valerio, B., and Bornand, M. (1927). Sur quelques maladies parasitaires des petits animaux domestiques observées dans le canton de Vaud. *Schweiz. Arch. Tierheilk.* **69**, 519–529.

Gauget, G. (1938). "Les Parasites du Cobaye." Vigot Frères, Paris.

Glazunova, Z. I. (1964a). [A reduction of the pathogenecity of *Leishmania enriettii* after 15-year maintenance in culture.] [Russian text; English summary] *Med. Parazitol. Parazit. Bolez.* **33**, 479–482.

Glazunova, Z. I. (1964b). [An experimental study of superinfection in leishmaniasis of guinea pigs.] [Russian text; English summary] *Med. Parazitol. Parazit. Bolez.* **33**, 643–650.

Glazunova, Z. I. (1965). [Allergic reactions in guinea-pigs upon repeated inoculation with *Leishmania enriettii*.] [Russian text; English summary.] *Med. Parazitol. Parazit. Bolez.* **34**, 582–585.

Gleiberman, S. E., and Belova, E. M. (1964). [General morphology of the cytopathogenic effect of *Leishmania* in tissue culture.] [Russian text; English summary.] *Med. Parazitol. Parazit. Bolez.* **34,** 650–654.

Goetz, O. (1960). Die Ätiologie der interstitiellen sogenannten plasmazellulären Pneumonie des jungen Säuglings. *Arch. Kinderheilk., Beih.* **41,** 1–73.

Grassé, P.-P. (1926). Contribution à l'étude flagellés parasites. *Arch. Zool. Exp. Gen.* **65**, 345–602.

Grassé, P.-P., and Faure, A. (1935). La reproduction de l'appareil parabasal du *Trichomonas caviae* Dav. *C. R. Acad. Sci.* **200**, 1493–1495.

Grassé, P.-P., and Faure, A. (1939). Quelques données nouvelles sur la cytologie et la reproduction de *Trichomonas caviae* Dav. *Bull. Biol. Fr. Belg.* **73**, 1–18.

Grassi, G. B. (1879). Dei protozoi parassiti e specialmente di quelli che sono nell'uomo. *Gazz. Med. Lomb.* **39**, 445–448.

Grassi, G. B. (1881). Note intorno ad alcuni parassiti dell'uomo. *Gazz. Osp. Clin.* **2**, 433–439.

Grassi, G. B. (1882). Intorno ad alcuni protisti endoparassitici ed appartenenti alle classi dei flagellati, lobosi, sporozoi e ciliati. Memoria di parassitologia comparata. *Atti. Soc. Ital. Sci. Natur.* **24,** 135–224.

Greenblatt, C. L., and Glaser, P. (1965). Temperature effect on *Leishmania enriettii in vitro. Exp. Parasitol.* **16**, 36–52.

Greenblatt, C. L., and Wetzel, B. K. (1966). Alterations in fatty acid metabolism and morphology of *Leishmania enriettii* exposed to elevated temperature. *J. Protozool.* **13**, 521–531.

Guérin, F. H., and Pons, R. (1925). Culture de *Blastocystis hominis* et des protozoaires parasites intestinaux de l'homme. *Arch. Inst. Pasteur Indochine* **2**, 213–221.

Guilbride, P. D. (1963). Attempts to adapt *Theileria parva* to laboratory animals. *Bull. Epizoot. Dis. Afr.* **11**, 283–287.

Guimarães, J. P. (1952). Observações sôbre a leishmaniose do cobaio. *Manguinhos Bol. Inst. Oswaldo Cruz, Rio de Janeiro* **1**, 4–5.

Gusev, V. F. (1934). Zur Frage der Coccidien der Einhufer. *Arch. Wiss. Prakt. Tierheilk.* **68**, 67–73.

Habermann, R. T., Williams, F. P., Jr., and Thorp, W. T. S. (1954). "Identification of some Internal Parasites of Laboratory Animals," Pub. Health Serv. Publ. No. 343. US Govt. Printing Office, Washington, D.C.

Haiba, M. H. (1953). "Studies on the Morphology and Biology of Giardia." Fouad I University Press, Cairo.

Haiba, M. H. (1956). Further study on the susceptibility of murines to human giardiiasis. *Z. Parasitenk.* **17**, 339–345.

Hardcastle, A. B. (1943). A check list and host-index of the species of the protozoan genus *Eimeria*. *Proc. Helminthol. Soc. Wash.* **10**, 35–69.

Hasselmann, G. E. (1918). Sôbre os ciliados dos mammiferos (Enterophryidae, nov. fam.). *Brazil-Med.* **32**, 81.

Hasselmann, G. E. (1924). Ciliados parasitos de *Cavia aperea*, Erxl. *Mem. Inst. Oswaldo Cruz* **17**, 229–235.

Hegner, R. W. (1923a). Giardias from wild rats and mice and *Giardia caviae* sp. n. from the guinea pig. *Amer. J. Hyg.* **3**, 345–349.

Hegner, R. W. (1923b). Giardias from wild rats and mice and *Giardia caviae* sp. n. from the guinea pig. *Collect. Pap., Sch. Hyg. Publ. Health Johns Hopkins Univ. (1923–1924)* **5**, 345–349.

Hegner, R. W. (1924a). *Giardia* and *Chilomastix* from monkeys, *Giardia* from the wild cat and *Balantidium* from the sheep. *J. Parasitol.* **11**, 75–78.

Hegner, R. W. (1924b). Infection experiments with *Trichomonas*. *Amer. J. Hyg.* **4**, 143–151.

Hegner, R. W. (1925). *Giardia felis* n. sp., from the domestic cat and giardias from birds. *Amer. J. Hyg.* **5**, 258–273.

Hegner, R. W. (1926a). Animal infections with the trophozoites of intestinal protozoa and their bearing on the functions of cysts. *Amer. J. Hyg.* **6**, 593–601.

Hegner, R. W. (1926b). *Endolimax caviae* n. sp., from the guinea-pig and *Endolimax janisae* n. sp. from the domestic fowl. *J. Parasitol.* **12**, 146–147.

Hegner, R. W. (1926c). *Giardia beckeri* n. sp. from the ground squirrel and *Endamoeba dipodomysi* n. sp. from the kangaroo rat. *J. Parasitol.* **12**, 203–206.

Hegner, R. W. (1927). "Host-Parasite Relations between Man and His Intestinal Protozoa." Century Co., New York.

Hegner, R. W. (1930). Host-parasite specificity in the genus *Giardia*. *In* "Problems and Methods of Research in Protozoology" (R. W. Hegner and J. M. Andrews, eds.), pp. 143–153. Macmillan, New York.

Hegner, R. W. (1934). Specificity in the genus *Balantidium* based on size and shape of body and macronucleus with descriptions of six new species. *Amer. J. Hyg.* **19**, 38–67.

Hegner, R. W., and Chu, H. J. (1930). A survey of protozoa parasitic in plants and animals of the Philippine Islands. *Philipp. J. Sci.* **43**, 451–482.

Hegner, R. W., and Schumaker, E. (1928). Some intestinal amoebae and flagellates from the chimpanzee, three-toed sloth, sheep, and guinea-pig. *J. Parasitol.* **15**, 31–37.

Hegner, R. W., and Taliaferro, W. H. (1924). "Human Protozoology." Macmillan, New York.

Heisch, R. B., Killick-Kendrick, R., Guy, M. W., and Dorrell, J. (1970). The development of trypanosomes, leishmaniae and ascitic tumour cells in the testicles of laboratory animals. *Trans. Roy. Soc. Trop. Med. Hyg.* **64**, 679–682.

Henry, D. P. (1932). Coccidiosis of the guinea pig. *Univ. Calif. Berkeley, Publ. Zool.* **37**, 211–268.

Herrer, A. (1964). Chagas' disease in Peru. I. The epidemiological importance of the guinea pig. *Trop. Geogr. Med.* **16**, 146–151.

Hertig, M., and McConnell, E. (1963). Experimental infection of Panamanian *Phlebotomus* sandflies with *Leishmania*. *Exp. Parasitol.* **14**, 92–106.

Heydorn, A. O., and Rommel, M. (1972). Beiträge zum Lebenszyklus der Sarkosporidien. II. Hund und Katze als Überträger der Sarkosporidien des Rindes. *Berlin. Muenchen. Tieraerztl. Wochenschr.* **85**, 121–123.

Hibler, C. P., Hammond, D. M., Caskey, F. H., Johnson, A. E., and Fitzgerald, P. R. (1960). The morphology and incidence of the trichomonads of swine, *Tritrichomonas suis* (Gruby and Delafond), *Tritrichomonas rotunda*, n. sp. and *Tritrichomonas buttreyi*, n. sp. *J. Protozool.* **7**, 159–171.

Hoare, C. A. (1972). The developmental stages of *Toxoplasma*. *J. Trop. Med. Hyg.* **75**, 56–58.

Hofman, V. H., and Hänichen, T. (1970). *Klossiella cobayae*–Nierenkokzidiose bei meerschweinchen. *Berlin. Muenchen. Tieraerztl. Wochenschr.* **83**, 151–153.

Holberton, D. V. (1973). Fine structure of the ventral disk apparatus and the mechanism of attachment in the flagellate *Giardia muris*. *J. Cell Sci.* **13**, 11–41.

Holbrook, A. A., and Frerichs, W. M. (1970). *Babesia mephitis* sp. n. (Protozoa: Piroplasmida), a hematozoan parasite of the striped skunk, *Mephitis mephitis*. *J. Parasitol.* **56**, 930–931.

Holmes, F. O. (1923). Observations on the cysts of *Endamoeba cobayae*. *J. Parasitol.* **10**, 47–50.

Honigberg, B. M. (1963). Evolutionary and systematic relationships in the flagellate order Trichomonadida Kirby. *J. Protozool.* **10**, 20–63.

Honigberg, B. M., and Davenport, H. A. (1954). Staining flagellate protozoa by various silver-protein compounds. *Stain Technol.* **29**, 241–246.

Honigberg, B. M., and Goldman, M. (1968). Immunologic analysis by quantitative fluorescent antibody methods of the effects of prolonged cultivation of *Trichomonas gallinae*. *J. Protozool.* **15**, 176–184.

Honigberg, B. M., Becker, R. DiM., Livingston, M. C., and McLure, M. T. (1964). The behavior and pathogenicity of two strains of *Trichomonas gallinae* in cell cultures. *J. Protozool.* **11**, 447–465.

Horton-Smith, C. (1958). Coccidiosis in domestic mammals. *Vet. Rec.* **70**, 256–262.

Horton-Smith, C., Taylor, E. L., and Turtle, E. E. (1940). Ammonia fumigation for coccidial disinfection. *Vet. Rec.* **52**, 829.

Houdemer, F. E. (1938). "Recherches de Parasitologie comparée Indochinoise." R. Bussière, Paris.

Hsu-Kuo, M. Y., Lien, J. C., and Cross, J. H. (1970). Studies on *Trypanosoma conorhini*. *Chin. J. Microbiol.* **3**, 148–149.

Hutchison, W. M., Dunachie, J. F., Siim, J. C., and Work, K. (1970). Coccidian-like nature of *Toxoplasma gondii*. *Brit. Med. J. 1970*, 142–144.

Jackson, G. J. (1962). On axenic cultures of certain protozoan and worm parasites of insects. *Trans. N. Y. Acad. Sci. [2]* **24**, 954–965.

Jackson, G. J. (1963). *Leishmania enriettii* leptomonads in various culture media, including defined and antibody containing ones. *Proc. Int. Congr. Protozool., 1st, 1961* Vol. 1, p. 549.

Jackson, L. (1920a). An intracellular protozoan parasite of the ducts of the salivary glands of the guinea-pig. *J. Infec. Dis.* **26**, 347–350.

Jackson, L. (1920b). An intracellular protozoan parasite of the ducts of the salivary glands of the guinea-pig. *Trans. Chicago Pathol. Soc.* **11**, 100–104.

Jacobs, L., Remington, J. S., and Melton, M. L. (1960). The resistance of the encysted form of *Toxoplasma gondii. J. Parasitol.* **46**, 11–21.

Jadin, J. B., and Wery, M. (1963). La culture des Trypanosomidae. *Ann. Soc. Belg. Med. Trop.* **43**, 831–842.

Jervis, H. R., Merrill, T. G., and Sprinz, H. (1966). Coccidiosis in the guinea pig small intestine due to a *Cryptosporidium. Amer. J. Vet. Res.* **27**, 408–414.

Jordan, J., and Mirick, G. S. (1955). An infectious hepatitis of undetermined origin in mice. I. Description of the disease. *J. Exp. Med.* **102**, 601–616.

Kallinikova, V. D. (1974). [Kinetoplast of trypanosomides and the organization levels of intracellular genetic systems.] [Russian text.] *Zhurnal Obsh. Biol.* **35**, 228–235.

Kallinikova, V. D. (1974). Kinetoplast of trypanosomides and the organization levels of intracellular genetic systems. Russian text. *Zhurnal Obsh. Biol.* **35**, 228–235.

Karapetyan, A. E. (1962). *In vitro* cultivation of *Giardia duodenalis. J. Parasitol.* **48**, 337–340.

Katiyar, R. D. (1953). Guinea-pig husbandry. *Indian Vet. J.* **29**, 330–340.

Kean, B. H., and Grocott, R. G. (1945). Sarcosporidiosis or toxoplasmosis in man and guinea-pig. *Amer. J. Pathol.* **21**, 467–483.

Kleeberg, H. H., and Steenken, W., Jr. (1963). Severe coccidiosis in guinea-pigs. *J. S. Afr. Vet. Med. Ass.* **34**, 49–52.

Kofoid, C. A., McNeil, E., and Bonestell, A. E. (1935). A comparison of the distribution of the intestinal protozoa of the Norway Rat, wood rat, and guinea pig with reference to the hydrogen ion concentrations as determined by the glass electrode. *Univ. Calif., Berkeley, Publ. Zool.* **41**, 1–8.

Kopperi, A. J. (1935). Ueber die nicht-pathogene Protozoenfauna des Vlinddarms einiger Nagetiere. *Suom. Elain-ja Kasvitiet. Seuran Vanamon Elaintieteellisia Julkaisuja* **3**, 1–92.

Krascheninnikow, S. (1958a). An improved method for purifying balantidia. *J. Parasitol.* **44**, 126–127.

Krascheninnikow, S. (1958b). Improvement of a device for purifying balantidia. *J. Parasitol.* **44**, 506.

Krascheninnikow, S. (1959). Abnormal infraciliatures of *Balantidium coli* and *B. caviae* (?) and some morphological observations on these species. *J. Protozool.* **6**, 61–68.

Krascheninnikow, S., and Jeska, E. L. (1961). Agar diffusion studies on the species specificity of *Balantidium coli, B. caviae* and *B. wenrichi. Immunology* **4**, 282–288.

Krascheninnikow, S., and Tiesler, E. (1959). Simple methods for purifying balantidia. *J. Protozool.* **6**, 309–310.

Krascheninnikow, S., and Wenrich, D. H. (1958). Some observations on the morphology and division of *Balantidium coli* and *Balantidium caviae* (?). *J. Protozool.* **5**, 196–202.

Krenn, E. (1936). Klossiellen bei Maus und Meerschweinchen. *Wein. Tieraerztl. Monatsschr.* **23**, 699–700.

Kretschmar, W. (1965). Immunität bei der *Leishmania enriettii*-Infektion des Meerschweinchens. *Z. Tropenmed. Parasitol.* **16**, 277–283.

Krishnan, R. (1968). Balantidiosis in a guinea pig. *Indian Vet. J.* **45**, 917–920.

Kučera, K., Vaněk, J., and Jírovec, O. (1971). Pneumozystose. *In* "Leitfaden der Zooanthroponosen" (E. Toppich and W. Kruger, eds.), pp. 279–294. VEB Verlag Volk und Gesundheit, Berlin.

Kuczynski, M. H. (1914). Untersuchungen an Trichomonaden. *Arch. Protistenk.* **33**, 119–204.

Kuczynski, M. H. (1918). Ueber die Teilungsvorgänge verschiedener Trichomonaden und ihre Organisation im allgemeinen. *Arch. Protistenk.* **39**, 107–146.

Kulasiri, C. (1960). The specificity of the Sabin-Feldman dye test with reference to protozoal infections. *J. Clin. Pathol.* **13**, 339–348.

Kulasiri, C. (1962). The isolation of *Toxoplasma gondii* Nicolle and Manceaux from some Ceylon rodents. *Ceylon J. Med. Sci.* **11**, 11–14.

Kulda, J., and Honigberg, B. M. (1969). Behavior and pathogenicity of *Tritrichomonas foetus* in chick liver cell cultures. *J. Protozool.* **16**, 479–495.

Kunstler, J. (1882). Sur cinq protozoaires parasites nouveaux. *C. R. Acad. Sci.* **95**, 347–349.

Kunstler, J. (1896). Recherches sur la morphologie du *Trichomonas intestinalis. C. R. Acad. Sci.* **123**, 839–842.

Labbé, A. (1899). "Sporozoa, 5 lief., Das Tierreich." von R. Friedländer und Sohn, Berlin.

Lainson, R. (1959). A note on the duration of *Toxoplasma* infection in the guinea pig. *Ann. Trop. Med. Parasitol.* **53**, 120–121.

Lapage, G. (1940). The study of coccidiosis [*Eimeria caviae* (Sheather, 1924)] in the guinea pig. *Vet J.* **96**, 144–154, 190–202, 242–254, and 280–295.

Laveran, C. L. A., and Mesnil, F. (1901). Sur la morphologie et la systématique des flagellés à membrane ondulante (genres *Trypanosoma* Gruby et *Trichomonas* Donné). *C. R. Acad. Sci.* **133**, 131–137.

Léger, M. (1918). Epizootie chez le cobaye paraissant due à une amibiase intestinale. *Bull. Soc. Pathol. Exot.* **11**, 163–166.

Leiva, L. (1921). Observations on *Chilomastix intestinalis* Kuczinski. *J. Parasitol.* **8**, 49–57.

Lemma, A., and Yau, P. (1973). Course of development of *Leishmania enriettii* infection in immunosuppressed guinea pigs. *Amer. J. Trop. Med. Hyg.* **22**, 477–481.

Lerche, M. (1921). Die Coccidiose der Schafe. *Arch. Protistenk.* **42**, 380–399.

Levaditi, C., Nicolau, S., and Schoen, R. (1923). L'agent étiologique de l'encéphalite épizootique du lapin (*Encephalitozoon cuniculi*). *C. R. Soc. Biol.* **89**, 984–986.

Levaditi, C., Nicolau, S., and Schoen, R. (1924). L'étiologie de l'encéphalite épizootique du lapin, dans ses rapports avec l'étude expérimentale de l'encéphalite léthargique *Encephalitozoon cuniculi,* (nov. spec.). *Ann. Inst. Pasteur, Paris* **38**, 651–712.

Levine, N. D. (1957). Protozoan diseases of laboratory animals. *Proc. Anim. Care Panel* **7**, 98–126.

Levine, N. D. (1973). "Protozoan Parasites of Domestic Animals and of Man," 2nd ed. Burgess, Minneapolis, Minnesota.

Levine, N. D., and Becker, E. R. (1933). A catalog and host-index of the species of the coccidian genus *Eimeria. Iowa State Coll. J. Sci.* **8**, 83–106.

Levine, N. D., and Ivens, V. (1965). "The Coccidian Parasites (Protozoa, Sporozoa) of Rodents." Univ. of Illinois Press, Urbana.

Lingard, A., and Jennings, E. (1904). A preliminary note on a piroplasmosis found in man and in some of the lower animals. *Indian Med. Gaz.* **39**, 161–165.

Litvenkova, E. A. (1969). Coccidia of wild mammals in Byelorussia. *Proc. Int. Congr. Protozool., 3rd, 1969* Vol. 3, pp. 340–341.

Long, P. L., and Burns Brown, W. (1972). The effect of methyl bromide on coccidial oocysts determined under controlled conditions. *Vet. Rec.* **90**, 562–567.

López-Neyra, C. R., and Suárez Peregrín, E. (1933). "Sindromes parasitarios en la región Granadina y estudio sobre el parasitismo intestinal humano. I. Estudio critico de los "Chilomastix" parásitos humanos y descripción de una especie nueva hallada en el intestino del hombre en Granada." Comisión permanente de investigaciones sanitarias, Dirección General de Sanidad, Madrid.

Lucas, M. S. (1932a). A study of *Cyathodinium piriforme.* An endozoic protozoan from the intestinal tract of the guinea pig. *Arch. Protistenk.* **77**, 64–72.

Lucas, M. S. (1932b). The cytoplasmic phases of rejuvenescence and fission in *Cyathodinium piriforme.* II. A type of fission heretofore undescribed for ciliates. *Arch. Protistenk.* **77**, 407–423.

Lwoff, A., and Nicolau, S. (1935). Le pouvoir pathogène de *Trichomonas foetus* pour le système nerveux central. *Bull. Soc. Pathol. Exot.* **28**, 277–281.

Lynch, K. M. (1922a). *Tricercomonas intestinalis* and *Enteromonas caviae* n. sp. and their growth in culture. *J. Parasitol.* **9**, 29–32.

Lynch, K. M. (1922b). Cultivation of *Trichomonas* and the question of differentiation of the flagellates. *J. Amer. Med. Ass.* **79**, 1130–1133.

Lynch, K. M. (1924). Notes on the natural and cultural growth of certain intestinal flagellates. *Amer. J. Trop. Med.* **4**, 537–545.

Machado, J. O. (1969). Observações carenciais no parasitismo pela *Leishmania enriettii.* I. Aspectos na carência da vitamina A. *Hospital (Rio de Janeiro)* **75**, 1927–1933.

Maciel, J. (1914). Novo parasita encontrado em rins de cobaya. *Ann. Paul. Med. Cir.* **3**, 48.

Makstenieks, O., and Verlinde, J. D. (1957). Toxoplasmosis in the Netherlands. Clinical interpretation of parasitological and serological examinations and epidemiological relationships between toxoplasmosis in man and animals. *Doc. Med. Geogr. Trop.* **9**, 213–224.

Mancilla, R., Naquira, C., and Lanas, C. (1965). Metabolism of glucose labelled with carbon-14 in *Leishmania enriettii. Nature (London)* **206**, 27–28.

Marciacq, Y., and Seed, J. R. (1970). Reduced levels of glycogen and glucose-6-phosphatase in livers of guinea pigs infected with *Trypanosoma gambiense. J. Infec. Dis.* **121**, 653–655.

Marcial-Rojas, R. A., ed. (1971). "Pathology of Protozoal and Helminthic Diseases." Williams & Wilkins, Baltimore, Maryland.

Mariani, G. (1941). Toxoplasmosis spontanea delle cavie ad Addis Ababa. *Riv. Biol. Colon.* **4**, 47–54.

Markham, F. S. (1937). Spontaneous *Toxoplasma* encephalitis in the guinea pig. *Amer. J. Hyg.* **26**, 193–196.

Maržan, B. (1952). [*Klossiella* infection of the kidney of white mice and guinea pigs.] [Croatian text; English summary.] *Vet. Arh.* **22**, 187–193.

Medina, H. (1946). Estudos sôbre leishmaniose. I. Primeiros casos de leishmaniose espontânea observados em cobáios. *Arq. Biol. Tecnol.* **1**, 39–74.

Medina, H. (1947a). Estudos sôbre leishmaniose. II. Sôbre a ocorrência de macrófages parasitados em divisão. *Arq. Biol. Tecnol.* **2**, 3–6.

Medina, H. (1947b). Estudos sôbre a leishmaniose. III. A leishmaniose do cobaio como elemento de prova dos medicamentos específicos. *Arq. Biol. Tecnol.* **2**, 7–20.

Mesnil, F. (1918). *Bull. Inst. Pasteur, Paris* **16**, 71.

Mettam, R. W. M. (1932). Extracts from annual report, 1931, of the veterinary pathologist, Entebbe. *Rep. Vet. Dep. Uganda Protect., 1931* pp. 16–20.

Meyer, E. A. (1970). Isolation and axenic cultivation of *Giardia* trophozoites from the rabbit, chinchilla and cat. *Exp. Parasitol.* **27**, 179–183.

Mieth, H. (1966). Tiefgefrierkonservierung vershiedener Blut- und Gewebeprotozoen in flüssigem Stickstoff. *Z. Tropenmed. Parasitol.* **17**, 103–108.

Miller, L. T., and Feldman, H. A. (1953). Incidence of antibodies for *Toxoplasma* among various animal species. *J. Infec. Dis.* **92**, 118–120.

Mooser, H. (1929). Tabardillo, an American variety of typhus. *J. Infec. Dis.* **44**, 186–193.

Mordlvilko, A. K. (1908). Proiskhozdenie iavleniia promezhutochnykh khoziaev u zhivotnykh parazitov. *Exhegodnik Zool. Muz. Imp. Akad. Nauk, Petrograd.* **13**, 129–220.

Morénas, L. (1938). Etude morphologie et biologique sur les flagellés intestinaux parasites des muridés. Etude comparative des flagellés du cobaye. *Ann. Univ. Lyon, Sci., Med.* [3] **1**, 1–234.

Morgan, B. B. (1943a). Inoculations of *Trichomonas foetus* (Protozoa) in guinea pigs. *Proc. Helminthol. Soc. Wash.* **10**, 26–29.

Morgan, B. B. (1943b). Host list of the genus *Trichomonas* (Protozoa: Flagellata). Part II. Host-parasite list. *Trans. Wis. Acad. Sci., Arts Lett.* **35**, 235–245.

Morini, E. G., Ruiz, G., and Colombo, R. G. (1959). Algunas observacianes sôbre la leishmaniosis experimental del cobayo. *Rev. Fac. Cienc. Vet. La Plata, Univ. Nac. La Plata* **1**, 19–27.

Mudrow-Reichenow, L. (1956). Spontanes Vorkommen von Amöben und Ciliaten bei Laboratoriumstieren. *Z. Tropenmed. Parasitol.*, **7**, 198–211.

Mühlpfordt, H. (1963). Ueber die Bedeutung und Feinstruktur des Blepharoplasten bei parasitischen Flagellaten. II. Teil. *Z. Tropenmed. Parasitol.* **14**, 475–501.

Mühlpfordt, H. (1964). Die Biologie normaler und experimentell abgewandelter Parasiten der Familie Trypansomidae: Ein Beitrag zur Klärung der Funktion des Kinetoplasten. *Angew. Parasitol.* **5**, 7–8.

Muniz, J., and Medina, H. (1948a). Leishmaniose tegumentar do cobaio (*Leishmania enriettii* n. sp.). *Hospital (Rio de Janeiro)* **33**, 7–25.

Muniz, J., and Medina, H. (1948b). Leishmaniose tegumentar do cobaio: *Leishmania enriettii* n. sp. *Arq. Biol. Tecnol.* **3**, 13–30.

Neiva, A., da Cunha, A. M., and Travassos, L. (1914). Contribuições Parazitolojicas. *Mem. Inst. Oswaldo Cruz* **6**, 180–191.

Nelson, E. C. (1935). Cultivation and cross-infection experiments with balantidia from pig, chimpanzee, guinea pig and *Macacus rhesus. Amer. J. Hyg.* **22**, 26–43.

Nery-Guimarães, F., Lage, H. A., Venancio, I. A., and Grynberg, N. F. (1969). Estudo comparativo da reação indireta de anticorpos fluorescentes em doença de Chagas, leishmanioses tegumentares e calasar com vários antígenos de "Leishmania" e "Trypanosoma." *Hospital (Rio de Janeiro)* **75**, 1811–1825.

Neu, H. C. (1967). Toxoplasmosis transmitted at autopsy. *J. Amer. Med. Ass.* **202**, 844–845.

Nicolau, S. (1932a). Infection toxoplasmique spontanée du cobaye. *C. R. Soc. Biol.* **100**, 676–678.

Nicolau, S. (1932b). Quelques propriétes d'un toxoplasme qui infecte spontanément les cobayes. *C. R. Soc. Biol.* **110**, 763–766.

Nicolau, S. (1933). Nouvelles recherches expérimentales sur le *Toxoplasma caviae C. R. Soc. Biol.* **113**, 706–708.

Nicolau, S., and Lwoff, A. (1935). L'action pathogène de *Trichomonas foetu* pour le système nerveux central. *Ann. Inst. Pasteur, Paris* **55**, 654–675.

Nie, D. (1948). The structure and division of *Chilomastix intestinalis* Kuczynski, with notes on similar forms in man and other vertebrates. *J. Morphol.* **82**, 287–329.

Nie, D. (1950). Morphology and taxonomy of the intestinal protozoa of the guinea pig, *Cavia porcella. J. Morphol.* **86**, 381–493.

Nomura, H. (1956). [Histochemical studies on intestinal protozoa. I. Studies on the distribution of phosphates in several species of trichomonads.] [Japanese text; English summary.] *Keio Igaku* **33**, 341–347.

Nomura, H. (1957). [Cytochemical studies on intestinal protozoa. II.

Morphological studies on the distribution of polysaccharides and lipoids, together with the demonstration of starch-splitting ferments in several species of trichomonads.] [Japanese text; English summary.] *Keio Igaku* **34**, 75–88.

Orio, J., Depoux, R., Ravisse, P., and Cassard, H. (1958). Contribution à l'étude de la toxoplasmose en Afrique Équatoriale. Enquête dans la population animale. *Bull. Soc. Pathol. Exot.* **51**, 607–615.

Otto, H. (1957). Befunde an Mausenieren bei Coccidiose (*Klossiella muris*). *Frankfurt. Z. Pathol.* **68**, 41–48.

Overdulve, J. P. (1970). The identity of *Toxoplasma* Nicolle and Manceaux, 1909 with *Isospora* Schneider, 1881 (I). *Proc., Kon. Ned. Akad. Wetensch. Ser. C* **73**, 129–151.

Pakes, S. P. (1974). Protozoal diseases. *In* "Biology of the Laboratory Rabbit" (R. E. Flatt, S. H. Weisbroth, and A. L. Kraus, eds.), pp. 263–286. Academic Press, New York.

Paraense, W. L. (1952a). Observações sôbre a leishmaniose du cobáia. *Manquinhos Bol. Inst. Oswaldo Cruz* **1**, 4–5.

Paraense, W. L. (1952b). Infection of the nasal mucosa in guinea pig leishmaniasis. *Ann. Acad. Brasil. Cienc.* **24**, 307–310.

Paraense, W. L. (1953). The spread of *Leishmania enriettii* through the body of the guinea pig. *Trans. Roy. Soc. Trop. Med. Hyg.* **47**, 556–560.

Paulin, J. J. (1967). A new ciliary component and its fate during resorption of cilia in *Cyathodinium piriforme. J. Protozool.* **14**, Suppl., 23.

Paulin, J. J. (1968). An investigation of the fine structure argyrome and morphogenesis in species of the enigmatic protozoan genus *Cyathodinium* da Cunha, 1914 (Ciliata, Trichostomatida). *Diss. Abstr.* **28**, Part I, 5252B.

Paulin, J. J. (1969). Some ultrastructural observations on division and reorganization in the enigmatic ciliate *Cyathodinium. Proc. Int. Congr. Protozool.*, 3rd, 1969 Vol. 3, pp. 68–69.

Paulin, J. J. (1973). The resorption of cilia in *Cyathodinium piriforme. J. Protozool.* **20**, 281–285.

Paulin, J. J., and Corliss, J. O. (1964). The somatic and oral infraciliature of the enigmatic ciliate *Cyathodinium piriforme. J. Protozool.* **11**, 438–444.

Paulin, J. J., and Corliss, J. O. (1969). Ultrastructural and other observations which suggest suctorian affinities for the taxonomically enigmatic ciliate *Cyathodinium. J. Protozool.* **16**, 216–223.

Paulin, J. J., and Krascheninnikow, S. (1973). An electron microscopic study of *Balantidium caviae.Acta Protozool.* **12**, 97–104.

Pearce, L. (1916). *Klossiella* infection of the guinea pig. *J. Exp. Med.* **23**, 431–442.

Pellérdy, L. P. (1965). "Coccidia and Coccidiosis." Akadémiai Kiadó, Budapest.

Pellérdy, L., and Dürr, U. (1969). Orale und parenterale Uebertrangungsversuche von Kokzidien auf nicht specifische Wirte. *Acta Vet. (Budapest)* **19**, 253–268.

Pereira, C., and de Almeida, W. F. (1940). Sôbre a verdadeira natureza das "formas ameboides," dos pretensos "cistos" e "formas degenerativas" no genero *Trichomonas* Donne, 1836. *Arq. Inst. Biol. (Sao Paulo* **11**, 347–366.

Pereira, C., and de Almeida, W. F. (1943a). Sôbre alguns preconceitos morfolgicos no genero *Trichomonas* Donne, 1836 a sua signifição taxonomica. *Arq. Inst. Biol. (Sao Paulo)* **14**, 195–206.

Pereira, C., and de Almeida, W. F. (1943b). Revisão das espécies de *Trichomonas* Donne, 1836 da galinha e do pombo domésticos. *Arq. Inst. Biol. (Sao Paulo)* **14**, 273–292.

Perrin, T. L. (1943a). Spontaneous and experimental encephalitozoon infection in laboratory animals. *Arch. Pathol.* **36**, 559–567.

Perrin, T. L. (1943b). *Toxoplasma* and *Encephalitozoon* in spontaneous and in experimental infections of animals. A comparative study. *Arch. Pathol.* **36**, 568–578.

Petri, M. (1966). The occurrence of *Nosema cuniculi* (*Encephalitozoon cuniculi*) in the cells of transplantable, malignant ascites tumours and its effect upon tumour and host. *Acta Pathol. Microbiol. Scand.* **66**, 13–30.

Pianese, G. (1901). Ueber ein protozoon des meerschweinchens. *Z. Hyg. Infektionskr.* **36**, 350–367.

Pinto, C. F. (1938). "Zoo-parasitos de interesse medico e veterinario." P. de Mello & Cia, Rio de Janeiro.

Porter, A. (1943). Report of the honorary parasitologist for 1941. *Proc. Zool. Soc. London, Ser. B* **112**, 136–137.

Preston, P. M., and Dumonde, D. C. (1971). Immunogenicity of a ribosomal antigen of *Leishmania enriettii. Trans. Roy. Soc. Trop. Med. Hyg.* **65**, 18–19.

Radwanski, Z. K., Bryceson, A. D. M., Preston, P. M., and Dumonde, D. C. (1974). Immunofluorescence studies of *Leishmania enriettii* infection in guinea pigs. *Trans. Roy. Soc. Trop. Med. Hyg.* **68**, 124–132.

Raether, W., and Seidenath, H. (1969). Infektiosität von Protozoen (Trypanosomen, Leishmanien, Plasmodien, Babesien) nach einer Konservierungszeit von 1000 Tagen in flüssigem Stickstoff. *Proc. Int. Congr. Protozool., 3rd, 1969* Vol. 3, pp. 218–219.

Rastegaieff, E. F. (1930). Zur Frage über Coccidien wilder Tiere. *Arch. Protistenk.* **71**, 377–404.

Rawal, B. D. (1959). Laboratory infection with *Toxoplasma. J. Clin. Pathol.* **12**, 59–61.

Ray, H., Banik, D. C., and Mondal, L. N. (1961). Giardial infection in a guinea pig. *Bull. Calcutta Sch. Trop. Med.* **9**, 154–155.

Ray, H. N., and Mitra, A. N. (1935). On the morphology of *Chilomitus caviae*, a flagellate from the caecum of guinea pig. *Proc. Indian Sci. Congr., 22nd, 1935* p. 315.

Rees, C. W. (1927). Balantidia from pigs and guinea-pigs; their viability, cyst production and cultivation. *Science* **66**, 89–91.

Reichenow, E. (1953). "Lehrbuch der Protozoenkunde," Vol. II. Fischer, Jena.

Rezai, H. R., Sher, S., and Gettner, S. (1969). *Leishmania tropica, L. donovani*,, and *L. enriettii*: Immune rabbit serum inhibitory in vitro. *Exp. Parasitol.* **26**, 257–263.

Rezai, H. R., Haghighi, P., and Ardehali, S. (1972). Histological appearance of the site of inoculation and lymph nodes of guinea pigs at various times after infection with *Leishmania enriettii. Trans. Roy. Soc. Trop. Med. Hyg.* **66**, 225–234.

Rezai, H., Gettner, S., and Behorouz, N. (1972). Anti-leishmanial activity of immune guinea-pig serum. *J. Med. Microbiol.* **5**, 371–375.

Ritchey, F. A. (1953). A cytological study of *Cyathodinium. Diss. Abstr.* **13**, 923–924.

Rommel, M., and Breuning, J. (1967). Untersuchungen über das Vorkommen von *Toxoplasma gondii* in der Milch einiger Tierarten und die Möglichkeit der laktogenen Infektion. *Berlin. Muenchen. Tieraerztl. Wochenschr.* **80**, 365–384.

Rommel, M., and Heydorn, A. O. (1972). Beiträge zum Lebenszyklus der Sarkosporidien. III. *Isospora hominis* (Railliet und Lucet, 1891) Wenyon, 1923, eine Dauerform der Sarkosporidien des Rindes und des Schweins. *Berlin. Muenchen. Tieraerztl. Wochenschr.* **85**, 143–145.

Rommel, M., Janitschke, K., Dalchow, W., Schulz, H.-P., Breuning, J., and Schein, E. (1968). Versuche zur Ubertrangung von *Toxoplasma gondii* durch parasitische Nematoden bei Schafen, Schweinen, Hunden, Katzen, Huhnern, und Mausen. *Berlin. Muenchen. Tieraerztl. Wochenschr.* **81**, 309–313.

Rommel, M., and Heydorn, A. O., and Gruber, F. (1972). Beiträge zum Lebenszyklus der Sarkosporidien. I. Die Sporozyste von *S. tenella* in den Fäzes der Katze. *Berlin. Muenchen. Tieraerztl. Wochenschr.* **85**, 101–105.

Ruge, H. (1951). *Encephalitozoon* beim Meerschweinchen. *Zentralbl. Bakteriol., Parasitenk., Infektionskr. Hyg., Abt. 1: Orig.* **156**, 543–544.

Ryšavý, B. (1954). Příspěvek k posnání kokcidií našich i dovezených obratlovců. *Cesk. Parazitol.* **1**, 131–174.

Sabin, A. B., and Olitsky, P. K. (1937). *Toxoplasma* and obligate intracellular parasitism. *Science* **85**, 336–338.

Sacchetti, G. (1903). Su alcune forme parassitarie nell'ovario di *Cavia cobaya. Boll. Soc. Natur. Napoli* **16**, 306.

Samuels, R. (1962). Agar techniques for colonizing and cloning trichomonads. *J. Protozool.* **9**, 103–107.

Sangiorgi, G. (1916). Di un coccidio parassita del rene della cavia. *Pathologica* **175**, 49–53.

Santos, U. M., and Perine, A. (1962). Efeitos da anfotericina B (Fungizone Squibb) sôbre tripanosomídeos. II. Estudo da resistência. *Hospital (Rio de Janeiro)* **62**, 383–388.

Saxe, L. H. (1954). Transfaunation studies on the host specificity of the enteric protozoa of rodents. *J. Protozool.* **1**, 220–230.

Scholtyseck, E., Mehlhorn, H., and Müller, B. E. G. (1973). Identifikation von Merozoiten der vier cystenbildenden Coccidien (*Sarcocystis, Toxoplasma, Besnoitia, Frenkelia*) auf Grund feinstruktureller Kriterien. *Z. Parasitenk.* **42**, 185–206.

Scott, M. J. (1927). Studies on the *Balantidium* from the guinea pig. *J. Morphol.* **44**, 417–465.

Seidelin, H. (1914). *Klossiella* sp. in the kidneys of a guinea pig. *Ann. Trop. Med. Parasitol.* **8**, 553–564.

Shadduck, J. A., and Pakes, S. P. (1971). Encephalitozoonosis (nosematosis) and toxoplasmosis. *Amer. J. Pathol.* **64**, 657–674.

Sheather, A. L. (1924). Coccidiosis in the guinea pig. *J. Comp. Pathol.* **37**, 243–246.

Sheffield, H. G., and Melton, M. L. (1970). *Toxoplasma gondii*: The oocyst, sporozoite, and infection of cultured cells. *Science* **167**, 892–893.

Simitch, T., Petrovitch, Z., and Lepech, T. (1954). Contribution à las connaissance de la biologie des Trichomonas. II. Différenciation de *T. microti* Wenrich et Saxe, 1950 et de *T. intestinalis* Leuckart, 1879, par leurs caractères biologiques. *Ann. Parasitol.* **29**, 199–205.

Simons, H. (1922). Ueber *Selenomonas palpitans* n. sp. *Zentralbl. Bakteriol., Parasitenk., Infektionskr. Hyg., Abt. 1: Orig* **87**, 50.

Smith, T., and Johnson, H. P. (1902). On a coccidium (*Klossiella muris*, gen. et spec. nov.) parasitic in the renal epithelium of the mouse. *J. Exp. Med.* **6**, 303–316.

Solovjev, M. M. (1968). [Morphological and biological pecularities of Lamblia in connection with their habitat on the brush border of intestinal epithelium.] [Russian text; English summary.] *Acta Protozool.* **6**, 365–376.

Soltys, M. A., and Woo, P. T. K. (1972). Immunological methods in diagnosis of protozoan diseases in man and domestic animals. *Z. Tropenmed. Parasitol.* **23**, 172–187.

Soresco, A., and Panaitesco, D. (1969). Contributions à l'étude de l'amibiase expérimentale du cobaye: Inoculation intrahépatique directe. *Arch. Roum. Pathol. Exp. Microbiol.* **28**, 669–673.

Sprague, V., and Vernick, S. H. (1971). The ultrastructure of *Encephalitozoon cuniculi* (Microsporidia, Nosematidae) and its taxonomic significance. *J. Protozool.* **18**, 560–569.

Steinmetz, P. (1921). Die Krankeheiten des Meerschweinchen und dessen Gesunderhaltung durch hygienische Massnahmen. *Deut. Tieraerztl. Wochenschr.* **29**, 372–373.

Steinmetz, P., and Lerche, M. (1923). Die Infektions–und Invasionskrankheiten des Meerschweinchens. *In* "Das Meerschweinchen" (H. Raebiger, ed.), pp. 82–147. von Schaper, Hannover.

Stewart, J. M., and Beck, J. S. (1967). Distribution of the DNA and the DNA-histone antigens in the nuclei of free-living and parasitic Sarcomastigophora. *J. Protozool.* **14**, 225–231.

Stojanov, D. P., and Cvetanov, J. L. (1965). Ueber die Klossiellose bei Meerschweinchen. *Z. Parasitenk.* **25**, 350–358.

Strada, F., and Traina, R. (1900). Ueber eine neue Form von infecktiöser Lungenkrankheit der Meerschweinchen. *Zentralbl. Bakteriol., Parasitenk., Infektionskr. Hyg., Abt., 1: Orig.* **28**, 635–648.

Takemura, S. (1932). On the cultivation of *Trichomonas caviae* (Davaine, 1875) and *Trichomonas vaginalis* (Donné, 1837) *in vitro*. [Japanese text; English summary.] *J. Med. Coll. Keijo* **2**, 106–124.

Takemura, S. (1933). On the cultivation of *Trichomonas caviae* and *Trichomonas vaginalis. Jap. J. Zool.* **5**, 21.

Takeuchi, A. (1971). Penetration of intestinal epithelium by various microorganisms. *Curr. Top. Pathol.* **54**, 1–27.

Takeuchi, A., and Phillips, B. P. (1972). Electron microscope study of experimental amoebiasis. Penetration of the colonic epithelium by *Entamoeba histolytica. Amer. J. Pathol.* **66**, 29A–30A.

Tanabe, M. (1925). A study of *Trichomonas* from the guinea-pig. *J. Parasitol.* **11**, 170–176.

Tempelis, C. H., and Lysenko, M. G. (1957). The production of hyaluronidase by *Balantidium coli. Exp. Parasitol.* **6**, 31–36.

Thomas, H. W., and Linton, S. F. (1904). A comparison of the animal reactions of the trypanosomes of Uganda and Congo Free State sleeping sickness with those of *Trypanosoma gambienese* (Dutton). *Lancet* **1**, 1337–1340.

Tôrres, C. M., Muniz, J., de Almeida Cardoso, R. A., and Duarte, E. (1948a). Caracteres do granuloma histiociatário na leishmaniose espontânea da cobaia. *Hospital (Rio de Janeiro)* **33**, 405–408.

Tôrres, C. M., Muniz, J., de Almeida Cardoso, R. A., and Duarte, E. (1948b). Reação peritesticular na leishmaniose espontânea da cobaia. *Hospital (Rio de Janeiro)* **33**, 835–843.

Travis, B. V. (1932). A discussion of synonymy in nomenclature of certain insect flagellates, with description of a new flagellate from the larvae of *Ligyrodes relictus* Say (Coleoptera, Scarabeidae). *Iowa State Coll. J. Sci.* **6**, 317–323.

Turk, J. L., and Bryceson, A. D. M. (1971). Immunological phenomena in leprosy and related diseases. *Advan. Immunol.* **13**, 209–266.

Twort, J. M., and Twort, C. C. (1932). Disease in relation to carcinogenic agents among 60,000 experimental mice. *J. Pathol. Bacteriol.* **35**, 219–242.

Tyzzer, E. E. (1907). A sporozoan found in the peptic glands of the common mouse. *Proc. Soc. Exp. Biol. Med.* **5**, 12–13.

Tyzzer, E. E. (1910). An extracellular coccidium, *Cryptosporidium muris* (gen. et sp. nov.), of the gastric glands of the common mouse. *J. Med. Res.* **23**, 487–509.

Tyzzer, E. E. (1912). *Cryptosporidium parvum* (sp. nov.), a coccidium found in the small intestine of the common mouse. *Arch. Protistenk.* **26**, 394–412.

Ulrich, M., Trujillo Ortiz, D., and Convit, J. (1968). The effect of fresh serum on the leptomonads of *Leishmania*. I. Preliminary report. *Trans. Roy. Soc. Trop. Med. Hyg.* **62**, 825–830.

Varela, G., Martínez Rodriguez, A. E., and Treviño Villaseñor, A. (1953). Toxoplasmosis en la República Mexicana. *Rev. Inst. Salubr. Enferm. Trop., Mex.* **13**, 217–222.

Vavra, J., and Kučera, K. (1970). *Pneumocystis carinii* Delanoë, its ultrastructure and ultrastructural affinities. *J. Protozool.* **17**, 463–483.

Vetterling, J. M., and Thompson, D. E. (1972). *Klossiella equi* Baumann, 1946 (Sporozoa: Eucoccidia: Adeleina) from equids. *J. Parasitol.* **58**, 589–594.

Vetterling, J. M., Takeuchi, A., and Madden, P. A. (1969). Ultrastructure of a species of *Cryptosporidium* from the guinea pig. *Proc. Int. Congr. Protozool., 3rd, 1969*, p. 77.

Vetterling, J. M., Jervis, H. R., Merrill, T. G., and Sprinz, H. (1971a). *Cryptosporidium wrairi* sp. n. from the guinea pig, *Cavia porcellus*, with an emendation of the genus. *J. Protozool.* **18**, 243–247.

Vetterling, J. M., Takeuchi, A., and Madden, P. A. (1971b). Ultrastructure of *Cryptosporidium wrairi* from the guinea pig. *J. Protozool.* **18**, 248–260.

Villágiová, I. (1962). Endoparaziti laboratórnych hlodavcov. *Cesk. Parazitol.* **9**, 423–429.

von Schuckmann, W. (1926). Ueber eine aus dem Darm eines Meerschweinchens gezüchete Amöbe. *Arb. Reichsgeshundheitsamte* **57**, 801–820.

Walker, E. L. (1908). The parasitic amoebae of the intestinal tract of man and other animals. *J. Med. Res.* **17**, 379–459.

Walker, E. L. (1909). Sporulation in the parasitic Ciliata. *Arch. Protistenk.* **17**, 297–306.

Wallace, G. D. (1971). Experimental transmission of *Toxoplasma gondii* by filth-flies. *Amer. J. Trop. Med. Hyg.* **20**, 411–413.

Wallace, G. D. (1973). *Sarcocystis* in mice inoculated with *Toxoplasma*-like oocysts from cat feces. *Science* **180**, 1375–1377.

Wang, C. C., and Nie, D. (1934). Notes on *Entamoeba muris* (Grassi) and *Trichomonas caviae* Davaine. *Proc. Pac. Sci. Congr., 5th, 1933*, Vol. 4, pp. 2991–2993.

Watson, J. M. (1946). The bionomics of coporphilic protozoa. *Biol. Rev. Cambridge Phil. Soc.* **21**, 121–139.

Weiland, G., and Kühn, D. (1970). Experimentelle *Toxoplasma*-Infektionen bei der Katze. II. Entwicklungstadien des Parasiten im Darm. *Berlin. Muenchen. Tieraerztl. Wochenschr.* **83**, 128–132.

Weissberger, H., Spira, D. T., and Zuckerman, A. (1973). Delayed hypersensitivity to various leishmania antigens in guinea pigs infected with *Leishmania enriettii*. *J. Protozool.* **20**, 534–535.

Wenrich, D. H. (1932). The relation of the protozoan flagellate, *Retortamonas gryllotalpae* (Grassi, 1879). Stiles, 1902 to the species of the genus *Embadomonas* Mackinnon, 1911. *Trans. Amer. Microsc. Soc.* **51**, 225–238.

Wenrich, D. H. (1935). Host-parasite relations between parasitic protozoa and their hosts. *Proc. Amer. Phil. Soc.* **75**, 605–650.

Wenrich, D. H. (1946). Culture experiments on intestinal flagellates. I. Trichomonad and other flagellates obtained from man and certain rodents. *J. Parasitol.* **32**, 40–53.

Wenrich, D. H. (1949). Protozoan parasites of the rat. *In* "The Rat in Laboratory Investigation" (E. J. Farris and J. Q. Griffith, eds.), pp. 542. Lippincott, Philadelphia, Pennsylvania.

Wenrich, D. H., and Saxe, L. H. (1950). *Trichomonas microti* n. sp. (Protozoa, Mastigophora). *J. Parasitol.* **36**, 261–269.

Wenyon, C. M. (1926). "Protozoology" Vols. I and II. W. Wood, New York.

Westphal, A. (1957). Experimentelle Infektionen des Meerschweinchens mit *Balantidium coli*. *Z. Tropenmed. Parasitol.* **8**, 288–294.

Westphal, A. (1971). Experimentelle Infektion der Maus und des Meerschweinchens mit *Balantidium coli*. *Z. Tropenmed. Parasitol.* **22**, 138–148.

Wetzel, J. C. (1972). Aspects of the immunopathology of *Leishmania donovani* infections in laboratory animals. *Diss. Abstr. Int. B* **32**, 5549B.

Wicktor, C. E. (1951). Stock inspection. *Annu. Rep. Los Angeles Co. Livestock Dep.* **37**, 13–27.

Witte, H. M., and Piekarski, G. (1970). Die Oocysten-Ausscheidung bei experimentell infizierten Katzen in Abhängigkeit vom *Toxoplasma*-Stamm. *Z. Parasitenk.* **33**, 358–360.

Wittfogel, H. (1935a). Ueber Züchtungs- und Kleintierversuche mit *Trichomonas vaginalis hominis.* Vorläufige Mitteilung. *Deut. Tieraerztl. Wochenschr.* **43**, 310–312.

Wittfogel, H. (1935b). Die Züchtung von *Trichomonas vaginalis hominis* und ihre Uebertragung auf kleine Versuchstiere. *Arch. Gynaekol.* **159**, 612–617.

Wittner, M., and Rosenbaum, R. M. (1970). Role of bacteria in modifying virulence of *Entamoeba histolytica*. Studies of amebae from axenic cultures. *Amer. J. Trop. Med. Hyg.* **19**, 755–761.

Wittner, M., Rosenbaum, R. M., and Einstein, A. (1971). Utilization of axenically grown strains of *Entamoeba histolytica* in providing further understanding of strain virulence. *J. Parasitol.* **57**, 44–45.

Wright, J. H., and Craighead, E. M. (1922). Infectious motor paralysis in young rabbits. *J. Exp. Med.* **36**, 135–140.

Yakimov, V. L. (1925a). Protistologische Beobachtungen. *Arch. Soc. Russe Protistol.* **2**, 247.

Yakimov, V. L. (1925b). Notes de parasitologie. *Ann. Soc. Belg. Med. Trop.* **5**, 127–235.

Yakimov, V. L. (1934). *Eimeria exigua* n. sp., eine neue Kaninchenkokzidie. *Zentralbl. Bakteriol., Parasitenk., Infektionskr. Hyg., Abt. 1: Orig.* **131**, 18–24.

Yakimov, V. L., and Gusev, V. F. (1935). Coccidiose des cobayes en Russie. *Bull Soc. Pathol. Exot.* **28**, 434–435.

Yakimov, V. L., Vasilevskaîa, V. I., Kornilov, M. T., and Tsvîetkov, N. A. (1921). Flagellés de l'intestin des animaux de laboratoire. *Bull. Soc. Pathol. Exot.* **14**, 558–564.

Yakimov, V. L., Senîushkina, V. P., and Machul'skiĭ, S. N. (1940). [Coccidiosis of guinea pigs in The USSR.] [Russian text] *Vestn. Mikrobiol. Epidemiol. Parazitol.* **17**, 390–401.

Zasukhin, D. N., and Kheisin, E. M. (1957). [Protozoan parasites of laboratory animals.] [Russian text.] *Tr. Inst. Zool., Akad. Nauk Kaz. SSR, Parazitol.* 7, 241–251.

Zeledón, R. (1959). Transaminases in four species of hemoflagellates. *J. Parasitol.* **45**, Suppl., 49.

Zeledón, R. (1960a). La aplicación de pruebas fisiológicas en el estudio taxonómico de tripanosómidos. *Libro Homenaje Caballero y Caballero* pp. 49–53.

Zeledón, R. (1960b). Comparative physiological studies on four species of hemoflagellates in culture. I. Endogenous respiration and respiration in the presence of glucose. *J. Protozool.* 7, 146–150.

Zeledón, R. (1960c). Comparative physiological studies on four species of hemoflagellates in culture. II. Effect of carbohydrates and related substances and some amino compounds on the respiration. *J. Parasitol.* **46**, 541–551.

Zeledón, R. (1960d). Comparative physiological studies on four species of hemoflagellates in culture. III. Effect of the Krebs' cycle intermediates on the respiration. *Rev. Biol. Trop.* **8**, 25–33.

Zeledón, R. (1960e). Comparative physiological studies on four species of hemoflagellates in culture. IV. Effect of metabolic inhibitors on the respiration. *Rev. Biol. Trop.* **8**, 181–195.

Zeledón, R. (1960f). Comparative physiological studies on four species of hemoflagellates in culture. V. Transaminases. *Rev. Brasil. Biol.* **20**, 409–414.

Zeledón, R., and Lizano, C. (1961). Infeccion experimental del cobayo con enfermedad de Chagas y leishmaniasis superpuesta (*L. enriettii*) y analisis electroforetico del suero. *Programa Gen. Resum. Trab. 2nd Congr. Latinoamer. 1st Nac. Microbiol.* p. 127.

Zeledón, R., and Lizano, C. (1962). Experimental infection of the guinea pig with Chagas' disease and superimposed leishmaniasis, and electrophorectic analysis of the serum. *Rev. Inst. Med. Trop. Sao Paulo* **4**, 124–129.

Chapter 13

Helminth Parasites

Richard B. Wescott

I. INTRODUCTION

Noninduced helminth infections are not often encountered in guinea pigs raised for biomedical research. In fact, *Paraspidodera uncinata* is the only helminth reported from guinea pigs with any degree of frequency and it rarely causes clinical disease.

Relative lack of natural helminth infections in guinea pigs might cause one to think that they are refractory to helminths and have few applications in experimental parasitology. This is not the case. The guinea pig can be infected with many important helminths of both man and domestic animals and serves as a valuable research animal for the parasitologist. Lack of noninduced infections actually is advantageous since use of this host is seldom complicated by unwanted internal parasites.

The intent of this chapter is to discuss the few natural helminth infections that do occur in sufficient detail so that they can be diagnosed and controlled and to introduce some of the more important applications of guinea pigs in experimental parasitology.

II. NATURAL INFECTIONS

A. *Paraspidodera uncinata*

This cecal worm has been reported on several occasions as a spontaneous infection in guinea pig colonies (Breza and Jurasek, 1965; Porter and Otto, 1934). Ordinarily, the infections are of little consequence. Although in one instance the parasite may have caused clinical disease.

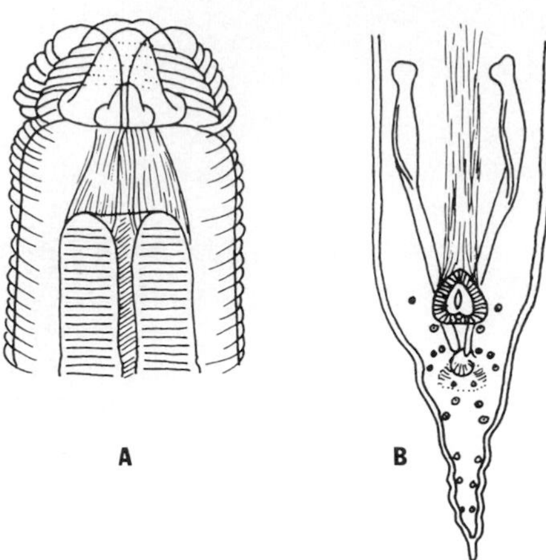

Fig. 1. Paraspidodera uncinata; (A) anterior extremity, dorsal view, (B) posterior extremity of male, ventral view. After Yorke and Maplestone (1962).

1. Morphology

Adult parasites are relatively small and are found on the mucosa of the cecum and colon. Males are from 11 to 22 mm long and about 300 μm in diameter. Females are from 16 to 28 mm long and 400 μm in diameter (Levine, 1968). Males have a preanal sucker and two spicules of equal length (Fig. 1, Yorke and Maplestone, 1962). The vulva of the female is just anterior to the middle of the body. Eggs are oval, have a thick shell, measure from 40 to 50 μm × 30 to 40 μm, and are unsegmented when laid.

2. Life Cycle

Adult females in the cecum and colon produce eggs that leave the host in the feces. These eggs do not hatch but become infective in 14 days or less at 28°C (Herlich and Dixon, 1965). Guinea pigs are infected by eating infective eggs, and parasites develop to maturity in 51 to 66 days (Porter and Otto, 1934). No migration beyond the mucosa of the gut occurs in the cycle.

3. Clinical Signs

No important clinical signs have been attributed to infection with this parasite.

4. Treatment and Control

Paraspidodera infection apparently can be eliminated from guinea pigs colonies by adequate sanitation. In the author's experience, infected animals usually are housed in facilities where bedding is not regularly changed and cages are not properly cleaned and sanitized. No anthelmintic has been suggested for elimination of this parasite. However, piperazine would probably be a logical choice if treatment were attempted, because this drug is relatively nontoxic and has activity against similar parasites.

B. *Fasciola* spp.

The only other noninduced helminth infection reported from guinea pigs is fascioliasis (Boray, 1969; Strauss and Heyneman, 1966). This disease was found to be related to feeding forage containing metacercaria of *Fasciola* spp. Although rare, it could appear as a clinical disease when commercial diets are supplemented with kale, hay, lettuce, or other vegetables raised in liver fluke-infested areas. This parasitism would be characterized by severe damage to the liver and will be discussed further as an experimental infection.

III. EXPERIMENTAL INFECTIONS

A. *Trichinella spiralis*

The guinea pig has probably been used more extensively as an experimental host for *T. spiralis* than for any other parasite. Trichina worm grows well in guinea pigs, and a considerable volume of research on host response to infection with *T. spiralis* has been done in the guinea pig (Cypess *et al.*, 1971; Ivey, 1964; Kim, 1966; Kim *et al.*, 1970; Sharp and Olson, 1962). This host–parasite system also has been used to study the effects of adult worms on digestion (Castro *et al.*, 1967) and larval stages on muscle function (Kozar *et al.*, 1965).

B. *Trichostrongylus colubriformis*

This parasite also appears to be well suited for study in the guinea pig. It develops to maturity in this host (Herlich, 1969), and the role of host response on distribution of adult parasites in the intestine has been investigated in guinea pigs (Connan, 1966). Other preliminary studies indicate the guinea pig can be useful in immunization experiments (Herlich, 1966; Poynter and Silverman, 1962) and studies involving alteration of intestinal function by developing parasites (Symons, 1970).

C. Lung Worms

Dictyocaulus viviparus (Cornwell and Jones, 1970, 1971; Douvres and Lucker, 1958), *D. filaria* (Casarosa, 1969;

Weiczorowski, 1965), *Metastrongylus apri* (Porter, 1937), and *Pneumostrongylus tenuis* (Anderson and Strelive, 1966; Spratt and Anderson, 1968) all have been studied in the guinea pig. To date, the most useful observations made in this host are related to testing of irradiated larval *D. viviparus* for viability (Cornwell and Jones, 1970) and effectiveness in preventing infection in vaccinated hosts (Cornwell and Jones, 1971). Work with *D. filaria* is less complete but this parasite also appears suitable for study in guinea pigs. *Pneumostrongylus tenuis* is a natural infection of moose and deer in which it occasionally invades the central nervous system. The parasite also invades the central nervous system of guinea pigs and this host has been suggested as an experimental model for the study of this aberrant migration (Anderson and Strelive, 1966; Spratt and Anderson, 1968).

D. Ascarids

Ascarids of dogs and swine have been studied in guinea pigs to a limited extent (Dobson *et al.*, 1971; Ivey, 1964; Jeska *et al.*, 1969; Krupp, 1956; Sharp and Olson, 1962). Immunoglobulins produced in response to *Ascaris suum* have been characterized in guinea pigs (Dobson *et al.*, 1971), and a modest amount of work has been done regarding cross-reactions of ascarids of dogs and swine in this host (Sharp and Olson, 1962).

E. *Fasciola hepatica*

Boray (1969) has reviewed the experimental use of guinea pigs in research on fascioliasis. He reported that this parasite produces severe disease in guinea pigs with 25 metacercaria causing mortality. However, some guinea pigs survived lesser exposures and patent infections were produced (Boray, 1969; Tewari, 1968). One reason guinea pigs have not been used more extensively as an experimental host for studying fascioliasis is that another, and perhaps superior, host is available in the laboratory rabbit (Boray, 1969; Dawes and Hughes, 1964).

F. Helminths of Laboratory Animals

A few helminths of other laboratory animals develop partially or completely in guinea pigs. These include *Nippostrongylus brasiliensis*–rats (Parker, 1961), *Obeliscoides cuniculi*–rabbits (Alicata, 1932), and *Strongyloides ratti*–rats (Sheldon and Otto, 1937). The guinea pig appears to offer no apparent advantage for study of these infections, hence, usage for this purpose probably will be limited in the future.

G. Other Helminths

There are a number of reports on the use of guinea pigs in the study of other metazoan parasites. The group includes *Schistosoma mansoni* (Abboud *et al.*, 1971; Akpom *et al.*, 1970; Schwartz and Alicata, 1931), *S. hematobium* (Sadun and Gore, 1970), *Brugia pahangi* (Ahmed, 1968), *Necator americanus* (Schwartz and Alicata, 1931), *Oesophagostomum dentatum* (Alicata, 1933a), *Hyostrongylus rubidis* (Alicata, 1933b), *Gongylonema pulchrum* (Lichtenfels, 1971), *Bunostomum trigonocephalum* (Srivastava and Subramanian, 1969), and *Linguatula serrata* (Khalil and Schacher, 1965). In most instances, the guinea pig does not appear to offer unique advantages as a host for these parasites. The application of guinea pigs to investigation of the schistosomes may be an exception. The importance of understanding host response in schistosomiasis may be of sufficient interest to encourage further application of the guinea pig as an experimental host to study this disease.

REFERENCES

Abboud, I. A., Hanna, L. S., and Ragab, H. A. (1971). Experimental ocular Schistosomiasis. *Brit. J. Ophthal. Mol.* **55**, 106–115.

Ahmed, S. S. (1968). The toxicity of 6-mercaptoupurine (6MP) to albino guinea pigs, and the determination of a workable dose of 6MP in the transmission of the filarial worm *Brugia pahangi* to albino guinea pigs. *J. Trop. Med. Hyg.* **71**, 241–242.

Akpom, C. A., Abdel-Wahab, M. F., and Warren, K. S. (1970). Comparison of formation of granulomata around eggs of *Schistosoma mansoni* in the mouse, guinea pig, rat, and hamster. *Amer. J. Trop. Med. Hyg.* **19**, 996–1000.

Alicata, J. E. (1932). Life history of the rabbit stomach worm, *Obeliscoides cuniculi. J. Agr. Res.* **44**, 401–419.

Alicata, J. E. (1933a). The development of the swine nodular worm, *Oesophagostomum dentatum*, in the guinea pig and rabbit. *J. Parasitol.* **20**, 73.

Alicata, J. E. (1933b). The development of the swine stomach worm, *Hyostrongylus rubidis*, in guinea pigs. *J. Parasitol.* **20**, 97.

Anderson, R. C., and Strelive, U. R. (1966). The transmission of *Pneumostrongylus tenuis* to guinea pigs. *Can. J. Zool.* **44**, 533–540.

Boray, J. C. (1969). Experimental fascioliasis in Australia. *Advan. Parasitol.* **7**, 95–210.

Breza, M., and Jurasek, V. (1965). Hromadny nalez nematoda *Paraspidodera unicata* (Rudolphi 1819) u morciat (*Cavia porcellus* L.). *Helminthol. Abstr.* **34**, 238.

Casarosa, L. (1969). Dictiocaulosi sperimentale della cavia da *Dictyocaulus filaria* (Rudolphi 1809). Indagini sulla vitalita e sulla crescita delle 3e larve di *Dictyocaulus filaria* irradiate mediante Co^{60} a vari livelli di R.I. (a 40.000 r ed a 50.000 r). *Helminthol. Abstr.* **38**, 200.

Castro, G. A., Olson, L. J., and Baker, R. D. (1967). Glucose malabsorption and intestinal histopathology in *Trichinella spiralis* infected guinea pigs. *J. Parasitol.* **53**, 595–612.

Connan, R. M. (1966). Experiments with *Trichostrongylus colubriformis* (Giles, 1892) in the guinea pig. I. The effect of the host response on the distribution of the parasites in the gut. *Parasitology* **56,** 521–530.

Cornwell, R. L., and Jones, R. M. (1970). Determination of viability and infectivity of *Dictyocaulus vivparus* larvae after storage. *Res. Vet. Sci.* **11,** 484–485.

Cornwell, R. L., and Jones, R. M. (1971). Immunity to *Dictyocaulus vivparus* infection in the guinea pig produced by normal and triethylene melamine-attenuated larvae. *J. Comp. Pathol.* **81,** 97–103.

Cypess, R., Larsh, J. E., and Pegram, C. (1971). Macrophage inhibition produced by guinea pig after sensitization with a larval antigen of *Trichinella spiralis. J. Parasitol.* **57,** 103–106.

Dawes, B., and Hughes, D. L. (1964). Fascioliasis: The invasive stages of *Fasciola hepatica* in mammalian hosts. *Advan. Parasitol.* **2,** 97–168.

Dobson, C., Morseth, D. J., and Soulsby, J. L. (1971). Immunoglobulin E-type antibodies induced by *Ascaris suum* infections in guinea pigs. *J. Immunol.* **106,** 128–133.

Douvres, F. W., and Lucker, J. T. (1958). The morphogenesis of the parasitic stages of the cattle lungworm, *Dictyocaulus vivparus,* in experimentally infected guinea pigs. *J. Parasitol.* **44,** Suppl. 28.

Herlich, H. (1966). Immunity to *Trichostrongylus colubriformis* in guinea pigs and lambs. *J. Parasitol.* **52,** 871–874.

Herlich, H. (1969). Dynamics of prepatent infections of guinea pigs with the ruminant parasite, *Trichostrongylus colubriformis* (Nematoda). *J. Parasitol.* **55,** 88–93.

Herlich, H., and Dixon, C. F. (1965). Growth and development of *Paraspidodera uncinata,* the cecal worm of the guinea pig. *J. Parasitol.* **51,** 300.

Ivey, M. H. (1964). Immediate hypersensitivity responses of guinea pigs infected with *Toxocara canis* or *Trichinella spirallis. J. Parasitol.* **50,** Suppl., 24.

Jeska, E. L., Williams, J. F., and Cox, D. F. (1969). *Ascaris suum:* Larval returns in rabbits, guinea pigs and mice after low-dose exposure to eggs. *Exp. Parasitol.* **26,** 187–192.

Khalil, G. M., and Schacher, J. F. (1965). *Linguatula serrata* in relation to halzoun and the marrar syndrome. *Amer. J. Trop. Med.* **14,** 736–746.

Kim, C. W. (1966). Delayed hypersensitivity to *Trichinella spiralis* antigens in irradiated guinea pigs. *J. Parasitol.* **52,** 722–726.

Kim, C. W., Jamuar, M. P., and Hamilton, L. D. (1970). Delayed hypersensitivity to *Trichinella spiralis.* III. Effect of repeated sensitization in donors and recipients. *J. Immunol.* **105,** 175–186.

Kozar, Z., Karpiak, S. E., and Krzyzanowski, M. (1965). Changes in the metabolism of the skeletal muscles of guinea pigs caused by the invasion of *Trichinella spiralis.* II. Effect of invasion on the metabolism of organic acids. *Acta Parasitol. Pol.* **13,** 271–274.

Krupp, J. (1956). Amebic invasion of the liver of guinea pigs infected with the larvae of a nematode *Toxacara canis. Exp. Parasitol.* **5,** 421–426.

Levine, N. D. (1968). "Nematode Parasites of Domestic Animals and of man." Burgess. Minneapolis, Minnesota.

Lichtenfels, J. R. (1971). Morphological variation in the gullet nematode, *Gongylonea pulchrum,* (Molin, 1875), from 8 species of definitive hosts with a consideration of *Gongylonema* from *Macaca* spp. *J. Parasitol.* **57,** 348–355.

Parker, J. C. (1961). Effect of cortisone on the resistance of the guinea pig to infection with the rat nematode, *Nippostrongylus brasiliensis. Exp. Parasitol.* **11,** 380–390.

Porter, D. A. (1937). An increase in the proportion of basophilic leukocytes in guinea pigs experimentally infected with swine lungworms. *J. Parasitol.* **23,** 73.

Porter, D. A., and Otto, G. F. (1934). The guinea pig nematode, *Paraspidodera uncinata. J. Parasitol.* **20,** 323.

Poynter, D., and Silverman, P. H. (1962). Some aspects of the disease produced in guinea pigs by *Trichostrongylus colubriformis* with observation on natural and artifically acquired immunity. *J. Parasitol.* **48,** Suppl., 52.

Sadun, E. H., and Gore, R. W. (1970). *Schistosoma mansoni* and *Schistosoma haematobium:* Homocytotrophic reagin-like antibodies in infections of man and experimental animals. *Exp. Parasitol.* **28,** 435–449.

Schwartz, B., and Alicata, J. E. (1931). Development of *Necator americanus* in guinea pigs. *J. Parasitol.* **18,** 54.

Sharp, A. D., and Olson, L. J. (1962). Hypersensitivity responses in *Toxocara-*, *Ascaris-*, and *Trichinella*-infected guinea pigs to homologous and heterologous challenge. *J. Parasitol.* **48,** 362–367.

Sheldon, A. J., and Otto, G. F. (1937). Infection of guinea pigs with *Strongyloides ratti. J. Parasitol.* **23,** 570.

Spratt, D. M., and Anderson, R. C. (1968). The guinea pig as an experimental host of the meningeal worm, *Pneumostrongylus tenius,* Doughtery. *J. Helminthol.* **42,** 139–155.

Srivastava, V. K., and Subramanian, G. (1969). Studies on *Bunostomum trigonocephalum* Rudolphi, 1808. V. Biology in abnormal hosts, mouse and guinea pig. *J. Helminthol.* **43,** 389–394.

Strauss, J. M., and Heyneman, D. (1966). Fatal ectopic fascioliasis in a guinea pig breeding colony from Malacca. *J. Parasitol.* **52,** 413.

Symons, L. E. (1970). Aspects of protein metabolism in intestinal nematode infections. *Gut* **11,** 980.

Tewari, H. C. (1968). Studies on experimental *Fasciola hepatica* infections in the guinea pig. *Ann. Trop. Med. Parasitol.* **62,** 495–501.

Wieczorowski, S. (1965). Studies on the adaptation of the sheep lungworm, *Dictyocaulus filaria,* to an abnormal host, the guinea pig. *Acta Parasitol. Pol.* **13,** 81–92.

Yorke, W., and Maplestone, P. A. (1962). "The Nematode Parasites of Vertebrates." Hafner, New York.

Chapter 14

The Arthropod Parasites of the Genus *Cavia*

N. C. Ronald and J. E. Wagner

I. INTRODUCTION

Arthropod parasites encountered on guinea pigs will depend on the species of guinea pig to be examined, whether the animal is from the wild or maintained in captivity and other animal species which may be maintained in the same rearing facility.

Among species of the genus *Cavia*, the laboratory guinea pig *Cavia porcellus* Linnaeus has been the most extensively studied. Therefore, the major emphasis of this chapter is related to the arthropod parasites of *Cavia porcellus* in the laboratory.

II. ARTHROPOD PARASITES OF THE GENUS *CAVIA*

The genus *Cavia* is widely distributed throughout South America. While numerous references exist on the arthropod parasites of *Cavia porcellus* few references exist for the parasites of other *Cavia* spp. Those references which have been located are presented in Table I.

Table I
Arthropod Parasites of the Genus *Cavia*

Cavia species[a]		Parasite	Reference
C. anolaine	Insecta		
	Gyropidae	*Gliricola distinctus*	Ewing, 1924; Hopkins, 1949; Hopkins and Clay, 1952
	Trimenoponidae	*Trimenopon hispidium*	Hopkins, 1949
C. aperea	Acarina		
	Macronyssidae	*Ornithonyssus bacoti*	Strandtmann and Wharton, 1958
		O. braziliensis	Strandtmann and Wharton, 1958
	Insecta		
	Hoplopleuridae	*Pterophthirus imitans*	Ferris, 1951
	Gyropidae	*Gliricola braziliensis*	Hopkins, 1949; Hopkins and Clay, 1952
		G. distinctus	Hopkins, 1949
		G. lindolphi	Hopkins, 1949; Hopkins and Clay, 1952
		G. porcelli	Hopkins, 1949; Hopkins and Clay, 1952
		Gyropus ovalis	Hopkins, 1949
	Trimenoponidae	*Trimenopon hispidium*	Hopkins and Clay, 1952
	Tungidae	*Hectopsylla suarezi*	Hopkins and Rothchild, 1953–1971; Cohrs *et al.*, 1958
	Pulcidae	*Pulex irritans*	Hopkins and Rothchild, 1953–1971
	Leptopsyllidae	*Leptopsylla seginis*	Hopkins and Rothchild, 1953–1971
C. cutleri	Insecta		
	Tungidae	*Hectopsylla eskeyi*	Hopkins and Rothchild, 1953–1971
C. pamparum	Insecta		
	Gyropidae	*Gyropus ovalis*	Hopkins, 1949
C. porcellus	Acarina		
	Demodicidae	*Demodex caviae*	Bacigalupo and Roveda, 1954
	Listrophoridae	*Chirodiscoides caviae*	Deoras and Patel, 1960; Sasa *et al.*, 1962; Patnaik, 1965; Blackmore and Owens, 1968; Wagner *et al.*, 1972
	Myocoptidae	*Myocoptes musculinus*	Sengbush, 1960
	Sarcoptidae	*Notoedres muris*	Sorenson *et al.*, 1963
		Sarcoptes scabiei	Cohrs *et al.*, 1958; Boch and Supperer, 1971
	Insecta		
	Gyropidae	*Gliricola lindolphi*	Hopkins, 1949
		G. porcelli	Ewing, 1924; Hopkins, 1949; Hopkins and Clay, 1952
		Gyropus ovalis	Ewing, 1924; Hopkins, 1949; Hopkins and Clay, 1952
	Trimenoponidae	*Trimenopon hispidium*	Hopkins, 1949; Hopkins and Clay, 1952
	Ceratophyllidae	*Nosophyllus fasciatus*	Cohrs *et al.*, 1958
	Pulicidae	*Pulex irritans*	Cohrs *et al.*, 1958
		Ctenocephalides felis	Cohrs *et al.*, 1958
	Rhopalopsyllidae	*Rhopalopsylla clavicola*	Cohrs *et al.*, 1958
	Tungidae	*Hectopsylla eskeyi*	Hopkins and Rothchild, 1953–1971
C. rufescens	Acarina		
	Laelaptidae	*Neoparalaelaps bispinosus*	Strandtmann and Wharton, 1958
	Insecta		
	Gyropidae	*Gliricola porcelli*	Ewing, 1924; Hopkins, 1949
		Gyropus ovalis	Ewing, 1924; Hopkins, 1949
		Paragliricola quadrisetosa	Ewing, 1924

[a]No attempt has been made to check the validity of the species of *Cavia*. Except for *Cavia porcellus* names appear as they do in the literature cites.

III. KEY TO THE ARTHROPOD PARASITES OF *CAVIA PORCELLUS* UNDER LABORATORY CONDITIONS

1a. Mouth parts mandibulate, body divided into 3 distinct regions (head, thorax, and abdomen), all stages with 3 pairs of legs ..... 2 Insecta
 b. Mouth parts chelicerate, no division of body regions, larvae with 3 pairs of legs, adults with 4 pairs of legs .... 4 Acarina
2a Head rounded, no more than 1 terminal claw on the legs, body setae fine 3
 b. Head triangular, 2 terminal claws on the legs, body setae coarse .... Trimenoponidae *Trimenopon hispidium* (Fig. 1)
3a. Labial palps 4 segmented, 6 pairs of spiracles located ventrolaterally lacking distinct spiracular plates, abdomen more oval than elongated .... Gyropidae *Gyropus ovalis* (Fig. 2)
 b. Labial palps 2 segmented, 5 pairs of spiracles located ventrally within distinct spiracular plates, abdomen distinctly elongated .... Gyropidae *Gliricola porcelli* (Fig. 3)
4a. Body elongate 5
 b. Body oval or round 6
5a. Body smooth, found free in the hair .... Listrophoridae *Chirodiscoides caviae* (Figs. 4A and B)
 b. Body annulate, embedded in eye muscles .. Demodicidae (Fig. 5)
6a. Legs 1 and 2 normal, leg 3 of male and legs 3 and 4 of female highly modified for clasping hair .... Myocoptidae *Myocoptes musculinus* (Figs. 6A and B)
 b. Legs 1 and 2 with a long unsegmented stalk ending in a bell-shaped sucker 7
7a. Dorsal skin striae broken by spinelike projections, anus located terminally .... Sarcoptidae *Sarcoptes scabiei* (Fig. 7)
 b. Dorsal skin striae not broken by spinelike projections, anus located dorsally .... Sarcoptidae *Notoedres muris* (Fig. 8)

IV. DESCRIPTIONS OF ARTHROPOD PARASITES OF *CAVIA PORCELLUS* UNDER LABORATORY CONDITIONS

A. Trimenoponidae

Trimenopon hispidium **(Burmeister, 1838)**

(Synonym: *Trimenopon jenningsi***)**

The family Trimenoponidae, herein represented by *T. hispidium* (Fig. 1), is unusual in that specimens of this family will key to the family Menoponidae in most textbooks of entomology. This discrepancy occurs because the family Trimenoponidae is small and many authors fail to discuss it. Since the family Menoponidae occurs only on birds (Borror and DeLong, 1966) confusion may result in inaccurate identification.

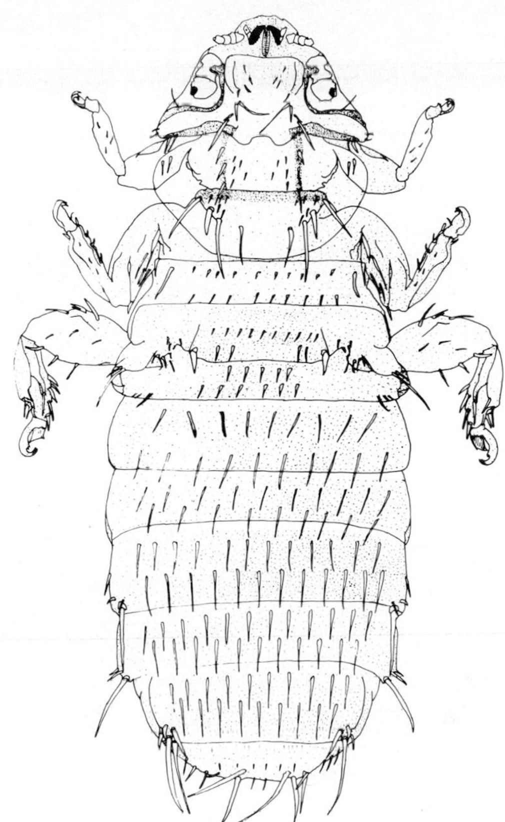

Fig. 1. Line drawing of *Trimenopon hispidium.*

a. Description. T. hispidium is approximately 1.25 mm long and has a maximum width of 0.5 mm. The head is broadly triangular and expanded behind the eyes. The antennae are club shaped and lie in grooves alongside the head. The legs are stout and terminate with two tarsal claws. The abdomen is composed of only five segments and the mesothorax is greatly reduced.

b. Significance. Lesions, resulting from infestations of *T. hispidium,* have not been reported. Consequently little is known of its life cycle and biology. This species has become so rare in colonies that specimens are very difficult to find. We have not observed it in several thousand necropsies of animals originating in the United States.

B. Gyropidae

The family Gyropidae is clearly delineated from other families of chewing lice because the tarsi of the mid and hind legs have either one or no claws, and the family is limited in nature to South American neotropical animals.

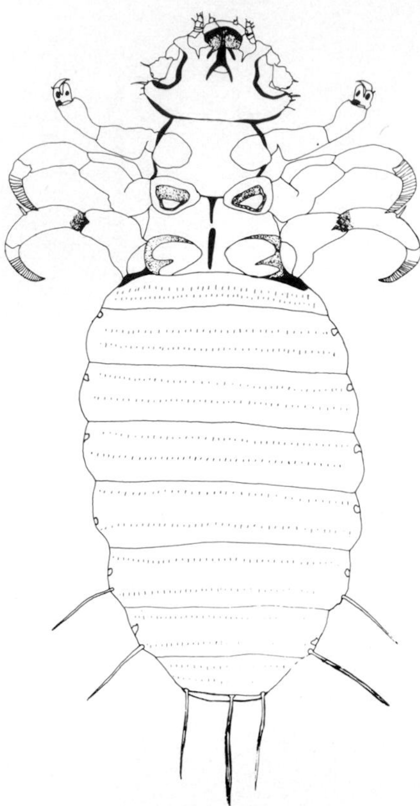

Fig. 2. Line drawing of *Gyropus ovalis.*

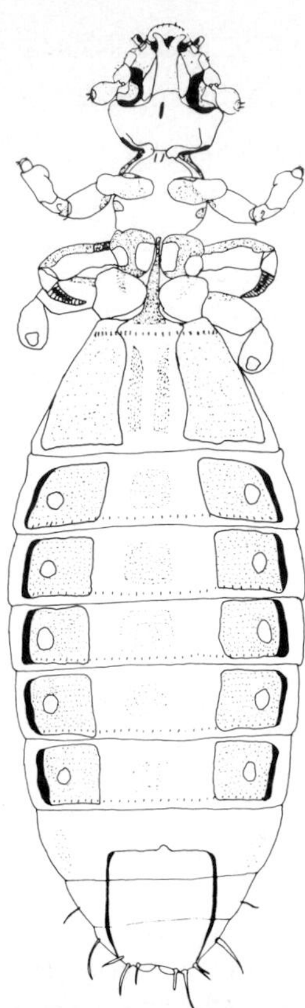

Fig. 3. Line drawing of *Gliricola porcelli.*

1. *Gyropus ovalis* Burmeister, 1838

Description *Gyropus ovalis* is 1 to 1.2 mm long and 0.5 mm in width (Sequy, 1944) (Fig. 2). The posterior portion of the head is broader than the anterior; however, the head is much less triangular than in *T. hispidium.* The antennae are club shaped and are nearly concealed. The maxillary palps have four segments which are easily discernable. The six pairs of abdominal spiracles are located ventrolaterally within poorly defined spiracular plates.

2. *Gliricola porcelli* (Schrank, 1878)

a. Description. *Gliricola porcelli* is 1 to 1.5 mm long and 0.3 to 0.44 mm in width (Sequy, 1944) (Fig. 3). The length of the head is slightly longer than the width and is more rounded than either *T. hispidium* or *G. ovalis.* The club-shaped antennae are nearly concealed. The maxillary palps have two segments and are easily discernable. The five pairs of abdominal spiracles are located ventrally within distinct spiracular plates.

b. Significance. *Gyropus ovalis* and *Gliricola porcelli* are commonly observed on guinea pigs from commercial breeding and laboratory facilities throughout the world as well as from individual pet guinea pigs. In our experience *G. porcelli* is observed more frequently than *G. ovalis.* Their life cycle is not well described; however, their feeding habits have been studied (Ewing, 1924). His observations indicated that *G. porcelli* is capable of using its mouthparts to abrade the skin to obtain cutaneous fluids. Ewing found no evidence "that the hairs of the pig was eaten or used in any way for food." Most infestations by gryopid lice are not accompanied by signs (Paterson, 1967). However, heavy infestations may result in alopecia and a rough hair coat because of excessive scratching (Owen, 1968).

C. Listrophoridae

Chirodiscoides caviae Hirst, 1917

(Synonyms: *Campylochirus caviiae, Indochirus utkalensis*)

The family Listrophoridae is a common family of fur mites which infest a wide variety of fur-bearing mammals. (Baker and Wharton, 1952). Krantz (1970) delineates the family Listrophoridae as being "soft-bodied; strongly striated, usually with a distinct prodorsal or prodonotal shield; mouth parts, legs I–II, III–IV or anterior coxal region modified for grasping hairs; empodial claws on legs I and II absent." Female genital openings are an inverted "V" or nearly transverse; genital discs are reduced or absent.

a. Description. *Chirodiscoides caviae* males measure 350 to 376 μm in length, and 130 to 147 μm in width (Fig. 4A); whereas the females measure 502 to 528 μm in length and 154 to 173 μm in width (Fig. 4B). The anterior portion of the body is triangular, which gives this species the appearance of having a distinct "head." The sternal shield is distinctly striated. All legs are modified for hair clasping; however, legs I and II are more distinctly modified than are legs III and IV.

b. Significance. *Chirodiscoides caviae* is a common parasite of the guinea pig, with a cosmopolitan distribution (Blackmore and Owens, 1968; Deoras and Patel, 1960, Patnaik, 1965; Sasa *et al.*, 1962; Wagner *et al.*, 1972).

Infestations with *C. caviae* vary from very light to extremely heavy. Light infestations are difficult to detect and easily overlooked on living animals. Infestations are normally found on dead animals after the carcass has cooled. (See Section V on ectoparasite recovery.) Parasites are frequently observed joined in pairs as if copulating. In this phenomenon a mature male is being carried continually by a nymphal female.

Although we have not associated lesions with *C. caviae* infestations, pruritis and alopecia have been observed with heavy infestations (Harrison and Daykin, 1965; Patnaik, 1965).

D. Demodicidae

Demodex caviae Bacigalupo and Roveda, 1954

The demodicid mites are small wormlike mites which inhabit the hair follicles of a wide range of mammalian hosts (Krantz,

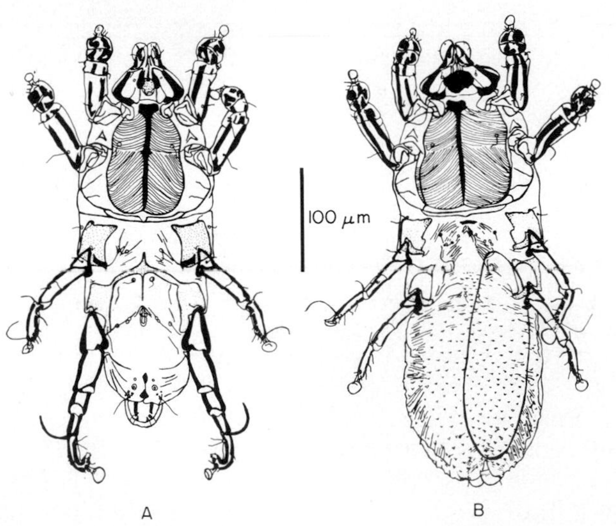

Fig. 4. Line drawing of *Chirodiscoides caviae.* A, male; B, female.

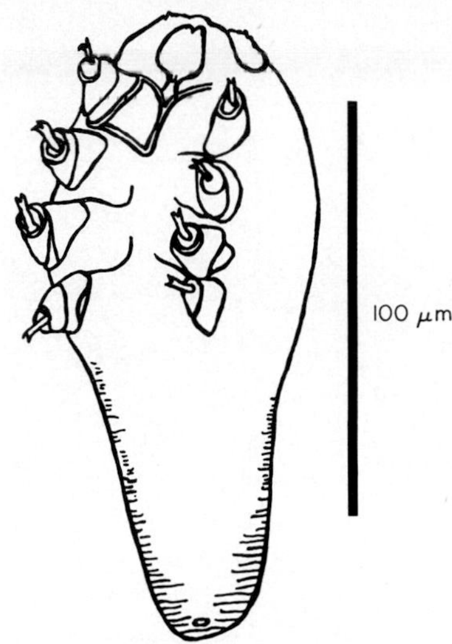

Fig. 5. Line drawing of *Demodex caviae.*

1970). *Demodex caviae* (Fig. 5) varies from this pattern in that this species has been found only in the "conjunctive muscle tissue" of the guinea pig (Bacigalupo and Roveda, 1954).

a. Description. *Demodex caviae* is 138 to 165 μm long by 65 to 69 μm wide. The abdomen is transversely striated. The stubby, five segmented legs are located close together on the anterior portion of the body.

b. Significance. There has been one report of *D. caviae* in guinea pigs (Bacigalupo and Roveda, 1954). However, no signs of infestation were observed in host animals. This information may lead one to believe that *D. caviae* may be widely distributed but overlooked. At this time further work is necessary to determine the incidence of this parasite and to determine whether *D. caviae* might be capable of causing conjunctivitis or other lesions in guinea pigs.

E. Myocoptidae

Myocoptes musculinus (Koch, 1844)

Species of the family Myocoptidae are common inhabitants of the fur of rodents throughout the world. Krantz (1970) lists their diagnostic characteristics as palps normally developed, legs III and IV modified for clasping hair, oval in shape, and tarsi without whiplike terminal setae.

a. Description. *Myocoptes musculinus* female (Fig. 6B) measure approximately 300 μm long and 130 μm wide, while the males (Fig. 6A) measure 185 μm long and 135 μm wide. Both sexes are striated, although the male is less strongly striated than the female. Legs III of the male and legs III and IV of the female are highly modified for grasping hair and

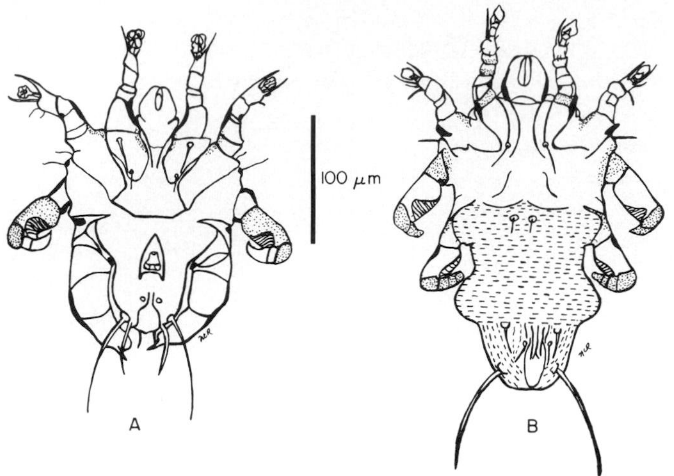

Fig. 6. Line drawing of *Myocoptes musculinus.* A, male; B, female.

resemble boxing gloves. Legs IV of the male are modified for clasping the female during copulation.

b. Significance. The literature contains only one reference to the occurrence of *M. musculinus* on the guinea pig (Sengbusch, 1960). Since *M. musculinus* is a common parasite of laboratory and wild mice (Baker *et al.*, 1956), this infestation probably was contracted from infested mice. *Myocoptes musculinus* infestations in mice often go unnoticed. Signs observed in mice are alopecia, erythema, pruritis, and dermatitis (Gambles, 1952; Watson, 1961). In the one reported case on myocoptic mange in guinea pigs, a suppurative mange was observed (Sengbusch, 1960).

Whether the transter of *M. musculinus* occurs with any frequency in facilities where both mice and guinea pigs are reared in close quarters requires further investigation. In the single case reported to date, the mites were found because a definite lesion was observed. Additional cases may occur where the parasite is present in low numbers. In such cases, the signs could be so slight as to go unnoticed.

F. Sarcoptidae

Species of the family Sarcoptidae are small, oval, burrowing mites which live in or on the skin of various mammals. According to Krantz (1970) the following features are diagnostic for the family: soft bodied, commonly rounded in shape; chelicerae reduced, chelate, palps simple. The legs are telescoped, terminating in empodial suckers or a series of terminal spinelike setae; legs IV occasionally absent.

Two species of sarcoptic mange mites have been associated with the guinea pig.

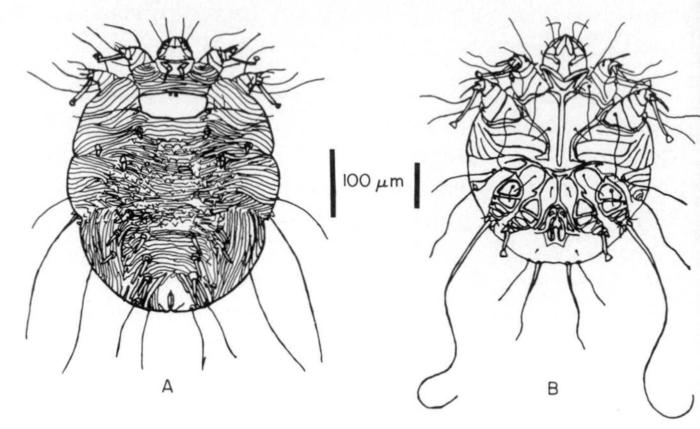

Fig. 7. Line drawing of *Sarcoptes scabiei.* A, female; B, male.

1. *Sarcoptes scabiei* (DeGeer, 1778)

Description: Females (Fig. 7A) are 380 μm long and 270 μm wide, males (Fig. 7B) 220 μm in length by 170 μm in width (Fain, 1968). Baker *et al.* (1956) described *S. scabiei* as being round with a pair of vertical setae on the anterior median margin of the propodosoma. The skin striations are broken by spinelike projections and the dorsal setae are strong and lanceolate. All legs are short; legs I and II end in long flaplike pretarsi; legs III and IV end in a single, long whiplike seta. The anus is located terminally.

2. *Notoedres muris* (Megnin, 1877)

a. Description. *Notoedres muris* females (Fig. 8A) are 400 μm in length by 350 μm in width. *Notoedres muris* is rounded as in *S. scabiei;* however, they lack the vertical setae on the anterior median margin of the propodosoma. The skin striations are not broken by projections as in *S. scabiei.* Legs I and

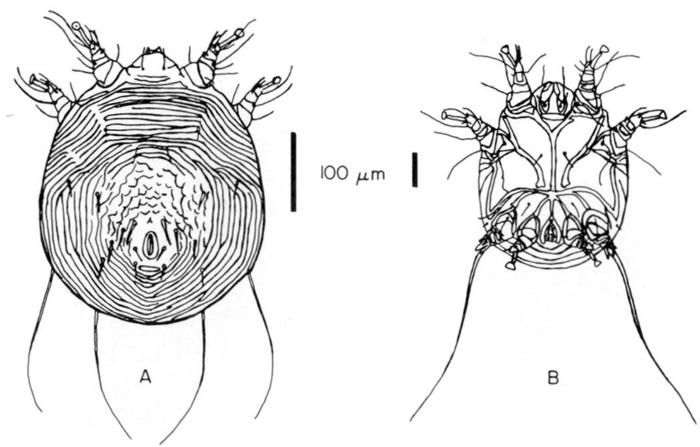

Fig. 8. Line drawing of *Notoedres muris.* A, female; B. male.

II are short, legs III and IV end in a simple whiplike seta. The anus is located dorsally.

b. Significance. There are only two reports which refer to sarcoptic mange in guinea pigs. Cohrs *et al.* (1958) stated that *S. scabiei* var. *cuniculi* can be transmitted from rabbits to guinea pigs via contact. Signs of the disease include brown scabs on the nose and lips, after which the lips become larger and thicker until the animal appears to have a "pig nose." The disease may be spread to other portions of the body by scratching. Young animals are particularly susceptible and the disease can occur epidemically with high mortality due to cachexia.

Notoedres muris infestation of guinea pigs has only been reported once. Sorenson *et al.* (1963) reported an epidemic of *N. muris* in guinea pig colony in Sao Paulo, Brazil. The epidemic occurred, in an animal rearing facility, subsequent to an outbreak of *N. muris* in rats maintained in the same facility. The lesions of *N. muris* on guinea pigs appeared as dark red surface crusts with a dark background located on the muzzle and around the eyes. Few mites were found in the lesions. Guinea pigs infested with *N. muris* recovered spontaneously during 18 months following the outbreak.

V. METHODS FOR THE DIAGNOSIS OF ECTOPARASITES

The method utilized to determine the presence of ectoparasites depends upon whether the animal is alive or dead; if dead, the length of time since death and whether the parasite is found free in the hair or embedded in tissue. Parting the hair of live animals is useful for detecting chewing lice on guinea pigs; however, this method is of less value in detection of ectoparasitic mites because of their minute size.

Postmortem recovery of ectoparasites can easily be accomplished in the following manner. The pelt is removed from the carcass and placed in a jar. The jar is then refrigerated for 30 to 45 minutes. The pelt is then allowed to warm to room temperature and examined with a dissecting microscope. As the pelt begins to warm, fur-inhabiting species will migrate to hair tips where they can be easily observed and collected. If alopecia or dermatitis is observed, deep skin scrapings are made and placed in 5.0% KOH and heated gently for 30 minutes to clear specimens from adjacent tissue.

Occasionally, an animal is received for necropsy which has been dead long enough that the ectoparasites will also be dead. In such a case the method of recovery of follicle-dwelling parasites is not affected. However, an alternative method of recovery for pelage parasites is required. Dead parasites can be recovered by removing the pelt from the animal and placing it in a 10% KOH solution. The KOH solution is heated until the fur can easily be scraped from the skin. The fur is then returned to the solution and boiled until completely dissolved. The KOH solution is allowed to cool and the parasites are allowed to sink to the bottom where they can be easily collected. These specimens will be well cleared and can be mounted immediately for identification.

VI. CONTROL OF ARTHROPOD PARASITES OF GUINEA PIGS

Data concerning the control of arthropod parasites of guinea pigs are sparse. Unfortunately, many citations recommend material such as lindane, BHC, and DDT which have come into general disfavor because of their long residual activity. Dichloro-divinyl phosphate resin vapor strips provides a recent advance in the control of ectoparasites of laboratory animals. Wagner (1969) found DDVP resin vapor strips to be effective in the control of *Myocoptes musculinus* (Koch) and *Myobia musculi* (Schranck) when the strips were placed on the tops of cages covered with air filters. Henderson (1973) obtained similar results with guinea pigs infested by *Chirodiscoides caviae.* We have also found this method to be effective for control of *Gliricola porcelli* of guinea pigs. Repeated applications may be necessary at appropriate times to kill subsequent hatches of eggs.

Published control recommendations are tabulated in Table II. No information has been published in regard to the development of resistance to insecticides by the ectoparasite species which parasitize the guinea pig. Therefore, any recommendation published for other animals should be effective for the control of ectoparasites of the guinea pig if adequate adjustment of dosage can be made. Personnel involved in the control of ectoparasites of any animal should realize that many of the recommended chemicals are organophosphates or carbamates which are cholinesterase inhibitors and can be harmful to both the animals and laboratory personnel if they are improperly handled.

In the event that pesticides cannot be used to control ectoparasitisms of guinea pigs, the use of corn oil to smother ectoparasites (Olewine, 1963) or silica-aerogel preparations that damage the cutile (Tarshis, 1967) and produce death by dehydration may be worthy of trial.

Infestations with ectoparasites may be an indication of a compromised health status. Parasitized animals should not be utilized in experiments. Newly arriving animals should be screened and infested sources avoided. Cesarian-derivation and barrier-sustentation of guinea pigs constitute the ideal eradication methods.

Table II
Recommended Controls for Arthropod Parasites of Guinea Pigs

Species	Recommended controls	References
Biting lice	DDT 0.1% dip	Boch and Supperer, 1971
Trimenopon hispidium	Lindane 0.1% dust or dip	Boch and Supperer, 1971
Gyropus ovalis	Malathion 0.1% spray	Boch and Supperer, 1971
Gliricola procelli	Co-Ral 0.1% spray	Boch and Supperer, 1971
	Nicotine extract 40% powder	Boch and Supperer, 1971
	Pyrethrium 0.2% powder	Boch and Supperer, 1971
	Carbaryl 0.5% powder	N. C. Ronald, unpublished data
	DDVP (vapona strip)	J. E. Wagner, unpublished data
Chirodiscoides caviae	BHC 0.1% spray	Boch and Supperer, 1971
	DDVP	N. C. Ronald and J. E. Wagner, unpublished data
Demodex caviae	None	
Myodoptes musculinus	BHC 0.1% dip	Boch and Supperer, 1971
	BHC 0.5% powder (repeat in 3 weeks)	Boch and Supperer, 1971
	Dimite 0.2% in 50% ETOH	Sengbush, 1960
	Aramite 2.0% dip	Sengbush, 1960
	Aramite 1.0% dip	Clark and Yunker, 1964
	Malathion 2.0%	Clark and Yunker, 1964
Sarcoptes scabei	Asuntol w.p. 0.15%	Boch and Supperer, 1971
	Lindane powder 0.02% (repeat in 3 weeks)	Boch and Supperer, 1971
Notoedres muris	Lindane dip 0.1%	Boch and Supperer, 1971

VII. THE GUINEA PIG IN ENTOMOLOGICAL RESEARCH

The guinea pig has been used as a source for blood feeding for a variety of insects, e.g., mosquitos (Ekis, 1971; French, 1972), fleas (Bar-Zeev and Gothilf, 1972), horse flies (Hafez *et al.*, 1972), tsetse flies (Turner, 1972), and ticks (Vorontsova and Grokhovskaya, 1971). Since the guinea pig can be used as a blood meal source for many insects and ticks, it can be effectively utilized for testing repellents (Bar-Zeev and Gothilf, 1972) and systemic insecticides (Clark and Cole, 1965, 1968).

The guinea pig has also been used as a model to study venoms from arthropods and has played a prominent role in determining that the venom of the brown recluse spider (*Loxosceles reclusus*) is the causative agent of necrotic arachnidism in the central United States (Atkins *et al.*, 1958).

VIII. SUMMARY

The guinea pig may become infested with several different arthropod ectoparasites. Most of these parasites are native to the guinea pig, and they are evolutionarily adjusted to the point where they cause a minimum of annoyance. A few species, e.g., *S. scabiei* and *N. muris,* have on occasion infested guinea pigs under laboratory conditions. Such crossover of evolutionarily unadapted species is usually accompanied by cutaneous lesions which can be easily observed.

Control of ectoparasites can be easily affected by the use of modern insecticides, if the applications are made in a proper sequence to kill all stages of the parasites. Pesticides are diverse in their mode of action and many are cholinesterase inhibitors. Pesticide selection should be made with care after consideration of their effect on experimental protocols.

REFERENCES

Atkins, J. A., Wingo, C. W., Sodeman, and Flynn, J. E. (1958). Necrotic arachnidism. *Amer. J. Trop. Med. Hyg.* **67,** 165–184.

Bacigalupo J., and Roveda, R. J. (1954). *Demodex caviae,* n. sp. *Rev. Med. Vet.* **36,** 149–153.

Baker, E. W., and Wharton, G. W. (1952). "An Introduction to Acarology." Macmillan, New York.

Baker, E. W., Evans, T. M., Gould, D. J., Hull, W. B., and Keegan, H. C. (1956). "A Manual of Parasitic Mites of Medical or Economic Importance." National Pest Control Association, New York.

Bar-Zeev, M., and Gothilf, S. (1972). Laboratory evaluation of flea repellents. *J. Med. Entomol.* **9,** 215–218.

Blackmore, D. K., and Owens, D. G. (1968). Ectoparasites: The significance in British wild rodents. *Symp. Zool. Soc. London* **24,** 197–220.

Boch, J., and Supperer, R. (1971). "Veterinärmedizinische Parasitologie." Parey, Berlin.

Borror, D. J., and DeLong, D. M. (1966). "An Introduction to the Study of Insects." Holt, New York.

Clark, G. M., and Yunker, C. E. (1964). Control of fur mites on mice in entomological laboratories. *Proc. Int. Congr. Acarol., 1st, 1963,* pp. 235–236.

Clark, P. H., and Cole, M. M. (1965). Laboratory evaluation of promising systematic insecticides in guinea pigs against oriental rat fleas. *J. Econ. Entomol.* **58,** 83–86.

Clark, P. H., and Cole, M. M. (1968). Systemic insecticides for control of oriental rat fleas: Tests in guinea pigs. *J. Econ. Entomol.* **61,** 420–423.

Cohrs, P., Jaffe, R., and Meessen, H. (1958). "Pathologie Der Laboratoriumstiere." Springer-Verlag, Berlin and New York.

Deoras, P. J., and Patel, K. K. (1960). Collection of parasites of laboratory animals. *Indian J. Entomol.* **22,** 7–14.

Eiks, G. (1971). Host acceptance of *Culex pipiens* (Culicidae: Diptera). *J. N. Y. Entomol. Soc.* **79,** 190–194.

Ewing, H. G. (1924). On the taxonomy, biology and distribution of the biting lice of the family gyropidae. *Proc. U.S. Nat. Mus.* **63,** Art. 20, 1–42.

Fain, A. (1968). Etude de la variabilité de *Sarcoptes scabiei* avec une revision des Sarcopidea. *Acta Zool. Pathol. Antiverpiensa* **47,** 3–196.

Ferris, G. F. (1951). "The Sucking Lice." Mem. Pac. Coast Entomol. Soc., San Francisco, California.

French, F. C. (1972). *Aedes aegypti* histopathology of immediate skin reactions of hypersensitive guinea pigs resulting from bites. *Exp. Parasitol.* **32,** 175–180.

Gambles, M. R. (1952). *Myocoptes musculinus* (Koch) and *Myobia musculi* (Schranck). Two species of mites commonly parasitizing the laboratory mouse. *Brit. Vet. J.* **108,** 194–203.

Hafez, M., El-Ziady, S., and Hefnawy, T. (1971). Studies on the feeding habits of female *Tabanus taeniola* (Deptera: Tabanidae). *Bull. Soc. Entomol. Egypte* **54,** 365–376.

Harrison, I. E., and Daykin, M. M. (1965). The biology and control of ectoparasites of laboratory animals with special reference to poultry parasites. *J. Inst. Anim. Tech.* **16,** 69–73.

Henderson, J. D. (1973). Treatment of cutaneous acariasis in the guinea pig. *J. Amer. Vet. Med. Ass.* **163,** 591–592.

Hopkins, G. H. E. (1949). The host associations of the lice of mammals. *Proc. Zool. Soc. London* **119,** 387–604.

Hopkins, G. H. E., and Clay, T. (1952). "A Check List of the Genera and Species of Mallophaga." Trustees of the British Museum of London, London.

Hopkins, G. H. E., and Rothchild, M. (1953–1971). "An Illustrated Catalogue of the Rothchild Collection of Fleas (*S. phonaptera*) in the British Museum (Natural History)," Vols. 1–7. Trustees of the British Museum, London.

Krantz, G. W. (1970). "A Manual of Acarology." O. S. U. Book Stores Inc., Corvallis, Oregon.

Olewine, D. A. (1963). An effective control of polyplax infestation without the use of insecticide. *Lab. Anim. Care.* **15,** 750–751.

Owen, D. (1968). Investigation. B. Parasitological studies, *Lab. Anim. Cent. News Lett.* **35,** 7–9.

Paterson, J. S. (1967). The guinea pig or cavy (*Cavia porcellus* L.). *In* "The UFAW Handbook on the Care and Management of Laboratory Animals" (UFAW staff, eds.), 3rd ed. pp. 241–287. Livingston and the Universities Federation for Animal Welfare, London.

Patnaik, M. M. (1965). On the validity of *Indochirus* utkalensis (Listrophoridae: Acarina). *J. Parasitol.* **51,** 301–302.

Sasa, M., Tanaka, H., Furui, M., and Takata, A. (1962). *In* "The Problems of Laboratory Animal Disease" (R.J.C. Harris, ed.), pp. 195–214. Academic Press, New York.

Sengbusch, H. G. (1960). Control of *Myocoptes musculinus* on guinea pigs. *J. Econ. Entomol.* **53,** 168.

Sequy, E. (1944). "Insectes Ectoparasites (Mallophaga, Anoplures, Siphonapteres) Faune de France." Lechevalier, Paris.

Sorenson, B., Saliba, A. M., and Neto, L. Z. (1963). Sarna em ratos e cobios. *Biologico* **29,** 232–234.

Strandtmann, R. W., and Wharton, G. W. (1958). "Manual of Mesostomatid Mites." Institute of Acarology, College Park, Maryland.

Tarshis, I. B. (1967). Control with a pyrethrin-silica aerogel insecticide of ectoparasites infesting animals and birds and their bedding. *18th Annu. Meet. Amer. Ass. Lab. Anim. Sci. Abstr.* No. 53.

Turner, D. A. (1972). Some differences in behavior of *Glossina morsitans* and *Glossina austeni* in an olfactometer. *Trans. Roy. Soc. Trop. Med. Hyg.* **66,** 314.

Vorontsova, T. A., and Grokhovskaya, I. M. (1971). Utilization of antibody neutralization test for detection of *Dermacentroxenus sibericus* in experimentally infected *Dermacentor pictus* ticks. *Med. Parazitol. Parazit. Bolez.* **40,** 581–584.

Wagner, J. E. (1969). Control of mouse ectoparasites with resin vapor strips containing vapona. *Lab. Anim. Care* **19,** 804–807.

Wagner, J. E., Al-Rabiai, S., and Rings, R. W. (1972). *Chirodiscoides caviae* infestation in guinea pigs. *Lab. Anim. Sci.* **22,** 750–752.

Watson, D. P. (1961). The effect of the mite *Myocoptes musculinus* (E. L. Koch, 1840) on the skin of the white laboratory mouse and its control. *Parasitology* **51,** 373–378.

Chapter 15

Neoplastic Diseases

Patrick J. Manning

I. INTRODUCTION

A. Prevalence of Neoplasms in Laboratory Guinea Pigs

Accurate estimates of the prevalence of neoplasia in any species must be based on complete necropsies and thorough microscopic examination of tissues of animals allowed to live their "natural" life span. Based upon these criteria there were few definitive reports on the prevalence of neoplasia in guinea pigs.

Shimkin and Mider (1940) stated that no neoplasms were seen in 15,000 guinea pigs of inbred strains 2, 13, and 35 or other guinea pigs born and observed for up to 5 years between 1916 and 1937. Papanicolaou and Olcott (1942) mentioned that only about 100 tumors were seen in over 7000 guinea pig necropsies for an incidence of approximately 1.4%; tumors were rare in animals less than 4 to 5 years of age. Notable was the report by Rogers and Blumenthal (1960) who examined 6000 guinea pigs of two inbred strains over a 10-year period. No animals were used for experimental purposes. All neoplasms were found in one strain (susceptible strain) and no tumors were seen in animals less than 3 years of age. Among

4000 guinea pigs in the tumor susceptible strain, 14 (0.4%) had tumors. However, since only 97 animals survived more than 3 years, the age-corrected incidence rate (14 of 97) was 14.4%. Mosinger (1961) reported neoplasms in five of 5540 guinea pigs necropsied at his institution. Some animals were not manipulated experimentally, whereas others were subjected to sundry experimental procedures such as induced infections, exposure to allergens, or exposure to silica dust. None was given hormones or compounds known to be carcinogenic. R. Ediger, R. Kovatch, and M. Rabstein (personal communication, 1974) compiled data on tumors seen over a 9-year period in a large production colony of Hartley strain guinea pigs. The colony was established from a nucleus of 500 Hartley strain breeder animals and was maintained at Fort Detrick, Maryland as a random bred closed colony. Tumor data were derived from approximately 8400 necropsies (estimated male to female ratio 1:3) of guinea pigs less than 27 months of age and 34 retired breeders (6 males and 28 females) greater than 27 months of age. In animals less than 27 months old, 63 tumors were seen for an incidence of 0.75%; whereas, 16 tumors occurred in 10 of the 34 retired breeders for an incidence of 29.4%. Three animals of the latter group had multiple primary neoplasms, the other 7 had single primary neoplasms.

These aforementioned reports, considered conjointly with published "case reports," strongly imply that aside from leukemia in certain inbred strains, neoplasia in guinea pigs was virtually nonexistent in animals less than 1 year of age. In some strains, animals more than 3 years of age had a high tumor incidence ranging from 14.4% in an inbred strain (Rogers and Blumenthal, 1960) to nearly 30% in a random bred strain (R. Ediger, R. Kovatch, and M. Rabstein, personal communication, 1974).

B. Tumor Inhibitory Properties of Guinea Pig Serum

Why the guinea pig seems less susceptible to cancer than other laboratory animals remains uncertain. Kidd (1953) demonstrated a principle in guinea pig serum which affected the growth of 3 transplanted lymphomas of rodents, lymphosarcoma $6C_3HED$ of C_3H mice, lymphoma II of strain A mice, and Murphy–Sturm lymphosarcoma of Wistar rats. The tumor inhibitory principle (TIP) had a variable effect on these tumors including partial or complete inhibition of tumor growth, increased latent period, or tumor regression. Pretreatment of lymphoma cells or recipient animals with guinea pig serum prior to transplantation had no effect on tumor growth. These findings were consonant with the conclusion that *in vivo* regression of lymphomas after injection of guinea pig serum was brought about through some action in which both guinea pig serum and tumor-bearing host participated. Further studies to characterize and isolate the TIP were largely unsuccessful but results indicated it probably was not complement, properdin, or a lipopolysaccharide (Herbut *et al.*, 1958) or the interaction of the TIP with recipient isoantibodies (Todd and Kidd, 1954; Kauffman and Kidd, 1956). Herbut *et al.* (1958) suggested that TIP may exert its effect through the properdin system of the tumor-bearing animal.

Could TIP account for the low prevalence of neoplasms in guinea pigs? Herbut *et al.* (1961) compared the TIP activity of sera from stock (random bred) guinea pigs with that of two inbred strains. One strain was tumor resistant and the other was tumor susceptible (Rogers and Blumenthal, 1960). The activity of TIP from serum of stock guinea pigs 1 year of age was much greater than that from aged (>4 years) animals of either inbred strain. However, serum TIP from 1-year-old guinea pigs from either inbred strain equaled the TIP activity present in sera of 1-year-old stock guinea pigs. Consequently, there was no demonstrable difference in the TIP activity among strains of guinea pigs tested and the decline in serum TIP activity with age was equiponderant in both inbred strains. The role that TIP may play on the prevalence of spontaneous cancer in guinea pigs is largely unsettled but deserves further investigation.

II. NEOPLASMS OF LABORATORY GUINEA PIGS

A. Tumors of the Integumentary System and Subcutis (Table I)

Neoplasms of the skin and subcutis were reported more often than in any other system except the lungs and accounted for 15.4% (47 of 306) of all reported tumors. A fibrosarcoma reported by Dickson (1915) was metastatic to the right axilla but tumor cells injected into young guinea pigs failed to grow. Wood (1916) described a fibrosarcoma of the right foreleg in an adult female guinea pig. The tumor weighed 60 gm and though not metastatic it invaded the ulna. First generation transplants were successful in 34 of 195 young guinea pigs, but subsequent transplants were less successful. Transplanted tumors were morphologically similar to the primary neoplasm except no areas of cartilage were seen as occurred in the original tumor. Leader (1937) mentioned two fibrosarcomas described by Lubarsch (1919); one occurred on the dorsum of a male guinea pig and the other arose in the cervical region of a female guinea pig. Metastasis occurred in the spleen of the male and in many visceral organs of the female. Both tumors were transplanted successfully in other guinea pigs, but the tumors regressed after the sixth generation transplant. Fibrosarcomas were also described by Nejedly and Straub (1957) and mentioned by Haagensen and Krehbiel (1936). Among the 14 tumors described by Rogers and Blumenthal (1960) one was a subcutaneous fibrolipoma.

Solitary sebaceous adenomas were reported by three investi-

Table I
Spontaneous Tumors of the Skin and Subcutis of the Guinea Pig

Tumor type	Number of animals	Reference
Fibrosarcoma (neck)	1	Dickson, 1915
Sebaceous adenoma (not stated)	1	Murray, 1916
Fibrosarcoma (foreleg)	1	Wood, 1916
Fibrosarcoma (dorsum; neck)	2	Lubarsch, 1919
Fibrosarcoma (subcutis)	1	Heim and Schwartz, 1931
Fibrosarcoma (not stated)	2	Haagensen and Krehbiel, 1936
Undifferentiated adenocarcinoma (ventral neck)	1	Heston and Deringer, 1952
Trichoepithelioma	1	Haranghy *et al.*, 1954
Fibrosarcoma (hind leg)	1	Nejedly and Straub, 1957
Fibrolipoma (abdomen)	1	Rogers and Blumenthal, 1960
Sebaceous adenoma (inguinal region)	1	Mosinger, 1961
Sebaceous adenoma	1	Lombard, 1960
Fibroma	1	Stenbeck, 1970
Trichofolliculoma (primarily lumber region)	29	Ediger *et al.*, 1971; R. Ediger, R. Kovatch, and M. Rabstein, personal communication (1974)
Lipoma	1	R. Ediger, R. Kovatch, and M. Rabstein, personal communication (1974)
Undifferentiated sarcoma	1	R. Ediger, R. Kovatch, and M. Rabstein, personal communication (1974)
Total	47	

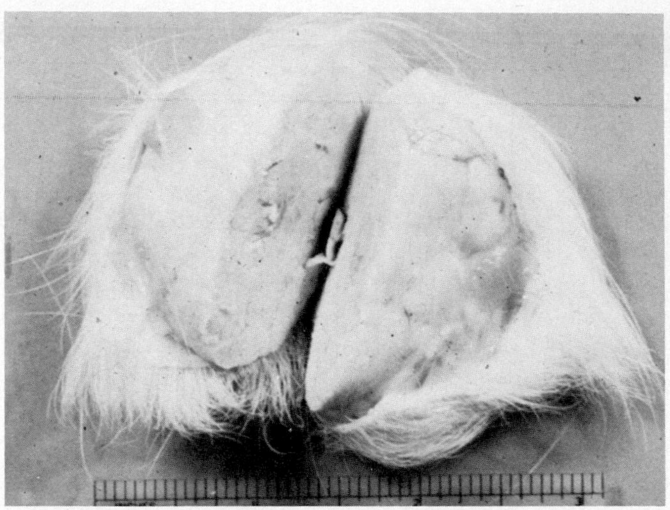

Fig. 1. Gross photograph of a trichofolliculoma in a Dunkin–Hartley guinea pig. (Courtesy Dr. Raymond Ediger.)

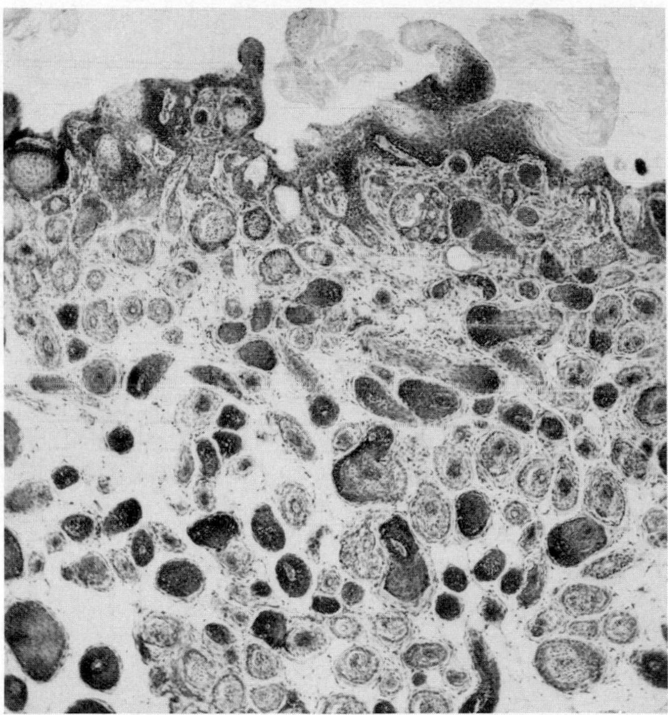

Fig. 2. Photomicrograph of trichofolliculoma shown in Fig. 1. Included is a portion of a multiloculated cyst, the lumen of which is at the top of the photograph. The wall of the cyst consists of stratified squamous epithelium and numerous abortive hair follicles. Hematoxylin and eosin. ×56. (Courtesy of Veterinary Pathology Division, Armed Forces Institute of Pathology.)

gators (Murray, 1916; Lombard, 1960; Mosinger, 1961) and one report described a trichoepithelioma (Haranghy *et al.*, 1954). Most conspicuous in this category are the contributions by Ediger *et al.* (1971; R. Ediger, R. Kovatch, and M. Rabstein, personal communication, 1974) who described 29 trichofolliculomas. In their initial report, Ediger *et al.* (1971) reported 21 trichofolliculomas noted at necropsy of 7670 Dunkin–Hartley guinea pigs. Affected animals were 6 weeks to 32 months of age and nine of the tumors were in males. Most tumors were confined to the hypodermis as unencapsulated multiloculated cysts lined by stratified squamous epithelium with abortive hair follicles (Figs. 1 and 2). The cysts contained keratin, hair, and sebum.

B. Tumors of the Cardiovascular System (Table II)

Tumors of the cardiovascular system were exceedingly rare and all reported cancers were in the heart. Athias (1937) reported a fibrosarcoma of the myocardium of a guinea

Table II
Spontaneous Tumors of the Cardiovascular System of the Guinea Pig

Tumor type	Number of animals	Reference
Fibrosarcoma (heart)	1	Athias, 1937
Mesenchymoma	4	McConnell and Ediger, 1968
Mesenchymoma (heart)	8	R. Ediger, R. Kovatch, and M. Rabstein, personal communication (1974)
Total	13	

pig that 110 days previously had been injected with methylcholanthrene intracerebrally. Benign mesenchymal mixed tumors (mesenchymomas) of the myocardium were described by McConnell and Ediger (1968) and an additional 8 animals from this colony have been similarly affected (R. Ediger, R. Kovatch, and M. Rabstein, personal communication, 1974). All affected guinea pigs were adult females. The tumors arose from the right atrium in 10 animals and were in the region of the right atrioventricular junction in the other two. Grossly, two tumors were yellow and circumscribed with a smooth to lobulated surface. Microscopically these tumors were comprised of well-differentiated mesodermal elements including fat, cartilage, and bone, as well as hematopoietic, myxomatous, angiomatous, and presumably smooth muscle tissues (Fig. 3). Mesenchymomas are believed to be dysontogenetic growths derived from pluripotent cells of primitive mesenchyme (Anderson, 1966). One or more of the tissue components may be malignant or they may all be benign. The occurrence of mesenchymomas in females of the Hartley strain strongly suggests that genetic factors play an important role in the development of this lesion.

Rhabdomyomatosis is a commonly encountered nonneoplastic lesion of the myocardium in guinea pigs. The condition is discussed here because some synonyms for this abnormality imply that it may be neoplastic. These synonyms include congenital rhabdomyoma, congenital glycogenic tumor, circumscribed glycogenic storage disease, nodular glycogenic degeneration, and nodular glycogenic infiltration. First described in the guinea pig by Hueper (1940), rhabdomyomatosis has since been reported by many investigators (Rooney, 1961; Argus and Hoch-ligeti, 1961; Vink, 1969; Cintorino and Luzi, 1970; R. Ediger, R. Kovatch, and M. Rabstein, personal communication, 1974). Myocardial rhabdomyomas in guinea pigs were identical microscopically to those described in man and since animals 3 to 20 weeks of age were reported to be most often affected, the lesions may be congenital. At necropsy these lesions were indistinct and pale whitish red in the ventricular and/or atrial myocardium or atrioventricular valves. They were often multiple and some subendocardial lesions

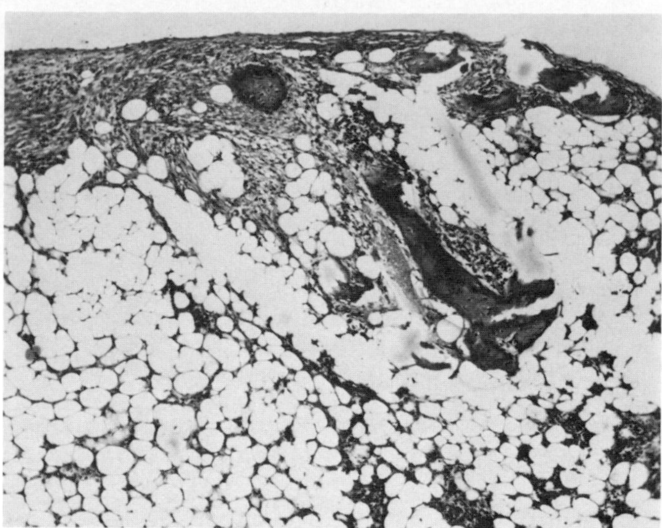

Fig. 3. Photomicrograph of a mesenchymoma from the right atrium of a guinea pig. Fat, bone, hematopoietic, and fibrous connective tissues are present. Hematoxylin and eosin. ×84. (Courtesy of Veterinary Pathology Division, Armed Forces Institute of Pathology.)

bulged slightly into the ventricle. The characteristic appearance by light microscopy consisted of a loose network of delicate fibrils supporting large vacuolated cells each with a central or peripherally located nucleus and abundant cytoplasm (Fig. 4). Some cells had a pink strandlike to granular material which along with the peripheral rim of cell cytoplasm was usually PAS positive. This material may radiate from the centrally placed nucleus to the cell border (spider cells) and occasionally it had an abortive striated appearance.

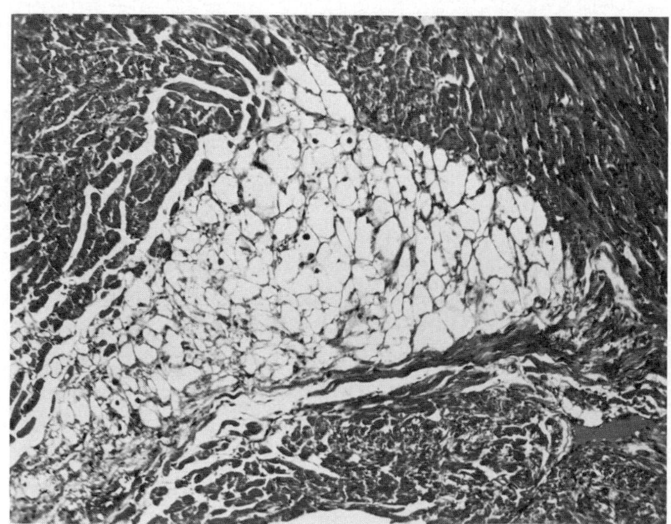

Fig. 4. Photomicrograph of a cardiac rhabdomyoma (circumscribed glycogen accumulation) in a guinea pig. Hematoxylin and eosin. ×105. (Courtesy of Veterinary Pathology Division, Armed Forces Institute of Pathology.)

Other stigmata that may accompany rhabdomyomatosis in man such as tuberous sclerosis of the brain and less often congenital abnormalities of other organs have not been reported in the guinea pig. The lesion may represent a form of von Gierke's disease (Hueper, 1940) but glycogen in primitive myocardial cells of rhabdomyomas was much more soluble in aqueous fixatives than glycogen stored in cells of normal parenchymatous tissues such as liver or myocardium. The high incidence rate of this lesion, particularly in closed colonies (Rooney, 1961; Vink, 1969; R. Ediger, R. Kovatch, and M. Rabstein, personal communication, 1974), suggests the guinea pig would be a very useful model for study of cardiac rhabdomyomatosis of man.

C. Tumors of the Respiratory System (Table III)

Pulmonary neoplasms accounted for nearly 35% of all reported tumors and were the most frequently reported solid tumors of guinea pigs. Eighty-seven of 105 reported pulmonary tumors were papillary adenomas and 56 of these were described by Spronck (1907) who observed these lesions at necropsy of 100 guinea pigs of the same strain. Most papillary adenomas were bronchogenic (Spronck, 1907) but some may be alveologenic (Franks and Chesterman, 1962). Bronchogenic papillary adenomas, when grossly visible, were small white circumscribed nodules consisting microscopically of numerous papillae of loose connective tissue covered by a single layer of hyperchromatic cuboidal epithelium. Similar lesions in distal bronchioles and alveoli consisted of adenomatous hyperplasia of hyperchromatic epithelical cells that formed fronds, papillae, and acini. Mitoses were rare and metastases were not reported. Fischer (1956) described pulmonary lesions among 120 guinea pigs with interstitial pneumonia. Included were descriptions of 18 adenomas, 17 adenocarcinomas, and 15 other guinea pigs had proliferation of alveolar epithelium.

The frequency of occurrence of pulmonary adenomatous lesions, their microscopic features, and resemblance to jagziekte and progressive ovine pneumonia have prompted investigators to question whether this condition is neoplastic and some prefer to use the term pulmonary adenomatosis.

Grumbach (1926) induced pulmonary adenomatosis in guinea pigs by injection of a diphtheroid bacillus, and both Grumbach (1926) and Cowdry and Marsh (1927) agreed that induced lesions in guinea pigs resembled those of jagziekte and progressive pneumonia of Montana sheep. The latter diseases are probably caused by viruses, but there is no evidence to support an infectious agent as the cause of similar appearing lesions in guinea pigs. The fact that pulmonary adenomatosis was induced by a diphtheroid bacillus and that lesions consisting in part of epithelial hyperplasia were associated with inflammatory changes or foreign bodies (Franks and Chesterman, 1962; Norris, 1947) supports the conclusion that epithelial hyperplasia and adenomatous changes may occur in the guinea pig lung in response to various stimuli. Consequently, localized pulmonary lesions of this type should probably not be considered neoplastic until further evidence is presented to substantiate this theory.

Table III
Spontaneous Tumors of the Respiratory System of Guinea Pigs

Tumor	Number of animals	Reference
Papillary adenoma	2	Sternberg, 1903
Papillary adenoma	56	Spronck, 1907
Bronchogenic adenocarcinoma	1	Goldberg, 1920
Papillary adenoma	1	Norris, 1947
Papillary adenoma	1	Heston and Deringer, 1952
Papillary adenoma	3	Lorenz *et al.*, 1954
Bronchogenic? adenoma	18	Fischer, 1956
Bronchogenic? adenocardinoma	17	Fischer, 1956
Papillary adenoma	1	Rogers and Blumenthal, 1960
Papillary adenoma	4	Franks and Chesterman, 1962
Adenoma	1	Toth, 1970
Total	105	

D. Tumors of the Alimentary System and Peritoneum (Table IV)

All reported neoplasms of the stomach were grossly visible on the greater curvature near the pylorus in guinea pigs 4 to 6

Table IV
Spontaneous Tumors of the Alimentary System and Peritoneum of Guinea Pigs

Tumor	Number of animals	Reference
Stomach		
Fibromyoma	1	Papanicolaou and Olcott, 1940
Leiomyoma	3	Papanicolaou and Olcott, 1942
Lipoma	1	Papanicolaou and Olcott, 1942
Intestine		
Fibroid	1	Lipschütz, 1941
Liposarcoma	1	Papanicolaou and Olcott, 1942
Peritoneum		
Fibrosarcoma	1	Heston and Deringer, 1952
Liver		
Liver cell adenoma	1	Rogers and Blumenthal, 1960
Cavernous hemangioma	1	Rogers and Blumenthal, 1960
Gallbladder		
Papilloma	1	Rogers and Blumenthal, 1960
Total	11	

years of age (Papanicolaou and Olcott, 1940, 1942). Except for one lipoma stomach tumors were derived mainly from smooth muscle which microscopically was arranged as nodules and whorls. Necrosis and hemorrhage occurred infrequently and in only one instance was the gastric mucosa altered.

The intestinal liposarcoma was a vascular, brittle tumor consisting of ovoid cells with cytoplasmic vacuoles. The mitotic index was low and the tumor was completely separated from the intestinal wall by normal adipose tissue (Papanicolaou and Olcott, 1942). Lipschütz (1941) mentioned a "fibroid tumor of the bowels."

All reported neoplasms of the liver and biliary system were described by Rogers and Blumenthal (1960). A cavernous hemangioma was grossly purple and consisted microscopically of numerous blood-filled vascular channels lined by a single layer of endothelium. In another guinea pig, a white hepatic nodule, a few millimeters in diameter, was a liver cell adenoma devoid of bile ducts and contained within a fibrous capsule. A third guinea pig had a small tumor on the gallbladder mucosa with microscopic characteristics of a papilloma, with tall hyperchromatic epithelial cells on slender connective tissue stalks.

E. Tumors of the Reproductive System (Table V)

1. Tumors of the Ovary

Not included as teratomas in Table V are embryonal structures within the ovary of guinea pigs described by Loeb who summarized his studies and described four new examples of this phenomenon in 1932. Because these structures could be misinterpreted as a neoplasm they deserve further comment. Parthenogenetic development of ova within the ovary occurs frequently in guinea pigs. Prior to follicular atresia, the ovum undergoes initial rudimentary divisions which in turn appear to induce intraovarian development of placental structures and embryonal structures. At maximum development the "embryonal placentoma" (Loeb, 1932) was a cavity lined by two cell layers. The outer layer consisted of giant cells, some of which were multinucleated, large, and hyperchromatic and an inner layer of cuboidal or cylindrical cells. Both cell layers were prototypes of chorionic epithelium and had a propensity to migrate perivascularly, penetrate vessel walls, replace vascular endothelium, and form syncytia. Hemorrhage and subsequent necrosis were common sequelae as a result of vascular and stromal invasion by these cells. The embryonal structure was distinct from the embryonal placentoma in that it resembled an anomalous embryo forced to develop in unfavorable conditions. Primitive formations derived in a restricted sense from ectoderm, entoderm, and mesoderm were often recognized. Tubular neural structures were readily recognized. Syncytia resembling normal trophoblasts occurred but they did not appear to migrate as extensively as those of the embryonal placentoma. The prevalence of this phenomenon is undoubtedly much greater than might be concluded from the number of reports in the literature for as emphasized by Loeb (1932) they were quite small and several sections of the ovary would be necessary to estimate their prevalence. They were also transitory, self-limiting, and resolved by fibrosis, and thus their former existence could not be recognized. These structures were seen in females less than 6 months of age and most were in guinea pigs less than 4 months of age (Loeb, 1932); estrogens appear to enhance their development (Mosinger, 1961).

Table V
Spontaneous Tumors of the Reproductive System of Guinea Pigs

Tumor	Number of animals	Reference
Ovary		
Teratoma	1	Montroni, 1930
Teratoma	1	Giordano, 1939
Teratoma	2	Athias, 1944
Teratoma	1	Wildi, 1949
Teratoma	1	Haranghy *et al.*, 1954
Cystadenoma	1	Lechner, 1958
Teratoma	1	Mosinger, 1961
Cystadenoma	1	Mosinger, 1961
Teratoma	2	Willis, 1962
Teratoma	10	Vink, 1970
Granulosa cell	1	Jain *et al.*, 1970
Teratoma	1	J. Wagner, personal communication, University of Missouri, Columbia, Missouri (1974)
Teratoma	3	R. Ediger, R. Kovatch, and M. Rabstein, personal communication (1974)
Cystadenoma	3	R. Ediger, R. Kovatch, and M. Rabstein, personal communication (1974)
Salpinx		
Adenoma	1	Toth, 1970
Uterus		
Sarcoma	1	Heim and Schwartz, 1931
Fibromyoma	1	Lipschütz, 1941
Leiomyoma (gross diagnosis)	1	Papanicolaou and Olcott, 1942
Myxofibroma	1	Lechner, 1958
Leiomyoma	2	Rogers and Blumenthal, 1960
Leiomyosarcoma	1	Rogers and Blumenthal, 1960
Adenomyoma	1	Rogers and Blumenthal, 1960
Fibrosarcoma	1	Rogers and Blumenthal, 1960
Myxosarcoma	1	Rogers and Blumenthal, 1960
Mesenchymal mixed tumor	1	Rogers and Blumenthal, 1960
Adenocarcinoma	2	Toth, 1970
Fibroma	1	Toth, 1970
Leiomyoma	1	R. Ediger, R. Kovatch, and M. Rabstein, personal communication (1974)
Testis		
Embryonal carcinoma	1	Rogers and Blumenthal, 1960
Total	46	

Teratomas accounted for nearly 80% of the 29 ovarian tumors (Table V). Teratomas are neoplasms composed of multiple tissues foreign to the part in which they arise. Ovarian teratomas are also believed to arise from parthenogenetic development of oocytes but the relationship between ovarian teratomas and the transitory placental and embryonic structures in young guinea pigs discussed previously is not known and appears not to have been explored experimentally. Montroni's report (1930) of an ovarian cystadenocarcinoma was actually a teratoma and the teratoma described by Giordano (1939) metastasized to the peritoneum. Athias (1944) described two ovarian teratomas, one in a young virgin female and the other in an adult female. The left ovary of the virgin animal was 8.5 × 7.5 cm and, microscopically, the tumor was composed of a variety of structures including neuroepithelial tubules, neurospongial tissue, ciliated and mucous cells, hair follicles, exocrine and endocrine glandular acini, and striated muscle, among other tissues. The teratoma in the adult female was smaller but of similar microscopic composition. A large teratoma of the right ovary in a pregnant guinea pig (Wildi, 1949) contained some tissue not previously recognized in other teratomas of guinea pigs including sympathetic ganglia, islets of adenohypophysial tissue, and thyroid gland. The teratoma of the left ovary described by Haranghy *et al.* (1954) weighed 16 gm; Mosinger (1961) mentioned one teratoma in an adult guinea pig. Unilateral ovarian teratomas were reported by Willis (1962) in two guinea pigs, one 9 weeks of age and the other 1 year of age. In the elder animal the tumor was metastatic to liver, omentum, peritoneum, and abdominal wall. The neoplasm was transplanted to other guinea pigs but tumor cells failed to survive the second generation transplant. R. Ediger, R. Kovatch, and M. Rabstein (personal communication, 1974) tabulated three ovarian teratomas from their extensive series (Fig. 5). Vink's contribution (1970) is also noteworthy because it accounts for nearly 35% of reported ovarian teratomas. The 10 teratomas seen by Vink were derived from 13,000 necropsies of a colony of random bred guinea pigs. Some animals died of intraperitoneal hemorrhage of the tumor though no tumor metastasized. He suggested that genetic factors may have had a significant effect on the number of teratomas in his colony.

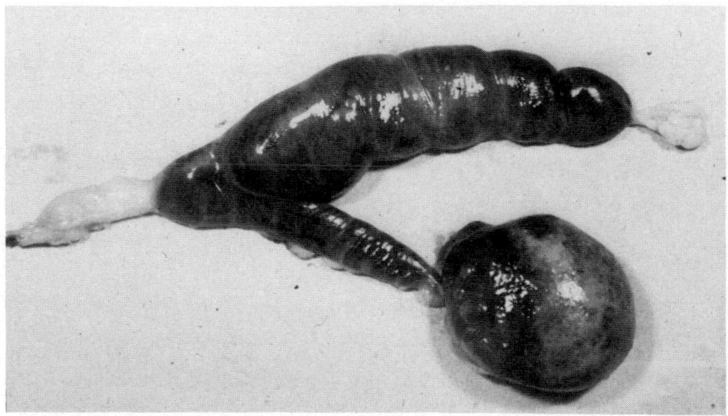

Fig. 5. Teratoma of the right ovary from an adult female guinea pig. The tumor was 5.5 cm × 4.5 cm × 3.0 cm. The enlarged uterine horn contained one normal fetus and three fetuses in various stages of resorption. (Courtesy Dr. Raymond Ediger.)

Other ovarian tumors included two cystadenomas (Lechner, 1958; Mosinger, 1961) and a granulosa cell tumor (Jain *et al.*, 1970). Two "cystomas" included in Blumenthal and Rogers review (1967) appeared in guinea pigs that were given the chemical carcinogen 2-acetylaminofluorene and I have not included them as spontaneous neoplasms.

2. Uterus

Fifteen uterine neoplasms are tabulated in Table V and among the seven tumors described by Rogers and Blumenthal (1960) four underwent sarcomatous transformation but none metastasized. The leiomyomas were discrete, encapsulated tumors composed of intermingling bundles of elongated smooth muscle cells; whereas, the leiomyosarcoma was also encapsulated but had numerous mitoses. The fibrosarcoma was confined to the serosa and the myxosarcoma consisted of loosely arranged spindle-shaped cells poorly demarcated from adjacent myometrium but did not extend through the serosa. Except for the presence of cystic endometrial glands among tumor cells the mesenchymal mixed tumor resembled the myxosarcoma.

3. Testis

The only reported tumor of the male reproductive system was an embryonal carcinoma of the left testis (Rogers and Blumenthal, 1960). A yellow-gray irregular nodule occupied nearly 70% of the testicle and consisted of small cells with scant vacuolated cytoplasm arranged compactly and less often as pseudoglands and papilloid structures.

F. Tumors of the Mammary Glands (Table VI)

Adenocarcinomas were the most frequently reported malignant mammary neoplasm and 3 of 9 adenocarcinomas were in male guinea pigs (Migunow, 1931; Twort and Twort, 1932). Nearly all the carcinomas were believed to be of ductal origin. Katase (1912) mentioned an adenocarcinoma of the breast. Metastastes occurred to the lungs and pleura in one instance (Sternberg, 1913) but tumor transplantation was not attempted. Jones (1916) successfully transplanted a mammary adenocarcinoma from an aged female to young guinea pigs. For three generations successive transplants resulted in a reduced latent period and more rapid tumor growth. One recipient had metastatic carcinoma in an inguinal lymph node and another had metastatic disease in a kidney and an inguinal

Table VI

Spontaneous Tumors of the Mammary Glands of Guinea Pigs

Tumor	Number of animals	References
Papillary cystadenoma	2	Apolant, 1908
Adenocarcinoma	1	Katase, 1912
Adenocarcinoma	1	Sternberg, 1913
Adenocarcinoma	1	Jones, 1916
Liposarcoma	1	Murray, 1916
Adenocarcinoma	1	Blumensaat and Champy, 1928
Adenocarcinoma	2 (males)	Migunow, 1931
Adenocarcinoma	1 (male)	Twort and Twort, 1932
Adenocarcinoma	1	Anderson and Lumbroso, 1933
Adenocarcinoma	1	Syverton, 1957
Adenofibroma	1	Mosinger, 1961
Adenocarcinoma	1	Toth, 1970
Adenoma	3	R. Ediger, R. Kovatch, and M. Rabstein, personal communication (1974)
Cystadenoma	1	R. Ediger, R. Kovatch, and M. Rabstein, personal communication (1974)
Papillary adenoma (ductal)	1	R. Ediger, R. Kovatch, and M. Rabstein, personal communication (1974)
Fibroadenoma	7	R. Ediger, R. Kovatch, and M. Rabstein, personal communication (1974)
Fibrocystadenoma	2	R. Ediger, R. Kovatch, and M. Rabstein, personal communication (1974)
Carcinosarcoma	1	R. Ediger, R. Kovatch, and M. Rabstein, personal communication (1974)
Papillary adenoma (teat canal)	1 (male)	R. Ediger, R. Kovatch, and M. Rabstein, personal communication (1974)
Total	30	

lymph node. The liposarcoma described by Murray (1916) arose in the region of the left mamma of an adult female. The tumor was transplanted successfully and though no metastases were seen one recipient had a tumor embolus in a pulmonary artery. A mammary adenocarcinoma mentioned by Miller *et al.* (1964) and tabulated by Blumenthal and Rogers (1967) appears to have been induced by *N*-hydroxyacetylaminofluorene and is not included as a spontaneous neoplasm. Sixteen of the 30 mammary tumors were seen in Hartley strain guinea pigs (R. Ediger, R. Kovatch, and M. Rabstein, personal communication, 1974). Fourteen of these tumors occurred in animals 10 to 26 months of age and 50% were fibroadenomas. The only malignant tumor in this category, a carcinosarcoma, metastasized to the kidney and spleen.

Table VII

Spontaneous Tumors of the Urinary System of Guinea Pigs

Tumor	Number of animals	Reference
Kidney		
Osteogenic sarcoma	1	Twort and Twort, 1932
Urinary bladder		
Anaplastic tumor	1	Heston and Deringer, 1952
Transitional cell carcinoma	2	R. Ediger, R. Kovatch, and M. Rabstein, personal communication (1974)
Epidermoid carcinoma	1	R. Ediger, R. Kovatch, and M. Rabstein, personal communication (1974)
Epidermoid papilloma	1	R. Ediger, R. Kovatch, and M. Rabstein, personal communication (1974)
Total	6	

G. Tumors of the Urinary System (Table VII)

The renal osteogenic sarcoma described by Twort and Twort (1932) was unusual in that it was one of the rare instances in which two primary morphologically malignant neoplasms were described in the same guinea pig. The animal, a 4-year-old male, also harbored a mammary adenocarcinoma. The renal osteosarcoma was necrotic, whitish, and surrounded by loculated hemorrhagic cysts. Microscopically, neoplastic spindle and polygonal cells were admixed with osteoclasts. An anaplastic tumor of the urinary bladder occurred in a strain 13 female, 28 months of age (Heston and Deringer, 1952). R. Ediger, R. Kovatch, and M. Rabstein, (personal communication, 1974) tabulated four tumors of the urinary bladder of guinea pigs. One, a transitional cell carcinoma, occurred in an animal less than 6 months of age, whereas the other three were seen in guinea pigs 69 months old. Metastases were not described although many of these tumors were morphologically malignant.

H. Tumors of the Endocrine System (Table VIII)

Endocrine neoplasms were among the rarest reported tumors of the guinea pig. Three were adequately described. An adrenal cortical carcinoma reported by Roskin (1930) was transplanted successfully for a number of generations. The original tumor was well differentiated with metastases to the mesentery and subcutis. Anaplastic foci developed after repeated transplantation.

Papanicolaou and Olcott (1940) described an adrenal cortical adenoma in a 7-year-old female guinea pig that also harbored a gastric fibromyoma. The right adrenal was enlarged four-fold. Centrally, the tumor consisted of compact lobules of reticular cells with dense nongranular cytoplasm and large hyperchromatic nuclei. Peripherally, tumor cells were arranged loosely, the cytoplasm was vacuolated and some cells were polynuclear. Franks and Chesterman (1962) mentioned an "adrenal tumor" in a 53-month-old male guinea pig that also had papillary adenomas of the lung. Not included in Table VIII are a number of adrenal cortical adenomas which occurred in male guinea pigs some years after neonatal castration (Spiegel, 1940). These lesions were most likely castration-induced hyperplastic nodules.

The only morphologically malignant thyroid tumor reported was described by Zarrin (1974). Grossly the tumor consisted of multiple masses in the right lower cervical region; the largest tumor was 35 mm long. Microscopically the tumor was of mixed composition with an epithelial element that resembled medullary (parafollicular) carcinoma and a spindle cell element with irregular bone trabeculae. Metastases were not seen. Lombard (1960) mentioned a thyroid tumor and R. Ediger, R. Kovatch, and M. Rabstein (personal communication, 1974) tabulated one thyroid adenoma in a 16-month-old Hartley strain guinea pig. Another thyroid adenoma included in Table VIII was noted at necropsy of an adult female guinea pig with an intestinal liposarcoma (Papanicolaou and Olcott, 1942).

Table VIII

Spontaneous Tumors of the Endocrine System of Guinea Pigs

Tumor	Number of animals	Reference
Adrenal		
Cortical carcinoma	1	Roskin, 1930
Cortical adenoma	1	Papanicolaou and Olcott, 1940
"Adrenal tumor"	1	Franks and Chesterman, 1962
Cortical adenoma	2	Toth, 1970
Thyroid		
Adenoma (gross only)	1	Papanicolaou and Olcott, 1942
"Tumor"	1	Lombard, 1960
Adenoma	1	R. Ediger, R. Kovatch, and M. Rabstein, personal communication (1974)
Carcinoma	1	Zarrin, 1974
Pancreas		
Islet cell adenoma	1	Toth, 1970
Total	10	

[a]R. Ediger, R. Kovatch, and M. Rabstein, personal communication (1974).

Table IX

Spontaneous Tumors of the Hemopoietic System of Guinea Pigs

Tumor	Number of animals	Reference
Lymphosarcoma (neck)	1	Dickson, 1915
Splenic sarcoma (lymphosarcoma?)	1	Kleinkuhner, 1916
Lymphosarcoma (neck)	1	Miguenz, 1918
Lymphosarcoma (heart)	1	Bender, 1925
"Splenoma" (lymphosarcoma?)	1	Guérin and Guérin, 1925
Lymphosarcoma with leukemia	1	Snijders, 1926
Lymphosarcoma (kidney)	1	Ball and Pagnon, 1935
Leukemia	4	Congdon and Lorenz, 1954
Leukemia	2	Lorenz *et al.*, 1954
Leukemia	1	Nadel, 1957
Leukemia	1	Rogers and Blumenthal, 1960
Leukemia	1	Ediger and Rabstein, 1968
Leukemia or lymphoblastic lymphosarcoma	4	R. Ediger, R. Kovatch, and M. Rabstein, personal communication (1974)
Lymphosarcoma	2	R. Ediger, R. Kovatch, and M. Rabstein, personal communication (1974)
Total	22	

I. Spontaneous Neoplasms of the Hemopoietic System and Lymphoreticular Systems (Table IX)

Certain inbred strains of guinea pigs have a relatively high incidence of leukemia associated with the presence of leukoviruses; this topic is discussed in Chapter 10. Aside from the aforementioned exception, hematopoietic and lymphoreticular neoplasms occurred sporadically and infrequently in guinea pigs. A succinct historical review of leukemia and lymphosarcoma of guinea pigs was included in the report of Congdon and Lorenz (1954). Two early reports (Dickson, 1915; Miguenz, 1918) described primary lymphosarcomas in the subcutis of the ventral neck and the latter author and his colleagues (Fischer and Kantor, 1919) transplanted the tumor in guinea pigs for more than 50 passages. Similarly, Bender (1925) and Ball and Pagnon (1935) reported primary lymphosarcomas of the heart and kidney, respectively.

Snijders (1926, 1927) described lymphoblastic leukemia with neoplastic infiltrates in many parenchymal organs of a guinea pig. The original neoplasm was transplanted to other guinea pigs in Sumatra and in Holland (Snijders, 1926, 1927; Tio Tjwan Gie, 1927). Four distinct morphological types of tumor developed in some guinea pigs injected with Snijders transplantable leukemia: (1) lymphoblastic leukemia, (2) aleukemic lymphadenosis, (3) lymphosarcoma, and (4) "lymphosarcoma resembling that of man." In those with leukemia, the white blood cell count sometimes reached several hundred thousand cells per cubic millimeter. Among the more commonly used strains of guinea pigs "spontaneous" leukemia has been described in strain 2 (Congdon and Lorenz, 1954) and the Hartley strain (Ediger and Rabstein, 1968; R. Ediger, R. Kovatch, and M. Rabstein, personal communication, 1974); the former authors transplanted neoplastic cells to other animals of the same inbred strain and all recipients contracted the disease. Leukemia, unlike many other types of neoplasia, appears to have its highest incidence in guinea pigs primarily between the ages of 2 and 4 years. The microscopic characteristics of the disease are described in Chapter 10 and were similar to those described for other rodents (Engelbreth-Holm, 1942).

J. Tumors of the Musculoskeletal System (Table X)

Kröning and Wepler (1938) reported a lipomyxofibroma invading the psoas muscle in a 3-year-old male guinea pig. An osteogenic sarcoma of the femur described by Leader (1937) invaded the tibia and fibula and metastasized to the lung in an adult male guinea pig. A chondrosarcoma of the right ilium with metastasis to the left mamma (Olcott and Papanicolaou, 1943) occurred in a 2.5-year-old female guinea pig. This tumor was morphologically atypical in that it consisted of nests of uniform tumor cells resembling undifferentiated mesenchyme. In most areas the intercellular substance was fibrillary but in other regions it resembled cartilage or osteoid. Similar tumor foci in the left mamma were believed to represent metastasis to a large lymph node. The neurogenic fibrosarcoma of the right maxilla described by Warren and Gates (1941) was transplanted subcutaneously to 20 stock guinea pigs and the tumor grew locally in six recipients; an additional 11 animals were injected with tumors from two of the six original recipients and tumors grew locally in two animals. Further transplants failed to grow. The transplantable osteochondrosarcoma reported by Laporte *et al.* (1962) was considerably more virulent. The original tumor arose near the proximal epiphysis of the right humerus and after a 3-month period of rapid growth it killed the host. Metastases were seen in the lungs, spleen, and right adrenal gland. From the years 1961 to 1963 this tumor was maintained through 11 generation transplants. Recipient guinea pigs were from either random bred or inbred

Table X
Spontaneous Tumors of the Musculoskeletal System of the Guinea Pig

Tumor	Number of animals	Reference
Osteogenic sarcoma (femur)	1	Leader, 1937
Lipomyxofibroma (psoas muscle)	1	Kröning and Wepler, 1938
Neurogenic fibrosarcoma (maxilla)	1	Warren and Gates, 1941
Chondrosarcoma (ilium)	1	Olcott and Papanicolaou, 1943
Osteochondrosarcoma	1	Laporte *et al.*, 1962
Enchondroma (rib)	1	R. Ediger, R. Kovatch, and M. Rabstein, personal communication, (1974)
Total	6	

strains and all inbred animals, including strain 2 guinea pigs, were totally resistant at first. However, once the tumor became established in neonatal animals, of any inbred strain, the tumor would readily grow in another animal of the same strain (Laporte and Sillard, 1963).

K. Tumors of Nerve Tissue and Nerve Sheaths (Table XI)

Among reported tumors of nerve tissue only one was in the central nervous system and that was a teratoma of the pons (Lutz, 1910). The tumor was quite small (< 5 mm) and was comprised of nerve tissue, glandular epithelium, muscle, bone and cartilage. The classification of the neoplasm described by Bablet and Bloch (1934) is uncertain. It was a large tumor (45 × 32 × 10 mm) attached by a pedicle to the inner abdominal wall adjacent to the stomach and intestines. Microscopically it was a complex anaplastic tumor with neuroid and neuroglial

Table XI
Spontaneous Tumors of Nerve Tissue and Nerve Sheaths of the Guinea Pig

Tumors	Number of animals	Reference
Teratoma (pons)	1	Lutz, 1910
Glioma (neurilemmoma) (inner abdominal wall)	1	Bablet and Bloch, 1934
Neurilemmoma (mesentery)	2	Papanicolaou and Olcott, 1942
Total	4	

tissues with zones of epitheloid cells. The author believed it was a malignant glioma (neurilemmoma). Two tumors of the distal small intestine were classified as neurilemmomas (Papanicolaou and Olcott, 1942). Both affected guinea pigs were females about 6 years of age. Microscopically the tumors resembled leiomyomas but the neoplastic cells were smaller and had denser nuclear chromatin than smooth muscle cells and their palisade arrangement was similar to Verocay bodies. In one animal, the intestinal neurilemmoma was accompanied by multiple neurilemmomas of the peritoneum and mesentery. Transplantation of tumors from the latter host to five guinea pigs was unsuccessful.

L. Unclassified Tumors and Tumors of Uncertain Origin or Location (Table XII)

Two tumors in these categories were included in the report by Papanicolaou and Olcott (1942). The abdominal leiomyoma occurred in a 6-year-old female guinea pig that also had an intestinal neurilemmoma. Grossly, the leiomyoma was a firm, pale, small tumor adjacent to but completely detached from the pyloric end of the stomach. The authors were uncertain of the diagnosis of fibrosarcoma that occurred in another 6-year-old female guinea pig with a liposarcoma attached to the small intestine. The tumor occurred at the point of adhesion of the left lung to the chest wall. They classified the tumor as a fibrosarcoma but speculated it may have been a reaction to metastasis of the abdominal tumor. An abdominal adenocarcinoma of unknown origin (Heston and Deringer, 1952) occurred in a strain 13 male 16 months of age. Mosinger (1961) mentioned an osteochondrosarcoma in the region of the urinary bladder of a guinea pig. The tumor contained zones resembling angiosarcoma and reticulum cell sarcoma.

M. Summary of Spontaneous Neoplasms (Table XIII)

Even if one considers the qualifying statements made in the introduction such as age, strain, and necropsy protocol considerations, the fact that only 306 neoplasms were tabulated from the literature substantiates the general conclusion that neoplasia occurs rarely in guinea pigs. This conclusion may have to be altered with the development of more sophisticated studies that include detailed clinical and necropsy examinations.

Among the 306 neoplasms tabulated in Table XIII nearly 35% were pulmonary adenomas or adenocarcinomas. The resemblance of these lesions to pulmonary adenomatosis and the propensity of lung tissue in guinea pigs to undergo hyperplastic and adenomatous changes in response to various stimuli render these diagnoses uncertain. If the pulmonary tumors are included in the calculation, the ratio of epithelial to mesenchy-

Table XII
Spontaneous Tumors of the Guinea Pig: UnclassifiedTumors and Tumors of Uncertain Origin or Location

Tumor	Number of animals	References
Carcinoma (uncertain origen)		Gouyon, 1876[a]
Sarcoma	1	Roffo, 1925
Unclassified tumor	1	Caranica, 1955
Fibrosarcoma (inner chest wall)	1	Papanicolaou and Olcott, 1942
Leiomyoma (adjacent to stomach)	1	Papanicolaou and Olcott, 1942
Adenocarcinoma (abcominal cavity)	1	Heston and Deringer, 1952
Osteochondrosarcoma (pelvic cavity)	1	Mosinger, 1961
Total	7	

[a]Cited by Heim and Schwartz (1931).

Table XIII
Summary of Spontaneous Neoplasms of Guinea Pigs

System	Number of tumors	% of total
Skin and subcutis	47	15.4
Cardiovascular	13	4.3
Respiratory	105	34.3
Alimentary and peritoneum	11	3.6
Reproductive	46	15.0
Mammary glands	30	9.8
Urinary	6	2.0
Endocrine	10	3.3
Hemopoietic	22	7.2
Musculoskeletal	6	2.0
Nervous	4	1.3
Uncertain origin[a]	6	2.0
Total	306	

[a]One unclassified tumor listed in Table XII omitted.

mal neoplasms is 2.2:1; the omission of the pulmonary lesions results in a ratio of nearly 1. Nearly 33% of the 306 tumors were morphologically malignant but metastasizes were rare.

Definitive studies on the influence of heredity on tumor incidence in guinea pigs have not been done but interestingly 79 tumors (∿26%) were seen in random bred Hartley strain guinea pigs (McConnell and Ediger, 1968; R. Ediger, R. Kovatch, and M. Rabstein, personal communication, 1974). The importance of age on the prevalence of neoplasia was emphasized by the data of Rogers and Blumenthal (1960) in which all tumors were seen in animals greater than 3 years of age. Similarly, a tumor incidence rate of nearly 30% occurred in 34 aged retired breeders of the Hartley strain (R. Ediger, R. Kovatch, and M. Rabstein, personal communication, 1974).

The rarity of naturally occurring tumors and the difficulty with which tumors are induced with carcinogens limit the usefulness of the guinea pig in many aspects of experimental oncology.

III. EXPERIMENTALLY INDUCED TUMORS OF GUINEA PIGS

Useful reviews of investigations in this area prior to 1961 were published by Blumenthal and Rogers (1962, 1967) whereas more recent literature was cited by Toth (1970) and Argus (1971). I shall discuss this topic in general terms only and the reader may consult bibliographies of the aforementioned authors for further information.

Guinea pigs are susceptible to the cancerogenic activity of a variety of agents including physical and chemical irritants, hydrocarbons and related compounds, and hormones, particularly estrogens.

The biliary system of guinea pigs is exquisitely susceptible to hyperplastic or neoplastic stimuli. Benign and malignant neoplasms of the biliary tract were readily induced in guinea pigs by placement of foreign bodies (choleliths, pebbles, string sutures) in the gallbladder and by administration of chemical irritants ("Pityrol," lanolin, pitch pellets). Though only one spontaneous tumor of the biliary tract was reported (Rogers and Blumenthal, 1960) adenomatous hyperplasia of bile ducts was a frequent sequelae to hepatic pseudotuberculosis (Mosinger, 1961) and other less specific experimental manipulations (Isidor, 1961).

Until about a decade ago guinea pigs were considered resistant to chemical carcinogenesis but since 1962 numerous reports indicate guinea pigs are susceptible to many different chemical carcinogens including ethyl carbamate, polycylic hydrocarbons [7, 12-dimethylbenz (*a*) anthracene, 3-methylcholanthrene, and benzopyrene among others], nitrosamine-type alkylating agents (diethylnitrosamine, dimethylnitrosamine, methylnitrosourea), and aflatoxin (Argus, 1971). In some instances the guinea pig is at least as susceptible as the mouse to the carcinogenicity of 7,12-dimethylbenz(*a*)-anthrene (DMBA) (Toth, 1970) and more susceptible than the rat to the oncogenic action of diethylnitrosamine (Toth, 1970; Gosh *et al.,* 1970). Subcutaneous injection of various hydrocarbons, excluding DMBA, resulted in 596 tumors of which 565 were sarcomas and the remainder were of epithelial origin (Blumenthal and Rogers, 1967). Conversely, DMBA injected subcutaneously induced a variety of malignant tumors at the site of injection and in various distant organs; only mesenchymal tumors were seen at the site of injection, whereas epithelial neoplasms predominated at sites distant from injection (Toth, 1970). Other investigators believe guinea pigs to be more resistant to chemical carcinogenesis than rats or rabbits. This appears to be particularly valid insofar as topical application is concerned because epidermal tumors were very difficult to induce and the few that have been reported required a minimum of 2 years of application and large doses of carcinogen (Stenbeck, 1970).

Prolonged estrogen administration has induced benign tumors in the uterus of guinea pigs including fibromas, fibromyomas, and leiomyomas. Gonadectomy of either sex at various ages potentiated the oncogenic effect of prolonged administration of estrogenic hormones (Lipschütz, 1950).

IV. CONCLUSIONS

This review serves to illustrate that the guinea pig possesses the capacity to develop a diversity of "spontaneous" neoplasms. If one assumes a maximum longevity for this species of 6 years, then most tumors begin to appear about midlife. Despite a fairly high prevalence of embryonal placentomas of the ovary, this lesion evidently does not progress to choriocarcinoma. Moreover, the incidence of malignant tumors in this species appears to be lower than in some other species even in the few inbred strains which have been studied. It might be possible to inbreed for tumor susceptibility as in the case of some mice strains, but this evidently has not been attempted.

Some investigators believe that guinea pigs are peculiarly resistant to the development of tumors, and a few have even searched for a serum factor which might explain the low incidence of spontaneous tumors. On the other hand, this species appears to be as susceptible to the carcinogenic effects of some chemicals as other species. Susceptibility to intraspecies transplantation of tumors, however, seems to be in an inconclusive state. Some studies show no significant difference between this and other species, but in other reports there appears to be an inordinately low number of successful "takes."

In light of recent observations regarding tumor immunity, it might be fruitful to study the various competencies of the guinea pig immune system compared to other species. An initial avenue of approach might be a study of the effects of various immunosuppressive agents on the incidence of spontaneous tumors. Good and Finstand (1969) believe that many chemical carcinogens exert their effect through immunosuppression, and the various reports on chemically induced carcinogenesis in guinea pigs may be a consequence of such a mechanism.

ADDENDUM

A report by Kitchen *et al.* (1975), described an additional thirteen neoplasms of guinea pigs. Mammary gland tumors accounted for four neoplasms, to include an adenoma, two adenocarcinomas, and a malignant mixed tumor. Additionally there were two lipomas, one Schwannoma, a uterine fibroma, three trichoepitheliomas, an undifferentiated carcinoma, and a histiocytic lymphosarcoma.

REFERENCES

Anderson, C., and Lumbroso, U. (1933). Note sur une 'néoproduction' intramammaire constatée chez un cobaye d'expériences. *Arch. Inst. Pasteur Tunis* **21**, 504–509.

Anderson, W. A. D. (1966). "Pathology," 5th ed., p. 438. Mosby, St. Louis, Missouri.

Apolant, H. (1908). Referat über die Genese des Carcinoma. *Verh. Deut. Ges. Pathol.* **12**, 3–12.

Argus, M. F. (1971). Susceptibility of the guinea pig to chemical carcinogenesis. *Cancer Res.* **31**, 917–918.

Argus, M. F., and Hoch-ligeti, C. (1961). Induction of malignant tumors in the guinea pig by oral administration of diethylnitrosamine. *J. Nat. Cancer Inst.* **30**, 533–551.

Athias, M. (1937). Sarcome du coeur chez un cobaye aprés injection, dans le cerveau, de méthylcholantrene. *C. R. Soc. Biol.* **126**, 583–587.

Athias, M. (1944). Deux cas d'embryome de L'ovaire chez le cobaye. *Arch Patol.* **16**, 267.

Bablet, J., and Bloch, F. (1934). Sur un cas de tumeur maligne spontanée du cobaye. *Bull. Ass. Fr. Etude Cancer* **23**, 686–696.

Ball, V., and Pagnon, F. (1935). Sarcome à cellules rondes du rein chez un cobaye. *Bull. Soc. Sci. Vet. Med. Comp. Lyon* **38**, 40.

Bender, I. (1925). Sarcoma of the heart in a guinea pig. *J. Cancer Res.* 384–387.

Blumensaat, C., and Champy, C. (1928). Un cas de tumeur mammaire chez le cobaye, coincident avec la présence de nématodes. *Bull. Ass. Fr. Etude Cancer* **17**, 716–723.

Blumenthal, H. T., and Rogers, J. B. (1962). Studies of guinea pig tumors. II. The induction of malignant tumors in guinea pigs by methylcholanthrene. *Cancer Res.* **22**, 1155–1162.

Blumenthal, H. T., and Rogers, J. B. (1967). Spontaneous and induced tumors in the guinea pig with special reference to the factor of age. *Progr. Exp. Tumor Res.* **9**, 261–285.

Caranica, N. (1955). Pathologie comparée des Tumeurs chez les jeunes Animaux. Ph.D. Thesis Vet., National Vet School. Alfort, France.

Cintorino, M., and Luzi, P. (1970). Myocardial rhabdomyomas in the guinea pig. *Bietr. Pathol.* **142**, 407–409.

Congdon, C. C., and Lorenz, E. (1954). Leukemia in guinea pigs. *Amer. J. Pathol.* **30**, 337–351.

Cowdry, E. V., and Marsh, H. (1927). The comparative pathology of South African jagziekte and Montana progressive pneumonia in sheep. *J. Exp. Med.* **45**, 571–585.

Dickson, E. C. (1915). Sarcoma occurring in guinea pig. *Proc. Soc. Exp. Biol. Med.* **13**, 26–27.

Ediger, R., and Rabstein, M. (1968). Spontaneous leukemia in a Hartley strain guinea pig. *J. Amer. Vet. Med. Ass.* **153**, 954–956.

Ediger, R., Dill, G. S., Jr., and Kovatch, R. M. (1971). Trichofolliculoma of the guinea pig. *J. Nat. Cancer Inst.* **46**, 517–23.

Engelbreth-Holm, J. (1942). "Spontaneous and Experimental Leukaemia in Animals," pp. 40–52. Oliver & Boyd, Edinburgh.

Fischer, G., and Kantor, L. (1919). Contribución al estudio del parentesco entre especies animales por métodos biólogicos. *Rev. Inst. Bacteriol. Buenos Aires,* **2**, 303–308.

Fischer, W. (1956). Adenomatose und Krebsbildung bei chronischen Pneumonie des Meerschweinchens. *Entral. Zbl. Pathol.* **94**, 555–562 (cited by Lombard, 1960).

Franks, L. M., and Chesterman, F. C. (1962). The pathology of tumors and other lesions of the guinea pig lung. *Brit. J. Cancer* **16**, 696–700.

Giordano, A. (1939). Un caso di teratoma spontaneo dell'ovaia in una cavia gravida. *Sperimentale* [5] **93**, 407–421.

Goldberg, S. A. (1920). The occurrence of epithelial tumors in the domesticated animals. *J. Amer. Vet. Med. Ass.* **58**, 47–63.

Good, R. A., and Finstand, J. (1969). Essential relationship between the lymphoid system, immunity and malignancy. *Nat. Cancer Inst., Monogr.* **31**, 41–58.

Gosh, H. H., Arcos, J. C., and Argus, M. F. (1970). On the unimpairable resistance of the guinea pig to dietary amino azo dye hepatocarcinogenesis. *Z. Krebsforsch.* **73**, 215–217.

Grumbach, A. (1926). Tumeurs epithdiales du pneumon chez le cobaye. á la suite d'injection d'un corynebacille diphthéroide. *Bull. Ass. Fr. Etude Cancer* **15**, 213–37.

Guérin, M., and Guérin, P. (1925). Contribution à l'étude de l'hérédité du cancer, basée sur l'observation d'un splénome malin chez le cobaye. *Neoplasmes* **4**, 276–286.

Haagensen, C. D., and Krehbiel, L. F. (1936). Liposarcoma produced by 1:2 benzpyrene. *Amer. J. Cancer* **27**, 474–484.

Haranghy, L., Gyorgyay, F., Antalffy, A., and Merie, G. (1954). Meerschweinchentumoren. *Acta Morphol.* **4**, 301–307 (cited by Rogers and Blumenthal, 1960).

Heim, F., and Schwartz, P. (1931). Die Spontantumoren der Meerschweinchen. *In* "Anatomie und Pathologie der Spontanerkrankugen der kleinen Laboratoriumstiere" (R. Jaff, ed.), pp. 734–739. Springer-Verglag, Berlin and New York (cited by Lipschütz, 1941).

Herbut, P. A., Kraemer, W. H., and Pillemer, L. (1958). The effects of components of guinea pig serum on lymphosarcoma $6C_3$HED in C_3H mice. *Blood* **13**, 733–739.

Herbut, P. A., Kraemer, W. H., McKeon, F. A., and Taylor, R. C. (1961). The effect of serums from tumor susceptible and nonsusceptible guinea pigs on lymphosarcoma $6C_3$HED in C_3H mice. *Amer. J. Pathol.* **38**, 387–391.

Heston, W. E., and Deringer, M. K. (1952). Introduction of pulmonary tumors in guinea pigs by intravenous injection of methylcholanthrene and dibenzanthracene. *J. Nat. Cancer Inst.* **13**, 705–718.

Hueper, W. C. (1940' Rhabdomyomatosis of the heart in a guinea pig. *Amer. J. Pathol.* **17**, 121–125.

Isidor, P. (1961). A propos des tumeurs spontanées des petits rangeurs: Les tumeurs du foic chez le cobaye adulte. *Bull. Ass. Fr. Etude Cancer* **48**, 46–48.

Jain, S. K., Singh, D. K., and Rao, U. R. K. (1970). Granulosa cell tumour in a guinea pig. *Indian Vet. J.* **47**, 563–564.

Jones, F. S. (1916). A transplantable carcinoma in the guinea pig. *J. Exp. Med.* **23**, 211–218.

Katase, E. (1912). Demonstration verschiedener Geschwülste bei Tieren. *Verh. Jap. Pathol. Ges.* **2**, 89 (cited by Leader, 1937).

Kauffmann, S. L., and Kidd, J. G. (1956). Effects of guinea pig serum on $6C_3$HED and $AKRL_1$ lymphoma cells implanted in various hosts. *Proc. Soc. Exp. Biol. Med.* **91**, 164–168.

Kidd, J. G. (1953). Regression of transplanted lymphomas *in vivo* by means of normal guinea pig serum. I. Course of transplanted cancer of various kinds in mice given guinea pig serum, horse serum or rabbit serum. II. Studies on the nature of the active serum constituent; histological mechanism of regression; tests for effects of guinea pig serum on lymphoma cells *in vitro*. Discussion. *J. Exp. Med.* **98**, 565–606.

Kitchen, D. N., Carlton, W. W., and Bickford A. A. A report of 14 spontaneous tumors of the guinea pig. (1975). *Lab. Anim. Sci.* **25**, 92–102.

Kleinkuhner, (1916). Les tumeurs spontanées du cobaye. Thesis Vet. University of Hanover, Germany (cited by Lombard, 1960).

Kröning, F., and Wepler, W. (1938). Ein histologisch beachtenswerter Tumor des Meerschweinchens. *Z. Krebsforsch.* **48**, 246–251.

Laporte, R., and Sillard, R. (1963). Immunological study of spontaneous osteochrodrosarcoma in the guinea pig. *Ann Inst. Pasteur, Paris* **105**, 838–848.

Laporte, R., Sillard, R., and Vallee, A. (1962). Spontaneous transmissible tumor in a guinea pig. *Ann. Inst. Pasteur, Paris* **103**, 299–302.

Leader, S. A. (1937). Osteogenic sarcoma of femur in guinea pig. *Amer. J. Cancer* **29**, 546–550.

Lechner, M. (1958). Spontantumoren bei Saügetieren Ein Beitrag zur vergleichenden Geschwulstforschung. Thesis Doct. Vet., University of Munich, (cited by Mosinger, 1961).

Lipschütz, A. (1941). Spontaneous fibromyoma in a female guinea pig. *Arch. Pathol.* **31**, 702–705.

Lipschütz, A. (1950). "Steroid Hormones and Tumors." Williams & Wilkins, Baltimore, Maryland.

Loeb, L. (1932). The parthenogenetic development of eggs in the ovary of the guinea pig. *Anat. Rec.* **51**, 373–408.

Lombard, C. H . (1960). La cancero-resistance du cobaye. *Bull. Ass. Fr. Etude Cancer* **48**, 217–235.

Lorenz, E., Jacobson, L. O., Heston, W. E., Shimkin, M., Eschenbrenner, M. K., Donger, J., and Schweistal, R. (1954). *In* "Biological Effects of External X and Gamma Irradiation" (R. E. Zirkle, ed.), pp. 24–148. McGraw-Hill, New York.

Lubarsch, O. (1919). Über spontane Impfsarkome bei Meerschweinchen. *Z. Krebsforsch.* **16**, 315–317 (cited by Leader, 1937).

Lutz, B. (1910). Ein Teratom am Kleinhirnbrückenwinkel beim Meerschweinchen. *Arb. Neurol. Inst. Univ. Wien.* **18**, 111–117.

McConnell, R. F., and Ediger, R. D. (1968). Benign mesenchymoma of the heart in the guinea pig. *Pathol. Vet.* **5**, 97–101.

Miguenz, C. (1918). Sarcoma espontaneo transplantable en el cobaye. *Rev. Inst. Bacteriol. Dep. Nac. Hig. (Argent.)* **1**, 147–154.

Migunow, B. I. (1931). Primäre spontane Neubildugen bei Versuchstieren. *Zentralbl. Allg. Pathol. Pathol. Anat.* **51**, 417–420.

Miller, E. C., Miller, J. A., and Enomoto, M. (1964). The comparative carcinogenicities of 2-acetylaminofluorene and its *n*-hydroxy metabolite in mice, hamsters and guinea pigs. *Cancer Res.* **24**, 2018–2026.

Montroni, L. (1930). Sopra algure particolarita istophathologische e istogenetiche di un adenocistcarcinoma ovarico della cavia. *Nuova Vet.* **8**, 235–239 (cited by Leader, 1937).

Mosinger, M. (1961). Sur la canceroréistance du cobaye. Premiere partie. Les spontanées du cobaye. *Bull. Ass. Fr. Etud. Cancer* **48**, 217–235.

Murray, J. A. (1916). A transplantable sarcoma of the guinea pig. *J. Pathol. Bacteriol.* **20**, 260–268.

Nadel, D. M. (1957). Transplantation of leukemia from inbred to non inbred guinea pigs. *J. Nat. Cancer Inst.* **19**, 351–359.

Nejedly, K., and Straub, R. (1957). Spontaneous spindle cell sarcoma in guinea pigs. *Neoplasma Brastisl.* **4**, 402–404.

Norris, R. F. (1947). Pulmonary adenomatosis resembling jagziekte in the guinea pig. *Arch. Pathol.* **43**, 553–558.

Olcott, C., and Papanicolaou, C. N. (1943). Studies of spontaneous tumors in guinea pigs. III. A chondrosarcoma of the iliac bone with metastasis to mammary region. *Cancer Res.* **3**, 321–325.

Papanicolaou, G. N., and Olcott, C. T. (1940). Studies of spontaneous tumors in guinea pigs. I. A fibromyoma of the stomach with adenoma (focal hyperplasia) of the right adrenal. *Amer. J. Cancer* **40**, 310–320.

Papanicolaou, G. N., and Olcott, C. T. (1942). Studies of spontaneous tumors in guinea pigs. II. Tumors of the stomach and intestine. *Arch. Pathol.* **34**, 218–228.

Roffo, A. H. (1925). Sobre un sarcoma transplantable en un cobaye. *Bol. Inst. Med. Exp. Estud. Trat. Cancer, Buenos Aires* **1**, 546–561.

Rogers, J. B., and Blumenthal, H. T. (1960): Studies on guinea pig tumors. I. Report on fourteen spontaneous guinea pig tumors, with a review of the literature. *Cancer Res.* **20**, 191–197.

Rooney, J. R. (1961). Rhabdomyomatosis in the heart of the guinea pig. *Cornell Vet.* **51**, 388–394.

Roskin, G. (1930). Eine bösartige Geschwulst beim Meerschweinchen zur vergleichenden Histologie und Cytologie der normalen und pathologischen Nebenniere. *Virchows Arch. Pathol. Anat. Physiol.* **277**, 466–488.

Shimkin, M. B., and Mider, G. B. (1940). Induction of tumors in guinea pigs with subcutaneously injected methylcholanthrene. *J. Nat. Cancer Inst.* **1**, 707–725.

Snijders, E. P. (1926). Over een overentbare leukaemie bij cavia's. *Ned. Tijdschr. Geneesk.* **70**, 1256–1261.

Snijders, E. P. (1927). Eenige resultaten van proefnemingen mit een overentbare cavia leukose. *Handel. Ned. Natuur-Geneesk. Congr.* **21**, 160–164.

Spiegel, A. (1940). Ueber das Auftreten von Geschwülsten der Nebennierenrinde mit vermännlichender Wirkung bei früh kastrierten Meerschweinchenmännchen. *Virchows Arch. Pathol. Anat. Physiol.* **305**, 366.

Spronck, C. H. H. (1907). Over adenoma distruens bij cavia cobaya: Eei bijdrage tot de erfelijkheid van kanker. *Ned. Tijdschr. Geneesk.* **1**, 1033–1040 (cited by Mosinger, 1961).

Stenbeck, F. (1970). Guinea pigs and carcinogens. *Acta Pathol. Microbiol. Scand., Sect. A* **78**, 192–204.

Sternberg, C. (1903). Adenomähnliche bildungen in der meerschweinchenlunge. *Verh. Deut. Pathol. Ges.* **6**, 134–136.

Sternberg, C. (1913). Ein adenokarzinom der mamma bei einem meerschweinchen. *Verh. Deut. Pathol. Ges.* **16**, 362–365.

Syverton, J. T. (1957). Immunology and cancer. *Ann. N. Y. Acad. Sci.* **69**, 525–856.

Tio Tjwan Gie. (1927). Over leukaemie bij dieren en over een overentbare cavialeukose. Inaugural Dissertation, Amsterdam.

Todd, J. E., and Kidd, J. G. (1954). Tests of isoantibodies active in conjunction with guinea pig serum against $6C_3$HED lymphoma cells. *Proc. Soc. Exp. Biol. Med.* **86**, 865–868.

Toth, B. (1970). Susceptibility of guinea pigs to chemical carcinogens: 7, 12-Dimethylbenz(*a*)anthrene and urethan. *Cancer Res.* **30**, 2583–2589.

Twort, C. C., and Twort, J. M. (1932). Sarcoma and carcinoma in a guinea pig. *J. Pathol. Bacteriol.* **35**, 976.

Vink, H. H. (1969). Rhabdomyomatosis (nodular glycogenic infiltration) of the heart in guinea pigs. *J. Pathol.* **97**, 331–334.

Vink, H. H. (1970). Ovarian teratomas in guinea pigs. *J. Pathol.* **102**, 180–182.

Warren, S., and Gates, O. (1941). Spontaneous and induced tumors of the guinea pig. *Cancer Res.* **1**, 65–68.

Wildi, E. (1949). Neoplasioes pluritissulaires dan les ovaries de un cobaye. *Rev. Can. Biol.* **462** (cited by Mosinger, 1961).

Willis, R. A. (1962). Ovarian teratomas in guinea pigs. *J. Pathol. Bacteriol.* **84**, 237–238.

Wood, F. C. A. (1916). A sarcoma in a guinea pig. *Proc. N. Y. Pathol. Soc.* **16**, 1–6.

Zarrin, Kh. (1974). Thyroid carcinoma of a guinea pig: A case report. *Lab. Anim.* **8**, 145–148.

Chapter 16

Miscellaneous Disease Conditions of Guinea Pigs

Joseph E. Wagner

I. INTRODUCTION

This chapter contains statements about a number of conditions and disease entities of guinea pigs which I and others have observed but which have been poorly described in the literature. Their mere mention in this chapter may be of some use to investigators and animal care personnel seeing these conditions in the future. If through listing these conditions I am compared to or criticized by others who subsequently study and better describe them, my goal will have been reached.

II. RESPIRATORY SYSTEM

A. Pulmonary Perivascular Lymphoid Nodules

Perivascular lymphoid nodules in the lungs of guinea pigs are a unique histological curiosity deserving further study. The nodules occur around smaller branches of the pulmonary arteries and veins. They have been reported as occurring in from 14 to 85% of guinea pigs of both sexes and all ages from 7 strains including one germfree animal (Thompson *et al.*, 1962). The nodules appear to enlarge with age and may be visible grossly as pinpoint, subpleural foci. What do they signify? Why are they there? Are they normal tissue? Do they occur in germfree animals? Are they a response to a chronic, low level infection? These are some of the questions to be answered by further study of this phenomenon. Meanwhile investigators examining guinea pig lungs should be aware of their existence.

B. Bony Spicules in Guinea Pig Lung

Kaufmann (1970) has reported observing bony spicules in the interstitium of aleveolar septa of the lungs of guinea pigs fed commercial diets. He suggested they were the result of metaplasia; however, the stimulus causing formation of bony spicules has not been determined.

III. DIGESTIVE SYSTEM

A. Malocclusion

Olson (1971) reported a case of malocclusion in a guinea pig. We have seen dozens of cases of malocclusion primarily of the premolar and anterior molar teeth. Typically malocclusion of both the maxillary and mandibular cheek teeth is more severe in the anterior-most teeth. Maxillary teeth overgrow laterally into the labial mucosa, while mandibular teeth overgrow to the lingual side. Guinea pigs, among other species of rodents, have open-rooted cheek teeth which grow continuously throughout life. The etiology of malocclusion has not been well studied in guinea pigs. Dietary and genetic factors would be worthy of further investigation. It is my impression that the condition is more common in animals receiving a poor diet, particularly pet animals. We have wondered if it could be a sequela of prolonged, subclinical vitamin C deficiency or due to an imbalance of minerals in the diet. Our observation that malocclusion is of relatively high incidence in inbred strain 13 guinea pigs suggests a genetic role.

Malocclusion of the lower premolars and anterior molars is frequently misdiagnosed, as it is difficult to see the molar teeth in a live guinea pig because of the looseness of the abundant buccal skin. Many times the condition is not diagnosed until there is secondary malocclusion of the incisors. Typically guinea pigs with cheek tooth malocclusion will have chronic weight loss. They may or may not show "slobbers." They "slobber" either because there is increased salivation or possibly they cannot swallow all saliva due to chronic irritation of the buccal mucosa. The mandibular premolars and anterior molars in some cases will impinge upon and even cross over the tongue possibly restricting its function. Typically, unattended animals slowly starve to death. We have had no experience in trying to correct molar malocclusion with dental technology and/or improved diet. Cutting the teeth to a normal level could be expected to temporarily alleviate the condition.

B. Gastric Ulcers

Gastric ulcers are fairly common. We recorded 15 cases from

1968 through 1973. Most were secondary to other disease processes, e.g., ketosis. One was a perforating ulcer. *Citrobacter* spp. was recovered from another.

C. Antibiotic "Toxicity"

Death following antibiotic administration is very common in guinea pigs. Contrary to early reports of toxicity, it is now believed to be due to an alterated intestinal bacterial flora from primarily gram-positive to primarily gram-negative followed by an enterocolitis and bacteremia. Hamre *et al.* (1943) first reported that penicillin was "toxic" to guinea pigs. Further reports have documented the lethality of penicillin to guinea pigs (Ambrus *et al.*, 1952; Boyd and Lloyd, 1965; Cormia *et al.*, 1947; DeSomer *et al.*, 1955; Eyssen *et al.*, 1957; Farrar and Kent, 1965; Schneierson and Perlman, 1956). Erythromycin (Eyssen *et al.*, 1957; Kaipainen and Faine, 1954), lincomycin (Gray *et al.*, 1964; Small, 1968), chlortetracycline (Ambrus *et al.*, 1952; DeSomer *et al.*, 1955; Eyssen *et al.*, 1957; Heilman, 1948), oxytetracycline (Carrere and Roux, 1951; Eyssen *et al.*, 1957; Small, 1968), streptomycin (Eyssen *et al.*, 1957), and bacitracin (DeSomer *et al.*, 1955; Eyssen *et al.*, 1957; Farrar *et al.*, 1966) are among antibiotics reported "toxic" for the guinea pig.

Eyssen *et al.* (1957) found that chloramphenicol orally at 60 mg daily was not toxic to guinea pigs. Formal *et al.* (1963) and Newton *et al.* (1964) found that penicillin was not toxic for germfree guinea pigs.

Based on literature review and personal experience it is apparent that guinea pigs should be treated with antibiotics only when one is reasonably sure the benefits will outweigh the risk. It also appears that broad-spectrum antibiotics would be preferred over those that may suppress certain intestinal flora and not others.

D. Cecitis

I have observed several hundred cases of an acute, necrotic cecitis or typhlocolitis in guinea pigs of all ages. The disease was generally fatal. Animals appeared healthy one day and are found dead the next. In our experience, it was most frequently detected in inbred strain 13 animals. The disease is reminiscent of the acute enterotoxemia syndrome caused by *Clostridia perfringens,* type E, reported by Madden *et al.* (1970) to occur in guinea pigs recently removed from germfree isolators. However, we have been able to culture clostridia organisms from only a few cases. Also, when detected by culture *C. perfringens* was usually present in small numbers.

Histological examination of affected cases has revealed absence of cecal absorbing epithelium with varying degress of necrosis of underlying mucosa. Direct smear examinations of affected mucosa revealed numerous organismal forms, many of which were spirochetes currently unclassified. We have found a similar syndrome in guinea pigs dying unexpectedly while undergoing a variety of experimental manipulations, particularly following corticosteroid injections, antibiotic injections, and starvation. Additionally guinea pigs in advanced pregnancy with and without ketosis will frequently have lesions of acute necrotic cecitis. This entire disease phenomenon of guinea pigs deserves addition study, particularly the role of anaerobic and other enteric flora in the etiology.

E. Impaction of Cecum

We have observed several guinea pigs at necropsy with obstruction of the cecal–colic orifice by wood shavings, a hair ball, or what appeared to be hard, inspissated fecal material.

F. Prolapsed Rectum and Vagina

Prolapsed rectum may occur concomitant with acute enteritis or around the time of parturition. Similarly, prolapsed vagina occasionally is associated with parturition.

G. Focal Coagulative Necrosis of the Liver

At necropsy it is not uncommon to see focal pale areas on the surface of the liver. They are not raised or depressed. They are sharply delineated and of irregular shape. In some cases the entire caudate lobe is involved. Upon incision the pale lesion usually extends deep into affected lobes. Microscopically the lesion is one of coagulative necrosis. We have not been able to ascertain the etiology of the condition, although we would have to suspect hepatic venous thrombosis as a likely cause. Perhaps endotoxins, diet and hyperlipemia, ketosis, the Shwartzman reaction, shock, and hemodynamic modifications are involved (Latour *et al.*, 1974a,b).

IV. UROGENITAL SYSTEM

A. Cystic Ovaries

Schoenbaum and Kopfer (1969) suggested that estrogenic substances in moldy hay were responsible for an unusually high incidence of cystic ovaries among breeding females in their colony. While I have seen several cases of cystic ovaries in guinea pigs, no etiological factors could be established.

B. Obstruction of the Urethra and Seminal Vesiculitis

I have seen at least 6 cases in which obstruction of the urethra with proteinaceous concretions was a contributing cause of death. The cases were all aged males. In several cases the urethral plug protruded from the external urethral orifice prior to necropsy. At necropsy the urinary bladder was distended, and urine could not be expressed by manual pressure in all cases. Microscopically the urethral plugs contained sperm and a highly eosinophilic hyaline matrix probably of seminal vesicular origin. There was usually minimal inflammatory reaction in surrounding urethral mucosa. These animals usually had *in vivo* coagulation of fluids in the seminal vesicles. In several cases coliforms or *Pseudomonas aeruginosa* were recovered from suppurative seminal vesicles.

C. Prepuce Infections

Male guinea pigs occasionally develop prepucial infections due to lodgment of foreign materials in the prepucial folds. Breeding males on bedding may be affected when pieces of bedding adhere to the moist prepuce following copulation and are drawn into the prepucial fornix where it may cause a foreign body reaction. Long-standing infections may cause adhesions and infertility.

D. Dystocia–Stillbirths–Ketosis

Guinea pigs as a species appear predisposed to high perinatal mortality. Infant perinatal mortality is the factor that many breeders mention as their greatest obstacle to better production. It is not clear whether dystocias and subsequent death of the sow are generally due to subclinical ketosis or not. Excluding cases of dystocia related to large fetuses (over 100 gm) generally observed when there are but one or two fetuses and those associated with breeding older sows, it is my impression that dystocias and stillbirths are a common sequela of subclinical ketosis. No doubt there are many interrelated reproductive physiological factors.

E. Chronic Interstitial Nephritis

Chronic interstitial nephritis is a commonly observed lesion of aged guinea pigs. I have been impressed with the high percent of aged pet guinea pigs that die of a wasting disease which we have ascribed to chronic renal disease. The lesion is more or less an incidental finding in research guinea pigs; however, research guinea pigs of my experience are rarely allowed to live a full life span as may be the case with pet guinea pigs.

Nephrosclerosis with increased blood pressure, resembling that in hypertensive human beings, has been described in Abyssinian and Hartley guinea pigs (Takeda and Grollman, 1970). The lesions were not inhibited by cyclophosphamide suggesting they were not autoimmune in origin. Steblay and Rudofsky (1971) reported on their studies of IgG and complement in glomerular lesions and other renal changes of aged guinea pigs.

V. MUSCULOSKELETAL SYSTEM

A. Diaphragmatic Hernia

The membranous diaphragm of the guinea pig appears very thin when viewed grossly. We have seen several cases wherein the stomach had totally or in part prolapsed into the thoracic cavity through a defect in the membranous diaphragm near the esophageal hiatus. It could not be determined for sure whether the condition was of congenital origin or acquired. Because they were breeder animals and had a history of either jumping or falling from cages 1 to 6 feet above the floor, we believed the condition was acquired.

B. Trauma

In our experience the most commonly encountered condition of traumatic origin is rear leg injury, generally of younger guinea pigs, usually due to improper wire flooring. A floor with rectangular openings 0.5 × 1.5 inches is preferred to a 2 mesh (0.5 inch) floor with square openings because the former greatly reduces the likelihood of leg injuries.

We have seen several cases of posterior paralysis due to broken backs or, in some instances, without visible skeletal lesions but with hemorrhage into the spinal cord, suggesting a "strained" back. Most cases have a history of fighting or falling from a cage.

A commonly observed sequella of bleeding via heart puncture in laboratory guinea pigs is death due to cardiac tamponade, or filling of the pericardial cavity with extravasated blood. Similarly blood can be found in the lungs, mediastinum, and pleural cavity following cardiac puncture. Based upon our observations of dozens of cases, guinea pigs that are latent carriers of *Diplococcus pneumoniae* will frequently die of a fibrinopurulent peritonitis, pericarditis, pleuritis, or meningitis following the injection of irritating substances into or the removal of fluids from body cavities.

C. Myopathy

On several occasions we have observed a subclinical myopathy that is rather generalized in skeletal muscles but particularly involves the larger muscle masses of the rear leg. The most commonly observed myopathy is accompanied by little if any inflammatory reaction and is characterized by generalized muscle degeneration of varied degree with swelling, loss of cross striations, fragmentation of fibers, and vacuolation. Unfortunately this is a lesion that in spite of the apparent frequency of its occurrence has not been well studied in the guinea pig. Although we have seen myopathies in dozens of guinea pigs from different experimental regimes, we are unable to suggest a common etiology. Others have similarily reported on guinea pig myopathies without establishing etiological associations (Webb, 1970; Saunders, 1958).

VI. SKIN AND SPECIAL SENSES SYSTEM

A. Alopecia

Alopecia develops to a degree in all guinea pigs in late pregnancy. The condition appears to be due to reduced anabolism of maternal skin associated with fetal growth. Older guinea pigs subjected to frequent pregnancy in an intensive breeding program (utilizing postpartum mating) will have more alopecia, particularly if pregnant with a large litter, than animals bred less intensively. Nutritional and genetic factors probably affect the degree of alopecia.

Around the time of weaning thinning of hair is common and seems to be associated with a period of transition in which more coarse guard hairs of adult fur are beginning to appear and "baby fur" is being lost.

B. Barbering

Barbering or hair biting is characterized by alopecia, usually in one or several subordinate animals in a pen. In some cases it can be distinguished by the irregular stepwise manner in which the hair has been bitten off. Juvenile animals in a large pen may be barbered excessively by adult animals. Many times one can determine whether an animal has barbered itself or been barbered by a cage mate by the pattern of the alopecia. Animals that barber themselves cannot reach the head, neck, and anterior shoulders with their mouth; therefore, these areas will be fully haired if the animal is self-barbered. Although hay and supplemental green vegetables are not customarily given laboratory guinea pigs in the United States, Paterson (1972) stated that long hay fed as a supplement prevents barbering and consumption of bedding.

C. Ear Chewing and Skin Lesions from Fighting

Ear chewing is believed to be a vice associated with excessive aggressiveness of one or more individuals in a cage or primary enclosure. Generally either no animals or most animals in a cage have affected ears. In breeding units ear chewing can usually be traced to overaggressiveness on the part of the male. Ear chewing interferes with identification of guinea pigs by ear tag or ear notch. Bite marks will resemble notches thus introducing confusion into an identification scheme. Animals with an ear chewing tendency also chew on ear tags so that numbers imprinted in soft metals or plastics are obliterated. Also ear tags may be pulled out or damaged so they fall out.

Dermatitis, bite wounds, scratches, and alopecia are also associated with excessive aggressiveness and fighting. Again a single animal can frequently be identified as responsible for most fighting. Elimination of that individual will frequently reduce or eliminate the problem. The maturity of animals constituting a newly formed cage group or harem is a determining factor in the predisposition of guinea pigs to fighting. Animals that are fully mature when placed together engage in much more fighting than animals grouped as adolescents. Retired breeders, particularly males, fight excessively when caged together following removal from breeding harems. Because of a tendency to be overly aggressive toward cage mates, it is recommended that retired breeder males be housed individually.

D. Circumanal Sebaceous Accumulations

Excessive accumulation of sebaceous secretions occurs in the folds of the circumanal and genital region in adult male guinea pigs. These folds must be cleaned periodically in older male guinea pigs to preclude infections and unpleasant odors. It is my impression that isolated and relatively old males are more susceptible to this condition than active young breeding males.

E. Hyperkeratosis of Food Pads

We have observed several cases of marked hyperkeratosis of the foot pad epithelium in guinea pigs. In some cases the horny growths approached 2 cm in length. All cases were in aged animals confined to laboratory cages. The etiology was not studied.

F. Cataracts

Cataracts are occasionally seen in young and adult guinea pigs. We have seen it in guinea pigs receiving what appears to be a balanced commercial diet. However, Reid and von Sallmann (1960) reported that at least 0.1% L-tryptophan in the diet was required to prevent cataracts.

G. Conjunctivitis

Guinea pigs are commonly presented with conjunctivitis. We have cultured coliforms, *Streptococcus zooepidemicus*, β-hemolytic *Streptococcus* spp., q-hemolytic *Streptococcus* spp., *Micrococcus* spp., *Staphylococcus aureus*, *Pasteurella multocida*, and *Proteus* spp. We have not done studies to determine which are primary pathogens and which may be secondary invaders from the environment. Chlamydial infections should also be viewed as a cause of conjunctivitis (Watson *et al.*, 1973; Murray *et al.*, 1973; Murray, 1964) as well as general systemic infections in newborn guinea pigs (Storz, 1964). Should we not also be looking for genital infections since these agents are such common inhabitants of the genital tracts of man and other animals? Similarly they cause abortions in man and animals (Storz and McKercher, 1962; Roberts *et al.*, 1967).

VII. CARDIOVASCULAR AND HEMATOPOIETIC SYSTEMS

Although not clearly a neoplasm, rhabdomyomatosis or nodular glycogenic infiltration of the heart has been covered in Chapter 15 of this treatise.

VIII. ENDOCRINE SYSTEM

A. Diabetes Mellitus

Munger and Lang (1973) reported on acute spontaneous diabetes mellitus characterized by hyperglycemia, glycosuria, elevated glucose tolerance tests, and plasma triglycerides in Abyssinian guinea pigs. It resembled human juvenile diabetes mellitus in that there was substantial degranulation of B-cells. The disease was contagious, i.e., passed from animal to animal by direct association.

B. Fatty Ingrowth of Pancreas

Fatty deposits in the pancreas increase markedly with age, as does the proportion of islet tissue. The proportions of exocrine pancreas appears to decrease with age when studied histologically. Investigators should be aware of these age-related histological changes when designing experiments.

IX. GENERAL

A. Amyloidosis

Amyloidosis of multiple organs, particularly the kidney, liver, spleen, and adrenal glands, is rather commonly found in guinea pigs indicating their relative tendency to form amyloid. We have seen generalized amyloidosis in guinea pigs with chronic pododermatitis and osteoarthritis caused by *S. aureus* (Taylor *et al.*, 1971).

B. Congenital Abnormalities

Congenital abnormalities in the guinea pig have been reported infrequently. Gupta (1972) reported a dermoid on the sclera of the eye and Brunschwig (1928) reported one from the cornea. Kaplun *et al.* (1972) reported a case of cojoined twins and cited a literature reference for another. Bland (1970) reported congenital abnormalities of the guinea pig uterus. I have seen a case of starvation from congenital mandibular agnathia in a 4-day-old strain 13 guinea pig.

C. Starvation and Water Deprivation

Starvation and water deprivation are commonly defined as occurring in an absence of feed and water. There is generally no excuse for deaths from these causes; however, animals may die from starvation and water deprivation when feeders appear full and water seems to be available. Some circumstances under which this may occur are listed below:

1. Water is provided via a device the animal is not familiar with or does not know how to operate. Guinea pigs reared on water provided in crocks may not learn to drink from a sipper tube or automatic watering device and die from water deprivation. Guinea pigs are notoriously naive in this regard.
2. Water devices may be placed so high or in such a location in the cage as to be inaccessible, particularly for smaller weanlings.
3. Water may be unpotable due to impurities or odors either in the container or the water itself.

4. Automatic watering valves become inoperable due to plugging with foreign objects or air locks. Also, nonfunctioning float valves will result in water deprivation. Similarly air locks in curved sipper tubes or plugged sipper tubes can cause water deprivation.

5. Territorialism on the part of dominant individuals may result in them successfully prohibiting less dominant animals from drinking or eating. One can prevent this by placing water and feed sources at opposite ends of the cage or pen. The latter arrangement also reduces contamination of watering containers and devices with food stuffs.

D. Miscellaneous

Although we have seen a variety of other disease processes or abnormalities in guinea pigs, either we have not had sufficient experience with them to comment further or they are of little significance. They include: medial mineralization of the aorta, visceral torsion, adrenal cortical degeneration and hemorrhage (usually secondary to other primary disease conditions), pancreatitis, chronic thyroiditis, anemia, fractures of many bones, and multiple iatrogenic abnormalities. The paucity of reports of guinea pig disease conditions of the kinds reported in this chapter exemplifies the need for further study and reporting of these conditions in this important research species.

ACKNOWLEDGMENT

This work supported in part by NIH Research Grant RR-00471 from the Division of Research Resources.

REFERENCES

Ambrus, C. M., Sideri, C. N., Johnson, G. C., and Harrison, J. W. E. (1952). Toxicity of penicillin and aureomycin in guinea pigs. *Antibiot. Chemother. (Washington, D.C.)* **2**, 521–527.

Bland, K. P. (1970). Congenital abnormalities of the uterus and their bearing on ovarian function (with three case reports on guinea pigs). *Vet. Rec.* **86**, 44–45.

Boyd, E. M., and Lloyd, G. R. (1965). Miminal oral doses of benzylpenicillin producing signs of toxicity in albino rats. *Arch. Int. Pharmacodyn. Ther.* **156**, 172–179.

Brunschwig, A. (1928). Dermoid of the cornea in the guinea pig. *Amer. J. Pathol.* **4**, 371–374.

Carrere, L., and Roux, J. (1951). Action de la terramycine sur la flore intestinale aérobic du cobaye et du chat. *Ann. Inst. Pasteur, Paris,* **81**, 352–355.

Cormia, F. E., Lewis, G. M., and Hopper, M. E. (1947). Toxicity of penicillin for the guinea pig. *J. Invest. Dermatol.* **9**, 261–267.

DeSomer, P., Van de Voorde, H., Eyssen, H., and Van Dijck, P. (1955). A study on penicillin toxicity in guinea pigs. *Antibiot. Chemother. (Washington, D.C.)* **5**, 463–469.

Eyssen, H., DeSomer, P., and Van Dijck, P. (1957). Further studies on antibiotic toxicity in guinea pigs. *Antibiot. Chemother. (Washington, D.C.)* **7**, 55–64.

Farrar, W. E., Jr., and Kent, T. H. (1965). Enteritis and coliform bacteremia in guinea pigs given penicillin. *Amer. J. Pathol.* **47**, 629–642.

Farrar, W. E., Jr., and Kent, T. H., and Elliot, V. B. (166). Lethal gram negative bacterial superinfection in guinea pigs given bacitracin. *J. Bacteriol.* **92**, 496–501.

Formal, S. B., Abrams, G. D., Schneider, H., and Laundy, R. (1963). Penicillin in germ-free guinea pigs. *Nature (London)* **198**, 712.

Gray, J. E., Purmalis, A., and Funstra, E. S. (1964). Animal toxicity studies of a new antibiotic, lincomycin. *Toxicol. Appl. Pharmacol.* **6**, 476–496.

Gupta, B. N. (1972). Scleral dermoid in a guinea pig. *Lab. Anim. Sci.* **22**, 919–921.

Hamre, D. M., Rake, G., McKee, C. M., and MacPhillany, H. B. (1943). The toxicity of penicillin as prepared for clinical use. *Amer. J. Med. Sci.* **206**, 642–652.

Heilman, F. R. (1948). Aureomycin in the treatment of experimental relapsing fever and *Leptospira icterohemorragiae. Proc. Staff Meet. Mayo Clin.* **23**, 569.

Kaipainen, W. J., and Faine, S. (1954). Toxicity of erythromycin. *Nature (London)* **174**, 969–970.

Kaplun, A., Shanir, B., and Kuttin, E. S. (1972). A case of guinea pig cojoined twins. *Lab. Anim. Sci.* **22**, 581–582.

Kaufmann, A. F. (1970). Bony spicules in guinea pig lung. *Lab. Anim. Care.* **20**, 1002–1003.

Latour, J. G., Leger, C., and Renaud, S. (1974a). Activation of Hageman factor and initiation of hepatic vein thrombosis in the hyperlipemic rat. *Amer. J. Pathol.* **76**, 179–192.

Latour, J. G., Leger, C., Renaud, S., and Simar, P. (1974b). On the mechanisms reponsible for selection of hepatic veins as target for thrombosis following injection of endotoxin in hyperlipemic rats. *Amer. J. Pathol.* **76**, 195–210.

Madden, D. L., Horton, R. E., and McCullough, N. B. (1970). Spontaneous infections in ex-germfree guinea pigs due to *Clostridium perfringens. Lab. Anim. Care* **20**, 454–455.

Munger, B. L., and Lang, C. M. (1973). Spontaneous diabetes mellitus in guinea pigs. *Lab. Invest.* **29**, 685–702.

Murray, E. S. (1964). Guinea pig inclusion conjunctivitis virus. *J. Infec. Dis.* **114**, 1–12.

Murray, E. S., Charbonnet, L. T., and MacDonald, A. B. (1973). Immunity to chlamydial infections of the eye. I. *J. Immunol.* **110**, 1518–1525.

Newton, W. L., Steinmen, H. G., and Brandriss, M. W. (1964). Absence of lethal effect of penicillin in germ-free guinea pigs. *J. Bacteriol.* **88**, 537–538.

Olson, G. A. (1971). Malocclusion of the cheek teeth of a guinea pig. *Lab. Anim. Dig.* **7**, 12–14.

Paterson, J. S. (1972). The guinea-pig or cavy. *In* "The Handbook on the Care and Management of Laboratory Animals," 4th ed., Ch. 19, pp. 223–241. Williams & Wilkins, Baltimore, Maryland.

Reid, M. E., and von Sallmann, L. (1960). Nutritional studies with the guinea pig. VI. Tryptophan (with ample dietary niacin). *J. Nutr.* **70**, 329–336.

Roberts, W., Grist, N. R., and Giroud, P. (1967). Human abortion associated with infection by ovine abortion agent. *Brit. Med. J.* **4**, 37.

Saunders, L. Z. (1958). Myositis in guinea pigs. *J. Nat. Cancer Inst.* **20**, 899.

Schneierson, S. S., and Perlman, E. (1956). Toxicity of penicillin for the syrian hamster. *Proc. Soc. Exp. Biol. Med.* **91**, 229–230.

Schoenbaum, M., and Klopfer, U. (1969). Cystic changes in the ovaries of guinea pigs. *Refuah Vet.* **26**, 118–121.

Small, J. D. (1968). Fatal enterocolitis in hamsters given lincomycin hydrochloride. *Lab. Anim. Care* **18**, 411–420.

Steblay, R. W., and Rudofsky, U. (1971). Spontaneous renal lesions and glomerular deposits of IgG and complement in guinea pigs. *J. Immunol.* **107**, 1192–1196.

Storz, J. (1964). Uber eine naturliche infektion eines Meerschweinchenbestandes mit einem erreger ans der Psittakose-Lymphogranuloma Gruppe, *Zentralbl. Bakteriol., Parasitenk., Infektionskr, Hyg. Abt. 1,* **193**, 432–445.

Storz, J., and McKercher, D. G. (1962). Etiological studies of epizootic bovine abortion. *Zentralbl. Veterinaermed.* **9**, 411–427.

Takeda, T., and Grollman, A. (1970). Spontaneously occurring renal disease in the guinea pig. *Amer. J. Pathol.* **60**, 103–118.

Taylor, J. L., Wagner, J. E., Owens, D. R., and Stuhlman, R. A. (1971). Chronic pododermatitis in guinea pigs. *Lab. Anim. Sci.* **21**, 944–945.

Thompson, S. W., Hunt, R. D., Fox, M. A., and Davis, C. L. (1962). Perivascular nodules of lymphoid cells in the lungs of normal guinea pigs. *Amer. J. Pathol.* **40**, 507–517.

Watson, R. R., MacDonald, A. B., Murray, E. S., and Modabbar, F. Z. (1973). Immunity to chlamydial infections of the eye. III. *J. Immunol.* **111**, 618–623.

Webb, J. N. (1970). Naturally occurring myopathy in guinea pigs. *J. Pathol.* **100**, 155–158.

Chapter 17

Nutrition, Nutritional Diseases, and Nutrition Research Applications

Juan M. Navia and Charles E. Hunt

I. INTRODUCTION

The guinea pig has been used extensively as an animal model because of its size, intermediate between the rat and the rabbit, its tractable nature, and some biochemical and metabolic characteristics that make it useful for nutrition research.

The guinea pig has great potential as a research animal, and as it becomes more widely used it is essential to understand its nutritional requirements and the interactions between nutrients that may affect its experimental response. Consequently, the aims of this chapter are:

(a) To compile and review the literature describing the nutrition of the guinea pig.

(b) To identify those areas where little or no information is available on specific nutritional requirements of the guinea pig.

(c) To describe and discuss nutritional diseases in the guinea pig and other diseases probably related to nutritional status.

(d) To indicate the advantages and limitations this rodent has as a model in research.

In accordance with these objectives the chapter is divided into three main sections. One section discusses in detail the nutritional requirements of the guinea pig, a second section deals with diseases of probable nutritional origin, and a third describes particular research applications related to nutritional characteristics of this animal model. In the latter section, the reported uses of the guinea pig are discussed and its potential usefulness and limitations are also considered.

Although knowledge of nutrition of the guinea pig is incomplete, the literature is extensive and we have attempted to be comprehensive rather than selective. There are two reasons for this approach: (1) in many areas not enough information has been obtained to justify a decision to reject the suggestions and hypotheses presented, and (2) no recent thorough review of the subject is available. Mannering's review (1949) of the vitamin requirements of the guinea pig and Reid's (1958) classic review of nutrition of this animal species represent the only attempts of this nature. The recent publication by the National Academy of Sciences–National Research Council (1972) on the nutrient requirements of laboratory animals contains a section on the guinea pig, which is based on Reid's studies and covers the literature to 1967.

II. NUTRITIONAL REQUIREMENTS AND DISEASES OF DEFICIENCY OR EXCESS

A. Use of Diets in Guinea Pig Research

1. Diets in Natural Habitat

The guinea pig is a New World mammal, found in the wild in Peru. It is a strictly herbivorous animal, and consumes large quantities of vegetation in its natural habitat. Their molar teeth are especially suited for grinding and continuously erupt. The guinea pig is classified together with the mouse, rat, and rabbit as a simple monogastric animal with a functional cecum. However, in contrast to the rat, mouse, and hamster, the entire stomach of the guinea pig is lined with glandular epithelium. Its intestine is, like that of the rabbit, somewhat specialized to allow development of a predominantly gram-positive bacterial flora which may contribute to the nutritional requirements of the host by some mechanisms such as direct absorption of bacterial metabolites and digestion and absorption of intestinal bacteria through coprophagy. A survey of the literature revealed occasional references to coprophagy in the guinea pig, but there have been few serious efforts to determine the contributions of fecal ingestion to the nutrition of this herbivore (Haltaline *et al.*, 1970; Hara, 1960; Hintz, 1969; Reid *et al.*, 1956; Worden and Slavin, 1944). This special characteristic of the guinea pig should be considered when a diet is designed for this animal.

In contrast to the rat and the mouse, which are omnivorous and eat practically any type of food as long as it supplies enough calories, the guinea pig learns early in life what type of feed he should consume (Lane-Petter, 1968) and these habits are changed in later life only with great difficulty. This fastidiousness in the choice of food, the special nutritional requirements and nutrient contributions from intestinal flora have made it difficult for investigators to use guinea pigs extensively in research. However, enough information has accumulated so that within a few years the nutritional and dietary peculiarities of the guinea pig will be understood and thereby allow more frequent use of this animal in experimentation.

2. Experimental Diets

a. Selection Criteria. The type of diet fed guinea pigs depends on the type of experiment being performed. In all cases the diet must be (1) palatable, to ensure adequate food intake, (2) nutritious, to supply nutrients essential for growth and development as well as to supply the nutritional reserves necessary to compensate for added demands due to physiological stresses or disease, and (3) safe, free of substances or microorganisms that may be toxic or cause infection. This last condition includes *stability* to prevent formation of breakdown products or losses in nutrients which may endanger the health of the animal.

Besides these general requirements, diets used in experimental situations must be (1) reproducible, to allow investigators to obtain precise results, and (2) flexible in its use, to allow for simple, uncomplicated change of one ingredient at a time, with assurance that no other factor has been affected.

b. Types of Diets. Diets for experimental animals can be divided according to the degree of complexity of their ingredients into:

i. Natural diets. Ingredients in these diets include: oats, soybean meal, hay, alfalfa, fresh cabbage or kale, yeast, molasses, phosphate, bone meal, and others. Stock diets are usually of this type and their composition, advantages and limitations have been discussed in several reports (Dean and Duell, 1963; National Academy of Sciences–National Research Council, 1972; Slanetz, 1943; Paterson, 1957). An example of such a diet is given in Table I.

ii. Purified diets. These diets contain ingredients which are fairly simple in composition such as casein or isolated soybean protein, pure cottonseed oil, sucrose, and synthetic vitamin and mineral mixtures made with pure chemicals. Such diets have been used successfully with young guinea pigs (Navia and Lopez, 1973; Reid and Briggs, 1953; Roine *et al.*, 1949; Seidel and Harper, 1960). Examples of these diets are presented in Table II.

iii. Chemically defined diets. These diets are made with pure amino acids, sugars, inorganic salts, essential fatty acids,

Table I
Composition of the National Institutes of Health Diet for Guinea Pigs[a]

Ingredient	Assumed dry matter (%)	Diet: Dry basis (%)	Diet: As fed (%)
Oats, whole, ground fine	89.7	17.64	17.70
Wheat, whole, ground fine	86.0	27.60	28.90
Alfalfa meal[b]	92.3	38.95	38.00
Soybean meal[c]	91.3	13.43	13.25
Vitamin D_2 premix (1,730,000 IU/kg)	94.0	0.10	0.10
Ascorbic acid	100.0	0.06	0.05
Sodium chloride, iodized	100.0	0.56	0.50
Limestone, ground	99.6	1.22	1.10
Dicalcium phosphate, min. of 0.2% fluorine	96.0	0.27	0.25
Delamix[d]	100.0	0.17	0.15
Total		100.00	100.00[e]

[a]Reprinted from National Academy of Sciences–National Research Council (1972).

[b]Dehydrated. 17% crude protein.

[c]Dehulled, solvent extracted, containing not less than 49% protein.

[d]A trace mineral mix produced by Limestone Products Co., Newton, N. J. Contains not less than 6% Mn; 2% Fe; 0.2% Cu; 0.12% I; 0.02% Co; 26.5% Ca.

[e]Finished product at time of delivery should conform to the following calculated standards (not less than): crude protein, 18%; crude fat, 2.25%; crude fiber, 13.50%; nitrogen-free extract (NFE), 48%; ash, 8.20%; calcium, 1.20%; phosphorus, 0.40%; sodium, 0.15%; iodine, 1 ppm; carotene, 80 ppm; niacin, 40 ppm; thiamine, 4 ppm; pantothenic acid, 15 ppm; riboflavin, 6 ppm; biotin, 0.15 ppm; α-tocopherol, 40 IU/gm; vitamin D, 2 IU/gm; vitamin C, 450 ppm.

and synthetic vitamins. Several formulations have been used successfully with rats (Ranhotra and Johnson, 1965; Rogers and Harper, 1965), but they have not been used in research with guinea pigs.

c. Preparation and Handling of Experimental Diets. Natural diets are useful to maintain caloric requirements of guinea pigs, because they are easy to prepare in large quantities and the cost is usually low. However, they have serious drawbacks when used in research because of: (1) the uncertainty as to their nutrient composition; (2) variation from batch to batch and from season to season (vitamin A, unless supplemented, is known to vary in feeds depending on the season); (3) difficulty in changing composition to study a particular nutrient; and (4) possible presence of hormones, antimetabolites, antibacterials, and toxins which may seriously interfere with the metabolism of the animal and change its experimental response (Harris, 1970).

Purified diets are better because they are easily prepared, they are reproducible and their composition can be changed easily to induce signs of deficiency or excess. The formulation and preparation of purified diets have been discussed in detail by Navia (1970).

The greatest disadvantage of purified diets for guinea pigs is palatability. Perhaps this factor has discouraged investigators from using the guinea pig as a model for nutritional research more than any other factor. Guinea pigs purchased from vendors are usually fed a pelleted natural diet and subsequently reject stubbornly a purified diet in powder form. Seeking to avoid these problems some investigators (Singh *et al.*, 1968) moisten the diet to obtain a more palatable thick paste, and others (Ostwald *et al.*, 1971) pellet the powdery diet to make it more palatable and minimize waste. Navia and Lopez (1973) formulated and tested a purified diet in gel form (Table III) which is readily accepted by both weanling and adult guinea pigs. This diet is basically a modification of the ones used by Roine *et al.* (1949) and Reid and Briggs (1953). It is palatable and nutritionally adequate as shown by body weight gains. Male Hra (HA) guinea pigs, weighing 250 gm when received from the vendors, weighed over 700 gm after 14 weeks of consuming the gel diet.

The gel diet is prepared by suspending 20 gm of agar in 500 ml of distilled water. Another 500 ml of distilled water is heated to a boil and the agar suspension is added to it. The agar suspension is then mixed with 980 gm of the dry purified ingredients and blended slowly to make a homogenous paste. This paste is poured into plastic molds (14 x 8 x 4 inches), allowed to cool for 1½ hours, covered with a plastic lid, and stored at 4°C. Prior to feeding, the gel is diced to about 1 cm size. This diet can be color coded with food colors to identify several experimental diets of different composition. This gel diet is useful for guinea pigs, but its composition can be changed to suit the nutritional needs of rabbits which also accept it readily.

B. Protein and Amino Acid Requirements

Protein supply is more a matter of quality than quantity because a dietary source of certain amino acids is essential for all nonruminant mammals since they cannot be synthesized from organic substrates. Woolley and Sprince (1945) observed that the guinea pig had an unusually high requirement for protein when casein was used in a semipurified diet. The best weight gains occurred when the diet contained 30% casein. Arginine, cystine, and glycine added to an 18% casein diet produced equivalent growth. These results were confirmed and extended to demonstrate that the most limiting essential amino acid in casein for the guinea pig was arginine (Heinicke *et al.*, 1955a,b; Reid and Mickelsen, 1963). In fact, as the

Table II
Examples of Satisfactory Purified Diets for Guinea Pigs[a]

Ingredient	Unit	Assumed dry matter (%)	Roine *et al.* (1949) diet Dry (per kg)	Roine *et al.* (1949) diet As fed (per kg)	Reid and Briggs (1953) diet Dry (per kg)	Reid and Briggs (1953) diet As fed (per kg)
Protein	gm	94.	333.	300.[b]	333.	300.[c]
Cornstarch	gm	–	–	–	222.	200.
Sucrose	gm	100.	483.	435.	114.	103.
Glucose	gm	100.	–	–	87.	78.
Gum arabic	gm	96.	167.	150.	–	–
Cellophane	gm	100.	–	–	17.	15.
Soybean oil	gm	100.	44.	40.	–	–
Corn oil	gm	100.	–	–	81.	73.
Salt mixture	gm	100.	44.	40.[d]	67.	60.[e]
Magnesium oxide	gm	100.	5.6	5.	5.6	5.
Potassium acetate	gm	100.	27.8	25.	28.	25.
Vitamin A acetate	mg	100.	–	–	6.7	6.
β-Carotene	mg	100.	13.	12.	–	–
Vitamin D_2 (calciferol)	mg	100.	0.09	0.08	0.04	0.04
Vitamin E (α-tocopherol)	mg	100.	133.	120.	–	–
Vitamin E (α-tocopherol acetate)	mg	100.	–	–	55.	50.
Vitamin K_3 (menadione)	mg	100.	2.2	2.	2.2	2.
Ascorbic acid	mg	100.	167.	150.[f]	2222.	2000.
Biotin	mg	100.	0.4	0.4	0.67	0.6
Calcium or sodium pantothenate	mg	100.	33.	30.	44.	40.
Choline chloride	gm	100.	3.3	3.	2.2	2.
Folic acid	mg	100.	3.3	3.	11.	10.
Inositol	gm	100.	2.2	2.	2.2	2.
Niacin	mg	100.	111.	100.	222.	200.
p-Aminobenzoic acid	mg	100.	111.	100.	–	–
Pyridoxine hydrochloride	mg	100.	11.	10.	18.	16.
Riboflavin	mg	100.	16.	14.	18.	16.
Thiamine hydrochloride	mg	100.	11.	10.	18.	16.
Vitamin B_{12}	mg	100.	–	–	0.04	0.04

[a]National Academy of Sciences–National Research Council (1972).
[b]To be supplied by casein.
[c]Thirty percent purified casein + 0.3% L-arginine hydrochloride, or 30% isolated soy protein + 0.5% DL-methionine, in this diet give similar growth.
[d]Salt mixture IV.
[e]The salt mixture of Fox and Briggs is preferred to that originally used in this diet.
[f]Ascorbic acid was fed separately at the rate of 12.5 mg per day and was not included in the diet.

casein content was decreased below 30%, arginine, methionine, and tryptophan became limiting in that order. Plant proteins contain generous amounts of arginine (Table IV), and the guinea pig, a herbivore, grows well on commercial diets which contain only 20% of a protein from plant sources such as alfalfa. The young guinea pig not only has a high requirement for arginine, but arginine present in casein is probably only 70–75% available. This estimate was verified in later studies which showed that supplementation of a 30% casein diet (1.26% arginine) with 0.3% L-arginine resulted in improved growth, although that level of casein should theoretically supply the arginine requirement.

Purified soybean protein is used widely in experimental diets for guinea pigs. It is adequate in arginine, but limiting in methionine (Table IV) at levels below 30% (Reid, 1966; Reid and Mickelsen, 1963). Actually, supplementation of a diet which contained 30% soybean protein, with 0.5% DL-methionine, stimulated growth considerably. Addition of 1.0% DL-methionine was required for maximal growth when soybean protein was at the 20% level.

A purified diet with 20% soy protein and various amino acids added to provide levels equivalent to those in 30% soy protein was used to determine methionine and cystine requirements of the young guinea pig (Reid, 1966). The sulfur-containing amino acid requirement of the young guinea pig fed a 20% soybean protein diet was supplied by adding 0.36%

Table III
Purified Gel Diet for Guinea Pigs[a]

Major ingredients	gm/kg diet
Casein[b]	300.0
DL-Methionine	2.0
Sucrose (confectioners)	431.4
Vitamin mix[c]	3.3
Choline, HCl	1.0
Mineral ingredients[d]	72.2
Cellulose[e]	130.1
Cottonseed oil[f]	40.0
Agar[g]	20.0

[a]From Navia and Lopez (1973).
[b]Casein (vitamin-free), General Biochemicals, Inc., Chagrin Falls, Ohio.
[c]Vitamin mix (gm/kg diet)–Water-soluble: thiamine, 0.01; riboflavin, 0.01; niacin, 0.05; inositol, 1.00; calcium pantothenate, 0.03; pyridoxine HCl, 0.01; folic acid, 0.01; vitamin B_{12} (triturated with mannitol at a concentration of 0.1%) 0.03; biotin, 0.0002; ascorbic acid, 2.00. Fat-soluble: vitamin A, 28,500 IU; vitamin D_2, 285 IU; *dl*-α-tocopherol, 0.04; menadione, 0.01.
[d]*Mineral ingredients* (gm/kg diet)–Salts: $KC_2O_2H_3$, 27.00; MgO, 5.00; $CaCO_3$, 14.50; $CaHPO_4$, 8.30; $MgSO_4$, 0.50; $MgCO_3$, 1.00; NaCl, 2.80; $Fe(PO_4)$, 1.60; KIO_3, 0.038; $MnSO_4 \cdot H_2O$, 0.80; $ZnSO_4 \cdot 7H_2O$, 0.025; $CuSO_4$, .036; $CoCl_2 \cdot 6H_2O$, 0.03; $AlK(SO_4)_2 \cdot 12H_2O$, 0.007; NaF, 0.04; KCl, 4.50, sucrose, 6.024.
[e]Cellulose; Alphacel, Nutritional Biochemicals, Cleveland, Ohio.
[f]Cottonseed oil; Wesson oil, Hunt-Wesson Foods, Inc., Fullerton, California.
[g]Agar, Nutritional Biochemicals, Cleveland, Ohio.

L-cystine and 0.35% L-methionine. The comparative nutritive value of the D and L-isomers of methionine also was determined with 20% soy protein diet supplemented with amino acids. Better growth was attained with 0.375% of the L-isomer than with 0.75% of the DL-form and growth was poor with addition of 0.375% of D-methionine (Reid, 1966). Thus, in contrast to findings in the chick (Fell *et al.*, 1959) and rat (Wretland and Rose, 1950), D-methionine is not as active as the L-isomer in the guinea pig.

Between 0.16 and 0.20% dietary tryptophan is required by growing guinea pigs. Signs of tryptophan deficiency were produced by feeding a diet with 10% each of soy protein and

Table IV
Approximate Amino Acid Composition of Some Milk and Plant Proteins

Amino acids (gm)[a]	Casein[b]	Lactalbumin[b]	Soy protein[c]	Cottonseed meal[b]	Peanut flour[b]
Arginine	3.9	3.0	8.3	11.2	11.3
Lysine	8.5	10.5	6.8	3.5	3.5
Tryptophan	1.3	2.5	1.0	1.3	0.8
Cystine	0.4	4.0	0.6	2.2	1.4
Methionine	3.5	2.6	1.0	1.7	0.8

[a]Calculated to 16 gm of nitrogen.
[b]Block and Bolling (1951).
[c]Skidmore Sales and Distributing Co., Inc., Cincinnati, Ohio.

gelatin, an amino acid mixture, and an ample supply (20 mg/100 gm diet) of niacin. Young animals fed the purified diet (0.108% L-tryptophan) did not grow well and had distended abdomens, alopecia, lens changes, and cataracts (Reid and von Sallmann, 1960). The addition of 0.03% L-tryptophan to the diet produced good growth, but complete protection from cataract was not obtained until 0.1% L-tryptophan was added. Thus, the requirement for tryptophan to prevent eye lesions was considerably greater than the requirement for maximal growth, a finding that is probably unique among animal species.

The qualitative and quantitative requirements of the guinea pig for other amino acids have not yet been determined. However, the availability of an adequate purified diet (Navia and Lopez, 1973) and the possibility of substituting an amino acid mixture for protein in a gel diet now make these studies feasible.

Enwonwu (1973a) studied protein malnutrition in guinea pigs fed a purified diet with 3% casein. Pair-fed control animals received a commercial ration. Animals fed the 3% protein diet rapidly developed clinical signs similar to the human kwashiorkor syndrome, including reduced activity, some hair loss, and extensive edema of the face and forelimbs. Protein-deficient guinea pigs also had reduced plasma total protein, albumin, plasma pool of essential amino acids, and mild fatty liver. The author concluded that young guinea pigs are suitable models for the study of human protein–calorie malnutrition (Enwonwu, 1973a).

C. Fat and Essential Fatty Acids

Young guinea pigs fed a purified diet with no fat gained less body weight than control animals fed the diet with 7.3% corn oil (Reid, 1954a,b; Reid and Martin, 1959). There was 40%

difference in weight after 28 weeks on experiment. Other signs included dermatitis, skin ulcers, fur loss, priapism, relative underdevelopment of spleen, testes, and gallbladder, enlargement of kidneys, liver, adrenals, and heart, and some deaths. A mild microcytic anemia developed in some guinea pigs. There was also a marked reduction in dienoic fatty acid content of lipids in serum and erthrocytes.

The quantitative requirement of the guinea pig for unsaturated fatty acid was determined by feeding purified diets containing various amounts of corn oil, safflower oil, or methyl linoleate (Reid *et al.*, 1964). Results showed that the guinea pig does well over a wide range of fat intake. Corn oil, at a level of 1% (1.89% of calories as linoleate), was adequate for growth and prevention of skin changes. When only pure methyl linoleate was fed, a level of 0.4% (1.31% of calories) was required to support maximal weight gains and prevent dermatitis.

D. Vitamin Requirements: Fat-Soluble

1. Vitamin A

a. Historical. Early investigators reported that guinea pigs required vitamin A and its deficiency produced either changes in the costochondral junctions (Tozar, 1921) or cessation of growth, weight loss, and occasionally corneal opacity (Book and Trevan, 1922). Wolbach and Howe (1928) realized that the diets used by earlier workers were nutritionally inadequate and studied vitamin A deficiency in guinea pigs with a purified basal diet. Guinea pigs 4 to 6 weeks of age were offered this basal diet plus orange juice for about 4 weeks. Only those that became accustomed to it and were gaining weight were selected for the experiments. The animals, which weighed approximately 550 gm, were then fed a diet made vitamin A-deficient by substituting lard for butter in the basal diet and reducing the amount of orange juice to a minimum. Guinea pigs on this dietary regime lived 66 to 710 days and the only external signs of vitamin A deficiency were cessation of growth, loss of weight, and desiccation of the ear margin. Other changes were edema, emaciation, atrophy of salivary glands and testes, and extensive squamous metaplasia of epithelium in the trachea, bronchi, urinary bladder, and uterus. The early and drastic changes in urinary bladder and uterus of guinea pigs have not been observed in vitamin A-deficient rats.

b. Metabolic and Physiological Considerations on Vitamin A Metabolism by the Guinea Pig. Early investigators studied absorption of vitamin A and carotene (Woytkiw and Esselbaugh, 1951) and its storage in the guinea pig (Bentley and Morgan, 1945; Chevallier and Choron, 1935, 1936). These studies indicated that after absorption, transport was mainly through the mesenteric lymphatic system, and portal venous transport of vitamin A or carotene was negligible. Bentley and Morgan (1945) studied vitamin A deficiency in the guinea pig using a simplified diet containing (%): casein, 25; cornstarch, 40; hydrogenated cottonseed oil, 3.5; Hubbel and Mendel, and Wakemann salts, 4; K_2CO_3, 0.5; wheat germ, 10; yeast, 10; and bran, 7. Like other investigators they had trouble with diet acceptance and growth was slow. A stock ration was fed for 2 weeks prior to feeding the experimental diet. This diet was made low in vitamin A by using hot alcohol-extracted casein in the formulation. Three or 4 weeks after young guinea pigs were fed the deficient diet, they showed xerophthalmia, weight loss, and died a few days after the eye lesions developed. Vitamin A storage was restricted mainly to the liver and carotene seemed to be less effective than vitamin A in increasing the levels of the vitamin in the liver. However, Chevallier and Choron (1935, 1936) found no difference between the ability of the rat and the guinea pig to store vitamin A from carotene.

Since the guinea pig is herbivorous, it is difficult to imagine any impairment of the ability to utilize carotene in this species. Recent studies with rats indicate clearly that utilization of carotenoids is dependent on protein intake. Deshmukh and Ganguly (1964) demonstrated that total liver vitamin A content was proportional to the level of dietary casein. Therefore, the intestinal conversion of β-carotene to vitamin A, at least in the rat, is related to protein intake. More recently, Kamath and Arnrich (1973) reported that rats fed a 10% protein diet incorporated 50% less ^{14}C-β-carotene into the retinyl ester fraction of the intestine than rats fed a diet containing 40% protein. These data support the evidence that the intestinal wall is an important site for the carotene–protein interaction and that conversion of carotene to vitamin A is largely protein dependent. Stereoconfiguration of the carotene in relation to liver storage of vitamin A was studied in rats by Sweeney and Marsh (1973). In general, higher levels of liver vitamin A were found by feeding all-*trans*-β-carotene than the all-*trans*-α-carotene. Transformation of the all *trans* into neo-B and neo-U could also take place in the intestinal lumen, thus affecting absorption and storage level.

Koyanagi and Odagiri (1961) reported that supplemental sulfur amino acids, such as methionine, in diets containing soybean meal as a source of protein increased the level of vitamin A in liver. Young *et al.* (1973) obtained significant increases in liver vitamin A when diets were supplemented with methionine or the level of protein was increased.

Absorption, storage, conversion, and utilization of carotenoids have been studied in the rat, but carotenoid metabolism in the guinea pig is unresolved. Diets in the past were often inadequate and protein status has been for the most part undetermined. Age and growth rate have a profound influence on the amount of liver vitamin A and these factors have not been sufficiently investigated in the guinea pig. It is essential to conduct further studies to bring better understanding of vitamin A and carotenoid metabolism in the guinea pig.

c. Signs of Hypovitaminosis A. Guinea pigs fed a vitamin A-deficient diet grow poorly and lose weight. Time of onset of these signs varies between 2 to 10 weeks depending on age, liver vitamin A content, and nutritional and metabolic status of the animals. Bentley and Morgan (1945) noted swelling and incrustations of eyelids and severe keratitis due to infection in animals that survived for longer periods of time.

Dowling and Wald (1958, 1960) elucidated the role of retinal in vision and indicated that retinoic acid could not be used as a precursor for retinal and therefore could not cure impaired vision produced by hypovitaminosis A. Howell *et al.* (1967) studied changes in tissues of guinea pigs fed a vitamin A-free diet in comparison to those receiving either a methyl retinoate or retinyl acetate supplement. Weanling guinea pigs fed a purified diet free of vitamin A showed within 3 to 4 weeks loss of body weight, incrustations in the eyelids, and dryness of the cornea (Reid and Briggs, 1953). Histologically, epithelia of various organs showed squamous metaplasia and some keratinization. Interestingly, 10 of 11 animals developed some form of pneumonia which may account for the dyspnea observed in these animals. Guinea pigs receiving the methyl retinoate or retinyl acetate supplements had no signs of hypovitaminosis A, and microscopic evaluation of many organs revealed no metaplasia. However, testes of guinea pigs fed retinoate had degenerated seminiferous tubules, and female guinea pigs from this group mated, but subsequently resorbed their fetuses.

Constriction of the pupil in response to light of guinea pigs supplemented with methyl retinoate was noticeable less after 100 days on the experimental diet in comparison to those given retinyl acetate, and by 150 days the pupils of deficient guinea pigs did not respond to the light stimulus. While changes were observed in the pupils, no retinopathy was observed even in guinea pigs that were on the diet for more than a year.

Wolbach (1954) described the effects of vitamin A deficiency on teeth of guinea pigs. The primary effect on incisors was mainly on odontogenic epithelium with incomplete differentiation of cells, loss of organization, and formation of defective dentin by atrophic odontoblasts. The incisors, therefore, had a distinctive appearance characterized by thickened dentin on the labial side and a thin dentin on the lingual and lateral sides.

d. Effects of Hypervitaminosis A. The effects of high doses of vitamin A on humans and experimental animals have been reviewed by Clark (1971). Naturally occurring hypervitaminosis A may result from consumption of liver from the polar bear or bearded seal. Most reports are of natural or accidental hypervitaminosis in man or experimental studies in the rat, dog, cat, pig, calf, and chicken. Few studies have dealt with effects of hypervitaminosis A on the guinea pig. Wolbach (1947) reported degenerative changes in the cartilagenous epiphyseal plates of long bones from guinea pigs that were fed excessive amounts of vitamin A. These changes were similar to those reported in the rat and dog. Besides rapid maturation of epiphyseal cartilage, there was increased bone resorption which interfered with normal remodeling.

Robens (1970) has described the teratogenic effects of hypervitaminosis A in the hamster and guinea pig. Administration of a single oral dose of 200,000 USP units/kg to pregnant guinea pigs during organogenesis (day 14 to 20) produced soft tissue and skeletal anomalies in the offspring. The most frequent defects recorded were agnathia, synotia, malpositioning of teeth, and microstomia. Administration of the same dose between day 17 and 20 frequently produced changes in the tibias and fibulas. Fetal growth was not affected by vitamin A excess. It is not clear what mechanisms explain the fetal malformations produced by an overdose of vitamin A organogenesis.

e. Requirements. Bentley and Morgan (1945) studied vitamin A storage in the guinea pig but did not obtain sufficient data to establish the vitamin A requirement. Howell *et al.* (1967) fed guinea pigs weighing approximately 200 gm a vitamin A-free diet and gave by pipette a twice weekly supplement of retinyl acetate (0.5 mg/animal). That dose is equivalent to 0.7 mg of retinyl acetate per kilogram of body weight per day. These guinea pigs apparently grew without showing deficiency signs.

Gil *et al.* (1968) reported on groups of five guinea pigs fed purified diets containing 0, 1.67, 3.3, 6.6, 9.9, or 330.0 mg vitamin A per kilogram of diet. Assuming an average intake of 30 gm of diet in the early stages of the experiment, the lowest vitamin A intake that gave an adequate growth response and some vitamin A storage in liver was 0.4 mg per kilogram of body weight per day. Guinea pigs consuming the diets containing either 6.6 or 9.9 mg of vitamin A/kg of diet showed the best body weight gains and the most liver storage of vitamin A in a period of 40 days.

It will be necessary to do more detailed studies in which factors such as age, sex, temperature, light cycle, protein intake, and infections are controlled and standardized in some manner to establish the actual requirement of vitamin A for the guinea pig. There are still insufficient data to determine the requirement under normal conditions as well as during certain physiologically stressful periods such as gestation, lactation, and growth. It should also be of great interest to determine the requirement under conditions of infections and trauma when the demands may be greatly increased.

2. Vitamin D

a. Historical. Early attempts to induce rickets in the guinea pig were, for the most part, unsuccessful (Randoin and Lecoq, 1930). These early studies suggested that the guinea pig did not require vitamin D. Emerique (1937) finally was able to induce rickets in guinea pigs with diets in which the calcium to phosphorous ratio was distorted by increasing the calcium content. He also reported a reversal of the deficiency by feeding irradiated ergosterol for 7 days.

Howe *et al.* (1940) attempted to determine if rickets could be induced in the guinea pig by diets low in calcium and vitamin D. Young guinea pigs were kept in a darkened room and fed a paste diet which contained (%): dextrin, 71; alcohol-extracted casein, 15; dried brewer's yeast, 6; butter fat, 5.9; and a calcium-free salt mixture, 2.1. In addition, each guinea pig received daily 10 gm lettuce, 50 mg ascorbic acid, and 0.05 mg carotene. The Ca and P content of the purified diet was 0.028% and 0.2%, respectively. Nine of twenty-one guinea pigs survived from 44 to 60 days. Growth was arrested soon after starting the experimental diet. Body weight was maintained until 1 or 2 weeks before death when the guinea pigs began to lose weight rapidly. Besides typical lesions in the zone of cartilage proliferation at the epiphyseal plate of long bones and ribs, the incisors exhibited a high degree of enamel hypoplasia. In certain areas there was failure of enamel deposition and in other areas irregular masses of enamel matrix appeared. The dentin also showed irregular, disorganized, and slow calcification.

Kodicek and Murray (1943) observed no signs of rickets in guinea pigs after 3 months of eating a diet with a normal Ca/P ratio, but deficient in vitamin D and C.

b. Metabolism of Vitamin D in Guinea Pigs. There are no recent reports on metabolism of vitamin D in guinea pigs. In view of present understanding of the biosynthesis of active metabolites of vitamin D, it is likely that the guinea pig has the necessary enzymes to convert cholecalciferol to 25-hydroxycholecalciferol in the liver, and, finally to 1,25-dihydroxycholecalciferol in the kidney. This is true for the rat, but not enough work has been done with the guinea pig to elucidate its vitamin D metabolism.

c. Signs of Hypovitaminosis D. From the sparse data reported in the literature using diets with an altered Ca/P ratio (Jones, 1971) it can be surmised that the main effect of vitamin D deficiency is deranged calcium metabolism, which interferes with growth and development of bones and teeth. Most of this work has been done on rats and further research is required to describe clearly the signs of hypovitaminosis D in the guinea pig.

d. Hypervitaminosis D. No reports were found describing the effects of acute or chronic vitamin D toxicity in the guinea pig. However, in view of the susceptibility of the guinea pig to soft tissue calcification (see Section III, B), studies of the effects of excess vitamin D need to be performed, especially with respect to Mg as well as Ca, P, and K metabolism.

e. Requirements. No vitamin D requirement has been established for guinea pigs, although purified diets usually contain between 1000 and 2000 IU/kg of diet. These levels seem to promote good growth without evidence of toxicity.

3. Vitamin E

a. Historical. Goettsch (1930) and Pappenheimer (1930) described diet-induced muscular dystrophy of the guinea pig, but the factor responsible for the dystrophic changes remained unknown. Madsen *et al.* (1933) continued studying the muscular changes that accompanied a dietary regime which included a generous administration of cod liver oil to goats, rabbits, and guinea pigs. The most significant change was fibrosis of skeletal and cardiac muscle which resulted in paralysis or stiffness. These changes were attributed to a toxic effect of the cod liver oil, as replacement of this oil by cottonseed oil containing vitamins A and D did not produce the characteristic "stiffness."

Wood and Hines (1937), aware that one of the diets used by Goettsch was deficient in vitamin E, and that such a deficiency in rats induced marked hypoplasia in the thyroid gland, conducted studies on the metabolic rate of guinea pigs kept on this low vitamin E diet. The metabolic rates were normal as determined by oxygen consumption measurements and did not, therefore, explain increased oxygen consumption in excised skeletal muscle from guinea pigs under similar dietary conditions. It remained for Shimotori *et al.* (1939) to show that vitamin E was related to the muscular dystrophy previously reported and that supplementation of a deficient diet with tocopherol (3 mg per os on alternate days) protected against development of signs of muscular dystrophy for 200 days during which time the guinea pigs showed normal values for muscle creatine. Soon after this, reports were published (Pappenheimer and Goettsch, 1941) indicating the essentiality of vitamin E for maintenance of normal muscle, and for successful completion of pregnancy, just as had been shown previously in the rat and mouse.

Pappenheimer and Schogoleff (1944) raised guinea pigs beyond sexual maturity on simplified vitamin E-deficient diets and, therefore, were able to study the role of vitamin E in preserving the integrity of the testes in this species. In these studies muscular dystrophy always preceded testicular degeneration.

In rats, degeneration of the testes has been reported to occur after only 40 or 50 days on a vitamin E-deficient diet, whereas such lesions in the testes of guinea pigs were observed after 130 days and advanced degeneration after 175 days.

b. Metabolic Reactions. Once vitamin E or tocopherol was shown to be related to the nutritional muscular dystrophy syndrome, several investigators attempted to evaluate the nature of the biochemical reactions, particularly in the dicarboxylic acid cycle in muscles of guinea pigs deprived of vitamin E. Barber *et al.* (1949) studied transamination between aspartic and α-ketoglutaric acids. They found that aspartic-glutamic transaminase activity of skeletal muscle from dystrophic guinea pigs fed a low vitamin E diet was one-half to two-thirds of that found in muscle homogenates from control animals. Pyridoxal phosphate (vitamin B_6) restored the activity in the homogenate. One question that challenges the credibility of most of this work is the extent to which partial starvation contributed to the loss of enzymes or reduced metabolic activity. It would seem necessary to do studies with guinea pigs which developed signs of muscular dystrophy, early in the course of the deficiency, to define which biochemical events lead to degeneration of skeletal muscle.

Because some investigators suggested that nutritional dystrophy could be due to a primary defect in myoglobin metabolism, Bender and Schottelius (1959) studied the effect of short-term vitamin E deficiency on guinea pig skeletal muscle metabolism. They fed weanling animals a diet containing low levels of vitamin E mixed in equal proportions with a commercial stock diet during the first 5 days to make it acceptable to young animals. On experimental day 0, animals in the control group received a ground commercial diet and the experimental and pair-fed animals were fed the experimental diet. The practice of giving different diets to control and experimental animals is regrettable but understandable, as most purified diets at that time did not produce optimum growth. This was clearly demonstrated in body weight increases of guinea pigs used by Bender and Schottelius (1959). While control animals (fed the commercial diet) gained 72 gm in 15 days, those fed the low E diet and supplemented with tocopherol gained only 14 gm, and the experimental animals (fed the low E diets) gained 12 gm. This clearly shows the importance of using acceptable and nutritious diets to separate and identify special factors under investigation. Under these experimental conditions an increase in myoglobin concentration in skeletal muscle occurred during the first 15 days on a vitamin E low diet, whereas in a subsequent study (Schottelius *et al.*, 1959) vitamin E deficiency precipitated a decrease in muscle myoglobin concentration. Reduced myoglobin concentration was observed before appearance of severe tissue lesions or elevated creatine excretion. Supplementation with vitamin E reduced the magnitude of the myoglobin change.

Other metabolic and biochemical parameters have been studied by Elmadfa and Feldheim (1971). Male guinea pigs weighing 240 gm were given a purified diet low in tocopherol which allowed them to survive for periods up to 19 weeks. No body weight differences were observed until the twelfth week, but creatine phosphokinase activity in skeletal muscle was reduced significantly after 2 weeks on the experimental diet, while serum creatine phosphokinase activity increased during the same period. At about 4 weeks creatine excretion in the urine increased and by the fifth and sixth week erythrocyte hemolysis increased significantly, reaching a maximum at 8 weeks. Soon thereafter the guinea pigs became prostrate and severe loss in body weight took place.

c. Signs of Hypovitaminosis E. Guinea pigs fed a palatable diet low in vitamin E and high in polyunsaturated fatty acids exhibit primarily degeneration of skeletal muscle which leads to partial paralysis and total prostration. In males the testes atrophy and develop degenerative changes in the seminiferous tubules and clumping or complete disappearance of spermatozoa and spermatids. In pregnant females, the absence of dietary vitamin E produces malformations and death of fetuses, which are frequently resorbed.

d. Vitamin E Requirements. The vitamin E requirement of guinea pigs is difficult to establish from available data. No studies define clearly in the guinea pig the relationship between polyunsaturated fatty acid (PUFA) intake and tocopherol requirement. Most diets were only partially acceptable to the animal so growth was not maximal. Shimotori *et al.* (1939) fed guinea pigs cod liver oil (1 ml per os) and tocopherol (3 mg per os) on alternate days for approximately 7 months. Pappenheimer and Goettsch (1941) reported that doses of 5 or 10 mg of tocopherol acetate given weekly to pregnant guinea pigs fed a diet containing 0.18% cod liver oil was sufficient to protect against skeletal muscle changes, but did not prevent resorption and death of fetuses.

Farmer *et al.* (1950) studied the vitamin E requirement of guinea pigs, but used a natural diet whose exact nutritional composition was not known. Under these conditions live births were obtained in primiparous animals given an average of 3 mg of tocopherol per day. In multipara this level reduced the incidence of hemorrhage and abortion and increased the percentage of live births. It is probable that the requirement is between 1.5 and 6.0 mg per day depending on PUFA intake, age, sex, and physiological stresses.

4. Vitamin K

Little experimental work has been done to study the deficiency signs and requirements of the guinea pig for vitamin K. Dam *et al* (1937) fed for 6 weeks a diet containing (%): vitamin A-free casein, 20; dried yeast, 15; sucrose, 62.3; mineral salts, 2.7; and cod liver oil, 4.0 to guinea pigs weighing about 250 gm. A daily supplement of 3 ml of lemon juice was given to ensure adequate vitamin C intake. These guinea pigs developed no hemorrhages and the clotting times did not vary appreciably. In view of the active intestinal flora of the guinea pig and its coprophagic habits it seems not to require dietary vitamin K. The actual nutritional needs of the guinea pig for vitamin K and the signs of hypovitaminosis K remain to be described and understood and perhaps use of germfree animals would facilitate this type of study.

E. Vitamin Requirements: Water-Soluble

1. Thiamine

a. Historical. Although Holst (1907) and Holst and Frolich (1907) attempted to induce the "polished rice disease," beriberi, in guinea pigs in the early 1900's, definitive studies of thiamine requirements in the guinea pig are much more recent. Reid (1954a) was first to produce uncomplicated thiamine deficiency in guinea pigs with a purified diet. In these and subsequent studies (Reid and Bieri, 1967; Liu *et al.*, 1967) it was found that young pigs fed a thiamine-deficient diet had poor appetites and weight gains, developed central nervous system disorders including tremors, lack of balance, and retraction of the head, and usually died within 3 to 4 weeks.

Stability of thiamine in purified diets is affected markedly by oxidizing agents such as K_2HPO_4 (Lyman and Elvehjem, 1951; Waibel *et al.*, 1954) and this factor was mainly responsible for overestimation of the requirement for thiamine by the guinea pig (National Academy of Science–National Research Council, 1962). Subsequent studies (Liu *et al.*, 1967; Reid and Bieri, 1967) demonstrated the effect of various salt mixtures on the stability of thiamine in guinea pig diets and have shown the requirement to be lower than was originally supposed. For example, young guinea pigs fed a diet with a salt mixture containing 18% K_2HPO_4 showed signs of thiamine deficiency even at a level of 6 mg/kg of diet (Reid and Bieri, 1967). However, 2 mg of thiamine/kg of diet was sufficient for growth and prevention of deficiency when a salt mixture which contained no K_2HPO_4 was used in the same diet. Liu and co-workers (1967) also demonstrated that composition of the mineral mix was a major factor in thiamine stability. The best mixture, in terms of thiamine stability, contained no K_2HPO_4 and allowed 94% thiamine retention after storage of diets for 4 weeks at 4°C.

b. Toxicity. One report described the peculiar effect of excess thiamine in scorbutic guinea pigs (Highet and West, 1946). The syndrome was produced experimentally by daily oral administration of 25 mg of thiamine during ascorbic acid depletion. When the animals developed scurvy, they were allowed to recover by feeding green food. The process was then repeated. Clinical signs of what was considered to be thiamine toxicity included in chronological order, weakness of jaw muscles and failure to masticate normally, rapid chewing motions, spastic contraction of jaw muscles, and excessive salivation. The animals became emaciated and died, but did not have the usual signs of scurvy at autopsy. There seems to be no explanation for this effect and it was not possible to produce the toxicity syndrome in guinea pigs fed adequate amounts of ascorbic acid.

c. Requirement. The requirement for thiamine by the guinea pig is probably less than the accepted level of 2 mg/kg of diet (Liu *et al.*, 1967; Reid and Bieri, 1967). However, considering the unstable nature of thiamine, purified diets should contain at least that much. The type of salt mix, storage conditions (temperature and humidity), and length of time in storage will markedly affect the final level of thiamine in the diet.

2. Riboflavin

There are only two reports of riboflavin deficiency in the guinea pig (Reid, 1954a; Hara, 1960) and the quantitative requirement for this vitamin has not been determined.

Reid (1954a) fed young guinea pigs a purified diet deficient in riboflavin and reported poor growth, rough hair coat, pale feet, nose, and ears, and death within 2 weeks. Microscopic lesions have been described also in young guinea pigs fed a riboflavin-deficient diet (Hara, 1960). Lesions included corneal vascularization, atrophy of skin, and chromatolysis and myelin degeneration in the pons and spinal cord. Myocardial alterations were hemorrhage and edema accompanied by vacuolar degeneration and atrophy.

3. Niacin

a. Deficiency. Although there were early attempts to study niacin (nicotinic acid) deficiency in the guinea pig (Fabianek, 1954; Harris and Raymond, 1939; Worden and Slavin, 1944), the only definitive studies have been done by Reid (1954a, 1961). Signs of niacin deficiency in young guinea pigs fed a 30% casein diet were seen within 3 to 4 weeks and approximately 50% died by the end of the sixth week in experiment. All deficient animals grew poorly, had pale feet, nose, and ears, poor appetites, drooling, anemia, and a tendency to diarrhea. There were no oral or ocular lesions and no dermatitis occurred.

b. Toxicity. Handler (1944) found that high levels of niacin (0.5–2.0%) in a diet which contained 20 % casein and 15% linseed meal were nontoxic to young guinea pigs. Unlike the rat, guinea pigs did not excrete the excess niacin as N^1-methylnicotinamide, a process which utilizes methyl groups to detoxify or prepare excess vitamin for excretion. In other experiments (Reid, 1961) a niacin level of 0.05% resulted in poor growth and mortalities when fed in a diet with 10% each of soybean protein and gelatin plus a supplement of all essential amino acids except tryptophan and arginine. This effect was alleviated by addition of 0.15% of DL-tryptophan. The reason for these differences in effect of high levels of niacin is unclear, but may be related to use of different sources and amount of protein.

c. Requirement. The guinea pig can produce niacin from tryptophan, and consequently its requirement is affected by quantity and quality of dietary protein, especially with regard to tryptophan content and availability. Reid (1961) thoroughly studied the niacin requirement of young guinea pigs in which she examined the interrelationships of these factors. Ten milligrams of niacin per kilogram of diet was adequate in a purified diet which contained 30% casein or 20% casein supplemented with 1% L-arginine. Maximum growth was obtained without addition of niacin when 30% soybean protein was used. When the purified diet contained 20% soybean protein and 0.5% of DL-methionine more than 10 mg of niacin/kg of diet was needed. There is less tryptophan in soybean protein than in casein (1.08 and 1.30%, respectively) and yet conversion of the amino acid to niacin seemed more efficient with the soybean protein (30% level).

4. Pyridoxine (Vitamin B_6)

a. Historical and Deficiency. Few investigators have reported on pyridoxine requirements in the guinea pig. Reid (1954a, 1964) described signs of deficiency induced by feeding purified diets containing 30% vitamin-free casein. When male guinea pigs less than a week old were fed a pyridoxine deficient diet only 15 out of 27 animals were alive after 8 weeks. Deficient animals grew poorly, but did not show any specific clinical signs of deficiency. Gross lesions at necropsy were nonspecific, including hemorrhages in the gastrointestinal tract, enlarged adrenals, pale spleens, and slightly fatty livers with apparent foci of necrosis. Most of these changes may be seen in guinea pigs that fail to eat for various reasons.

The effect of pyridoxine deficiency on phagocytosis in mature male guinea pigs has been studied by van Bijsterveld (1971a,b). In these experiments deoxypyridoxine was added to the deficient diet to suppress uptake of residual pyridoxine. *In vitro* phagocytic activity of myeloid cells from pyridoxine-deficient animals was decreased significantly as compared with controls. In similar studies the bactericidal capacity of phagocytes and histochemically detectable myeloperoxidase from pyridoxine-deficient guinea pigs were decreased. Phagocytosis was shown to be unaffected by deoxypyridoxine.

b. Requirement. The requirement of the growing guinea pig for pyridoxine, based on weight gain and general appearance, seems to be 2 to 3 mg/kg of diet (Reid, 1964).

5. Folic Acid (Pteroylglutamic Acid, Vitamin B_c)

a. Deficiency. Wooley and Sprince (1945) first demonstrated a requirement for folic acid (pteroylglutamic acid) in guinea pigs fed a purified diet. Animals which received 0.5 μg of folic acid daily became lethargic, lost weight, and died within 5 weeks. Profuse salivation and terminal convulsions occurred in many deficient animals.

Additional studies confirmed the need of the guinea pig for folic acid and documented the effects of deficiency in this species (Mannering, 1949; Reid, 1953, 1954a; Reid *et al.*, 1956; Woodruff *et al.*, 1953). Young guinea pigs are especially susceptible to folate deficiency. They grew poorly, and within 2 to 3 weeks they developed anemia and leukopenia. Hemoglobin and hematocrit values were reduced, there was a marked decrease in numbers of erythrocytes and leukocytes in peripheral blood and the bone marrow was aplastic. At necropsy fatty liver and adrenal hemorrhages were seen.

Faulkner and associates (1958) pair-fed guinea pigs a folic acid deficient diet and studied myoglobin content of skeletal muscle after onset of hematological signs of deficiency. Folic acid-deficient animals were anemic and had a greater concentration of myoglobin in their muscles than did the pair-fed control guinea pigs; the authors suggested that there were basic differences in the synthesis or degradation of the heme respiratory pigments in this species. However, production of all blood cells by bone marrow is depressed markedly in folic acid-deficient animals and the reduced hemoglobin levels may be simply a reflection of this effect (fewer cells to synthesize and carry hemoglobin), whereas increased myoglobin concentration in muscle could represent an attempt to compensate for tissue hypoxia due to anemia.

Guinea pigs are normally resistant to fatal infection with *Shigella flexneri.* However, when young guinea pigs were fed a folic acid-deficient diet and subsequently were given viable *S. flexneri* intragastrically 89% succumbed, whereas only 17% of control animals fed the folic acid-supplemented diet died (Haltaline *et al.*, 1970). The majority of infected deficient animals died within 24 hours and bacteremia correlated strongly with fatal outcome. The mechanism by which folic acid deficiency increased susceptibility was not identified although factors such as decreased caloric intake (animals fed an optimal stock ration and infected died) or relative leukopenia in deficient animals before and after challenge must be considered.

b. Requirement. Several studies have shown that young guinea pigs fed purified diets have an unusually high requirement for folic acid (Mannering, 1949; Reid, 1954a; Reid *et al.*, 1956; Woodruff *et al.*, 1953). Reid and associates (1956) fed several levels of folic acid (0–40 mg/kg of diet) to young guinea pigs and found that survival was improved in groups fed 2 or 3 mg as compared to 0 or 1 mg but maximum growth and leukocyte production was attained at the 6 mg level. The optimal level for young guinea pigs fed a purified diet is probably between 3 and 6 mg/kg.

Several factors may modify the dietary requirement for folic acid in the guinea pig. There are various brief reports in the literature concerning coprophagy in the guinea pig, but the actual extent of this practice in these animals is unknown. Reid and associates (1956) observed coprophagy during their experiments and assumed that improvement in growth and hematological values in guinea pigs fed only 2 mg of folic acid per kilogram of diet beyond 6 weeks could be accounted for in this way.

Folic acid sufficiency is also influenced by dietary para-aminobenzoic acid (PABA). Thus, Wichmann *et al.* (1954) reported that guinea pigs fed a diet which contained PABA did not need supplemental folic acid. Their animals were about 3 weeks old at the beginning of the experiment. Other workers (Woodruff *et al.*, 1953) fed a basal diet which supplied 100 mg PABA/kg and found that addition of 3 mg of folic acid prevented hematological changes and was adequate for growth. These findings are in contrast to those of Reid *et al.* (1956) in which a diet devoid of PABA required addition of 6 mg folic acid per kilogram to attain normal blood values and maximal growth.

In conclusion, there is good evidence that the very young guinea pig requires 3 to 6 mg folic acid per kilogram of purified diet. However, the requirement may be modified by age, intestinal synthesis, coprophagy, and intake of PABA. The apparent decreased requirement as guinea pigs mature may be related to establishment of a folic acid producing intestinal flora, coprophagy, and decreased need due to reduced rate of growth.

6. Pantothenic Acid

a. Deficiency. Pantothenic acid is an essential nutrient for the guinea pig although it has received limited attention in experimental studies. Young guinea pigs fed a purified pantothenic acid deficient diet quickly developed signs of deficiency such as decreased growth rate, anorexia, weight loss, rough coat, diarrhea, weakness, and death (Reid and Briggs, 1954). Coat pigmentation was unaffected, but at autopsy the adrenals were enlarged, and sometimes hyperemic or hemorrhagic. Adult guinea pigs are also sensitive to pantothenate deficiency. All thirteen adults in an experimental group died within 10 to 41 days when fed a pantothenic acid-deficient diet (Hurley *et al.*, 1965). Many of these animals had adrenal and gastrointestinal hemorrhages.

Reid and Briggs (1954) tested the possible relationship between dietary ascorbic acid levels and pantothenate requirement. Large amounts of ascorbic acid (0.5 or 2.0% of diet) did not increase survival time of young guinea pigs fed the diet lacking in pantothenic acid. Furthermore, ascorbic acid (0.1 or 1.0%) did not significantly affect weight gain or survival of young guinea pigs fed diets with suboptimal (10 mg/kg) or optimal (29 mg/kg) levels of pantothenic acid. These results contrast with those reported from studies in the rat where 2% dietary ascorbic acid prevented signs of pantothenate deficiency (Daft, 1951; Daft and Schwarz, 1952; Reid and Briggs, 1954).

The effect of varying pantothenic acid intake during gestation in the guinea pig has been studied by Hurley and associates (1965). When a complete diet was fed to guinea pigs, a sharp rise in bound pantothenic acid and coenzyme A (CoA) occurred in fetal liver at 58 days of gestation and reached a maximum 4 days after birth (Hurley and Volkert, 1965). A transitory deficiency of pantothenate during the ninth or tenth weeks of gestation often resulted in abortion and/or death of the mother and increased body fat and decreased pantothenic acid in liver of newborns. These experiments suggest that the fetal guinea pig has its greatest requirement for pantothenic acid about 1 week before birth (Hurley *et al.*, 1965).

b. Requirement. The young guinea pig has a high requirement for pantothenic acid, approximately 20 mg/kg of dry diet (Reid and Briggs, 1954). The adult requirement is not known, but may be close to that for the young animals since pregnant or nonpregnant adults can be depleted in a short period (Hurley *et al.*, 1965).

7. Choline

a. Historical. Mammalian tissues can synthesize choline, and many nutrients contribute to production of this substance. Choline, hydroxyethyltrimethylammonium hydroxide, is synthesized by successive methylations of aminoethanol (phosphatidylaminoethanol). Methionine is the major methyl donor in mammalian tissues and therefore the quality and quantity of protein in diets are important. Also, the methionine–homocysteine system can serve in transfer of newly synthesized methyl groups from formate in a series of reactions involving folic acid and vitamin B_{12} (Griffith and Nyc, 1971). For these reasons it is difficult to produce choline deficiency in most laboratory animals by feeding diets adequate in methionine, folic acid and vitamin B_{12} and devoid of choline.

The effects of choline and methyl donor deficiency have been studied in many animal species since Best and Huntsman (1934) first demonstrated the lipotropic action of choline in the rat. The laboratory rat has been the principal test animal for choline studies and appears to be unique in that the weanling rat develops fatal hemorrhagic necrosis of the renal cortex when deprived of dietary choline and an adequate supply of other sources of methyl groups. The change commonly associated with experimental choline deficiency in many species is accumulation of fat in liver. The entire subject of choline metabolism and deficiency has been reviewed comprehensively by Griffith and Nyc (1971).

b. Choline Metabolism. Choline synthesis and the role of various nutrients, such as methionine, folic acid, and vitamin B_{12}, have not been completely elucidated in the guinea pig and species differences have been reported. For example, the rat seems capable of *de novo* synthesis of choline from aminoethanol and a source of labile methyl groups (Griffith and Nyc, 1971). However, the chick (Jukes *et al.*, 1945; Schaefer *et al.*, 1951) and guinea pig (Reid, 1955; Young and Lucas, 1957) are practically unable to convert aminoethanol to monomethylaminoethanol (MME), but both species effectively utilize MME for choline synthesis when a source of labile methyl such as betaine or methionine is available in the diet (Reid, 1955; Young and Lucas, 1957; Young *et al.*, 1954).

In Reid's studies (1955) a 30% casein diet deficient in choline did not seem to provide sufficient methionine for transmethylation of MME and other synthetic processes. However, other workers (Kobayashi, 1970) fed a similar diet and addition of 0.117% MME resulted in growth equivalent to that of the choline-supplemented control group. The reason for this difference is not apparent since Reid's diet was adequate in folic acid and vitamin B_{12} (10 and 0.04 mg/kg of diet, respectively). The nutrient requirements of the guinea pig are especially critical during the first 2 weeks of life, and age differences at onset of these studies may account for the different results. Reid's animals were less than 1 week old (90 to 115 gm), whereas, Kobayashi's were at least 2 weeks old (140 to 190 gm) when first fed the experimental diets.

Methionine has a choline-sparing effect, and diets used to induce choline deficiency must be low in methionine. Peanut meal and soy protein are even more limiting in methionine than casein (Table IV). Interestingly, choline deficiency was induced in guinea pigs fed an adequate level (30%) of casein (Kobayashi, 1970; Reid, 1955), whereas the usual practice is to lower the level of protein and use methionine-limiting combinations (peanut meal and soy protein).

Cystine, in contrast to methionine, had a marked antilipotropic activity in rats (Beeston and Channon, 1936; Griffith and Wade, 1940; Tucker and Eckstein, 1937). This effect has not been reported in the guinea pig. In fact, Reid (1955) reported that L-cystine and DL-homocystine were slightly beneficial in a diet that lacked choline.

c. Deficiency. There are conflicting reports in the literature concerning success of inducing choline deficiency in guinea pigs. The factors involved probably include age (weight) of the animals when started on experiment and the presence or absence of dietary constituents that contribute to choline synthesis.

Handler (1949) fed several different semipurified diets to weanling guinea pigs and young rats. These diets were deficient in choline and contained various combinations of casein, peanut meal, and amino acid supplements. The rats developed fatty livers, but signs of choline deficiency were not observed in guinea pigs fed the same diets. These results were considered compatible with a slow rate of choline turnover in guinea pigs due to a lack of hepatic choline oxidase activity in this species (Bernheim and Bernheim, 1938). Other workers, however, have found low, but measurable choline oxidase activity in guinea pig liver and kidney (Mazzone and Williams, 1957).

Signs of choline deficiency in young guinea pigs have been reported by Reid (1954a, 1955). Guinea pigs, from 2 to 4 days of age, were fed a 30% casein diet deficient in choline, but adequate in folic acid and vitamin B_{12}. They grew poorly, developed anemia and muscular weakness, and at necropsy had some adrenal and subcutaneous hemorrhages. There were no renal hemorrhages and no marked fatty infiltration of liver.

An attempt to induce choline deficiency in mature (550 gm) male guinea pigs met with little success (Casseleman and Williams, 1954). The diets were fed for periods up to 160 days and the deficient animals gained less weight, but apparently had no gross signs of choline deficiency. There were many fine droplets of fat in the centrilobular region of livers from the choline-deficient animals.

d. Requirement. Reid (1955) fed young guinea pigs a purified diet supplemented with many levels of choline ranging from 0 to 5 gm/kg. At levels of 1.0 to 1.5 gm of choline chloride per kilogram of diet there were no deaths and maximal growth was attained.

8. Ascorbic Acid (Vitamin C)

a. Historical. Scurvy (hypovitaminosis C) has been recognized since early times, particularly infantile scurvy. The characteristic abnormalities in the epiphyses of long bones, the costochondral junctions and changes in the gums and teeth of human beings have been studied since the beginning of this century, but were not reproduced in experimental animals. Holst and Frolich (1907) produced by dietary means these same alterations in the guinea pig and finally related them to antiscorbutic foods by curing the disease when these substances were added to the diet. Later Hart and Lessing (1913, cited in Zilva and Wells, 1919) used the monkey as an experimental animal and reproduced the scorbutic syndrome. Harden and Zilva (1919) showed that a monkey with signs of scurvy could also be cured by feeding an antiscorbutic agent. Today we understand that of all experimental animals commonly used in research, only the primates, the guinea pig, the red vented bulbul bird, and some species of fruit-eating bats of India depend on food sources to fulfill their strict requirement for ascorbic acid (Roy and Guha, 1958).

Zilva and Wells (1919) studied the changes in teeth of guinea pigs during various stages of scurvy and found fibrosis of the pulp and derangement of odontoblasts. These changes appeared before other microscopic signs of the disease. Waugh and King (1932a,b) demonstrated that administration of 0.5 mg of ascorbic acid per day prevented development of signs of scurvy in most guinea pigs. This identified ascorbic acid as a component of the antiscorbutic foods, such as citrus fruits, and as the constituent responsible for the curative and preventive effects of these foods.

b. Biochemistry and Metabolism of Ascorbic Acid. Most animals synthesize ascorbic acid from glucose via the glucuronic pathway, but guinea pigs and other animals mentioned previously require dietary ascorbic acid because they are genetically deficient in *l*-gulonolactone oxidase. In guinea pigs, ascorbic acid turnover is rapid and tissue storage is insufficient for periods of inadequate intake. For these reasons it is mandatory that ascorbic acid be supplied frequently. Zilva (1941) studied the influence of intermittent consumption of vitamin C on the development of scurvy. Guinea pigs receiving 2 mg of ascorbic acid daily or 4 mg every other day or 6 mg every third day responded equally well without signs of scurvy, but guinea pigs receiving 14 mg of ascorbic acid once a week grew poorly and some had signs of scurvy. The response of the animals to intermittent feeding of ascorbate was similar regardless of whether they were "saturated" with ascorbic acid prior to the experiment. The distribution of ascorbic acid in tissues seems to be similar in most species: The concentration in adrenal cortex is highest; in pituitary, corpus luteum, glandular cells of the intestinal tract, and leukocytes the concentration is also high; pancreas, liver, thymus, kidney, and spleen are intermediate; and muscle is fairly low in ascorbate. Kuether and associates (1944) found that tissue concentrations of ascorbic acid in guinea pigs in such organs as liver, spleen, kidney, adrenal, and muscle were related to amount ingested and blood concentrations.

Membrane permeability of some tissues may determine the intracellular concentration of ascorbate. The transport of ascorbic acid into the eye, for example, is highly selective (Linner and Nordstrom, 1969) and is dependent on configuration of the molecule. A high plasma concentration of D-isoascorbic acid is required to reach normal isoascorbate concentration in the aqueous humor. The concentration is usually higher in the posterior than in the anterior chamber both of which exceed the concentration in blood, thus suggesting active transport across the ciliary processes. In most biological systems only the oxidized form of ascorbic acid, dehydroascorbic acid, seems to readily cross membranes whereas in the guinea pig both ascorbic acid and dehydroascorbic acid seem to enter the eye (Hughes and Hurley, 1970). This behavior is similar to that reported by Hornig *et al.* (1971), who studied the uptake and release of [1-^{14}C] ascorbic acid and [1-^{14}C] dehydroascorbic acid by guinea pig erythrocytes. Their results suggest that the erythrocyte membrane from either normal or ascorbic acid deficient animals was permeable to both ascorbic acid and dehydroascorbic acid in either direction. The eye lens of the guinea pig is special in that the uptake of D-araboascorbic acid (isoascorbic acid) is not significantly different from that of L-xyloascorbic acid (vitamin C), the form which preferentially crosses biological membranes (Hughes and Hurley, 1970). Retention and loss of ascorbic acid by the different tissues of guinea pigs fed scorbutigenic diets vary considerably. The adrenals, spleen, and aqueous humor lost ascorbate rapidly, while loss from the brain and eye lens was slower (Hughes *et al.*, 1971a,b). After 14 days on the scorbutigenic diet the ascorbate levels in these tissues were 25% of the initial concentrations, while organs such as the adrenals and the spleen were 5% of the original.

Hughes and Jones (1971) found no difference among young male and female guinea pigs in the ascorbic acid concentration of the adrenal glands and spleen. Older animals, however, had lower levels of ascorbic acid in spleen, adrenals, and eye lens, and higher levels in the brain than young animals. These investigators compared the retention of a dose of ascorbic acid given either orally or intramuscularly and concluded that reduced gastrointestinal absorption is in part responsible for the low ascorbate concentration in some organs in the guinea pig.

The question of whether some guinea pigs may produce endogenous ascorbic acid requires more investigation. Stone (1966) suggested that the requirement for ascorbic acid is a genetic disease ("hypoascorbemia"). Williams and Deason (1967) reported that guinea pigs fed a vitamin C-free diet varied widely in response with most animals losing weight rapidly while others maintained their weights for long periods of time. Odumosu and Wilson (1971) fed female guinea pigs (Duncan–Hartley) a scorbutigenic diet and concluded that some female guinea pigs could readjust their ascorbic acid metabolism and compensate for the influence of a possible defective gene responsible for the hypoascorbemia suggested by Stone (1966). If this is a reality, then it would affect the use of the guinea pig as an experimental animal in various types of research, for such accommodation to ascorbic acid metabolism would also bring undesirable variability in their biological response to experimental treatments. This aspect of ascorbic acid metabolism in the guinea pig requires further investigation.

c. Deficiency (Scurvy). The best known and understood effects of ascorbic acid deficiency in the guinea pig are related to defects in collagen synthesis. Ascorbic acid is essential in the hydroxylase reactions in the formation of hydroxyproline and hydroxylysine in the collagen molecule (Stone and Meister, 1962; Udenfriend, 1966). Impaired synthesis of this ubiquitous molecule has widespread effects in the organism including enlarged costochondral junctions, disturbed epiphyseal growth centers of long bones, bone loss, altered dentin, and gingivitis. Experimental evidence has shown that growth and maintenance of connective tissue in skin (Barnes *et al.*, 1969a,b, 1970), fetal tissues (Rivers *et al.*, 1970), and repairing wounds depend on a supply of ascorbic acid in the guinea pig. The characteristic hemorrhages in subcutaneous tissues, joints, skeletal muscle, and intestine of scorbutic guinea pigs are partly the result of defective connective tissue maintenance. An impaired clotting mechanism, as indicated by increased prothrombin time, probably also contributes to hemorrhaging in vitamin C deficiency.

Ascorbic acid deficiency seems to promote the accumulation of cholesterol in liver, not through increased cholesterol synthesis from acetate (Ginter and Nemic, 1969) but probably through a decreased catabolism of cholesterol to bile acids (Ginter *et al.*, 1971a). The high content of ascorbic acid in the adrenal glands which enlarge (up to 2½ times) during scurvy and the decreased ascorbic acid content of adrenals under the effect of stress, such as caging (Hughes and Nicholas, 1971) or injections of ACTH, all indicate a functional relationship between vitamin C and the adrenals.

Ascorbic acid apparently plays an important role in the metabolism of several amino acids (Baker, 1967). Although the evidence is somewhat conflicting, increased concentrations of some amino acids and reduced concentrations of others have been reported in serum and other tissues of scorbutic guinea pigs. Hornig and co-workers (1971) reported an increased proline concentration in serum after 8 days of feeding ascorbic acid-deficient diet, whereas there was a general increase in amino acid levels by 16 to 18 days. Others (Barnes *et al.*, 1969a; Enwonwu, 1973b) reported reduced serum and liver levels of glycine and histidine. Serum concentrations of tyrosine are increased in scorbutic guinea pigs (Enwonwu, 1973b; Hornig *et al.*, 1971), and the apparent defect in metabolism of this amino acid is reflected in excretion of large amounts of the intermediary metabolite *p*-hydroxyphenyl pyruvate in the urine (Goswami and Knox, 1963). Early clinical signs of vitamin C deficiency in the guinea pig are reduced food intake and weight loss. Consequently, any study of tissue amino acid levels during scurvy must be interpreted in light of drastically altered energy (Barnes *et al.*, 1969a) and protein metabolism.

Deficiency signs of ascorbic acid in the guinea pig depend on many factors such as type and composition of experimental diet, age, sex, pregnancy or lactation, and stress factors such as exercise, space, and temperature. The first signs are microscopic and involve changes in odontoblasts and the epiphyseal plates of long bones in young animals. Weakness, lassitude, and anorexia bring about a decrease in body weight, anemia, and widespread hemorrhages which finally end, 3 to 4 weeks later, in death of the animal either from starvation and the described changes or from secondary infections to which they are quite susceptible during this time.

d. Requirement. The requirement of ascorbic acid for the guinea pig has been difficult to determine because of uncertainty as to: the quality of the diet, type of parameter to be used, nutritional and biochemical interactions which may modify the requirement, and the physiological and environmental conditions of the guinea pigs. Early studies of the vitamin C requirement were plagued by use of inadequate diets which were either unacceptable or nutritionally incomplete for the guinea pig. The result was that starvation and other nutrient deficiency signs prevented a clear evaluation of the vitamin C needs of the guinea pig.

Mannering (1949) described the different parameters and the amount of ascorbic acid suggested to avoid appearance of deficiency signs. Table V shows a range of requirement values extending from 0.4 to 25 mg per day depending on the experimental conditions used by the investigator and the parameter of choice. Pfander and Mitchell (1952) used adrenal weight per unit of body weight and odontoblast height as criteria to determine the ascorbic acid requirement in male guinea pigs with weights ranging from 110 to 840 gm, and, they found it to be approximately 0.7 mg/100 gm of body weight. No excretion of ascorbic acid in the urine was detected when 7 mg of ascorbic acid per kilogram of body weight was

Table V
Ascorbic Acid Requirement of the Guinea Pig[a]

Criterion of deficiency	Daily requirement[b] (mg)
Growth	0.4 to 2.0
Macroscopic scurvy	0.5
Microscopic scurvy	1.3 to 2.5
Odontoblast growth	2
Wound healing	2
Bone regeneration	2[c]
Serum phosphatase	0.23
Reproduction	2 to 5
Prolonged survival	5 or less
Tissue saturation	25 to 50

[a]From Mannering (1949).
[b]Per animal (oral) unless otherwise indicated (animals weighing 250 to 350 gm were customarily utilized.
[c]Parenteral.

fed. The comparable requirement for a man weighing 70 kg would be 490 mg, which is more than ten times higher than that recommended by RDA tables. This is difficult to explain and might be accounted for by (1) a difference in the metabolic conservation of the vitamin, (2) the possibility that man is capable of synthesizing some ascorbic acid, but not sufficient to meet his requirement, (3) other substances substitute for ascorbic acid in human metabolic reactions, or (4) the human requirement should be reconsidered. The disparity between guinea pigs and human beings deserves further research effort.

F. Mineral Requirements

1. Calcium

a. Historical and Deficiency. There have been few studies of calcium metabolism in the guinea pig, although many reports describe the relationship of Ca to P, Mg, and K. A form of rickets was produced in young guinea pigs by feeding a semipurified diet low in Ca (0.028%) and vitamin D (Howe *et al.*, 1940). Nine of 21 animals that survived up to 60 days developed rachitic lesions in teeth and epiphyses of ribs and long bones. However, the diet was low in protein (15% casein) and there were no control animals, so it is difficult to determine whether the lesions developed solely as a result of low Ca or vitamin D intake.

Studies on the relationship of dietary Ca to Mg deficiency or excess demonstrated that excess Ca increased the requirement for Mg (Morris and O'Dell, 1963; O'Dell *et al.*, 1960) and accentuated signs of Mg deficiency, although with high levels of Mg, excess calcium was only slightly detrimental. Morris and O'Dell (1963) suggested that Ca–Mg antagonism may be important because the guinea pig has a high apparent absorption of Ca and quickly excretes any excess via the kidneys (O'Dell *et al.*, 1957). This latter mechanism probably is related to the finding that guinea pigs utilize cations rather than ammonia to neutralize and excrete acid in the urine (O'Dell *et al.*, 1956).

b. Requirement. Specific studies of the Ca requirement for guinea pigs apparently have not been done. However, when other elements, particularly P and Mg, are present in normal quantities, a level of 0.8 to 1.0% of Ca in the diet seems adequate (Morris and O'Dell, 1963; O'Dell *et al.*, 1960).

2. Phosphorus

Relationship to Other Elements and to Soft Tissue Calcification. Many publications support the concept that the level of phosphorus in guinea pig diets is critical with respect to acid–base balance and soft tissue calcification and also modifies requirements for other elements. Hogan and Regan (1946) implicated P excess as a cause of soft tissue calcification in the guinea pig. These findings were confirmed when 90% of guinea pigs fed a diet with 0.8% Ca and 0.9% P developed soft tissue mineral deposts whereas the incidence was <10% when the diet contained only 0.5% P (Hogan *et al.*, 1950). In further experiments supplemental Mg and K prevented the effects of excess dietary P, including soft tissue calcification (House and Hogan, 1955). The authors concluded that P was the determining mineral in development of soft tissue calcification when the diet is limiting in Mg and K. The effects of excess P and the alleviating effect of supplemental Mg and K were partially explained by the observation that the guinea pig excretes relatively little ammonia via the kidneys and consequently is very sensitive to an acid diet (O'Dell *et al.*, 1956). Thus, high P diets resulted in low urine pH and plasma CO_2 capacity and high blood inorganic phosphorus. O'Dell *et al.* (1957) reported that excess dietary P resulted in negative Ca, Mg, and K balance and absorption of Ca and Mg by animals fed 1.8% dietary P was about 50% of the value obtained for those fed 0.4% P. Excess dietary P increased the requirement for Mg (Morris and O'Dell, 1963; O'Dell *et al.*, 1960). For example, guinea pigs fed a purified diet with 0.9% Ca and 0.4% P required 80 mg of Mg/100 gm of diet, whereas those fed 1.7% P in the same diet required 240 mg/100 gm. Furthermore, as demonstrated in previous experiments (House and Hogan, 1955) excess Mg prevented the injurious effect of excess P (O'Dell *et al.*, 1960).

Evidence from experiments discussed above clearly indicates the importance of careful control of P content of experimental diets in guinea pig studies.

3. Magnesium

a. Historical and Deficiency. The importance of magnesium in guinea pig nutrition has been especially pertinent in relation to soft tissue calcification and other elements, such as phosphorus. Roine *et al.* (1949) demonstrated the beneficial effect of Mg, potassium (K), and gum arabic in a purified diet fed to growing guinea pigs. House and Hogan (1955) confirmed the finding (Hogan and Regan, 1946) that excess phosphate was harmful to the guinea pig and showed that Mg and K supplements prevented the effects of excess P, such as soft tissue calcification. Other experiments revealed that Mg, with Na or K, was particularly effective in alleviating the alterations in acid–base balance induced in guinea pigs by feeding excess phosphate (O'Dell *et al.*, 1956). Excess P results in negative Mg balance in the guinea pig, mainly due to decreased absorption of Mg (O'Dell *et al.*, 1957). Apparently the guinea pig absorbs normally a high percentage of dietary Mg and the excess is eliminated via the kidneys. Excretion of cations, such as Mg, represents an important mechanism for maintaining acid–base balance since the guinea pig excretes very little ammonia through the kidneys (O'Dell *et al.*, 1956).

Clinical signs of deficiency in young guinea pigs fed purified diets limiting in Mg include poor weight gains, hair loss, decreased activity, poor muscular coordination and stiffness of rear limbs, elevated serum phosphorus, and anemia (Maynard *et al.*, 1958; O'Dell *et al.*, 1960; Morris and O'Dell, 1963). Signs of central nervous system disturbance, which characterize Mg deficiency in some species, were uncommon in guinea pigs (Grace and O'Dell, 1970a; O'Dell *et al.*, 1960), with the exception of one study in which tetany was reported (Thompson *et al.*, 1964). Gross tissue changes at necropsy were enlarged pale kidneys and white foci and streaks in liver, and, in chronically deficient animals, defective incisors which were darkened, eroded, and soft (Maynard *et al.*, 1958; O'Dell *et al.*, 1960). Soft tissue calcification (see Section III, B) is associated with Mg deficiency in several animal species and may be observed grossly and microscopically in tissues of Mg-deficient guinea pigs. Maynard and associates (1958) reported that kidneys of Mg-deficient guinea pigs contained excess Ca and subsequent studies (Morris and O'Dell, 1961) demonstrated a quantitative increase in ash, Ca, and P content of kidney, skeletal muscle, and heart.

Studies to evaluate the distribution of water and certain cations in muscle tissue of the Mg-deficient guinea pig have shown that Mg has an important role in maintenance of electrolyte distribution (Grace and O'Dell, 1970a). Extra- and intracellular Mg was reduced to about 20 and 80% of control values, respectively. Intracellular potassium was decreased also, while the sodium level was elevated in muscle of Mg-deficient animals. A significant increase in total water in skeletal muscle was associated with these changes in cation distribution. Grace and O'Dell (1970a) discussed the failure of the Na pump as a possible explanation of these results. This pump removes Na from the cell and maintains high intracellular potassium. The source of energy for this operation is adenosine triphosphate (ATP) which is cleaved by Mg-dependent (Na^+–K^+)-ATPase.

Studies of the relation of polyribosome structure to Mg deficiency in guinea pigs revealed dissociation to smaller aggregates as compared with *ad libitum* or pair-fed control animals (Grace and O'Dell, 1970b). However, this effect was nonspecific because altered polysome structure also occurred in animals on restricted quantities of an adequate diet. Grace and O'Dell (1970b) concluded that Mg deficiency probably affected appetite and/or membrane transport of nutrients, thereby limiting metabolites essential for polysome integrity.

Excess P and Ca independently increased the minimal Mg requirement and their effects were additive (Morris and O'Dell, 1963). These and previous studies (O'Dell *et al.*, 1960) showed that, not only do P and Ca modify the requirement for Mg but, also, the guinea pig will tolerate a wide range of Ca:P ratios if Mg is adequate.

Grace and O'Dell (1970a) reported a significant physiological interaction between Mg and K in the guinea pig. A diet suboptimal in Mg, with addition of K above the requirement stimulated growth. When Mg-deficient diets were fed, supplemental dietary K extended survival time, reduced mortality, lowered blood P, and decreased the Ca concentration of muscle.

Fluoride also has been reported to alleviate Mg deficiency in the guinea pig. Addition of 100 or 200 ppm of F to a diet with only 0.04% Mg improved growth, increased serum Mg significantly, reduced the incidence of soft tissue calcification, and reduced mean Ca concentration in kidney, heart, and liver. The authors suggested that F may have reduced the Mg requirement since it reduced soft tissue calcification, stimulated growth, and increased the concentration of Mg in serum and bone (Pyke *et al.*, 1967).

b. Requirement. The requirement for Mg depends on the level of certain other elements in the diet (as discussed above). When Ca and P were present at a level of 0.9 and 0.4%, respectively, a level of 0.08% Mg was adequate (O'Dell *et al.*, 1960). Morris and O'Dell (1961, 1963) reported that 0.3% Mg in purified diets is more than adequate for growth and allows for some variation in the Ca:P ratio.

c. Toxicity. Relatively high levels of Mg had no adverse effect on guinea pigs when calcium was not a limiting factor in the diet (Morris and O'Dell, 1963). If phosphorus was in excess of Ca (1.7 and 0.9%, respectively) then 1.2% Mg was toxic, resulting in decreased growth and deaths, but if Ca and P both were high the toxic effects of Mg were alleviated.

4. Potassium

a. Historical and Deficiency. Booth *et al.* (1949) found that the growth rate of guinea pigs fed purified diets was improved when ash from a natural type diet or alfalfa was substituted for mineral mix. The factor(s) responsible for this effect was not identified. In other studies (Roine *et al.*, 1949) it was shown that purified diets supplemented with potassium acetate, magnesium oxide, and gum arabic were superior in promoting growth in young guinea pigs. Subsequent work revealed that gum arabic contains considerable K and Mg (House and Hogan, 1955) and is quite well digested by the guinea pig (O'Dell *et al.*, 1957), factors which probably account for its observed beneficial effects.

Potassium and other cations counteracted the adverse effects of excess P on acid–base balance in guinea pigs (O'Dell *et al.*, 1956). Growth was subnormal at even low levels of P if supplemental K and Mg were not provided. Potassium, Na, Mg, and Ca had about equal efficacy in alleviating the effects of a high P diet and the effect was proportional to the quantity added. Combinations of K and Mg or Na and Mg were, however, most beneficial.

Potassium deficiency *per se* has been studied in the guinea pig on a very limited basis. Young guinea pigs fed a potassium deficient diet had reduced body weight gains, and membrane potentials in striated muscle cells were higher than in control animals (Luderitz *et al.,* 1971). These effects were accompanied by a significant, apparently quantitative increase in (Na^+-K^+)-ATPase activity in heart muscle cells (Bolte *et al.,* 1971; Erdmann *et al.,* 1971).

b. Requirement. The guinea pig's need for a generous supply of cations to offset an inability to conserve fixed base (O'Dell *et al.,* 1956) probably accounts for the supposed high requirement (1.4% of the diet) for potassium by this species (National Academy of Sciences–National Research Council, 1962). More recent evidence indicates that the actual requirement is much less that 1.4% when sufficient quantities of other dietary cations are present (Grace and O'Dell, 1968). Mortality was 100% within 4 weeks when young guinea pigs were fed a purified diet (30% casein) which supplied excess cations but only 0.1% potassium. The requirement for maximal growth under these circumstances was 0.4 to 0.5% of K in the diet as potassium acetate (Grace and O'Dell, 1968). These studies confirmed the finding that excess cations are essential in the diet of the guinea pig (O'Dell *et al.,* 1956) and demonstrated again that the level of certain elements in the diet may modify the apparent requirement of another element.

5. Manganese

Young female guinea pigs were reared and maintained on a semipurified diet (30% casein) of low (<2–3 ppm) Mn content (Everson, 1968; Everson *et al.,* 1959; Everson and Shrader, 1968). The animals were fed the low Mn diet throughout one or more pregnancies and the offspring were fed the same diet and used to study Mn deficiency. The effects of maternal deficiency were reduced litter size, abortions or stillbirths, and all living young had signs of ataxia which persisted in animals kept alive for 2–3 months (Everson *et al.,* 1959). Depletion of tissue Mn would appear simple in normal guinea pigs, because the amount in liver, for example, is relatively low in newborn guinea pigs, rabbits, and rats (Lorenzen and Smith, 1947).

Congenital Mn deficiency results in morphological and metabolic defects in pancreatic islets and cartilage. The pancreas of guinea pigs born to Mn-deficient mothers was often hypoplastic or aplastic and, in hypoplastic glands, there were fewer but larger islets (Shrader and Everson, 1968). Some of these Mn-deficient guinea pigs survived to become adults. Glucose tolerance tests were performed on mature deficient and control guinea pigs, and the deficient animals had a diabetic-type glucose curve indicative of reduced capacity to utilize glucose (Everson and Shrader, 1968). Feeding a Mn-supplemented diet corrected the response to glucose load (Everson and Shrader, 1968) and increased the number of islets and granulation of beta cells (Shrader and Everson, 1968). Other evidence of an effect of Mn on carbohydrate metabolism has been obtained by analysis of certain free sugars and sugar alcohols in urine of Mn-deficient guinea pigs at birth. The deficient animals excreted only one-third as much myoinositol as controls (Everson, 1968), a finding that may have important implications since myoinositol can act as a precursor of free glucuronic acid (Hollman and Touster, 1964).

Manganese is essential in the biosynthesis of acid mucopolysaccharides (AMPS) in cartilage (Leach, 1967; Leach and Muenster, 1962). Congenital skeletal deformities such as missing or flattened ribs and joint enlargement have been observed in offspring of Mn-deficient guinea pigs. The AMPS content of rib and epiphyseal cartilage was reduced in deficient animals (Tsai and Everson, 1967). Other studies have produced histochemical evidence that failure of otolith development in the semicircular canals of Mn-deficient guinea pigs is related to a defect in synthesis of AMPS (Shrader and Everson, 1967).

It is apparent from these studies on the congenitally deficient guinea pig that Mn has important roles in several aspects of carbohydrate metabolism. Additional studies are needed to pinpoint the action of Mn in these various roles in the guinea pig.

6. Copper

Effects of Deficiency. Everson and associates (1967, 1968) induced copper (Cu) deficiency in the newborn guinea pig by rearing and maintaining females on a Cu-deficient diet throughout pregnancy. The Cu-deficient offspring grew slowly; some became moribund or died suddenly during the first postpartum month. Intrathoracic or intraabdominal hemorrhage and aortic aneurisms were found in these animals at necropsy. The elastin content of aorta from Cu-deficient guinea pigs was markedly reduced at 28 days of age. These vascular lesions resemble those in Cu-deficient chicks (Carlton and Henderson, 1963; O'Dell *et al.,* 1961) and pigs (Shields *et al.,* 1962). These lesions have been explained on the basis of a requirement for Cu in the synthesis of elastin cross-links (Partridge, 1966).

Severely affected newborn Cu-deficient guinea pigs showed various signs of central nervous system disturbance including abnormal head movements, ataxia, and body tremor (Everson *et al.,* 1967). At necropsy some animals had hemorrhages in the brain, cerebral edema, and agenesis of cerebellar folia. Histological evaluation and chemical analyses indicated a failure in myelination throughout the brain of Cu-deficient guinea pigs (Everson *et al.*, 1968). These studies have shown that, although the fetal and neonatal guinea pig responds somewhat differently to Cu deprivation than the lamb (Barlow, 1963), it nevertheless has good potential as a model for nutritionally induced central nervous system disorders.

7. Zinc

a. Requirements. Little information is available on the requirements and metabolism of zinc in the guinea pig. Weanling 200 gm guinea pigs fed a purified gel diet containing approximately 19 ppm of zinc seem to do well, gaining in body weight (Navia and Lopez, 1973). However, this is a marginal amount and much better body weight gains are obtained with diets that contain 75 to 100 ppm of Zn^{2+} as zinc sulfate.

McBean *et al.* (1972) fed a zinc-deficient diet (1.2 ppm) to guinea pigs and observed a decreased zinc level in the plasma and femur compared with tissues from guinea pigs fed a diet containing 164 ppm Zn.

The guinea pig, like the rat, tolerates high levels of dietary zinc. Lopez *et al.* (1970) fed guinea pigs a gel diet with 2000 ppm of zinc and observed no ill effects, although final body weights after 20 days on this diet were slightly lower than guinea pigs receiving 75 ppm of zinc. Retention of zinc in bones was extremely high. Tibia bone ash of guinea pigs fed 2000 ppm of zinc in the diet had a mean content of 1300 ppm while control animals had approximately 400 ppm of zinc. Zinc retention in guinea pigs is affected by phosphate levels in the diet as, in this same study, a group of guinea pigs receiving 2000 ppm of zinc and 2% KH_2PO_4 in the diet had a mean content of 700 ppm in tibia bone ash.

b. Metabolism. Zinc sulfate in a purified diet at 100 ppm of Zn^{2+} is sufficient to meet growth demands and stress demands such as those imposed by fracturing a leg. Lopez *et al.* (1973) studied the metabolic balance of zinc in guinea pigs stressed by fracturing the tibia. Two groups were used; one received basal diet containing 19 ppm of Zn and the others received the basal diet supplemented with 100 ppm of Zn as zinc sulfate. Retention of zinc in the latter was approximately 67% of the intake at the beginning of the experiment. Eight days postfracture, guinea pigs receiving 19 ppm zinc had a negative zinc balance (−200% of intake) which persisted until termination of the experiment 35 days later. Those given the supplement maintained a positive zinc balance throughout the postfracture period. Zinc losses were primarily through the feces, where zinc was found to be higher in concentration than in feces of guinea pigs receiving the marginal levels of zinc in the diet. No information is available on the source of fecal zinc and on the mechanisms which elicit such a response in the guinea pig.

III. DISEASES OF PROBABLE NUTRITIONAL ORIGIN

A. Ketosis or Pregnancy Toxemia in the Guinea Pig

1. Historical

Female guinea pigs, several other species of animals, and human beings are susceptible to toxemia syndromes associated with pregnancy. These disorders are of interest in animals because of disease in pregnant women and for economic reasons. The clinical and pathological manifestations of pregnancy toxemias differ somewhat in all species affected. The disease in women usually occurs late in gestation and is characterized by hypertension, edema, often with proteinuria, and may be accompanied by anuria, convulsions, and coma (Assali, 1954). Pregnancy toxemia in sheep, both natural and experimentally induced, has many features in common with the disease in women, such as higher frequency with obesity and multiple pregnancy, central nervous system disturbance, reduced renal function, and rapid recovery after delivery (Assali *et al.*, 1960). The pregnancy toxemias which occur in other animal species, including the cow (Stevenson and Wilson, 1963), goat (Gilyard and Gilyard, 1935), horse (Williams, 1890), and rabbit (Green, 1937, 1938), have less features in common with the disease in women.

Smith (1913) was first to report a pregnancy toxemia syndrome in the guinea pig. The animals became ill suddenly, shortly before or after parturition, and died within 1 to 2 days. At autopsy they had empty stomachs and extremely fatty livers. Young guinea pigs were never affected but several breeding males developed a similar syndrome on one occasion. Other reports described naturally occurring (Foley, 1942; Rogers *et al.*, 1951) and experimentally induced (Bergman and Sellers, 1960; Ganaway and Allen, 1971; Sauer, 1961, 1963) pregnancy toxemia or ketosis in the guinea pig.

2. Etiology

No single factor has been incriminated as the specific cause of pregnancy ketosis in the guinea pig. The disorder is considered a metabolic disease associated with several contributing factors such as age, sex, diet, obesity, fasting, exercise, parity, fetal load, and heredity. Naturally occurring ketosis in the guinea pig has been seen only in adults and most frequently in females during late pregnancy (Foley, 1942; Ganaway and Allen, 1971; Rogers *et al.*, 1951). Consequently, a discussion of etiological factors must take into account any peculiarities of the adult laboratory guinea pig, particularly those that might be accentuated in late pregnancy.

Smith (1913) originally suggested that compromised pulmonary ventilation, from reduced fresh air and reduced thoracic volume because of the gravid uterus, might contribute to development of ketosis. This possibility was never thoroughly investigated, although pneumonia occurred in some cases (Smith, 1913; Foley, 1942). These authors also thought that infection and bacterial toxins might be involved as a cause of ketosis. However, attempts to culture organisms from viscera of affected dams with no apparent infection or to transmit the disease with tissue suspensions were unsuccessful.

Inadequate diet also contributes to development of pregnancy ketosis in the guinea pig. Smith (1913) found that the majority of cases occurred in winter and realized that the diet contained minimal "greens" during that season. The possible role of toxic substances in the diet was ruled out to Foley's (1942) satisfaction, but the question of nutritional deficiency or imbalance has never been satisfactorily resolved because no studies reported have utilized purified diets (quality and quantity of all ingredients known and controlled). In every case natural-type commercial rations were fed, often supplemented with cabbage or other green vegetables. It may well be that diet, obesity, lack of exercise, and fasting (stress) are key factors in the development of pregnancy ketosis in the guinea pig. In their natural habitat these animals are herbivores and forage for food. Laboratory guinea pigs are confined and fed prepared (concentrated) rations *ad libitum,* which often lead to obesity unless they are in a breeding colony which demands high productivity (Ganaway and Allen, 1971). Furthermore, the guinea pig will voluntarily fast if stressed by shipping, etc. Dietary restriction during late pregnancy caused abortion and, in some sows, a condition resembling pregnancy toxemia (Edwards, 1966). Ganaway and Allen (1971) indicated that the combined effects of obesity and fasting in late pregnancy were critical in producing pregnancy ketosis in the guinea pig. In this regard, obesity is known to predispose to pregnancy toxemia in women (Tracy and Miller, 1969) and sheep (Clark, 1943; Clark *et al.,* 1943) and the disease can be largely prevented in the ewe by careful management and avoidance of stress in late pregnancy that might result in failure to eat (Parry and Shelley, 1961).

In induced ketosis in the guinea pig fasting in late pregnancy resulted in the most severe disease syndrome (Bergman and Sellers, 1960; Ganaway and Allen, 1971; Sauer, 1961). Clinical signs of fasting ketosis in pregnant guinea pigs were similar to those of the spontaneously occurring disease and included depression, hypoglycemia, muscle spasms, prostration, convulsions, and death within 1 to 4 days after a 48- to 72-hour fast (Bergman and Sellers, 1960). Females carrying 3 or more mature fetuses developed the most severe clinical signs.

Rogers *et al.* (1951) studied heredity as a factor of possible importance in pregnancy ketosis of the guinea pig. They maintained an isolated colony separated into families considered susceptible or nonsusceptible to pregnancy ketosis depending on whether the maternal ancestor died with pregnancy toxemia or some other cause, respectively. Pregnancy ketosis was diagnosed on the basis of microscopic changes in the adrenal cortex, namely, decreased lipid content and necrosis in the zona fasiculata, although others have not found these changes in their studies (Ganaway and Allen, 1971). These families of guinea pigs subsequently were inbred. During the study there were 25 maternal deaths resulting from pregnancy ketosis among 190 females from 16 susceptible families, whereas no deaths were attributed to the disease in 96 females from 11 nonsusceptible families. The death rate (13.1%) from pregnancy ketosis in the susceptible females was considered consistent with a Mendelian recessive mode of inheritance (Rogers *et al.,* 1951). Clinical signs of pregnancy ketosis were not reported. However, blood glucose concentrations were reduced throughout the last half of gestation in dams from both groups and were reduced further in those which developed ketosis. Green (1937, 1938) reported a form of pregnancy toxemia in rabbits, which differed clinically from that seen in guinea pigs. Toxemia was limited to the progeny of a certain group of males and females. In fact, on the basis of parental relation, the incidence was confined to 22% of the female population, and approximately 50% of these died with the toxemia syndrome. No confirming reports of pregnancy toxemia in the rabbit have appeared which perhaps substantiates Green's proposal that the disorder was genetic in origin (Green, 1938).

No specific cause of pregnancy ketosis in the guinea pig has been positively identified. Reports of the natural and induced disease implicate a number of factors, most of which indicate that the guinea pig in late pregnancy is metabolically unstable. The slightest stress may result in failure to eat, accentuating preexisting hypoglycemia associated with pregnancy, and precipitating mobilization of lipid and development of ketosis which, in contrast to simple starvation ketosis, is almost always irreversible (Smith, 1913; Rogers *et al.,* 1951; Ganaway and Allen, 1971). Specific nutrients have not been investigated in relation to pregnancy ketosis although obesity was shown to be a predisposing factor (Ganaway and Allen, 1971; Sauer, 1961, 1963) and possibly heredity is also involved (Rogers *et al.,* 1951).

3. Incidence

Pregnancy ketosis, as the name implies, is generally a disease of adult female guinea pigs which occurs sporadically in late pregnancy. In Foley's studies (1942) the incidence was highest among dams in their first or second pregnancy; however, ketosis has been induced in obese virgin females (Ganaway and Allen, 1971). There are no reports on the incidence of pregnancy ketosis in guinea pigs in their natural habitat.

4. Clinical Signs

In the naturally occurring disease one may observe the following signs within 7 to 10 days of parturition (Ganaway and Allen, 1971; Smith, 1913). The first signs of illness are a sudden quietness accompanied by ruffled coat, adipsia, anorexia, and weight loss. Within 48 hours the animal becomes motionless, is unaffected by sound, and gradually becomes prostrate and dyspneic. Clonic spasms of voluntary muscles also may be seen during the course of the illness. The syndrome usually terminates in death within 2 to 5 days of onset.

Rogers *et al.* (1951) determined blood glucose concentrations in pregnant and nonpregnant guinea pigs and in sows with pregnancy ketosis. Levels averaged 108 mg% in nonpregnant fed females. The level decreased to approximately 80 mg% during pregnancy and was reduced further to 50 mg% in dams with pregnancy ketosis. Bergman and Sellers (1960) also reported hypoglycemia in pregnant guinea pigs. These authors used a 72-hour fast to induce ketosis in pregnant dams and found, in agreement with Rogers *et al.* (1951), a further reduction in blood glucose. Bergman and Sellers (1960) also demonstrated a marked rise in blood acetone associated with development of ketosis. Nonpregnant fasted females did not develop the hypoglycemia or acetonemia that occurred in the pregnant animals.

Urine of guinea pigs with pregnancy ketosis was acidic (pH = 5 to 6; normal pH = 9) and contained protein (Ganaway and Allen, 1971).

Most clinical findings discussed previously have been observed also in pregnant guinea pigs with ketosis induced by fasting (Bergman and Sellers, 1960; Ganaway and Allen, 1971).

5. Pathology of Pregnancy Ketosis

The most striking gross lesion in guinea pigs which have died with pregnancy ketosis is fatty liver (Foley, 1942; Ganaway and Allen, 1971; Smith, 1913). The liver may be pale yellow to orange, enlarged, and friable. There is usually evidence of excess lipid in other tissues, such as lactescent blood and yellow kidneys. Affected animals characteristically have an empty stomach and abundant fat depots. Some workers found gross evidence of pulmonary congestion and pneumonia in many cases (Foley, 1942; Smith, 1913). Adrenal glands of pregnant guinea pigs with naturally occurring or induced (fasting) ketosis were enlarged and sometimes hemorrhagic (Bergman and Sellers, 1960; Rogers *et al.*, 1951; Ganaway and Allen, 1971).

Rogers *et al.* (1951) claimed that the most characteristic microscopic changes in pregnancy toxemia were necrosis and lipid depletion in the zona fasiculata of adrenal glands. Other workers either have overlooked this lesion or have not found it (Ganaway and Allen, 1971). Microscopic findings in other tissues essentially confirm the gross changes (Foley, 1942; Ganaway and Allen, 1971; Rogers *et al.*, 1951; Smith, 1913). Variable fatty change occurs in cells of liver, lungs, and kidneys. The liver is generally most severely affected, but with no particular pattern of involvement with respect to lobular architecture. Microscopic lesions in other organs are not seen consistently.

6. Biochemistry of Pregnancy Ketosis

Sauer (1961, 1963) produced ketosis by fasting guinea pigs in late pregnancy. The disease syndrome was characterized by apparent rapid mobilization of depot fat with increased levels of fatty acids in plasma and liver. The hyperlipemia was, however, suppressed as ketonemia developed and there was no evidence that synthesis of fatty acids was increased. Utilization of acetate appeared unimpaired because total CO_2 from injected [1-C^{14}]acetate was not altered in fasting pregnant guinea pigs with ketosis. Also, whereas fatty acid synthesis was not increased, specific activity and percent of incorporation of [1-C^{14}]into liver sterols were increased in the ketotic group. Sauer interpreted these findings as evidence in favor of increased ketogenesis rather than decreased utilization of ketone bodies during fasting ketosis.

7. Prevention and Control

The studies of Ganaway and Allen (1971) are enlightening with regard to possible measures for prevention of ketosis in pregnant guinea pigs. They found no ketosis among 40 primiparous pregnant guinea pigs of normal weight (about 500 gm). However, the incidence approached 50% when obese (about 900 gm) primiparous guinea pigs were stressed in late pregnancy. Another factor of probable importance is the stress induced by moving sows or changing the diet. Animals will sometimes refuse to eat or drink after being moved and this may increase the severity of hypoglycemia that already exists in late pregnancy (Bergman and Sellers, 1960; Rogers *et al.*, 1951). In the studies referred to above (Ganaway and Allen, 1971) obese pregnant sows were stressed by moving them to new quarters and/or withholding a cabbage supplement. Interestingly, withholding cabbage alone produced as high an incidence of ketosis (50%) as the combined measures. Cabbage is rich in ascorbic acid and the guinea pig has a high requirement and rapid turnover of this vitamin, which may be affected by pregnancy and stress. However, depriving guinea pigs of this succulent food may in itself have been sufficient stress to induce ketosis.

Presently, the best approach to prevent pregnancy ketosis in the guinea pig is to avoid obesity. This can be accomplished by controlling food intake and by breeding the females when they weigh 450 to 500 gm and thereafter continuing to demand high productivity from the colony (Ganaway and Allen, 1971).

8. Conclusions

Pregnancy ketosis affects mainly late pregnant sows, although ketosis has been induced in obese virgin females. Ketosis is characterized clinically by rapid onset, inappetence, depression, and death within 2 to 5 days. Other features include hypoglycemia, lipemia, ketonemia, aciduria, and proteinuria. Lesions associated with pregnancy ketosis are nonspecific. The liver is usually markedly fatty and the adrenal glands are enlarged and may have hemorrhages and cortical necrosis. No single etiological agent has been identified. Experimental evidence indicates that obesity and stress, especially fasting, in late pregnancy may induce the syndrome.

As Bergman and Sellers (1960) have suggested, the susceptibility of late pregnant guinea pigs to ketosis may be related to hypoglycemia because blood glucose concentrations are reduced 20 to 30 mg% below normal. This circumstance, combined with a fetal load, obesity, and sensitivity to stress with resultant fasting, provides a metabolically unstable state and frequently ketosis. The roles played by the endocrine system, ascorbic acid, and metabolites other than glucose remain to be elucidated.

B. Metastatic or Soft Tissue Calcification and the Wrist Stiffness Syndrome

1. Historical

The guinea pig is apparently especially susceptible to soft tissue calcification (STC) and this phenomenon, in association with wrist stiffness (WS), was recognized as a disease of nutritional origin even when first observed. Wulzen and Bahrs (1941) reported WS and STC in guinea pigs fed a diet based on skim milk. These problems were the subject of many subsequent investigations and no consensus was reached as to whether WS and STC were separate entities or part of the same syndrome (Petering *et al.*, 1948; Smith *et al.*, 1949). In retrospect, it seems likely that WS and STC were related phenomena; however, in the literature of the past 15 to 20 years WS is seldom mentioned whereas STC has received considerable attention. Many efforts were made to isolate and identify a specific antistiffness factor during the 1940's (van Wagtendonk and Wulzen, 1950). Again, in retrospect, it appears that the WS–STC syndrome was not the result of deficiency of a single nutrient, but probably due to feeding a diet which was marginal with respect to supply of some nutrients and/or imbalanced with respect to others. The WS–STC syndrome in the guinea pig is a prime example of the importance of providing an adequate balanced diet as a prerequisite to performing metabolic studies in any laboratory animal.

2. Clinical Signs and Etiology

The WS–STC syndrome, as observed by Wulzen and Bahrs (1941) and others (van Wagendonk and Wulzen, 1950), was characterized by poor growth, muscular stiffness (especially forelegs), abnormal posture, bony deformities, abnormal growth of teeth, calcification of many soft tissues, slight anemia, elevated serum phosphorus, and death. The original diet consisted of skim milk supplemented with copper, iron, carotene, and orange juice with iodized salt and straw available *ad libitum* (Wulzen and Bahrs, 1941). This diet, and variations of it, was used by several investigators to study different aspects of the WS–STC syndrome. Not all workers reproduced the disease with the milk diet (Homburg and Reed, 1945; Kon *et al.*, 1946). Others produced WS with entirely different diets (Oleson *et al.*, 1947; Petering *et al.*, 1948) but did not report STC in their experimental animals. Except for Petering *et al.* (1948), early investigators did not incorporate a mineral mix in their diets. The skim milk diet of van Wagtendonk and Wulzen (1950) contained about 1% P and Ca and probably suboptimal magnesium. Subsequent studies showed clearly that these minerals and potassium have important interrelationships in the guinea pig and are critical with respect to development of soft tissue calcification.

Early evidence that the mineral content of the diet was critical in development of STC came from studies by Hogan and Regan (1946) and Hogan *et al.* (1950). Young guinea pigs were fed semipurified diets in which the amount of phosphorus was varied. Animals fed a diet with 0.8% Ca and 0.9% P grew poorly, developed sore and stiff wrists, and, after five months, had small white foci of calcium phosphate deposits on the foot pads. Mineral deposits also occurred in the spinal column, skeletal muscle, gastrointestinal tract, and soft tissue near the elbows and ribs. The quantity of ash in muscle, heart, lungs, liver, and stomach was much greater than normal. Neither unprocessed cream nor cane molasses, both of which were reported to contain antistiffness factor (van Wagtendonk and Wulzen, 1950), had curative effects in these experiments (Hogan *et al.*, 1950). Magnesium was not mentioned in these experiments, but it was demonstrated later that Mg and K prevented the effects of excess phosphorus (House and Hogan, 1955). Furthermore, high levels of dietary P decreased Mg absorption (O'Dell *et al.*, 1957) and increased the Mg requirement of the guinea pig (O'Dell *et al.*, 1960). It is important to remember, with regard to interrelationships between Ca, P, Mg, and K, that the guinea pig uses cations rather than ammonia to neutralize excess acid excreted by the kidney (O'Dell *et al.*, 1956). This factor plays an important role in the occurrence of STC in guinea pigs since any imbalance of mineral intake (e.g., P excess) may affect acid–base balance. Many changes associated with the WS syndrome, as reported by Wulzen and Bahrs (1941) and others (van Wagtendonk and Wulzen, 1950), were similar to those of experimental Mg deficiency. Uncomplicated magnesium deficiency in guinea pigs resulted in retarded growth, abnormal gait and posture (muscle stiffness), soft tissue calcification, anemia, and increased serum phosphorus (Maynard *et al.*, 1958; O'Dell *et al.*, 1960).

3. Conclusion

These studies and others designed to examine the role of Ca, P, Mg, and K in the guinea pig (see Section II, F) all indicate that the STC syndrome is directly related to the mineral constituents of the diet. Careful control of dietary Ca, P, Mg, and K is imperative for maintenance of acid–base balance and prevention of soft tissue calcification. STC still occurs in guinea pigs fed commercial rations (Galloway *et al.*, 1964; Sparschu and Christie, 1968), which indicates that further improvements could be made in these diets through application of knowledge gained from studies of mineral metabolism in this species. Other factors may be of importance in STC in the guinea pig. For example, excess vitamin D is known to cause calcification of vascular and other tissues in several animal species. However, little is known about the metabolism or requirement of vitamin D in the guinea pig, let alone the effects of excess.

4. Plant Toxicity and Soft Tissue Calcification

The guinea pig was used in studies of the poisonous plant *Solanum malacoxylon* because of its size and known susceptibility to STC (Camberos *et al.*, 1970). Ingestion of this plant results in anorexia, weight loss, stiffness of the legs, and massive STC, and this toxicity has been responsible for losses of thousands of cattle and sheep in Argentina. Mature young guinea pigs fed air-dried leaves or an aqueous extract of leaves from *Solanum malacoxylon* developed signs of toxicity within one to several weeks. These included anorexia, failure to gain weight, and death. There was gross evidence of calcification in heart, aorta, and skeletal muscle, and, microscopically, mineral deposits were seen also in kidney, spleen, and liver. The reason for STC in guinea pigs fed the poisonous plant was not determined. The observed changes have many features in common with phosphorus excess or magnesium deficiency and may be due to a mineral inbalance or to the presence of provitamin D substances that enhance calcification.

C. "Slobbers" in the Guinea Pig

"Slobbers" is a descriptive term for a problem in guinea pigs that probably has a variety of causes related to improper diet and/or faulty dentition. The guinea pig's teeth continue to erupt throughout life and any interference with normal wear and occlusion may lead to malocclusion and resultant difficulty with prehension and swallowing. These problems would naturally be accompanied by inability to drink efficiently or to retain saliva, which in herbivores flows profusely.

Pirtle and McKee (1951) reported an epizootic among guinea pigs in a colony maintained for tuberculosis testing. The most consistent sign was continual dampness around the mouth, chin, and ventral region of the neck. The usual course included inappetence, weight loss, and death within 6 days. Attempts to transmit the disease produced inconsistent results and no etiological agent was identified. Diet and condition of the oral cavity was not mentioned in these studies. "Slobbers" has been reported in guinea pigs fed a practical diet (Parke's Diet 18) and kale, and the syndrome was associated with dental overgrowth and histological changes in teeth (Paterson, 1957). Profuse salivation with slobbering was observed also in guinea pigs fed a purified diet deficient in folic acid (Reid *et al.*, 1956).

Chronic fluorosis was thought to be the probable cause of "slobbers" among guinea pigs in colonies in Australia (Hard and Atkinson, 1967). Signs of illness were similar to those reported previously including weight loss, depression and reduced food intake, drooling, and dysphagia. At necropsy fat depots were depleted and there was little food in the gastrointestinal tract. The lower molars were overgrown in a lingual direction whereas the upper molars were excessively worn with resultant malocclusion. Histological changes included hypoplasia and variability in thickness of molar enamel with cyst formation. The authors thought that the signs and lesions observed in these guinea pigs were suggestive of chronic fluorosis and subacute scurvy. This may have been the case, but no mention was made of type of diet fed or analyses of diet or tissues from animals with the disease.

The examples referred to above serve to illustrate the point that the guinea pig is susceptible to development of dental problems which result in difficult prehension and deglutition with resultant gradual starvation and death. Accompanying this syndrome there is uncontrolled loss of fluid from the mouth because of inefficient drinking and salivation. It is not known for certain whether the cause of this syndrome is related to nutrient deficiencies or excesses or the presence of toxic substances in the diet.

IV. SPECIAL USES OF THE GUINEA PIG AS AN EXPERIMENTAL ANIMAL MODEL

Studies Related to Ascorbic Acid Requirements

1. Connective Tissue Studies with Guinea Pigs

a. Collagen Biosynthesis. The guinea pig has been uniquely useful as an animal model to study the role of ascorbic acid in collagen biosynthesis. Boucek and Noble (1955) described a method in which pieces of sterile polyvinyl sponge (Ivalon) were implanted aseptically in the subcutis. A fibrous capsule grows around the sponge consisting mainly of loose fibrous connective tissue. Gould (1958, 1960) used this method to study collagen. Guinea pigs weighing 250 to 300 gm were fed a scorbutigenic diet and after 7 days the polyvinyl sponge was inserted aseptically into the subcutis. At various intervals after insertion, the sponges were collected; collagen in the sponge was extracted in acetone and gelatinized in water. This method was widely used and enabled investigators to obtain a considerable amount of collagen under fairly normal conditions.

Investigators previously used other methods to quantitate fibroplasia induced by wrapping one or both kidneys in Cellophane (Robertson, 1950, 1952), or injecting a colloidal mixture containing Irish moss into the subcutis (Robertson and Schwartz, 1953). Other approaches have been used to study collagen synthesis in guinea pigs such as incision wounds (Schwartz, 1970) which are either evaluated chemically for collagen synthesis or physically by determining the tensile strength of the scar tissue as a measure of healing under various nutritional conditions.

b. Studies of Normal Collagen and Proteoglycans in Guinea Pigs. The rat has been used extensively in studies of osteolathyrism produced by feeding β-aminopropionitrile or aminoacetonitrile, but the guinea pig has not been widely used in studies of intramolecular cross-linking in collagen. Recent studies on guinea pig skin collagen have focused on the isolation and characterization of peptides from the α_1 and α_2 chains. Clark and Bornstein (1972) isolated the α_1 and α_2 chains and cleaved them into peptides by a cyanobromide (CNBr) technique which breaks polypeptide chains at methionine sites. In contrast to the collagens of other species such as the rat, these polypeptide chains show a different number and distribution of methionyl residues. The α_1 chain is missing a methionine in the sequence homologous to peptide 1-CB7 of other species. The α_2 chain contains two additional methionines in the sequence homologous to peptide 2-CB4 of other species. Other than these differences guinea pig skin collagen is similar to other collagens in overall amino acid composition and molecular weight.

The guinea pig also has been useful in studying the effects of scurvy on skin acid mucopolysaccharides (Boumans and Mier, 1970), on elastin (Barnes *et al.*, 1969b), and on epiphyseal cartilage (Bonucci, 1970), but the greatest use has been in connection with collagen studies (Gould, 1968).

2. Studies Related to Bones and Teeth

a. Bone Induction. The guinea pig is a useful animal for the study of bone and ectopic calcification and there are several reasons for this. First is the requirement that the guinea pig has for ascorbic acid, a nutrient essential to the biosynthesis of collagen, a major component of the organic matrix of bone. This categorizes these animals with primates, including man who also requires vitamin C in the diet. The second advantage is the ease with which the guinea pig forms bone tissue extraneous to the skeletal tissue (ectopically). Several reports (see Section III) have described spontaneous calcification of joints, the middle ear, and other sites. Third, the animal is larger than the rat but smaller than most primates, and is easy to handle and the cost is low in comparison to primates.

Experimentally, bone formation can be induced in a variety of ways such as (a) stress or traumatic agents; and (b) use of other tissue cells such as epithelium of various types. Heiven *et al.* (1949) produced ecotopic cartilage and calcification in muscle of rabbits with such agents as alcohol and local irradiation. Bridges and Pritchard (1958) implanted small pieces of muscle pretreated with alcohol and induced the formation of cartilage beneath the kidney capsule of rabbits. This cartilage was subsequently replaced by bone.

Osteoplasia induced by implantation of bone into soft tissue is feasible. The implanted bone may be intact (Urist and McLean, 1952), treated with dilute HCl (Urist, 1965; Urist *et al.*, 1972), or enclosed in a Millipore chamber, in which case newly formed bone develops on the outer surface of the chamber (Goldhaber, 1961). The investigations of Urist and co-workers have shown that the guinea pig is especially suited for the study of bone morphogenetic potential. Excised long bones of adult guinea pigs were prepared for implantation by excising the epiphyses and soft tissue; the marrow is scraped and the cortical bone is demineralized in cold 0.6 *N* HCl. When this treated tissue is implanted in the anterior abdominal wall muscle of an autologous or allogeneric guinea pig new bone develops under the influence of a bone morphogenetic constituent which is probably a noncollagenous protein or a peptide. Such studies in the guinea pig are of great importance to understanding bone formation in healing fractures, repair of evulsive wounds, and replacement of lost alveolar height in periodontal disease.

Bone induction also has been studied in the guinea pig with transplants of transitional epithelium. Huggins (1931) described bone induction by the epithelium of the urinary tract. Friedenstein (1968) used the guinea pig extensively in this work in which autotransplants and allogeneric transplants of bladder mucosa induce osteogenesis within 10 days in most (90%) cases. The inductive activity of transitional epithelium is also high in cats, lower in rats and mice, and least in rabbits. This is an active area of research in which the guinea pig has found wide use because of its great responsiveness to bone formation under a variety of experimental situations.

b. Studies on Tooth Extraction Healing. Healing of extraction wounds has been studied with a variety of experimental animal models such as monkeys (Simpson, 1960), dogs (Huebsch and Hansen, 1969), rats (Huebsch *et al.*, 1952; Johansen, 1970), and guinea pigs (Johansen and Gilhaus-Moe, 1969; Lopez *et al.*, 1971). The guinea pig has again been quite useful for this purpose because of its requirement for ascorbic acid, as well as for the ease with which the incisors, particularly the lower incisors, can be extracted. The molars are unsuitable for this purpose because they are continuously erupting and possess a type of cartilagenous tissue which is unique to the guinea pig. Healing of extraction wounds in man, guinea pigs, and other experimental animals is similar and consists of (1) formation of blood clot in the alveolus; (2) organization of the clot; (3) replacement of granulation tissue by connective tissue; (4) transformation of the young connective tissue into osteoid; and (5) appearance of young bone and gradual maturation to normal bone.

Johansen and Gilhaus-Moe (1969) studied the repair of extraction sites in guinea pigs with autoradiography of cells labeled with [^{3}H]thymidine. Labeled fibroblasts and endothelial cells were present among the fractured fibers of the periodontium 24 hours after extraction. Forty-eight hours later, fibroblasts and endothelial cells were within the clot and 5 days after extraction the periodontal membrane remnants and granulation tissue were indistinguishable.

As a corollary of this type of work on extraction healing a method has been devised to study early bone formation in guinea pigs without the use of inducing agents. Extraction of the lower incisor leaves an alveolus about 2 cm long and about 4 mm in diameter. This space, when undisturbed, fills with bone about 20 days after tooth extraction. This behavior of the alveolar bone suggested a novel approach for the study of bone formation in guinea pig.

Most model systems of bone formation rely on either bone induction procedures described previously or the production of a bone defect or lesion which will then repair with the formation of new bone. Such approaches involve fracturing long bones or surgical production of bony defects in experimental animals. Some limitations of such approaches are the lack of reproducibility of the stress and the problem encountered in collecting the new bone formed which is always contaminated with the original intact bone. This poses no special problem if the specimen is examined histologically, where a clear distinction can be seen between the newly formed bone and old bone, but it may seriously affect results if the healing is evaluated chemically. Several approaches have been devised to allow only the recovery of the repairing osseous tissue from the site of injury. Battistone *et al.* (1972) studied the effect of a zinc-containing chelate on the healing of a guinea pig bone injury. A bone plug (about 2 mm in diameter) was removed from the tibia with a trephine. At specified time intervals the guinea pigs were sacrificed and the lesion was resampled with the trephine to obtain the repairing osseous tissue.

The alveolar space left by the extraction of the lower incisor was utilized by Lopez and associates (1970) to recover developing connective tissue. Small cylinders of a polyvinyl sponge were implanted in the alveolar socket of guinea pigs after extraction and later removed after various periods of implantation. The polyvinyl sponges seemed to delay the healing process and produced a foreign body reaction. Lopez *et al.* (1970) modified this system and implanted a rolled Dacron patch in the guinea pig incisor extraction site. Examination of the Dacron cloth 14 days after implantation with the scanning electron microscope revealed a dense proliferation of fibroblasts and fibers coursing in all directions. Histological examination was not feasible because of the resilient properties of the Dacron material. Klouda and Navia (1974) further refined this procedure by implanting a nylon mesh tube in the extraction site of guinea pig incisors. This model met the following criteria of an ideal *in vivo* model system for the study of bone formation: (1) the experimental animal should be metabolically similar to man, i.e., requirement for ascorbic acid; (2) bony defect should be reproducible; (3) the implantation should not significantly delay bone healing; (4) sufficient quantities of newly formed bone should be recovered free of previously formed bone; and (5) the implant should be of such consistency that it allows histological evaluation *in situ* and easy recovery of repairing bone for quantitative evalution. Bone was found to develop inside the tube in close opposition with the nylon fibers and completely filled the tube in 10 to 12 days.

The guinea pig has been used frequently to study normal bone activity (Soni, 1968) or fractured bones (Kodicek and Murray, 1943; Tanzer *et al.*, 1973). Methods used to evaluate the healing process have included histological evaluation, autoradiography, microradiography, tetracycline labeling, and many other techniques. Healing studies of soft tissues in guinea pigs have focused mainly on skin wounds. Repair of cutaneous wounds in guinea pigs has been an effective approach to study the mechanism of healing and fibrosis.

Because ascorbic acid, as indicated previously, is necessary for connective tissue formation, and because the guinea pig requires the vitamin, this animal has been used extensively in wound healing studies (Gillman, 1968; Ross, 1964; Schwartz, 1970).

3. Ascorbic Acid–Cholesterol Interrelationship

Scorbutic guinea pigs show atheromatous changes in the aorta (Willis, 1957). To study this phenomenon, Ginter *et al.* (1968) fed guinea pigs a scorbutigenic diet supplemented with 0.5 mg of vitamin C daily to produce a chronic hypovitaminosis in which the tissue level of ascorbic acid was below normal and yet the animals developed no overt signs of scurvy. With this model, Ginter and associates (1969) studied the effect of chronic hypovitaminosis C on the metabolism of cholesterol and atherogenesis. Guinea pigs were fed daily amounts of 0.5, 5, or 50 mg of ascorbic acid in a scorbutic diet supplemented with 0.3% cholesterol during 140 days. Their results indicated that chronic vitamin C deficiency in guinea pigs was associated with increased accumulation of cholesterol in several tissues, particularly the liver. A daily dose of 5 mg of ascorbic acid, which generally is sufficient to meet the vitamin C needs of the guinea pig, was not sufficient to meet the requirement when cholesterol was added to the diet. The mechanism for this behavior was not understood and they investigated whether absorption of exogenous cholesterol was increased. Their studies showed that this was not the case, for gastrointestinal absorption of [4-^{14}C]cholesterol was found to be reduced significantly in guinea pigs with chronic vitamin C deficiency. The possibility that increased oxidation of [1-^{14}C]acetate to liver cholesterol would occur under these same circumstances was investigated also (Ginter and Nemic, 1969) and found not to be altered significantly. Rabbits and albino rats, which are capable of synthesizing ascorbic acid, showed an accumulation of vitamin C and an increased elimination in the urine when fed cholesterol (Ginter, 1970) thus suggesting that under the influence of a cholesterol load there was an increased synthesis of ascorbic acid. In guinea pigs with mild hypovitaminosis C more [4-^{14}C] cholesterol was present in blood serum, thoracic aorta, and the bile acid fraction in liver and gallbladder bile than in control groups (Ginter *et al.*, 1971b). Thus, impaired catabolism of cholesterol to bile acids may be a factor in cholesterol accumulation in tissues such as liver and aorta. The significance of this to man and its role in atherosclerosis (Ginter, 1971) and other problems such as colelithiasis have not been definitely shown, but the guinea pig has been valuable in elucidating some of the mechanisms involved in the pathogenesis of atherosclerosis and offers the potential to explore other interactions with mineral elements such as Fe^{2+} (Brodie *et al.*, 1954; Matkovics *et al.*, 1965).

4. Cholesterol–Anemia Interrelationship

Guinea pigs fed a diet with 1% cholesterol develop severe anemia within 50 to 60 days (Okey and Greaves, 1939). The anemia results from hemolysis of erythrocytes (RBC) and is accompanied by hyperplasia of bone marrow, splenomegaly, and enlarged and fatty livers (Okey, 1944; Okey and Greaves, 1939; Ostwald *et al.*, 1966; Ostwald and Shannon, 1964). Increasing the dietary levels of protein, fat, choline, vitamin E, or ascorbic acid had not protective effect against development of anemia (Ostwald *et al.*, 1971). Splenectomy had no effect on development and progression of the anemia (Kennedy and Okey, 1947). Cholesterol-fed anemic guinea pigs had greatly increased amounts of esterified and nonesterified cholesterol in plasma, livers, and spleens and a threefold increase in cholesterol and lipid content of RBC (Ostwald *et al.*, 1966). Other studies have shown altered ratios of phospholipid classes in plasma, liver, and RBC of cholesterol-fed anemic guinea pigs (Ostwald *et al.*, 1970). Also, plasma of guinea pigs fed a control diet contained no detectable high density lipoproteins whereas in response to feeding 1% cholesterol a significant high density lipoprotein fraction appeared in the plasma (Puppione *et al.*, 1971). Subsequent studies confirmed the presence of unusual lipoprotein species in plasma of cholesterol-fed guinea pigs and showed that these were associated with a particular peptide that was not detected in lipoprotein of controls (Sardet *et al*, 1972).

The basic question related to the induction of anemia in cholesterol-fed guinea pigs has not been answered explicitly. Further studies are needed to determine whether production of defective RBC (e.g., altered lipid composition) or decreased resistance to lysis in the presence of altered plasma lipids, or both, is responsible for massive hemolysis of erythrocytes.

V. CONCLUSION

In this chapter we compiled and reviewed the literature on the nutrition and nutritional characteristics which favor the use of this laboratory animal as a research model. Review of the published data seems to merit the following general conclusions.

There are certain characteristics of the guinea pig which limits its use in certain areas of research:

1. The long fetal life of the guinea pig is responsible for its high degree of development at birth and makes it less useful than the rat for postnatal growth and development studies.
2. The gram-positive flora of the intestine is easily altered by antibiotics and studies involving systemic antibacterial compounds are not usually successful.

3. The guinea pig is highly fastidious in its choice of diet and does not lend itself to studies in which drastic dietary changes are necessary, unless a diet which is acceptable to the animal is used.

4. The requirement for many nutrients is not clearly understood, also interactions between different nutrients are not understood and this has interfered with the formulation of nutritionally adequate diets.

5. Certain habits such as coprophagy and anatomical considerations of the gastrointestinal tract (glandular stomach and medium sized cecum) may modify the nutritional behavior of the guinea pig and set it apart from the rat and rabbit. The degree of coprophagy which guinea pigs practice and the contribution of the intestinal flora to their nutrition is unknown and should be carefully investigated with present day methodology.

6. The cost of the animal today is higher than that of other rodents. This factor, along with the maintenance cost may discourage investigators from using the numbers of guinea pigs required for statistically meaningful experiments.

There also are characteristics of the guinea pig which make it particularly useful in research, e.g.,

1. The most significant characteristic is the requirement for vitamin C which places it in a category with man and other primates. This requirement makes the guinea pig a useful model for: (a) nutritional studies pertaining to vitamin C metabolism, i.e., vitamin activity of analogs, metabolic pathways, turnover rates, tissue distribution and others; (b) collagen studies—biosynthesis of collagen, amino acid and cross-linkage studies, derangement of collagen formation; (c) skin studies, particularly wound healing, scar formation, collagen–mucopolysaccharide interaction in dermal tissues, and metabolism of buccal mucosa; (d) bone studies, such as healing of tooth extractions, fractures, and early calcification of osteoid tissue; (e) atherosclerosis studies; especially those involving the role of vitamin C and cholesterol deposition in tissues; (f) adrenal–pituatary studies directed to the study of stress, corticosteroid biosynthesis, effects of ACTH, and others; and (g) hydroxylating reactions where ascorbic seems to play a role (e.g., drug toxicity, corticoid production, trytophan metabolism).

2. Germfree guinea pigs have been produced successfully so that the above-mentioned uses can be investigated in the absence of bacteria and viruses. The germfree animal should provide great advantages for gaining an understanding of the role of bacteria in many of the nutritional aspects of the guinea pig.

3. Its size, smaller than primates but larger than the rat or mouse, makes it especially useful in studies where experimental manipulations are difficult and where moderate tissue samples are required.

The guinea pig has a definite potential as an animal model in research, but further understanding of its nutritional and dietary characteristics must be obtained before this potential can be fully realized.

ACKNOWLEDGMENTS

This work was supported in part by Grants DE 02670 and RR 00463 of the National Institutes of Health.

REFERENCES

Assali, N. S. (1954). Toxemia of pregnancy. *Ciba Clin. Symp.* **6,** 3–20.

Assali, N. S., Longo, L. D., and Holm, L. W. (1960). Toxemia-like syndromes in animals, spontaneous and experimental. *Obstet. Gynecol. Survey* **15,** 151–181.

Baker, E. M. (1967). Vitamin C requirements in stress. *Amer. J. Clin. Nutr.* **20,** 583–590.

Barber, M. A., Basinski, D. H., and Mattill, H. A. (1949). Transamination in the muscles of animals deprived of vitamin E. *J. Biol. Chem.* **181,** 17–21.

Barlow, R. M. (1963). Further observations on swayback. I. Transitional pathology. *J. Comp. Pathol.* **73,** 51–67.

Barnes, M. J., Constable, B. J., and Kodicek, E. (1969a). Excretion of hydroxyproline and other amino acids in scorbutic guinea pigs. *Biochim. Biophys. Acta* **184,** 358–365.

Barnes, M. J., Constable, B. J., and Kodicek, E. (1969b). Studies *in vivo* on the biosynthesis of collagen and elastin in ascorbic acid-deficient guinea pigs. *Biochem. J.* **113,** 387–397.

Barnes, M. J., Constable, B. J., Morton, L. F., and Kodicek, E. (1970). Studies *in vivo* on the biosynthesis of collagen and elastin in ascorbic acid-deficient guinea pigs. Evidence for the formation and degradation of a partially hydroxylated collagen. *Biochem. J.* **119,** 575–585.

Battistone, G., Rubin, M., Cutright, D. E., Miller, R. A., and Harmuth-Hoene, A. E. (1972). Zinc and bone healing: Effect of zinc cysteamine-*N*-acetic acid on the healing of experimentally injured guinea pig bone. *Oral. Surg., Oral Med. Oral Pathol.* **34,** 542–552.

Beeston, A. W., and Channon, H. J. (1936). Cystine and the dietary production of fatty livers. *Biochem. J.* **30,** 280–284.

Bender, A. D., and Schottelius, D. D. (1959). Effect of short term vitamin E deficiency on guinea pig skeletal muscle myoglobin. *Amer. J. Physiol.* **197,** 491.

Bentley, L. S., and Morgan, A. F. (1945). Vitamin A and carotene in the nutrition of the guinea pig. *J. Nutr.* **30,** 159–168.

Bergman, E. N., and Sellers, A. F. (1960). Comparison of fasting ketosis in pregnant and nonpregnant guinea pigs. *Amer. J. Physiol.* **198,** 1083–1086.

Bernheim, F., and Bernheim, M. L. C. (1938). The choline oxidase of liver. *Amer. J. Physiol.* **121,** 55–60.

Best, C. H. and Huntsman, M. E. (1934). The effect of choline on the liver fats of rats in various states of nutrition. *J. Physiol. (London)* **83,** 255–274.

Block, R. J., and Bolling, D. (1951). "The Amino Acid Composition of Proteins and Foods." Thomas, Springfield, Illinois.

Bolte, H. D., Erdmann, E., and Luederitz, B. (1971). Sodium ion plus potassium on ATPase activity of ventricular heart muscle in potassium deficiency. *Circulation* **44,** Suppl., 121–132.

Bonucci, E. (1970). Fine structure of experimental epiphyseal cartilage in experimental scurvy. *J. Pathol.* **102,** 219–227.

Book, E., and Trevan, J. (1922). The food value of mangolds and the effects of deficiency of vitamin A on guinea pigs. *Biochem. J.* **16,** 780–791.

Booth, A. N., Elvehjem, C. A., and Hart, E. B. (1949). The importance of bulk in the nutrition of the guinea pig. *J. Nutr.* **37,** 263–274.

Boucek, R. J., and Noble, N. L. (1955). Connective tissue; techniques for its isolation and study. *AMA Arch. Pathol.* **59,** 553–558.

Boumans, P. J., and Mier, P. D. (1970). Cutaneous acid mucopolysaccharides in ascorbic acid deficiency. *Dermatologica* **141,** 234–238.

Bridges, J. B., and Prichard, J. J. (1958). Bone and cartilage induction in the rabbit. *J. Anat.* **92,** 28–38.

Brodie, B. B., Axelrod, J., Shore, P. A., and Udenfriend, S. (1954). Ascorbic acid in aromatic hydroxylation. II. Products formed by reaction of substrate with ascorbic acid, ferrous ion, and oxygen. *J. Biol. Chem.* **208,** 741–750.

Camberos, H. R., Davis, G. K., Djafar, M. I., and Simpson, C. F. (1970). Soft tissue calcification in guinea pigs fed the poisonous plant *Solanum malacoxylon. Amer. J. Vet. Res.* **31,** 685–696.

Carlton, W. W., and Henderson, W. (1963). Cardiovascular lesions in experimental copper deficiency in chickens. *J. Nutr.* **81,** 200–208.

Casselman, W. G. B., and Williams, G. R. (1954). Choline deficiency in the guinea pig. *Nature (London)* **173,** 210–211.

Chevallier, A., and Choron, Y. (1935). Sur la teneur du foie en vitamine A et ses variations. *C. R. Soc. Biol.* **120,** 1223–1225.

Chevallier, A., and Choron, Y. (1936). Accumulation of vitamin A reserves in the guinea pig. *C. R. Soc. Biol.* **121,** 1015–1016.

Clark, C. C., and Bornstein, P. (1972). Cyanogen bromide clevage of guinea pig skin collagen. Isolation and characterization of peptides from the $\alpha 1$ and $\alpha 2$ chains. *Biochemistry* **11,** 1468–1474.

Clark, L. (1971). Hypervitaminosis A: A review. *Aust. Vet. J.* **47,** 568–571.

Clark, R. (1943). Domsiekte or pregnancy disease in sheep. IV. The effect of obesity on the reaction of sheep to a suddent reduction in diet. *Onderstepoort J. Vet. Sci. Anim. Ind.* **18,** 279–288.

Clark, R., Groenewald, J., and Malan, J. (1943). Domsiekte or pregnancy disease in sheep. III. *Onderstepoort J. Vet. Sci. Anim. Ind.* **18,** 263–278.

Daft, F. S. (1951). Effect of vitamin C on pantothenic acid-deficient rats. *Fed. Proc., Fed. Amer. Soc. Biol.* **10,** 380.

Daft, F. S., and Schwarz, K. (1952). Prevention of certain B-vitamin deficiencies with ascorbic acid or antibiotics. *Fed. Proc., Fed. Amer. Soc. Exp. Biol.* **11,** 200–201.

Dam, H., Schonheyder, F., and Lewis, L. (1937). The requirement for vitamin K of some different species of animals. *Biochem. J.* **31,** 22–27.

Dean, D. J., and Duell, C. (1963). Diets without green food for guinea pigs. *Lab. Anim. Care* **13,** 191–196.

Deshmukh, D. S., and Ganguly, J. (1964). Effect of dietary protein contents on the intestinal conversion of β-carotene to vitamin A in rats. *Indian J. Biochem.* **1,** 204–207.

Dowling, J. E., and Wald, G. (1958). Vitamin A deficiency and night blindness. *Proc. Nat. Acad. Sci. U.S.* **44,** 648–661.

Dowling, J. E., and Wald, G. (1960). The biological function of vitamin A acid, *Proc. Nat. Acad. Sci.* **46,** 587–608.

Edwards, M. J. (1966). Prenatal loss of fetuses and abortion in guinea pigs. *Nature (London)* **210,** 223–224.

Elmadfa, I., and Feldheim, W. (1971). Enzyme activity, metabolites and clinically demonstrable changes in guinea pigs in tocopherol deficiency. *Int. J. Vitam. Nutr. Res.* **41,** 490–503.

Emerique, L. (1937). Experimental rickets in the guinea pig. *C. R. Soc. Biol.* **205,** 879–882.

Enwonwu, C. O. (1973a). Experimental protein-calorie malnutrition in the guinea pig and evaluation of the role of ascorbic acid status. *Lab. Invest.* **29,** 17–26.

Enwonwu, C. O. (1973b). Alterations in ninhydrin-positive substances and cytoplasmic protein synthesis in the brains of ascorbic acid deficient guinea pigs. *J. Neurochem.* **21,** 69–78.

Erdmann, E., Bolte, H. D., and Luderitz, B. (1971). The (Na^+ + K^+)-ATPase activity of guinea pigs heart muscle in potassium deficiency. *Arch. Biochem. Biophys.* **145,** 121–125.

Everson, G. J. (1968). Preliminary study of carbohydrates in the urine of manganese-deficient guinea pigs at birth. *J. Nutr.* **96,** 283–288.

Everson, G. J., and Shrader, R. E. (1968). Abnormal glucose tolerance in manganese-deficient guinea pigs. *J. Nutr.* **94,** 89–94.

Everson, G. J., Hurley, L. S., and Geiger, J. F. (1959). Manganese deficiency in the guinea pig. *J. Nutr.* **68,** 49–56.

Everson, G. J., Tsai, H. C., and Wang, T. (1967). Copper deficiency in the guinea pig. *J. Nutr.* **93,** 533–540.

Everson, G. J., Shrader, R. E., and Wang, T. (1968). Chemical and morphological changes in the brains of copper-deficient guinea pigs. *J. Nutr.* **96,** 115–125.

Fabianek, J. (1954). Observations on guinea pigs fed a purified artificial diet devoid of nicotinic acid. *Bull. Soc. Chim. Biol.* **36,** 1009–1014.

Farmer, F. A., Mutch, B. C., Bell, J. M., Woolsey, L. D., and Crampton, E. W. (1950). The vitamin E requirement of guinea pigs. *J. Nutr.* **42,** 309–318.

Faulkner, W. R., Blood, F. R., and Darby, W. J. (1958). Effect of folic acid deficiency on myoglobin concentration in skeletal muscle of the guinea pig. *J. Nutr.* **66,** 361–366.

Fell, R. V., Wilkinson, W. S., and Watts, A. B. (1959). The utilization in the chick of D-and L-amino acids in liquid and dry diets. *Poultry Sci.* **38,** 1203.

Foley, E. J. (1942). Toxemia of pregnancy in the guinea pig. *J. Exp. Med.* **75,** 539–546.

Friedenstein, A. Y. (1968). Induction of bone tissue by transitional epithelium. *Clin. Orthop.* **59,** 21–37.

Galloway, J. H., Glover, D., and Fox. W. C. (1964). Relationship of diet and age to metastatic calcification in guinea pigs. *Lab. Anim. Care* **14,** 6–12.

Ganaway, J. R., and Allen, A. M. (1971). Obesity predisposes to pregnancy toxemia (ketosis) of guinea pigs. *Lab. Anim. Sci.* **21,** 40–44.

Gil, A., Briggs, G. M., Typpo, J., and MacKinney, G. (1968). Vitamin A requirement of the guinea pig. *J. Nutr.* **96,** 359–362.

Gillman, T. (1968). On some aspects of collagen formation in localized repair and in diffuse fibrotic reactions in injury. *In* "Treatise on Collagen" (B. S. Gould, ed.), Vol. 2, Part B, pp. 373–406. Academic Press, New York.

Gilyard, A. T., and Gilyard, R. T. (1935). Acetonemia in goats. *Cornell Vet.* **25,** 201–202.

Ginter, E. (1970). Effect of dietary cholesterol on vitamin C metabolism in laboratory animals. *Acta Med. (Budapest)* **27,** 23–29.

Ginter, E. (1971). Vitamin C deficiency and gallstone formation. *Lancet* **2,** 1198–1199.

Ginter, E., and Nemic, R. (1969). Metabolism of (1-14C)acetate in guinea pigs with chronic vitamin C hyposaturation. *J. Atheroscler. Res.* **10,** 373–376.

Ginter, E., Bobek, P., and Orecka, M. (1968). Model of chronic hypovitaminosis C in guinea pigs. *Int. J. Vitam. Res.* **38**, 104–106.

Ginter, E., Babala, J., and Cerven, J. (1969). The effect of chronic hypovitaminosis C on the metabolism of cholesterol and atherogenesis in guinea pigs. *J. Atheroscler. Res.* **10**, 341–352.

Ginter, E., Cerven, J., Nemic, R., and Mikus, L. (1971a). Lowered cholesterol catabolism in guinea pigs with chronic ascorbic acid deficiency. *Amer. J. Clin. Nutr.* **24**, 1238–1245.

Ginter, E., Zloch, Z., Cerven, J., Nemic, R., and Babala, J. (1971b). Metabolism of L-ascorbic acid-1-14-C in guinea pigs with alimentary cholesterol atheromatosis. *J. Nutr.* **101**, 197–204.

Goettsch, M. (1930). The dietary producton of dystrophy of the voluntary muscles. *Proc. Soc. Exp. Biol. Med.* **27**, 564–567.

Goldhaber, P. (1961). Osteogenic induction across millipore filters *in vivo*. *Science* **133**, 2065–2067.

Goswami, M. N. D., and Knox, W. E. (1963). An evaluation of the role of ascorbic acid in the regulation of tyrosine metabolism. *J. Chronic Dis.* **16**, 363–371.

Gould, B. S. (1958). Biosynthesis of collagen. III. The direct action of ascorbic acid on hydroxyproline and collagen formation in subcutaneous polyvinyl sponge implants in guinea pigs. *J. Biol. Chem.* **232**, 637–649.

Gould, B. S. (1960). Ascorbic acid and collagen fiber formation. *Vitam. Horm. (New York)* **18**, 89–120.

Gould, B. S. (1968). Collagen biosynthesis. *In* "Treatise on Collagen" (B. S. Gould, ed.), Vol. 2, Part A, pp. 139–188. Academic Press, New York.

Grace, N. D., and O'Dell, B. L. (1968). Potassium requirement of the weanling guinea pig. *J. Nutr.* **94**, 166–170.

Grace, N. D., and O'Dell, B. L. (1970a). Effect of magnesium deficiency on the distribution of water and cations in the muscle of the guinea pig. *J. Nutr.* **100**, 45–50.

Grace, N. D., and O'Dell, B. L. (1970b). Relation of polysome structure to ribonuclease and ribonuclease inhibitor activities in livers of magnesium-deficient guinea pigs. *Can. J. Biochem.* **48**, 21–26.

Green, H. S. N. (1937). Toxemia of pregnancy in the rabbit. I. Clinical manifestations and pathology. *J. Exp. Med.* **65**, 809–832.

Green, H. S. N. (1938). Toxemia of pregnancy in the rabbit. II. Etiological considerations with special reference to hereditary factors. *J. Exp. Med.* **67**, 369–388.

Griffith, W. H., and Nyc, J. F. (1971). *In* "The Vitamins" (W. H. Sebrell, Jr. and R. S. Harris, eds.), 2nd ed., Vol. 3, pp. 3–123. Academic Press, New York.

Griffith, W. H., and Wade, N. J. (1940). The interrelationship of choline, cystine, and methionine in the occurrence and prevention of hemorrhagic degeneration in young rats. *J. Biol. Chem.* **132**, 627–637.

Haltaline, K. C., Nelson, J. D., and Woodman, E. B. (1970). Fatal shigella infection induced by folic acid deficiency in young guinea pigs. *J. Infec. Dis.* **121**, 275–287.

Handler, P. (1944). The effect of excessive nicotinamide feeding on rabbits and guinea pigs. *J. Biol. Chem.* **154**, 203–206.

Handler, P. (1949). Response of guinea pigs to diets deficient in choline. *Proc. Soc. Exp. Biol. Med.* **70**, 70–73.

Hara, H. (1960). Pathologic study on riboflavin deficiency in guinea pigs. *J. Vitaminol. (Kyoto)* **6**, 24–42.

Hard, G. C., and Atkinson, F. F. V. (1967). "Slobbers" in laboratory guinea pigs as a form of chronic fluorosis. *J. Pathol. Bacteriol.* **94**, 95–102.

Harden, A., and Zilva, S. S. (1919). Experimental scurvy in monkeys. *J. Pathol. Bacteriol.* **22**, 246–251.

Harris, L. J. and Raymond, W. D. (1939). Assessment of the level of nutrition. A method of the estimation of nicotinic acid in urine. *Biochem. J.* **33**, 2037–2051.

Harris, R. S. (1970). Natural versus purified diets in research with nonhuman primates. *In* "Feeding and Nutrition of Nonhuman Primates" (R. S. Harris, ed.). Academic Press, New York.

Heinicke, H. R., Harper, A. E., and Elvehjem, C. A. (1955a). Protein and amino acid requirements of the guinea pig. I. Effect of carbohydrate, protein level and amino acid supplementation. *J. Nutr.* **57**, 483–496.

Heinicke, H. R., Harper, A. E., and Elvehjem, C. A. (1955b). Protein and amino acid requirements of the guinea pig. II. Effect of age, potassium and magnesium and type of protein. *J. Nutr.* **58**, 269–280.

Heiven, J. (1949). The experimental production of ectopic cartilage and bone in the muscle of rabbits. *J. Bone Joint Surg. Amer. Vol. 31,* 765–775.

Highet, D. M., and West, E. S. (1946). Toxic effects in scorbutic guinea pigs produced by large doses of thiamine. *Proc. Soc. Exp. Biol. Med.* **63**, 482–483.

Hintz, H. F. (1969). Effect of coprophagy on digestion and mineral excretion in the guinea pig. *J. Nutr.* **99**, 375–378.

Hogan, A. G., and Regan, W. O. (1946). Diet and calcium phosphate deposits in guinea pigs. *Fed. Proc., Fed. Amer. Soc. Exp. Biol.* **5**, 138.

Hogan, A. G., Regan, W. O., and House, W. B. (1950). Calcium phosphate deposits in guinea pigs and the phosphorus content of the diet. *J. Nutr.* **41**, 203–213.

Hollmann, S., and Touster, O. (1964). "Non-Glycolytic Pathways of Metabolism of Glucose." Academic Press, New York.

Holst, A. (1907). Experimental studies relative to "Ship-beri-beri" and scurvy. I. Introduction. *J. Hyg.* **7**, 619–633.

Holst, A., and Frolich, T. (1907). Experimental studies relative to "Ship-beri-beri" and scurvy. II. On the etiology of scurvy. *J. Hyg.* **7**, 634–671.

Homburg, E., and Reed, C. I. (1945). An effort to demonstrate wrist stiffness in guinea pigs on a deficient diet. *Fed. Proc., Fed. Amer. Soc. Exp. Biol.* **4**, 34–35.

Hornig, D., Weber, F., and Wiss, O. (1971). The effect of vitamin C depletion on the free amino acid content in blood plasma of the guinea pig. *Int. J. Vitam. Nutr. Res.* **41**, 86–89.

House, W. B., and Hogan, A. G. (1955). Injury to guinea pigs that follows a high intake of phosphates. *J. Nutr.* **55**, 507–517.

Howe, P. R., Wesson, L. G., Boyle, P. E., and Wolbach, S. B. (1940). Low calcium rickets in the guinea pig. *Proc. Soc. Exp. Biol. Med.* **45**, 298–301.

Howell, J. M., Thompson, J. N., and Pitt, G. A. J. (1967). Changes in the tissues of guinea pigs fed on a diet free from vitamin A, but containing methyl retinoate. *Brit. J. Nutr.* **21**, 37–42.

Huebsch, R. F., and Hansen, L. S. (1969). A histological study of extraction wounds in dogs. *Oral Surg., Oral Med. Oral Pathol.* **28**, 187–196.

Huebsch, R. F., Coleman, R. D., Frandsen, A. M., and Becks, H. I. (1952). The healing process following molar extraction. I. Normal male rats. *Oral Surg., Oral Med. Oral Pathol.* **5**, 864–876.

Huggins, C. (1931). The formation of bone under the influence of epithelium of the urinary tract. *Arch. Surg. (Chicago)* **22**, 377–408.

Hughes, R. E., and Hurley, R. J. (1970). *In vitro* uptake of ascorbic acid by the guinea pig eye lens. *Exp. Eye Res.* **9**, 175–180.

Hughes, R. E., and Jones, P. R. (1971). The influence of sex and age on the deposition of L-xyloascorbic acid in tissue of guinea pigs. *Brit. J. Nutr.* **25**, 77–83.

Hughes, R. E., and Nicholas, P. (1971). Effects of caging on the ascorbic acid content of the adrenal glands of the guinea pig and gerbil. *Life Sci., Part II* **10,** 53–55.

Hughes, R. E., Hurley, R. J., and Jones, P. R. (1971a). Retention of ascorbic acid by the guinea pig eye lens. *Exp. Eye Res.* **12,** 39–43.

Hughes, R. E., Hurley, R. J., and Jones, P. R. (1971b). The retention of ascorbic acid by guinea pig tissues. *Brit. J. Nutr.* **26,** 433–438.

Hurley, L. S., and Volkert, N. E. (1965). Pantothenic acid and coenzyme A in the developing guinea pig liver. *Biochim. Biophys. Acta* **104,** 372–376.

Hurley, L. S., Volkert, N. E., and Eichner, J. T. (1965). Pantothenic acid deficiency in pregnant and non-pregnant guinea pigs, with special reference to effects on the fetus. *J. Nutr.* **86,** 201–208.

Johansen, J. R. (1970). Repair of the post-extraction alveolus in the Wistar rat. *Acta Odontol. Scand.* **28,** 441–461.

Johansen, J. R., and Gilhaus-Moe, O. (1969). Repair of the post-extraction alveolus in the guinea pig. *Acta Odontol. Scand.* **27,** 249–262.

Jones, J. H. (1971). Vitamin D. Deficiency effects in animals. *In* "The Vitamins" (W. H. Sebrell, Jr., and R. S. Harris, eds.), 2nd ed., Vol. 3, Chapter X. Academic Press, New York.

Jukes, T. H., Oleson, J. J., and Dornbush, A. C. (1945). Observations on monomethylaminoethanol and dimethylaminoethanol. *J. Nutr.* **30,** 219–223.

Kamath, S. K., and Arnrich, L. (1973). Effect of dietary protein on the intestinal biosynthesis of retinal from ^{14}C-β carotene in rats. *J. Nutr.* **103,** 202–206.

Kennedy, B., and Okey, R. (1947). Lipid metabolism and development of anemia in splenectomized guinea pigs fed cholesterol. *Amer. J. Physiol.* **149,** 1–6.

Klouda, G., and Navia, J. M. (1974). An improved model system for the study of bone repair. *Calcif. Tissue Res.* **14,** 245–249.

Kobayashi, M. (1970). Studies on the phospholipid metabolism in choline deficient guinea pigs. II. Effects of feeding on a *N*-methylethanolamine-supplemented diet. *J. Vitaminol. (Kyoto)* **16,** 119–128.

Kodicek, E., and Murray, P. D. F. (1943). Influence of a prolonged partial deficiency of vitamin C on the recovery of guinea pigs from injury to bones and muscles. *Nature (London)* **151,** 395.

Kon, S. K., Bird, M. J., Coates, M. E., Mullen, J. E. C., and Shepheard, E. E. (1946). Failure to demonstrate wrist stiffness in guinea pigs receiving skim milk diets. *Arch. Biochem.* **11,** 371–373.

Koyanagi, T., and Odagiri, S. (1961). Effects of the sulfur amino acids on the vitamin A content in liver of rats. *Nature (London)* **192,** 168–169.

Kuether, C. A., Telford, I. R., and Roe, J. H. (1944). The relation of the blood level of ascorbic acid to the tissue concentrations of this vitamin and to the histology of the incisor teeth in the guinea pig. *J. Nutr.* **28,** 347–358.

Lane-Petter, W. (1968). Cannibalism in rats and mice. *Proc. Roy. Soc. Med.* **61,** 1295–1296.

Leach, R. M. (1967). Role of manganese in the synthesis of mucopolysaccharides. *Fed. Proc., Fed. Amer. Soc. Exp. Biol.* **26,** Part 1, 118–120.

Leach, R. M., Jr., and Muenster, A. M. (1962). Studies on the role of manganese in bone formation. I. Effect upon the mucopolysaccharide content of chick bone. *J. Nutr.* **78,** 51–56.

Linner, E., and Nordstrom, K. (1969). Transfer of D-isoascorbic acid and L-ascorbic acid into guinea pigs eyes. *Doc. Ophthalmol.* **26,** 164–170.

Liu, K. C., Typpo, J. T., Lu, J. Y., and Briggs, G. M. (1967). Thiamine requirement of the guinea pig and the effect of salt mixtures in the diets on thiamine stability. *J. Nutr.* **93,** 480–484.

Lopez, H., Latham, M., Navia, J. M., and Martinez, J. G. (1970). Effect of dietary zinc and phosphate supplements on composition of healing bone. *Int. Ass. Dent. Res. Proc.* Abstract No. 81, p. 69.

Lopez, H., Latham, M., Navia, J. M., and Shackleford, J. (1971). Effect of zinc and phosphate dietary supplements on experimental extraction wounds. *Int. Ass. Dent. Res. Proc.* Abstract No. 379, p. 147.

Lopez, H., Isbell, P., Anderson, J., and Navia, J. M. (1973). The metabolism of zinc during bone fracture healing. *Int. Ass. Dent. Res. Proc.* Abstract No. 94, p. 82.

Lorenzen, E. J., and Smith, S. E. (1947). Copper and manganese storage in the rat, rabbit, and guinea pig. *J. Nutr.* **33,** 143–154.

Luderitz, B., Bolte, H. D., and Steinbeck, G. (1971). Single fiber potentials and cellular cation-concentration of the heart ventricle in chronic potassium deficiency. *Klin. Wochenshr.* **49,** 369–371.

Lyman, R. L., and Elvehjem, C. A. (1951). The lability of thiamine in certain purified rations. *Proc. Soc. Exp. Biol. Med.* **77,** 813–816.

McBean, L. D., Smith, J. C., and Halsted, J. A. (1972). Zinc deficiency in guinea pigs. *Proc. Soc. Exp. Biol. Med.* **140,** 1207–1209.

Madsen, L. L., McCay, C. M., and Maynard, L. A. (1933). Possible relationship between cod liver oil and muscular degeneration of herbivora fed synthetic diets. *Proc. Soc. Exp. Biol. Med.* **30,** 1434.

Mannering, G. J. (1949). Vitamin requirements of the guinea pig. *Vitam. Horm. (New York)* **7,** 201–221.

Matkovics, B., Pénzes, P., and Göndös, G. (1965). The *in vitro* transformation of deoxycholic acid into cholic acid with ferroascorbate system. *Steroids* **5,** 451–457.

Maynard, L. A., Boggs, D., Fisk, G., and Sequin, D. (1958). Dietary mineral interrelations as a cause of soft tissue calcification in guinea pigs. *J. Nutr.* **64,** 85–97.

Mazzone, H. M., and Williams, J. N., Jr. (1957). Monometric studies on guinea pig choline oxidase. *Proc. Soc. Exp. Biol. Med.* **94,** 183–185

Morris, E. R., and O'Dell, B. L. (1961). Magnesium deficiency in the guinea pig. Mineral composition of tissues and distribution of acid-soluble phosphorus. *J. Nutr.* **75,** 77–85.

Morris, E. R., and O'Dell, B. L. (1963). Relationship of excess calcium and phosphorus to magnesium requirement and toxicity in guinea pigs. *J. Nutr.* **81,** 175–181.

National Academy of Sciences–National Research Council. (1962). "Nutrient Requirements of Laboratory Animals," Publ. No. 990. NAS–NRC, Washington, D.C.

National Academy of Sciences–National Research Council. (1972). "Nutrient Requirements of Laboratory Animals," Publ. No. 0-309-02028-x. NAS–NRC, Washington, D.C.

Navia, J. M. (1970). The preparation, use and nutrient stability of non-human primate diets. *In* "Feeding and Nutrition of Non-Human Primates" (R. S. Harris, ed.), pp. 277–297. Academic Press, New York.

Navia, J. M., and Lopez, H. (1973). A purified gel diet for guinea pigs. *Lab. Anim. Sci.* **23,** 111–114.

O'Dell, B. L., Vandepopuliere, J. M., Morris, E. R., and Hogan, A. G. (1956). Effect of a high phosphorus diet on acid-base balance in guinea pigs. *Proc. Soc. Exp. Biol. Med.* **91,** 220–223.

O'Dell, B. L., Morris, E. R., Pickett, E. E., and Hogan, A. G. (1957). Diet composition and mineral balance in guinea pigs. *J. Nutr.* **63,** 65–77.

O'Dell, B. L., Morris, E. R., and Regan, W. O. (1960). Magnesium requirements of guinea pigs and rats. Effect of calcium and phosphorus and symptoms of magnesium deficiency. *J. Nutr.* **70,** 103–110.

O'Dell, B. O., Hardwick, B. C., Reynolds, G., and Savage, J. E. (1961). Connective tissue defect in the chick resulting from copper deficiency. *Proc. Soc. Exp. Biol. Med.* **108,** 402–405.

Odumosu, A., and Wilson, C. W. (1971). Metabolic availability of ascorbic acid in female guinea pigs. *Brit. J. Pharmacol.* **42,** 637P–638P.

Okey, R. (1944). Cholesterol injury in the guinea pig. *J. Biol. Chem.* **156,** 179–190.

Okey, R., and Greaves, V. D. (1939). Anemia caused by feeding cholesterol to guinea pigs. *J. Biol. Chem.* **129,** 111–123.

Oleson, J. J., Van Donk, E. C., Bernstein, S., Dorfman, L., and Subbarow, Y. (1947). Steroids and the stiffness syndrome in guinea pigs. *J. Biol. Chem.* **171,** 1–7.

Ostwald, R., and Shannon, A. (1964). Composition of tissue lipids and anemia of guinea pigs in response to dietary cholesterol. *Biochem. J.* **91,** 146–154.

Ostwald, R., Darwish, O., Irwin, D., and Okey, R. (1966). Bone marrow composition of cholesterol-fed guinea pigs. *Proc. Soc. Exp. Biol. Med.* **123,** 220–224.

Ostwald, R., Yamanaka, W., and Light, M. (1970). The phospholipids of liver, plasma, and red cells in normal and cholesterol-fed anemic guinea pigs. *Proc. Soc. Exp. Biol. Med.* **134,** 814–820.

Ostwald, R., Yamanaka, W., Irwin, D., Hansma, H., Light, M., and Tom, K. (1971). Effects of dietary modifications on cholesterol-induced anemia in guinea pigs. *J. Nutr.* **101,** 699–712.

Pappenheimer, A. M. (1930). Pathological changes in the skeletal muscles produced by dietary means. *Proc. Soc. Exp. Biol. Med.* **27,** 567–568.

Pappenheimer, A. M., and Goettsch, M. (1941). Death of embryos in guinea pigs on diets low in vitamin E. *Proc. Soc. Exp. Biol. Med.* **47,** 268–270.

Pappenheimer, A. M., and Schogoleff, C. (1944). The testis in vitamin E deficiency guinea pigs. *Amer. J. Pathol.* **20,** 239–244.

Parry, H. B., and Shelley, H. (1961). Experimental induction and control of "Toxemia of Pregnancy" in sheep. *Pathol. Microbiol.* **24,** 681.

Partridge, S. M. (1966). Biosynthesis and nature of elastin structures. *Fed. Proc., Fed. Amer. Soc. Exp. Biol.* **25,** 1023–1029.

Paterson, J. S. (1957). The role of an adequate diet in the production of healthy guinea pigs. *Proc. Nutr. Soc.* **16,** 83–87.

Petering, H. G., Stubberfield, L., and Delor, R. A. (1948). Studies on the guinea pig factor of Wulzen and van Wagtendonk. *Arch. Biochem.* **18,** 487–494.

Pfander, W. H., and Mitchell, H. H. (1952). The ascorbic acid requirement of the guinea pig when adrenal weight and odontoblast height are used as criteria. *J. Nutr.* **47,** 503–523.

Pirtle, E. C., and McKee, A. P. (1951). An epizootic of unknown etiology in guinea pigs. *Proc. Soc. Exp. Biol. Med.* **77,** 425–429.

Puppione, D. L., Sardet, C., Yamanaka, W., Ostwald, R., and Nichols, A. V. (1971). Plasma lipoproteins of cholesterol-fed guinea pigs. *Biochim. Biophys. Acta* **231,** 295–301.

Pyke, R. E., Hockstra, W. C., and Phillips, P. H. (1967). Effects of fluoride on magnesium deficiency in guinea pigs. *J. Nutr.* **92,** 311–316.

Randoin, L., and Lecoq, M. (1930). Is it possible to produce experimental rickets in the guinea pig? *C. R. Soc. Biol.* **191,** 732–734.

Ranhotra, G. S., and Johnson, B. C. (1965). Effect of feeding different amino acid diets on growth rate and nitrogen retention of weanling rats. *Proc. Soc. Exp. Biol. Med.* **118,** 1197–1201.

Reid, M. E. (1953). Development of a synthetic diet for young guinea pigs and its use in the production of B vitamin deficiencies. *Fed. Proc., Fed. Amer. Soc. Exp. Biol.* **12,** 472.

Reid, M. E. (1954a). Nutritional studies with the guinea pig. B-vitamins other than pantothenic acid. *Proc. Soc. Exp. Biol. Med.* **85,** 547–550.

Reid, M. E. (1954b). Production and counteraction of a fatty acid deficiency in the guinea pig. *Proc. Soc. Exp. Biol. Med.* **86,** 708–709.

Reid, M. E. (1955). Nutritional studies in the guinea pig. III. Choline. *J. Nutr.* **56,** 215–229.

Reid, M. E. (1958). "The Guinea Pig in Research," Publ. No. 557. Dr. Henry J. Klaunberg, Human Factors Research Bureau, Inc., 2349 Coral Way, Miami 45, Florida.

Reid, M. E. (1961). Nutritional studies with the guinea pig. VII. Niacin. *J. Nutr.* **75,** 279–286.

Reid, M. E. (1964). Nutritional studies with the guinea pig. XI. Pyridoxine. *Proc. Soc. Exp. Biol. Med.* **116,** 289–292.

Reid, M. E. (1966). Methionine and cystine requirements of the young guinea pig. *J. Nutr.* **88,** 397–402.

Reid, M. E., and Bieri, J. G. (1967). Nutritional studies with the guinea pig. VIII. Thiamine. *Proc. Soc. Exp. Biol. Med.* **126,** 11–13.

Reid, M. E., and Briggs, G. M. (1953). Development of a semi-synthetic diet for young guinea pigs. *J. Nutr.* **51,** 341–354.

Reid, M. E., and Briggs, G. M. (1954). Nutritional studies with the guinea pig. II. Pantothenic acid. *J. Nutr.* **52,** 507–518.

Reid, M. E., and Martin, M. G. (1959). Nutritional studies with the guinea pig. V. Effects of deficiency of fat or unsaturated fatty acids. *J. Nutr.* **67,** 611–622.

Reid, M. E., and Mickelsen, O. (1963). Nutritional studies with the guinea pig. VIII. Effect of different proteins, with and without amino acid supplements on growth. *J. Nutr.* **80,** 25–32.

Reid, M. E., and von Sallmann, L. (1960). Nutritional studies with the guinea pig. VI. Tryptophan (with ample dietary niacin). *J. Nutr.* **70,** 329–336.

Reid, M. E., Martin, M. G., and Briggs, G. M. (1956). Nutritional studies with the guinea pig. IV. Folic acid. *J. Nutr.* **59,** 103–119.

Reid, M. E., Bieri, J. G., Plack, P. A., and Andrews, E. L. (1964). Nutritional studies with the guinea pig. X. Determination of the linoleic acid requirement. *J. Nutr.* **82,** 401–408.

Rivers, J. M., Krook, L., and Cormier, A. (1970). Biochemical and histological study of guinea pig fetal and uterine tissue in ascorbic acid deficiency. *J. Nutr.* **100,** 217–227.

Robens, J. R. (1970). Teratogenic effects of hypervitaminosis A in the hamster and the guinea pig. *Toxicol. Appl. Pharmacol.* **16,** 88–99.

Robertson, W. van B. (1950). Concentration of collagen in guinea pig tissues in acute and prolonged scurvy. *J. Biol. Chem.* **187,** 673–677.

Robertson, W. van B. (1952). The effect of ascorbic acid deficiency on the collagen concentration of newly induced fibrous tissue. *J. Biol. Chem.* **196,** 403–408.

Robertson, W. van B., and Schwartz, B. (1953). Ascorbic acid and the formation of collagen. *J. Biol. Chem.* **201,** 689–696.

Rogers, J. B., Vanloon, E. J., and Beattie, M. F. (1951). Familial incidence of a toxemia of pregnancy in the guinea pig. *J. Exp. Zool.* **117,** 247–258.

Rogers, Q. R., and Harper, A. E. (1965). Amino acid diets and maximal growth in the rat. *J. Nutr.* **87,** 267–273.

Roine, P., Booth, A. N., Elvehjem, C. A., and Hart, E. B. (1949). "Importance of Potassium and Magnesium in Nutrition of the Guinea Pig." Department of Biochemistry, College of Agriculture, University of Wisconsin, Madison.

Ross, R. (1964). Chapter IX. Studies of Collagen Formation in Healing Wounds. *Advan. Biol. Skin* **5,** 144–164.

Roy, R. N., and Guha, B. C. (1958). Species different in regard to the biosynthesis of ascorbic acid. *Nature (London)* **182,** 319–320.

Sardet, C., Hansma, H., and Ostwald, R. (1972). Characterization of guinea pig plasma lipoproteins. The appearance of new lipoproteins in response to dietary cholesterol. *J. Lipid Res.* **13,** 624–639.

Sauer, F. (1961). Acetate metabolism in experimental ketosis of guinea pigs. *Can. J. Biochem. Physiol.* **39,** 739–746.
Sauer, F. (1963). Fasting ketosis in the pregnant guinea pig. *Ann. N. Y. Acad. Sci.* **104,** 787–798.
Schaefer, A. E., Salmon, W. D., and Strength, D. R. (1951). The influence of vitamin B_{12} on the utilization of choline precursors by the chick. *J. Nutr.* **44,** 305–311.
Schottelius, B. A., Schottelius, D. D., and Bender, A. D. (1959). Effect of vitamin E on myoglobin content of guinea pig skeletal muscle. *Proc. Soc. Exp. Biol. Med.* **102,** 581–583.
Schwartz, P. L. (1970). Ascorbic acid in wound healing–a review. *J. Amer. Diet. Ass.* **56,** 497–503.
Seidel, J. C., and Harper, A. E. (1960). Some observations on vitamin E deficiency in the guinea pig. *J. Nutr.* **70,** 147–155.
Shields, G. S., Coulson, W. F., Kimball, D. A., Carnes, W. H., Cartwright, G. E., and Wintrobe, M. M. (1962). Studies on copper metabolism. XXXII. Cardiovascular lesions in copper-deficient swine. *Amer. J. Pathol.* **41,** 603–621.
Shimotori, N., Emerson, G. A., and Evan, N. M. (1939). Role of vitamin E in the prevention of muscular dystrophy in guinea pigs reared on synthetic rations. *Science* **90,** 89.
Shrader, R. E., and Everson, G. J. (1967). Anomalous development of otoliths associated with postural defects in manganese-deficient guinea pigs. *J. Nutr.* **91,** 453–459.
Shrader, R. E., and Everson, G. J. (1968). Pancreatic pathology in manganese-deficient guinea pigs. *J. Nutr.* **94,** 269–281.
Simpson, H. E. (1960). Experimental investigation into the healing of extraction wounds in macacus rhesus monkeys. *J. Oral Surg., Anesth. Hosp. Dent. Serv.* **18,** 391–399.
Singh, K. D., Morris, E. R., Regan, W. O., and O'Dell, B. L. (1968). An unrecognized nutrient for the guinea pig. *J. Nutr.* **94,** 534–542.
Slanetz, C. A. (1943). The adequacy of improved stock diets for laboratory animals. *Amer. J. Vet. Res.* **4,** 182–189.
Smith, S. E., Williams, M. A., Bauer, A. C., and Maynard, L. A. (1949). The wrist stiffness syndrome in guinea pigs. *J. Nutr.* **38,** 87–96.
Smith, T. (1913). Some bacteriological and environmental factors in the pneumonias of lower animals with special reference to the guinea pig. *J. Med. Res.* **29,** 291–323.
Soni, N. N. (1968). Quantitative study of bone activity in alveolar and femoral bone of the guinea pig. *J. Dent. Res.* **47,** 584–589.
Sparschu, G. L., and Christie, R. J. (1968). Metastatic calcification in a guinea pig colony: A pathological survey. *Lab. Anim. Care* **18,** 520–526.
Stevenson, D. E., and Wilson, A. A. (1963). Bovine ketosis. *In* "Metabolic Disorders of Domestic Animals," pp. 115–121. Davis, Philadelphia, Pennsylvania.
Stone, I. (1966). Hypoascorbemia, the genetic disease causing the human requirement for exogenous ascorbic acid. *Perspect. Biol. Med.* **10,** 133–134.
Stone, N., and Meister, A. (1962). Function of ascorbic acid in the conversion of proline to collagen hydroxyproline. *Nature (London)* **194,** 555–557.
Sweeney, J. P., and Marsh, A. C. (1973). Liver storage of vitamin A in rats fed carotene stereoisomers. *J. Nutr.* **103,** 20–25.
Tanzer, F. S., Lopez, H., Isbell, P., and Navia, J. M. (1973). Calcitonin studies of bone healing using a quantitative chlortetracycline assay. *Int. Ass. Dent. Res.* Abstract No. 93, p. 82.
Thompson, D. J., Heintz, J. F., and Phillips, P. H. (1964). Effect of magnesium, fluoride, and ascorbic acid on metabolism of connective tissue. *J. Nutr.* **84,** 27–30.
Tozar, F. M. (1921). The effect on the guinea pig of deprivation of vitamin A and of the antiscorbutic factor, with special reference to the condition of the costochondral junctions of the ribs. *J. Pathol. Bacteriol.* **24,** 306–324.
Tracy, T. A., and Miller, G. L. (1969). Obstetric problems of the massively obese. *Obstet. Gynecol.* **33,** 204–208.
Tsai, H. C. C., and Everson, G. J. (1967). Effect of manganese deficiency on the acid mucopoly-saccharides in the cartilage of guinea pigs. *J. Nutr.* **91,** 447–452.
Tucker, H. F., and Eckstein, H. C. (1937). The effect of supplementary methionine and cystine on the production of fatty livers by diet. *J. Biol. Chem.* **121,** 479–484.
Undenfriend, S. (1966). Formation of hydroxyproline in collagen. *Science* **152,** 1335–1340.
Urist, M. R. (1965). Bone: Formation by autoinduction. *Science* **150,** 893–899.
Urist, M. R., and McLean, F. C. (1952). Osteogenic potency and new bone formation by induction in transplants to the anterior chamber of the eye. *J. Bone Joint Surg., Amer. Vol.* **34,** 443 and 470.
Urist, M. R., Iwata, H., and Strates, B. S. (1972). Bone morphogenetic protein and proteinase in guinea pigs. *Clin. Orthop.* **85,** 275–290.
van Bijsterveld, O. P. (1971a). *In vitro* phagocytosis in pyridoxine deficiency. *J. Med. Microbiol.* **4,** 165–170.
van Bijsterveld, O. P. (1971b). The digestive capacity of pyridoxine-deficient phagocytes *in vitro*. *J. Med. Microbiol.* **4,** 337–342.
van Wagtendonk, W. J., and Wulzen, R. (1950). Physiological and chemical aspects of the antistiffness factor essential for guinea pigs. *Vitam. Horm. (New York)* **8,** 69–125.
Waibel, P. E., Bird, H. R., and Baumann, C. A. (1954). Effects of salts on the instability of thiamine in purified chick diets. *J. Nutr.* **52,** 273–283.
Waugh, W. A., and King, C. G. (1932a). Isolation and identification of vitamin C. *J. Biol. Chem.* **97,** 325–331.
Waugh, W. A., and King, C. G. (1932b). The vitamin C activity of hexuronic acid from suprarenal glands. *Science* **76,** 630–631.
Wichmann, K., Salminen, M. and Roine, P. (1954). Intestinal synthesis of folic acid and biotin in the guinea pig. *Suom. Kemistilehti B* **27,** 5.
Williams, R. J., and Deason, G. (1967). Individuality in vitamin C needs. *Proc. Nat. Acad. Sci U.S.* **57,** 1638–1641.
Williams, W. L. (1890). Parturient eclampsia in the mare. *Amer. Vet. Rev.* **14,** 559–571.
Willis, G. C. (1957). The reversibility of atherosclerosis. *J. Can. Med. Ass.* **77,** 106–110.
Wolbach, S. B. (1947). Vitamin A deficiency and excess in relation to skeletal growth. *J. Bone Joint Surg.* **29,** 171–192.
Wolbach, S. B. (1954). VII. Effects of vitamin A deficiency and hypervitaminosis A in animals. *In* "The Vitamins" (W. H. Sebrell, Jr. and R. S. Harris, eds.), Vol. 1, p. 106. Academic Press, New York.
Wolbach, S. B., and Howe, P. R. (1928). Vitamin A deficiency in the guinea pig. *Arch. Pathol.* **5,** 239–253.
Wood, E. L., and Hines, H. M. (1937). Effect of vitamin E deficient and muscular dystrophy producing diet on metabolism of guinea pigs. *Proc. Soc. Exp. Biol. Med.* **36,** 746–747.
Woodruff, C. W., Clark, S. L., Jr., and Bridgeforth, E. B. (1953). Folic acid deficiency in the guinea pig. *J. Nutr.* **51,** 23–34.
Wooley, D. W., and Sprince, H. (1945). The nature of some new dietary factors required by guinea pigs. *J. Biol. Chem.* **157,** 447–453.
Worden, A. N., and Slavin, G. (1944). Nicotinic acid deficiency in the pig and guinea pig. I. The effects of a pellagra-producing diet upon these species. *J. Comp. Pathol. Ther.* **54,** 77–87.
Woytkiw, L., and Esselbaugh, N. C. (1951). Vitamin A and carotene absorption in the guinea pig. *J. Nutr.* **43,** 451–458.

Wretland, K. A., and Rose, W. C. (1950). Methionine requirement for growth and utilization of its optical isomers. *J. Biol. Chem.* **187**, 697–701.

Wulzen, R. and Bahrs, A. M. (1941). Effects of milk diets on guinea pigs. *Amer. J. Physiol.* **133**, 500.

Young, M. L., Mitchell, G. V., and Seward, C. R. (1973). Effect of protein and methionine on vitamin A liver storage in rats fed D.D.T. *J. Nutr.* **103**, 218–224.

Young, R. J., and Lucas, C. C. (1957). Choline deficiency in the guinea pig. *Can. J. Biochem. Physiol.* **35**, 1–6.

Young, R. J., Norris, L. C., and Heuser, G. F. (1954). The utilization by B_{12} deficient chicks of monomethyl-aminoethanol, homocystine and betaine as precursors of choline and methionine. *J. Nutr.* **53**, 233–248.

Zilva, S. S. (1941). The influence of intermittent consumption of vitamin C on the development of scurvy. *Biochem. J.* **35**, 1240–1245.

Zilva, S. S., and Wells, F. M. (1919). Changes in the teeth of the guinea pig produced by a scorbutic diet. *Proc. Roy. Soc., Ser. B* **90**, 505–512.

Chapter 18

Toxicology and Teratology

Richard M. Hoar

I. INTRODUCTION

Guinea pigs are accepted widely as a suitable model for either toxicity or teratology studies. They are readily available, of convenient size, grow rapidly, and have been used extensively as an experimental animal in a wide variety of biological research. Their long gestation period of 68 days, with its trimester characteristics, provides an opportunity for separation of toxic or teratogenic effects on the embryo from those upon the fetus and allows investigation of a fetus with an essentially mature central nervous system prior to delivery. Other special characteristics of the guinea pig will be discussed as the literature encompassing the toxicological and teratological responses of guinea pigs is reviewed in the following pages.

II. TOXICOLOGY

A. Inhalation Studies

The toxicity of various compounds or air pollutants may be evaluated by inhalation studies. The well-known sensitivity of the respiratory system of the guinea pig has provided a basis for studies of inhalation phenomena including bronchospasms, asthma, and reactions to dust and particle behavior. Such studies are usually conducted in a small exposure chamber into which the material under investigation is introduced in a vapor or as particulate matter. There are various techniques for introducing the materials into the chamber (Rector *et al.*, 1966) and for measuring air flow and chamber or tissue concentrations (Amdur *et al.*, 1952; Rose *et al.*, 1970). In addition, Amdur and Mead (1956) developed a technique for measuring several aspects of respiration in unanesthetized guinea pigs within an exposure chamber and reported normal values for tidal volume, respiratory rate, minute volume, resistance, and compliance (Amdur and Mead, 1958).

1. Irritating Vapors

Amdur (1957) studied the influence of particulate matter upon the irritability of toxic gases and demonstrated that while a 1-hour exposure to sulfur dioxide increased pulmonary flow resistance (P.F.R.), the addition of an aerosol of submicrometer dimensions, whether it be an irritant (sulfuric acid mist) or inert (sodium chloride), increased P.F.R. in a manner greater than a simple additive effect. Particle sizes greater than submicrometer did not have this effect. Amdur *et al.* (1952) had previously demonstrated that sulfuric acid mist alone produced laryngeal spasms first and then deep-seated lung damage. The laryngeal response resulted in high mortality and depended more upon concentration than length of exposure while lung damage was more dependent upon the total dosage than upon concentration alone. Pattle *et al.* (1956) suggested that the response of guinea pigs to sulfuric acid should include bronchoconstriction as well as laryngeal spasm; however, Amdur (1958) indicated that response of the respiratory apparatus depended upon particle size of the sulfuric acid mist until concentration levels were reached that induced reactions only in the upper respiratory tract. The response to ethylene oxide, a decrease in pulmonary compliance and an increase in pulmonary resistance, was not produced by bronchial constriction, but rather by obstruction of the "bronchial tree" with secretions (Amdur and Mead, 1956), thus suggesting another factor in mortality observed following exposure of guinea pigs to irritating gases or air pollutants. Amdur (1959) continued her studies of irritant gases and found that of those studied the most irritating gas was formic acid followed by formaldehyde, acetic acid, and sulfur dioxide. When combined with a sodium chloride aerosol, the response to sulfur dioxide and to formaldehyde was potentiated (Amdur, 1959, 1960) while the response to acetic and formic acids was unchanged (Amdur, 1959, 1960, 1961).

The effect of histamine aerosols was qualitatively different from the irritant gases discussed above (Amdur, 1966), increasing pulmonary flow resistance, and decreasing compliance tidal volume and minute volume with respiratory frequency dependent upon both concentration and length of exposure. Reduction of histamine-induced bronchospasms was employed as a measure of bronchodilator effects of sympathomimetic amines. Ten percent CO_2 in air decreased bronchoconstrictor activity of histamine and at the same time decreased the effectiveness of some bronchodilators; in particular, ethylnoradrenaline (less effective), phenylephrine amphetamine and tyramine (inactive), and ephedrine which became a potentiator of the constrictor action of histamine (Atkinson *et al.*, 1970). Acetylcholine, methacholine, nicotine, a muscarine-like compound 5-methylfurfuryltrimethylammonium (Furmethide), and 5-hydroxytryptamine aerosols are also bronchoconstrictors in guinea pigs. Herxheimer (1956) found that atropine, propantheline, and hexamethonium antagonize all these bronchoconstrictors.

Low concentrations of ozone (1.06 ppm per hour by volume) given a total of 268 days over 433 calendar days increased the mortality rate of guinea pigs from 40 to 71% (Stokinger *et al.*, 1957). Deaths were attributed to chronic bronchitis, bronchiolitis, and pneumonia induced by ozone. Preexposure to 1 to 5 ppm of ozone for 2 hours increased susceptibility of guinea pigs to the lethal effects of histamine (Easton and Murphy, 1967). On the other hand, Murphy *et al.* (1964) demonstrated while preexposure to low concentrations of ozone produced a tolerance to its lethal effects, it did not change the respiratory patterns during breathing low concentrations of ozone. Rose *et al.* (1970) did not significantly alter carbon monoxide lethality by elevating atmospheric pressure in an exposure chamber.

Inhalation studies of paint thinner (mineral spirits) conducted with guinea pigs produced an increased mortality rate of 27 to 79% depending on concentration which could not be explained by hematological, pathological, and biochemical examinations (Rector *et al.*, 1966). Further studies of "mineral spirits" (Jenkins *et al.*, 1971) indicated that higher levels of ascorbic acid in diets reduced mortality; males were more susceptible than females and there were strain differences in mortality. Difficulties associated with trichlorethylene (TCE) anesthesia and detection of dichloroacetylene (DCA), a degradation product of TCE, in very low concentrations within the "atmosphere" of nuclear submarines prompted a study of these vapors as mixtures of DCA-TCE or DCA-ether (Siegel *et al.*, 1971). Following a 4-hour exposure a "mixture containing TCE was approximately 4 times as toxic as that containing ether," the LC_{50} being 15 ppm for DCA-TCE and 52 ppm for DCA-ether.

2. Irritating Particles

Occupational diseases and the effects of air polluted with particulate matter may be studied with guinea pigs and inhalation chambers. Stokinger *et al.* (1950) demonstrated the lethality of inhaled beryllium sulfate. Levy and Higgins (1965) injected a single dose of zinc silicate or zinc beryllium silicate intratracheally and studied resultant lesions in the lungs. Beryllium salt produced more severe lesions with some injury still present 15 months later. Nordberg and Serenius (1969) demonstrated that inhalation of mercury vapors resulted in much higher concentrations of mercury in the brain of guinea pigs than was attained by injection. Amdur and Corn (1963) demonstrated that zinc ammonium sulfate aerosols increased pulmonary flow resistance in guinea pigs exposed for only 1 hour to its particles. Experimental asbestosis was studied in guinea pigs using chrysotile asbestos dust in an inhalation chamber (Gross and de Treville, 1967), and early results indicated that, as in the rat, this type of asbestosis is nonprogressive and localized in the short respiratory bronchioles and adjoining alveolar ducts. Davis (1970a,b,c) studied the development of pleural granulomas following intrapleural injection of chrysotile asbestos dust, fine glass fibers, or ceramic aluminum silicate (Davis *et al.*, 1970) in guinea pigs and reported a wide range of histological and ultrastructural characteristics as well as long-term effects which included fibrosis and eventual calcification of granulomas.

Religa and Máslinski (1971) suggested that the activation of histamine synthesis and release in guinea pig lungs exposed to silica dust may "play an important role in the pathogenesis and symptomatology of silicosis." Silicosis, pneumoconiosis, and chronic obstructive bronchopulmonary disease are common among those in dusty environments. Whether these disease states may predispose an individual to emphysema was investigated by Gross *et al.* (1968). Dusts of various types were introduced by intratracheal injections, and emphysema was produced by chronic exposure to NO_2 or by the intratracheal injection of papain. The authors concluded that pneumoconiotic lesions "did not determine the location of emphysema whether experimentally produced (guinea pigs, rats and hamsters) or naturally occurring (hamsters)."

3. Anesthetics

Chenoweth (1971) reported chronic exposure (7 hours, 5 days/week × 5–6 weeks) to subanesthetic levels of diethyl ether caused no deleterious effects while halothane and methoxyflurane produced weight loss and liver damage. Confirmation came from studies in which guinea pigs exposed to 1% halothane for an hour (light surgical anesthesia) from 1 to 5 times exhibited no visible untoward effects; however, hepatic lesions were seen which increased in severeity with increased exposure to halothane (Hughes and Lang, 1972).

Geddes *et al.* (1972) determined the distribution of halothane-^{82}Br in both maternal and fetal tissues of guinea pigs following exposure to a 0.5% concentration of the vapor for from 5 to 45 minutes. They demonstrated that the fetal liver plays an important role in the distribution of halothane within the fetus for the fetal liver had more than twice that found in the maternal liver while the fetal and maternal brains had similar halothane levels. Similarly, the importance of the fetal liver in preventing the fetal brain from exposure to high concentrations of thiopental was demonstrated by Finster *et al.* (1972a). However, lidocaine crossed the placenta rapidly producing high concentrations in the fetal heart and brain and a concentration in the fetal liver higher than that of the dam (Finster *et al.*, 1972b).

4. Tranquilizers

Bergström *et al.* (1963) reported that effects of thalidomide upon cortical activity of the guinea pig brain depended somewhat upon its age. Administration at 46–55 days gestation produced electrical silence, at 55–62 days there were "silent intervals interspersed between intervals of irregular slow wave activity," while at or near term fetuses, neonates, and adults exhibited similar responses. Berté *et al.* (1968) demonstrated that oxazepam crosses the guinea pig placenta although appearing in a lower concentration in the fetus. Chlordiazepoxide was found to have antihistaminic activity while both oxazepam and diazepam were found to be inactive (Gluckman, 1965).

5. Fetal Effects—General

If, as has been seen, anesthetics and tranquilizers cross the placental barrier in guinea pigs, then it follows that they may have a direct as well as an indirect effect (maternal) on the fetus which could be deleterious. Further, interference with maternal respiration or cord vessels should produce a fetal response. Thus, Windle and Becker (1941) found that a subanesthetic dose of Nembutal* given to the dam produced uncontrolled respiration and hypercapnia in the fetus; a response which following delivery, an atmosphere of air alone could not prevent, CO_2 made worse, but oxygen corrected. In this regard it is interesting to note the work of Glass *et al.* (1944) who measured the ability of guinea pigs to resist anoxia produced by an atmosphere of nitrogen. Fetuses, just prior to delivery, continued breathing for 6 minutes; neonates, at 12 hours after birth, continued breathing for 4.5 minutes; and adults lasted only 3 minutes. Fetal brain effects, as measured by a decreased amplitude of EEG potentials, were induced by maternal injections of sodium pentobarbital (Becker *et al.*, 1958; Rosen and McLaughlin, 1966a,b), thiopental (Rosen, 1967b); or thiogenal (Bergström *et al.*, 1966); meperidine (Bleyer and Rosen, 1968); by maternal exposure to ether (Bergström *et al.*, 1966; Bergström, 1962; Rosen, 1967b) or nitrogen gas (Bergström, 1962); by clamping of the maternal trachea (Rosen, 1967a; Rosen and McLaughlin, 1966b); or by oral administration of alcohol to the dam (Bergström *et al.*, 1965).

6. Fetal Effects—Asphyxia Neonatorum

The guinea pig is equally suited to studies of asphyxia neonatorum with its associated high incidence of stillbirths, neonatal deaths, and neurological disorders. The gestation period can be accurately timed, its placentation is comparable to that in man, its survival time under anoxia at term resembles the human neonate and is shorter than many other species. However, its nervous system is more highly developed at birth than that of the human neonate thus making the effects of anoxia easier to initiate, recognize, and describe (Becker and Donnell, 1952). Asphyxia induced near term by clamping either uterine or umbilical vessels produced an uneven expansion of the lungs and caused aspiration of amniotic fluid (Whitehead *et al.*, 1942). The cardiovascular responses of fetal guinea pigs to asphyxia were investigated by Greenfield and Shepherd (1953) whose work indicated that temporary occlusion of the umbilical vessels or uterine vessels resulted in slowing of the fetal heart, an effect which could be mimicked

*Abbott Laboratories, North Chicago, Illinois, 60064.

by giving the dam low O_2 mixtures, or abolished by fetal atropine injections. These effects were absent in fetuses that weigh less than 20 to 35 gm thus suggesting an age factor could be involved. Guinea pigs rendered hypoxic just prior to delivery lost more weight immediately following birth and subsequently failed to gain weight as did their littermate controls. They all exhibited symptoms of neural damage such as tremors, lack of coordination, flaccid paralysis (hindlimbs), spastic paralysis (forelimbs), and facial motor weakness. The degree and location of the impairment varied between animals, but showed no correlation with duration of anoxia (Windle and Becker, 1943). Their central nervous systems exhibited histopathological changes including edema, chromatolysis, petechial hemorrhages, enlarged ventricles, and loss of neurons and myelinated fibers (Windle and Becker, 1943; Windle *et al.*, 1944). Neurological damage was also manifested in neonates subjected to anoxia by their behavior in simple problem solving using a specially constructed problem box. They made more errors originally and required extensive retraining following an initial learning experience (Becker and Donnell, 1952).

B. Dermal and Oral Toxicity

1. Skin Sensitization

The skin sensitization capability of various compounds was first demonstrated in guinea pigs by Landsteiner and Jacobs (1935, 1936). Using substituted benzene compounds they demonstrated development of a true allergic reaction following sensitization of the skin. As additional studies suggested from these findings were pursued, it became evident that skin could be sensitized by administration of a chemical either topically, intradermally, or intraperitoneally, confirming the work of Sulzberger (1930). Chase (1941) demonstrated guinea pigs could inherit differing susceptibilities to substances such as 2,4-dinitrochlorobenzene or poison ivy; the reactivity to poison ivy having already been demonstrated by Simon *et al.* (1934), Rackemann and Simon (1934), and Simon (1936). Rothberg (1970) reported on the skin-sensitizing capacity of several riot control agents administered by the intradermal or topical route or both. He noted that neither α-bromo-α-tolunitrile nor 10-chloro-5,10-dihydrophenarsazine produced skin sensitivity when administered intradermally. However, both α-chloracetophenone and *O*-chlorobenzylidene malononitrile produced skin sensitization when administered either intradermally or topically.

In 1944 Draize *et al.* reported that, although there appeared to be some individual variation, 0.5 ml of a 30% solution of DDT/kg/day (150 mg/kg/day) in dimethylphthalate was absorbed by both intact and abraided skin producing anorexia, weight loss, tremors, clonic convulsions, and, in some cases, death. However, Dunn *et al.* (1946) could not repeat the results of Draize *et al.* and suggested that the previous responses were due to contaminants. Kar and Dikshith (1970), on the other hand, reported a sharp decrease in the level of almost all amino acids in the skin, increased keratinization, and disruption of the basal layer following dermal application of DDT, suggesting the earlier work of Draize *et al.* (1944) had merit.

2. Oral

Oral administration of DDD and DDT at doses of 500 mg/kg/day and 150 mg/kg/day, respectively, for 1 or 2 weeks, first stimulated and then decreased cortisol production in guinea pigs (Balazs, 1969). St. Omer (1970), in a review article, indicated that the oral LD_{50} of DDT for this species was 400 mg/kg in oil. The LD_{50}, reported for other insecticides, were as follows: lindane, 127 mg/kg; aldrin, 33 mg/kg; and dieldrin, 25 mg/kg. Uzoukwu and Sleight (1972) stated that the median lethal dose of dieldrin following oral administration was about 45 mg/kg. These same investigators reported that dieldrin in the feed (100 ppm) caused abortions and was found in the fetuses. Davies *et al* (1959) suggested that following poisoning by the organophosphate sarin, injections (im) of the soluble methanesulphonate (2-hydroxyiminomethyl-*N*-methylpridinium plus atropine sulfate) proved to be quite efficacious in guinea pigs raising the LD_{50} from 0.048 to 3.81 mg/kg. Fleisher *et al.* (1970) extended these studies, examining the effects of atropine, various oximes, and mecamylamine on sarin poisoning, increasing the LD_{50} as much as 18.5-fold with various combinations. Finally, it should be noted that perhaps the most toxic of the herbicides is dioxin, its LD_{50} in guinea pigs being 0.0006 mg/kg (Anonymous, 1971).

Early studies of lead poisoning in guinea pigs indicated very quickly that their response was typical and included degenerative changes in the kidney epithelium, chronic focal atrophy of the liver and effusions into serous cavities (Ophüls, 1915). However, degeneration of germ cells produced by lead acetate (Weller, 1916) was not transferred to their descendants (Colin, 1931), although lead administration increased the frequency of abortions in females from Family 2, an inbred strain. Following earlier investigators, Fullerton (1966) examined the effects of the oral administration of lead acetate upon nerve conduction velocity. The results were varied, the death rate being difficult to assess and reduced nerve conduction velocity and/or paralysis of the hind limbs occurring in only a few animals. However, reduced conductance velocity was seen only in those animals which exhibited segmental demyelination. Similarly, it appears that defects and vertigo which accompany plumbism are associated with segmental demyelination and axonal degeneration of the VIII nerve (Goździk-Żolnierkiewicz and Moszyński, 1969). Secchi *et al.* (1970) compared enzymatic activity of kidneys made ischemic by partial constriction of the renal artery with that of kidneys damaged by a daily dose of 120 mg/kg of lead nitrate delivered by gastric intubation. The results suggested that lead produced renal damage through tissue hypoxia. Bielecka (1972) demonstrated that the guinea pig was a good experimental model for investigation of pathological aminoaciduria resulting from oral administration of lead acetate. She discovered the urinary excretion of alanine, glycine, aspartate, and glutamate was proportional to the dosage of lead received. Thus, aspartate and glycine levels increased at the middle (9 mg/kg) and high (12 mg/kg) levels of lead, glutamate at the high dose, and alanine at all three doses. Bielecka and Jeske (1972) continued this research with guinea pigs in a study of agents which protect against lead poisoning. All animals survived a daily oral dose of 12 mg/kg lead acetate when they received a liver protein hydrolysate im. The mechanism of this prophylactic action is unknown, but they suggest it may promote synthesis of body proteins, resynthesis of lead-inhibited enzymes, or enrichment of the initial pool of heme synthesis precursors or perhaps all three.

Combination of some metals with a second substance can enhance the deleterious effects of the metal. Desselberger and Wegener (1971) demonstrated the ethyl alcohol or cobalt given separately were nonlethal to guinea pigs, but when given in combination most of the animals died within a few weeks. The suggestion of synergism was strengthened by morphological changes within the myocardium, liver, and pancreas and by the general unspecific decrease in resistance (increase in severe infections) which accompanied the combined treatment.

The toxic reaction produced in guinea pigs by contact with or consumption of certain plants ranges from skin sensitization to poison ivy (Rackemann and Simon, 1934; Simon *et al.*, 1934; Simon, 1936) to lathyrism (osteo- and neuro-) which follows the ingestion of seeds of various varieties of the genus *Lathyrus.* A neurotoxin, β-*N*-oxalyl-L-α,β-diaminopropionic acid (OX-Dapro), derived from several of the species of *Lathyrus,* will produce neurological symptoms such as ataxia, torticollis, or sudden jerking movements (Rao *et al.*, 1969). Other toxic plants studied in guinea pigs include *Solanum malacoxylon,* an Argentinian plant which produces soft tissue calcification and death (Camberos *et al.*, 1970); *Crotalaria spectabilis* seeds which are often incorporated into ground commercial diets and can produce congested and necrotic livers, copious amounts of ascitic fluid, and focal areas of pneumonia (Carlton, 1967) and *Swainsona galegifolia.* The latter produces vacuolation of circulating lymphocytes (Huxtable and Gibson, 1970) as well as vacuolar lesions in the neurons of the central nervous system, kidneys, and livers (Huxtable, 1969) which appear to be single "membrane-bound" structures upon electron microscopic examination (Huxtable, 1970). Groundnut toxicity, which Paget (1954) first labeled "exudative hepatitis" and described as a dietary deficiency [a toxicity later correctly attributed to a plant by Paterson and Crook (1962)], is actually a noninfectious disease of guinea pigs which produced gross edema and pathological changes in the liver and pancreas. Wogan and Pong (1970) described the small number of fungi with the capability of producing aflatoxins that cause liver necrosis and death.

Penicillin toxicity for guinea pigs was established by Hamré *et al.* (1943). As little as 70–120 mg/kg iv produced death. Heilman and Herrell (1944) reported a similar response to from 1000 to 5000 units of penicillin and noted that the toxic effects they observed appeared to be identical to those reported by Hamré *et al.* (1943). Similarly, Hauduroy and Rosset (1948) and Stuart and Slavin (1951) while testing the effectiveness of penicillin in experimental tuberculosis in guinea pigs found the antibiotic to be extremely toxic. Cormia *et al.* (1947), reporting the toxicity of penicillin, stated that 1000 units of penicillin G given subcutaneously produced a characteristic adrenal necrosis while Stevens and Gray (1953) noted that the mortality was increased by intraperitoneal injections of adrenal cortical extract and cortisone. However, Ambrus *et al.* (1952) felt that the toxic effects were due to an allergic reaction. Subsequently, it was suggested by de Somer *et al.* (1955) that the toxicity was due to the overgrowth of gram-negative bacteria, with their accompanying toxins, in the intestinal tract. These authors modified their position later (Eyssen *et al.*, 1957) by suggesting that although the initial disorder must reside in the gastrointestinal tract, probably the intestinal flora, the mode of action was not clear and might even be accompanied by the development of resistance to high doses followed by the return of sensitivity 3 months later. This developed sensitivity to penicillin, when it occurred during pregnancy, resulted in a hypersensitivity to penicillin by the progeny (Chenchikova and Matron, 1970).

Other antibiotics, with few exceptions, are also toxic when given to guinea pigs. Bacitracin given orally at a dosage of 1000 units per animal was lethal (de Somer *et al.*, 1955; Eyssen *et al.*, 1957). Chlortetracycline (20 mg orally) and streptomycin (60 mg orally) were toxic while chloramphenicol (60 mg/day for 2 weeks) was not (Eyssen *et al.*, 1957). Although Roine and Ettala (1952) reported losses of 6 to 9 animals within 10 days on a diet of 100 mg aureomycin/kg of diet, Ambrus *et al.* (1952) reported that only 30% of the guinea pigs receiving 10 mg/kg of aureomycin orally died, and Altemeier *et al.* (1950) stated that 10–20 mg/kg/day given im for 4 days was not toxic. These same authors (Altemeier *et al.*, 1950) stated that toxicity observed following im injections of chloromycetin was due to glycols used as vehicles.

III. TERATOLOGY

A. Introduction

As in general toxicity studies, among animals commonly employed in investigations of congenital malformations, the guinea pig has unique characteristics. It occupies a position intermediate between rats and mice on the one hand and primates and man on the other. For example, its endocrine control of reproduction is similar to that of man even to its trimester characteristics and yet pregnancy is preceded by estrus. Its placenta appears to be capable of endocrine activity and yet it is labyrinthine and its functions are supplemented by an everted yolk sac exposed to uterine secretions. Estrus, ovulation, and fertilization can be accurately timed as with most rodents and data are available defining or describing many aspects of gestation and embryonic development. For example, normal resorption activity involves the loss of approximately 5.8 to 6.3% of implanted embryos as determined by differences between the number of implantation sites and functioning corpora lutea (Hoar and King, 1967; Hoar, 1969). Normal embryonic development of the guinea pig through gestation day 26 was described by Scott (1937). Tables presented by Draper (1920) and Ibsen (1928) give size data for timed pregnancies and the work of Ibsen (1928) includes weights of placentas, deciduae basales, fetal membranes, amniotic fluid, and maternal uteri. The development of the external form correlated with the weight and length of guinea pig embryos between the ages of 11 and 20 days of gestation was described by Harman and Prickett (1931/1932) and between the ages of 21 and 35 days of gestation by Harman and Dobrovolny (1932/1933). The ossification of the entire skeleton was detailed by Petri (1935), while Harman and Saffry (1934) presented the skeletal development of anterior limb from the 25-day embryo to 161 days postnatally. Their efforts were extended by Rajtová (1966, 1967, 1968). In addition, Goy *et al.* (1957) defined stillbirth and abortion in guinea pigs, demonstrating that the length of gestation varied inversely with the number of offspring in the litter. Their definition provided mathematical limits within which one could expect normal litters with live offspring and outside of which one could expect deaths due to abortion (early) or stillbirths (late).

B. Malformations

1. Induced

Malformations have been induced in guinea pigs in a variety of ways. Thalidomide given ip in a saline suspension or orally by gastric tube or in dry feed for three consecutive generations produced a "conspicuous number of cleft palates and deformities of the outer ear and shortened limbs" as well as reducing the litter size, increasing prenatal deaths, and producing smaller offspring particularly from those mothers fed thalidomide in the diet (Arbab-Zadeh, 1965). However, if 2 mg of thalidomide was mixed with human serum (1:50) derived from pooled blood obtained from parents of "Contergan" children and injected ip from 3 days prior to mating until 15 days after mating, the offspring displayed external and internal malformations similar to those observed in man such as aplasia and bone atrophy of the forelimbs (Arbab-Zadeh, 1965).

The azo dye, trypan blue, produced deleterious effects upon the fetus. Pregnant guinea pigs received a single subcutaneous injection of 2 ml of 1% trypan on a single day during the period of days 6 through 13 of gestation and their offspring were recovered on day 30 of gestation or allowed to deliver. A generalized response seen at 30 days included an increased resorption rate, growth retardation, and gross abnormalities with maximal abnormalities (57%) resulting from injection on day 11. Every embryo from treated females was affected by the dye, the response varying from shorter crown–rump length to gross abnormalities. The malformations displayed included: cyst of the anterior thoracic wall (49.3%), spina bifida (33.8%), microphthalmia (5.6%), hydrocephaly (4.2%), edema (2.8%) meningocele (1.4%), and miscellaneous (2.8%). Fifty percent of retarded and/or malformed embryos displayed a posterior cleft palate. Treated females allowed to deliver had a reduced litter size, their offspring displaying only those abnormalities (5.3%) which were compatible with life (Hoar and Salem, 1961).

Hypervitaminosis A produced malformations. Giroud and Martinet (1959a,b) gave pregnant guinea pigs 50,000 IU of vitamin A on days 12 through 14 of gestation and reported an increased number of abortions, resorptions, and a case of mandibular fissure combined with a bifid tongue. Robens (1970) gave guinea pigs 200,000 USP units/kg of vitamin A palmitate as a single dose on selected days (14 through 20) during organogenesis. Most of the females were allowed to deliver although some were sacrificed at 50 days of gestation. Multiple defects, involving primarily the head region, were seen in 60.8% of offspring born following maternal treatment on days 14 through 16. Missing coccygeal vertebrae and agnathia, involving 38.5% of offspring, were seen following treatment on day 17 of gestation. Limb defects (37.2%) were the principle abnormalities resulting from treatment on days 18 through 20, while only 1 of 226 control offspring was abnormal (conjoined twins, 0.4%). Fetal growth was not affected and it is unlikely that fetal death was elevated because the average litter size was not reduced.

The pesticide, carbaryl, a carbamate cholinesterase inhibitor, was teratogenic when given orally in gelatin capsules at a dosage of approximately 300 mg/kg on either days 11 through 20 inclusive or singly on days 11 through 20 of gestation (Table I). When single doses were given on selected days, malformations were produced only on days 12 through 16 of gestation (Robens, 1969). The defects in treated animals were skeletal, mostly in cervical vertebrae. In addition, it was noted that "two fetuses from a litter treated on day 13 had no kidneys or genital organs; one of these also had fused thoracic

Table I
Effects of Carbaryl in the Guinea Pig
(300 mg/kg/day)

Treatment (oral doses)	Gestation days	Maternal deaths (%)	Average litter size	Fetal mortality (%)	Number malformed
Control	–	–	3.4	9.5	2 (1.9%)
Multiple	11–20	38	2.9	17.5	11 (23.9%)
Single	11, 17–20	9	3.7	2.7	–
Single	12–16	3	3.7	7.6	9 (9.8%)

vertebrae and ribs. The 2 terata in the controls were a cervical vertebra anomaly in 1 fetus and a third lower incisor and a bifid tongue in another." It should also be noted that multiple treatment increased maternal deaths and fetal mortality while reducing litter size (Table I). Contrasting results were obtained by Weil *et al.* (1973) who were unable to produce malformations with carbaryl at either 300 mg/kg in the diet or 200 mg/kg given by oral intubation.

Edwards (1967, 1969a,b) examined effects of hyperthermia applied early in gestation on reproduction and fetal development in guinea pigs. He noted that resorptions appeared to be most common following hyperthermia on about days 11 to 15, while abortions, occurring at a mean of 32.4 ± 4.85 days of gestation, appeared most frequently (83%) following hypothermia on days 11 through 18. Of 251 offspring recovered at delivery the following malformations were noted: microencephaly (41%), hypoplastic digits (13%), exomphalos (7%), talipes (4%), hypoplastic incisors (4%), cataract (3%), renal agenesis (2%), and amyoplasia (2%). A detailed investigation of prenatal retardation of brain growth at various times during gestation was conducted (Edwards, 1969c). The incidence of reduced brain weight and microencephaly increased most following hyperthermia for 4 or 8 days during days 15 through 32 of gestation. For 2 successive days of hyperthermia the effects were most marked on days 20 and 21, and 22 and 23 of gestation. Particularly on day 21 these effects could be produced if maternal body temperature was elevated more than 2.5°C. These studies of hyperthermia in guinea pigs were continued with a report on the production of clubfoot (Edwards, 1971). The defect was most frequent following hyperthermia at days 18 through 25 of gestation and was usually associated with defects of the spinal cord which included defects of the central canal and increases in width of the gray commissure.

Abnormal levels of adrenocortical hormones will produce congenital malformations. Adrenalectomy of mated females, the second adrenal being removed within 10 hours after mating, resulted in an increased resorption rate (48.9%) and an elevated percent of abnormal fetuses (28.5%) at day 30 of gestation (Table II). Although no frequencies were given, the areas affected included the central nervous system (myelomeningocele and syringomyelomeningocele), anterior body wall (abdominal eventration and umbilical hernia), subcutaneous collections of fluids (hematocele, hydrocele, and edema), and the head region (open eyelid and cleft palate) (Hoar and Salem, 1962). Similarly, pregnant guinea pigs, injected subcutaneously with either 0.3 or 0.6 mg/100 gm body weight hydrocortisone twice a day on days 16 and 17 of gestation, exhibited an elevated resorption and abnormality rate (Table II). The abnormalities produced were similar to those seen following maternal adrenalectomy and included open eyelids, edema, abdominal eventration, umbilical hernia, reduced weight, cleft palate, syringomyelomeningocele, syndactyly, and twisted limbs (Hoar, 1962).

Table II
Abnormal Adrenocortical Levels and Malformations in Guinea Pigs

Adults		Embryos		
Treatment	Abortions	Resorbed	Abnormal	Normal
Control	0/14	7.1% (3/42)	–	100% (39/39)
0.3 mg hydrocortisone (2×/day, days 16–17)	0/8	9.0% (2/22)	65.0% (13/20)	35.0% (7/20)
0.6 mg hydrocortisone (2×/day, days 16–17)	4/26	13.3% (8/60)	63.4% (33/52)	36.6% (20/52)
Adrenalectomy	0/32	48.9% (47/96)	28.5% (14/49)	71.5% (35/49)

Synthetic steroids including both androgens and progestens will induce masculinized female offspring if given during gestation. Testosterone proprionate administered to pregnant guinea pigs as an initial injection of 5 mg on day 10, 15, 18, or 24 of gestation and 1 mg daily thereafter until day 68 produced female offspring with masculinized external genitalia indistinguishable macroscopically from those of newborn males (Phoenix *et al.,* 1959). Goy *et al.* (1964), during additional investigations of this phenomenon, indicated that treatment could be limited to days 25 through 40 of gestation, the dosage of testosterone proprionate being 5 mg daily for the first 6 days and 1 mg daily thereafter. Buño *et al.* (1967) injected guinea pig fetuses subcutaneously following laparotomy late in gestation with 10 mg testosterone proprionate in 0.2 ml of sesame oil and found that 4 of the 7 newborn females exhibited a hypertrophic clitoris. Foote *et al.* (1968) examined the effects of synthetic progestogens and testosterone on fetal genital development. Treatment consisted of daily subcutaneous injections of 1 mg hormone in 0.2 ml sesame oil per animal from day 18 through day 60 of gestation. Testosterone and 19-nor-17α-ethynyltestosterone (Norlutin)* produced clitoral enlargement. Medroxyprogesterone acetate produced masculinized external genitalia and "wolffian duct-like structures as well as bundles of tissue resembling prostate glands." Progesterone injections (1 mg daily) produced no masculinization.

The effects of ionizing radiation upon the production of malformations are somewhat contradictory. Kosaka (1928) could find no gross malformations following irradiation of the pregnant guinea pig; however, microscopic lesions were seen in many organs (German summary of a Japanese paper). On the other hand, Osipovskiy and Kunicheva (1959) and Osipovskiy *et al.* (1963) found malformations in three generations of guinea pigs following cobalt irradiation of the male and female progenitors with 225 or 450 R a month before breeding. Abnormalities involved the eyes, teeth, skeleton, and central nervous system and appeared with increasing frequency during the three generations studied (7.6, 36.2, and 55.7%). Nelson *et al.* (1969) reported bilateral infolding of the retina in 63.5% of the embryos exposed to 15 μCi ^{131}I per day orally for 6 days during early pregnancy; the most sensitive period being days 15–20.

Everson and Wang (1967) were able to induce varying degrees of agenesis of the cerebellar folia and decreased vascularity of the cerebral cortex in offspring from dams fed a copper-deficient diet. Chase *et al.* (1971) were able to demonstrate that maternal malnutrition had significant effects on intrauterine brain growth as indicated by reduced brain weights, cellularity, protein, cholesterol, cerebroside, and sulfatide contents. At least some of these effects could be eliminated by adequate postnatal nutrition; however, brain weight and cellularity were still diminished in the mature cerebella.

2. Spontaneous

Malformations may be induced as the result of environmental manipulation as decribed above or be of spontaneous genetic origin as described in the chapter on guinea pig genetics (Chapter 8). In addition, spontaneously occurring defects of probable genetic origin, but of rare or single incidence, have been reported. Although arthrogryposis and myelodysplasia can be induced in guinea pigs (*vide supra*), these defects can also appear spontaneously (Doige and Olfert, 1974). A single case of cyclopia was reported by Hoeve (1938). In addition, dermoids have been associated with the cornea (Brunschwig, 1928) or sclera (Chan, 1932; Gupta, 1972). Hueper (1941) reported one case of rhabdomyomatosis of the heart of a guinea pig which he considered to be a "congenital tissue malformation with blastomatoid characteristics." Vink (1969) reported 22 cases of rhabdomyomatosis of the heart found during autopsy of 1400 randomly bred guinea pigs and suggested that the lesion might be congenital in origin. Radav (1960) reported that hypocatalasemia in guinea pigs is a recessive character and is hereditarily transmitted and not sex-linked. Bland (1970) described two cases of congenital absence of one uterine horn and one animal in which the "left horn was distended with fluid and 'blind' due to the absence of endometrium and myometrium at the cervical end." A case of conjoined twins was reported by Kaplun *et al.* (1972). The two bodies were joined at the atlantal vertebrae and exhibited a single head and each had four distinct limbs. This defect was the first of its type seen among 12,000 births in his colony since 1962 thus suggesting a frequency of 0.008% which appears more realistic than the 0.4% suggested by the data of Robens (1970). A more recent report of conjoined twins is that of Capel-Edwards and Eveleigh (1974). A single case of opocephaly (ears fused below the mandible, single orbit, no nose, no month) in a litter of two pups was reported by Bujard (1919). Gatz and Allen (1961) reported that two females and one male produced seven litters in which 11 of 25 offspring exhibited amelia accompanied by brain and renal defects. One second generation female, bred to her father, produced additional amelic offspring. Scher and Weisbroth (1974) reported a single instance of unilateral renal and urogenital tract aplasia in an 8-week-old female guinea pig and Gupta and Feldman (1975) described 3 cases of bilateral renal agenesis in neonatal guinea pigs.

*Parke, Davis and Company, Detroit, Michigan 48232.

REFERENCES

Altemeier, W. A., McMurrin, J. A., and Alt, L. P. (1950). Chloromycetin and aureomycin in experimental gas gangrene. *Surgery* **28,** 621–631.

Ambrus, C. M., Sideri, C. N., Johnson, G., and Harrisson, J. W. E. (1952). Toxicity of penicillin and aureomycin in guinea pigs. *Antibiot. Chemother.* **2,** 521–527.

Amdur, M. O. (1957). The influence of aerosols on the respiratory response of guinea pigs to sulfur dioxide. *Amer. Ind. Hyg. Ass., Quart.* **18,** 149–155.

Amdur, M. O. (1958). The respiratory response of guinea pigs to sulfuric acid mist. *AMA Arch. Ind. Health* **18,** 407–414.

Amdur, M. O. (1959). The physiological response of guinea pigs to atmospheric pollutants. *Int. J. Air Pollut.* **1,** 170–183.

Amdur, M. O. (1960). The response of guinea pigs to the inhalation of formaldehyde and formic acid alone and with a sodium chloride aerosol. *Int. J. Air Pollut.* **3,** 201–220.

Amdur, M. O. (1961). The respiratory response of guinea pigs to the inhalation of acetic acid vapor. *Amer. Ind. Hyg. Ass., J.* **22,** 1–4.

Amdur, M. O. (1966). The respiratory response of guinea pigs to histamine aerosol. *Arch. Environ. Health* **13,** 29–37.

Amdur, M. O., and Corn, M. (1963). The irritant potency of zinc ammonium sulfate of different particle sizes. *Amer. Ind. Hyg. Ass., J.* **24,** 326–333.

Amdur, M. O., and Mead, J. (1956). The respiratory response of guinea pigs to inhalation of ethylene oxide. *AMA Arch. Ind. Health* **14,** 553–559.

Amdur, M. O., and Mead, J. (1958). Mechanics of respiration in unanesthetized guinea pigs. *Amer. J. Physiol.* **192,** 364–368.

Amdur, M. O., Schulz, R. Z., and Drinker, P. (1952). Toxicity of sulfuric acid mist to guinea pigs. *AMA Arch. Ind. Hyg. Occup. Med.* **5,** 318–329.

Anonymous (1971). Herbicide commission reports extensive damage. *Nature (London)* **229,** 223–224.

Arbab-Zadeh, von A. (1965). Tierversuche mit Thalidomid und Thalidomid-Serum-Mischung. *Med. Klin. (Munich)* **60,** 1733–1736.

Atkinson, J. M., Pun, L.-Q., and Rand, M. (1970). The effect of directly and indirectly acting sympathomimetic amines on bronchospasm in the guinea-pig during CO_2 inhalation. *J. Pharm. Pharmacol.* **22,** 488–495.

Balazs, T. (1969). Effects of DDD and DDT on the production and metabolism of adrenocortical steroids in guinea pigs and dogs. *Amer. J. Vet. Res.* **30,** 1535–1540.

Becker, R. F., and Donnell, W. (1952). Learning behavior in guinea pigs subjected to asphyxia at birth. *J. Comp. Physiol. Psychol.* **45,** 153–162.

Becker, R. F., Flannagan, E., and King, J. E. (1958). The fate of offspring from mothers receiving sodium pentobarbital before delivery. *Neurology* **8,** 776–782.

Bergström, R. M. (1962). Brain and muscle potentials from intrauterine foetus in unnarcotized conscious animals. *Nature (London)* **195,** 1004–1005.

Bergström, R. M., Bergström, L., Putkonen, P., and Sainio, K. (1963). The effects of thalidomide on the electrical activity of the brain in the intrauterine guinea-pig foetus. *Med. Exp.* **11,** 119–127.

Bergström, R. M., Sainio, K., and Taalas, J. (1965). The effect of alcohol on the electrocorticogram of the intra-uterine guinea pig fetus. *Electroencephalogr. Clin. Neurophysiol.* **19,** 614.

Bergström, R. M., Stenberg, D., Yokinen, Y., and Järvi, K. (1966). The effect of anaesthetics on the electrocorticogram of the intrauterine guinea pig foetus. *Med. Pharmacol. Exp.* **15,** 79–84.

Berté, F., Benzi, G., Manzo, L., and Hokari, S. (1968). Investigation on tissue distribution and metabolism of oxazepam in pregnant guinea-pig and rat. *Arch. Int. Pharmacodyn. Ther.* **173,** 377–381.

Bielecka, W. (1972). Urinary excretion of alanine, glycine, aspartic acid and glutamic acid of guinea pigs poisoned with lead. *Acta Pol. Pharm.* **29,** 104–112.

Bielecka, W., and Jeske, J. (1972). Effects of the liver protein hydrolysate on blood hemoglobin and urinary coproporphyrins in guinea pigs poisoned with lead. *Acta Pol. Pharm.* **29,** 113–118.

Bland, K. P. (1970). Congenital abnormalities of the uterus and their bearing on ovarian function (with three case reports on guinea-pigs). *Vet. Rec.* **86,** 44–45.

Bleyer, W. A., and Rosen, M. G. (1968). Meperidine-induced changes in the maternal and fetal electroencephalograms of the guinea pig. *Electroencephalogr. Clin. Neurophysiol.* **24,** 249–258.

Brunschwig, A. (1928). A dermoid of the cornea in a guinea pig. *Amer. J. Pathol.* **4,** 371–374.

Bujard, E. (1919). A propos d'un cas d'opocéphalie chez le cobaye: Les synotocyclopes et les strophocéphales. *C. R. Soc. Physiol. Genève* **36,** 43–50.

Buño, W., Dominquez, R., and Carlevaro, E. (1967). Effects of testosterone proprionate on guinea-pig foetuses. *Anat. Rec.* **157,** 352.

Camberos, H. R., Davis, G. K., Djafar, M. I., and Simpson, C. F. (1970). Soft tissue calcification in guinea pigs fed the poisonous plant *Solanum malacoxylon*. *Amer. J. Vet. Res.* **31,** 685–696.

Capel-Edwards, K., and Eveleigh, J. R. (1974). A case of guinea-pig conjoined young. *Lab. Anim.* **8,** 35–37.

Carlton, W. W. (1967). Crotalaria intoxication in guinea pigs. *J. Amer. Vet. Med. Ass.* **151,** 845–855.

Chan, E. (1932). A corneo-scleral dermoid in a guinea pig. *Amer. J. Ophthalmol.* **15,** 525–526.

Chase, H. P., Dabiere, C. S., Welch, N. N., and O'Brien, D. (1971). Intrauterine undernutrition and brain development. *Pediatrics* **47,** 491–500.

Chase, M. W. (1941). Inheritance in guinea pigs of the susceptibility to skin sensitization with simple chemical compounds. *J. Exp. Med.* **73,** 711–726.

Chenchikova, E. P., and Matron, N. D. (1970). Effect of mother sensibilization with penicillin on sensitivity of progeny to it in experiments with guinea pigs. *Antibiotiki* **15,** 281–284.

Chenoweth, M. B. (1971). Chronic toxicity of inhalational anaesthetics. *Ann. Roy. Coll. Surg. Engl.* **48,** 79.

Colin, E. C. (1931). A comparison of the descendants of lead-poisoned male guinea-pigs with those from untreated animals of the same closely inbred strains. *J. Exp. Zool.* **60,** 427–484.

Cormia, F. E., Lewis, G. M., and Hopper, M. E. (1947). Toxicity of penicillin for the guinea pig. *J. Invest. Dermatol.* **9,** 261–267.

Davies, D. R., Green, A. L., and Willey, G. L. (1959). 2-hydroxyiminomethyl-*N*-methylpyridinium methanesulphonate and atropine in the treatment of severe organophosphate poisoning. *Brit. J. Pharmacol. Chemother.* **14,** 5–8.

Davis, J. M. G. (1970a). Asbestos dust as a nucleation center in the calcification of old fibrous tissue lesions, and the possible association of this process to the formation of asbestos bodies. *Exp. Mol. Pathol.* **12,** 133–147.

Davis, J. M. G. (1970b). The long term fibrogenic effects of chrysotile and crocidolite asbestos dust injected into the pleural cavity of experimental animals. *Brit. J. Exp. Pathol.* **51,** 617–627.

Davis, J. M. G. (1970c). Further observations on the ultrastructure and chemistry of the formation of asbestos bodies. *Exp. Mol. Pathol.* **13,** 346–358.

Davis, J. M. G., Gross, P., and de Treville, R. T. P. (1970). "Ferruginous bodies" in guinea pigs. Fine structure produced experimentally from minerals other than asbestos. *Arch. Pathol.* **89,** 364–373.

de Somer, P., van de Voorde, H., Eyssen, H., and van Dÿck, P. (1955). A study on penicillin toxicity in guinea pigs. *Antibiot. Chemother.* **5,** 463–469.

Desselberger, U., and Wegener, H.-H. (1971). Experimentelle Untersuchungen am Meerschweinchen zur Alkohol -, Kobalt - und kombinierten Alkohol - Kobalt - Intoxikation. *Beitr. Pathol.* **142,** 150–176.

Doige, C. E., and Olfert, E. D. (1974). Arthrogryposis and myelodysplasia in a guinea pig. *Lab. Anim. Sci.* **24,** 103–104.

Draize, J. H., Nelson, A. A., and Calvery, H. O. (1944). The percutaneous absorption of DDT (2,2-bis (*p*-chlorophenyl) 1,1,1-trichloroethane) in laboratory animals. *J. Pharmacol. Exp. Ther.* **82,** 159–166.

Draper, R. L. (1920). The prenatal growth of the guinea-pig. *Anat. Rec.* **18,** 369–392.

Dunn, J. E., Dunn, R. C., and Smith, B. S. (1946). Skin-sensitizing properties of DDT for the guinea pig. *Pub. Health Rep.* **61,** 1614–1620.

Easton, R. E., and Murphy, S. D. (1967). Experimental ozone pre-exposure and histamine. Effect on the acute toxicity and respiratory function effects of histamine in guinea pigs. *Arch. Environ. Health* **15,** 160–166.

Edwards, M. J. (1957). Congenital defects in guinea pigs, following induced hyperthermia during gestation. *Arch. Pathol.* **84,** 42–48.

Edwards, M. J. (1969a). Congenital defects in guinea pigs: Fetal resorptions, abortions, and malformations following induced hyperthermia during early gestation. *Teratology* **2,** 313–328.

Edwards, M. J. (1969b). Hyperthermia and congenital malformations in guinea-pigs. *Aust. Vet. J.* **45,** 189–193.

Edwards, M. J. (1969c). Congenital defects in guinea pigs: Prenatal retardation of brain growth of guinea pigs following hyperthermia during gestation. *Teratology* **2,** 329–336.

Edwards, M. J. (1971). The experimental production of clubfoot in guinea-pigs by maternal hyperthermia during gestation. *J. Pathol.* **103,** 49–53.

Everson, G. J., and Wang, T. I. (1967). Copper deficiency in the guinea pig and related brain abnormalities. *Fed. Proc., Fed. Amer. Soc. Exp. Biol.* **26,** 633.

Eyssen, H., de Somer, P., and van Dÿck, P. (1957). Further studies on antibiotic toxicity in guinea pigs. *Antibiot. Chemother.* **7,** 55–64.

Finster, M., Morishima, H. O., Mark, L. C., Perel, J. M., Dayton, P. G., and James, L. S. (1972a). Tissue thiopental concentrations in the fetus and newborn. *Anesthesiology* **36,** 155–158.

Finster, M., Morishima, H. O., Boyes, R. N., and Covino, B. G. (1972b). The placental transfer of lidocaine and its uptake by fetal tissues. *Anesthesiology* **36,** 159–163.

Fleisher, J. H., Harris, L. W., Miller, G. R., Thomas, N. C., and Cliff, W. J. (1970). Antagonism of Sarin poisoning in rats and guinea pigs by atropine, oximes and mecamylamine. *Toxical. Appl. Pharmacol.* **16,** 40–47.

Foote, W. D., Foote, W. C., and Foote, L. H. (1968). Influence of certain natural and synthetic steroids on genital development in guinea pigs. *Fert. Steril.* **19,** 606–615.

Fullerton, P. M. (1966). Chronic peripheral neuropathy produced by lead poisoning in guinea-pigs. *J. Neuropathol. Exp. Neurol.* **25,** 214–236.

Gatz, A. J., and Allen, L. (1961). A study of amelus guinea pigs. *Anat. Rec.* **139,** 302.

Geddes, I. C., Brand, L., Finster, M., and Mark, L. (1972). Distribution of halothane-^{82}Br in maternal and foetal guinea pig tissues. *Brit. J. Anaesth.* **44,** 542–547.

Giroud, A., and Martinet, M. (1959a). Tératogénèse par hypervitaminosis A chez le rat, la souris, le cobaye et le lapin. *Arch. Fr. Pediat.* **16,** 971–975.

Giroud, A., and Martinet, M. (1959b). Extension à plusieurs espèces de Mammifères des malformations embryonnaires par hypervitaminose A. *C. R. Soc. Biol.* **153,** 201–202.

Glass, H. G., Snyder, F. F., and Webster, E., (1944). The rate of decline in resistance to anoxia of rabbits, dogs and guinea pigs from the onset of viability to adult life. *Amer. J. Physiol.* **140,** 609–615.

Gluckman, M. I. (1965). Pharmacology of oxazepam (Serax), a new anti-anxiety agent. *Curr. Ther. Res.* **7,** 721–740.

Goy, R. W., Hoar, R. M., and Young, W. C. (1957). Length of gestation in the guinea pig with data on the frequency and time of abortion and stillbirth. *Anat. Rec.* **128,** 747–758.

Goy, R. W., Bridson, W. E., and Young, W. C. (1964). Period of maximal susceptibility of the prenatal female guinea pig to masculinizing actions of testosterone proprionate. *J. Comp. Physiol. Psychol.* **57,** 166–174.

Goździk-Żolnierkiewicz, T., and Moszyński, B. (1969). VIII nerve in experimental lead poisoning. *Acta Oto-Laryngol.* **68,** 85–89.

Greenfield, A. D. M., and Shepherd, J. T. (1953). Cardiovascular responses to asphyxia in the foetal guinea-pig. *J. Physiol. (London)* **120,** 538–549.

Gross, P., and de Treville, R. T. P. (1967). Experimental asbestosis. Studies on the progressiveness of the pulmonary fibrosis caused by chrysotile dust. *Arch. Environ. Health* **15,** 638–649.

Gross, P., de Treville, R. T. P., Babyak, M. A., Kaschak, M., and Tolker, E. B. (1968). Experimental emphysema. Effect of chronic nitrogen dioxide exposure and papain on normal and pneumoconiotic lungs. *Arch. Environ. Health* **16,** 51–58.

Gupta, B. N. (1972). Scleral dermoid in a guinea pig. *Lab. Anim. Sci.* **22,** 919–921.

Gupta, B. N., and Feldman, D. B. (1975). Renal agenesis in the guinea pig and opossum. *Lab. Anim. Sci.* **25,** 238–240.

Hamre, D. M., Rake, G., McKee, C. M., and MacPhillamy, H. B. (1943). The toxicity of penicillin as prepared for clinical use. *Amer. J. Med. Sci.* **206,** 642–652.

Harman, M. T., and Dobrovolny, M. P. (1932/1933). The development of the external form of the guinea-pig (*Cavia cobaya*) between the ages of 21 days and 35 days of gestation. *J. Morphol.* **54,** 493–515.

Harman, M. T., and Prickett, M. (1931/1932). The development of the external form of the guinea-pig. (*Cavia cobaya*) between the ages of eleven days and twenty days of gestation. *Amer. J. Anat.* **49,** 351–378.

Harman, M. T., and Saffry, O. B. (1934). The skeletal development of the anterior limb of the guinea pig, *Cavia cobaya Cuv.,* from the 25-day embryo to the 161-day postnatal guinea-pig. *Amer. J. Anat.* **54,** 315–327.

Hauduroy, P. and Rosset, W. (1948). A própos de l'action accélératrice de la pénicilline sur la tuberculose expérimentale du cobaye. *Ann. Inst. Pasteur, Paris* **75,** 67–69.

Heilman, F. R. and Herrell, W. E. (1944). Penicillin in the treatment of experimental *Leptospirosis icterohaemorrhagica* (Weil's disease). *Proc. Staff Meet. Mayo Clin.* **19,** 89–99.

Herxheimer, H. (1956). Bronchconstrictor agents and their antagonists in the intact guinea-pig. *Arch. Int. Pharmacodyn. Ther.* **106,** 371–380.

Hoar, R. M. (1962). Similarity of congenital malformations produced by hydrocortisone to those produced by adrenalectomy in guinea pigs. *Anat. Rec.* **144,** 155–164.

Hoar, R. M. (1969). Resorption in guinea pigs as estimated by counting corpora lutea: The problem of twinning. *Teratology* **2,** 187–190.

Hoar, R. M., and King, T. J. (1967). Further observations on resorption in guinea pigs following injections of trypan blue. *Anat. Rec.* **157,** 617–620.

Hoar, R. M., and Salem, A. J. (1961). Time of teratogenic action of trypan blue in guinea pigs. *Anat. Rec.* **141,** 173–182.

Hoar, R. M., and Salem, A. J. (1962). The production of congenital malformations in guinea pigs by adrenalectomy. *Anat. Rec.* **143,** 157–168.

Hueper, W. C. (1941). Rhabdomyomatosis of the heart in a guinea pig. *Amer. J. Pathol.* **17,** 121–125.

Hughes, H. C., and Lang, C. M. (1972). Hepatic necrosis produced by repeated administration of halothane to guinea pigs. *Anesthesiology* **36,** 466–471.

Huxtable, C. R. (1969). Experimental reproduction and histo-pathology of *Swainsona galegifolia* poisoning in the guinea-pig. *Aust. J. Exp. Biol. Med. Sci.* **47,** 339–347.

Huxtable, C. R. (1970). Ultrastructural changes caused by *Swainsona galegifolia* poisoning in the guinea-pig. *Aust. J. Exp. Biol. Med. Sci.* **48,** 71–80.

Hustable, C. R., and Gibson A. (1970). Vacuolation of circulating lymphocytes in guinea-pigs and cattle ingesting *Swainsona galegifolia. Aust. Vet. J.* **46,** 446–448.

Ibsen, H. L. (1928). Prenantal growth in guinea-pigs with special reference to environmental factors affecting weight at birth. *J. Exp. Zool.* **51,** 51–91.

Jenkins, C. J., Jr., Coon, R. A., Lyon, J. P., and Siegel, J. (1971). Effect on experimental animals of long-term inhalation exposure to mineral spirits. II. Dietary, sex and strain influences in guinea pigs. *Toxicol. Appl. Pharmacol.* **18,** 53–59.

Kaplun, A., Shamir, B., and Kuttin, E. S. (1972). A case of guinea pig conjoined twins. *Lab. Anim. Sci.* **22,** 581–582.

Kar, P. P., and Dikshith, T. S. S. (1970). Dermal toxicity of DDT. *Experientia* **26,** 634–635.

Kosaka, S. (1928). Der Einfluss der Röntgenstrahlen auf die Feten. IV. Mitteilung Untersuchen an Meerschweinchen. (In Japanese with German summary.) *Okayama Igakkai Zasshi* **40,** 2214–2234.

Landsteiner, K., and Jacobs, J. (1935). Studies on the sensitization of animals with simple chemical compounds. *J. Exp. Med.* **61,** 643–657.

Landsteiner, K., and Jacobs, J. (1936). Studies on the sensitization of animals with simple chemical compounds. II. *J. Exp. Med.* **64,** 625–639.

Levy, B. M., and Higgins, G. M. (1965). Reactions within the lungs of guinea pigs to the intratracheal administration of zinc beryllium silicate. *Amer. Ind. Hyg. Ass. J.* **26,** 227–235.

Murphy, S. D., Ulrich, C. E., Frankowitz, S. H., and Xintaras, C. (1964). Altered function in animals inhaling low concentrations of ozone and nitrogen dioxide. *Amer. Ind. Hyg. Ass., J.* **25,** 246–253.

Nelson, N. S., Stara, J. F., and Hoar, R. M. (1969). *In* "Radiation Biology of the Fetal and Juvenile Mammal" (M. R. Sikov and D. D. Mahlum, eds.), No. 17, pp. 45–62. AEC Symp. Ser.

Nordberg, G. F., and Serenius, F. (1969). Distribution of inorganic mercury in the guinea pig brain. *Acta Pharmacol. Toxicol.* **27,** 269–283.

Ophüls, W. (1915). Chronic lead-poisoning in guinea-pigs: With special reference to nephritis, cirrhosis and polyserositis. *Amer. J. Med. Sci.* **150,** 518–541.

Osipovskiy, A. I., and Kunicheva, G. S. (1959). Developmental anomalies in the offspring of guinea pigs irradiated by gamma-rays and the inheritance of them by a number of generations. *Med. Radiol.* **4,** 65–76.

Osipovskiy, A. I., Afanas'ev, Y. I., Pauper, A. I., and Sukhanov, Y. S. (1963). Central nervous system developmental anomalies and deformities in successive generations of gamma-ray-irradiated animals. (In Russian; English translation AEC-tr-5434.) *Radiobiologia* **3,** 120–127.

Paget, G. E. (1954). Exudative hepatitis in guinea-pigs. *J. Pathol. Bacteriol.* **67,** 393–400.

Paterson, J. S., and Crook, J. C. (1962). Groundnut toxicity as the cause of exudative hepatitis (oedema disease) of guinea-pigs. *Vet. Rec.* **74,** 639–640.

Pattle, R. E., Burgess, F., and Cullumbine, H. (1956). The effects of a cold environment and of ammonia on the toxicity of sulfuric acid mist to guinea pigs. *J. Pathol. Bacteriol.* **72,** 219–232.

Petri, C. (1935). Die Entwicklung des Skeletts von Cavia. Medical Dissertation, Zürich.

Phoenix, C. H., Goy, R. W., Gerall, A. A., and Young, W. C. (1959). Organizing action of prenatally administered testosterone propri-onate on the tissues mediating mating behavior in the female guinea pig. *Endocrinology* **65,** 369–382.

Rackemann, F. M., and Simon, F. A. (1934). The sensitization of guinea pigs to poison ivy. *Science* **79,** 334.

Radav, T. (1960). Inheritance of hypocatalasemia in guinea-pigs. *J. Genet.* **57,** 169–172.

Rajtová, V. (1966). Skeletogeny in the guinea-pig. I. Prenatal and postnatal ossification of the forelimb skeleton. *Folia Morphol. (Prague)* **14,** 99–106.

Rajtová, V. (1967). The development of the skeleton in the guinea-pig. II. The morphogenesis of the carpus in the guinea-pig (*Cavia porcellus*). *Folia Morphol. (Prague)* **15,** 132–139.

Rajtová, V. (1968). Development of the skeleton in the guinea pig. IV. Morphogenesis of the tarsus in the guinea pig (*Cavia porcellus*). *Folia Morphol. (Prague)* **16,** 162–170.

Rao, S. L. N., Malathi, K., and Sarma, P. S. (1969). Lathyrism. *World Rev. Nutr. Diet.* **10,** 214–238.

Rector, D. E., Steadman, B. L., Jones, R. A., and Siegel, J. (1966). Effects on experimental animals of long-term inhalation exposure to mineral spirits. *Toxicol. Appl. Pharmacol.* **9,** 257–268.

Religa, Z., and Maślinski, Cz. (1971). Histamine metabolism in experimental silicosis. II. *In vivo* experiments in guinea pigs. *Life Sci.* **10,** 257–271.

Robens, J. F. (1969). Teratologic studies of carbaryl, diazinon, norea, disulfiram, and thiram in small laboratory animals. *Toxicol. Appl. Pharmacol.* **15,** 152–163.

Robens, J. F. (1970). Teratogenic effects of hypervitaminosis A in the hamster and the guinea pig. *Toxicol. Appl. Pharmacol.* **16,** 88–99.

Roine, P., and Ettala, T. (1952). Toxicity of aureomycin in guinea pigs. *Nature (London)* **169,** 1014.

Rose, C. S., Jones, R. A., Jenkins, L. L., Jr., and Siegel, J. (1970). The acute hyperbaric toxicity of carbon monoxide. *Toxicol. Appl. Pharmacol.* **17,** 752–760.

Rosen, M. G. (1967a). Effects of asphyxia on the fetal brain. *Obstet. Gynecol.* **29,** 687–693.

Rosen, M. G. (1967b). Fetal electroencephalographic studies of the placental transfer of thiopental and ether. *Obstet. Gynecol.* **30,** 560–567.

Rosen, M. G., and McLaughlin, A. (1966a). Maternal and fetal electro-encephalography in the guinea pig. *Amer. J. Obstet. Gynecol.* **95,** 997–1000.

Rosen, M. G., and McLaughlin, A. (1966b). Fetal and maternal electro-encephalography in the guinea pig. *Exp. Neurol.* **16,** 181–190.

Rothberg, S. (1970). Skin sensitization potential of the riot control agents BBC, DM, CN and CS in guinea pigs. *Mil. Med.* **135,** 552–556.

St. Omer, V. V. (1970). Chronic and acute toxicity of the chlorinated hydrocarbon insecticides in mammals and birds. *Can. Vet. J.* **11,** 215–226.

Scher, S., and Weisbroth, S. H. (1974). Unilateral renal and urogenital tract aplasia in a guinea pig. (*Cavia porcellus*). *Lab. Anim. Sci.* **24,** 370–371.

Scott, J. P. (1937). The embryology of the guinea pig. I. A table of normal development. *Amer. J. Anat.* **60,** 397–432.

Secchi, G. C., Alessio, L., and Cirla, A. (1970). The effect of experimental lead poisoning on some enzymatic activities of the kidney. *Clin. Chim. Acta* **27,** 467–474.

Siegel, J., Jones, R. A., Coon, R. A., and Lyon, J. P. (1971). Effects on experimental animals of acute, repeated and continuous inhalation exposures to dichloroacetylene mixtures. *Toxicol. Appl. Pharmacol.* **18,** 168–174.

Simon, F. A. (1936). Observations on poison ivy hypersensitiveness in guinea pigs. *J. Immunol.* **30,** 275–286.

Simon, F. A., Simon, M. G., Rackemann, F. M., and Dienes, L. (1934). The sensitization of guinea pigs to poison ivy. *J. Immunol.* **27,** 113–123.

Stevens, K. M., and Gray, I. (1953). Studies on penicillin toxicity in guinea pigs. *Antibiot. Chemother.* **3,** 731–740.

Stokinger, H. E., Sprague, G. F., III, Hall, R. H., Ashenburg, N. J., Scott, J. K., and Steadman, L. T. (1950). Acute inhalation toxicity of beryllium. I. Four definitive studies of beryllium sulfate at exposure concentrations of 100, 50, 10 and 1 mg. per cubic meter. *AMA Arch. Ind. Hyg. Occup. Med.* **1,** 379–397.

Stokinger, H. E., Wagner, W. D., and Dobrogorski, O. J. (1957). Ozone toxicity studies. III. Chronic injury to lungs of animals following exposure at a low level. *AMA Arch. Ind. Health* **16,** 514–522.

Stuart, P., and Slavin, G. (1951). Toxicity of penicillin to guinea pigs. *Nature (London)* **167,** 319–320.

Sulzberger, M. B. (1930). Arsphenamine hypersensitiveness in guinea-pigs. II. Experiments demonstrating the role of the skin, both as originator and as site of the hypersensitiveness. *Arch. Dermatol. Syph.* **22,** 839–840.

Uzoukwu, M. B. A., and Sleight, S. D. (1972). Dieldrin toxicosis: Fetotoxicosis, tissue concentrations, and microscopic and ultrastructural changes in guinea pigs. *Amer. J. Vet. Res.* **33,** 579–583.

van der Hoeve, J. (1938). Cyclopie. *Ned. Tijdschr. Geneesk.* **82,** 134–142.

Vink, H. H. (1969). Rhabdomyomatosis (nodular glycogenic infiltration) of the heart in guinea-pigs. *J. Pathol.* **97,** 331–334.

Weil, C. S., Woodside, M. D., Bernard, J. B., Condra, N. I., King, J. M., and Carpenter, C. P. (1973). Comparative effect of carbaryl on rat reproduction and guinea pig teratology when fed either in the diet or by stomach intubation. *Toxicol. Appl. Pharmacol.* **26,** 621–638.

Weller, C. V. (1916). Histological study of the testes of guinea-pigs showing lead blastophthoria. Preliminary report. *Proc. Soc. Exp. Biol. Med.* **14,** 14–24.

Whitehead, W. H., Windle, W. F., and Becker, R. F. (1942). Changes in lung structure during aspiration of amniotic fluid and during air-breathing at birth. *Anat. Rec.* **83,** 255–265.

Windle, W. F., and Becker, R. F. (1941). Role of carbon dioxide in resuscitation at birth after asphyxia and after nembutal anesthesia. An experimental study in the cat and guinea pig. *Amer. J. Obstet. Gynecol.* **42,** 852–858.

Windle, W. F., and Becker, R. F. (1943). Asphyxia neonatarum. An experimental study in the guinea pig. *Amer. J. Obstet. Gynecol.* **45,** 183–200.

Windle, W. F., Becker, R. F., and Weil, A. (1944). Alterations in brain structure after asphyxiation at birth. *J. Neuropathol. Exp. Neurol.* **3,** 224–238.

Wogan, G. N., and Pong, R. S. (1970). Aflatoxins. *Ann. N. Y. Acad. Sci.* **174,** 623–635.

Chapter 19

Auditory Research

James G. McCormick and Alfred L. Nuttall

I. INTRODUCTION

The two most often used animals in otologic research are the guinea pig and the cat. Because of the vast amount of otologic research and manifold nature of the studies in which the guinea pig has been used, we have not attempted to bring the entire subject up to date, and thus the present discussion is somewhat limited in scope. We have highlighted areas of investigation in which the guinea pig has been used as an important animal model. Given the nature of this publicaton we were restricted, within any given area of study, from mentioning important works done on the cat or some other animal.

We have directed our chapter largely to investigators with a new interest in otologic research. We discuss why the guinea pig is an excellent subject in this area of endeavor, give examples of the many types of otologic research applications of the guinea pig, and provide a reasonable core of literature which may help lead to other significant contributions. For more comprehensive reviews of the literature in general, the reader will find valuable such works as Wever's "Theory of Hearing" (1949), "Physiological Acoustics" by Wever and Lawrence (1954), and "The Auditory Periphery: Biophysics and Physiology" (Dallos, 1973).

II. CHOICE OF THE GUINEA PIG FOR OTOLOGIC RESEARCH

An investigator planning to use the guinea pig for the study of an otologic problem will benefit from a large amount of published baseline anatomical and physiological data in the literature. In addition, the guinea pig is readily available, easy to maintain, very amenable to handling, and is inexpensive.

One must be cautious, however, to obtain animals free of any form of otitis. We have studied the ears of close to 1000 guinea pigs, and our success in obtaining animals free of observable otitis has varied. Transport of guinea pigs over long distances particularly in cold weather predisposes guinea pigs to otitis media. A healthy guinea pig breeding colony free of the aforementioned diseases is a prerequisite for otologic research.

It is always best to use young animals about 350 gm in weight. Older animals usually have a higher incidence of otitis, and the bone enclosing the middle ear space becomes thicker and more difficult to enter surgically.

Streptococcal infection can cause an abscess of the mandibular lymph nodes which may not directly affect the middle ears of the guinea pig, but this disease can complicate surgical procedures in the neck, especially cannulation of the jugular veins. This condition seems to be quite contagious, so when and if it strikes, you must dispose of all animals in contact with the afflicted stock. Cervical lymphadenitis and associated diseases are discussed in Chapter 9.

The anatomy of the guinea pig ear and associated structures makes it ideal for otologic studies. A postauricular surgical approach to the middle ear presents no major blood vessels or muscles, and the boney lateral wall of the middle ear is easily penetrated with the point of a scalpel. The petrous bone (otic capsule) of the guinea pig is easily entered and dissected away, without drilling, to expose the inner ear structures. These procedures are greatly facilitated by the fact that the otic capsule of the guinea pig is not embedded in the temporal bone of the skull, instead it protrudes into the middle ear space. Many more hours are required to expose the inner ear structures in the cat, monkey, or man (Johnsson and Hawkins, 1967; Hawkins and Johnsson, 1968).

An inner ear whole mount dissection of the guinea pig inner ear can be performed in approximately 2 hours, and the anatomical perspective which the dissector obtains is invaluable. Professor Joseph E. Hawkins, Jr. of the Kresge Hearing Research Institute at the University of Michigan has used the guinea pig extensively in teaching this aspect of the anatomy with great success.

III. PRELIMINARY EXAMINATION OF THE GUINEA PIG

Certain procedures are useful to eliminate the possibility of using a guinea pig with otitis media or inner ear deafness. First, the Preyer reflex should be checked by observing a cocking of the pinnae of the ears in response to a short signal from a Galton whistle (Preyer, 1890). If a Galton whistle is not available, the response can be tested by placing the guinea pig in a box so that he cannot see the experimenter while the experimenter claps his hands sharply. Animals without a good Preyer response are unsuitable for ear studies. Next, the external ear canal and tympanic membrane should be examined in detail. For this procedure a good operating microscope with a light source in line with the lens optics is much preferred over an otoscope because magnification and illumination of the microscope are far superior to those of the otoscope. The eardrum should be free of inflammation or other defects, and one can observe if the middle ear is free of fluid or exudate. A 2-mm ear speculum greatly facilitates this procedure, and at the same time the condition of the eardrum is checked, the ear canal can be cleaned. This examination is best done prior to surgery after induction of anesthesia.

If 15 minutes of immobilization of the guinea pig for examination is desired, intramuscular injection (50 mg/kg) of ketamine (Vetalar–ketamine hydrochloride–100 mg per ml, Parke-Davis) is ideal (Chen *et al.,* 1969). We have successfully examined over 100 guinea pigs with this agent. The margin of safety is very good. Much lower doses in primates like man and monkey (6 mg/kg) will produce good analgesia for surgery, however, we have not obtained good analgesia in the guinea pig even with doses as high as 70 mg/kg. Guinea pigs are up and well on the way to recovery about one-half hour after injection.

IV. SURGERY AND ANESTHESIA

In auditory research for acute procedures on the guinea pig it is especially desirable to utilize a long-acting anesthetic agent. This is necessitated by two common requirements in auditory research. First, after the induction of anesthesia and the positioning of the animal for the experiment, it is usually important not to move the animal, even by an amount as small as might be required in giving multiple injections of an anesthetic agent. Second, auditory research usually dictates that the experimental animal be enclosed in a soundproof electrostatically shielded room. These rooms usually do not allow the experimenter to closely observe the animal's condition with regard to depth of anesthesia.

The first point noted above is exemplified in Fig. 1. An anesthetized guinea pig has a cannula placed in his external ear canal for the delivery of a sound stimulus to the eardrum. A slight movement of the animal during the experiment might alter the position of the sound cannula relative to the eardrum, and this in turn could alter the intensity of the sound stimulus

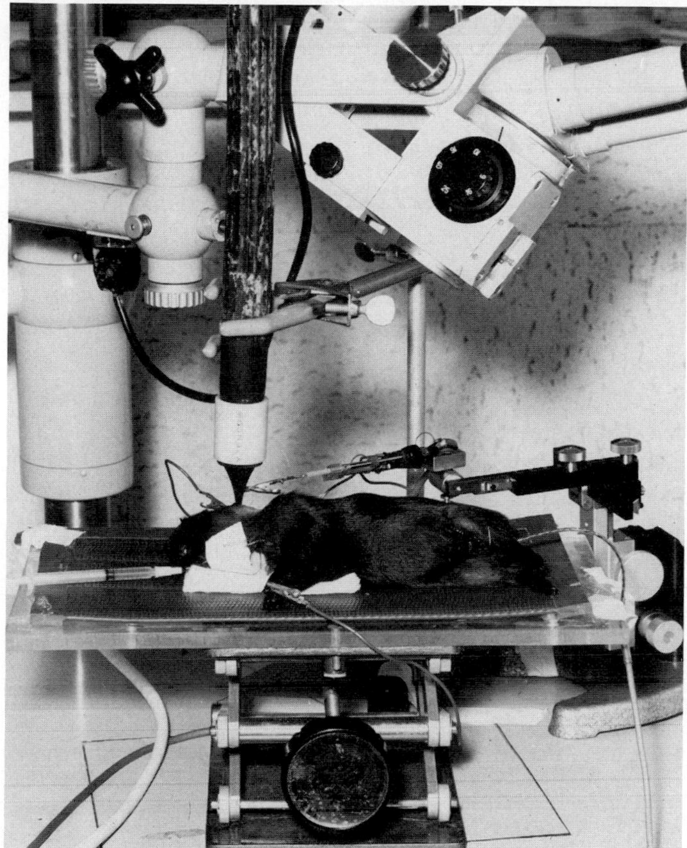

Fig. 1. Anesthetized guinea pig prepared for recording AC cochlear potentials. A sound delivery cannula is placed in the external ear canal, and the jugular vein is cannulated for drug administration. The rectal thermometer leads to a unit (not shown) which triggers the heating blanket under the guinea pig to maintain normal body temperature. The dissection microscope is used to position an electrode (in micromanipulator) on the inner ear round window membrane.

presented to the eardrum or there might even be a danger of rupturing the eardrum with the cannula. It is not uncommon to have an experiment which requires maintaining a surgically anesthetized guinea pig in the position shown in Fig. 1 for more than 24 hours (McCormick *et al.*, 1973). For this type of work one can use Dial* with urethane for anesthesia. This compound is a mixture of diallylbarbituric acid (to facilitate induction) and urethane (for prolonged anesthesia with little or no requirement for additional maintenance doses). It is given in an approximate dose of 0.5 ml/kg.

In several hundred guinea pig ear operations, we have successfully used 20% urethane alone given intraperitoneally in an approximate dose of 10 ml/kg. The 20% urethane can be mixed in normal (0.9%) saline. The urethane crystals are available from several different drug companies, one such source being the Merck Drug Company in Rahway, New Jersey. Larger older animals may not tolerate 10 ml/kg and we usually given an animal 5 to 7 mg/kg, wait 15 to 20 minutes, and then give additional urethane as indicated. After the initial induction with urethane anesthesia 0.05 ml of atropine sulfate (0.4 mg per ml by Lilly and Company, Indianapolis, Indiana) is given intramuscularly.

Often there is a delicate balance between surgical anesthesia and respiratory arrest. To facilitate surgery, or while waiting for completion of urethane induction, Xylocaine injections can be used for local anesthesia. If the guinea pig stops breathing, artificial respiration (pumping rhythmically on the chest) will often restore breathing. The heart of the guinea pig usually beats for several minutes after the cessation of breathing, unlike the rabbit in which cardiac arrest ensues almost immediately after breathing stops. In cases of anesthetic overdose with a valuable animal preparation, a respiratory stimulant, Mikedimide 3% (3,3-methylethylgutarmide by Parlam Corporation, Englewood, New Jersey) can be given intravenously to effect. Usually mikedimide is given on a milligram per milligram basis with the anesthetic dose used.

For emergency or routine experimental administration of intravenous drugs, guinea pig jugular veins can be cannulated with a small size catheter drawn even smaller in a flame. The jugular veins are readily exposed on either side of the tracheotomy site in the guinea pig.

For ear surgery on the guinea pig, it is especially desirable to do a tracheotomy. When manipulating the head for a good view of the middle or inner ear it is very easy to twist the neck in such a manner that will cut off respiration. Tracheotomy also helps to prevent respiratory acidosis, decreasing respiratory dead space and resistance to compensate for reduced tidal volume with anesthetic depression. Tracheotomy tubes can be cut from plastic tubing usually with an outside diameter of around 2 mm. Unwanted fluid buildup in the respiratory tree can be readily aspirated with a small number 3 French sucker tip.

The tracheotomy provides a connection point for a respirator. When anesthesia is not deep enough to suppress middle ear muscle activity some investigators supplement anesthesia with a muscle relaxant necessitating controlled artificial respiration. Controlled respiration should be used with care in the guinea pig so that venous return to the heart is not compromised due to excessive intrathoracic pressure.

Chronic surgery on the guinea pig's ear, in our experience, requires sterile procedures to prevent subsequent middle ear infection. For smooth induction and good recovery from anesthesia, we use Innovar* premedication in an intramuscular dose of 1 ml/kg. The Innovar injection is followed in a few minutes by an intraperitoneal injection of Nembutal in a dose of 25 mg/kg.

*Ciba Pharmaceutical Co., Summit, New Jersey.

*McNeil Laboratories, Fort Washington, Pennsylvania.

For good physiological maintenance, the body temperature of the guinea pig should be kept at 37°C. An ideal situation is shown in Fig. 1 where the anesthetized guinea pig is placed on a direct current heating blanket (to prevent AC interference in electrode pickup systems) which is automatically turned on and off as needed by a telethermometer hooked to a rectal thermometer in the guinea pig.

In addition to controlling body temperature during surgery and anesthesia for general physiological maintenance, it is necessary to keep this factor constant since electrical function of the ear varies with changes in the body temperature (Gulick and Cutt, 1960, 1962; Cutt and Gulick, 1960).

Figure 1 also shows the guinea pig with a tracheotomy, a cannula for drug administration in the jugular vein, and the left pinna of the ear cut off for better insertion of a sound cannula. This particular animal has a silver wire electrode placed on his round window (not shown) for recording cochlear potentials, and the operating microscope is positioned over the animal.

Finally, when operating on the ear of the guinea pig or any other animal, mechanical drills should not be used because their vibration may damage delicate inner ear structures. Rongeurs and picks should be used instead of drills. Also, to avoid potential inner ear damage, heat cautery rather than electrocautery is used to control hemorrhage.

V. THE BEHAVIORAL ABSOLUTE HEARING THRESHOLD

Otologic research in the guinea pig must include fundamental studies of the performance of the intact hearing mechanism in the normal alert animal. A commonly used hearing evaluation test is the pinna reflex, also known as the Preyer reflex. When the guinea pig is presented a loud sound [e.g., 100 dB sound pressure level RE 2×10^{-4} dynes/cm^2 (SPL)], there occurs a bilateral reflex jerk of the auricles to the onset of the tone or transient acoustic signal (Preyer, 1890). The reflex is a function of the frequency and intensity of the sound and, thus, functions as a hearing test. Gerstner (1942) quantified and standardized the pinna reflex but other investigators report the test to be an unreliable measure of hearing threshold (Wever, 1949; Rüedi, 1954).

Guinea pigs are difficult to train in the conventional avoidance behavioral situation because they become catatonic in response to discomfort and/or fear. Catatonia, however, can be used as a measure of perceptual threshold when, for example, the animal stops working at the behavioral task in response to a tone. Auditory thresholds also have been obtained by observing changes in respiration (Upton, 1929; Horton, 1933; Alexander and O'Brien, 1954; Sherrick and Bilger, 1959), and by cessation in chewing (Miller and Murray, 1962). One very unusual measurement technique was reported by Anderson and Wedenberg (1965), where sounds produced changes in a very regular cold-induced shivering pattern. Other shivering experiments on guinea pigs have been reported by Ernston (1972) and Crifó (1972). Crifó also reports finding a difference between the auditory thresholds of albino and pigmented guinea pigs, the albino being more sensitive. This difference was not found in a comparison of round window cochlear potentials from the two strains (Nuttall, 1974a).

In a recent report, Heffner *et al.* (1971) obtained the guinea pig auditory threshold by suppression of a conditioned response. Their animals were trained to lick a spout for a water reward. When steady lick rates were established, the animal was given tone followed by electric shock stimuli. The animal soon learns that the tone serves as a warning for impending shock and, thus, changes the lick rate on hearing the tone. The guinea pig auditory threshold for frequencies between 55 Hz and 50 kHz is given in Fig. 2 along with thresholds of man and several common laboratory mammals for comparison. Note that the guinea pig's high frequency range is about one octave higher than that of man but the latter is more sensitive at low frequencies.

It may also be possible to use another type of contingency behavior training to determine the auditory threshold, that of positive (reward) reinforcement. The only reported use of the food reward technique is the tonal discrimination testing of Herington and Gundlach (1933). These authors discussed the great difficulty of balancing motivation and obtaining the desired training, against the low dietary requirements of the

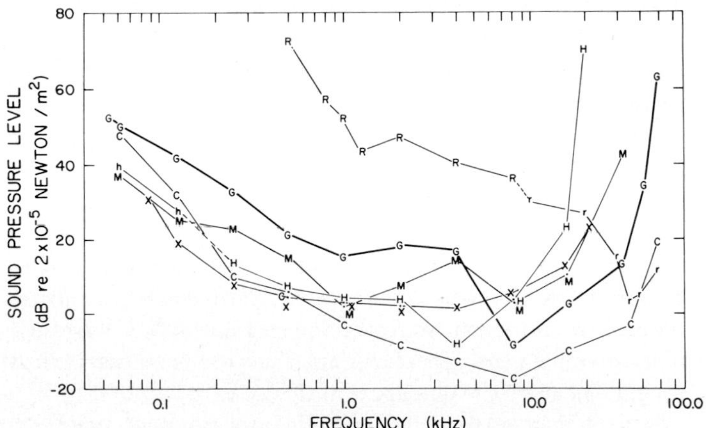

Fig. 2. The behavioral hearing threshold of the guinea pig compared to man and several common laboratory mammals. G, guinea pig (from Heffner *et al.*, 1971); H, human (from Masterton *et al.*, 1969); h, human (from Sivian and White, 1933); C, cat (from Neff and Hind, 1955); R, rat (from Gourevitch, 1965); r, rat (from Gourevitch and Hack, 1966); M, *Macaca* monkey (from Stebbins, 1966); X, chinchilla (from Miller, 1970).

guinea pig. Hope remains for positive reinforcement, however, because it is reported that the guinea pig will work for carrot juice without food or water deprivation (Gundy, 1959). Additionally, graduate students at this Institute (Kresge Hearing Research Institute) have found the same guinea pig partiality to aqueous solutions of sucrose.

VI. MIDDLE EAR AND COCHLEAR MECHANICS

The middle ear is an impedance matching mechanism that transmits acoustic energy from air into the inner ear fluids with improved efficiency over the air–fluid boundry. In the middle ear experimentation which has taken place over the last 100 years since Helmholtz's 1868 treatise, the guinea pig has shared the experimental limelight with the cat, rabbit, and human cadaver temporal bone specimens. Nevertheless, a number of crucial ear biomechanic experiments have been done with the guinea pig.

Two kinds of measurements are typically made on the middle ear mechanism to determine its acoustic properties. First, the measurement of input impedance is one way of assessing the function of the intact ear. These measurements are made with an acoustic impedance bridge or other special instrumentation. By dismantling various parts of the middle ear (e.g., opening the auditory bulla or breaking the ossicular chain), the relative contributions of these parts to the overall input function can be determined (Mundie, 1962; Zwislocki, 1963). The specific acoustic input impedance (magnitude and phase) is given for a typical intact guinea pig ear by the graph of Fig. 3. The low frequency portion is nearly a straight line with the phase leveling out to a value of minus 90°. This means that the mechanical system becomes dominated by elastic reactance (compliance or stiffness) at these low frequencies and much of the stiffness is from the contributions of the closed volume of the middle ear and the elastic properties of the tympanic membrane.

The second measurement is the transfer function or sound transmission characteristic of the middle ear. This function can be defined as the ratio of stapes footplate movement to sound pressure at the tympanic membrane and is often measured with the bulla open. The function which has been determined for the guinea pig is qualitatively similar to that found for the cat and human middle ear, and was modeled with minus 12 dB/octave low pass filer type characteristics (Nuttall, 1974b). Johnstone and Taylor (1972) made direct measurements of the transfer function using the Mössbauer technique (i.e., velocity Doppler shift in radiation from a radioactive source placed on the stapes) in the guinea pig with similar results as above except that the high frequency slope was a value between −6 and −12/dB octave.

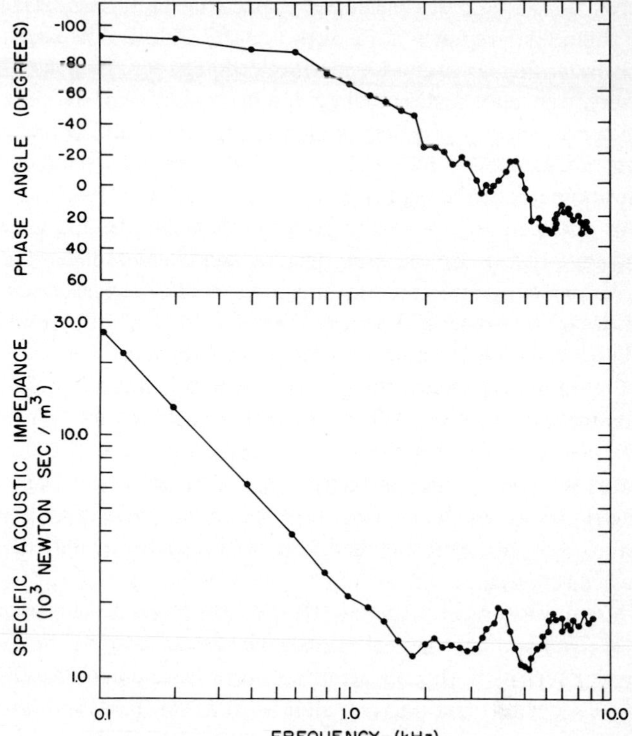

Fig. 3. The typical acoustic input impedance of the intact guinea pig ear (from Mundie, 1962).

Another aspect of middle ear mechanics is the action of the tympanic muscles. In the guinea pig, effects of the stapedius and tensor tympani muscles on sound transmission through the middle ear were evaluated by Wiggers (1937) and Nuttall (1974c). The tensor tympani caused the greatest changes, up to 30 dB of transmission attenuation for frequencies below 300 Hz. At higher frequencies an appreciable phase shift up to 100° can occur, and there is a range of frequencies near 2 kHz where both muscles produced a slight increase in sound transmission efficiency.

Cochlear mechanics, a research area of great current interest, has been studied mainly in the squirrel monkey, guinea pig, and the temporal bone of man. von Békésy (1947), by means of an optical technique, first observed the traveling wave on the basilar membrane of the guinea pig. Using von Békésy's results, Greenwood (1961, 1962) compared the guinea pig tuning curve width to that of man, chicken, and elephant, showing that even though the length of the basilar membrane changes, the width of the tuning curve remains a constant fraction of the length. The place of maximal vibration of the basilar membrane for different frequencies in guinea pigs was shown histologically after destructive overstimulation with sound by Lurie *et al.* (1944).

Using the Mössbauer technique in the guinea pig, Johnstone and Boyle (1967) and Johnstone and Taylor (1970) have found a fairly sharp localized displacement of the basilar membrane in response to acoustic energy. Plotted as basilar membrane displacement for constant stapes input against frequency, the curves show a low frequency slope of 10 to 24 dB/octave and high frequency slope of up to −200 dB/octave (maximum displacement point 17 kHz). These data indicate that some of the tuning seen in single units of the auditory nerve can, perhaps, be accounted for by mechanical frequency analysis. Further aspects of middle ear and cochlear mechanics are discussed by Johnstone and Taylor (1970) and in the review by Johnstone and Sellick (1972).

Recently, some very worthwhile studies have been done of basilar membrane vibrations in the guinea pig using a new laser light method for the analysis of microvibrations (Kohllöffel, 1972a,b). Cochlear mechanics of the guinea pig have also been examined recently by Kohllöffel (1971) in which he uses a multielectrode technique for the study of the potential distribution along the basilar membrane in the basal one-half turn of scala tympani.

The guinea pig is well suited to the above middle and inner ear studies because the auditory structures are relatively more accessible than in other mammals. Middle ear components are easily observed and manipulated within the large auditory bulla. All turns of the cochlea are available for study, covered only by the thin bony shield of the otic capsule.

VII. HISTOLOGY

The guinea pig has been a valuable subject for all types of middle and inner ear histology. Various procedures for histological preparation of inner ear tissue will not be discussed, but adequate fixation of the tissue is imperative and is preferably accomplished in the live animal either by systemic injection or local perfusion of the ear. If the temporal bones are removed, one must guard against transmitting a fracture force from the skull proper to the temporal bone when using Rongeurs. A small saw is probably safer for use in this regard.

An example of the cross-sectional anatomy from the upper portion of the basal coil of the cochlea of a guinea pig is shown in Fig. 4. This work is by Professor Joseph Hawkins, Jr., and it is an updated and modified version of a work originally published by him in 1966. This type of preparation could be made from a cochlea which was fixed, decalcified, and embedded in celloidin.

Excellent examples and a discussion of the use of the guinea pig for whole-mount histological "surface preparations" are given by Hawkins (1965). In this technique the ear is usually perfused locally with a fixative flushed slowly through the perilymph via the oval and round windows. After fixation, the bone of the otic capsule is removed by hand dissection under an operating microscope. To quote Hawkins "... whole-mounts of segments of the organ of Corti are dissected from the cochlea and mounted in glycerol or other suitable medium, for viewing by phase-contrast illumination. They provide a view of Corti's organ such as might be enjoyed by a micro-ornithoid observer perched on Reissner's membrane."

The guinea pig has also been studied with transmission and scanning electron microscopy. Figure 5 is a scanning electron micrograph of the hair cells of the guinea pig made by Professor Hawkins and provided to us from his unpublished collection. For additional examples of scanning electron microscopy on the guinea pig ear, see Bredberg *et al.* (1970, 1972). A sample of transmission electron microscopy on the guinea pig ear appears in Fig. 12 by Hawkins (1971).

Terayama *et al.* (1968) have completed a transmission electron microscopic study of the postganglionic sympathetic fibers in the guinea pig cochlea. This work was carried out to supplement earlier fluorescent histochemical investigations by them on the guinea pig. An excellent light and scanning electron microscopic study of the degeneration and distribution of efferent nerve fibers in the guinea pig organ of Corti has been performed by Wright and Preston (1973). Smith and Haglan (1973) have used Golgi stains on the guinea pig organ of Corti. With this method they studied the branching of the cochlear and efferent nerve fibers. Additional examples of scanning and transmission electron microscopy of the guinea pig inner ear are contained in papers by Dr. Lim and his colleagues (Lim, 1972; Lim and Lane, 1969a,b).

VIII. LABYRINTHINE FLUIDS AND BIOCHEMISTRY OF THE INNER EAR

Biochemical research using the guinea pig ear is far too diverse to receive even a token mention in the space available here. We feel that the reader will be best served if directed to the several books and reviews which can provide a basis for further investigation of the biochemical aspects of hearing. Many studies that we cite do not deal solely with the guinea pig, but research using this animal is strongly represented. Three books which include very useful discussions of chemistry, especially the histochemistry and histopathology, including methods, are those of Rauch (1964), Vinnikov and Titova (1964), and Schätzle (1971). A more general treatment of biochemical topics is to be found in Paparella (1970).

The content and maintenance of the labyrinthine fluids have received considerable attention over the years. Some fluid compartments of the ear have yet to be sampled directly (e.g., the fluid spaces of the organ of Corti) because the technical expertise is not available. One relevant publication is the excellent monograph by Vosteen (1971), who discusses ion

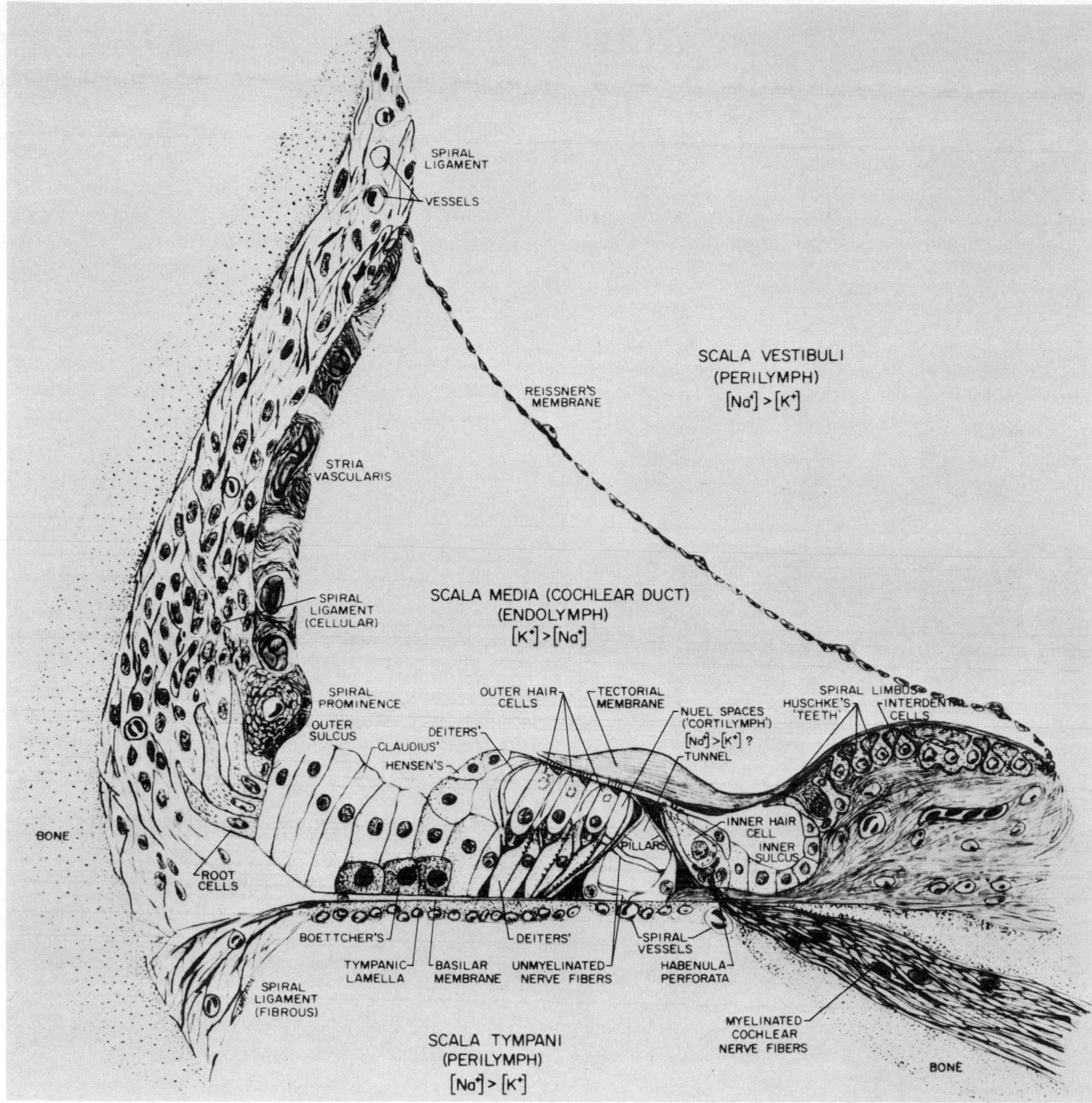

Fig. 4. A cross-sectional view of the basal turn of the guinea pig cochlear duct. The view in this drawing is typical of material prepared with celloidin embedding and photographed through the light microscope. (Updated by Professor Hawkins from an original published in 1966.)

transport in depth and includes some of the studies of Ilberg on inner ear membrane permeability (von Ilberg and Vosteen, 1969). Further reports by Ilberg delineate the various fluid compartments of the inner ear using the diffusion and transport of thorium dioxide particles as a tracer (von Ilberg, 1968a–d; von Ilberg *et al.*, 1968). Other tracer studies, reviewed by Duvall and Sutherland (1972), make use of horseradish peroxidase to study labyrinthine membrane activity and passive transport. Yet another publication on membrane permeability, by Meyer zum Gottesberg *et al.* (1965), also includes work on oxygen consumption and protein metabolism. The concentrations of inorganic ions in the ear are discussed in some of the above articles, while a recent paper by Eggemann *et al.* (1970) reports the heavy metal content of the guinea pig inner ear.

Lawrence (1965, 1968), in discussing the fluid balance in the

Fig. 5. A scanning electron micrograph of the tops of some of the hair cells in the guinea pig inner ear. The W-shaped hair tufts of the three outer hair cell rows are at the bottom of the plate, and the tufts of the inner hair cells are at the top. One hair cell is missing from the middle outer row, but this occurrence is typical of normal material. (Micrograph courtesy of Professor Joseph E. Hawkins, Jr.)

inner ear of the guinea pig and mammals in general, has reiterated an important basic tenet proposed by Naftalin and Harrison (1958). In Fig. 4, it is noted that the sodium concentration in the perilymph is greater than the concentration of potassium. The reverse is true in the scala media. Regarding this matter, Fig. 6 from Lawrence (1968) depicts the concept of Naftalin and Harrison that the perilymph is formed by the supra stria vessels above Reissner's membrane, where sodium exceeds the concentration of potassium. Then perilymph diffuses through Reissner's membrane to be modified in ionic content to form endolymph which contains a greater concentration of potassium than sodium. Malfunction of this proposed system could be a potential etiological factor for Meniere's disease.

Suga *et al.* (1970a,b) and Nakashima *et al.* (1970b) studied changes in the sodium and potassium concentration of the guinea pig endolymph during intense sound stimulation and asphyxia. With either intense sound stimulation or asphyxia, sodium concentration was increased and potassium concentration was decreased. In a further study, Nakashima *et al.* (1970a) showed that intense sound stimulation slightly decreased the sodium concentration and slightly increased the potassium concentration in the perilymph of the scala vestibuli, but the sodium and potassium concentration in the scala tympani did not change appreciably.

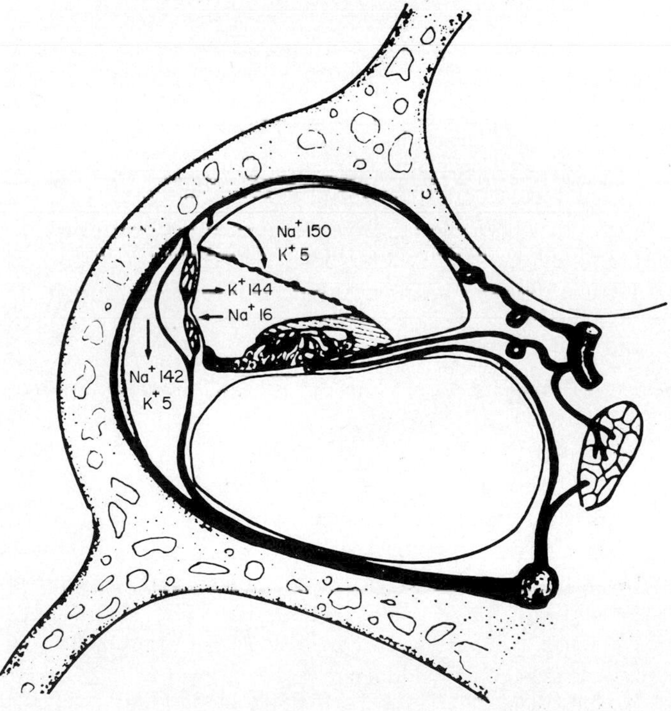

Fig. 6. The concept of Naftalin and Harrison that the perilymph is formed by the supra stria vessels above Reissner's membrane, where sodium exceeds the concentration of potassium (values are given in mEq/liter). The perilymph diffuses through Reissner's membrane to be modified in ionic content to from endolymph which contains a greater concentration of potassium than sodium.

Changes in ionic chemistry have also been shown in the inner ear of the guinea pig associated with administration of ototoxic drugs. For example, Mendelsohn and Katzenberg (1972) have studied the effect of kanamycin on the cation content of the endolymph, and alterations in the sodium and potassium concentrations of the labyrinthine fluids have been reported following the administration of ethacrynic acid (Wilson and Juhn, 1970; Cohn *et al.*, 1971).

IX. ROUND WINDOW AC COCHLEAR POTENTIALS

The technique of recording round window AC cochlear potentials is probably the most useful research method ever employed in the field of physiological acoustics. Credit for the development of this procedure belongs to Professor E. G. Wever of Princeton University. The fundamentals and theory associated with AC cochlear potentials are described in great detail in the book "Physiological Acoustics" by Wever and Lawrence (1954). This work is certainly one of the most outstanding scholarly contributions to the American scientific literature. A more recent review of the AC cochlear potentials has been written by Wever (1966).

AC cochlear potentials recorded at the round window membrane represent the output of the sensory hair cells of the organ of Corti when the ear is stimulated by sounds in the environment (Wever, 1959). The AC potentials follow (within the frequency range of the particular species) the frequency of sound used to stimulate the ear. Also, within the dynamic range of the ear, the cochlear potentials increase in an orderly manner with increases in sound intensity. Once an investigator has determined the normal AC output of an ear for so much sound pressure to the eardrum, he can then determine quantitatively how much gain or loss of sensory cell function is caused by any given manipulation of the middle ear mechanics or inner ear physiology.

The guinea pig has been extremely popular for use in AC round window experiments. One of the main reasons for this is the ease with which the round window of the guinea pig can be exposed surgically. A well-trained person can operate and place an electrode on the round window of the guinea pig in 10 minutes. A typical set-up for recording the AC round window potentials of the guinea pig is shown in Fig. 1.

Any investigator wishing to check the accuracy of his equipment and surgical preparation for the baseline cochlear potential sensitivity data for the guinea pig shown in Fig. 7. (Wever *et al.*, 1963). With reference to the intensity functions of the guinea pig AC potentials, most investigators routinely measure

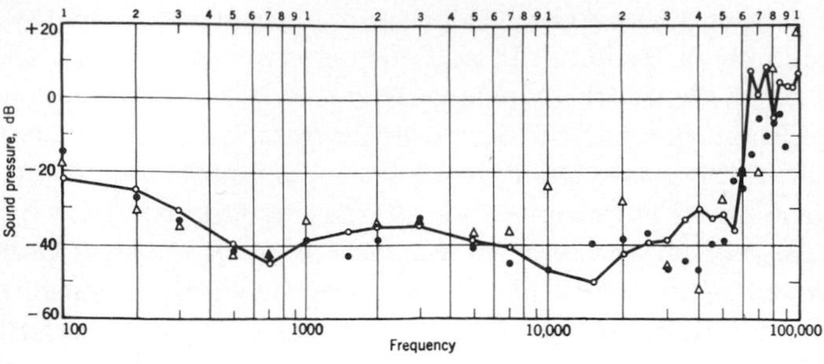

Fig. 7. AC round window cochlear potential sensitivity functions for three guinea pig ears, as indicated by the different kinds of points. Each point represents the sound pressure, in decibels relative to 1 dyne per cm², required to produce a potential of 1 μV at the indicated frequency (after Wever *et al.*, 1963).

the maximum output obtainable with a 1000 Hz tone and then again with a 10 kHz tone. For 1000 Hz a healthy guinea pig ear will give a maximum output of 1000 μV root mean square (rms). If a result below 500 μV rms is obtained at 1000 Hz it is probably best to eliminate the animal from the experimental protocol since the number of viable inner ear sensory hair cells is probably below normal. At the Bowman Gray School of Medicine we have had occasional guinea pig 1000 Hz outputs as high as 2600 μV rms. A good output for a guinea pig at 10 kHz would be in the range of 200 to 400 μV rms.

The first study of the intensity functions of the round window cochlear potential were recorded from the guinea pig by Wever and Bray in 1936. Since this original work, the expansion of the literature utilizing AC round window cochlear potential recordings has been massive. Numerous examples are contained in various sections of this chapter. The particulars of recording AC cochlear potentials from locations in the cochlea other than the round window are described by Dallos *et al.* (1971).

X. AC POTENTIALS DUE TO LOCAL BASILAR MEMBRANE VIBRATION

By using a vibrating microprobe it is possible to impart discrete and local vibration to accessible areas of the basilar membrane. The guinea pig is particularly well suited for the local vibration studies because it is possible to dissect away a portion of the otic capsule in the round window area. This exposes a length of the scala tympani side of the basilar membrane for direct visual observation and/or placement of electrodes and vibration probes. It is also possible to remove the apex of the cochlea exposing the scala vestibuli side of the organ of Corti in an upper turn.

von Békésy (1951), employing a vibrating microelectrode (i.e., responses of the tissue to mechanical vibration of the electrode were recorded by the electrode itself) in the guinea pig, determined that the AC cochlear potential is proportional to basilar membrane displacement and that displacements along an axis radially out from the modiolus were more effective producers of cochlear potentials than tangential (longitudinal) displacements. In a later study, von Békésy (1953) explored cochlear potential sensitivity to the shearing motion of the tectorial membrane, using a vibrating probe.

More recently, Lawrence *et al.* (1974) used a vibrating microprobe to obtain locally generated cochlear potentials in the basal or first turn of the guinea pig cochlea. With an electrode probing the organ of Corti, the local cochlear potential was compared to remotely generated cochlear potentials at the same frequency (from stapes vibration of the perilymph). They found the maximum response from local vibration at the basilar membrane and the interface of the organ of Corti with endolymph.

XI. DC POTENTIALS OF THE INNER EAR

The guinea pig has played a major role in the discovery and investigation of direct current (DC) potentials of the cochlea because the exposed otic capsule affords a better access to inner structures than in many other animals.

Unlike AC potentials, the measurement of DC resting potentials requires the use of electrodes which tend not to polarize and that have very small tips. These requirements limit the electrode choice to electrolyte-filled glass micropipettes. By using such an electrode on the guinea pig organ of Corti, von Békésy (1952) discovered the positive endolymphatic potential (EP). The fluid in the membranous labyrinth (scala media) was found to be 50 to 80 mV positive relative to the perilymph of the scala tympani or tissues of the head.

The EP magnitude can be changed by application of sound, pressure, asphyxic hypoxia, or oxidative metabolism inhibitors to the inner ear. Sound causes the potential to decrease in magnitude (Misrahy *et al.*, 1958b; Rice and Shinabarger, 1960), whereas positive and negative pressure applied to the scala vestibuli increase and decrease EP, respectively (Tasaki *et al.*, 1954). With 2–3 minutes of hypoxia the endolymphatic potential reveals itself as having two components. One component is a steady negative potential of up to −40 mV (Konishi *et al.*, 1961; Fernandez, 1955) which is thought to be a potassium ion diffusion potential (this view is summarized in the review of Johnstone and Sellick, 1972). The other component is a positive potential which may be an electrogenic potential because it is susceptible to metabolic inhibitors (Morizono and Johnstone, 1968; Konishi and Kelsey, 1968; Kuijpers and Bonting, 1970a,b).

A second resting potential of the inner ear is intracellular negative potential. von Békésy (1952), using the guinea pig, observed a polarization of −40 mV in Hensens', Claudius', and other cells of the organ of Corti. Subsequent investigators have found negative potentials ranging to −90 mV (Tasaki *et al.*, 1954; Davis, 1958; Butler *et al.*, 1962a,b). There are also fluid-filled spaces in the organ of Corti (e.g., Nuell's spaces and the tunnel of Corti) which were thought to exhibit large negative DC potentials (Butler, 1965), but a recent study by Lawrence *et al.* (1974) has demonstrated that the spaces are nearly at the same potential as the perilymph of the scala tympani, i.e., zero or slightly negative. Thus, it can be shown the potential map given by an electrode, passing through the organ of Corti from the scala tympani to the scala media, is somewhat specific for a given area or structure within the organ of Corti (Lawrence and Nuttall, 1970; Lawrence *et al.*, 1974). As an example, in the guinea pig, Fig. 8 illustrates the DC potential plotted against micrometers as a microelectrode penetrates Corti's organ. The large negative potential represents the intracellular potential of the Claudius cell area while the jump to a large positive represents the endolymphatic potential as the electrode enters the scala media.

A third DC potential which can be recorded from the inner ear is the summating potential (SP). This potential was discovered by Davis *et al.* (1950) in the guinea pig and is manifested as a DC offset which occurs concurrent with the AC response of the ear to a tone burst. The summating potential is most easily produced by high frequency tones and its magnitude is a function of the sound intensity. Various procedures which affect the size of the summating potential in guinea pigs were reported by Misrahy *et al.* (1957). The summating potential has been attributed to the hair cells of the organ of Corti (Davis *et al.*, 1958). An extensive and up-to-date treatment of the SP is given in the reports of (Dallos *et al.*, 1972; Durant and Dallos, 1972). The AC and DC potentials of the inner ear of the guinea pig as well as other animals are described more thoroughly in a review by Wever (1966), and in the textbook by Dallos (1973).

All of the bioelectric potentials found in the guinea pig compare favorably to the findings from other animals. Thus the guinea pig inner ear, which is relatively accessible for study and manipulation, appears to be a representative model of the mammalian ear.

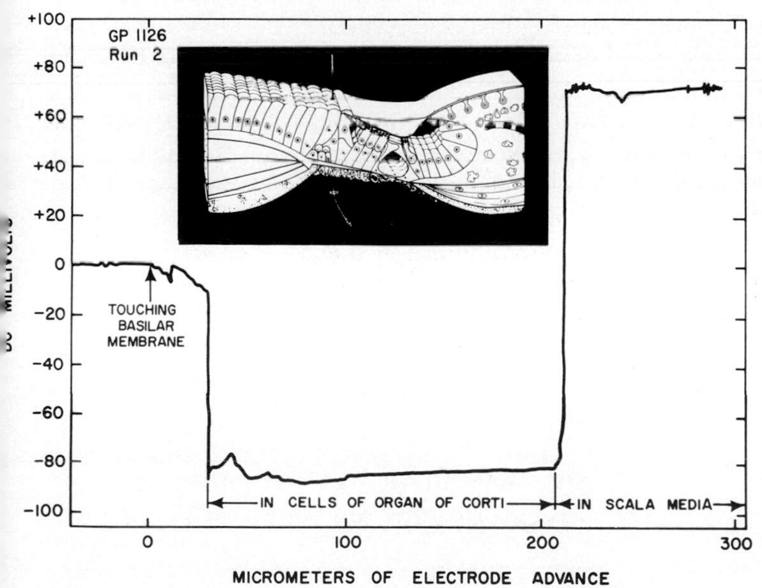

Fig. 8. An example of the DC potential map that is produced when a microelectrode passes through the organ of Corti in the region of Claudius cells. The negative potential represents intracellular cytoplasm while the positive potential is the endolymph of scala media.

XII. STUDIES OF THE ACOUSTIC NERVE AND EVENTS MORE CENTRAL

Auditory information which has been encoded can be observed at three basic levels of the nervous system: nerve, brainstem, and auditory cortex. At the peripheral end, the response of the auditory nerve (VIII cranial nerve) can be recorded as a whole nerve action potential (AP) (Fig. 9) or as the activity of a single nerve fiber (Fig. 10).

The AP is a bioelectric potential which may be picked up by an electrode placed in, on, or near the cochlea. The potential is produced in response to fast rise time acoustic transients or noise bursts and is most easily recorded when the electrode is in the perilymph or on the round window of the cochlea. Since AP magnitude is small, it is sometimes necessary to improve the signal to noise ratio by using computer averaging techniques, especially if the electrode is remote from the

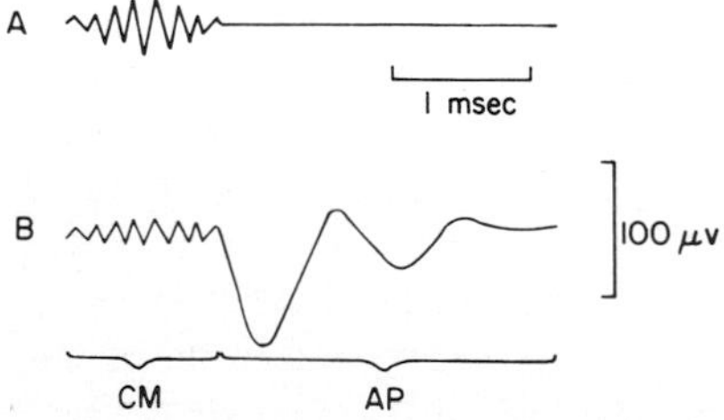

Fig. 9. A schematic representation of the whole nerve action potential (AP), in response to a short acoustic tone burst, as would be recorded by a round window electrode. (A) The acoustic tone burst presented to the external ear. (B) AC cochlear potential response followed by the AP.

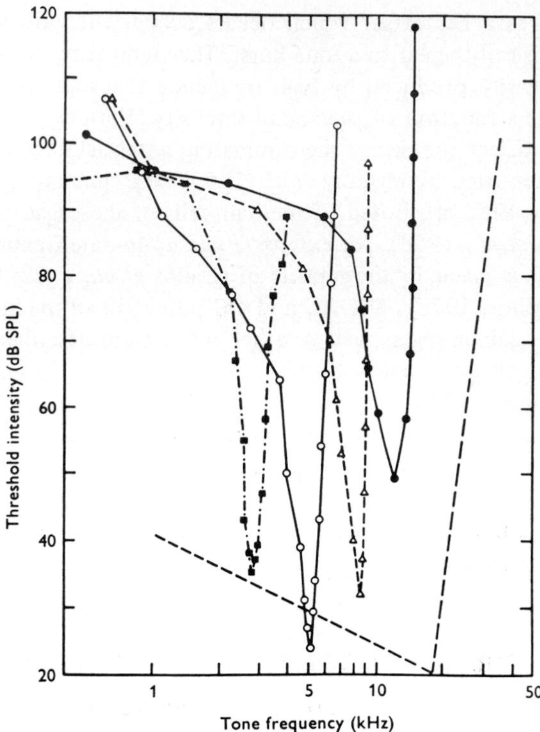

Fig. 10. Response areas of individual eighth nerve fibers (open and closed symbols); note the extremely sharp slope of the high frequency side of each curve as compared with the Johnstone and Boyle (1967) basilar membrane response curve (lower dashed line) (by permission; from Evans, 1970a).

cochlea. AP is believed to be an electrical summation of many spiral ganglion cells firing with some synchrony to the acoustic transient stimulus. This bioelectric signal is easily obtained from the inner ears of any of the commonly used experimental animals, so the guinea pig has not particularly received a large amount of the attention. There are experiments where the guinea pig may be a good experimental subject, e.g., correlation AP changes with histologically determined cochlear nerve distribution changes resulting from noise or ototoxic agents because surface preparation histology of the organ of Corti is easily accomplished. Impulses were first recorded from the acoustic nerve of the guinea pig by Professor E. G. Wever in 1931. An extensive study of the AP in the guinea pig was made by Teas *et al.* (1962). Earlier work on AP can be found in reports by Davis *et al.* (1950), Tasaki *et al.* (1952), Tasaki and Fernandez (1952), and Tasaki (1954).

It is also possible to observe the firing of single units of the auditory nerve by inserting a microelectrode into the nerve body or its axon. Such an experiment is an extremely important step in the study of auditory encoding and processing. The first successful auditory single unit recordings were made by Tasaki (1954) in the guinea pig. Evans (1970a,b, 1972) has expanded and improved single fiber measurements, showing the guinea pig auditory fiber response areas to be much like those of the cat and monkey which are now more commonly used for this kind of experiment.

Studies of acoustic centers in the brainstem and auditory cortex are usually performed on larger mammals than the guinea pig. This has resulted in a situation where much is known about the peripheral auditory end organ of the guinea pig but relatively little about central processing. Certainly part of the problem is the small size of the pertinent neural structures and this is coupled with the lace of a sterotaxic atlas for the guinea pig brainstem, a crucial tool for exploring the subdivisions of the acoustic pathways.

Most brainstem experiments have been measurements of second-order neuron responses in the cochlear nucleus. The early work is represented by the reports of Galambos and Davis (1943), Galambos (1944), and Tasaki and Davis (1955). In recent years most of the research in this area using the guinea pig has been done by Pfalz (1962a,b, 1966, 1969a,b) and co-workers (Pfalz and Pirsig, 1966; Pirsig and Pfalz, 1966, 1967; Pirsig, *et al.,* 1968; Pirsig, 1968). Wusterfeld and Gleiss (1969) also have recorded medulla responses to acoustic stimulation.

Another aspect of brainstem research is investigation of efferent innervation of the cochlea by electrical stimulation of the crossed olivocochlear bundle. Such stimulation has resulted in suppression of neural activity in the auditory portion of the VIII nerve (Konishi and Slepian, 1971; Daigneault and Stopp, 1971). An extensive electrophysiological study of the efferent system is that of Teas *et al.* (1972). Whereas, pharmacological studies on the olivocochlear bundle in the guinea pig have been performed by Tanaka and Katsuki (1966) and Konishi (1972).

One observable sign of the final stage of auditory processing is the slow wave evoked cortical response. The guinea pig is hardly the most widely used specimen for this research, yet one can find a few reports which further demonstrate the usefulness and versatility of this animal (Kern *et al.,* 1969a,b; Zoellner and Stange, 1967). A report by Scibetta and Rosen (1969) suggests the use of evoked potentials, in fetal guinea pigs, to study the maturation of the fetal brain (see also Section XVI).

XIII. VASCULAR ANATOMY AND PHYSIOLOGY OF THE INNER EAR

The guinea pig has been and continues to be a very important model for the study of the vascular function and related oxygen availability in the inner ear. One reason for this is the previously mentioned fact that the cochlea of the guinea pig protrudes into the middle ear space making it more accessible for study. Workers such as Perlman and Kimura (1955, 1957) and Nomura (1961) have developed techniques for fenestrating the lateral wall of the guinea pig cochlea for the study of the blood flow in the small vessels of the spiral ligament and stria vascularis (cf. structures of Fig. 4).

Another reason for interest in the study of the microcirculation of the inner ear of the guinea pig is the fact that this animal along with man is the only one known so far to consistently have the outer spiral vessel or vas spirale beneath the basilar membrane (see Figs. 4 and 11). In most mammals this vessel is present only in the embryonic stage. The vessel does not exist in the adult cat or rabbit (Axelsson and Lind, 1973), and the vas spirale only exists irregularly throughout the monkeys (Axelsson, 1974).

Professor Merle Lawrence and his colleagues at the Kresge Hearing Research Institute at the University of Michigan have developed very sophisticated means for the direct observation of the physiology of the vas spirale and basilar membrane vessels in the guinea pig. Observation and filming of the vessels are carried out with a microscope positioned over the round window of the guinea pig cochlea (Lawrence, 1970, 1971, 1973a; Lawrence and Clapper, 1972; see Fig. 11).

Through the physiological studies noted above as well as pathological studies on the effects of interference with the terminal blood supply of the organ of Corti in the guinea pig (Lawrence, 1966), Lawrence and his co-workers have demonstrated that the blood supply to the basilar membrane and perhaps also the capillaries on the tympanic lip of the spiral osseous lamina and in the limbus are most important for the immediate metabolic maintenance of the sensory hair cells. On the other hand the vessels of the stria vascularis and spiral ligament seem to have more to do with the long-term maintenance of cochlear function. This view has been strengthened by a study of the oxygen availability in the tunnel of Corti measured by microelectrodes placed through the round window of the guinea pig (Lawrence and Nuttall, 1972).

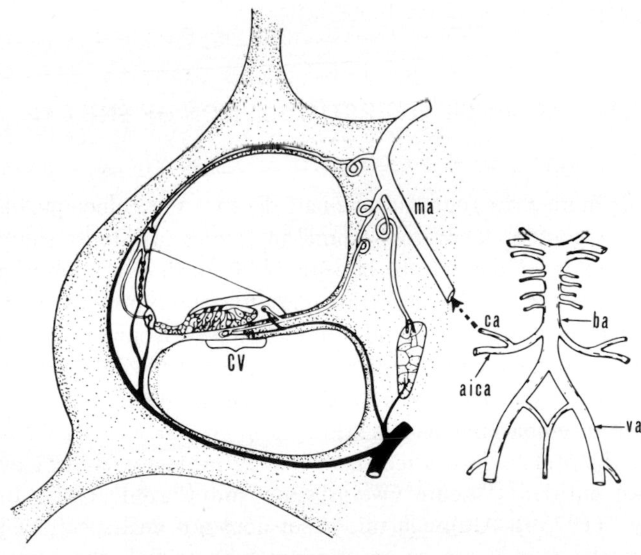

Fig. 11. Schematic drawing of the blood supply to the scala media. The area marked CV indicates the region of view for the motion picture camera photography which Lawrence accomplished in the basal region of the guinea pig. ma, Modiolar arteriole; ca, cochlear artery; ba, basilar artery; aica, anterior inferior cerebellar artery; va, vertebral artery (after Lawrence, 1971).

With regard to the above tenet, McCormick *et al.* (1973), while studying diving deafness in the guinea pig, found marked loss of sensory hair cells and AC cochlear potentials associated with probable loss of basilar membrane circulation and near normal stria vascularis, supporting the view of Lawrence. Other literature bearing on this question is discussed in a monograph by Axelsson (1968, pp. 112–113).

In addition to the intracochlear oxygen measurements in the guinea pig carried out by Lawrence and Nuttall (1972), Misrahy *et al.* (1958a,b) have studied oxygen availability to various stimuli, especially anoxia, with microelectrodes placed in the scala media. Koide *et al.* (1959) measured the oxygen usage of excised guinea pig labyrinthine tissue in a closed reaction vessel. One investigator, Okumura (1970) found reduction of perilymphatic oxygen tension had little effect on AC cochlear potentials.

Several other reports are in the literature concerning cochlear function under metabolic impairment in the guinea pig. Notable examples are listed here. Butler *et al.* (1962a,b) conducted work which investigated the relationships of the AC cochlear potential to the evoked potential, and their experiments on perfusing the anoxic cochlea led them to question the idea that cochlear potentials are highly sensitive to oxygen deprivation. Honrubia *et al.* (1965) observed the maintenance of cochlear potentials in the guinea pig during asphyxia with artificial perfusion of the cochlea. Morizono and Johnstone (1968) described their technique developed for perfusing the guinea pig's cochlea. Also changes in the cochlear potentials as a result of asphyxic, ischemic, and histotoxic anoxia, together with the effects of different hematocrit and flow rates were described. Tsunoo and Perlman (1969) studied cochlear respiration in the guinea pig with systemic hypoxia and perfusion of the scala tympani in the basal turn with sodium cyanide. Misrahy (1958) altered the scala tympani oxygen concentration enzymatically. The effect of chemical substances upon the electrical responses of the cochlea, especially the application of sodium chloride to the round window membrane of the guinea pig, was reviewed and studied by Wever and Bray (1937). Mayahara and Perlman (1972) studied the cochlear microcirculation and oxygen transport in the guinea pig cochlea with variations of the velocity of flow, the oxygen content, and oxygen tension of the blood. They found that all of these factors affected the transport of oxygen from the cochlear microcirculation into the cells and fluids of the inner ear.

The work and review by Axelsson (1968) is an excellent monograph entitled: "The Vascular Anatomy of the Cochlea in the Guinea Pig and in Man." Axelsson has also published papers on the cochlear blood vessels in guinea pigs of different ages (1971), on the cochlear vascular anatomy in a strain of the waltzing guinea pig (Axelsson and Ernston, 1972), the healing of the external cochlear wall in the guinea pig after mechanical injury (Axelsson and Hallén, 1973), and a demonstration of the cochlear vessels in the guinea pig by contrast injection (Axelsson, 1972). The work of Axelsson will be particularly important for workers wishing to interpret guinea pig inner ear research in the light of possible human application.

Further important studies of the guinea pig are brought out in the book: "Vascular Disorders and Hearing Defects" (de Lorenzo, 1973). Although referenced in this publication two additional important studies of the vascular anatomy in the guinea pig are by Nabeya (1923) and Smith (1951).

When a clinical otolaryngologist is faced with a case of sudden deafness in a person with a suspected vascular etiology it is helpful to have knowledge of basic physiological studies of cochlear arterial and venous obstruction so that one may understand the limits of the potential use of such agents as vasodilators, anticoagulants, and fibrinolytic agents. Several such basic works have been carried out in the guinea pig. Perlman (1952) reported on experimental occlusion of the inferior cochlear vein in the guinea pig. Kimura and Perlman (1956) studied extensive venous obstruction of the labyrinth, and Perlman and Kimura (1957) produced experimental obstruction of the venous drainage and arterial supply of the inner ear of the guinea pig. In 1958 Kimura and Perlman went on to study further arterial obstruction of the labyrinth. A sequel to this paper appeared in 1959 by Perlman *et al.* (1959b). These works all defined the histological changes produced in the inner ear with venous or arterial obstructions for various time intervals. It is interesting to note that the investigations of Perlman and his colleagues with surgical interference with the inner ear blood supply produced results very similar to nonsurgical diving induced deafness observed by McCormick, and his co-workers (1973). McCormick postulated that decompression sickness may produce hypercoagulation, embolic, and thrombotic problems which precipitate a loss of cochlear function. Both McCormick *et al.* (1973) and Perlman and Kimura (1957) found loss of vestibular function and electrical activity of the cochlea. Both groups also noted the production of hemorrhage in the inner ear.

Another report of experimental microembolization of cochlear vessels has been made by Suga *et al.* (1970b). This group produced microembolization in the guinea pig with a suspension of barium sulfate. Suga's group has also been interested in the effects of labyrinthine vasodilators and the behavior of the cochlear blood flow in the guinea pig (Snow and Suga, 1973; Suga and Snow, 1969c; Morimitsu *et al.*, 1965).

Suga and his colleagues measured changes in the cochlear blood flow of the guinea pig with the use of an electrical impedance plethysmograph. Furthermore, their work reviewed the evidence for cholinergic (see also Suga and Snow, 1969b) and adrenergic control (see also Suga and Snow, 1969a) of cochlear blood flow in the guinea pig. Perlman *et al.* (1963) have studied blood flow velocity changes in the guinea pig stria vascularis and spiral ligament as a function of variations in carotid blood pressure produced by the administration of epinephrine, morepinephrine, vasopressin, and serotonin. However, Perlman *et al.* (1959) found that the cochlear vessels were resistant to changes in diameter even under the powerful vasomotor stimulation produced by profound rapid hypothermia. Adrenergic innervation of the cochlea of the guinea pig has been reviewed by Terayama *et al.* (1966).

The innervation of the cochlear receptor in general and in the guinea pig, including considerations of the autonomic nervous system has been reported (c.f. Spoendlin, 1973). Some earlier work on cochlear potentials and stimulation of the sympathetic nervous system in the guinea pig is noted by Seymour and Tappin (1953). However for this type of work Seymour found the cat to be a more suitable surgical preparation than the guinea pig.

As a last note of interest in this section, Morizono *et al.* (1968) have measured the cochlear blood volume in the guinea pig with ^{51}Cr-labeled red blood cells.

XIV. ACOUSTIC OVERSTIMULATION OF THE EAR

For more than four and one-half decades the guinea pig has been a popular laboratory animal in studies of intense sound stimulation of the ear. To be sure, many of these studies have been directed toward answering questions about how the inner ear can be damaged by loud sounds in the environment, but in addition several workers have also cleverly utilized this paradigm to get at matters of normal cochlear mechanics.

Before embarking on experiments in this area it would be most helpful to read a recent review by Professor Merle Lawrence entitled: "Acute Overpressure and Chronic Noise Injury" (1973b). Although this paper does not deal specifically with the guinea pig as an experimental animal, the terms, methods, and basic physiology relative to the field are described.

Many excellent studies of high level sound stimulation in the guinea pig are in the literature. Professor E. G. Wever of Princeton University along with some of his colleagues has reported a series of papers in this area, and a review of their works will undoubtedly provide one with an appreciation for well-controlled highly productive experiments with the guinea pig.

In 1934 Horton did a behavioral experiment with the guinea pig in which he found a marked sensitivity impairment as a result of stimulation with loud pure tones. The impairment not only appeared in the range of the stimulation frequency, but extended to some degree over all tones tested postintense stimulation. The next year, Wever *et al.* (1935) in some of the same animals confirmed the above findings with a study of the AC round window cochlear potentials. Further, it was noted that: "It is probable that when a tone attains an intensity of 100 dB or more, it involves practically the entire extent of the basilar membrane and allied structures. It should be added, however, that these results do not indicate a correspondingly great spread for tones of more moderate intensity."

In 1936, using the guinea pig as an animal model, Wever and Bray investigated the functional relationship between the AC cochlear potential and sound intensity and the changes in this relationship as frequency varies. A linear relationship between sound intensity and electric response was noted with a culmination "overload" or nonlinearity at high intensity. Wever, collaborating with Bray and Lawrence (1940) carried out other experiments on the guinea pig which found the locus of distortion or "overload" to be the inner ear as opposed to the middle ear.

Smith, while at Princeton University in 1947, studied the histological damage to intense pure tone exposed guinea pig inner ears. Microscopic tissue alterations were somewhat more widespread for low tone stimulation than high, but electrical measurements indicated general broad loss of function for high and low frequency stimulation. The injurious effect of a high frequency tone was more extensively examined by Smith and Wever (1949), and they found significantly less insult over the low tone range of the cochlea for high frequency stimulation as opposed to low frequency stimulation. In 1949 Wever and Lawrence published another guinea pig investigation with pertinent application to the problems of the locus and spread of response over the basilar membrane. The work of Alexander and O'Brien on high tone stimulation and hearing loss in the guinea pig (1954) has already been mentioned in Section V. In 1955 Wever and Lawrence made another report on the patterns of injury produced by overstimulation of the guinea pig ear. This work confirmed earlier efforts by the Princeton group and especially sighted the finding that "With rare exceptions, the maximum responses to any tone are much less impaired than the sensitivity, and the maximums are more seriously affected for the low tones." Other important views on cochlear distortion are brought out by Worthington and Dallos (1971). Lawrence (1958) continued studies of functional changes in inner ear deafness, and in 1964 he reported on some of the histological changes in the inner ear with loud sound stimulation. Overstimulation of the guinea pig ear by Lawrence and Yantis (1957) revealed that permanent loss can depend largely on the ear's ability to recover. The ability of Reissner's membrane to repair itself was also discussed.

An excellent example of ultrastructural and surface preparation changes with acoustic trauma in the guinea pig is made by Spoendlin and Brun (1973). Ultrastructural changes in the inner ear with high intensity noise stimulation are reported by Engstrom and Ades (1961).

Ionic changes in the inner ear fluids with intense sound stimulation were mentioned in Section VIII (Snow *et al.*, 1971; Nakashima *et al.*, 1970a,b).

Falk *et al.* (1974) have carried out noise-induced inner ear damage in newborn and adult guinea pigs and they found the younger animals more prone toward dysfunction. Inner ear function after impulse noise was compared with performance and structural changes after high intensity pure tones by Poche *et al.* (1969).

A most interesting finding in the guinea pig was Hawkins' production of vasoconstriction in noise-induced hearing loss (1971). He found swelling of the endothelial cells in the microcirculation of the inner ear (see Fig. 12). This phenomenon was first reported by Lawrence *et al.* (1967) from experiments using guinea pigs. Undoubtedly such changes produce an impairment in the rheology of the ear's vascular bed. Thus Hawkins' finding may be related to the work of Kellerhals (1972) in which he noted less hair cell loss after noise exposure in guinea pigs pretreated with low molecular weight dextran. Studies which show protection of the ear from deafness with drugs are extremely rare and this is certainly an exciting field for further study. McCormick *et al.* (1973) demonstrated a protective effect of heparin for diving induced deafness, but loud sound was not a factor. Another study of cochlear blood flow in the guinea pig during acoustic trauma was made by Perlman and Kimura (1962).

XV. OTOTOXICITY

The guinea pig is an important animal model for ototoxicity studies. This field deals with efforts to elucidate the pathophysiology of drugs which cause deafness and vestibular disorders. Principally involved are the aminoglycosidic antibiotics, including neomycin, gentamicin, and other members of the streptomycin family. Some diuretics such as ethacrynic acid are ototoxic. These agents all lead to permanent deafness; however, transient dysfunction can be caused by quinine and salicylates.

For the past 25 years Professor Joseph E. Hawkins, Jr. has been a leader in ototoxicity research. Recently Dr. Hawkins has written three papers which summarize the literature and

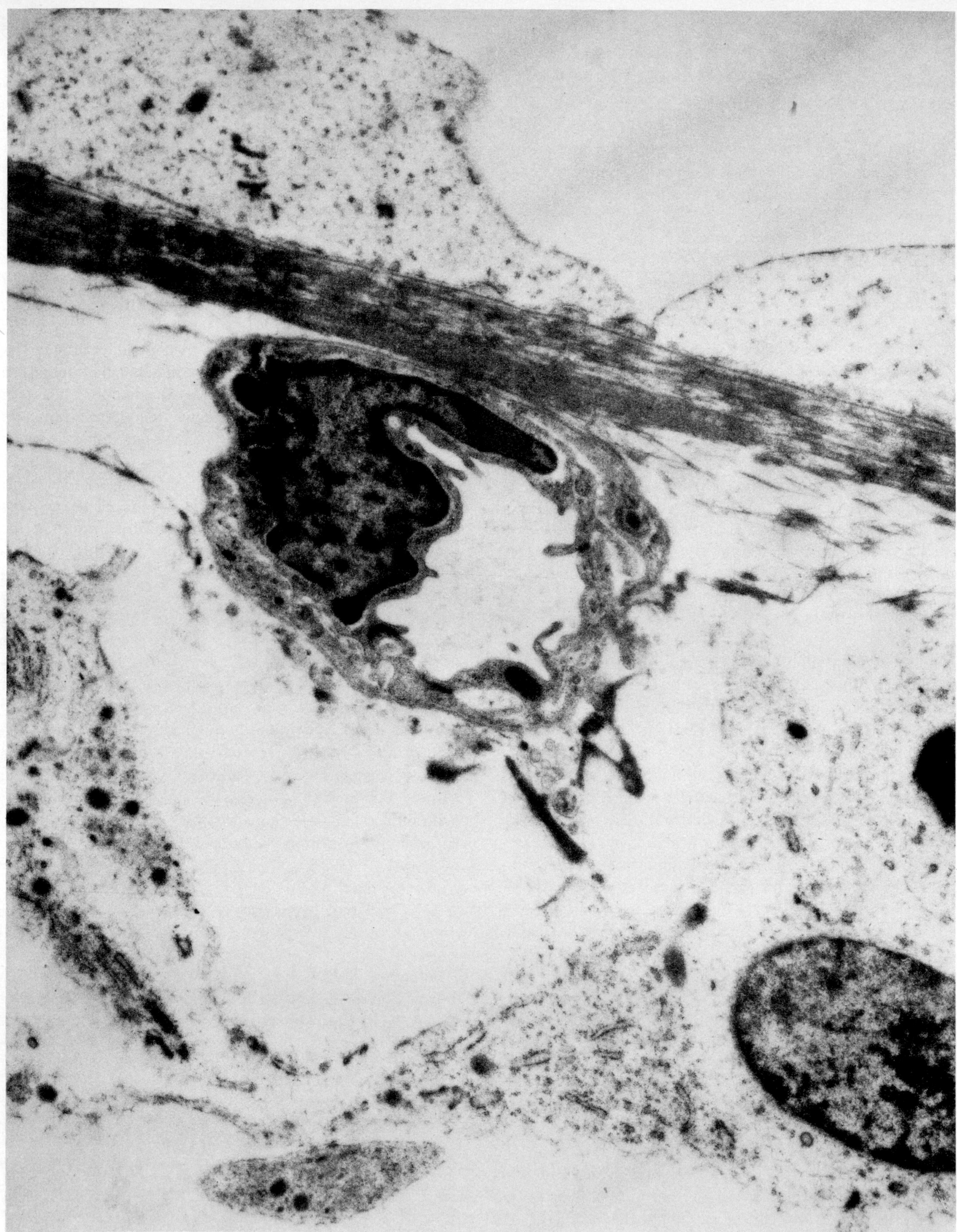

Fig. 12. A transmission electron micrograph of swollen endothelial cell enroaching on the lumen of the outer spiral vessel beneath the tunnel of Corti in the upper second turn. The guinea pig ear was exposed to noise of 118 to 120 dB for 110 hours in all. The amount of lumen remaining open in the vessel is about 3 μm (after Hawkins, 1971).

bring up-to-date current theories on the matter. His works are full of references to many key findings made with the guinea pig, especially several plates depicting vascular pathology associated with the syndrome (Hawkins, 1970, 1973a,b).

The first of the above three papers (Hawkins, 1970) covers the biochemical aspects of ototoxicity. The theme of the biochemical monograph includes ototoxic mechanisms (Hawkins, 1973b). Here Hawkins strongly argues that "the primary ototoxic action of the aminoglycosides is on the secretory and reabsorptive tissues (in the ear), and that the destruction of the sensory cells is secondary to the resulting disruption of the micro-homeostasis." This theme was also emphasized in the earlier work of Hawkins *et al.* (1950). Further, Hawkins notes that the ototoxic process is relatively slow, postulating a hemato–labyrinthine barrier for drugs given by normal clinical routes. However, a possible direct toxic action of drugs on the sensory hair cells is allowed for with direct application to the round window membrane (Spoendlin, 1966). In a study carried out at the Bowman Gray School of Medicine, McCurdy *et al.* (1974) found that the ototoxic effect of ethacrynic acid on the guinea pig could be doubled by performing a bilateral nephrectomy. This maneuver must certainly accelerate the altered permeability of the hemato–labyrinthine barrier by maintaining higher drug blood levels.

Hawkins (1973a) goes on to point out the similarity between the histopathology of inner ear deafness due to aging, noise, and ototoxic drugs. In Section XIV on acoustic overstimulation of the ear, it was already noted that Hawkins (1971) found occlusion of the inner ear microcirculation with swollen endothelial cells after loud noise stimulation. The same finding depicted in Fig. 12 was also reported for quinidine intoxication. This mechanism originally delineated in the guinea pig is a possible explanation for the temporary effects of quinine, salicylates, and temporary threshold shift with noise exposure. However, Hawkins (1975) has recently questioned the prevalence of this phenomenon in nonhuman primates.

An earlier review paper entitled "Effect of Some Ototoxic Drugs upon the Pattern and Innervation of Cochlear Sensory Cells in the Guinea Pig" was published by Kohonen (1965). In addition to this review and those of Hawkins, the reader may be interested in a representative sampling of papers in the area for methodology.

The work of Mendelsohn and Katzenberg (1972) on the effect of kanamycin on the cation content of the endolymph was already mentioned in Section VIII. The ethacrynic acid studies of Wilson and Juhn (1970) and Cohn *et al.* (1971) were also in that section. Using the electron microscope, Quick and Duvall (1970) made a study of the early changes in the cochlear duct from ethacrynic acid. Kohonen *et al.* (1970) ran an electrophysiological and histological experiment with ethacrynic acid.

Kanamycin investigations to determine dosage levels in the ear and other organs were carried out by Stupp *et al.* (1967). Kaneko *et al.* (1970) looked at Reissner's membrane after kanamycin administration, and Dayal *et al.* (1971) studied the combined effects of noise and kanamycin.

Comparative tests of gentamicin ototoxicity using guinea pigs and other animals have been completed by Hawkins *et al.* (1969). Holz *et al.* (1968) claim to have reduced the ototoxicity of streptomycin sulfate in the guinea pig with the administration of ozothin, a compound of hydrosoluble oxidation products of oleum terebinthinal (turpentine oil) (West Germany). Work on salicylate ototoxicity in the guinea pig has been published by Wilpizeski and Tanaka (1967, 1970) and McPherson and Miller (1974).

XVI. PERINATAL MATURATION OF AUDITORY FUNCTION

In the guinea pig as in other mammals that have been studied, the development of the AC round window cochlear potential precedes the maturation of the eighth nerve action potential and other higher auditory nervous system responses to sound (Romand, 1971; Romand *et al.*, 1971). With a study utilizing cochlear potential and eighth nerve action potential recording as well as light and electron microscopy, Pujol and Hilding (1973) made an investigation of the development of auditory anatomy and physiology in the guinea pig. In addition these people did similar comparative perinatal work on other common mammalian species.

As they reviewed the literature in the light of their current efforts, Pujol and Hilding (1973) noted that the AC round window cochlear potential first can be recorded from the guinea pig with intense sound stimulation at 15 days before birth. (Gestation of the guinea pig was estimated at 63 days.) The AC cochlear potential response becomes normal about 4 days before birth. The action potential of the eighth nerve first appears with a high threshold about 24 hours after the cochlear potential and begins to look normal a few days after birth. The total frequency range of the guinea pig cochlear potential and eighth nerve action potential is mature at birth (Pujol and Hilding, 1973; Romand, 1971).

XVII. CONCLUSION

From the sampling of studies presented in this chapter it should be evident that the guinea pig has been an extremely important animal model in physiological acoustics over the past 50 years. References sighted here will hopefully open the door for the reader to the rest of this voluminous literature.

ACKNOWLEDGMENTS

We thank Professor Merle Lawrence and Dr. Charles G. Wright for valuable discussions of various aspects of this chapter. We are most grateful to Professor Joseph Hawkins, Jr. for allowing us to use his unpublished scanning electron micrograph (Fig. 5), the updated version of a light histology inner ear cross section (Fig. 4), and his previously published plate (Fig. 12). Special thanks are due to Miss Gloria Gamble for typing the manuscript. Research and laboratory experience which contributed to background for the writing of this chapter were supported in part by Office of Naval Research #N00014-72-A-0429-0001 with partial support from the Naval Bureau of Medicine and Surgery. Navy support was to Dr. McCormick. Dr. Nuttall's contributions were supported in part by a grant from the John A. Hartford Foundation and by Public Health Service Grant NS-05785.

REFERENCES

Alexander, I. E., and O.Brien, T. F., Jr., (1954). High-tone stimulation and hearing loss. *Proc. Nat. Acad. Sci. U.S.* **40,** 848–852.

Anderson, H., and Wedenberg, E. A. (1965). A new method for hearing tests in the guinea pig. *Acta Oto-Laryngol.* **60,** 375–393.

Axelsson, A. (1968). The vascular anatomy of the cochlea in the guinea pig and in man. *Acta Oto-Laryngol., Suppl.* **243,** 1–134.

Axelsson, A. (1971). The cochlear blood vessels in guinea pigs of different ages. *Acta Oto-Laryngol.* **72,** 172–181.

Axelsson, A. (1972). The demonstration of the cochlear vessels in the guinea pig by contrast injection. *J. Laryngol. Otol.* **86,** 121–128.

Axelsson, A. (1974). The vascular anatomy of the rhesus monkey cochlea. *Acta Oto-Laryngol.* **77,** 381–392.

Axelsson, A. and Ernstson, S. (1972). Cochlear vascular anatomy in a strain of the waltzing guinea pig. *Acta Oto-Laryngol.* **74,** 172–182.

Axelsson, A., and Hallén, O. (1973). The healing of the external cochlear wall in the guinea pig after mechanical injury. *Acta Oto-Laryngol.* **76,** 136–148.

Axelsson, A. and Lind, A. (1973). The capillary areas in the rabbit cochlea. *Acta Oto-Laryngol.* **76,** 254–267.

Bredberg, G., Lindeman, H. H., Ades, H. W., West, R., and Engström, H. (1970). Scanning electron microscopy of the organ of Corti. *Science* **170,** 861–863.

Bredberg, G., Ades, H. W., and Engström, H. (1972). Scanning electron microscopy of the normal and pathologically altered organ of Corti. *Acta Oto-Laryngol., Suppl.* **301,** 3–48.

Butler, R. A. (1965). Some experimental observations on the DC resting potentials in the guinea pig cochlea. *J. Acoust. Soc. Amer.* **37,** 429–433.

Butler, R. A., Honrubia, V., Johnstone, B. M., and Fernandez, C. (1962a). LVI. Cochlear function under metabolic impairment. *Ann. Otol., Rhinol., & Laryngol.* **71,** 648–656.

Butler, R. A., Honrubia, V., Johnstone, B. M., and Fernandez, C. (1962b). Cochlear function under metabolic impairment. *Trans. Amer. Otol. Soc.* **50,** 50–60.

Chen, G., Ensor, C. R., and Bohner, B. (1969). The pharmacology of 2-(ethylamino)-2-(2-thineyl)-cyclohexanone. HCI (CI-634). *J. Pharmacol. Exp. Ther.* **168,** 171–179.

Cohn, E. S., Gordes, E. H., and Brusilow, S. W. (1971). Ethacrynic acid effect on the composition of cochlear fluids. *Science* **171,** 910–911.

Crifò, S. (1973). Shiver-audiometry in the conditioned guinea pig, (simplified Anderson-Wedenberg test.) *Acta Oto-Laryngol.* **75,** 38–44.

Cutt, R. A., and Gulick, W. L. (1960). The effects of abnormal body temperature upon the ear: Heating. *Ann. Otol., Rhinol., & Laryngol.* **69,** 997–1006.

Daigneault, E. A., and Stopp, P. E. (1971). A study of the influence of the olivocochlear bundle on the N_1 responses to repeated pulses. Letters to Ed. *J. Acoust. Soc. Amer.* **49,** 1896–1897.

Dallos, P. (1973). "The Auditory Periphery: Biophysics and Physiology." Academic Press, New York.

Dallos, P., Schoeny, Z. G., and Cheatham, M. A. (1971). On the limitations of cochlear-microphonic measurements. *J. Acoust. Soc. Amer.* **49,** No. 4, Part 2, 1144–1154.

Dallos, P., Schoeny, Z. G., and Cheatham, M. A. (1972). Cochlear summating potentials: Descriptive aspects. *Acta Oto-Laryngol., Suppl.* **302,** 1–46.

Davis, H. (1958). A Mechano-electrical theory of cochlear action. *Ann. Otol., Rhinol., & Laryngol.* **67,** 789–801.

Davis, H., Fernandez, C., and McAuliffe, D. R. (1950). The excitatory process in the cochlea. *Proc. Nat. Acad. Sci. U.S.* **36,** 580–587.

Davis, H., Deatherage, B. H., Rosenblut, B., Fernandez, C., Kimura, R., and Smith, C. A. (1958). Modification of cochlear potentials produced by streptomycin poisoning and by extensive venous obstruction. *Laryngoscope* **68,** 596–627.

Dayal, V. S., Kokshanian, A., and Mitchell, D. P. (1971). Combined effects of noise and kanamycin. *Ann. Otol., Rhinol., & Laryngol.* **80,** 897.

de Lorenzo, A. J. D. (1973). "Vascular Disorders and Hearing Defects" (based on the Proceedings of a Workshop, Baltimore, Maryland, April 13–14, 1972), pp. 1–357. University Park Press, Maryland.

Durant, J. D., and Dallos, P. (1972). Influence of direct current polarization of the cochlear partition on the summating potentials. *J. Acoust. Soc. Amer.* **52,** 542–551.

Duvall, A. J., and Sutherland, C. R. (1972). Cochlear transport of horseradish peroxidase. *Ann. Otol., Rhinol., & Laryngol.* **81,** 705–714.

Eggemann, G., Reeschig, M., and Matschiner, H. (1970). Eine Untersucheeng über Schluermetalle im Innenohr des Meerschweinchen. *Arch. Klin, Exp. Ohren Nasen Kehlkopfheilkd.* **197,** 134–141.

Engström, H., and Ades, H. W. (1961). Effect of high-intensity noise on inner ear sensory epithelia. *Acta Oto-Laryngol., Suppl.* **158,** 219–228.

Ernstson, S. (1972). Cochlear physiology and hair cell population in a strain of the waltzing guinea pig. *Acta Oto-Laryngol., Suppl.* **297,** 5–24.

Evans, E. F. (1970a). Narrow 'tuning' of cochlear nerve fiber responses in the guinea pig. *J. Physiol. (London)* **206,** 14–15P.

Evans, E. F. (1970b). Narrow 'tuning' of the responses of cochlear nerve fibers emanating from the exposed basilar membrane. *J. Physiol. (London)* **208,** 75P–76P.

Evans, E. F. (1972). The frequency response and other properties of single fibers in the guinea pig cochlear nerve. *J. Physiol. (London)* **226,** 263–287.

Falk, S. A., Cook, R. O., Haseman, J. K., and Sanders, G. M. (1974). Noise-induced inner ear damage in newborn and adult guinea pigs. *Laryngoscope* **84,** 444–453.

Fernandez, C. (1955). The effect of oxygen lack on cochlear potential. *Ann. Otol., Rhinol., & Laryngol.* **64,** 1193–1203.

Galambos, R. (1944). Inhibition of activity in single auditory nerve fibers by acoustic stimulation. *J. Neurophysiol.* **7,** 287–303.

Galambos, R., and Davis, H. (1943). The responses of single auditory nerve fibers to acoustic stimulation. *J. Neurophysiol.* **6,** 39–58.

Gerstner, H. (1942). Die Schallstärkeschwelle des Preyerschen Ohrmuschelreflexes als Quantitatives Hörprüfverfahren an Meerschweinchen. *Pfluegers Arch. Gesamte Physiol. Menschen Tiere* **246**, 265.

Gourevitch, G. (1965). Auditory masking in the rat. *J. Acoust. Soc. Amer.* **37**, 439–443.

Gourevitch, G., and Hack, M. H. (1966). Audibility in the rat. *J. Comp. Physiol. Psychol.* **62**, 289–291.

Greenwood, D. D. (1961). Critical bandwidth and the frequency coordinates of the basilar membrane. *J. Acoust. Soc. Amer.* **33**, 1344–1356.

Greenwood, D. D. (1962). Approximate calculation of the dimensions of traveling-wave envelopes in four species. *J. Acoust. Soc. Amer.* **34**, 1364–1369.

Gulick, W. L., and Cutt, R. A. (1960). The effects of abnormal body temperature upon the ear: Cooling. *Ann. Otol., Rhinol., & Laryngol.* **69**, 35–50.

Gulick, W. L., and Cutt, R. A. (1962). Intracochlear temperature and the cochlear response. *Ann. Otol., Rhinol., & Laryngol.* **71**, 331.

Gundy, R. F. (1959). Some techniques in operant conditioning of the guinea pig. *J. Exp. Anal. Behav.* **2**, 86.

Hawkins, J. E., Jr., (1965). Cytoarchitectural basis of the cochlear transducer. *Cold Spring Harbor Symp. Quant. Biol.* **30**, 147–157.

Hawkins, J. E., Jr., (1966). Hearing: Anatomy and acoustics. *In* "The Physiological Basis of Medical Practice" (N. B. Taylor, ed.), pp. 375–394. Williams & Wilkins, Baltimore, Maryland.

Hawkins, J. E., Jr.(1970. Biochemical aspects of ototoxicity. *In* "Biochemical Mechanisms in Hearing and Deafness" (M. M. Paparella, ed.), pp. 323–339. Thomas, Springfield, Illinois.

Hawkins, J. E., Jr. (1971). The role of vasoconstriction in noise-induced hearing loss. *Ann. Otol., Rhinol., & Laryngol.* **80**, 903.

Hawkins, J. E., Jr. (1973a). Comparative otopathology: Aging, noise, and ototoxic drugs. *Advan. Oto-Rhino-Laryngol.* **20**, 125–141.

Hawkins, J. E., Jr. (1973b). Ototoxic mechanisms, a working hypothesis. *Audiology* **12**, 383–393.

Hawkins, J. E., Jr. (1975). Circulation of the inner ear. *In* "The Oto-Larynogologic Clinics of North America—Symposium on Fluctuant Hearing Loss" (J. J. Shea, ed.). Saunders, Philadelphia, Pennsylvania.

Hawkins, J. E., Jr. and Johnsson, L. (1968). Light microscopic observations of the inner ear in man and monkey. *Ann. Otol., Rhinol., & Laryngol.* **77**, 608.

Hawkins, J. E., Jr., Boxer, G. E., and Jelinek, V. C. (1950). Concentration of streptomycin in brain and other tissues of cats after acute and chronic intoxication. *Proc. Soc. Exp. Biol. Med.* **75**, 759–761.

Hawkins, J. E., Jr., Johnsson, L. G., and Aran, J. M. (1969). Comparative tests of gentamicin ototoxicity. *J. Infec. Dis.* **119**, No. 4, 417–426.

Heffner, R., Heffner, H., and Masterton, B. (1971). Behavioral measurements of absolute and frequency difference thresholds in guinea pig. *J. Acoust. Soc. Amer.* **49**, 1888–1895.

Helmholtz, H. L. F. (1868). Die Mechanik der Gehorknochelchen und des Trommelfells. *Pfluegers Arch. Gesamte Physiol. Menschen Tiere* **1**, 1–60.

Herington, G. B., and Gundlach, R. H. (1933). How well can guinea pigs hear tones?. *J. Comp. Psychol.* **16**, 287.

Holz, E., Stange, G., Soda, T., and Beck, C. (1968). Decrease of ototoxicity of streptomycin sulfate. *Arch. Otolaryngol.* **87**, 359–363.

Honrubia, V., Johnstone, B. M., and Butler, R. A. (1965). Maintenance of cochlear potentials during asphyxia. *Acta Oto-Laryngol.* **60**, 105–112.

Horton, G. P. (1933). A quantitative study of hearing in the guinea pig. *J. Comp. Psychol.* **15**, 59.

Horton, G. P. (1934). The effect of intense and prolonged acoustical stimulation on the auditory sensitivity of guinea pigs. *J. Comp. Psychol.* **18**, 405–417.

Johnsson, L.-G., and Hawkins, J. E., Jr. (1967). A direct approach to cochlear anatomy and pathology in man. *Arch. Otolaryngol.* **85**, 599–613.

Johnstone, B. M., and Boyle, A. J. F. (1967). Basilar membrane vibration examined with the Mössbauer technique. *Science* **158**, 389–390.

Johnstone, B. M., and Sellick, P. M. (1972). The peripheral auditory apparatus. *Quart. Rev. Biophys.* **5**, 1–58.

Johnstone, B. M., and Taylor, K. J. (1970). Mechanical aspects of cochlear function. *In* "Frequency Analysis and Periodicity Detection in Hearing" (R. Plomp and G. F. Smooreburg, eds.), pp. 81–93. Sijthoff, Leiden, Netherlands.

Johnstone, B. M., and Taylor, K. J. (1971). Physiology of the middle ear transmission system. *J. Otolaryngol. Soc. Aust.* **3**, 225–228.

Kaneko, Y., Nakagawa, T., and Tanaka, K. (1970). Reissner's membrane after kanamycin administration. *Arch. Otolaryngol.* **92**, 457–462.

Kellerhals, B. (1972). Acoustic trauma and cochlear microcirculation. *Advan. Oto-Rhino-Laryngol.* **18**, 91–168.

Kern, E. B., Cody, T. R., and Bickford, R. G. (1969a). Neurogenic components of the averaged response evoked by clicks in guinea pigs. *Mayo Clin. Proc.* **44**, 886–899.

Kern, E. B., Cody, T. R., and Bickford, R. G. (1969b). Vertex response thresholds to pure tones in guinea pigs. *Arch. Otolaryngol.* **90**, 315–325.

Kimura, R., and Perlman, H. B. (1956). XXVII. Extensive venous obstruction of the labyrinth. *Ann. Otol.* **65**, 332–350.

Kimura, R., and Perlman, H. B. (1958). Arterial obstruction of the labyrinth. Part I. Cochlear changes. *Ann. Otol., Rhinol., & Laryngol.* **67**, 5–40.

Kohllöffel, L. U. E. (1971). Studies of the distribution of cochlear potentials along the basilar membrane. *Acta Oto-Laryngol., Suppl.* **288**, 7–66.

Kohllöffel, L. U. E. (1972a). A study of basilar membrane vibrations I. Fuzziness-detection: A new method for the analysis of microvibrations with laser light. *Acustica* **27**, 49–65.

Kohllöffel, L. U. E. (1972b). A study of basilar membrane vibrations. II. The vibratory amplitude and phase pattern along the basilar membrane (post-mortem). *Acustica* **27**, 66–81.

Kohonen, A. (1965). Effect of some ototoxic drugs upon the pattern and innervation of cochlear sensory cells in the guinea pig. *Acta Oto-Laryngol., Suppl.* **208**, 1.

Kohonen, A., Jauhiainen, T., and Tarkkanen, J. (1970). Experimental deafness causes by etachrynic acid. *Acta Oto-Laryngol.* **70**, 187–189.

Koide, Y., Yoshinda, M., and Konno, M. (1959). The effect of cutting the labyrinthine artery on the oxygen tension in the labyrinth. *Ann. Otol.* **68**, 164–169.

Konishi, T. (1972). Action of tubocurarine and atropine on the crossed olivocochlear bundles. *Acta Oto-Laryngol.* **74**, 252–264.

Konishi, T., and Kelsey, E. (1968). Effect of cyanide on cochlear potentials. *Acta Oto-Laryngol.* **65**, 381–390.

Konishi, T., and Slepian, J. (1971). Effects of electric stimulation of the crossed olivocochlear bundle on cochlear potentials recorded with intracochlear electrodes in guinea pigs. *J. Acoust. Soc. Amer.* **49**, 1762.

Konishi, T., Butler, R. A., and Fernandez, C. (1961). Effect of anoxia on cochlea potentials. *J. Acoust. Soc. Amer.* **33,** 349–356.

Kuijpers, W., and Bonting, S. O. (1970a). The cochlear potential. I. The effect of ouabain on cochlear potentials of the guinea pig. *Pfluegers Arch. Gesamte Physiol. Menschen Tiere* **320,** 348–358.

Kuijpers, W., and Bonting, S. L. (1970b). The cochlear potential. II. The nature of the cochlear resting potential. *Pfluegers Arch. Gesamte Physiol. Menschen Tiere* **320,** 359–372.

Lawrence, M. (1958). Functional changes in inner ear deafness. *Ann. Otol., Rhinol., & Laryngol.* **67,** No. 3, 802.

Lawrence, M. (1964). Current concepts of the mechanism of occupational hearing loss. *Amer. Ind. Hyg. Ass., J.* **25,** 269–273.

Lawrence, M. (1965). Fluid balance in the inner ear. *Ann. Otol., Rhinol., & Laryngol.* **74,** 486.

Lawrence, M. (1966). Effects of interference with terminal blood supply on organ of Corti. *Laryngoscope.* **76,** 1318–1337.

Lawrence, M. (1968). Theories of the cause of hydrops. *Otolaryngol. Clin. N. Amer.,* 353–362.

Lawrence, M. (1970). Circulation in the capillaries of the basilar membrane. *Laryngoscope* **80,** 1364–1375.

Lawrence, M. (1971). Blood flow through the basilar membrane capillaries. *Acta Oto-Laryngol.* **71,** 106–114.

Lawrence, M. (1973a). *In vivo* studies of the microcirculation. *Advan. Oto-Rhino-Laryngol.* **20,** 244–255.

Lawrence, M. (1973b). Acute overpressure and chronic noise injury. *Prac. Med.* **9,** 1–21.

Lawrence, M., and Clapper, M. P. (1972). Analysis of flow pattern in Vas Spirale. *Acta Oto-Laryngol.* **73,** 94–103.

Lawrence, M., and Nuttall, A. L. (1970). Electrophysiology of the organ of Corti. *In* "Biochemical Mechanisms in Hearing and Deafness" (M.M. Paparella, ed.), pp. 83–96. Thomas, Springfield, Illinois.

Lawrence, M., and Nuttall, A. L. (1972). Oxygen availability in tunnel of Corti measured by microelectrode. *J. Acoust. Soc. Amer.* **52,** 566–573.

Lawrence, M., Gonzalez, G., and Hawkins, J. E., Jr. Some physiologic factors in noise-induced hearing loss. *Amer. Ind. Hyg. Ass. J.* **28,** 425–430

Lawrence, M., and Yantis, P. A. (1957). Individual differences in functional recovery and structural repair following overstimulation of the guinea pig ear. *Ann. Otol., Rhinol., & Laryngol.* **66,** 596–621.

Lawrence, M., Nuttall, A. L., and Clapper, M. P. (1974). Electrical potentials and fluid boundaries within the organ of Corti. *J. Acoust. Soc. Amer.* **55,** 122–138.

Lim, D. J. (1972). Fine morphology of the tectorial membrane: Its relationship to the organ of Corti. *Arch. Otolaryngol.* **96,** 199–215.

Lim, D. J., and Lane, W. C. (1969a). Cochlear sensory epithelium: A scanning electron microscopic observation. *Ann. Otol., Rhinol., & Laryngol.* **78,** 827–842.

Lim, D. J., and Lane, W. C. (1969b). Three dimensional observation of the inner ear with the scanning electron microscope. *Trans. Amer. Acad. Ophthalmol. Otolaryngol.* **73,** 842–871.

Lurie, M. H., Davis, H., and Hawkins, J. E., Jr. (1944). Acoustic trauma of the organ of Corti in the guinea pig. *Laryngoscope* **54,** 375–386.

McCormick, J. G., Philbrick, T., Holland, W., and Harrill, J. A. (1973). Diving induced sensori-neural deafness: Prophylactic use of heparin and preliminary histopathology results. *Laryngoscope* **83,** 1483–1501.

McCurdy, J. A., Jr., McCormick, J.G., and Harrill, J. A. (1974). Ototoxicity of ethacrynic acid in the anuric guinea pig. *Arch. Otolaryngol.* **100,** 143–147.

McPherson, D. L., and Miller, J. M. (1974). Choline salicylate: Effects of cochlear function. *Arch. Otolaryngol.* **99,** 304–308.

Masterton, B., Heffner, H., and Rauizza, R. (1969). The evolution of human hearing. *J. Acoust. Soc. Amer.* **45,** 966–985.

Mayahara, T., and Perlman, H. B. (1972). Cochlear microcirculation and oxygen transport. *Laryngoscope* **82,** 578–597.

Mendelsohn, M., and Katzenberg, I. (1972). The effect of kanamycin on the cation content of the endolymph. *Laryngoscope* **82,** 397–403.

Meyer zum Gottesberg, Rauch, A. S., and Koburg, E. (1965). Unterschiede in Metabolismos der einzelnen Schneckenwindungen. *Acta Oto-Laryngol.* **59,** 1–6.

Miller, J. D. (1970). Audibility curve of the chinchilla. *J. Acoust. Soc. Amer.* **48,** 513–523.

Miller, J. D., and Murray, F. (1962). Behavioral audiometry with guinea pigs. *Central Institute for the Deaf Periodic Progress Report.* **5,** 16. St. Louis, Missouri.

Misrahy, G. A. (1958). Effects of intra cochlear injection of glucose-glucoseoxydase on the DC potential, microphonics and action potential of the cochlea of guinea pigs. *J. Acoust. Soc. Amer.* **30,** 688.

Misrahy, G. A., Shinabarger, E. W. and Hildreth, K. M. (1957). Studies on factors affecting the summating potential. *Wright Air Development Center Technical Report* **57,** 704–730.

Misrahy, G. A., Hildreth, K. M., and Shinabarger, E. W. (1958a). Endolymphatic oxygen tension in the cochlea of the guinea pig. *J. Acoust. Soc. Amer.* **30,** 247–250.

Misrahy, G. A., Shinabarger, E. W., and Arnold, J. E. (1958b). Changes in cochlear endolymphatic oxygen availability, action potential, and microphonics during and following asphyxia, hypoxia, and exposure to loud sounds. *J. Acoust. Soc. Amer.* **30,** 701–704.

Morimitsu, T., Matsuo, K., and Suga, F. (1965). II. Behavior of the cochlear blood flow. *Ann. Otol.* **74,** 22–32.

Morizono, T., and Johnstone, B. M. (1968). Vascular perfusion technique applied to the guinea pig cochlea. *J. Oto-Laryngological Soc. Aust.* **2,** No. 3, 34–44.

Morizono, T., Johnstone, B. M., and Kaldor, I. (1968). Cochlear blood volume in the guinea pig measured with Cr^{51} labelled red blood cells. *Otol. Fukuoka* **14,** 82–89.

Mundie, A. R. (1962). "The Impedance of the Ear–A variable Quantity," Rep. No. 576. U. S. Army Med. Res. Lab., Ft. Knox, Kentucky.

Nabeya, D. (1923). A study in the comparative anatomy of the blood-vascular system of the internal ear in Mammalia and in *Homo.* (In Japanese.) *Acta Sch. Med. Univ. Kioto* **6,** 1–153.

Naftalin, L., and Harrison, M. S. (1958). Circulation of labyrinthine fluids. *J. Laryngol.* **72,** 118–136.

Nakashima, T., Meiring, N. L., and Snow, J. B., Jr. (1970a). Cations in the endolymph of the guinea pig with noise-induced deafness. *Surg. Forum* **21,** 489–491.

Nakashima, T., Sullivan, M. J., Snow, J. B., Jr., and Suga, F. (1970b). Sodium potassium changes in inner ear fluids. *Arch. Otolaryngol.* **92,** 1–6.

Neff, W. D., and Hind, J. E. (1955). Auditory thresholds of the cat. *J. Acoust. Soc. Amer.* **27,** 480–483.

Nomura, Y. (1961). LXXV. Observations on the microcirculation of the cochlea, an experimental study. *Ann. Otol., Rhinol., & Laryngol.* **70,** 1037–1054.

Nuttall, A. L. (1974a). Comparison of cochlear microphonic potentials from albino and pigmented guinea pigs. *Acta Oto-Laryngol.* **(in press).**

Nuttall, A. L. (1974b). Measurements of the guinea pig middle-ear transfer characteristic. *J. Acoust. Soc. Amer.* **56,** 1231–1238.

Nuttall, A. L. (1974c). Tympanic muscle effects on middle-ear transfer characteristic. *J. Acoust. Soc. Amer.* **56,** 1239–1247.

Okumura, H. (1970). Perilymph as a medium of oxygen supply for the organ of Corti. *Arch. Klin. Exp. Ohren-Nasen-Kehlkopfheilkd.* **195,** 257–265.

Paparella, M. M., ed. (1970). "Biochemical Mechanisms in Hearing and Deafness," Res. Otol. Int. Symp. Thomas, Springfield, Illinois.

Perlman, H. B. (1952). III. Experimental occlusion of the inferior cochlear vein. *Ann. Otol.* **61,** 33–44.

Perlman, H. B., and Kimura, R. S. (1955). CVI. Observations of the living blood vessels of the cochlea (part of a symposium on blood circulation). *Ann. Otol.* **64,** 1176–1192.

Perlman, H. B., and Kimura, R. S. (1957). XLIII. Experimental obstruction of venous drainage and arterial supply of the inner ear. *Ann. Otol.* **66,** 537–546.

Perlman, H. B., and Kimura, R. S. (1962). Cochlear blood flow in acoustic trauma. *Acta Oto-Laryngol.* **54,** 99–110.

Perlman, H. B., Kimura, R. S., and Butler, R. A. (1959a). LVIII. Cochlear blood flow during hypothermia. *Ann. Otol., Rhinol., & Laryngol.* **68,** 803–815.

Perlman, H. B., Kimura, R. S., and Fernandez, C. (1959b). Experiments on temporary obstruction of the internal auditory artery. *Laryngoscope* **69,** 591–613.

Perlman, H. B., Tsunoo, M., and Spence, A. (1963). Cochlear blood flow and function: Effect of pressor agents. *Acta Oto-Laryngol.* **56,** 587.

Pfalz, R. K. S. (1962a). Centrifugal inhibition of afferent secondary neurons in the cochlear nucleus by sound. *J. Acoust. Soc. Amer.* **34,** 1472–1477.

Pfalz, R. K. S. (1962b). Einfluss schallgereizter efferenter Horbahnanteile Auf den de afferentierten Nucleus Cochlearis (Meerschweinchen). *Pfluegers Arch. Gesamte Physiol. Menschen Tiere* **274,** 533–552.

Pfalz, R. K. S. (1966). Gekreuzte, zentrifugale Hommungen und Erregungen im Nucleus cochlearis durch lange Klickfolgen (Meerschweinchen). *Arch. Klin. Exp. Ohren-Nasen- Kehlkopfheilkd.* **186,** 9–19.

Pfalz, R. K. S. (1969a). The ventral cochlear nucleus: the significance of the crossed inhibitory pathways towards the nucleus for directional hearing. *Advan. Oto-Rhino-Laryngol.* **16,** 1–94.

Pfalz, R. K. S. (1969b). Absence of a function for the cross olivocochlear bundle under physiological conditions. *Arch. Klin. Exp. Ohren-Nasen-Kehlkopfheilkd.* **193,** 89–100.

Pfalz, R. K. S., and Pirsig, W. (1966). Compound afferent action potentials of the cochlear nucleus evoked electrically–inhibition due to acoustic stimulation of the contralateral cochlea (guinea pig). *Ann. Otol.* **75,** 1077–1087.

Pirsig, W. (1968).Region, Zelltypen und Synapsen im ventralen Nucleus cochlearis des Meerschweinchem. *Arch. Klin. Exp. Ohren-Nasen-Kehlkopfheilkd.* **192,** 333–350.

Pirsig, W., and Pfalz, R. (1966). Die Wirkung gekreuzter auditorischer Efferenzen aut elektrisch erregt worden waren (Meerschweinchen). *Arch. Klin. Exp. Ohren-Nasen- Kehlkopfheilkd.* **187,** 595–599.

Pirsig, W., and Pfalz, R. (1967). Neurons in Nucleus cochlearis ventralis, die von homolateral durch electrishcen Reiz an der Schnecken basis windung erregt warden Zontrifugale Hemmung duroh contralaterale Beschallung (Meerschweinchen). *Arch. Klin. Exp. Ohren-Nasen-Kehlkopfheilkd.* **189,** 135–157.

Pirsig, W., Pfalz, R., and Sadanage, M. (1968). Postsynaptic auditory crossed efferent inhabition in the ventral cochlear nucleus and its blocking by strychnine nitrate (guinea pig). *Kumamoto Med. J.* **21,** 75–82.

Poche, L. B., Jr., Stockwell, C. W., and Ades, H. W. (1969). Cochlear hair-cell damage in guinea pigs after exposure to impulse noise. *J. Acoust. Soc. Amer.* **46,** No. 4, Part 2, 947–951.

Preyer, W. (1890). "Die Seele des Kindes: Beobachtungen über die geistige Entwickelung des Menschen in den ersten Lebensjahren." T. Grieben, Leipzig.

Pujol, R., and Hilding, D. (1973). Anatomy and physiology of the onset of auditory function. *Acta Oto-Laryngol.* **76,** 1–10.

Quick, C. A., and Duvall, A. J. (1970). Early changes in the cochlear duct from ethacrynic acid: An electronmicroscopic evaluation. *Laryngoscope* **80,** No. 6, 954–965.

Rauch, S. (1964). "Biochemie des Hörogans Einführung in Methoden und Ergebnisse." Thieme, Stuttgart.

Rice, E. A., and Shinabarger, E. W. (1960). Studies on the Endolymphatic DC Potential of the Guinea Pig's Cochlea. *Wright Air Development Center Technical Report* **60,** 162–170.

Romand, R. (1971). Maturation des potentiels cochléaires dans la période périnatale chez le chat et chez le cobaye. *J. Physiol. (Paris)* **63,** 763–782.

Romand, R., Granier, M. R., and Pujol, R. (1971). Potentiels cochléaires chez le cobaye dans la période prénatale. *J. Physiol. (Paris)* **63,** 280–281.

Rüedi, L. (1954). Different types and degrees of acoustic trauma by experimental exposure of the human and animal ear to pure tones and noise. *Ann. Otol.* **63,** 702.

Schätzle, W. (1971). "Histochemie des Innenohres." Urban & Schwarzenberg, Munich.

Scibetta, J. J., and Rosen, M. G. (1969). Response evoked by sound in the fetal guinea pig. *Obstet. Gynecol.* **33,** 830–836.

Seymour, J. C., and Tappin, J. W. (1953). Some aspects of the sympathetic nervous system in relation to the inner ear. *Acta Oto-Laryngol.* **43,** 618–635.

Sherrick, C. E., Jr., and Bilger, R. C. (1959). Auditory sensitivity of the guinea pig to low frequency tones. *Percept. Mot. Skills* **9,** 339.

Sivian, L. J., and White, S. D. (1933). On minimum audible sound fields. *J. Acoust. Soc. Amer.* **4,** 288.

Smith, C. A. (1951). Capillary areas of the cochlea in the guinea pig. *Laryngoscope* **61,** 1073–1095.

Smith, C. A., and Haglan, B. J. (1973). Golgi stains on the guinea pig organ of Corti. *Acta Oto-Laryngol.* **75,** 203–210.

Smith, K. R. (1947). The problem of stimulation deafness. II. Histological changes in the cochlea as a function of tonal frequency. *J. Exp. Psychol.* **37,** 304–317.

Smith, K. R., and Wever, E. G. (1949). The problem of stimulation deafness. Ill. The functional histological effects of a high-frequency stimulus. *J. Exp. Psychol.* **39,** 238–241.

Snow, J. B., Jr., and Suga, F. (1973). Labyrinthine vasodilators. *Arch. Otolaryngol.* **97,** 365–370.

Snow, J. B., Jr., Suga, F., Sullivan, M. J., Nakashima, T., Leonard, J. E., and Meiring, N. L. (1971). Pathophysiologic responses of the inner ear to intense sound. *Ann. Otol., Rhinol., & Laryngol.* **80,** 871.

Spoendlin, H. (1966). The ototoxicity of streptomycin. *Pract. Oto-Rhino-Laryngol.* **28,** 305–322.

Spoendlin, H. (1973). The innervation of the cochlear receptor. *In* "Basic Mechanisms in Hearing" (A. R. Moller, ed.), pp. 185–234. Academic Press, New York.

Spoendlin, H., and Brun, J. P. (1973). Relation of structural damage to exposure time and intensity in acoustic trauma. *Acta Oto-Laryngol.* **75,** 220–226.

Stebbins, W. C. (1966). Auditory reaction time and the derivation of equal loudness contours for the monkey. *J. Exp. Anal. Behav.* **7,** 135.

Stupp, H., Rauch, S., Sous, H., Brun, J. P., and Lagler, F. (1967). Kanamycin dosage and levels in ear and other organs. *Arch. Otolaryngol.* **86,** 63–69.

Suga, F., and Snow, J. B., Jr. (1969a). Adrenergic control of cochlear blood flow. *Ann. Otol., Rhinol., & Laryngol.* **78,** 358–374.

Suga, F., and Snow, J. B., Jr. (1969b). Colinergic control of cochlear blood flow. *Ann. Otol., Rhinol., & Laryngol.* **78,** 1081–1090.

Suga, F., and Snow, J. B., Jr. (1969c). Cochlear blood flow in response vasodilating drugs and some related agents. *Laryngoscope* **9,** 1956–1979.

Suga, F., Nakashima, T., and Snow, J. B., Jr. (1970a). Sodium and potassium ions in endolymph: *In vivo* measurements with glass microelectrodes. *Arch. Otolaryngol.* 37–43.

Suga, F., Preston, J., and Snow, J. B., Jr., (1970b). Experimental microembolization of cochlear vessels. *Arch. Otolaryngol.* **92,** 213–220.

Tanaka, Y., and Katsuki, Y. (1966). Pharmacological investigations of cochlear responses and of olivocochlear inhibition. *J. Neurophysiol.* **29,** 94.

Tasaki, I. (1954). Nerve impulses in individual auditory nerve fibers of guinea pig. *J. Neurophysiol.* **17,** 97–122.

Tasaki, I., and Davis, H. (1955). Electric responses of individual nerve elements in cochlear, nucleus to sound stimulation (guinea pig). *J. Neurophysiol.* **18,** 151–158.

Tasaki, I., and Fernandez, C. (1952). Modification of cochlear microphonics and action potentials by KCl solution and by direct currents. *J. Neurophysiol.* **15,** 497–512.

Tasaki, I., Davis, H., and Legouix, J. P. (1952). Space-time patterns of the cochlear microphonics (guinea pig) as recorded by differential electrodes. *J. Acoust. Soc. Amer.* **24,** 502–519.

Tasaki, I., Davis, H., and Eldredge, D. H. (1954). Exploration of cochlear potentials in guinea pig with a microelectrode. *J. Acoust. Soc. Amer.* **26,** 765–773.

Teas, D. C., Edlredge, D. H., and Davis, H. (1962). Cochlear responses to acoutic transients: An interpretation of whole-nerve action potentials. *J. Acoust. Soc. Amer.* **34,** 1438–1359.

Teas, D. C., Konishi, T., and Nelson, D. W. (1972). Electro physiological studies on the spatial distribution of the crossed olivocochlear bundle along the guinea pig cochlea. *J. Acoust. Soc. Amer.* **51,** 1256–1264.

Terayama, Y., Holz, E., and Beck, C. (1966). V. Adrenergic innervation of the cochlea. *Ann. Otol., Rhinol., & Laryngol.* **75,** 69–86.

Terayama, Y., Yamamoto, K., and Sakamoto, T. (1968), XCIII. Electron microscopic observations on the postganglionic sympathetic fibers in the guinea pig cochlea. *Ann. Otol., Rhinol., & Laryngol.* **77,** 1152–1170.

Tsunoo, M., and Perlman, H. B. (1969). Respiration of the cochlea and function. *Acta Oto-Laryngol.* **67,** 17–23.

Upton, M. (1929). Auditory sensitivity of guinea pigs. *Amer. J. Psychol.* **41,** 412.

Vinnikov, Ya. A., and Titova, L. K. (1964). "The Organ of Corti–Its Histapathology and Histochemistry." Consultants Bureau, New York.

von Békésy, G. (1947). Variation of phase along the basilar membrane with sinusoidal vibrations. *J. Acoust. Soc. Amer.* **19,** 452–460. 452–460.

von Békésy, G. (1951). Microphonics produced by touching the Cochlear partition with a vibrating electrode. *J. Acoust. Soc. Amer.* **23,** 29–35.

von Békésy, G. (1952). DC resting potentials inside the cochlear partition. *J. Acoust. Soc. Amer.* **24,** 72–76.

von Békésy, G. (1953). Shearing microphonics produced by vibrations near the inner and outer hair cells. *J. Acoust. Soc. Amer.* **25,** 786–790.

von Ilberg, C. (1968a). Elektronenmikroskopische Untersuchung uber Meerschweinschnecke 1. Mitteilung. *Arch. Klin. Exp. Ohren-, Nasen-, Kehlkopfheilkd.* **190,** 415–425.

von Ilberg, C. (1968b). Elektronenmikroskopische Untersuchung uber Meerschweinschnecke 2. Mitteilung. *Arch. Klin. Exp. Ohren,- Nasen,- Kehlkopfheilkd.* **190,** 426–438.

von Ilberg, C. (1968c). Elektronenmikroskopische Untersuchung uber Meerschweinschnecke 3. Mitteilung. *Arch. Klin. Exp. Ohren-, Nasen-, Kehlkopfheilkd.* **192,** 163–175.

von Ilberg, C. (1968d). Elektronenmikroskopische Untersuchung uber Meerschweinschnecke 4. Mitteilung. *Arch. Klin. Exp. Ohren-, Nasen-, Kehlkopfheilkd.* **192,** 384–400.

von Ilberg, C., and Vosteen, K. H. (1969). Permeability of the inner ear membranes. *Acta Oto-Laryngol.* **67,** 165–170

von Ilberg, C., Spoendlin, H., and Vosteen, K. H. (1968). Die Ultrastruktur und Funktion des Sulcus spiralis externus und der Prominentia spiralis der Meorschweinchenschenecke. Darstellung mittles Thorotrast. *Arch. Klin Exp. Ohren-, Nasen-, Kehlkopfheilkd.* **192,** 124–136.

Vosteen, K. H. (1971). Passive and active transport in the inner ear. *Transl. Beltone Inst. Hear. Res.* **No. 24, 1**–30.

Wever, E. G. (1931). Impulses from the acoustic nerve of the guinea pig, rabbit and rat. *Amer. J. Psychol.* **43,** 457–462.

Wever, E. G. (1949). "Theory of Hearing." Wiley, New York.

Wever, E. G. (1959). The cochlear potentials and their relation to hearing. *Ann. Otol., Rhinol., & Laryngol.* **68,** 975.

Wever, E. G. (1966). Electrical potentials of the cochlea. *Physiol. Rev.* **46,** No. 1, 102–127.

Wever, E. G., and Bray, C. W. (1936). The nature of acoustic response: The relation between sound intensity and the magnitude of responses in the cochlea. *J. Exp. Psychol.* **19,** 129–143.

Wever, E. G., and Bray, C. W. (1937). The effects of chemical substances upon the electrical responses of the cochlea. I. The application of sodium chloride to the round window membrane. *Ann. Otol., Rhinol., & Laryngol.* **46,** 291–302.

Wever, E. G., and Lawrence, M. (1949). The patterns of response in the cochlea. *J. Acoust. Soc. Amer.* **21,** No. 2, 127–134.

Wever, E. G., and Lawrence, M. (1954). "Physiological Acoustics." Princeton Univ. Press, Princeton, New Jersey.

Wever, E. G., and Lawrence, M. (1955). Patterns of injury produced by overstimulation of the ear. *J. Acoust. Soc. Amer.* **27,** No. 5, 853–858.

Wever, E. G., Bray, C. W., and Horton, G. P. (1935). Localization in the cochlea as studied by the stimulation deafness method. *Ann. Otol., Rhinol., & Laryngol.* **44,** 772.

Wever, E. G., Bray, C. W., and Lawrence, M. (1940). The locus of distortion in the ear. *J. Acoust. Soc. Amer.* **11,** No. 4, 427–433.

Wever, E. G., Vernon, J. A., and Peterson, E. A. (1963). The high-frequency sensitivity of the guinea pig ear. *Proc. Nat. Acad. Sci.* **49,** No. 3, 319–322.

Wiggers, H. C. (1937). The functions of the intra-aural muscles. *Amer. J. Physiol.* **120,** 771–790.

Wilpizeski, C., and Tanaka, Y. (1967). Recent animal contributions to the study of salicylate ototoxicity. *Del. Med. J.* **pp. 90**–93.

Wilpizeski, C., and Tanaka, Y. (1970). Cochlear microphonic and action potential thresholds during acute salicylism. *79th Acoust. Soc. Amer., 1970,* pp. 1–6.

Wilson, K. S., and Juhn, S. K. (1970). The effect of ethacrynic acid on perilymph Na and K. *Pract. Oto-Rhino-Laryngol.* **32,** 279–287.

Worthington, D. W., and Dallos, P. (1971). Spatial patterns of cochlear difference tones. *J. Acoust. Soc. Amer.* **49,** No. 6, Part 2, 1818–1830.

Wright, C. G., and Preston, R. E. (1973). Degeneration and distribution of efferent nerve fibers in the guinea pig organ of Corti. A light and scanning electron microscopic study. *Brain Res.* **58,** 37–59.

Wusterfeld, E., and Gleiss, H. (1969). Das medullare Acusticusgebiet und seine Reaktion auf Reintonbeschallung (Meerschweinchen). *Verh. Anat. Ges.* **63,** 447–459.

Zoellner, F., and Strange, G. (1967). Augmentation of the compound action potentials of the acoustic nerve by isolated damage of central auditory pathways. *Int. Audiol.* **6,** 369–374.

Zwislocki, J. (1963). Analysis of the middle-ear function. Part II. Guinea pig ear. *J. Acoust. Soc. Amer.* **35,** No. 7, 1034–1040.

Subject Index

F

G

N

Q

R

V

W

X

Y

Z

B
C 8
D 9
E 0
F 1
G 2
H 3
I 4
J 5